Law of Internet Speech

2005 Supplement to the Second Edition

Madeleine Schachter

CAROLINA ACADEMIC PRESS
Durham, North Carolina

ISBN: 1-59460-171-2

Carolina Academic Press
700 Kent Street
Durham, North Carolina 27701
Telephone (919) 489-7486
Fax (919) 493-5668
E-mail: cap@cap-press.com
www.cap-press.com

Table of Contents

Preface

Technological advances, policy formulation, and legal developments continue to flourish in the realm of Internet speech. This second edition of the Supplement, which goes to press in mid-2005,* is designed to replace the earlier Supplement and augment the materials both in the second edition of the accompanying casebook, *Law of Internet Speech,* which went to press in mid-2002, and the first Supplement, which went to press in mid-2003. While exhaustive review of all aspects of the law of Internet speech simply is not feasible, the Supplement, like the text, includes materials that are noteworthy for their analysis, because courts have referred to or relied on them, or in light of the media attention they have garnered. (Occasionally, matters that have received increased attention because of appellate or other developments are included in the Supplement even if they preceded publication of the casebook.)

The Supplement utilizes stylistic conventions similar to those in the *Law of Internet Speech* casebook. Thus, footnotes, headings, and citations to case records have been selectively omitted, and other stylistic modifications have been made to court decisions and other sources, in order to promote consistency and facilitate review. Footnotes within cases, to the extent they have been included in this Supplement, correspond to the footnote numbers in the published reports. References herein to "*Law of Internet Speech*" denote the second edition of *Law of Internet Speech* by the author, published by Carolina Academic Press in 2003.

The author is an in-house attorney at Time Warner Book Group, Inc. (which is part of Time Warner Inc.), and an Adjunct Professor at the Fordham University School of Law. As is the case with the accompanying text, the materials included in this Supplement, which contain divergent viewpoints, are intended to serve as an intellectual catalyst to provoke discussion and thought. To the extent views are inferred, nothing herein should be construed as expressing the views of anyone other than the author or as constituting legal advice.

---

* The materials included in this edition of the Supplement primarily consist of developments through May, 2005. Exceptions include the decision issued by the U.S. Supreme Court in June 2005 in *Metro-Goldwyn-Mayer Studios, Inc. v. Grokster, Ltd., see* Supplement *infra* at 358; and references to developments in June 2005 in *In re Grand Jury Subpoena, Judith Miller, see* Supplement *infra* at 72; and in *1-800 Contacts, Inc. v. WhenU.com, see* Supplement *infra* at 450-51.

CHAPTER I
FUNDAMENTAL PRINCIPLES OF FREE SPEECH AND THE INTERNET

Values Served By the First Amendment

insert the following in the fourth full paragraph after the citation to Planned Parenthood of Columbia/Willamette Inc. v. American Coalition of Life on page 5 of Law of Internet Speech:

aff'd in part, vacated in part, remanded in part, 298 F.3d 1058 (9th Cir. 2002), *cert. denied,* 123 S. Ct. 2367 (2003); *see* Supplement *infra* at 99.

* * * * *

The Nature of the Internet

insert the following after the first sentence in the second full paragraph on page 20 of Law of Internet Speech:

Some have endeavored to analyze the geography of Internet address space by visualizing geographical patterns of ownership of blocks of Internet addresses. *See Analysing the Geography of Internet Address Space, available at* <http://www.geog.ucl.ac.uk/casa/martin/internetspace/>.

* * * * *

insert the following at the end of page 33 of Law of Internet Speech:

Notes and Questions

1. In January 2005, the Pew Internet & American Life Project released findings based on a survey it had conducted of technology experts and scholars to "evaluate where the network is headed in the next ten years." Pew Internet & American Life Project, *The Future of the Internet* (Jan. 9, 2005), *available at* <http://www.pewinternet.org/pdfs/PIP_Future_of_Internet.pdf>. When the experts were asked to rate the amount of change likely to occur in various institutions in the next decade, they "predicted the most radical change in news and publishing organizations and the least amount of change in religious institutions." *Id.* at ii. In addition, some experts reflected that "[t]he dissemination of information will increasingly become the dissemination of drivel. As more and more 'data' is posted on the internet, there will be increasingly less 'information.'" *Id.* at iii.

Historically, a number of editorial functions have been performed by press entities. Newspapers, magazines, books, and other media have gathered information, screened and assessed the credibility of sources, and prioritized and ordered content. As persons and groups that are not members of institutionalized press entities proliferate on the World Wide Web, how might recipients of information evaluate the credibility and reliability of content?

2. According to one study, "[o]n a typical day at the end of 2004, some 70 million American adults logged onto the Internet to use email, get news, access government information, check out health and medical information, participate in auctions, book travel reservations, research their genealogy, gamble, seek out romantic partners, and engage in countless other activities. That represents a 37 percent increase from the 51 million Americans who were online on an

average day in 2000 when the Pew Internet & American Life Project began its study of online life." Lee Rainie and John Horrigan, Pew Internet & American Life Project, *Reports: Internet Evolution: A Decade of Adoption: How the Internet Has Woven Itself Into American Life* (Jan. 25, 2005), *available at* <http://www.pewinternet.org/PPF/r/148/report_ display.asp>.

3. With respect to the increasing use of blogs, *see* Supplement *infra* at 77.

* * * * * *

Is There a Dichotomy Between Freedom of Speech and Freedom of the Press?

Characterizing "The Press"

insert the following after the heading Characterizing "The Press" on page 54 of Law of Internet Speech:

As the U.S. District Court for the Southern District of New York observed, examples of the journalistic ethic of preserving the identity of confidential sources may be found as early as the colonial period.

> Benjamin Franklin's older brother James refused to disclose the identity of the author of a story published in his newspaper to a committee of the legislature and was jailed for a month as a result. In 1812, an editor for The Alexandria Herald refused to identify the sources of a news story and received a contempt citation from Congress. The earliest reported case in the courts did not occur until 1848, when a reporter was jailed for contempt of the Senate upon refusing to disclose who had given him a copy of a secret draft of a proposed treaty to end the Mexican-American War. In 1857, a correspondent for *The Times* was imprisoned when he refused to reveal to a select committee of the House the identities of the House members who had told him that some of their colleagues were taking bribes. The issue of reporters preserving the confidentiality of their sources came to the forefront again during the Depression, when the publication of stories on municipal corruption and labor unrest brought reporters to the witness stand, and prompted several states to adopt statutory protections for reporters. More recently, the 1969 trial of the "Chicago 7" and investigations of other anti-war activities during the Viet Nam war gave rise to renewed attention to confidential sources in the years preceding the Watergate scandal.

New York Times Co. v. Gonzales, No. 04 Civ. 7677 (RWS), 2005 U.S. Dist. LEXIS 2642, at *20 n.28 (S.D.N.Y. Feb. 24, 2005) (citations omitted).

* * * * *

substitute the following for first full paragraph on page 55 of Law of Internet Speech:

In *Blum v. Schlegel,* a law student was served with a subpoena seeking production of a tape recording of an interview with the school's associate dean that was used to prepare an article for the school newspaper. 150 F.R.D. 42, 43 (W.D.N.Y. 1993), *aff'd,* 18 F.3d 1005 (2d Cir. 1994). The plaintiff argued that the New York Shield Law was inapposite to the student because he did not qualify as a "professional journalist" working "for gain or livelihood." 150 F.R.D. at 44; *see also* N.Y. Civ. Rts. L. § 79-h(a)(6). The court stated, "If state law governed this question, Plaintiff may well be correct. However, at least in this area, the federal privilege appears broader than the protection of the Shield Law." 150 F.R.D. at 44 (citations omitted). Ultimately, "whether a person is a professional journalist is irrelevant. The question is how the person asserting the privilege intended to use the information gathered." *Id.* at 45. Therefore, "although prior experience as a professional journalist may be persuasive evidence of present intent to gather for the purpose of dissemination, it is not the *sine qua non*. The burden indeed may be sustained by one who is a novice in the field." *Id.* (quoting *von Bulow by Auersperg v. von Bulow,* 811 F.2d 136, 144 (2d Cir.), *cert. denied,* 481 U.S. 1015 (1987)).

In *In re Fitch, Inc.,* 330 F.3d 104 (2d Cir. 2003), the Second Circuit considered an order finding the movant in contempt for its refusal to comply with a subpoena. The movant, Fitch, Inc., was a financial rating agency that, for a fee, analyzed and rated securities and debt offerings on behalf of such clients as corporations or banks that planned to issue a security. Clients engaged Fitch to rate their securities in order to facilitate their sale to investors and to reap regulatory benefits from favorable ratings. In this action, a savings bank had a dispute with one of its long-time brokers. The bank discovered facts that led it to believe that the broker and Fitch had extensive communications relating to its transactions. The bank alleged that the broker had relied on information it received from Fitch when it made certain marketing representations to potential investors regarding the level of risk and the anticipated rate of return on the investment.

Fitch refused to produce documents or submit to depositions, citing New York's Shield Law, N.Y. Civ. Rts. L. § 79-h (McKinney 2002). *See* 330 F.3d at 108. In support of its position, Fitch pointed out that it conducted research, gathered facts, and performed analysis "directed towards matters of general public concern, just like any journalist, and note[d] that it ma[de] its information available on its web site to the general public." *Id.* at 109. The U.S. Court of Appeals for the Second Circuit rejected the argument, however. Scrutinizing Fitch's newsgathering activities, the appellate court was influenced by the fact that Fitch "report[ed]" only on specific transactions for which it had been retained and "cover[ed]" only its own clients. *Id.* The Second Circuit emphasized that its ruling was narrow but declined to find that Fitch was entitled to assert the journalistic privilege with respect to the information at issue. *Id.* at 111.

Would the outcome of the decision have been different if Fitch had occasionally disseminated to the public more general analyses of industry trends and published conclusions about companies with which it had no commercial relationship? Would such activities have buttressed Fitch's claim of privilege?

In January 2003, the U.S. District Court for the District of Columbia held that the Electronic Privacy Information Center ("EPIC") was appropriately classified as a "representative of the news media" by the U.S. Department of Defense for purposes of Freedom of Information Act ("FOIA") requests. *Electronic Privacy Information Ctr. v. Department of Defense,* 241 F. Supp. 2d 5 (D.D.C. 2003). Accordingly, EPIC is entitled to preferred status with respect to fees relating to FOIA requests. The ruling was contrary to the determination by the Department of Defense that EPIC was not a member of the news media because it was not organized or operated to publish news to the public. *See id.* at 7. EPIC pointed out that it regularly published a bi-weekly electronic newsletter and prints and distributes books on privacy, technology, and civil liberties issues. *Id.* The court noted:

EPIC gleans the information it publishes in its books from a wide variety of sources, including FOIA requests, state and federal courts, government agencies, universities, international groups, law reviews, interest groups, and even other news sources. EPIC researches issues on privacy and civil liberties, reports on this information, analyzes relevant data, evaluates the newsworthiness of material and puts the facts and issues into context, publishing and distributing this "news" through the sale of its books to the public. All these activities are hallmarks of publishing, news, and journalism. As EPIC explained, "[a]ny information that is obtained as a result of this [FOIA] request will be disseminated through these publications and others." Hence, EPIC "gathers information of potential interest to a segment of the public, uses its editorial skills to turn the raw material into a distinct work, and distributes that work to an audience."

Id. at 11-12 (quoting EPIC and *National Sec. Archive v. Department of Defense,* 880 F.2d 1381, 1387 (D.C. Cir. 1989)) (footnote omitted). The fact that EPIC's newsletter was disseminated via the Internet to subscribers' e-mail addresses did not change the analysis because, among other reasons, the applicable regulation anticipates technological advancements, recognizing that "'as traditional methods of news delivery evolve (e.g., electronic dissemination of newspapers through telecommunications services), such alternative media would be included in [the news media] category.'" *Id.* (quoting 32 C.F.R. § 286.28(e)(7)(i) (2002)).

When one man criticized administrators of the Seattle, Washington senior citizens' home in which he had lived, his on-line postings led to claims of harassment. Paul Trummel served more than three months, including nearly a month in solitary confinement, for defying a court order to de-post the names and addresses of administrators, notwithstanding that they were gathered from public records. Ultimately, Trummel complied with the order. "Valiant local investigative journalist or cranky fanatical stalker?," asked the *Columbia Journalism Review.* Sharlee DiMenichi, *Law: Who's a Reporter?,* Colum. Journalism Rev. (Sept./Oct. 2002) at 9.

* * * * *

insert the following before In re: Michael A. Cusumano and David B. Yoffie [United States of America v. Microsoft Corporation] on page 56 of Law of Internet Speech:

Notes and Questions

1. In the wake of a spate of subpoenas issued to reporters seeking disclosure of confidential sources, *see Law of Internet Speech* at 34; Supplement *infra* at 31, various press entities have announced tighter controls on the use of anonymous sources. *The New York Times,* for example, requires that the identity of every unidentified source must be known to at least one editor, and *USA Today* similarly requires that all anonymous sources must be identified to a managing editor. *See* Lorne Manly, *Big News Media Join in Push to Limit Use of Unidentified Sources,* N.Y. Times, May 23, 2005, at C1. *Newsweek* stated that it would confine its use of anonymous sources to instances in which a top editor of the magazine had approved their use. *Newsweek Tightens Sourcing After Koran Story,* Reuters (May 22, 2005). "'The cryptic phrase "sources said" will never again be the sole attribution for a story in *Newsweek.*'" *Id.* (quoting Richard Smith, Chairman and Editor-in-Chief of *Newsweek*).

What are the implications for the senior editors to whom the identities of confidential sources are disclosed who receive subpoenas? Might a senior editor prefer to ask preliminary questions about the nature of the report before requiring a reporter to divulge the source, or inquire about potential alternative sources that might go on the record?

2. Ethical guidelines proposed by the Associated Press devote considerable attention to the use of anonymous sources, stating that they may be used only if the material is informational, rather than a matter of opinion or speculation; with approval of a news manager; and when the manager has been apprised of the source's identity. The policy also requires identification of an anonymous source as specifically as possible, as opposed to mere references to the individual as "a source." Furthermore, the anonymous source should not be cited elsewhere in the story as someone who had declined comment. In addition, the policy requires that all articles that rely on anonymous sources carry a byline. *See, e.g.,* Joe Strupp, *Proposed AP Ethics Policy Draws Some Guild Concerns,* Editor & Publisher (Dec. 21, 2004), *available at* <http://www.editorandpublisher.com/eandp/news/article_display.jsp?vnu_content_id=10007 40863>.

3. Some Web publishers have endeavored to increase readership by enlisting local residents to assist in gathering information about local news. *See, e.g.,* Leslie Walker, *On Local Sites, Everyone's a Journalist,* Wash. Post (Dec. 9, 2004) at E-01, *available at* <http://www. washingtonpost.com/wp-dyn/articles/A46519-004Dec8.html>. "'With cheaper digital cameras and cell phones that can also shoot video, more and more regular people ... will start becoming citizen-journalists.'" Jeffrey Ressner, *See Me, Blog Me,* Time, Apr. 19, 2004, at 98 (quoting Steve Garfield, a video blogger or "vlogger"). Are participating residents members of "the press"?

4. In Greensboro, North Carolina, a local newspaper with a daily circulation of just under 100,000 "embarked on a journalistic experiment," known as its "Town Square" project, to create an on-line community for readers. *See* Martin Miller, *Paper's Aim: Building Blog for Success,* L.A. Times, May 23, 2005, at E1. Yet when a Ventura County, California newspaper was "[b]ombarded by vicious online postings concerning race and immigration, [it] ... pulled the plug on a virtual bulletin board that invited readers to comment on stories that appeared on the paper's website." Fred Alvarez and Tonya Alanez, *Paper Cuts Off Website Forum,* L.A. Times, May 21, 2005, at B1.

5. One daily California newspaper launched a community web-site by utilizing one editor and relying predominantly on reader contributions. *See id.* Some on-line photo services, such as Flickr, "offer[ ] users the ability to upload, store and organize digital photos, as well as to automatically post camera-phone shots to a blog." Daniel Terdiman, *Photo Site a Hit With Bloggers,* Wired News.com (Dec. 9, 2004), *available at* <http://www.wired. com/news/culture/0,1284,65958,00.html>. In addition, users can annotate posted photographs. *See id.* "When bombs went off in Jakarta, Indonesia, in September, CNN.com readers weren't the first to know. Instead, members of Flickr, an online photo service, were among the very earliest to see pictures of what had happened." *Id.* This enabled visitors to promptly receive newsworthy information. The site's mission also has been characterized as "'trying to capture the conversations that people have about photos....'" *Id.* (quoting Caterina Fake, a co-founder of Flickr). Is this site a press entity?

* * * * *

insert the following before "The Press" and Internet Publications on page 58 of Law of Internet Speech:

MICHAEL MCKEVITT, Plaintiff-Appellee
v.
ABDON PALLASCH, *et al.,* Defendants-Appellants

United States Court of Appeals for the Seventh Circuit

Nos. 03-2753, 03-2754, 339 F.3d 530

August 8, 2003

Michael McKevitt is being prosecuted in Ireland for membership in a banned organization and directing terrorism. He asked the district court for an order pursuant to 28 U.S.C. § 1782 to produce tape recordings that he thinks will be useful to him in the cross-examination of David Rupert, who according to McKevitt's motion is the key witness for the prosecution. The district court obliged. Its order is directed against a group of journalists who have a contract to write Rupert's biography and who in the course of their research for the biography interviewed him; the tape recordings that they made of the interviews and are in their possession are the recordings sought in McKevitt's motion. The journalists appealed from the district court's order and asked us to stay it, which we refused to do, and the recordings were turned over to McKevitt. We now explain why we refused to issue the stay. Ordinarily the explaining could await the decision of the appeal, but not in this case, because the denial of the stay, and the resulting disclosure of the recordings to McKevitt, mooted the appeal. *Publicis Communication v. True North Communications, Inc.,* 206 F.3d 725, 727-28 (7th Cir. 2000); *compare United States v. Administrative Enterprises, Inc.,* 46 F.3d 670, 671 (7th Cir. 1995). By the time an order could be obtained and executed against McKevitt commanding the return of the recordings, he would have memorialized the information contained in them and the information would inevitably become public at his trial. The appeal was not yet moot, however, when we denied the stay, and there is no irregularity in a court's explaining the ground of a decision after the decision itself has been made ending the case. *See, e.g., FoodComm Int'l v. Barry,* 328 F.3d 300, 302 (7th Cir. 2003); *Dela Rosa v. Scottsdale Memorial Health Systems, Inc.,* 136 F.3d 1241, 1242 (9th Cir. 1998); *Dant v. District of Columbia,* 264 U.S. App. D.C. 284, 829 F.2d 69, 73 (D.C. Cir. 1987).

Section 1782(a) of the Judicial Code authorizes federal district courts to order the production of evidentiary materials for use in foreign legal proceedings, provided the materials are not privileged. The defendants claim that the tapes in question are protected from compelled disclosure by a federal common law reporter's privilege rooted in the First Amendment. *See* Fed. R. 501. Although the Supreme Court in *Branzburg v. Hayes,* 408 U.S. 665, 33 L. Ed. 2d 626, 92 S. Ct. 2646 (1972), declined to recognize such a privilege, Justice Powell, whose vote was essential to the 5-4 decision rejecting the claim of privilege, stated in a concurring opinion that such a claim should be decided on a case-by-case basis by balancing the freedom of the press against the obligation to assist in criminal proceedings. *Id.* at 709-10. Since the dissenting Justices would have gone further than Justice Powell in recognition of the reporter's privilege, and preferred his position to that of the majority opinion (for they said that his "enigmatic concurring opinion gives some hope of a more

18

flexible view in the future," *id.* at 725), maybe his opinion should be taken to state the view of the majority of the Justices – though this is uncertain, because Justice Powell purported to join Justice White's "majority" opinion.

A large number of cases conclude, rather surprisingly in light of *Branzburg*, that there is a reporter's privilege, though they do not agree on its scope. *See, e.g., In re Madden*, 151 F.3d 125, 128-29 (3d Cir. 1998); *United States v. Smith*, 135 F.3d 963, 971 (5th Cir. 1998); *Shoen v. Shoen*, 5 F.3d 1289, 1292-93 (9th Cir. 1993); *In re Shain*, 978 F.2d 850, 852 (4th Cir. 1992); *United States v. LaRouche Campaign*, 841 F.2d 1176, 1181-82 (1st Cir. 1988); *von Bulow v. von Bulow*, 811 F.2d 136, 142 (2d Cir. 1987); *United States v. Caporale*, 806 F.2d 1487, 1504 (11th Cir. 1986). A few cases refuse to recognize the privilege, at least in cases, which *Branzburg* was but this case is not, that involve grand jury inquiries. *In re Grand Jury Proceedings*, 5 F.3d 397, 402-03 (9th Cir. 1993); *In re Grand Jury Proceedings*, 810 F.2d 580, 584-86 (6th Cir. 1987). Our court has not taken sides.

Some of the cases that recognize the privilege, such as *Madden*, essentially ignore *Branzburg*, *see* 151 F.3d at 128; some treat the "majority" opinion in *Branzburg* as actually just a plurality opinion, such as *Smith*, *see* 135 F.3d at 968-69; some audaciously declare that *Branzburg* actually created a reporter's privilege, such as *Shoen*, 5 F.3d at 1292, and *von Bulow v. von Bulow*, *supra*, 811 F.2d at 142; *see also* cases cited in *Schoen* 5 F.3d at 1292 n.5, and *Farr v. Pitchess*, 522 F.2d 464, 467-68 (9th Cir. 1975). The approaches that these decisions take to the issue of privilege can certainly be questioned. *See In re Grand Jury Proceedings*, *supra*, 810 F.2d at 584-86. A more important point, however, is that the Constitution is not the only source of evidentiary privileges, as the Supreme Court noted in *Branzburg* with reference to the reporter's privilege itself. 408 U.S. at 689, 706. And while the cases we have cited do not cite other possible sources of the privilege besides the First Amendment and one of them, *LaRouche*, actually denies, though without explaining why, that there might be a federal common law privilege for journalists that was not based on the First Amendment, *see* 841 F.2d at 1178 n.4; *see also In re Grand Jury Proceedings*, *supra*, 5 F.3d at 402-03, other cases do cut the reporter's privilege free from the First Amendment. *See United States v. Cuthbertson*, 630 F.2d 139, 146 n.1 (2d Cir. 1980); *In re Grand Jury Proceedings*, *supra*, 810 F.2d at 586-88; *cf. Gonzales v. National Broadcasting Co.*, 194 F.3d 29, 36 n.2 (2d Cir. 1999).

The federal interest in cooperating in the criminal proceedings of friendly foreign nations is obvious; and it is likewise obvious that the news-gathering and reporting activities of the press are inhibited when a reporter cannot assure a confidential source of confidentiality. Yet that was *Branzburg* and it is evident from the result in that case that the interest of the press in maintaining the confidentiality of sources is not absolute. There is no conceivable interest in confidentiality in the present case. Not only is the source (Rupert) known, but he has indicated that he does not object to the disclosure of the tapes of his interviews to McKevitt.

Some cases that recognize a reporter's privilege suggest that it can sometimes shield information in a reporter's possession that comes from a nonconfidential source; in addition to the *Madden*, *Schoen*, and *La Rouche* cases cited above *see Gonzales v. National Broadcasting Co.*, *supra*, 194 F.3d at 33; *United States v. Burke*, 700 F.2d 70, 76, 78 (2d Cir. 1983); *United States v. Cuthbertson*, *supra*, 630 F.2d at 147. Others disagree. *United States v. Smith*, *supra*, 135 F.3d at 972; *In re Grand Jury Proceedings*, *supra*, 810 F.2d at 584-85. The cases that extend the privilege to nonconfidential sources express concern with harassment, burden, using the press as an investigative arm of government, and so forth; *see* the *Gonzalez*, *LaRouche*, and *Cuthbertson* opinions. Since these considerations were rejected by *Branzburg* even in the context of a confidential source, these courts may be skating on thin ice.

Illinois has enacted a statutory version of the reporter's privilege. 735 I.L.C.S. 5/8-901; *Desai v. Hersh*, 954 F.2d 1408, 1412 (7th Cir. 1992). But it has no application to this case. Section 1782(a) of the Judicial Code provides that "a person may not be compelled to give his testimony or statement or to produce a document or other thing in violation of any *legally applicable* privilege" (emphasis added). State-law privileges are not "legally applicable" in federal-question cases like this one. Fed. R. Evid. 501; *Patterson v. Caterpillar, Inc.*, 70 F.3d 503, 506 (7th Cir. 1995). In any event, while the reporters' motion included a citation to the Illinois statute as part of a string cite, it failed to discuss, even minimally, why the statute should apply here. As a result, even if the statute were applicable, the reporters waived reliance on it. *Hojnacki v. Klein-Acosta*, 285 F.3d 544, 549 (7th Cir. 2002).

It seems to us that rather than speaking of privilege, courts should simply make sure that a subpoena *duces tecum* directed to the media, like any other subpoena *duces tecum*, is reasonable in the circumstances, which is the general criterion for judicial review of subpoenas. Fed. R. Crim. P. 17I; *CSC Holdings, Inc. v. Redisi*, 309 F.3d 988, 993 (7th Cir. 2002); *EEOC v. Sidley Austin Brown & Wood*, 315 F.3d 696, 700 (7th Cir. 2002). We do not see why there need to be special criteria merely because the possessor of the documents or other evidence sought is a journalist. *See Cohen v. Cowles Media Co.*, 501 U.S. 663, 669, 115 L. Ed. 2d 586, 111 S. Ct. 2513 (1991); *New York Times Co. v. Jascalevich*, 439 U.S. 1317, 1322, 58 L. Ed. 2d 25, 99 S. Ct. 6 (1978); *cf. United States v. Ahn*, 343 U.S. App. D.C. 392, 231 F.3d 26, 37 (D.C. Cir. 2000). The approach we are suggesting has support in *Branzburg* itself, where the Court stated that "grand jury investigations if instituted or conducted other than in good faith, would pose wholly different issues for resolution under the First Amendment. Official harassment of the press undertaken not for purposes of law enforcement but to disrupt a reporter's relationship with his news sources would have no justification. Grand juries are subject to judicial control and subpoenas to motions to quash. We do not expect courts will forget that grand juries must operate within the limits of the First Amendment as well as the Fifth." 408 U.S. at 707-08.

When the information in the reporter's possession does not come from a confidential source, it is difficult to see what possible bearing the First Amendment could have on the question of compelled disclosure. If anything, the parties to this case are reversed from the perspective of freedom of the press, which seeks to encourage publication rather than secrecy. *Florida Star v. B.J.F.*, 491 U.S. 524, 533-34, 105 L. Ed. 2d 443, 109 S. Ct. 2603 (1989). Rupert *wants* the information disclosed; it is the reporters, paradoxically, who want it secreted. The reason they want it secreted is that the biography of him that they are planning to write will be less marketable the more information in it that has already been made public.

In other words, the reporters are concerned about McKevitt's "appropriating" their intellectual property in the tape recordings and by doing so reducing the value of that property. Disputes over intellectual property, as the Supreme Court just reminded us, are not profitably conducted in the idiom of the First Amendment. *Eldred v. Ashcroft*, 537 U.S. 186, 123 S. Ct. 769, 788-89, 154 L. Ed. 2d 683 (2003). They are the subject of specialized bodies of law regulating intellectual property, such as copyright law or, of particular relevance here, the common law of misappropriation, most famously exemplified by *International News Service v. Associated Press*, 248 U.S. 215, 63 L. Ed. 211, 39 S. Ct. 68 (1918). That decision no longer is legally authoritative because it was based on the federal courts' subsequently abandoned authority to formulate common law principles in suits arising under state law though litigated in federal court. But the doctrine it announced has been adopted as the common law of a number of states, including Illinois, *Board of Trade v. Dow Jones & Co.*, 98 Ill. 2d 109, 456 N.E.2d 84, 88, 74 Ill. Dec. 582 (Ill. 1983), and could in any event influence the formulation of federal common law evidentiary privileges.

The Associated Press and the International News Service competed in gathering news to be published in newspapers. Barred during much of World War I by British and French censors from sending war dispatches to the United States, INS would paraphrase AP's war dispatches published in east coast newspapers and was able to publish the paraphrases in west coast newspapers at the same hour because of the difference in time zones, and in east coast newspapers only a few hours later. There was no copyright infringement, because INS was copying the facts reported in AP's dispatches rather than the dispatches themselves and anyway AP had not bothered to copyright its dispatches. Nevertheless in *International News Service v. Associated Press* the Supreme Court held that AP was entitled to enjoin INS's copying as a form of unfair competition, since INS was trying to reap where AP had sown.

The present case is sharply different, since McKevitt has no commercial motive in "stealing" the defendant reporters' work product. And yet to the extent that such "thefts" can be anticipated, the incentive to gather information, in this case for the projected biography, will be diminished, just as INS's copying AP's dispatches might have impaired AP's incentive to incur the expense of gathering news about the war. Recent cases, however in recognition of the nebulousness of misappropriation doctrine, place tight limitations on it. This is how the Second Circuit, in an influential opinion interpreting New York common law, stated the elements of the doctrine: "(i) the plaintiff generates or collects information at some cost or expense; (ii) the value of the information is highly time-sensitive; (iii) the defendant's use of the information constitutes free-riding on the plaintiff's costly efforts to generate or collect it; (iv) the defendant's use of the information is in direct competition with a product or service offered by the plaintiff; (v) the ability of other parties to free-ride on the efforts of the plaintiff would so reduce the incentive to produce the product or service that its existence or quality could be substantially threatened." *National Basketball Association v. Motorola, Inc.*, 105 F.3d 841, 852 (2d Cir. 1997) (citations omitted). The meat is in (v), with (i) through (iv) identifying the conditions in which the criterion stated in (v) is likely to be satisfied. It seems, then, that legal protection for the gathering of facts is available only when unauthorized copying of the facts gathered is likely to deter the plaintiff, or others similarly situated, from gathering and disseminating those facts.

We are far from that in the present case. No showing has been made, or would be plausible, that the reporters will have to abandon the Rupert biography if the information contained in the recordings of their interviews with him is made public. It is a consideration that a district court might properly consider in deciding on a challenge to a subpoena, but it would add nothing to the court's consideration to analyze it in legal categories drawn from the First Amendment. And in this case it provides no support for the reporters' claim.

The district judge's grant of the order to produce the tape recordings for use in the Irish trial was clearly sound, and so the stay of the order was properly denied. The appeal is dismissed as moot.

* * * * *

21

LINDA R. TRIPP, Plaintiff

v.

DEPARTMENT OF DEFENSE, *et al.,* Defendants

United States District Court for the District of Columbia

Civil Action No. 01-157 (EGS) [48-1], 284 F. Supp. 2d 50

September 30, 2003

MEMORANDUM OPINION AND ORDER

In this action, plaintiff Linda Tripp alleges that the United States Department of Defense ("DOD") violated the Privacy Act, 5. U.S.C. § 552a (2003), as well as the Administrative Procedures Act ("APA"), 5 U.S.C. § 551 *et seq.* (2003) and 5 U.S.C. § 701 *et seq.* (2003), by releasing information related to her application for employment at the George Marshall Center in Germany to the Department of Defense publication *Stars and Stripes*. The issue now before the Court is whether Ms. Sandra Jontz, a reporter for the DOD Armed Forces Newspaper *Stars and Stripes*, is entitled to invoke the "reporter's privilege" in response to plaintiff's discovery requests regarding her sources for the article at issue.

I. BACKGROUND

… In or about October 2000, Plaintiff applied for a position as Deputy Director of the Conference Center at the George C. Marshall European Center for Security Studies, a Department of Defense research and training institute located in Gamusch, Germany.[1] Several months after she submitted her application, plaintiff was notified that she had been certified as one of the top qualified applicants for the position. She subsequently contacted the Marshall Center by telephone to inquire as to the job application process, and spoke to Mr. Robert Kennedy, the Marshall Center Director. Plaintiff contends that during that conversation she did not give Mr. Kennedy or anyone else the authority to disclose to any third parties information related to her job application.

Plaintiff was scheduled for an interview at the Marshall Center on January 23, 2001. When she arrived at the Center, she was handed a copy of that day's *Stars and Stripes* newspaper, which featured an article titled "Linda Tripp up for Job at Marshall Center" and authored by Ms. Jontz. Plaintiff alleges that this article was published in the European and Pacific print editions of *Stars and Stripes*, the on-line edition of the European edition of *Stars and Stripes*, and in the electronic "Early Bird" on-line and e-mail publication distributed by DOD. In the article Jontz identified a number of sources, including: unnamed "center officials;" Marshall Center Director Robert Kennedy; an unnamed "Pentagon spokeswoman;" and unnamed "sources close to the Center." Ultimately, plaintiff was not selected for the Deputy Director position at the Marshal Center.

---

[1] At the time of her application for employment at the Marshall Center, plaintiff was employed with the Office of Public Affairs at DoD. Because plaintiff was a non-career, Schedule C political appointee, she was terminated from this position on January 20, 2001, at the conclusion of the Clinton administration.

Plaintiff commenced this action on January 25, 2001, alleging that DOD officials violated her Privacy Act rights by disclosing information contained in a Privacy Act system of records to *Stars and Stripes*. Plaintiff also claims that DOD failed to make necessary efforts to ensure the accuracy of the released information, to establish adequate rules for personnel with respect to the Privacy Act, and to establish sufficient safeguards to prevent unauthorized disclosures. ...

On July 25, 2002, Tripp served a notice of deposition and request for documents on Defendant DOD, seeking the production of DOD-employee Sandra Jontz for deposition testimony, as well as Jontz' notes, sources' names, drafts, and any document relating directly or indirectly to Linda Tripp. ... The DOD subsequently informed plaintiff by letter received after an October 7, 2002 status hearing in this case, that DOD was asserting "the reporter's privilege" with respect to "any information relating to Ms. Jontz' newsgathering sources" for the *Stars and Stripes* article at issue.

On October 22, 2002, Ms. Jontz, who is not a party to this action, filed a motion for a protective order pursuant to Fed. R. Civ. P. 26(c), officially objecting to Plaintiff's discovery request. In so doing, Jontz asserted the "reporter's privilege" with respect to Plaintiff's discovery of "any information relating to Ms. Jontz' newsgathering sources for the January 23, 2001 *Stars and Stripes* article at issue" without "first attempting to obtain discovery from alternate sources," and further requested that plaintiff withdraw the discovery request. Failing that, Jontz asks the Court for a protective order barring plaintiff from seeking discovery regarding her newsgathering activities. ...

II. First Amendment "Reporter's Privilege"

The Federal Rules of Civil Procedure provide that "parties may obtain discovery regarding any matter, not privileged, which is relevant to the subject matter involved in the pending action," reflecting the "fundamental principle that ... the public has a right to know every [person's] evidence," Fed. R. Civ. P. 26(b)(1); *see Hutira v. Islamic Republic of Iran*, 211 F. Supp. 2d 115, 117 (D.D.C. 2002). Under the First Amendment, reporters enjoy a qualified privilege against compelled disclosure of sources and information obtained through news gathering activities.[2] *Clyburn v. News World Communications, Inc.*, 284 U.S. App.

---

[2] The District of Columbia's "Free Flow of Information Act of 1992," applicable in diversity actions, provides statutory protection to members of the news media. It provides, in relevant parts:

> no judicial ... body ... shall compel any person who is or has been employed by the news media and acting in an official news gathering or news disseminating capacity to disclose:
>
> (1) The source of any news or information procured by the person while employed by the news media and acting in an official news gathering capacity, whether or not the source has been promised confidentiality....
>
> if the court finds that the party seeking the news or information established by clear and convincing evidence that:
>
> (1) The news or information is relevant to a significant legal issue before a judicial ... body;

D.C. 212, 903 F.2d 29, 35 (D.C. Cir. 1990); *Zerilli v. Smith*, 211 U.S. App. D.C. 116, 656 F.2d 705, 711 (D.C. Cir. 1981) *Hutira v. Islamic Republic of Iran*, 211 F. Supp. 2d at 118; *Blumenthal v. Drudge*, 186 F.R.D. 236, 244 (D.D.C. 1999). While the D.C. Circuit has never ruled directly on the issue, other Circuits, as well as District Courts within this Circuit, have concluded that the qualified "reporter's privilege" protects both confidential and non-confidential information obtained by the reporter during the course of the reporter's newsgathering efforts. *See Hutira*, 211 F. Supp. 2d at 121-122; *NLRB v. Mortensen*, 701 F. Supp. 244, 247 (D.D.C. 1988); *see also Gonzales v. NBC, Inc.*, 194 F.3d 29, 33-36 (2d. Cir. 1999); *United States v. LaRouche*, 841 F.2d 1176, 1182 (1st Cir. 1988). One District Court has held that the privilege protects not only the sources of a reporter's information, but also a reporter's notes, diaries, and any other material generated in connection with the editorial process. *See Maughan v. NL Indus.*, 524 F. Supp. 93, 95 (D.D.C. 1981).

Although the reporter bears the burden of demonstrating the applicability of the privilege, *Hutira*, 211 F. Supp. 2d at 120-121, "in the ordinary case the civil litigant's interest in disclosure should yield to the journalist's privilege." *Zerilli*, 656 F.2d at 712. "The privilege is not absolute, however, and may be abrogated upon sufficient showing by the party seeking the information." *Hutira v. Islamic Republic of Iran*, 211 F. Supp. 2d at 118. Once a court determines that the reporter's privilege is properly invoked, it must "look to the facts of the particular case, balancing 'the public interest in protecting the reporter's sources against the private interest in compelling disclosure.'" *Id.* at 118-119. The following factors are to be considered when deciding whether to uphold the privilege:

1) whether the information sought "goes to the heart of" the case;

2) efforts made by the party seeking disclosure to obtain the information from an alternative source and the availability of the information from such an alternative source;

3) whether the journalist from whom disclosure is sought is a party to the action;

[Except]

4) whether the information sought is confidential or non-confidential in nature.

See id. at 119, 120. In assessing claims of "reporter's privilege" "courts will be mindful of the *preferred position* of the First Amendment and the importance of a rigorous press." *Zerilli*, 656 F.2d at 711-12; *Grunseth v. Marriott Corp.*, 868 F. Supp. at 335.

---

(2) The news or information could not, with due diligence, be obtained by any alternative means;

(3) There is an overriding public interest in the disclosure.

D.C. Code Ann. §§ 16-4702 -16-4704 (2002); *Grunseth v. Marriott Corporation*, 868 F. Supp. 333, 336 (D.D.C. 1994).

Before turning to consideration of these factors, however, the Court must first determine whether *Stars and Stripes* is the type of publication to which the reporter's privilege is intended to apply, and whether Ms. Jontz is a journalist as that term is used in the relevant jurisprudence.

A. *Status of Stars and Stripes*

In her response to Ms. Jontz' motion, plaintiff argues that the *Stars and Stripes* does not qualify as a "newspaper," and thus its employees are not entitled to First Amendment protections, including the right to assert the "reporter's privilege." Plaintiff specifically alleges that *Stars and Stripes* is a government-controlled internal information organization under the control of, and operated by, the employees of the DOD, and therefore cannot invoke First Amendment protections reserved for the "press." Therefore, Plaintiff alleges that Jontz, as an employee of *Stars and Stripes*, is not entitled to invoke the "reporter's privilege" to avoid Plaintiff's discovery request. DOD responds that, although *Stars and Stripes* is published by the DOD and its audience consists primarily of members of the "armed forces community," it is also "every bit a newspaper in the traditional sense," and as such enjoys "the full protection of the First Amendment."

The Supreme Court has long held that the notion of the "press" should be given a broad meaning, stating that "the press in its historic connotation comprehends every sort of publication which affords a vehicle of information and opinion." *Lovell v. City of Griffin*, 303 U.S. 444, 452, 58 S. Ct. 666, 82 L. Ed. 949 (1938). The D.C. Circuit has never directly addressed the question of whether *Stars and Stripes* is a publication protected by the First Amendment. Nor has it provided any guidance as to what characteristics should bring a publication within the scope of the First Amendment. Nevertheless, it appears that, as a general rule, courts refer to *Stars and Stripes* as a newspaper, or more generally as part of the "media." *See United States v. New*, 50 M.J. 729, 734 (U.S. Army Crim. App. 1999) (referring to the *Stars and Stripes* "newspaper"); *United States v. Creer*, 1997 CCA LEXIS 277, No. NMCM96-00469, 1997 WL 658741, at *2 (N.M. Crim. App. Apr. 9, 1997) (unpublished opinion) (referring to the *Stars and Stripes* when discussing "newspaper" coverage of an event damaging to the military's reputation in Japan); *United States v. Grzeganek*, 841 F. Supp. 1169, 1170 (S.D. Fl. 1993) (referring to the *Stars and Stripes* along with *USA Today*, the *International Herald Tribune*, *CNN*, and the *New York Times* as the "media"); *Freedman v. Turnage*, 646 F. Supp. 1460, 1461 (W.D.N.Y. 1986).

Plaintiff cites no authority supporting her position with respect to *Stars and Stripes* First Amendment "status," as it were, instead relying entirely on statements made on the DOD World Wide Web site regarding the role of the American Forces Information Services ("AFIS"). Essentially, Plaintiff's argument is that because the AFIS' primary goal is to "promote and sustain individual and unit military readiness, quality of life, and morale throughout the Department of Defense," any employee working for an AFIS publication is necessarily not entitled to the First Amendment protections afforded to reporters engaged in objective "newsgathering."

Jontz responds that the *Stars and Stripes* is "much the same as any other commercial newspaper" and therefore qualifies for First Amendment protections. Jontz correctly points out that both the DOD and Congress intend for the *Stars and Stripes* to operate like other commercial newspapers, and enjoy First Amendment protections and prohibitions. While it is true that *Stars and Stripes* is within DOD control, the legislative history of the National Defense Authorization Act reveals that Congress intended the information gathered by editors and reporters and published in *Stars and Stripes* to be free of interference from the DOD chain of command, provided it is balanced, accurate, and of interest to the readership. Report of the Committee on Armed Services, House of Representatives, on the National Defense Authorization Act for Fiscal Years 1990-1991, H.R. 2461, Report 101-121 (July 1, 1989). Moreover, Congress has expressly stated that articles in *Stars and Stripes* should "enjoy the full protection of the First Amendment, and military personnel on the frontiers of freedom must enjoy their first amendment rights." *Id.* Additionally, the DOD directive establishing the procedures and assigning the responsibilities for *Stars and Stripes* states:

> The *Stars and Stripes* is an unofficial, abstracted collection of commercial news and opinion available to commercial newspapers in the United States, [and also contains] *Stars and Stripes* editorial staff-generated DOD, command, and local news and information. The *Stars and Stripes* provides this information to the members of the Department of Defense and their family members serving overseas, as do commercial daily newspapers that are published and sold throughout the United States in keeping with the principles of the First Amendment of the U.S. Constitution. DOD Directive 5122.11, § 4.6.2 (Oct. 5, 1993).

The DOD's intent is further evidenced by DOD directives stating that "the *Stars and Stripes* does not represent the official position of the U.S. government, the DOD, or the Unified Combatant Command," and that *Stars and Stripes* reporters enjoy no special access to the military. While the Plaintiff is correct when she alleges that the *Stars and Stripes* is owned and controlled by the DOD and "operated by AFIS, the principal internal information organization within the DOD, the Director of AFIS' responsibilities do not extend to the editorial operations of *Stars and Stripes*. Furthermore, the current *Stars and Stripes* Editorial Director has stated in a sworn affidavit that *Stars and Stripes* is editorially independent, largely financially independent, and is often the only source of uncensored information about the military available to service members. The relevant case law, recent legislative history, recent DOD Directives, and affidavit of *Stars and Stripes* Editorial Director all support Jontz' contention that the *Stars and Stripes* and its employees should be afforded First Amendment protections. In the absence of any authority to the contrary, the Court concludes that *Stars and Stripes* is a newspaper for the purposes of First Amendment analysis.

B. *Jontz' Right to Invoke the Reporter's Privilege*

Plaintiff next submits that Jontz, as an employee of the DOD, is not entitled to invoke the "reporter's privilege." However, the D.C. Circuit has held that the "reporter's privilege' must encompass all newsgathering efforts, not simply those for newspapers." *United States v. Hubbard*, 493 F. Supp. 202, 205 (D.C. 1979). Since *Hubbard*, a District Court within this Circuit has held, in a case involving a publisher and editor of a bi-weekly newsletter, that:

> the protections which the First Amendment extends to newsgathering activities are not restricted to those who identify themselves as journalists by education, employment, or other such criteria ... the privilege is not limited to the writers of large established newspapers and media enterprises but is equally applicable to the sole publisher of a newsletter or other writing or paper distributed to the public to inform, to comment, or to criticize....

Liberty Lobby, Inc. v. Rees, 111 F.R.D. 19, 20 (D.D.C. 1986). In holding the privilege to be applicable on the facts before it, the court relied on evidence of ongoing publishing and distribution of the newsletter for "many years" and the recognition of its publisher and editor as a journalist by others. *Id.* at 21.

While this Circuit has not articulated a standard to be applied when an individual's actions rise to the level of "newsgathering" for purposes of entitling the reporter to assert the "reporter's privilege," recent District Court opinions have expressed support for a test adopted in the Third and Ninth Circuits under which, in order to invoke the privilege, a reporter must demonstrate that (1) the information was obtained for the purpose of dissemination to the public; and (2) the reporter had this intent at the time the information was obtained. *Hutira,* 211 F. Supp. 2d at 120-121 (citing *Shoen v. Shoen*, 5 F.3d 1289, 1293-1294 (9th Cir. 1993)); *Alexander v. F.B.I.*, 186 F.R.D. 21, 49-50 (D.D.C. 1998); *see also Titan Sports, Inc. v. Turner Broad. Sys. (In re Madden)*, 151 F.3d 125, 129-130 (3d Cir. 1998). One D.C. District Court has described the intent-based test as follows:

> whether a person is a journalist, and thus protected by the privilege, must be determined by the person's intent at the inception of the information-gathering process. ... [T]he individual claiming the privilege must demonstrate, through competent evidence, the intent to use material B sought, gathered, or received B to disseminate information to the public and that such intent existed at the inception of the newsgathering process. This requires an intent-based factual inquiry to be made by the district court. ... [P]rior experience as a professional journalist may be persuasive evidence of present intent to gather for the purpose of dissemination. ... [T]he primary relationship between the one seeking to invoke the privilege and his sources must have as its basis the intent to disseminate the information to the public garnered from that relationship.

Alexander v. FBI, 186 F.R.D. at 50 (quoting *von Bulow v. von Bulow*, 811 F.2d 136, 142, 144-45 (2d Cir. 1987)). However, in none of these cases was it alleged that the publication or journalist asserting the privilege was associated with any government agency. One sister District Court has also found that a person's prior experience as a professional journalist is persuasive evidence of present intent to gather for the purpose of dissemination. *Alexander,* 186 F.R.D. at 50.

It appears from the record now before the Court that Jontz engaged in newsgathering while preparing the Tripp article. The article itself indicates that Jontz interviewed a number of individuals while researching Tripp's employment with the DOD and her application to the Marshall Center, an activity which is a "fundamental aspect" of investigative journalism. *See Mgmt. Info. Tech., Inc. v. Alyeska Pipeline Serv. Co.*, 151 F.R.D. 471, 476 (D.D.C. 1993). Moreover, plaintiff's own document request suggests that Jontz engaged in traditional newsgathering activities such as keeping notes. Additionally, it is beyond dispute that Jontz' article qualifies as a "writing distributed to the public to inform." *See Liberty Lobby*, 111 F.R.D. at 20. Therefore, Jontz' duties at *Stars and Stripes* appear to fall within the scope of "newsgathering."

While Jontz has not directly alleged that she obtained information regarding Tripp's application with the intent to disseminate the information to the public, the fact that she was employed in a journalistic capacity is sufficient to meet her burden on this issue. *See Alexander v. FBI*, 186 F.R.D. at 50. Jontz has engaged in traditional journalistic activities as a reporter for *Stars and Stripes*, an organization whose sole purpose is to disseminate commercial news and information to individuals involved in the military. Plaintiff offers no alternative explanation, nor is any explanation found in the record, for why Jontz would have obtained information regarding Tripp's Marshall Center application. Accordingly, this Court finds that Jontz' efforts during her research for the Tripp article were "newsgathering activities" for which she is entitled to invoke the "reporter's privilege."

Plaintiff maintains that such a finding is not dispositive, arguing that, notwithstanding the existence of the privilege, Jontz violated the Privacy Act by using her position as an employee of the DOD to obtain information regarding Tripp's current employment with the DOD and application for the Marshall Center position, which she then kept in a system of records, i.e. her notes, and distributed to the public via the *Stars and Stripes* article. Without passing on its merits, this argument is irrelevant to the Court's determination of whether Jontz, as an employee of the *Stars and Stripes*, has a general right to assert the "reporter's privilege" with respect to sources and information she obtains during her newsgathering efforts. It does have some relevance to the final question before the Court, namely whether Plaintiff's need for the information can overcome the qualified "reporter's privilege."

C. *Balance of Interests*

In order for a party seeking discovery to overcome the "reporter's privilege" he or she must prove that (1) the information sought goes to the "heart of the matter;" and (2) that he or she has exhausted all reasonable alternatives available to him or her to obtain the information. *See generally Zerilli*, 656 F.2d at 704-706; *Hutira*, 211 F. Supp. 2d at 119; *Tavoulareas v. Piro*, 93 F.R.D. 11, 16 (D.D.C. 1981).

The Court need not engage in an exhaustive analysis of the public and private interests at stake in this case. As a general rule, no matter how strongly the other factors weigh in favor of the party seeking news gathering information from a journalist, where, as here, the party seeking to compel disclosure has made no effort whatsoever, or insufficient efforts, to obtain the information sought from alternative sources, or has made conclusory claims that the information cannot be obtained from other sources, courts in this Circuit have uniformly upheld the reporter's privilege and refused to compel disclosure of information related to news gathering activities. *See Clyburn v. News World Communications*, 284 U.S. App. D.C. 212, 903 F.2d 29, 35 (D.C. Cir. 1990) *Zerilli v. Smith*, 211 U.S. App. D.C. 116, 656 F.2d 705, 714-715 (D.C. Cir. 1981); *Hutira*, 211, F. Supp. at 121-22; *Alexander v. FBI*, 186, F.R.D. 21, 1998 WL 1049005 at *1 (D.D.C. May 28, 1998); *Grunseth*, 868 F. Supp. at 335; *Liberty Lobby, Inc. v. Rees*, 111 F.R.D. 19, 22-23 (D.D.C. 1986). It should be noted that in several of these cases there appear to have been a discrete or limited number of possible alternative sources for the information sought, either ascertainable directly from a news article or provided by a party, to which the party seeking disclosure could be required to turn. *See, e.g. Zerilli*, 656 F.2d at 708 (Justice Department provided a list of employees who knew most about the information alleged to have been disclosed in violation of the Privacy Act, as well as a list of all government officials who had access to the information); *Hutira*, 211 F. Supp. at 122 (other individuals discussed in the article); *Liberty Lobby*, 111 F.R.D. at 22 (defendant revealed "numerous names individuals who purportedly had information about the alleged relationship," of which 10 or 12 remained alive); *Maughan v. NL Industries*, 524 F. Supp. 93,

94 (D.D.C. 1981) (plaintiffs were available for discovery and were sufficient source of information regarding when they became aware of facts at issue); *see also Carey v. Hume*, 160 U.S. App. D.C. 365, 492 F.2d 631, 638-39 (D.C. Cir. 1972) (privilege was *not* upheld where reporter provided only "vague" "guidemarks" as to who sources could be, and party seeking information therefore had "no reasonable basis to know where to begin"). Nevertheless, courts have found that the fact that a party "may have considerable difficulty obtaining the information ... does not, however relieve ... the party of [the burden] of trying initially to obtain the information elsewhere." *Hutira*, 211, F. Supp. at 122.

DOD asserts that the deposition of Ms. Jontz is not the only means available to plaintiff to obtain the identity of the person who disclosed the information in question to *Stars and Stripes*. DOD maintains that it has provided plaintiff with a "clear and alternate path" to obtain the information sought from Ms. Jontz by suggesting the deposition of Lt. Col. Michael B. Glenn, the personnel manager at the Marshall Center who oversaw the application process for the position for which plaintiff applied. According to defendants, Lt. Col. Glenn could provide plaintiff with information relating to the identities of persons who may have had knowledge or access to information alleged to have been improperly disclosed, as well as information regarding what documents may have contained the information in question. This information would in turn assist plaintiff in assessing whether the information disclosed in the article was contained within a "system of records." Alternatively, defendants suggest that plaintiff could serve written discovery requests for information within Lt. Col. Glenn's possession.

Plaintiff insists that it is unfair to require her to conduct extensive discovery in an effort to seek out the potential sources for the information contained in the *Stars and Stripes* article from a seemingly endless set of possibilities, particularly where only Ms. Jontz and her anonymous sources are likely to have access to the information plaintiff seeks. She emphasizes that, in the cases cited by DOD for the proposition that depositions of numerous other witnesses was an acceptable alternative source, the number of potential alternative sources of information was significantly limited.

Plaintiff further contends that there is no reasonable alternative source for the information she seeks to obtain from Ms. Jontz. In support of this contention, plaintiff points to evidence submitted by defendant which suggests that Ms. Jontz knew of the information alleged to have been improperly disclosed *before* she contacted the Marshall center. She submits that, in light of this information, Lt. Col. Glenn's deposition, which would touch only on information available through the Marshall Center, cannot serve as a reasonable substitute for that of Ms. Jontz, because it could not reveal who Ms. Jontz spoke to before calling the Center. Furthermore, plaintiff emphasizes that the article itself refers to a "Pentagon spokeswoman," about whom an employee of the Marshall Center is unlikely to be able to provide information central to plaintiff's claim.

Without reaching the merits of plaintiff's arguments, the fact remains that with the exception of deposing Lt. Col. Glenn, plaintiff has not even attempted to obtain the information requested from other sources, and therefore has not met the exhaustion requirement set forth by relevant case law. The D.C. Circuit has held that "efforts made by the litigants to obtain the information from alternative sources is ... of central importance ... reporters should be compelled to disclose their sources only after the litigant has shown that he has exhausted every reasonable source of information." *Zerilli*, 656 F.2d at 713; *see also Hutira*, 211 F. Supp. 2d at 122; *Blumenthal v. Drudge*, 186 F.R.D. at 244. The Circuit stated in *Zerilli* that "appellants cannot escape their obligation to exhaust alternative sources simply because they feared that deposing Justice Department employees would be time-consuming, costly, and unproductive." *Id.* When considering what a reasonable burden to impose on the Plaintiff prior to compelling a reporter to disclose the reporter's source would be, the Circuit has suggested that the taking of 25 depositions would be a reasonable prerequisite to compelled disclosure. *Carey*, 492 F.2d at 639; *see also Zerilli*, 656 F.2d at 714 (suggesting that 60 depositions is a reasonable burden to impose on a Plaintiff). Additionally, as a District Court within this Circuit stated in *Tavoulareas*, "making disclosure of sources the end point of discovery rather than the beginning serves that additional purpose of assuring a context in which the Court can meaningfully assess whether the identities of the sources are crucial, important, or even relevant to the plaintiff's case before issuing an order compelling their disclosure." 93 F.R.D. at 17. Only when the journalist appears to be the only individual with the relevant and critical information has the journalist been required to disclose the source of the information. *See PPM America v. Marriott Corp.*, 152 F.R.D. 32, 34-36 (S.D.N.Y. 1993); *N.L.R.B. v. Mortenson*, 701 F. Supp. at 248.

Plaintiff has engaged in minimal discovery, choosing instead to directly seek Jontz' deposition. While the Plaintiff submits that Jontz' deposition will "narrow some of the plaintiff's discovery," and that there is no one else with the access to the relevant information, the D.C. Circuit has summarily rejected these arguments in favor of upholding the "reporter's privilege." *See, e.g., Clyburn v. News World Communications, Inc.*, No. CIV.A. 86-1149, 1988 WL 489658, at *7 (D.D.C. April 14, 1988) (stating that Plaintiff's futility argument is "without any legal basis"), *aff'd*, 284 U.S. App. D.C. 212, 903 F.2d 29 (D.C. Cir. 1990). The DOD had identified Glenn, the personnel manager for the Directorate of the Conference Center at the Marshall Center, and whom the plaintiff has now deposed, as someone who may be able to assist the Plaintiff by identifying the names of individuals who may have had knowledge of Tripp's application. Since Ms. Jontz' motion for a protective order was filed, plaintiff has not informed the Court that this deposition was futile. Plaintiff could also depose employees in the DOD and Office of Personnel Management's personnel and records departments, as well as Marshall Center employees who have access to personnel files or employment applications, in an effort to determine who may have provided information to Jontz prior to her call to the Center.

It is therefore clear that plaintiff has not exhausted all reasonable alternative sources of information regarding Jontz' sources, and cannot, at this stage in the litigation, overcome Jontz' assertion of "reporter's privilege." Accordingly, the Court will grant the motion for a protective order. To be sure, plaintiff remains free to seek reconsideration of the Court's Order upon completion of further discovery.

III. Conclusion

Upon careful consideration of the pending motion for a protective Order, the responses and reply thereto, the governing statutory and case law, and the entire record herein, it is by the Court hereby ORDERED that the motion is hereby GRANTED, and Ms. Sandra Jontz is entitled to invoke the reporter's privilege in response to plaintiff's discovery requests regarding her sources for the article at issue.

* * * * *

IN RE: GRAND JURY SUBPOENA, JUDITH MILLER

United States Court of Appeals for the District of Columbia Circuit

No. 04-3138, Consolidated with 04-3139, 04-3140, 397 F.3d 964

February 15, 2005

An investigative reporter for the *New York Times*; the White House correspondent for the weekly news magazine Time; and Time, Inc., the publisher of Time, appeal from orders of the District Court for the District of Columbia finding all three appellants in civil contempt for refusing to give evidence in response to grand jury subpoenas served by Special Counsel Patrick J. Fitzgerald. Appellants assert that the information concealed by them, specifically the identity of confidential sources, is protected by a reporter's privilege arising from the First Amendment, or failing that, by federal common law privilege. The District Court held that neither the First Amendment nor the federal common law provides protection for journalists' confidential sources in the context of a grand jury investigation. For the reasons set forth below, we agree with the District Court that there is no First Amendment privilege protecting the evidence sought. We further conclude that if any such common law privilege exists, it is not absolute, and in this case has been overcome by the filings of the Special Counsel with the District Court. We further conclude that other assignments of error raised by appellants are without merit. We therefore affirm the decision of the District Court.

I. Background

According to the briefs and record before us, the controversy giving rise to this litigation began with a political and news media controversy over a sixteen-word sentence in the State of the Union Address of President George W. Bush on January 28, 2003. In that address, President Bush stated: "The British government has learned that Saddam Hussein recently sought significant quantities of uranium from Africa." The ensuing public controversy focused not on the British source of the alleged information, but rather on the accuracy of the proposition that Saddam Hussein had sought uranium, a key ingredient in the development of nuclear weaponry, from Africa. Many publications on the subject followed. On July 6, 2003, the *New York Times* published an op-ed piece by former Ambassador Joseph Wilson, in which he claimed to have been sent to Niger in 2002 by the Central Intelligence Agency ("CIA") in response to inquiries from Vice President Cheney to investigate whether Iraq had been seeking to purchase uranium from Niger. Wilson claimed that he had conducted the requested investigation and reported on his return that there was no credible evidence that any such effort had been made.

On July 14, 2003, columnist Robert Novak published a column in the *Chicago Sun-Times* in which he asserted that the decision to send Wilson to Niger had been made "routinely without Director George Tenet's knowledge," and, most significant to the present litigation, that "two senior administration officials" told him that Wilson's selection was at the suggestion of Wilson's wife, Valerie Plame, whom Novak described as a CIA "operative on weapons of mass destruction." Robert Novak, *The Mission to Niger*, Chi. Sun-Times, July 14, 2003, at 31. After Novak's column was published, various media accounts reported that other reporters had been told by government officials that Wilson's wife worked at the CIA monitoring weapons of mass destruction, and that she was involved in her husband's selection

31

for the mission to Niger. One such article, published by Time.com on July 17, 2003, was authored in part by appellant Matthew Cooper. That article stated that:

> Some government officials have noted to *Time* in interviews ... that Wilson's wife, Valerie Plame, is a CIA official who monitors the proliferation of weapons of mass destruction ... [and] have suggested that she was involved in the husband's being dispatched to Niger to investigate reports that Saddam Hussein's government had sought to purchase large quantities of uranium ore....

Matthew Cooper, *et al., A War on Wilson?*, Time.com, *at* <http://www.time.com/time/ nation/article/0,8599,465270,00.html> (Dec. 13, 2004). Other media accounts reported that "two top White House officials called at least six Washington journalists and disclosed the identity and occupation of Wilson's wife." Mike Allen & Dana Priest, *Bush Administration is Focus of Inquiry; CIA Agent's Identity was Leaked to Media*, Wash. Post, Sept. 28, 2003, at A1. The Department of Justice undertook an investigation into whether government employees had violated federal law by the unauthorized disclosure of the identity of a CIA agent. *See, e.g.,* 50 U.S.C. § 421 (criminalizing, *inter alia*, disclosure of the identity of a covert agent by anyone having had authorized access to classified information). ...

In cooperation with Special Counsel [Patrick J.] Fitzgerald, the grand jury conducted an extensive investigation. On May 21, 2004, a grand jury subpoena was issued to appellant Matthew Cooper, seeking testimony and documents related to two specific articles.... [In addition,] on August 12 and August 14, grand jury subpoenas were issued to Judith Miller, seeking documents and testimony related to conversations between her and a specified government official "occurring from on or about July 6, 2003, to on or about July 13, 2003, ... concerning Valerie Plame Wilson (whether referred to by name or by description as the wife of Ambassador Wilson) or concerning Iraqi efforts to obtain uranium." ...

The appellants['] ... first claim is that the First Amendment affords journalists a constitutional right to conceal their confidential sources even against the subpoenas of grand juries. Secondly, they claim that reporters enjoy an evidentiary privilege under the common law to conceal confidential sources. Adjunct to this claim, while denying that the privilege is less than absolute, they argue that if the privilege is in fact qualified, the United States has not overcome the privilege. Thirdly, appellants argue that their due process rights were violated by the Special Counsel's *ex parte* and *in camera* submission of evidence to the court to establish that the United States had overcome any qualified privilege. Finally, they argue that the Special Counsel failed to comply with Department of Justice guidelines for the issuance of subpoenas to journalists, and that the failure to comply is an independent ground for reversal of their contempt conviction. Finding no grounds for relief under the First Amendment, due process clause, or Department of Justice guidelines, and persuaded that any common law privilege that exists would be overcome in this case, we affirm the judgment of the District Court for the reasons set out more fully below.

II. Analysis

A. *The First Amendment Claim*

... [T]here is no material factual distinction between the petitions before the Supreme Court in *Branzburg* and the appeals before us today. Each of the reporters in *Branzburg* claimed to have received communications from sources in confidence, just as the journalists before us claimed to have done. At least one of the petitioners in *Branzburg* had witnessed the commission of crimes. On the record before us, there is at least sufficient allegation to warrant grand jury inquiry that one or both journalists received information concerning the identity of a covert operative of the United States from government employees acting in violation of the law by making the disclosure. Each petitioner in *Branzburg* and each journalist before us claimed or claims the protection of a First Amendment reporter's privilege. The Supreme Court in no uncertain terms rejected the existence of such a privilege. As we said at the outset of this discussion, the Supreme Court has already decided the First Amendment issue before us today.

In rejecting the claim of privilege, the Supreme Court made its reasoning transparent and forceful. The High Court recognized that "the grand jury's authority to subpoena witnesses is not only historic ... but essential to its task." 408 U.S. at 688 (citation omitted). The grand juries and the courts operate under the "longstanding principle that 'the public has a right to every man's evidence,' except for those persons protected by constitutional, common law, or statutory privilege." *Id.* (citations and internal punctuation omitted). The Court then noted that "the only testimonial privilege for unofficial witnesses that is rooted in the Federal Constitution is the Fifth Amendment privilege against compelled self-incrimination." *Id.* at 689-90. The Court then expressly declined "to create another by interpreting the First Amendment to grant newsmen a testimonial privilege that other citizens do not enjoy." *Id.* at 690. In language as relevant to the alleged illegal disclosure of the identity of covert agents as it was to the alleged illegal processing of hashish, the Court stated that it could not "seriously entertain the notion that the First Amendment protects a newsman's agreement to conceal the criminal conduct of his source, or evidence thereof, on the theory that it is better to write about a crime than to do something about it." *Id.* at 692.

Lest there be any mistake as to the breadth of the rejection of the claimed First Amendment privilege, the High Court went on to recognize that "there remain those situations where a source is not engaged in criminal conduct but has information suggesting illegal conduct by others." *Id.* at 693. As to this category of informants, the Court was equally adamant in rejecting the claim of First Amendment privilege:

> We cannot accept the argument that the public interest in possible
> future news about crime from undisclosed, unverified sources must
> take precedence over the public interest in pursuing and prosecuting
> those crimes reported to the press by informants and in thus deterring
> the commission of such crimes in the future.

Id. at 695.

... We have pressed appellants for some distinction between the facts before the Supreme Court in *Branzburg* and those before us today. They have offered none, nor have we independently found any. Unquestionably, the Supreme Court decided in *Branzburg* that there is no First Amendment privilege protecting journalists from appearing before a grand jury or from testifying before a grand jury or otherwise providing evidence to a grand jury regardless of any confidence promised by the reporter to any source. The Highest Court has spoken and never revisited the question. Without doubt, that is the end of the matter. ...

B. *The Common Law Privilege*

Appellants argue that even if there is no First Amendment privilege protecting their confidential source information, we should recognize a privilege under federal common law, arguing that regardless of whether a federal common law privilege protecting reporters existed in 1972 when *Branzburg* was decided, in the intervening years much has changed. While appellants argue for an absolute privilege under the common law, they wisely recognize the possibility that a court not recognizing such an absolute privilege might nonetheless find a qualified privilege. They therefore also argue that if there is a qualified privilege, then the government has not overcome that qualified privilege. The Court is not of one mind on the existence of a common law privilege. Judge Sentelle would hold that there is no such common law privilege for reasons set forth in a separate opinion. Judge Tatel would hold that there is such a common law privilege. Judge Henderson believes that we need not, and therefore should not, reach that question. However, all believe that if there is any such privilege, it is not absolute and may be overcome by an appropriate showing. All further believe, for the reasons set forth in the separate opinion of Judge Tatel, that if such a privilege applies here, it has been overcome. Therefore, the common law privilege, even if one exists, does not warrant reversal.

C. *The Due Process Argument*

While appellants insist that their privilege is absolute, they assert a secondary line of argument that if their privilege is conditional, then their due process rights have been violated by the refusal of the Special Counsel and the District Court to provide them access to the Special Counsel's secret evidentiary submissions in support of the enforcement of the subpoenas. This argument is without merit. As appellants themselves admit in their brief, this circuit has recognized that "a district court can ensure that [grand jury] secrecy is protected by provisions for sealed, or when necessary *ex parte*, filings." *In re Sealed Case*, 326 U.S. App. D.C. 276, 121 F.3d 729, 757 (D.C. Cir. 1997). Indeed, the rule of grand jury secrecy is so well established that we have noted that "there is a plethora of authority recognizing that the grand jury context presents an unusual setting where privacy and secrecy are the norm." *In re Sealed Case*, 339 U.S. App. D.C. 309, 199 F.3d 522, 526 (D.C. Cir. 2000) (collecting authorities).

As the Supreme Court has reminded us on occasion, "the grand jury is an institution separate from the courts." *United States v. Williams*, 504 U.S. 36, 47, 118 L. Ed. 2d 352, 112 S. Ct. 1735 (1992). The function of that separate institution is to "serve as a kind of buffer or referee between the government and the people." *Id.* The function of the grand jury "depends on 'maintaining the secrecy of the grand jury proceedings in the federal courts.'" *In re Sealed Case*, 199 F.3d at 526 (quoting *United States v. Procter & Gamble Co.*, 356 U.S. 677, 681, 2 L. Ed. 2d 1077, 78 S. Ct. 983 (1958)). The authorities collected in *In re Sealed Case* recite the broad variety of circumstances in which the courts have upheld this grand jury secrecy, a secrecy that has been the persistent rule for grand jury proceedings for at least four hundred years. *See Douglas Oil v. Petrol Stops Northwest*, 441 U.S. 211, 218 n.9, 60 L. Ed. 2d 156, 99 S. Ct. 1667 (1979) ("Since the 17th century, grand jury proceedings have been closed to the public, and records of such proceedings have been kept from the public eye.").

In the *Douglas Oil* decision, the Supreme Court catalogs multiple reasons for preserving the ancient secrecy of the grand jury:

(1) disclosure of pre-indictment proceedings would make many prospective witnesses "hesitant to come forward voluntarily, knowing that those against whom they testify would be aware of that testimony;" (2) witnesses who did appear "would be less likely to testify fully and frankly as they would be open to retribution as well as inducements;" and (3) there "would be the risk that those about to be indicted would flee or would try to influence individual grand jurors to vote against indictment."

In re North (Omnibus Order), 305 U.S. App. D.C. 23, 16 F.3d 1234, 1242 (D.C. Cir., Spec. Div., 1994) (quoting *Douglas Oil Co.*, 441 U.S. at 218-19).

... Assuming for the sake of this case that the general rule of grand jury secrecy is not sufficient to justify the District Court's use of *in camera* and *ex parte* proceedings, we further note that we have approved the use of such a procedure in other cases raising privilege claims. In *In re Sealed Case No. 98-377*, 331 U.S. App. D.C. 385, 151 F.3d 1059 (D.C. Cir. 1998), a case, like this one, involving the use of *in camera* and *ex parte* proceedings in the context of a Rule 6(e) motion by the government, we upheld their use, and in so doing, relied, at least in part, on precedent established in privilege analysis. We observed there that "courts often use *in camera*, *ex parte* proceedings to determine the propriety of a crime fraud exception to the attorney-client privilege when such proceedings are necessary to ensure the secrecy of ongoing grand jury proceedings." *Id.* at 1075 (citing *In re Grand Jury*, 35 V.I. 516, 103 F.3d 1140, 1145 (3d Cir.), *cert. denied sub nom. Roe v. United States*, 520 U.S. 1253, 138 L. Ed. 2d 177, 117 S. Ct. 2412 (1997)). Having previously noted the propriety of the procedures to protect the well-established attorney-client privilege, we are persuaded that a similar protection of grand jury secrecy is appropriate to protect whatever privilege, if any, may exist between a reporter and a confidential source.

We affirm the District Court's ruling on the maintenance of the seal of grand jury secrecy.

D. *Department of Justice Guidelines*

In their final argument for reversal of the District Court's contempt finding, appellants contend that the Special Counsel did not comply with the Department of Justice guidelines for issuing subpoenas to news media and that such failure provides an independent basis for reversal. The District Court expressed its doubt that the DOJ guidelines were enforceable, but found that even if they were, Special Counsel had fully complied with the guidelines. Because we conclude that the guidelines create no enforceable right, we need not reach the question of the Special Counsel's compliance.

The guidelines in question are set forth in 28 C.F.R. § 50.10 and the United States Attorney's Manual, § 9-2.161. Those guidelines provide that subpoenas for testimony by news media must be approved by the Attorney General, a requirement not pertinent in the present case as the Special Counsel had received delegation of all the Attorney General's authority, and should meet the following standards:

(a) "In criminal cases, there should be reasonable grounds to believe, based on information obtained from nonmedia sources, that a crime has occurred, and that the information sought is essential to a successful investigation-particularly with reference to establishing guilt or innocence. The subpoena should not be used to obtain peripheral, nonessential, or speculative information." 28 C.F.R. § 50.10(f)(1).

(b)   Before issuing a subpoena to a member of the news media, all reasonable efforts should be made to obtain the desired information from alternative sources. *Id.* at §§ 50.10(b), 50.10(f)(3);

(c)   Wherever possible, subpoenas should be directed at information regarding a limited subject matter and a reasonably limited period of time. Subpoenas should avoid requiring production of a large volume of unpublished materials and provide reasonable notice of the demand for documents. *Id.* at § 50.10(f)(6);

(d)   "The use of subpoenas to members of the news media should, except under exigent circumstances, be limited to the verification of published information and to such surrounding circumstances as relate to the accuracy of the published information." *Id.* at § 50.10(f)(4); and

(e)   When issuance of a subpoena to a member of the media is contemplated, the government shall pursue negotiations with the relevant media organization. The negotiations should seek accommodation of the interests of the grand jury and the media. Where the nature of the investigation permits, the government should make clear what its needs are in a particular case as well as its willingness to respond to particular problems of the media. *Id.* at § 50.10(c).

However, as the District Court correctly observed, the guidelines expressly state that they do "not create or recognize any legally enforceable right in any person." *Id.* at § 50.10(n). This reservation has been upheld by several federal appellate and district courts. *See In re Special Proceedings*, 373 F.3d 37, 44 n.3 (1st Cir. 2004) (noting that DOJ guidelines state that they do not create legally enforceable rights); *In re Grand Jury Subpoena American Broadcasting Companies, Inc.*, 947 F. Supp. 1314, 1322 (D. Ark. 1996) (declining to quash subpoena based on failure to comply with DOJ regulations, on ground that regulations, by their own terms, confer no rights on media witnesses). *See also In re Grand Jury Proceedings No. 92-4*, 42 F.3d 876, 880 (4th Cir. 1994) (holding that special prosecutor's failure to comply with guidelines regarding issuance of subpoenas to attorney, even if applicable, were not enforceable by witness through motion to quash). The guidelines, not required by any constitutional or statutory provision, *see In re Special Proceedings*, 373 F.3d at 44 n.3, exist to guide the Department's exercise of its discretion in determining whether and when to seek the issuance of subpoenas to reporters, not to confer substantive or procedural benefits upon individual media personnel. *See In re Shain*, 978 F.2d 850, 853 (4th Cir. 1992) (holding reporters have no right to seek enforcement of DOJ guidelines before being compelled to testify) (citing *United States v. Caceres*, 440 U.S. 741, 59 L. Ed. 2d 733, 99 S. Ct. 1465 (1979) (exclusionary rule not applicable to evidence obtained in violation of internal IRS regulations governing electronic surveillance)); *In re Grand Jury Proceedings No. 92-4*, 42 F.3d at 880 (following *In re Shain*, 978 F.2d at 854).

... It is well established that the exercise of prosecutorial discretion is at the very core of the executive function. Courts consistently hesitate to attempt a review of the executive's exercise of that function. *See, e.g., United States v. Armstrong,* 517 U.S. 456, 464-65, 134 L. Ed. 2d 687, 116 S. Ct. 1480 (1996). Federal prosecutors have "broad discretion to enforce the Nation's criminal laws." *Id.* at 464 (internal punctuation and citations omitted). The prosecutor's discretion arises from their designation "as the President's delegates to help him discharge his constitutional responsibility to 'take care that the laws be faithfully executed.'" *Id.* (quoting U.S. Const. art. II, § 3). Given the nature of the guidelines themselves, and the function they govern, we conclude that the guidelines provide no enforceable rights to any individuals, but merely guide the discretion of the prosecutors. We therefore need not reach the question of the Special Counsel's compliance with the guidelines, and again we affirm the decision of the District Court.

III. Conclusion

For the reasons set forth above, the judgment of the District Court is affirmed.

SENTELLE, *Circuit Judge, concurring.*

As noted in the opinion of the court, I write separately to express my differing basis for affirming the District Court on the common law privilege issue. I would hold that reporters refusing to testify before grand juries as to their "confidential sources" enjoy no common law privilege beyond the protection against harassing grand juries conducting groundless investigations that is available to all other citizens. While I understand, and do not actually disagree with, the conclusion of my colleagues that any such privilege enjoyed by the reporters has been overcome by the showing of the United States, and that we therefore need not determine whether such privilege exists, I find this ordering of issues a bit disturbing. To me, the question of the existence of such privilege *vel non* is logically anterior to the quantum of proof necessary to overcome it. While I understand Judge Henderson's theory that she cannot support a privilege afforded by the common law which would not be overcome by the quantum of proof offered by the government, I think it more logical to not reach the quantum question in the absence of a determination as to the existence of the privilege than to proceed the other way around. That said, I fully join the conclusion that we should affirm the District Court's decision to hold the appellants in contempt, unswayed by their claim of protection of common law privilege. I write separately only to explain my reasons for rejecting the theory that such a privilege is known to the common law.

I base my rejection of the common law privilege theory on foundations of precedent, policy, and separation of powers. As to precedent, I find *Branzburg v. Hayes,* 408 U.S. 665, 33 L. Ed. 2d 626, 92 S. Ct. 2646 (1972), to be as dispositive of the question of common law privilege as it is of a First Amendment privilege. While *Branzburg* generally is cited for its constitutional implications, the *Branzburg* Court repeatedly discussed the privilege question in common law terms as well as constitutional. Indeed, the majority opinion by Justice White includes the phrase "common law" no fewer than eight times. More significant than the fact that the Court frequently spoke of the common law is what the Court had to say about it: "at common law, courts consistently refuse to recognize the existence of any privilege authorizing a newsman to refuse to reveal confidential information to a grand jury." *Id.* at 685 (collecting cases).

... Because the Supreme Court rejected the common law privilege, I think it would be at least presumptuous if not overreaching for us to now adopt the privilege. ...

The Supreme Court has rejected a common law privilege for reporters subpoenaed to give evidence to grand juries. In my view that rejection stands unless and until the Supreme Court itself overrules that part of *Branzburg*. Although the appellants argue that other changes in the law since *Branzburg* should lead to an opposite result, I think that argument should appropriately be made to the Supreme Court, not the lower courts.

Even if appellants are correct that we would have the power to adopt such a privilege in the face of the *Branzburg* precedent, I nonetheless would not accept that invitation. Appellants' argument for our authority to adopt the new privilege begins with the Federal Rules of Evidence. Rule 501, enacted by Congress in the Federal Rules of Evidence in 1975, three years after *Branzburg*, rejected an enumeration of specific federal privileges and provided that privileges in federal criminal cases "shall be governed by the principles of the common law as they may be interpreted by the courts of the United States in the light of reason and experience." Although the rules became effective after *Branzburg*, Rule 501 does not effect any change in the authority of federal courts to adopt evidentiary privileges. Before the enactment of the Federal Rules of Evidence, the authority of the federal courts to adopt common law privileges was governed by case law. The relevant case law provided for precisely the same authority as Congress enacted in the rules. Indeed, the language of the rule is drawn directly from case law governing at the time of *Branzburg*. The Supreme Court expressly held in *Wolfle v. United States*, 291 U.S. 7, 78 L. Ed. 617, 54 S. Ct. 279 (1934), that

> the rules governing the competence of witnesses in criminal trials in the federal courts are not necessarily restricted to those local rules enforced at the time of the admission into the union of the particular state where the trial takes place, but are *governed by common law principles as interpreted and applied by the federal courts in the light of reason and experience.*

291 U.S. 7, 12, 78 L. Ed. 617, 54 S. Ct. 279 (1934) (citing *Funk v. United States*, 290 U.S. 371, 78 L. Ed. 369, 54 S. Ct. 212 (1933)) (emphasis added). Given the venerable origins of the language used in Rule 501, it cannot be said that the courts have more power to adopt privileges today than at the time of *Branzburg*. The power is precisely the same. Thus, the enactment of Rule 501 cannot by itself work any change in the law which should empower us to depart from the Supreme Court's clear precedent in *Branzburg*.

....[R]easons of policy and separation of powers counsel against our exercising that authority. While I concede that the adoption of the "shield" by legislation rather than judicial fiat does not prevent the change being considered by the courts in assessing the common law, I find the adoption of the privilege by the legislatures of the states instructive as to how the federal government should proceed, if at all, to adopt the privilege. The statutes differ greatly as to the scope of the privilege, and as to the identity of persons entitled to the protection of the privilege. We have alluded in the majority opinion to the differing decisions of courts as to civil, criminal, and grand jury proceedings. There is also a more fundamental policy question involved in the crafting of such a privilege.

The Supreme Court itself in *Branzburg* noted the difficult and vexing nature of this question, observing that applying such privilege would make it necessary to define those categories of newsmen who qualify for the privilege, a questionable procedure in light of the traditional doctrine that liberty of the press is the right of the lonely pamphleteer who uses carbon paper or a mimeograph just as much as of the large metropolitan publisher who utilizes the latest photocomposition methods.

408 U.S. at 704. The Supreme Court went on to observe that "freedom of the press is a 'fundamental personal right ... not confined to newspapers and periodicals. It necessarily embraces pamphlets and leaflets.... The press in its historic connotation comprehends every sort of publication which affords a vehicle of information and opinion.'" *Id.* (quoting *Lovell v. Griffin*, 303 U.S. 444, 450, 452, 82 L. Ed. 949, 58 S. Ct. 666 (1938)). Are we then to create a privilege that protects only those reporters employed by *Time Magazine*, the *New York Times*, and other media giants, or do we extend that protection as well to the owner of a desktop printer producing a weekly newsletter to inform his neighbors, lodge brothers, co-religionists, or co-conspirators? Perhaps more to the point today, does the privilege also protect the proprietor of a web log: the stereotypical "blogger" sitting in his pajamas at his personal computer posting on the World Wide Web his best product to inform whoever happens to browse his way? If not, why not? How could one draw a distinction consistent with the court's vision of a broadly granted personal right? If so, then would it not be possible for a government official wishing to engage in the sort of unlawful leaking under investigation in the present controversy to call a trusted friend or a political ally, advise him to set up a web log (which I understand takes about three minutes) and then leak to him under a promise of confidentiality the information which the law forbids the official to disclose?

The state legislatures have dealt with this vexing question of entitlement to the privilege in a variety of ways. Some are quite restrictive. Alabama limits its protection to "persons engaged in, connected with, or employed on any newspaper, radio broadcasting station or television station, while engaged in a newsgathering capacity." Ala. Code § 12-21-142. Alaska's statutes protect only the "reporter," a category limited to "persons regularly engaged in the business of collecting or writing news for publication or presentation to the public, through a news organization." Alaska Stat. § 09.25.300. The statutory privilege in Arizona protects "a person engaged in newspaper, radio, television or reportorial work, or connected with or employed by a newspaper or radio or television station...." Ariz. Rev. Stat. § 12-2237. Arkansas's legislature has declared the privilege applicable to "any editor, reporter, or other writer for any newspaper, periodical, or radio station, or publisher of any newspaper or periodical, or manager or owner of any radio station...." Ark. Code Ann. § 16-85-510. Delaware is perhaps the most specific, protecting a "reporter," which

means any journalist, scholar, educator, polemicist, or other individual who either: (a) At the time he or she obtained the information that is sought was earning his or her principal livelihood by, or in each of the preceding 3 weeks or 4 of the preceding 8 weeks had spent at least 20 hours engaged in the practice of, obtaining or preparing information for dissemination with the aid of facilities for the mass reproduction of words, sounds, or images in a form available to the general public; or (b) Obtained the information that is sought while serving in the capacity of an agent, assistant, employee, or supervisor of an individual who qualifies as a reporter under subparagraph a.

Del. Code Ann. tit. 10 § 4320. Presumably, states such as these would provide the privilege only to the "established" press.

Others are quite inclusive. The Nebraska legislature, for example, has declared:

> (1) That the policy of the State of Nebraska is to insure the free flow of news and other information to the public, and that those who gather, write, or edit information for the public or disseminate information to the public may perform these vital functions only in a free and unfettered atmosphere; (2) That such persons shall not be inhibited, directly or indirectly, by governmental restraint or sanction imposed by governmental process, but rather that they shall be encouraged to gather, write, edit, or disseminate news or other information vigorously so that the public may be fully informed.

Neb. Rev. Stat. § 20-144. To that end, it protects any "medium of communication" which term "shall include, *but not be limited to*, any newspaper, magazine, other periodical, book, pamphlet, news service, wire service, news or feature syndicate, broadcast station or network, or cable television system." *Id.* at § 20-145(2) (emphasis added).

In defining the persons protected by that privilege, Nebraska tells us that "Person shall mean any individual, partnership, limited liability company, corporation, association, or other legal entity existing under or authorized by the law of the United States, any state or possession of the United States, the District of Columbia, the Commonwealth of Puerto Rico, or any foreign country." *Id.* at 20-145(7). Presumably, then, Nebraska, perhaps more in keeping with the spirit of the recent revolutionaries who gave us the First Amendment, protects the pamphleteer at the rented printer, and the blogger at the PC, as well as the giant corporation with its New York publishing house.

The variety of legislative choices among the states only serves to heighten the concern expressed by the majority in *Branzburg*. *See* 408 U.S. at 704. This concern is reinforced by examination of the *Jaffee* decision, upon which appellants rely. In *Jaffee*, the Supreme Court extended a federal privilege "to confidential communications made to licensed social workers in the course of psychotherapy." 518 U.S. at 15. There is little definitional problem with the application of this privilege. The court need only ask: Does this "social worker" have a license? If the answer is "yes," then the privilege applies; if it's "no," the privilege does not. If the courts extend the privilege only to a defined group of reporters, are we in danger of creating a "licensed" or "established" press? If we do so, have we run afoul of the breadth of the freedom of the press, that "fundamental personal right" for which the Court in *Branzburg* expressed its concern? 408 U.S. at 704. Conversely, if we extend that privilege to the easily created blog, or the ill-defined pamphleteer, have we defeated legitimate investigative ends of grand juries in cases like the leak of intelligence involved in the present investigation?

Nor does the identity of the protected persons constitute the only difficult policy decision. *Branzburg* enumerates several concerns. For example, does "the public interest and possible future news about crime from undisclosed, unverified sources ... take precedence over the public interest in pursuing and prosecuting those crimes reported to the press by informants and in thus deterring the commission of such crimes in the future"? *Id.* at 695. Do "agreements to conceal information relevant to the commission of crime avail little to recommend them from the standpoint of public policy"? *Id.* at 696. What are we to do with the historic common law recognition of "a duty to raise the 'hue and cry' and report felonies to the authorities"? *Id.* (*see also* authorities collected in *id.* at 696 n.34). Should we be creating immunity from prosecution for "misprision" of a felony -- that is, the concealment of a felony? *Id.* at 696.

Should the privilege be absolute or limited? If limited, how limited? Without attempting to catalog, I note that the state statutes provide a variety of answers to that policy question. Therefore, if such a decision requires the resolution of so many difficult policy questions, many of them beyond the normal compass of a single case or controversy such as those with which the courts regularly deal, doesn't that decision smack of legislation more than adjudication? Here, I think the experience of the states is most instructive. The creation of a reporter's privilege, if it is to be done at all, looks more like a legislative than an adjudicative decision. I suggest that the media as a whole, or at least those elements of the media concerned about this privilege, would better address those concerns to the Article I legislative branch for presentment to the Article II executive than to the Article III courts.

For all the reasons set forth above, I would hold that there is no common law privilege protecting reporters or any other news media personnel, no matter how defined, from the reach of grand jury subpoenas on claim of confidentiality.

HENDERSON, *Circuit Judge, concurring*

I write separately to emphasize that adherence to the principle of judicial restraint -- patience in judicial decision-making -- would produce a better result in II.B of the majority opinion. Because my colleagues and I agree that any federal common-law reporter's privilege that may exist is not absolute and that the Special Counsel's evidence defeats whatever privilege we may fashion, we need not, and therefore should not, decide anything more today than that the Special Counsel's evidentiary proffer overcomes any hurdle, however high, a federal common-law reporter's privilege may erect.

In our circuit it is a venerable practice, and one frequently observed, to assume *arguendo* the answer to one question -- *e.g.*, whether to recognize a federal common-law reporter's privilege -- in order to resolve a given case by answering another and equally dispositive one -- *e.g.*, whether *any* privilege would protect these reporters. Although both of my colleagues question the logic of this approach here, it is a mode of decision-making they themselves have often used. In this case, however, they employ two divergent forms of "wide-angle adjudication." *See* Harry T. Edwards, *The Role of the Judge in Modern Society: Some Reflections on Current Practices in Federal Appellate Adjudication*, 32 CLEV. ST. L. REV. 385, 414 (1983-84). Judge Sentelle would hold that a reporter enjoys no federal common-law privilege to refuse to provide a *bona fide* grand jury with relevant documents and testimony while Judge Tatel would fix the contours of a qualified reporter's privilege by using a novel multi-factor balancing test only to conclude that it helps these reporters not at all.

While I am convinced that we need not, and therefore should not, go further than to conclude, as did the district court, that the Special Counsel's showing decides the case, I feel compelled to comment briefly on my colleagues' opposing conclusions if only to make clear why I think it unwise to advance either of them. I cannot agree with Judge Sentelle's conclusion that the United States Supreme Court has answered the question we now avoid. *Branzburg v. Hayes* addressed only "whether requiring newsmen to appear and testify before state or federal grand juries abridges the freedom of speech and press guaranteed by the *First Amendment*" and "held that *it* does not." 408 U.S. 665, 667, 33 L. Ed. 2d 626, 92 S. Ct. 2646 (1972) (emphases added). The boundaries of constitutional law and common law do not necessarily coincide, however, and while we are unquestionably bound by *Branzburg*'s rejection of a reporter's privilege rooted in the First Amendment, we are not bound by *Branzburg*'s commentary on the state of the common law in 1972. Federal Rule of Evidence 501, which came into being nearly three years after *Branzburg*, authorizes federal courts to develop testimonial privileges "in the light of reason and experience," allowing for the often evolving state of the common law. *See* Fed. R. Evid. 501; *Trammel v. United States*, 445 U.S. 40, 47, 63 L. Ed. 2d 186, 100 S. Ct. 906 (1980) ("In rejecting the proposed Rules and enacting Rule 501, Congress manifested an affirmative intention not to freeze the law of privilege."); *see id.* ("The Federal Rules of Evidence acknowledge the authority of the federal courts to continue the evolutionary development of testimonial privileges."). Judge Sentelle's view also discounts the fact that, even as they rejected a reporter's First Amendment right to withhold testimony from a bona fide grand jury, both the *Branzburg* majority opinion as well as Justice Powell's separate concurrence hint ambiguously at the existence of some special protection for reporters stemming from their significant role in sustaining our republican form of government.

At the same time, I am far less eager a federal common-law pioneer than Judge Tatel as I find less comfort than he in riding *Jaffee v. Redmond*, 518 U.S. 1, 135 L. Ed. 2d 337, 116 S. Ct. 1923 (1996), into the testimonial privilege frontier. Just as Rule 501 imposes no "freeze" on the development of the common law, *see Univ. of Penn. v. EEOC*, 493 U.S. 182, 189, 107 L. Ed. 2d 571, 110 S. Ct. 577 (1990); *Trammel*, 445 U.S. at 47, it likewise does not authorize federal courts to mint testimonial privileges for any group -- including the "journalistic class," as Judge Sentelle dubs it, -- that demands one. The Supreme Court has warned that testimonial privileges "are not lightly created nor expansively construed, for they are in derogation of the search for truth." *United States v. Nixon*, 418 U.S. 683, 710, 41 L. Ed. 2d 1039, 94 S. Ct. 3090 (1974); *see Branzburg*, 408 U.S. at 690; *see also Jaffee*, 518 U.S. at 21 (Scalia, J., dissenting). Accordingly, we should proceed as cautiously as possible "when erecting barriers between us and the truth," *id.* recognizing that the Legislature remains the more appropriate institution to reconcile the competing interests -- prosecuting criminal acts versus constricting the flow of information to the public -- that inform any reporter's privilege to withhold relevant information from a bona fide grand jury. *See Univ. of Penn.*, 493 U.S. at 189.

Because *Jaffee* sits rather awkwardly within a jurisprudence marked by a fairly uniform disinclination to announce new privileges or even expand existing ones, and even though it enjoyed the support of an overwhelming majority, I am hesitant to apply its methodology to a case that does not require us to do so. While it would not be the first of its kind, *see Lemon v. Kurtzman*, 403 U.S. 602, 29 L. Ed. 2d 745, 91 S. Ct. 2105 (1971) ("*Lemon* test"); *cf. Elk Grove Unified Sch. Dist. v. Newdow*, 159 L. Ed. 2d 98, __ U.S. __, 124 S. Ct. 2301, 2327 n.1 (2004) ("We have selectively invoked particular tests, such as the '*Lemon* test,' with predictable outcomes." (internal citation omitted)) (Thomas, J., concurring in judgment), the type of multi-factor balancing test Judge Tatel proposes seems, at least to me, to lack analytical rigor because its application to this case is foreordained. Indeed, I am not convinced that a balancing test that requires more than an evaluation of the essentiality of the information to the prosecution and the exhaustion of available alternative sources thereof is either useful or appropriate. While Judge Tatel makes the centerpiece of his test the balancing of "the public interest in compelling disclosure, measured by the harm the leak caused, against the public interest in newsgathering, measured by the leaked information's value," this court (in the civil context), the United States Department of Justice and the lone district court that has recognized a federal common-law reporter's privilege in the grand jury context have declined to consider either of these factors in deciding whether to recognize a reporter's exemption from compulsory process. There is a good reason for this: I suspect that balancing "harm" against "news value" may prove unproductive because in most of the projected scenarios -- leaks of information involving, for example, military operations, national security, policy choices or political adversaries -- the two interests overlap. Furthermore, *Branzburg* warns of the risk inherent in the judicial assessment of the importance of prosecuting particular crimes. *See* 408 U.S. at 706 ("By requiring testimony from a reporter in investigations involving some crimes but not in others, [the courts] would be making a value judgment that a legislature had declined to make, since in each case the criminal law involved would represent a considered legislative judgment, not constitutionally suspect, of what conduct is liable to criminal prosecution. The task of judges, like other officials outside the legislative branch, is not to make the law but to uphold it in accordance with their oaths."). And any evaluation of the importance of newsgathering keyed to its perceived "benefit" to the public, seems antithetical to our nation's abiding commitment to the uninhibited trade in ideas. *See, e.g., Riley v. National Federation of Blind, Inc.,* 487 U.S. 781, 790-91, 101 L. Ed. 2d 669, 108 S. Ct. 2667 (1988) ("The First Amendment mandates that we presume that speakers, not the government, know best both what they want to say and how to say it."); *Cohen v. California,* 403 U.S. 15, 24, 29 L. Ed. 2d 284, 91 S. Ct. 1780 (1971) ("The constitutional right of free expression is ... designed and intended to remove governmental restraints from the arena of public discussion, putting the decision as to what views shall be voiced largely into the hands of each of us."); *McConnell v. FEC,* 251 F. Supp. 2d 176, 266 (D.D.C. 2003) ("The First Amendment delegates to the populace at large the responsibility of conducting an 'uninhibited, robust, and wide-open' debate." (quoting *New York Times Co. v. Sullivan,* 376 U.S. 254, 270, 11 L. Ed. 2d 686, 84 S. Ct. 710 (1964))); *cf. Gertz v. Welch, Inc.,* 418 U.S. 323, 346, 41 L. Ed. 2d 789, 94 S. Ct. 2997 (1974). Moreover, to attempt to establish the contours of a reporter's privilege here would tend, unnecessarily, to leave a future panel less maneuverability in a case that might require just that to achieve justice. On this score, Judge Tatel levels the identical charge against my approach, but I fail to see how declining to decide whether a reporter's privilege exists or to define its contours could confine a future panel.

For the foregoing reasons, I am convinced that the court would chart the best course by charting the narrowest one and, accordingly, concur only in the judgment with respect to II.B of the majority opinion. In all other respects, I fully concur.

TATEL, *Circuit Judge,* concurring in the judgment

This case involves a clash between two truth-seeking institutions: the grand jury and the press. On the one hand, the grand jury, a body "deeply rooted in Anglo-American history" and guaranteed by the Fifth Amendment, *see United States v. Calandra,* 414 U.S. 338, 342-43, 38 L. Ed. 2d 561, 94 S. Ct. 613 (1974), holds "broad powers" to collect evidence through judicially enforceable subpoenas. *See United States v. Sells Eng'g, Inc.,* 463 U.S. 418, 423-24, 77 L. Ed. 2d 743, 103 S. Ct. 3133 (1983). "Without thorough and effective investigation, the grand jury would be unable either to ferret out crimes deserving of prosecution, or to screen out charges not warranting prosecution." *Id.* at 424. On the other hand, the press, shielded by the First Amendment, "has been a mighty catalyst in awakening public interest in governmental affairs, exposing corruption among public officers and employees and generally informing the citizenry of public events and occurrences." *Estes v. Texas*, 381 U.S. 532, 539, 14 L. Ed. 2d 543, 85 S. Ct. 1628 (1965). Using language we have quoted with approval, *see Carey v. Hume*, 160 U.S. App. D.C. 365, 492 F.2d 631, 634-35 (D.C. Cir. 1974), the Second Circuit aptly described this conflict between press freedom and the rule of law: "Freedom of the press, hard-won over the centuries by men of courage, is basic to a free society. But basic too are courts of justice, armed with the power to discover truth. The concept that it is the duty of a witness to testify in a court of law has roots fully as deep in our history as does the guarantee of a free press." *Garland v. Torre*, 259 F.2d 545, 548 (2d Cir. 1958).

Because I agree that the balance in this case, which involves the alleged exposure of a covert agent, favors compelling the reporters' testimony, I join the judgment of the court. I write separately, however, because I find *Branzburg v. Hayes*, 408 U.S. 665, 33 L. Ed. 2d 626, 92 S. Ct. 2646 (1972), more ambiguous than do my colleagues and because I believe that the consensus of forty-nine states plus the District of Columbia -- and even the Department of Justice -- would require us to protect reporters' sources as a matter of federal common law were the leak at issue either less harmful or more newsworthy.

I.

Although I join the court's rejection of appellants' First Amendment argument, I am uncertain that *Branzburg* offers "no support" for a constitutional reporter privilege in the grand jury context. To be sure, *Branzburg* upheld the enforcement of subpoenas seeking confidential source information, including notes and testimony about interviews and observations at a militant group's headquarters. *See* 408 U.S. at 672-77. Yet even the *Branzburg* majority declared that "news gathering is not without its First Amendment protections," *id.* at 707, a phrase we have interpreted (albeit in dictum) to "indicate[] that a qualified privilege would be available in some circumstances even where a reporter is called before a grand jury to testify," *Zerilli v. Smith*, 211 U.S. App. D.C. 116, 656 F.2d 705, 711 (D.C. Cir. 1981). *Branzburg*'s caveat, placed in a discussion of "official harassment of the press" and "grand jury investigations ... instituted or conducted other than in good faith," *Branzburg*, 408 U.S. at 707-08, seems to refer only to journalists' power to quash "unreasonable or oppressive" subpoenas, *see* Fed. R. Crim. P. 17(c)(2). But given that any witness -- journalist or otherwise -- may challenge such a subpoena, the majority must have meant, at the very least, that the First Amendment demands a broader notion of "harassment" for journalists than for other witnesses. Reinforcing that view, the majority added, "We do not expect courts will forget that grand juries must operate within the limits of the First Amendment as well as the Fifth." *Branzburg*, 408 U.S. at 708. That prediction, too, would appear meaningless if no First Amendment safeguards existed for subpoenaed reporters.

Then there is Justice Powell's "enigmatic concurring opinion." *Id.* at 725 (Stewart, J., dissenting). Though providing the majority's essential fifth vote, he wrote separately to outline a "case-by-case" approach, *see id.* at 710 (Powell, J., concurring), that fits uncomfortably, to say the least, with the majority's categorical rejection of the reporters' claims. Emphasizing "the limited nature of the Court's holding," *id.* at 709, he wrote:

> The asserted claim to privilege should be judged on its facts by the striking of a proper balance between freedom of the press and the obligation of all citizens to give relevant testimony with respect to criminal conduct. The balance of these vital constitutional and societal

interests on a case-by-case basis accords with the tried and traditional way of adjudicating such questions.

Id. at 710. "In short," Justice Powell concluded, "the courts will be available to newsmen under circumstances where legitimate First Amendment interests require protection." *Id.* Even more than the majority opinion, this language places limits on grand jury authority to demand information about source identities -- though, again, the precise extent of those limits seems unclear.

Given *Branzburg*'s internal confusion and the "obvious First Amendment problems" involved in "compelling a reporter to disclose the identity of a confidential source," *Zerilli*, 656 F.2d at 710, it is hardly surprising that lower courts have, as Chief Judge Hogan put it, "chipped away at the holding of *Branzburg*," finding constitutional protections for reporters in "various factual scenarios different than those presented in *Branzburg*." *In re Special Counsel Investigation*, 332 F. Supp. 2d 26, 31 (D.D.C. 2004). We ourselves have affirmed the denial of a criminal defense subpoena on grounds that the defendant "failed to carry his burden" of "demonstrating that the reporters' qualified privilege should be overcome." *United States v. Ahn*, 343 U.S. App. D.C. 392, 231 F.3d 26, 37 (D.C. Cir. 2000). In civil litigation, moreover, we have held that the First Amendment requires courts to "look to the facts on a case-by-case basis in the course of weighing the need for the testimony in question against the claims of the newsman that the public's right to know is impaired." *Carey*, 492 F.2d at 636; *see also Zerilli*, 656 F.2d at 707 (affirming the denial of a motion to compel discovery because "in this case the First Amendment interest in protecting a news reporter's sources outweighs the interest in compelled disclosure"). Other circuits have reached similar conclusions. *See, e.g., United States v. LaRouche Campaign*, 841 F.2d 1176, 1180-81 (1st Cir. 1988) (acknowledging First Amendment limits on criminal defense subpoenas directed at news organizations); *United States v. Burke*, 700 F.2d 70, 76-77 (2d Cir. 1983) (extending a First Amendment reporter privilege developed in civil cases to a criminal defense subpoena); *Bruno & Stillman, Inc. v. Globe Newspaper Co.*, 633 F.2d 583, 593-99 (1st Cir. 1980) (describing First Amendment limits on discovery of reporters' sources in civil litigation); *Silkwood v. Kerr-McGee Corp.*, 563 F.2d 433, 436-37 (10th Cir. 1977) (indicating that a qualified newsgathering privilege "is no longer in doubt"); *but see In re Grand Jury Proceedings*, 810 F.2d 580, 584-85 (6th Cir. 1987) (rejecting claims of First Amendment privilege in grand jury proceedings).

In this case, however, our hands are tied for two independent reasons. First, although this circuit has limited *Branzburg* in other contexts, *see Zerilli*, 656 F.2d at 707; *Carey*, 492 F.2d at 636; *Ahn*, 231 F.3d at 37, with respect to criminal investigations we have twice construed that decision broadly. In *Reporters Committee for Freedom of the Press v. AT&T*, 192 U.S. App. D.C. 376, 593 F.2d 1030 (D.C. Cir. 1978), which addressed a First Amendment challenge regarding access to journalists' phone records and describing *Branzburg* as foreclosing "case-by-case consideration," we declared, "Good faith investigation interests *always* override a journalist's interest in protecting his source." *Id.* at 1049 (emphasis added). Echoing this broad view, we have also described *Branzburg* as "squarely rejecting" a claim to "general immunity, qualified or otherwise, from grand jury questioning." *See In re Possible Violations of 18 U.S.C. 371, 641, 1503*, 84 U.S. App. D.C. 82, 564 F.2d 567, 571 (D.C. Cir. 1977). In this circuit, then, absent any indication of bad faith, I see no grounds for a First Amendment challenge to the subpoenas at issue here.

Second, although *Branzburg* involved militants and drug dealers rather than government leakers, the factual parallels between that case and this one preclude us from quashing the subpoenas on constitutional grounds. If, as *Branzburg* concludes, the First Amendment permits compulsion of reporters' testimony about individuals manufacturing drugs or plotting against the government, *see* 408 U.S. at 667-69, 675-77, all information the government could have obtained from an undercover investigation of its own, the case for a constitutional privilege appears weak indeed with respect to leaks, which in all likelihood will be extremely difficult to prove without the reporter's aid. Thus, if *Branzburg* is to be limited or distinguished in the circumstances of this case, we must leave that task to the Supreme Court.

II.

But *Branzburg* is not the end of the story. In 1975 -- three years after *Branzburg* -- Congress enacted Rule 501 of the Federal Rules of Evidence, authorizing federal courts to develop evidentiary privileges in federal question cases according to "the principles of the common law as they may be interpreted ... in the light of reason and experience." Fed. R. Evid. 501; *see also* Pub. L. No. 93-595, 88 Stat. 1926 (1975). Given *Branzburg's* instruction that "Congress has freedom to determine whether a statutory newsman's privilege is necessary and desirable and to fashion standards and rules as narrow or broad as deemed necessary to deal with the evil discerned," 408 U.S. at 706, Rule 501's delegation of congressional authority requires that we look anew at the "necessity and desirability" of the reporter privilege -- though from a common law perspective.

Under Rule 501, that common lawmaking obligation exists whether or not, absent the rule's delegation, Congress would be "the more appropriate institution to reconcile the competing interests ... that inform any reporter's privilege to withhold relevant information from a bona fide grand jury." (Henderson, J., concurring) (citing *Univ. of Pa. v. EEOC*, 493 U.S. 182, 189, 107 L. Ed. 2d 571, 110 S. Ct. 577 (1990)); *but see* (Sentelle, J., concurring) (observing that even before Rule 501, case law provided federal courts with "precisely the same authority" to recognize common law privileges) (citing *Wolfle v. United States*, 291 U.S. 7, 12, 78 L. Ed. 617, 54 S. Ct. 279 (1934)); *Univ. of Pa.*, 493 U.S. at 189 (declining to recognize a privilege "where it appears that Congress has considered the relevant competing concerns but has not provided the privilege itself"). As the Supreme Court has explained, "Rule 501 was adopted precisely because Congress wished to leave privilege questions to the courts rather than attempt to codify them." *United States v. Weber Aircraft Corp.*, 465 U.S. 792, 803 n.25, 79 L. Ed. 2d 814, 104 S. Ct. 1488 (1984). Thus, subject of course to congressional override, we must assess the arguments for and against the claimed privilege, just as the Supreme Court has done in cases recognizing common law privileges since 1975. *See, e.g., Jaffee v. Redmond*, 518 U.S. 1, 15, 135 L. Ed. 2d 337, 116 S. Ct. 1923 (1996) (psychotherapist-patient); *Upjohn Co. v. United States*, 449 U.S. 383, 389, 66 L. Ed. 2d 584, 101 S. Ct. 677 (1981) (attorney-client); *Trammel v. United States*, 445 U.S. 40, 51, 63 L. Ed. 2d 186, 100 S. Ct. 906 (1980) (confidential marital communications).

In this case, just as *Jaffee v. Redmond* recognized a common law psychotherapist privilege based on "the uniform judgment of the States," 518 U.S. at 14, I believe that "reason and experience" dictate a privilege for reporters' confidential sources -- albeit a qualified one. Guided by *Jaffee's* reasoning, I reach this conclusion by considering first whether "reason and experience" justify recognizing a privilege at all, and if so whether the privilege should be qualified or absolute and whether it should cover the communications at issue in this case.

... Unless we conclude, as does Judge Sentelle (Sentelle, J., concurring), and as did the district court, *see In re Special Counsel Investigation*, 338 F. Supp. 2d 16, 18-19 (D.D.C. 2004), that no privilege exists, we cannot resolve this case without adopting *some* standard. Judge Henderson criticizes my approach, but she never indicates what standard she would apply, except to state that "the Special Counsel's evidentiary proffer overcomes any hurdle, however high, a federal common-law reporter's privilege may erect." (Henderson, J., concurring). To reach even that conclusion, however, one must explain why federal common law cannot support any higher "hurdle," such as an absolute privilege for source identities, which exists in the District of Columbia and several states, *see, e.g.,* D.C. Code Ann. §§ 16-4702, 16-4703(b); 42 Pa. Cons. Stat. § 5942; Ala. Code § 12-21-142, or a privilege that applies unless non-disclosure "will cause a miscarriage of justice," N.D. Cent. Code § 31-01-06.2; *see also* Minn. Stat. § 595.024; N.M. Stat. Ann. § 38-6-7. Without ruling out all such plausible alternatives that would allow the reporters to prevail, how could one know that they cannot prevail here? And without selecting some other test based on *Jaffee* and Rule 501, how could one know that no such alternatives are plausible?

Because the *Jaffee* analysis is thus essential to resolving this case (assuming a privilege exists), our frequent practice of avoiding non-essential issues is inapplicable. ...

Accordingly, given that we must apply some test to the government's showing, if we simply assume the privilege exists but our assumption is wrong, then we will have reached out to establish a framework for a non-existent claim--an undertaking hardly consistent with principles of judicial restraint. Indeed, our decision would establish a precedent, potentially binding on future panels, regarding the scope of the assumed privilege, even though resolving that question was entirely unnecessary. Therefore, I think it imperative to decide as a threshold matter whether the privilege exists, turning only afterwards to the privilege's specific contours.

In this case, moreover, the issue of the privilege's existence is fully briefed, and resolving it definitively will provide critical guidance in similar situations in the future. ...

Existence of the Privilege

Under *Jaffee*, the common law analysis starts with the interests that call for recognizing a privilege. *See* 518 U.S. at 11. If, as the Supreme Court held there, "the mental health of our citizenry is a public good of transcendent importance," *id.* -- one that trumps the "fundamental maxim that the public has a right to every man's evidence," *id.* at 9 (internal quotation marks and ellipsis omitted) -- then surely press freedom is no less important, given journalism's vital role in our democracy. Indeed, while the *Jaffee* dissenters questioned psychotherapy's "indispensable role in the maintenance of the citizenry's mental health," *see id.* at 22 (Scalia, J., dissenting), the First Amendment's express protection for "freedom ... of the press" forecloses any debate about that institution's "important role in the discussion of public affairs," *Mills v. Alabama*, 384 U.S. 214, 219, 16 L. Ed. 2d 484, 86 S. Ct. 1434 (1966). "Whatever differences may exist about interpretations of the First Amendment, there is practically universal agreement that a major purpose of that Amendment was to protect the free discussion of governmental affairs." *Brown v. Hartlage*, 456 U.S. 45, 52, 71 L. Ed. 2d 732, 102 S. Ct. 1523 (1982) (quoting *Mills*, 384 U.S. at 218-19).

....[A]s with other privileges, "the likely evidentiary benefit that would result from the denial of the privilege is modest." [*Jaffee*, 518 U.S. at 12.] At the same time, although suppression of some leaks is surely desirable (a point to which I shall return), the public harm that would flow from undermining all source relationships would be immense. For example, appellant Judith Miller tells us that her Pulitzer Prize-winning articles on Osama bin Laden's terrorist network relied on "information received from confidential sources at the highest levels of our government." Likewise, appellant Matthew Cooper maintains that his reports for "*Time*'s four million-plus readers about White House policy in Iraq, the chances of passage of major legislation such as Budget and Energy Bills, and the Clinton White House" would have been impossible without confidentiality. Insofar as such stories exemplify the press's role "as a constitutionally chosen means for keeping officials elected by the people responsible to all the people whom they were elected to serve," *Mills*, 384 U.S. at 219, "reason and experience" support protecting newsgathering methods crucial to their genesis. Acknowledging as much in *Zerilli*, we emphasized that "compelling a reporter to disclose the identity of a source may significantly interfere with this news gathering ability" and weaken "a vital source of information," leaving citizens "far less able to make informed political, social, and economic choices." 656 F.2d at 711.

....[T]he special counsel's confidence that exposing sources will have no effect on newsgathering is unjustified. Citing the "'symbiotic' relationships between journalists and public officials," the special counsel presumes that leaks will go on with or without the privilege. Not only does this contradict the Justice Department's own guidelines, which expressly recognize that revealing confidential sources can "impair the news gathering function," 28 C.F.R. § 50.10, but the available evidence suggests the special counsel is wrong. As anyone with even a passing interest in news knows, reporters routinely rely on sources speaking on condition of anonymity -- a strong indication that leakers demand such protection. Besides, for all the reasons that lead me to conclude that a privilege exists, reporters and their editors, attorneys, and sources probably believe the same, making it speculative indeed for the special counsel to suppose that dashing that expectation of confidentiality would have no effect on newsgathering.

Turning next, as did *Jaffee*, to the consensus among states, I find support for the privilege at least as strong for journalists as for psychotherapists. Just as in *Jaffee*, where "the fact that all 50 states and the District of Columbia have enacted into law some form of psychotherapist privilege" favored an exercise of federal common lawmaking, *see* 518 U.S. at 12, so here undisputed evidence that forty-nine states plus the District of Columbia offer at least qualified protection to reporters' sources confirms that "'reason and experience' support recognition of the privilege," *id.* at 13. Indeed, given these state laws, "denial of the federal privilege ... would frustrate the purposes of the state legislation" by exposing confidences protected under state law to discovery in federal courts. *See id.*

Making the case for a privilege here even stronger than in *Jaffee*, federal authorities also favor recognizing a privilege for reporters' confidential sources. As noted earlier, we ourselves have limited discovery of reporters' sources in both civil and criminal litigation, *see Zerilli*, 656 F.2d at 707; *Carey*, 492 F.2d at 636; *Ahn*, 231 F.3d at 37, as have other federal courts, *see, e.g., Bruno & Stillman*, 633 F.2d at 593-99; *Burke*, 700 F.2d at 76-77; *Silkwood*, 563 F.2d at 436-37, including some acting on the basis of Rule 501, *see, e.g., Riley v. City of Chester*, 612 F.2d 708, 715 (3d Cir. 1979) (recognizing a qualified common law privilege in civil litigation); *but see In re Grand Jury Proceedings*, 5 F.3d 397, 398 (9th Cir. 1993) (holding that no "scholar's privilege" exists under the First Amendment or common law). In addition, the Justice Department guidelines (though privately unenforceable, for reasons the court explains) establish a federal policy of protecting "news media from forms of compulsory process, whether civil or criminal, which might impair the news gathering function." 28 C.F.R. § 50.10. Denial of the privilege, then, would not only buck the clear policy of virtually all states, but would also contradict regulations binding on the federal government's own lawyers. ...

In sum, "reason and experience," as evidenced by the laws of forty-nine states and the District of Columbia, as well as federal courts and the federal government, support recognition of a privilege for reporters' confidential sources. To disregard this modern consensus in favor of decades-old views, as the special counsel urges, would not only imperil vital newsgathering, but also shirk the common law function assigned by Rule 501 and "freeze the law of privilege" contrary to Congress's wishes, *see Trammel*, 445 U.S. at 47.

Scope of the Privilege

The next step, according to *Jaffee*, is to determine what principles govern the privilege's application in this case. *See Jaffee*, 518 U.S. at 15-16 (deciding first that a psychotherapist privilege exists and only then addressing whether the privilege applies to social workers). ...

As to the scope of the privilege, ... I agree with the special counsel that protection for source identities cannot be absolute. Leaks similar to the crime suspected here (exposure of a covert agent) apparently caused the deaths of several CIA operatives in the late 1970s and early 1980s, including the agency's Athens station chief. *See Haig v. Agee*, 453 U.S. 280, 284-85, 69 L. Ed. 2d 640, 101 S. Ct. 2766 & n.7, 453 U.S. 280, 69 L.Ed. 2d 640, 101 S. Ct. 2766 (1981). Other leaks -- the design for a top secret nuclear weapon, for example, or plans for an imminent military strike -- could be even more damaging, causing harm far in excess of their news value. In such cases, the reporter privilege must give way. Just as attorney-client communications "made for the purpose of getting advice for the commission of a fraud or crime" serve no public interest and receive no privilege, *see United States v. Zolin*, 491 U.S. 554, 563, 105 L. Ed. 2d 469, 109 S. Ct. 2619 (1989) (internal quotation marks omitted), neither should courts protect sources whose leaks harm national security while providing minimal benefit to public debate.

Of course, in some cases a leak's value may far exceed its harm, thus calling into question the law enforcement rationale for disrupting reporter-source relationships. For example, assuming Miller's prize-winning Osama bin Laden series caused no significant harm, I find it difficult to see how one could justify compelling her to disclose her sources, given the obvious benefit of alerting the public to then-underappreciated threats from al Qaeda. News reports about a recent budget controversy regarding a super-secret satellite program inspire another example (though I know nothing about the dispute's details and express no view as to its merits). *See, e.g.*, Dan Eggen & Walter Pincus, *Justice Reviews Request for Probe of Satellite Reports*, Wash. Post, Dec. 16, 2004, at A3; Douglas Jehl, *New Spy Plan Said to Involve Satellite System*, N.Y. Times, Dec. 12, 2004, at A1. Despite the necessary secrecy of intelligence-gathering methods, it seems hard to imagine how the harm in leaking generic descriptions of such a program could outweigh the benefit of informing the public about billions of dollars wasted on technology considered duplicative and unnecessary by leading Senators from both parties. In contrast to the nuclear weapon and military strike examples mentioned above, cases like these appear to involve a balance of harm and news value that strongly favors protecting newsgathering methods.

Given these contrasting examples, much as our civil cases balance "the public interest in protecting the reporter's sources against the private interest in compelling disclosure," *Zerilli*, 656 F.2d at 712; *see also Carey*, 492 F.2d at 634-36, so must the reporter privilege account for the varying interests at stake in different source relationships. ...

In leak cases, then, courts applying the privilege must consider not only the government's need for the information and exhaustion of alternative sources, but also the two competing public interests lying at the heart of the balancing test. Specifically, the court must weigh the public interest in compelling disclosure, measured by the harm the leak caused, against the public interest in newsgathering, measured by the leaked information's value. That framework allows authorities seeking to punish a leak to access key evidence when the leaked information does more harm than good, such as in the nuclear weapon and military strike examples, while preventing discovery when no public interest supports it, as would appear to be the case with Miller's Osama bin Laden articles. Though flexible, these standards (contrary to the special counsel's claim) are hardly unmanageable. Indeed, the Supreme Court employs a similar requirement of "legitimate news interest," meaning "value and concern to the public at the time of publication," in assessing restrictions on government employee speech. *See City of San Diego v. Roe*, 160 L. Ed. 2d 410, __ U.S. __, 125 S. Ct. 521, 526 (2004) (*per curiam*). ... [J]ust as courts determine the admissibility of hearsay or the balance between probative value and unfair prejudice under Rule 403, so with respect to this issue must courts weigh factors bearing on the privilege.

Moreover, in addition to these principles applicable to the judicial role in any evidentiary dispute, the dynamics of leak inquiries afford a particularly compelling reason for judicial scrutiny of prosecutorial judgments regarding a leak's harm and news value. Because leak cases typically require the government to investigate itself, if leaks reveal mistakes that high-level officials would have preferred to keep secret, the administration may pursue the source with excessive zeal, regardless of the leaked information's public value. ... [Certain] considerations -- the special counsel's political independence, his lack of a docket, and the concomitant risk of overzealousness -- weigh against his claim to deference in balancing harm against news value.

....[T]he special counsel argues that waivers signed by suspected sources represent an "additional factor" favoring compulsion of the reporters' testimony. As the reporters point out, however, numerous cases (including persuasive district court decisions from this circuit) indicate that only reporters, not sources, may waive the privilege. *See, e.g.*, *United States v. Cuthbertson*, 630 F.2d 139, 147 (3d Cir. 1980); *Palandjian v. Pahlavi*, 103 F.R.D. 410, 413 (D.D.C. 1984); *Anderson v. Nixon*, 444 F. Supp. 1195, 1198-99 (D.D.C. 1978). ...

As this case law recognizes, a source's waiver is irrelevant to the reasons for the privilege. Because the government could demand waivers -- perhaps even before any leak occurs -- as a condition of employment, a privilege subject to waiver may, again, amount to no privilege at all, even in those leak cases where protecting the confidential source is most compelling. Moreover, although the attorney-client and psychotherapist privileges are waivable by clients and patients, respectively, *see, e.g.*, *In re Sealed Case*, 278 U.S. App. D.C. 188, 877 F.2d 976, 980 (D.C. Cir. 1989) (attorney-client); *Jaffee*, 518 U.S. at 15 n.14 (psychotherapist), that is because those privileges exist to prevent disclosure of sensitive matters related to legal and psychological counseling, *see, e.g.*, *Swidler & Berlin*, 524 U.S. at 407-08; *Jaffee*, 518 U.S. at 10-11, a rationale that vanishes when the source authorizes disclosure. In contrast, the reporter privilege safeguards public dissemination of information--the *reporter's* enterprise, not the source's.

Consistent with that purpose, the privilege belongs to the reporter. Not only are journalists best able to judge the imperatives of newsgathering, but while the source's interest is limited to the particular case, the reporter's interest aligns with the public, for journalists must cultivate relationships with other sources who might keep mum if waiving confidentiality at the government's behest could lead to their exposure. Indeed, as compared to counseling-related privileges, the privilege against spousal testimony represents a better analogy. Just as under *Trammel*'s waiver theory testifying spouses, regardless of the other spouse's wishes, may judge for themselves whether their testimony will undermine "marital harmony," *see Trammel*, 445 U.S. at 44-45, 52-53, so should journalists -- the experts in newsgathering -- base the decision to testify on their own assessment of the consequences, unconstrained by their source's waiver (provided other requirements of the privilege are met).

... For their part, appellants insist that a qualified privilege fails to provide the certainty their work requires because sources are unlikely to disclose information without an advance guarantee of secrecy. In particular, they argue that journalists cannot balance a leak's harm against its news value until they know what information the source will reveal, by which time it is too late to prevent disclosure. True enough, but journalists are not the ones who must perform the balancing; sources are. Indeed, the point of the qualified privilege is to create disincentives for the source -- disincentives that not only promote the public interest, but may also protect journalists from exploitation by government officials seeking publication of damaging secrets for partisan advantage. Like other recipients of potentially privileged communications -- say, attorneys or psychotherapists -- the reporter can at most alert the source to the limits of confidentiality, leaving the judgment of what to say to the source. While the resulting deterrent effect may cost the press some leads, little harm will result, for if the disincentives work as they should, the information sources refrain from revealing will lack significant news value in the first place.

In any event, although *Jaffee* said that "making the promise of confidentiality contingent upon a trial judge's later evaluation ... [will] eviscerate the effectiveness of the privilege," 518 U.S. at 17, the clash of fundamental interests at stake when the government seeks discovery of a reporter's sources precludes a categorical approach. *See Zerilli*, 656 F.2d at 712 n.46 (rejecting arguments for greater "specificity" as to the scope of the First Amendment privilege in civil litigation). And as we explained in *Zerilli*, the "deterrence effect" on beneficial newsgathering will be small if courts make clear that the privilege is "overridden only in rare circumstances." *See id.* at 712 & n.46.

In short, the question in this case is whether Miller's and Cooper's sources released information more harmful than newsworthy. If so, then the public interest in punishing the wrongdoers -- and deterring future leaks -- outweighs any burden on newsgathering, and no privilege covers the communication (provided, of course, that the special counsel demonstrates necessity and exhaustion of alternative evidentiary sources).

III.

Applying this standard to the facts of this case, and considering first only the public record, I have no doubt that the leak at issue was a serious matter. Authorized "to investigate and prosecute violations of any federal criminal laws related to the underlying alleged unauthorized disclosure, as well as federal crimes committed in the course of, and with intent to interfere with, [his] investigation, such as perjury, obstruction of justice, destruction of evidence, and intimidation of witnesses," *see* Letter from James B. Comey, Acting Attorney General, to Patrick J. Fitzgerald, United States Attorney, Northern District of Illinois (Feb. 6, 2004), the special counsel is attempting to discover the origins of press reports describing Valerie Plame as a CIA operative monitoring weapons of mass destruction. These reports appeared after Plame's husband, former Ambassador Joseph Wilson, wrote in a *New York Times* op-ed column that his findings on an official mission to Niger in 2002 cast doubt on

President Bush's assertion in his January 2003 State of the Union address that Iraq "recently sought significant quantities of uranium from Africa." *See id.* at 3.

An alleged covert agent, Plame evidently traveled overseas on clandestine missions beginning nearly two decades ago. *See, e.g.,* Richard Leiby & Dana Priest, *The Spy Next Door; Valerie Wilson, Ideal Mom, Was Also the Ideal Cover*, Wash. Post, Oct. 8, 2003, at A1. Her exposure, therefore, not only may have jeopardized any covert activities of her own, but also may have endangered friends and associates from whom she might have gathered information in the past. Acting to criminalize such exposure of secret agents, *see* 50 U.S.C. § 421, Congress has identified that behavior's "intolerable" consequences: "the loss of vital human intelligence which our policymakers need, the great cost to the American taxpayer of replacing intelligence resources lost due to such disclosures, and the greatly increased risk of harm which continuing disclosures force intelligence officers and sources to endure." S. Rep. No. 97-201, at 10-11 (1981), *reprinted in* 1982 U.S.C.C.A.N. 145, 154-55.

The leak of Plame's apparent employment, moreover, had marginal news value. To be sure, insofar as Plame's CIA relationship may have helped explain her husband's selection for the Niger trip, that information could bear on her husband's credibility and thus contribute to public debate over the president's "sixteen words." Compared to the damage of undermining covert intelligence-gathering, however, this slight news value cannot, in my view, justify privileging the leaker's identity.

Turning now to the classified material, I agree with the special counsel that *ex parte* review presents no due process difficulty. To be sure, grand jury secrecy is not absolute. As Rule 6(e) itself provides, courts may "authorize disclosure ... of a grand jury matter ... preliminarily to or in connection with a judicial proceeding." Fed. R. Crim. P. 6(e)(3)(E). In addition, as the reporters point out, even apart from *United States v. Dinsio*, 468 F.2d 1392 (9th Cir. 1973), now superceded by *United States v. Mara*, 410 U.S. 19, 35 L. Ed. 2d 99, 93 S. Ct. 774 (1973), *see* majority op. at 19 (citing *In re Braughton*, 520 F.2d 765, 767 (9th Cir. 1975)), the Second and Ninth Circuits have held that due process requires an "uninhibited adversary hearing" in civil contempt proceedings, *see United States v. Alter*, 482 F.2d 1016, 1024 (9th Cir. 1973) (internal quotation marks omitted); *In the Matter of Kitchen*, 706 F.2d 1266, 1272 (2d Cir. 1983) (internal quotation marks omitted), including "the right to confront all the government's evidence, both documentary and testimonial, unless particular and compelling reasons peculiar to the grand jury function require some curtailment of [that] right," *Kitchen*, 706 F.2d at 1272.

In this circuit, however, we have approved the use of "*in camera, ex parte* proceedings to determine the propriety of a grand jury subpoena or the existence of a crime-fraud exception to the attorney-client privilege when such proceedings are necessary to ensure the secrecy of ongoing grand jury proceedings." *In re Sealed Case No. 98-3077*, 331 U.S. App. D.C. 385, 151 F.3d 1059, 1075 (D.C. Cir. 1998) (*per curiam*). Just as due process poses no barrier to forcing an attorney to testify based on the court's examination of evidence, unseen by the lawyer, that the client sought legal advice in pursuit of a crime, neither does it preclude compulsion of a reporter's testimony based on a comparable review of evidence, likewise unseen by the reporter, that a source engaged in a harmful leak. In fact, appellants' protests notwithstanding, *ex parte* review protects their interests, as it allows the government to present -- and the court to demand -- a far more extensive showing than would otherwise be possible given the need for grand jury secrecy discussed in the court's opinion.

That said, without benefit of the adversarial process, we must take care to ensure that the special counsel has met his burden of demonstrating that the information is both critical and unobtainable from any other source. Having carefully scrutinized his voluminous classified filings, I believe that he has.

With respect to Miller, * * * * * [REDACTED] * * * * *

Regarding Cooper, * * * * * [REDACTED] * * * * *

In sum, based on an exhaustive investigation, the special counsel has established the need for Miller's and Cooper's testimony. Thus, considering the gravity of the suspected crime and the low value of the leaked information, no privilege bars the subpoenas.

One last point. In concluding that no privilege applies in this case, I have assigned no importance to the fact that neither Cooper nor Miller, perhaps recognizing the irresponsible (and quite possibly illegal) nature of the leaks at issue, revealed Plame's employment, though Cooper wrote about it after Novak's column appeared. Contrary to the reporters' view, this apparent self-restraint spares Miller and Cooper no obligation to testify. Narrowly drawn limitations on the public's right to evidence, testimonial privileges apply "only where necessary to achieve [their] purpose," *Fisher v. United States*, 425 U.S. 391, 403, 48 L. Ed. 2d 39, 96 S. Ct. 1569 (1976), and in this case the privilege's purpose is to promote dissemination of useful information. It thus makes no difference how these reporters responded to the information they received, any more than it matters whether an attorney drops a client who seeks criminal advice (communication subject to the crime-fraud exception) or a psychotherapist seeks to dissuade homicidal plans revealed during counseling (information *Jaffee* suggested would not be privileged, *see* 518 U.S. at 18 n.19). In all such cases, because the communication is unworthy of protection, recipients' reactions are irrelevant to whether their testimony may be compelled in an investigation of the source.

Indeed, Cooper's own *Time*.com article illustrates this point. True, his story revealed a suspicious confluence of leaks, contributing to the outcry that led to this investigation. Yet the article had that effect precisely because the leaked information -- Plame's covert status -- lacked significant news value. In essence, seeking protection for sources whose nefariousness he himself exposed, Cooper asks us to protect criminal leaks so that he can write about the crime. The greater public interest lies in preventing the leak to begin with. Had Cooper based his report on leaks *about* the leaks -- say, from a whistleblower who revealed the plot against Wilson--the situation would be different. Because in that case the source would not have revealed the name of a covert agent, but instead revealed the fact that others had done so, the balance of news value and harm would shift in favor of protecting the whistleblower. Yet it appears Cooper relied on the Plame leaks themselves, drawing the inference of sinister motive on his own. Accordingly, his story itself makes the case for punishing the leakers. While requiring Cooper to testify may discourage future leaks, discouraging leaks of this kind is precisely what the public interest requires.

IV.

I conclude, as I began, with the tensions at work in this case. Here, two reporters and a news magazine, informants to the public, seek to keep a grand jury uninformed. Representing two equally fundamental principles -- rule of law and free speech -- the special counsel and the reporters both aim to facilitate fully informed and accurate decision-making by those they serve: the grand jury and the electorate. To this court falls the task of balancing the two sides' concerns.

As James Madison explained, "[A] people who mean to be their own Governors must arm themselves with the power which knowledge gives." *See In re Lindsey*, 331 U.S. App. D.C. 246, 148 F.3d 1100, 1109 (D.C. Cir. 1998) (quoting Letter from James Madison to W.T. Barry (Aug. 4, 1822), *in* 9 *The Writings of James Madison* 103 (Gaillard Hunt ed., 1910)). Consistent with that maxim, "[a] free press is indispensable to the workings of our democratic society," *Associated Press v. United States*, 326 U.S. 1, 28, 89 L. Ed. 2013, 65 S. Ct. 1416 (1945) (Frankfurter, J., concurring), and because confidential sources are essential to the workings of the press -- a practical reality that virtually all states and the federal government now acknowledge -- I believe that "reason and experience" compel recognition of a privilege for reporters' sources. That said, because "liberty can only be exercised in a system of law which safeguards order," *Cox v. Louisiana*, 379 U.S. 559, 574, 13 L. Ed. 2d 487, 85 S. Ct. 476 (1965), the privilege must give way to imperatives of law enforcement in exceptional cases.

Were the leak at issue in this case less harmful to national security or more vital to public debate, or had the special counsel failed to demonstrate the grand jury's need for the reporters' evidence, I might have supported the motion to quash. Because identifying appellants' sources instead appears essential to remedying a serious breach of public trust, I join in affirming the district court's orders compelling their testimony.

* * * * *

IN RE: GRAND JURY SUBPOENA, JUDITH MILLER

United States Court of Appeals for the District of Columbia Circuit

No. 04-3138 Consolidated with 04-3139, 04-3140, 2005 U.S. App. LEXIS 6608

April 19, 2005

Order

Appellants' petition for rehearing *en banc*, the response thereto, and the brief of *amici curiae* in support of appellants have been circulated to the full court. The taking of a vote was requested. Thereafter, a majority of the judges of the court in regular, active service did not vote in favor of the petition. Upon consideration of the foregoing and the emergency motion for expedited consideration of the petition for rehearing *en banc*, it is

ORDERED that the petition for rehearing *en banc* be denied. It is

FURTHER ORDERED that the emergency motion for expedited consideration of the petition for rehearing *en banc* be dismissed as moot.

Per Curiam

TATEL, *Circuit Judge*, concurring in the denial of rehearing *en banc*:

Although *en banc* review is "not favored," Fed. R. App. P. 35(a), and although all three panel members agreed on the result in this case -- i.e., that two subpoenaed reporters can be compelled to give grand jury testimony -- petitioners seek reconsideration of three issues: their assertion of a common law privilege under Federal Rule of Evidence 501; their claim to First Amendment protection; and their due process challenge to the district court's use of *ex parte* evidence.

Regarding the common law issue, while I believe that "reason and experience," Fed. R. Evid. 501, support a qualified privilege for reporters' confidential sources, *see In re Grand Jury Subpoena, Judith Miller*, 397 F.3d 964, 989 (D.C. Cir. 2005) (Tatel, J., concurring), I concur in the court's denial of *en banc* review. Judge Henderson's opinion -- which, as the narrowest supporting the result, is the controlling decision of the court--determined neither whether any common law privilege exists nor what standard would govern its application if it did. *See id.* at 981-82 (Henderson, J., concurring); *see also id.* at 976-77 (Sentelle, J., concurring); *id.* at 989-91 (Tatel, J., concurring). Hence, future panels of this court remain free to recognize any privilege (or no privilege) consistent with the result in this case, and those panels may, as necessary, clarify the standards governing reporter-source relationships. Given that the panel here agreed unanimously on the result, this particular case presents no question of "exceptional importance" in the sense required by our rule on *en banc* review. Fed. R. App. P. 35(a)(2).

En banc review is likewise unnecessary with respect to the First Amendment issue. True, this court's decisions interpreting *Branzburg v. Hayes*, 408 U.S. 665, 33 L. Ed. 2d 626, 92 S. Ct. 2646 (1972), are somewhat conflicted. For example, we have stated in civil litigation that "compelling a reporter to disclose the identity of a confidential source raises obvious First Amendment problems," *Zerilli v. Smith*, 211 U.S. App. D.C. 116, 656 F.2d 705, 710 (D.C. Cir. 1981), while maintaining with respect to grand juries that "[a] newsman can claim no general immunity, qualified or otherwise," unless "questions are put in bad faith for the purpose of harassment," *In re Possible Violations of 18 U.S.C. 371, 641, 1503*, 184 U.S. App. D.C. 82, 564 F.2d 567, 571 (D.C. Cir. 1977). But factual similarities between this case and *Branzburg* prevent this court from recognizing a First Amendment privilege here. *See In re Grand Jury Subpoena*, 397 F.3d at 988 (Tatel, J., concurring). Only the Supreme Court can limit or distinguish *Branzburg* on these facts.

Finally, petitioners offer no compelling reason to reconsider the panel's ruling on the due process issue. Claiming a right to review evidence used to find them in contempt, petitioners object to the district court's and panel's reliance on *ex parte* submissions to determine that any conceivable privilege was overcome. But barring an absolute privilege – something no federal common law decision endorses and that *Branzburg* forecloses as a First Amendment matter -- reporters either enjoy no privilege, in which case compelling their testimony requires no evidence at all, or they hold a qualified privilege, that is, a privilege subject to exceptions, much like the crime-fraud exception to the attorney-client privilege, *see, e.g., United States v. Zolin*, 491 U.S. 554, 563, 105 L. Ed. 2d 469, 109 S. Ct. 2619 (1989), and the imminent-harm exception for psychotherapist-patient communications, *see Jaffee v. Redmond*, 518 U.S. 1, 18 n.19, 135 L. Ed. 2d 337, 116 S. Ct. 1923 (1996). If the privilege is qualified, then *ex parte* review, far from violating due process, affords a critical protection to journalists: it permits the court to demand a detailed showing by the government that it has satisfied the criteria for overcoming the privilege.

I certainly understand petitioners' preference for reviewing the evidence themselves, but given the "'indispensable secrecy of grand jury proceedings,'" *United States v. R. Enterprises, Inc.*, 498 U.S. 292, 299, 112 L. Ed. 2d 795, 111 S. Ct. 722 (1991) (quoting *United States v. Johnson*, 28764 C.B. 995, 319 U.S. 503, 513, 87 L. Ed. 1546, 63 S. Ct. 1233, 1943 C.B. 995 (1943)), it can hardly represent an abuse of discretion for the district court to deny them that option. Telling one grand jury witness what another has said not only risks tainting the later testimony (not to mention enabling perjury or collusion), but may also embarrass or even endanger witnesses, as well as tarnish the reputations of suspects whom the grand jury ultimately declines to indict. Strong guarantees of secrecy are therefore critical if grand juries are to obtain the candid testimony essential to ferreting out the truth. *See generally In re Grand Jury Subpoena*, 397 F.3d at 973-74 (discussing reasons for grand jury secrecy). Accordingly, we have approved of *ex parte* review in applying the crime-fraud exception to the attorney-client privilege -- a context precisely analogous to application of a qualified reporter privilege. *See id.* at 1002 (Tatel, J., concurring) (citing *In re Sealed Case No. 98-3077*, 331 U.S. App. D.C. 385, 151 F.3d 1059, 1075 (D.C. Cir. 1998) (*per curiam*)).

Attempting to manufacture a circuit conflict on this issue, petitioners cite language in *United States v. Alter*, 482 F.2d 1016 (9th Cir. 1973), and *In the Matter of Kitchen*, 706 F.2d 1266 (2d Cir. 1983), contemplating an "uninhibited adversary hearing" in civil contempt proceedings. *See Alter*, 482 F.2d at 1024; *Kitchen*, 706 F.2d at 1272. Yet neither case remotely resembles this one. *Alter* dealt with alleged illegal surveillance of discussions between a grand jury witness and his attorney, a matter requiring no review of secret grand jury materials, *see* 482 F.2d at 1024-25, and *Kitchen* involved contempt findings based on the alleged implausibility of a witness's claimed failure of memory -- a situation more akin to punishment for perjury than evaluation of a privilege claim, *see Kitchen*, 706 F.2d at 1272 (identifying a need for "heightened" procedural protection "when a case is in the grey area between contempt and perjury"). Nor do petitioners' other authorities involve compulsion of testimony due to failure of an asserted privilege. While expressing caution regarding use of secret evidence, they deal, respectively, with retraction of security clearance, punishment for false testimony, and denial of visas. *See Greene v. McElroy*, 360 U.S. 474, 3 L. Ed. 2d 1377, 79 S. Ct. 1400 (1959); *In re Oliver*, 333 U.S. 257, 92 L. Ed. 682, 68 S. Ct. 499 (1948); *Abourezk v. Reagan*, 251 U.S. App. D.C. 355, 785 F.2d 1043 (D.C. Cir. 1986), *aff'd by an equally divided court*, 484 U.S. 1, 98 L. Ed. 2d 1, 108 S. Ct. 252 (1987). Unlike in those cases, the disputed evidence here relates to the government's conduct of its investigation, not the witness's own conduct. Moreover, again unlike in those cases, the reporters here face only a coercive penalty, not punishment for past actions. To avoid incarceration, they need not persuade the district judge that any accusation against them is false; they need only abandon their unlawful resistance and testify before the grand jury. *See Int'l Union, UMW v. Bagwell*, 512 U.S. 821, 828, 129 L. Ed. 2d 642, 114 S. Ct. 2552 (1994).

The better analogy is *R. Enterprises*, where the Supreme Court approved of *ex parte* proceedings to determine the reasonableness of grand jury subpoenas. Although denial of a reasonableness-based motion to quash may expose witnesses to coercive measures (including incarceration) no less than denial of a claimed privilege, the Court observed that "to ensure that subpoenas are not routinely challenged as a form of discovery, a district court may require that the Government reveal the subject of the investigation to the trial court *in camera*, so that the court may determine whether the motion to quash has a reasonable prospect for success before it discloses the subject matter to the challenging party." *R. Enterprises*, 498 U.S. at 302; *cf. Abourezk*, 785 F.2d at 1061 (describing in camera review of subpoenaed evidence "for the limited purpose of determining whether the asserted privilege is genuinely applicable" as a "notable" exception to the rule against secret evidence).

In short, because none of petitioners' claims meets our high standard for reconsideration by the *en banc* court, I join in denying their petition.

* * * * *

THE NEW YORK TIMES COMPANY, Plaintiff

v.

ALBERTO GONZALES, in his official capacity as Attorney General of the United States, and THE UNITED STATES OF AMERICA, Defendants

United States District Court for the Southern District of New York

04 Civ. 7677 (RWS), 2005 U.S. Dist. LEXIS 2642

February 24, 2005

The defendants Alberto Gonzales ("Gonzales") in his official capacity as Attorney General of the United States and the United States of America (collectively, the "government") have moved under Rule 12, Fed. R. Civ. P., to dismiss the complaint of The New York Times Company ("*The Times*") seeking a declaratory judgment concerning the confidentiality of telephone records for two of its reporters, which records are held by a third-party telephone company. *The Times* has moved for summary judgment under Rule 56, Fed. R. Civ. P., seeking certain of the relief sought in its complaint. The government has cross-moved for summary judgment dismissing the complaint. Upon the facts found to be undisputed and the conclusions of law set forth below, the government's motion to dismiss is denied, its cross-motion for summary judgment is granted in part and denied in part, and the motion of *The Times* is granted in part and denied in part.

The Issues Presented

These motions present competing considerations of the role of secrecy in our society. Secrecy may well be seen as the enemy of freedom when it conceals facts important to public understanding. Yet here, both sides seek to enforce secrecy, albeit from dramatically different perspectives. The government, through a grand jury proceeding, seeks to investigate, and perhaps to prosecute, an alleged breach of a government secret, namely, the timing of the seizure of assets and Federal Bureau of Investigation ("FBI") searches of the offices of two Islamic charities in the fall of 2001. *The Times*, in opposing the government's efforts, seeks to keep confidential the identity of the sources known to two of its reporters who wrote articles during the same period. ...

In order to gather information on sensitive topics, reporters, particularly those investigating stories that implicate our government and public officials, often depend upon confidential sources. In the words of Max Frankel, the former Executive Editor of *The Times*, offered some thirty years ago in connection with the Pentagon Papers case[4]:

> In the field of foreign affairs, only rarely does our Government give full public information to the press for the direct purpose of simply informing the people. For the most part, the press obtains significant information bearing on foreign policy only because it has managed to make itself a party to confidential materials, and of value in transmitting those materials from government to other branches and offices of government as well as the public at large. This is why the press has been wisely and correctly called The Fourth Branch of Government.

Just as the ability of the press to report on issues of significance often depends on information obtained from others, so too is the ability of federal prosecutors to investigate and enforce the nation's criminal laws dependent upon the power of the federal prosecutor to obtain, at times through compulsion, testimony and evidence necessary to determine whether a crime has been committed. It is axiomatic that, in seeking such testimony and evidence, the prosecutor acts on behalf of the public and in furtherance of the "strong national interest in the effective enforcement of its criminal laws." *United States v. Davis*, 767 F.2d 1025, 1035 (2d Cir. 1985) (citations omitted). Indeed, it is a fundamental and "ancient proposition of law," *United States v. Nixon*, 418 U.S. 683, 709, 41 L. Ed. 2d 1039, 94 S. Ct. 3090 (1973), that "'the public ... has a right to every man's evidence,' except for those persons protected by a constitutional, common-law, or statutory privilege." *Branzburg v. Hayes*, 408 U.S. 665, 688, 33 L. Ed. 2d 626, 92 S. Ct. 2646 (1972) (citations omitted and alteration in original).

Here presented by the motions and cross-motion are the conflicting interests of the press and the federal criminal justice system -- each institution, in turn, representing distinct interests of the public -- under the particular circumstances presented by the parties to this litigation.

By this action, *The Times* seeks a declaratory judgment that the telephone records of two reporters employed by *The Times*, Judith Miller ("Miller") and Philip Shenon ("Shenon"), relating to time periods of twenty-three and eighteen days, respectively, during the months following September 11, 2001, are protected against compelled disclosure by the First Amendment to the U.S. Constitution, federal common law and the guidelines of the U.S. Department of Justice ("DOJ") set forth in 28 C.F.R. § 50.10 (the "Guidelines").

The telephone records at issue, held by an unidentified third-party telephone company or companies, are being sought by the government as part of an investigation to uncover the identity of one or more government employees who purportedly "leaked" information to Miller and Shenon relating to the government's plans to block the assets and search the

---

[4] In *New York Times Co. v. United States*, 403 U.S. 713, 29 L. Ed. 2d 822, 91 S. Ct. 2140 (1971) (*per curiam*), familiarly known as the Pentagon Papers case, the government sought to enjoin *The Times* and the Washington Post from publishing the contents of a classified study entitled "History of U.S. Decision-Making Process on Viet Nam Policy." The Supreme Court ruled that the government had not met its heavy burden to establish justification for such prior restraint. *See New York Times*, 403 U.S. at 714.

offices of two Islamic charity organizations in the fall of 2001. According to *The Times*, the disclosure of the telephone records at issue would not only constitute an unacceptable violation of the privacy of both Miller and Shenon but would also likely reveal the identities of dozens of confidential sources who are of no relevance to the government's investigation. … It is the government's position that the relief sought by *The Times* is both unwarranted and inappropriate, as the grant of such relief would permit a federal district court of the Southern District of New York to interfere with and potentially enjoin an investigation currently being conducted by a federal grand jury in the Northern District of Illinois, thereby encroaching on the authority of the Chief Judge of that district. …

Discussion

….*The Times* has asserted that the government has failed to comply with the DOJ's Guidelines with regard to the telephone records sought here and that, as a result, the government should be barred from seeking or obtaining those telephone records. The Guidelines in question, set forth in 28 C.F.R. § 50.10, address, *inter alia*, the issuance of subpoenas to members of the media by the DOJ and the issuance of subpoenas for telephone records of members of the media. …

Initially announced in 1970 in what then-Attorney General John N. Mitchell termed an effort "to prohibit federal law enforcement officers from annexing the media as an investigative arm," and subsequently amended in 1980 to provide protection for telephone records of members of the media, the Guidelines reflect a fundamental concern with "striking the proper balance between the public's interest in the free dissemination of ideas and information and the public's interest in effective law enforcement and the fair administration of justice." 28 C.F.R. § 50.10(a); *see also* 28 C.F.R. § 50.10(m) (noting "the intent of this Section to protect freedom of the press, news gathering functions, and news media sources….").

This concern was expressly articulated in the Guidelines' preamble:

> Because freedom of the press can be no broader than the freedom of reporters to investigate and report the news, the prosecutorial power of the government should not be used in such a way that it impairs a reporter's responsibility to cover as broadly as possible controversial public issues. This policy statement is thus intended to provide protection for the news media from forms of compulsory process, whether civil or criminal, which might impair the news gathering function.

28 C.F.R. § 50.10. In accordance with the stated interests, the Guidelines are to be "adhered to by all members of the Department in all cases" in order to balance "the concern that the Department of Justice has for the work of the news media and the Department's obligation to the fair administration of justice…." 28 C.F.R. § 50.10.

By their terms, the Guidelines require members of the DOJ not to issue subpoenas to members of the news media in criminal cases before: (1) negotiations with the media members concerned have been pursued, during which negotiations the government has clarified its needs in the case and its willingness to respond to the media member's concerns; and (2) the Attorney General has authorized the subpoena. *See* 28 C.F.R. § 50.10(c) & (e). The Guidelines further caution that "all reasonable attempts should be made to obtain information from alternative sources before considering issuing a subpoena to a member of the news media...." 28 C.F.R. § 50.10(b).

In criminal cases, a request for the authorization of the Attorney General to issue a subpoena to members of the news media is to be guided by the principle that,

> There should be reasonable grounds to believe, based on information obtained from nonmedia sources, that a crime has occurred, and that the information sought is essential to a successful investigation -- particularly with reference to directly establishing guilt or innocence. The subpoena should not be used to obtain peripheral, nonessential, or speculative information.

28 C.F.R. § 50.10(f)(1). In addition, requests for authorization are subject to the principle that, absent "exigent circumstances," subpoenas to members of the media "should ... be limited to the verification of published information and to such surrounding circumstances as relate to the accuracy of the published information." 28 C.F.R. § 50.10(f)(4). Moreover,

> Subpoenas should, wherever possible, be directed at material information regarding a limited subject matter, should cover a reasonably limited period of time, and should avoid requiring production of a large volume of unpublished material. They should give reasonable and timely notice of the demand for documents.

28 C.F.R. § 50.10(f)(6).

With respect to subpoenas for the telephone records of a member of the media, the Guidelines provide that, prior to seeking a subpoena, the government should have pursued all reasonable alternative investigation steps and that no subpoena may be issued absent the Attorney General's express authorization. *See* 28 C.F.R. § 50.10(b), (e) & (g)(1). Where such authorization is being sought,

> There should be reasonable ground to believe that a crime has been committed and that the information sought is essential to the successful investigation of that crime. The subpoena should be as narrowly drawn as possible; it should be directed at relevant information regarding a limited subject matter and should cover a reasonably limited time period.

28 C.F.R. § 50.10(g)(1). The Guidelines direct that negotiations with the affected member of the media shall be pursued in all cases in which a subpoena for telephone records is contemplated if it is determined that such negotiations would not pose a substantial threat to the integrity of the underlying investigation. *See* 28 C.F.R. § 50.10(d). They further direct that timely notice of the Attorney General's determination to authorize a subpoena for telephone records and the DOJ's intent to issue a subpoena shall be provided to the media member where such negotiations have occurred. *See* 28 C.F.R. § 50.10(g)(2). There is no requirement that further notice concerning the actual issuance of the subpoena be provided to the media member with whom negotiations have occurred. *But cf.* 28 C.F.R. § 50.10(g)(3) (providing that, when a subpoena for telephone records has been issued without prior notice, "notification of the subpoena shall be given the member of the news media as soon thereafter

as it is determined that such notification will no longer pose a clear and substantial threat to the integrity of the investigation"). ...

While the Guidelines at issue here announce the DOJ's "intent[ ] to provide protection for the news media from forms of compulsory process," 28 C.F.R. § 50.10, and its further intent "to protect freedom of the press, news gathering functions, and news media sources," 28 C.F.R. § 50.10(m), these expressions of intent simply reflect the goals underlying the DOJ's policy with respect to the exercise of prosecutorial discretion in the context of dealings with members of the media. *See In re Grand Jury Subpoena, Judith Miller*, 2005 U.S. App. LEXIS 2494, 2005 WL 350745, at *12 (concluding that the Guidelines "merely guide the discretion of the prosecutors"). It is neither the nature nor the purpose of the Guidelines to confer a legally enforceable benefit or right in any person, as they expressly acknowledge, *see* 28 C.F.R. § 50.10(n), rendering *Ruiz* and its progeny inapposite. *See In re Grand Jury Subpoena, Judith Miller*, 2005 U.S. App. LEXIS 2494, 2005 WL 350745, at *12.

Because the Guidelines are just that -- touchstones to assist the DOJ in its exercise of prosecutorial discretion -- and confer no substantive rights or protections such as may be privately enforced, the government's motion for summary judgment as to [this count] is granted, and *The Times*' motion for summary judgment as to that same count is denied.

... A. There Is A Qualified Reporter's Privilege Under The First Amendment

....[T]he Second Circuit, based on *Branzburg* [*v. Hayes,* 408 U.S. 665, 33 L. Ed. 2d 626, 92 S. Ct. 2646 (1972),] has recognized a qualified First Amendment privilege, applicable in civil actions and in all phases of a criminal prosecution, that protects reporters from compelled disclosure of confidential sources. *See Burke,* 700 F.2d at 77. Pursuant to this qualified privilege, the party seeking disclosure must make "a clear and specific showing that the sought information is: [1] highly material and relevant, [2] necessary or critical to the maintenance of the claim, and [3] not obtainable from other available sources." *Id.* at 76-77 (quoting *In re Petroleum Products,* 680 F.2d at 7 (citing *Baker,* 470 F.2d at 783-85)). The burden to overcome the qualified privilege is diminished where: (1) the party seeking discovery is a criminal defendant, *see Gonzales,* 194 F.3d at 34 n.3 (interpreting *Cutler,* 6 F.3d at 73) or (2) the sought materials are nonconfidential. *See id.* at 30.

The government's contentions that this qualified privilege should not be applied in the context of a grand jury investigation do not overcome the conclusions set forth above. ....[T]he interpretation of *Branzburg* urged by the government is contrary to the view adopted by the Second Circuit and the courts of this district.

....[T]he government has not offered a principled basis for concluding that the qualified First Amendment reporter's privilege applies in the context of a criminal trial but not in the context of a grand jury investigation. The Second Circuit has stated repeatedly that the application of the privilege (i.e., the weight to be afforded to the interests militating for and against compelled disclosure) depends on the legal context in which the disclosure is sought. ... [Earlier decisions,] each of which was based on interpretation of *Branzburg*, were premised on the assumption that a qualified First Amendment privilege exists that requires case-by-case balancing. The scope of the reporter's privilege may vary depending on the context, but whether there is a qualified privilege rooted in the First Amendment is not dependent on the nature of the case.

As set forth above, *The Times* has demonstrated that there exists a qualified First Amendment reporter's privilege with respect to confidential sources.

B. There Is A Qualified Reporter's Privilege Under The Common Law

In addition to the constitutional protection discussed above, *The Times* has invoked the federal common law, which, *The Times* asserts, would provide an independent basis for granting summary judgment in favor of *The Times*.[23] Specifically, *The Times* has urged that a common law reporter's privilege protecting confidential sources should be recognized under Rule 501, Fed. R. Evid., in accordance with the methodology for recognizing privileges under Rule 501 set forth by the Supreme Court in *Jaffee v. Redmond*, 518 U.S. 1, 135 L. Ed. 2d 337, 116 S. Ct. 1923 (1996). According to the government, no basis to recognize a federal common law reporter's privilege as to confidential sources exists, particularly in light of the holding and reasoning of *Branzburg v. Hayes*, 408 U.S. 665, 33 L. Ed. 2d 626, 92 S. Ct. 2646 (1972).

1. Rule 501 and the Recognition of Federal Common Law Privileges

Three years after *Branzburg* was decided, Congress enacted the Federal Rules of Evidence. Among the Rules adopted was Rule 501, which provides, in relevant part:

> Except as otherwise required by the Constitution of the United States or provided by Act of Congress or in rules prescribed by the Supreme Court pursuant to statutory authority, the privilege of a witness, person, government, state, or political subdivision thereof shall be governed by the principles of the common law as they may be interpreted by the courts of the United States in the light of reason and experience.

Fed. R. Evid. 501. ...

Pursuant to Rule 501, the recognition and application of testimonial or other evidentiary privileges are governed by "the principles of the common law," as interpreted "in the light of reason and experience." Fed. R. Evid. 501. ...

Thus, to determine "in light of reason and experience, Fed. R. Evid. 501, whether an asserted privilege promotes sufficiently important interests so as to outweigh the countervailing need for probative evidence, the Court considers four factors, as set forth in *Jaffee:* (1) whether the asserted privilege would serve significant private interests; (2) whether the privilege would serve significant public interests; (3) whether those interests outweigh any evidentiary benefit that would result from rejection of the privilege proposed; and (4) whether the privilege has been widely recognized by the states. *See Jaffee*, 518 U.S. at 10-13; *see also* In re Special Counsel Investigation, 338 F. Supp. 2d 16, 18 (D.D.C. 2004) (acknowledging that *Jaffee* "articulates the analysis courts should undertake when determining whether to recognize a common law privilege under Rule 501"), *aff'd on other grounds by In re Grand Jury Subpoena, Judith Miller*, F.3d , 2005 U.S. App. LEXIS 2494, 2005 WL 350745 (D.C. Cir. Feb. 15, 2005). The language and broad applicability of Rule 501 suggests, and *Jaffee* confirms, that in determining whether to recognize a privilege

---

[23] "'Federal common law' ... means any federal rule of decision that is not mandated on the face of some authoritative federal text -- whether or not that rule can be described as the product of 'interpretation' in either a conventional or an unconventional sense." Thomas W. Merrill, *The Common Law Powers of Federal Courts*, 52 U. Chi. L. Rev. 1, 5 (1985) (footnote omitted).

through consideration of the various factors identified above, a court should not distinguish between criminal and civil cases, or between criminal trials and grand jury proceedings. *See also Cuthbertson*, 630 F.2d at 147.

State precedent and the existence of consensus among the states are of particular importance in considering whether to recognize a privilege under Rule 501....

2. A Qualified Common Law Reporter's Privilege Is Recognized Under Rule 501

....[As t]he Court of Appeals for the Third Circuit [observed] ... in *Riley v. City of Chester*, 612 F.2d 708 (3d Cir. 1979), explaining that,

> The strong public policy which supports the unfettered communication to the public of information, comment and opinion and the Constitutional dimension of that policy, expressly recognized in *Branzburg v. Hayes*, lead us to conclude that journalists have a federal common law privilege, albeit qualified, to refuse to divulge their sources. Such a privilege has also been recognized by many other courts which have considered this question following the decision in *Branzburg v. Hayes*.

Riley, 612 F.2d at 715 (collecting cases). ... Since that time, the courts of other circuits have repeatedly recognized the existence of a common law reporter's privilege, specifically denominated as such, in various contexts. *See, e.g., United States v. Foote*, 2002 U.S. Dist. LEXIS 14818, No. 00-CR-20091-01 (KHV), 2002 WL 1822407, at *2 (D. Kan. Aug. 8, 2002) (explaining that the Tenth Circuit has recognized "a qualified federal common law 'journalist's privilege'") (footnote omitted); *Howard v. Antilla*, 191 F.R.D. 39, 42 (D.N.H. 1999) (construing the First Circuit's opinion in *Bruno & Stillman, Inc. v. Globe Newspaper Co.*, 633 F.2d 583 (1st Cir. 1980), "to have fashioned a federal common law qualified privilege rule based on the First Amendment because the state jurisdictions involved had not codified a newsman's privilege and their common law focused on the First Amendment origins of any such protection"); *McCarty v. Bankers Ins. Co.*, 195 F.R.D. 39, 44 (N.D. Fla. 1998) (stating that "the federal courts, including the Eleventh Circuit, and the district courts therein have overwhelmingly recognized a qualified privilege for journalists which allows them to resist compelled disclosure of their professional news gathering efforts and results, whether published or not"); *Cinel v. Connick*, 792 F. Supp. 492, 499 (E.D. La. 1992) (concluding that the federal common law reporter's privilege recognized in the Fifth Circuit does not protect against the compelled disclosure of information unrelated to confidential sources). *But cf. In re Grand Jury Proceedings*, 5 F.3d at 403 (expressing disinclination to "undermine" *Branzburg* by recognizing a federal common law reporter's privilege in the context of grand jury proceedings). Most recently, the District of Columbia Circuit affirmed the lower court's ruling in *In re Special Counsel Proceeding*, 338 F. Supp. 2d 16 (D.D.C. 2004) (concluding that no federal common law privilege existed in the context of a grand jury proceeding), without reaching any determination as to the existence of a common law reporter's privilege. *See In re Grand Jury Subpoena, Judith Miller*, 2005 U.S. App. LEXIS 2494, 2005 WL 350745, at *9 ("The Court is not of one mind on the existence of a common law privilege. ... However, all believe that if there is any such privilege, it is not absolute and may be overcome by an appropriate showing.").

The Second Circuit, in addition to recognizing a qualified reporter's privilege arising under the First Amendment, as set forth above, has suggested that such a privilege may also be "rooted in federal common law," *Gonzales*, 194 F.3d at 35 n.6, and several of the courts of this district have proceeded on an assumption that a qualified reporter's privilege exists on just such a basis. *See, e.g., Pugh v. Avis Rent A Car Sys.*, 1997 U.S. Dist. LEXIS 16671, No. M8-85, 1997 WL 669876, at *3 (S.D.N.Y. Oct. 28, 1997) (noting that "under federal common law journalists possess a qualified privilege not to disclose information prepared or obtained in connection with a news story....") (citing *Burke,* 700 F.2d at 76-78); *In re Waldholz (In re ICN/Viratek Sec. Litig.),* 1996 U.S. Dist. LEXIS 9648, No. 87 Civ. 4296 (KMW), 1996 WL 389261, at *2 (S.D.N.Y. July 11, 1996) (stating that, "under federal common law, journalists enjoy a qualified, but not an absolute, privilege with respect to information gathered in connection with the publication of an article.") (citing, *inter alia, Burke,* 700 F.2d at 76-78). ...

Turning, therefore, to the first factor identified in *Jaffee,* it is concluded here upon the record set forth above that the recognition of a reporter's privilege would serve significant private interests by permitting investigative reporters to continue to secure information from confidential sources with greater assurance that they would not be compelled to reveal the information obtained or the source of that information or run the risk of court-imposed sanctions, either option posing a threat to the reporters' ability to obtain confidential information in the future or to publish investigative stories at all. As the facts set forth above establish, disclosure of the identity of confidential sources would greatly hinder reporters' ability to gather and report news in the future. ...

... The second *Jaffee* factor to be weighed is whether the privilege would serve important public interests. Insofar as the full and unhampered reporting of the news depends, at least in part and for the reasons just stated, upon the ability of reporters to offer confidential protection to would-be sources, the reporter's privilege asserted by *The Times* does serve such interests. Although the reporting of Carl Bernstein and Bob Woodward, who exposed the Watergate scandal based in part on information obtained from a confidential source known only as "Deep Throat," is the most celebrated example of the use of information obtained from a confidential source to report on matters of public concern, further examples abound, from the revelation of information and photographs concerning the abuses at Abu Ghraib prison in Iraq, obtained by The Washington Post from confidential sources, *see* Scott Higham & Joe Stephens, *New Details of Prison Abuse Emerge; Abu Ghraib Detainees' Statements Describe Sexual Humiliation And Savage Beatings*, Wash. Post, May 21, 2004, at A1; Today (NBC television broadcast, May 21, 2004), to the numerous revelations cited in the affidavit of Jack Nelson, expert witness for *The Times*, including reports on the pardon of President Nixon, allegedly improper activities by administration officials during the Carter presidency, the Iran/Contra affair, and the Monica Lewinsky scandal, all made possible through the use of confidential sources. News reports based upon information obtained from confidential sources have sparked investigations into organized crime, *see* Carl C. Monk, *Evidentiary Privilege for Journalists' Sources: Theory and Statutory Protection*, 51 Mo. L. Rev 1, 13 (1986), environmental and safety hazards related to nuclear power plants, and financial misconduct by elected officials, *see* Committee on Communications & Media Law, Association of the Bar of the City of New York, *The Federal Common Law of Journalists' Privilege: A Position Paper,* at 15-16 (2004), *available at* http://www.abcny.org/ (last visited Feb. 22, 2005) ("Position Paper"), to cite only a few additional examples of issues of indisputable public concern. Similarly, between September 24, 2001 and December 31, 2001, Shenon and Miller wrote seventy-eight articles for *The Times* on topics ranging from continued threats from Al Qaeda to the government's preparedness for the attacks of September 11, 2001, and from the investigation of the anthrax attacks in the months following September 11, 2001 to the government's investigation of GRF and HLF, dozens of which articles likewise contain information attributed to confidential sources. ...

The third *Jaffee* factor to be considered is whether the significant private and public interests that would be served by recognition of the privilege proposed outweigh any evidentiary benefit that would result from rejection of that privilege. ... In the absence of recognition of the reporter's privilege advocated by *The Times*, the government stands to enjoy an evidentiary benefit in this particular case. More generally, however, the record here has established, and the reason and experience of the numerous courts and state legislatures which have recognized or adopted protections for reporters vis-a-vis confidential sources affirm, that in the absence of a recognized privilege fewer sources will provide information of a sensitive nature to reporters where doing so places them at risk of losing their job or otherwise incurring some penalty should they be identified. ...

Reason dictates here, as in *Jaffee,* that the likelihood that whistle-blowing or other provision of sensitive information would decrease were the reporter's privilege unequivocally rejected by this and other courts is particularly strong where it is obvious that the circumstances that give rise to the revelation of any such sensitive information are likely to result in litigation or, as here, a governmental investigation. Moreover, as was the case in *Jaffee,* were the existence of the reporter's privilege denied, the very transfer of information from would-be confidential sources to reporters would be less likely, if not, as the *Jaffee* Court concluded, "unlikely," to occur at all, rendering the probable evidentiary benefit from the denial of the privilege modest at best when viewed, per *Jaffee,* outside the confines of the particular case at hand.

... Contrary to *The Times'* suggestion, however, this privilege is no more absolute than the privilege arising from the First Amendment discussed above. While this Court is mindful of the view expressed in *Jaffee* that "the participants in ... confidential conversations 'must be able to predict with some degree of certainty whether particular discussions will be protected,'" and that "'an uncertain privilege, or one which purports to be certain but results in widely varying applications by the courts, is little better than no privilege at all,'" *Jaffee*, 518 U.S. at 17-18 (quoting *Upjohn Co. v United States*, 449 U.S. 383, 393, 66 L. Ed. 2d 584, 101 S. Ct. 677 (1981)), those federal courts to have recognized a common law reporter's privilege as such have uniformly concluded that an absolute privilege is not appropriate, *see, e.g., Cuthbertson*, 630 F.2d at 146-48; *Riley*, 612 F.2d at 715; *Foote*, 2002 U.S. Dist. LEXIS 14818, 2002 WL 1822407, at *2; *McCarty,* 195 F.R.D. at 44; *Cinel*, 792 F. Supp. at 499; *cf. In re Grand Jury Subpoena, Judith Miller*, 2005 U.S. App. LEXIS 2494, 2005 WL 350745, at *1 (reaching no decision as to the existence of a common law reporter's privilege, but holding that if such a privilege exists, "it is not absolute"), as have those courts of this circuit and elsewhere which have recognized a First Amendment reporter's privilege, as documented above. In view of the unanimity of judicial reason and experience in this regard, the desirability of congruence between the First Amendment privilege recognized in this circuit and the federal common law privilege recognized here, and the predictability of circumstances in which the public interests served by the reporter's privilege might be overshadowed by other, more compelling public interests, no basis is found here to recognize anything more than a qualified privilege.

This recognition of a qualified reporter's privilege with respect to confidential sources is consonant with the conclusions reached by the courts or legislatures of forty-eight states as well as the District of Columbia on the issue of a reporter's privilege against compelled disclosure, a fact of some significance under *Jaffee*. "Shield laws," by which reporters have been afforded varying degrees of protection against compelled disclosure of, *inter alia,* confidential sources, have been adopted in thirty-one states, including Alabama, Alaska, Arizona, Arkansas, California, Colorado, Delaware, Florida, Georgia, Illinois, Indiana, Kentucky, Louisiana, Maryland, Michigan, Minnesota, Montana, Nebraska, Nevada, New Jersey, New Mexico, New York, North Carolina, North Dakota, Ohio, Oklahoma, Oregon, Pennsylvania, Rhode Island, South Carolina and Tennessee, as well as the District of Columbia,[34] and California's Constitution was amended in 1980 to add specific protections for reporters.[35] Judicial decisions in several of these same states, including Florida, Louisiana, Michigan, New York and Oklahoma, have also interpreted either the federal or state constitutions as giving rise to a qualified reporter's privilege.[36]

---

[34] *See* Ala. Code § 12-21-142; Alaska Stat. § 09.25.300 *et seq.*; Ariz. Rev. Stat. §§ 12-2214, 12-2237; Ark. Code Ann. § 6-85-510; Cal. Evid. Code § 1070; Colo. Rev. Stat. §§ 13-90-119, 24-72.5-101 *et seq.;* Del. Code Ann. tit. 10, § 4320 *et seq.;* D.C. Code Ann. § 16-4701 *et seq.;* Fla. Stat. Ann. § 90.5015; Ga. Code Ann. § 24-9-30; 735 Ill. Comp. Stat. Ann. § 5/8-901 *et seq.;* Ind. Code Ann. § 34-46-4-1 *et seq.*; Ky. Rev. Stat. Ann. § 421.100; La. Rev. Stat. Ann. § 45:1451 *et seq.;* Md. Code. Ann., Cts. & Jud. Proc. § 9-112; Mich. Compl. Laws Ann. §§ 767.5a, 767A.6; Minn. Stat. Ann. § 595.021 *et seq.;* Mont. Code Ann. § 26-1-902 *et seq.*; Neb. Rev. Stat. § 20-144 *et seq.*; Nev. Rev. Stat. Ann. §§ 49.275, 49.385; N.J. Stat. Ann. §§ 2A:84A-21.1 *et seq.*, 2A:84A-29; N.Y. Civ. Rights Law § 79-h; N.C. Gen. Stat. § 8-53.11; N.D. Cent. Code § 31-01-06.2; Ohio Rev. Code Ann. §§ 2739.04, 2739.12; Okla. Stat. Ann. tit. 12, § 2506; Or. Rev. Stat. § 44.510 *et seq.*; 42 Pa. Cons. Stat. Ann. § 5942; R.I. Gen. Laws § 9-19.1-1 *et seq.*; S.C. Code Ann. § 19-11-100; Tenn. Code Ann. § 24-1-208. A shield law adopted in New Mexico in 1973, presently codified at N.M. Stat. Ann. § 8-6-7, was held to be an invalid exercise of legislative power by the state's highest court, *see Ammerman v. Hubbard Broadcasting, Inc.,* 89 N.M. 307, 551 P.2d 1354, 1358-59 (N.M. 1976), which subsequently created a rule of evidence embodying just such a privilege. *See* N.M.R. Evid. 11-514; *see generally* Daniel M. Faber, Comment, *Coopting the Journalist's Privilege: Of Sources and Spray Paint,* 23 N.M.L. Rev. 435, 440 (1993) (describing the history of the reporter's privilege in New Mexico).

[35] *See* Cal. Const., Art. I, § 2(b) (declaring that reporters could not be adjudged in contempt for refusing to disclose the source of any information). Although neither California's Constitution nor its shield law, *see* Cal. Evid. Code § 1070, refers specifically to a privilege *per se*, "since contempt is generally the only effective remedy against a non-party witness, the California enactments grant such witnesses virtually absolute protection against compelled disclosure." *Mitchell v. Superior Court*, 37 Cal. 3d 268, 690 P.2d 625, 628, 208 Cal. Rptr. 152 (Cal. 1984).

[36] *See Morgan v. State*, 337 So. 2d 951, 956 (Fla. 1976) (recognizing a qualified reporter's privilege arising under the First Amendment to the U.S. Constitution against the forced revelation of sources); *In re Grand Jury Proceedings (Ridenhour),* 520 So. 2d 372, 376 (La. 1988) (recognizing a qualified privilege arising under the federal constitution against forced testimony before a grand jury*); In re Photo Marketing Asso. International*, 120 Mich. App. 527, 327 N.W.2d 515, 517-18 (Mich. Ct. App. 1982) (recognizing a qualified privilege arising under the First Amendment); *O'Neill v. Oakgrove Constr., Inc.,* 71 N.Y.2d 521, 523 N.E.2d 277, 277-78, 528 N.Y.S.2d 1 (N.Y. 1988) (recognizing a qualified privilege arising under the federal and the state constitutions for non-confidential materials); *Taylor v. Miskovsky,* 1981 OK 143, 640 P.2d 959, 961-62 (Okla. 1981) (recognizing a qualified First Amendment privilege and concluding that the privilege was embodied in the state's shield law*). But see In re WTHR-TV,* 693 N.E.2d 1, 13 (Ind. 1998) (rejecting arguments for a qualified reporter's privilege arising under the federal constitution related to non-confidential materials); *Vaughn v. State*, 259 Ga. 325, 381 S.E.2d 30, 31 (Ga. 1989) (concluding that the Georgia Constitution offers no protection to reporters from compelled disclosure of confidential sources).

In fourteen of the remaining nineteen states, including Idaho, Iowa, Kansas, Maine, Massachusetts, Missouri, New Hampshire, South Dakota, Texas, Vermont, Virginia, Washington, West Virginia and Wisconsin, a reporter's privilege has been recognized by either the state's highest court or an appeals court in civil or criminal proceedings, including, in several instances, grand jury proceedings.[37] In addition, lower courts in Connecticut, Mississippi and Utah have recognized a reporter's privilege in both civil and criminal contexts.[38] Of the two remaining states, the courts and legislature of Wyoming have remained silent on the issue,[39] as have those of Hawaii since *Branzburg* was issued.[40]

---

[37] *See, e.g., State v. Salsbury,* 129 Idaho 307, 924 P.2d 208, 213 (Idaho 1996) (criminal); *In re Wright,* 108 Idaho 418, 700 P.2d 40, 41 (Idaho 1985) (criminal); *Winegard v. Oxberger,* 258 N.W.2d 847, 850 (Iowa 1977) (civil); *Kansas v. Sandstrom,* 224 Kan. 573, 581 P.2d 812, 814-15 (Kan. 1978) (criminal); *In re Letellier,* 578 A.2d 722, 726-27 (Me. 1990) (grand jury); *In re John Doe Grand Jury Investigation,* 410 Mass. 596, 574 N.E.2d 373, 375 (Mass. 1991) (grand jury); *Sinnott v. Boston Retirement Bd.,* 402 Mass. 581, 524 N.E.2d 100 (Mass. 1988) (civil); *Ayash v. Dana-Farber Cancer Inst.,* 46 Mass. App. Ct. 384, 706 N.E.2d 316, 319 (Mass. App. Ct. 1999) (civil); *Missouri ex rel. Classic III, Inc. v. Ely,* 954 S.W.2d 650, 654-55 (Mo. Ct. App. 1997) (civil); *State v. Siel,* 122 N.H. 254, 444 A.2d 499, 502-03 (N.H. 1982) (criminal); *Opinion of the Justices,* 117 N.H. 386, 373 A.2d 644, 647 (N.H. 1977) (civil statutory proceeding); *Hopewell v. Midcontinent Broadcasting Corp.,* 538 N.W.2d 780, 781-82 (S.D. 1995) (civil); *Dallas Morning News Co. v. Garcia,* 822 S.W.2d 675, 678 (Tex. App. 1991) (civil); *Vermont v. St. Peter,* 132 Vt. 266, 315 A.2d 254, 256 (Vt. 1974) (criminal); *Brown v. Commonwealth,* 214 Va. 755, 204 S.E.2d 429, 431 (Va. 1974) (criminal); *Clemente v. Clemente,* 56 Va. Cir. 530, 530 (Va. Cir. 2001) (civil); *Clampitt v. Thurston County.,* 98 Wn.2d 638, 658 P.2d 641, 642 (Wash. 1983) (civil); *Senear v. Daily Journal-American,* 97 Wn.2d 148, 641 P.2d 1180, 1181, 1183 (Wash. 1982) (civil); *State v. Rinaldo,* 36 Wn. App. 86, 673 P.2d 614 (Wash. Ct. App. 1983) (criminal), *aff'd on other grounds,* 102 Wn.2d 749, 689 P.2d 392 (Wash. 1984); *West Virginia ex rel. Charleston Mail Ass'n v. Ranson,* 200 W. Va. 5, 488 S.E.2d 5, 10-11 (W. Va. 1997) (criminal); *West Virginia ex rel. Hudok v. Henry,* 182 W. Va. 500, 389 S.E.2d 188, 192-93 (W. Va. 1989) (civil); *Zelenka v. State,* 83 Wis. 2d 601, 266 N.W.2d 279, 287 (Wis. 1978) (criminal); *Kurzynski v. Spaeth,* 196 Wis. 2d 182, 538 N.W.2d 554, 557-58 (Wis. Ct. App. 1995) (civil); *State v. Knops,* 49 Wis. 2d 647, 183 N.W.2d 93, 99 (Wis. Ct. App. 1971) (grand jury).

[38] *See Connecticut State Bd. of Labor Relations v. Fagin,* 33 Conn. Supp. 204, 370 A.2d 1095, 1097-98 (Conn. Super. Ct. 1976) (civil); *Pope v. Village Apartments, Ltd.,* No. 92-71-436 CV (Miss. 1st Cir. Ct. Jan. 23, 1995) (unpublished opinion) (civil); *In re Grand Jury Subpoena,* No. 38,664 (Miss. 2d Cir. Ct. Oct. 4, 1989) (unpublished opinion) (grand jury); *Mississippi v. Hand,* No. CR89-49-C (T-2) (Miss. 1st Cir. Ct. July 31, 1990) (unpublished opinion) (grand jury); *Lester v. Draper,* No. 000906048 (Utah 3d Dist. Ct. Jan. 16, 2002) (unpublished opinion) (civil); *Utah v. Koolmo,* No. 981905396 (Utah 3d Dist. Ct. Mar. 29, 1999) (unpublished opinion) (criminal). *See also* Edward L. Carter, Note, *Reporter's Privilege in Utah,* 18 B.Y.U. J. Pub. L. 163, 174-79 (2003) (describing six Utah trial court decisions recognizing a qualified reporter's privilege, four of which involved subpoenas from prosecutors); The Reporters Committee for Freedom of the Press, *The Reporter's Privilege Compendium (2002),* available at http://www.rcfp.org/privilege/index.html (last visited Feb. 22, 2005) (collecting additional unpublished trial privilege orders from Mississippi court recognizing a qualified under Fifth Circuit jurisprudence).

[39] *See generally* The Reporters Committee for Freedom of the Press, *The Reporter's Privilege Compendium (2002),* available at http://www.rcfp.org/privilege/index.html (last visited Feb. 22, 2005) (noting that anecdotal evidence suggests that few subpoenas have been issued to news organizations or reporters in Wyoming and that those few subpoenas issued usually ask the reporter to testify that his or her story was accurate).

As the *Jaffee* court observed with respect to a psychotherapist-patient privilege, "the existence of a consensus among the States indicates that 'reason and experience' support recognition of the privilege," *Jaffee*, 518 U.S. at 13, and the near unanimous consensus of the states as to the importance of offering qualified, and in some cases absolute, protection to reporters with respect to confidential sources leads to the same conclusion here. Furthermore, while the adoption in New York of an absolute protection concerning information obtained or received in confidence does not compel the recognition of a similarly absolute rule here, the fact that New York as well as Illinois (the location of the grand jury at issue here) are among those states to have adopted statutory protections for reporters with respect to confidential sources is particularly relevant to the determination of whether such a protection should be recognized here. ... This relevance stems from recognition of the fact that, were the privilege advocated here rejected, the degree to which confidential sources could be protected would be rendered uncertain, thereby lessening the likelihood that such sources will cooperate and undercutting the very benefit to the public that New York, like so many other states, sought to bestow through its shield law. Thus, here, as in Jaffee, denial of the privilege "would frustrate the purposes of the state legislation that was enacted to foster these confidential communications." *Jaffee,* 518 U.S. at 13 (noting, with respect to the psychotherapist-patient privilege, that "any State's promise of confidentiality would have little value if the patient were aware that the privilege would not be honored in a federal court") (footnote omitted).

... The fact that a federal shield law has not been enacted by Congress in the decades since *Branzburg* issued does not, as the government has argued, provide a clear indication that the recognition of such a privilege is unnecessary.[45] As the Supreme Court has recognized, the "significance of subsequent congressional action or inaction necessarily varies with the circumstances," *United States v. Wells,* 519 U.S. 482, 495, 137 L. Ed. 2d 107, 117 S. Ct. 921 (1997), and the government has suggested no basis upon which it might be concluded that Congress' silence in this regard is particularly meaningful.

... Finally, the government has argued that a reporter's privilege should not be recognized under the federal common law because the precise contours of such a privilege would be difficult to fashion. Although the development of parameters concerning the application of a privilege under the federal common law will doubtless encounter certain interpretive hurdles, the possibility of interpretive disputes does not counsel against recognition of a qualified privilege at all, particularly where guidance may be derived from

---

[40] *Compare Appeal of Goodfader*, 45 Haw. 317, 367 P.2d 472, 480-83 (Haw. 1961) (declining to recognize an evidentiary reporter's privilege where no statutory authority for such a privilege existed and noting that "we have not been convinced that there is a First Amendment protection available"), *with DeRoburt v. Gannett Co.,* 507 F. Supp. 880, 883 (D. Haw. 1981) (recognizing a qualified reporter's privilege derived from the First Amendment to the U.S. Constitution).

[45] Federal shield laws have been proposed on numerous occasions, most recently in February 2005. *See* 151 Cong. Rec. S1344-02, at S1344 (Feb. 14, 2005) (introducing S. 369); 151 Cong. Rec. S1199-02, at S1215 (Feb. 9, 2005) (introducing S. 340); 151 Cong. Rec. H290-06, at H290 (Feb. 2, 2005) (introducing H.R. 581); *see also* Theodore Campagnolo, *The Conflict Between State Press Shield Laws and Federal Criminal Proceedings: The Rule 501 Blues,* 38 Gonz. L. Rev. 445, 470-72 (2002/2003) (describing the introduction in both the House and the Senate of a number of bills and resolutions aimed at creating a federal reporter's privilege following the announcement of *Branzburg).*

the ample body of legislation and jurisprudence of the states as well as from the First Amendment and federal common law caselaw of the federal courts. As the *Jaffee* Court emphasized, a rule, such as Rule 501, "that authorizes the recognition of new privileges on a case-by-case basis makes it appropriate to define the details of new privileges in a like manner." *Jaffee,* 518 U.S. at 18.

Accordingly, for the reasons stated, there is a qualified federal common law reporter's privilege with respect to the protection of confidential sources.

C. The Government Has Not Overcome The Qualified Reporter's Privilege

1. Third Party Telephone Records Are Protected By The Qualified Reporter's Privilege

The government argues that the qualified reporter's privilege, whether deriving from the First Amendment or arising under federal common law, does not extend to telephone records held by third-party telephone providers because such records "will not identify any confidential source ... but rather, at best, will supply leads which, with additional investigation, will enable the government to identify the source of the subject disclosure."

In support of this argument, the government relies heavily on a single decision from the District of Columbia Circuit. *See Reporters Committee for Freedom of the Press v. AT&T,* 192 U.S. App. D.C. 376, 593 F.2d 1030 (D.C. Cir. 1978). The Reporters Committee court considered, *inter alia,* whether journalists are "entitled under the First Amendment to prior notice of toll-call-record subpoenas issued in the course of felony investigations." *Id.* at 1046. Based on its view that *Branzburg* recognized no First Amendment privilege, the Reporters Committee court concluded that "the Government's good faith inspection of [a reporter's] telephone companies' toll call records does not infringe on plaintiffs' First Amendment rights, because that Amendment guarantees no freedom from such investigation." *Id.* at 1051-52.

Because the Second Circuit has interpreted *Branzburg* as recognizing a First Amendment qualified privilege, *Reporters Committee* is inapposite. Moreover, *The Times'* First Amendment interest in records held by third parties is well supported. ....[T]he First Amendment interest at issue, i.e., the protection of newsgathering that depends on information obtained from confidential sources, is the same whether the government compels testimony from *The Times'* reporters concerning the names of their confidential sources or instead compels production from third parties of records evidencing telephone communication between such reporters and their confidential sources. Therefore, the telephone records are protected by the qualified reporter's privilege. ...

2. The Government Has Not Made The Requisite Showing Necessary To Overcome The Qualified Reporter's Privilege

... In the present context, where the identities of the reporters' confidential sources are sought pursuant to a grand jury investigation, the interests militating in favor of disclosure are substantial.

But even in this context, in order to overcome the qualified reporter's privilege, the government must first demonstrate that the *Petroleum Products* test has been satisfied. That is, the government must "make a clear and specific showing that the subpoenaed documents are '[1] highly material and relevant, [2] necessary or critical to the maintenance of the claim, and [3] not obtainable from other available sources.'" *Burke,* 700 F.2d at 77 (quoting *In re Petroleum Products,* 680 F.2d at 7). The government has failed to make this threshold showing.

The government argues that Rule 6(e), Fed. R. Crim. P., prevents it from proffering evidence to this Court to demonstrate that it has satisfied the *Petroleum Products* test. As discussed in greater detail above, Rule 6(e) authorizes the court in the district where the grand jury convened to order disclosure of secret grand jury information "in connection with a judicial proceeding." Fed. R. Crim. P. 6(e)(3)(E)(i). No materials to overcome the privilege have been transferred under seal to this Court. *See* Fed. R. Crim. P. 6(e)(3)(G).

a. There Has Been No Showing Of The Materiality, Relevance and Necessity of the Subpoenaed Documents

The government has not disputed that the subpoena at issue will capture a substantial number of records of confidential communications that are irrelevant to the investigation at issue in this case. Nor has the government demonstrated that it has complied with the requirement, imposed by the First Amendment and provided for by the Guidelines, that its subpoena be drawn as narrowly as possible. Rather, the government merely asserts that "it is obvious from the nature of the investigation ... and the nature of the information sought," that it has satisfied the three-part *Petroleum Products* test. Such conclusory assertions are insufficient to satisfy the first two prongs of the *Petroleum Products* test.

b. There Has Been No Showing That The Sought Information Is Unavailable From Other Sources

The government has not sought to demonstrate that it has exhausted all reasonable alternative sources of the identities of government officials who made the alleged unauthorized disclosures to Miller and Shenon. Nor has the government stated whether it has interviewed all government employees with access to the "leaked" information, whether it has examined the telephone records of all such employees, or what other steps it has taken that would avoid the need to engage in the contemplated invasion into the protected relationship between reporter and confidential source. The only evidence submitted by the government in this regard is the statement of Fitzgerald that the government "reasonably exhausted alternative investigative means." This conclusory statement lacks sufficient specificity and clarity to satisfy *Petroleum Products* and *Burke.*

... The *Petroleum Products* court emphasized the significant lengths that a party seeking disclosure of a reporter's confidential sources must go to demonstrate that it has exhausted all other available investigative means. *See, e.g., In re Petroleum Products,* 680 F.2d at 9 (holding that mere fact that 100 witnesses had been deposed was not sufficient to establish that available sources had been exhausted). As the Second Circuit explained:

> Justice Brennan has suggested that the harm caused by requiring the taking of 65 depositions did not "outweigh the unpalatable choice that civil contempt would impose upon the" reporter ordered to disclose the names of his confidential source. *In re Roche,* [448 U.S. 1312, 1316, 65 L. Ed. 2d 1103, 101 S. Ct. 4] (1980) (Brennan, J. in chambers). Likewise, the District of Columbia Circuit recently recognized that "an alternative requiring the taking of as many as 60 depositions might be

a reasonable prerequisite to compelled disclosure." *Zerilli v. Smith*, 211 U.S. App. D.C. 116, 656 F.2d 705, 714 (D.C. Cir. 1981).

Id. at 9 n.12. The government has not satisfied this heavy burden.

Finally, it should be noted that the government has tacitly acknowledged that it possesses the wherewithal to search its own internal records for the identities of the suspected leakers:

> If the investigation identified telephone calls from a government agency telephone extension to the *New York Times* reporter, the Government could question the official(s) who placed the telephone call(s). The *New York Times* could not quarrel with the government's ability to examine its own telephone records.

Based on the foregoing, the government has failed to satisfy the third prong of the Petroleum Products test. Since the government has failed to carry its burden with respect to the three prongs of the *Petroleum Products* test, it has established no basis for overcoming *The Times'* qualified reporter's privilege.

> 3. Other Factors Militate Against Invasion of *The Times'* Qualified Reporter's Privilege

The government's failure to demonstrate compliance with the Guidelines also weighs against disclosure of the sought records. *See* 28 C.F.R. § 50.10(g)(1). Specifically, the government has declined to make any meaningful showing that (1) the subpoena is as narrowly drawn as possible, (2) that it covers a reasonable period of time, and (3) that the government pursued all reasonable alternative investigation steps prior to issuance of the subpoena. *See id.; see also In re Williams,* 766 F. Supp. at 371 (stating that the government's compliance with the Guidelines is relevant to the question of whether it has established a basis for overcoming a qualified reporter's privilege against compelled disclosure of confidential sources.).

....[S]ince the government has failed to make the requisite *Petroleum Products* showing, the Court need not reach the difficult question of how to properly balance the legitimate, competing interests of the parties.

To deny the relief sought by *The Times* under these circumstances, i.e., without any showing on the part of the government that the sought records are necessary, relevant, material and unavailable from other sources, has the potential to significantly affect the reporting of news based upon information provided by confidential sources. The record before this Court has demonstrated that the reporters at issue relied upon the promise of confidentiality to gather information concerning issues of paramount national importance -- e.g., the nation's preparedness for the attacks of September 11, the government's efforts to combat Al Qaeda post-September 11, and the risk posed to the American people by biological weapons. The government has failed to demonstrate that the balance of the competing interests weighs in its favor. ...

Conclusion

The Court has balanced the interests of the free press and the government under these facts and authorities. That balance requires maintaining the secrecy of the confidential sources of Miller and Shenon.

Accordingly, on the facts and conclusions set forth above, the motion of the government to dismiss the complaint of *The Times* is denied. The government's cross-motion for summary judgment is granted with respect to Count IV of *The Times'* complaint, and is otherwise denied. *The Times'* motion for summary judgment is granted as to Counts II and III of the complaint, and is otherwise denied.

It is so ordered.

* * * * *

In *In re Grand Jury Subpoena, Judith Miller*, the U.S. Court of Appeals for the District of Columbia Circuit, referring to *Branzburg*, declared that the U.S. Supreme Court had "in no uncertain terms rejected the existence of a [reporter's] privilege." 397 F.3d 964, 969 (D.C. Cir. 2005). By contrast, in *New York Times v. Gonzales*, the U.S. District Court for the Southern District of New York noted that, based on *Branzburg*, courts within the U.S. Court of Appeals for the Second Circuit "have recognized the existence of a qualified reporters' privileged derived from the First Amendment;" the New York federal court concluded that "the Second Circuit, based on *Branzburg*, [likewise] has recognized a qualified First Amendment privilege, applicable in civil actions and in all phases of a criminal prosecution that protects reporters from compelled disclosure of confidential sources." No. 04 Civ. 7677 (RWS), 2005 U.S. Dist. LEXIS 2642 at *92, *94 (S.D.N.Y. Feb. 24, 2005) (citations omitted). The disparity in rulings was among the points made in connection with the petition for a writ of *certiorari* to the U.S. Supreme Court.

The reporters were supported in their petition by, among others, an *amici curiae* brief filed by 39 states and the District of Columbia. *See* Brief *Amici Curiae* of the States of Oklahoma, *et al.*, in Support of Petitioners, *Miller v. United States of America*, Nos. 04-1507 & 04-1508 (filed May 27, 2005). Appearing through the states' respective attorneys general, the *amici* argued that the appellate decision conflicted with the recognition of a reporter's privilege by 49 states and the District of Columbia. *See id.* at 2, 3. "A federal policy that allows journalists to be imprisoned for engaging in the same conduct that these State privileges encourage and protect 'buck[s] the clear policy of virtually all states,' and undermines both the purpose of the shield laws, and the policy determinations of the State courts and legislatures that adopted them." *Id.* at 2-3 (citations omitted). The *amici* argued that they have a vital interest in the issue beyond concerns about protecting the integrity of their state shield laws. "Uncertainty and confusion – exemplified by the split in the federal courts of appeals and by the fractured panel opinions below – have marked this area of the law in the three decades that have passed since th[e Supreme] Court decided *Branzburg* and the Congress enacted Rule 501 of the Federal Rules of Evidence. This increasing conflict has undercut the State shield laws just as much as the absence of a federal privilege." *Id.* at 3.

On June 27, 2005, the U.S. Supreme Court denied the petition for *certioriari*, however. Nos. 04-1507, 04, 1508, 2005 U.S. LEXIS 5190, 5191 (U.S. June 27, 2005). A few days later, Time Inc. announced that it would comply with the lower court's order requiring it to deliver documents to the grand jury. Norman Pearlstine, Editor-in-Chief of *Time*, stated, "The same Constitution that protects the freedom of the press requires obedience to final decisions of the courts and respect for their rulings and judgments. That Time Inc. strongly disagrees with the courts provides no immunity. The innumerable Supreme Court decisions in which even Presidents have followed orders with which they strongly disagreed evidences that our nation lives by the rule of law and that none of us is above it." *See, e.g.,* Poynter Online, *Time Inc. to Comply with Court Order in Plame Case,* (June 30, 2005) (quoting Norman Pearlstine), *available at* <http://poynter.org/forum/view_post.asp?id=9778>. On July 6, 2005, Judge Thomas F. Hogan ordered *New York Times* reporter Judith Miller to be jailed immediately after she refused again to cooperate with the grand jury. *See* Adam Liptak and Maria Newman, *New York Times Reporter is Jailed for Keeping Source Secret,* N.Y. Times, July 6, 2005, *available at* <http://www.nytimes.com/2005/07/06/politics/06cnd-leak.html?hp&ex=1120708800&en=0cf3bf4cb26d50fb&ei=5094&partner=homepage>. Time reporter Matt Cooper agreed to testify after his source released him from promises of confidentiality. *See id.*

* * * * *

Notes and Questions

1.   How might access to a confidential source assist a reporter not only in gathering newsworthy information, but also in evaluating the credibility of other sources whom the reporter has consulted?

2.   As courts consider journalists' arguments about privilege, should a court expect a proffer of empirical evidence to support the need for a privilege?

In *Branzburg v. Hayes,* Justice Stewart, dissenting, cited an affidavit submitted by veteran CBS anchor Walter Cronkite, who stated, "'In doing my work, I (and those who assist me) depend constantly on information, ideas, leads and opinions received in confidence. Such material is essential in digging out newsworthy facts and, equally important, in assessing the importance and analyzing the significance of public events.'" 408 U.S. 665, 730 n.8 (1972) (Stewart, J., dissenting) (quoting Walter Cronkite). Justice Stewart also took note of "surveys among reporters and editors [that] indicate that the promise of nondisclosure is necessary for many types of news gathering." *Id.* at 731.

Three decades later, in *In re Grand Jury Subpoena, Judith Miller,* Judge Tatel, concurring in the judgment, acknowledged Special Counsel Patrick Fitzgerald's observation that, with the exception of affidavits and citations to two articles in their reply brief, the reporters had presented no empirical evidence that denial of the privilege would "'have a significant impact on the free flow of information protected by the First Amendment.'" 397 F.3d 964, 992 (D.C. Cir. 2005) (Tatel, J., concurring in the judgment) (quoting appellee's brief). But he also noted that:

> [T]he Supreme Court has never required proponents of a privilege to adduce scientific studies demonstrating the privilege's benefits. Rather, as the ... dissenters [in *Jaffee v. Redmond,* 518 U.S. 1, 22-23 (1996) (Scalia, J., dissenting),] pointed out, the empirical question – "[h]ow likely is it that a person will be deterred from seeking psychological counseling, or from being completely truthful in the course of such counseling, because of fear of later disclosure in litigation?" -- was one "[t]he Court [did] not attempt to answer." [*Id.*] Instead, following the wise precept that common sense need not be "the mere handmaiden of

social science data or expert testimonials," *Amatel v. Reno*, 332 U.S. App. D.C. 191, 156 F.3d 192, 199 (D.C. Cir. 1998), *Jaffee* relied on the traditional common law process: it examined the logical prerequisites of the confidential relationship, taking into account the policy and experience of parallel jurisdictions. *See Jaffee*, 518 U.S. at 10 (reasoning that given the need for "frank and complete disclosure of facts, emotions, memories, and fears" in psychotherapy, "the mere possibility of disclosure may impede development of the confidential relationship necessary for successful treatment").

397 F.3d at 992 (Tatel, J., concurring in the judgment).

In *New York Times Co. v. Gonzales,* the U.S. District Court for the Southern District of New York observed that *New York Times* reporters testified that without information they obtained on the condition that the identity of their sources would be kept confidential, the journalists would not have been able to report on such important matters of public concern "as the threat posed by international terrorists, the prospect of germ warfare, efforts to reorganize the United States' intelligence agencies, and plans to expand law enforcement's powers to conduct surveillance." One *New York Times* reporter stated that without the protection afforded by a recognized privilege, "[r]eporters and editors might eliminate information obtained from confidential sources from news reports if publication might result in subpoenas to themselves or their telephone companies. On some sensitive topics, the only available sources of information are confidential sources; the press might simply avoid reporting on these topics altogether." No. 04 Civ. 7677 (RWS), 2005 U.S. Dist. LEXIS 2642 at *114-*115 (S.D.N.Y. Feb. 24, 2005) (quoting Philip Shenon).

Are there any other reasonable means of proffering evidence of the nexus between the existence of the privilege and the ability to obtain information from sources who do not want to disclose their identities? As Judge Tatel observed, "[l]ike psychotherapists, as well as attorneys and spouses, all of whom enjoy privileges under Rule 501, reporters 'depend[ ] upon an atmosphere of confidence and trust.'" *In re Grand Jury Subpoena, Judith Miller,* 397 F.3d at 991 (Tatel, J., concurring in the judgment) (citations omitted). Judge Tatel logically concluded that "just as mental patients who fear 'embarrassment or disgrace,' will 'surely be chilled' in seeking therapy, so will sources who fear identification avoid revealing information that could get them in trouble." *Id.* (quoting *Jaffee v. Redmond,* 518 U.S. at 12). Accordingly, privileges have been founded upon the recognition of benefits inherent in candid disclosures of confidential information, as well as on acknowledgement of the inevitable deterrent effect that compulsory disclosure will have on such disclosures. "Reason dictates," *New York Times Co. v. Gonzales,* 04 Civ. 7677 (RWS), 2005 U.S. Dist. LEXIS 2642 at *127, that prospective confidential sources would be chilled and newsgathering impeded if privilege protections are denied the press.

3. The pursuit by Special Counsel Patrick Fitzgerald of *The New York Times* reporter Judith Miller and *Time* reporter Matthew Cooper has been questioned, not only because it raises journalistic and privilege questions, but also because it appears that Fitzgerald has otherwise concluded his investigation. One commentator surmised that the "continuing legal squeeze" by Fitzgerald on Miller and Cooper to reveal their sources may derive less from an investigation into the leak and more from inquiry into possible perjury by a senior administration official. David Ignatius, *A Leak's Wider Ripples,* Wash. Post, May 13, 2005 at A23. Such an inquiry raises interesting journalistic questions. "Does a reporter's confidentiality agreement extend to protecting a cover-up? ….[T]his case raises the

74

possibility that one of the senior administration officials who talked with Cooper or Miller has denied doing so, under oath. Otherwise, Fitzgerald would have been finished months ago." *Id.*

4. Judge Tatel, concurring in *In re Grand Jury Subpoena, Judith Miller,* 397 F.3d 964, 1004 (D.C. Cir. 2005) (Tatel, J., concurring in the judgment), weighed the harm caused by the leak of the identity of an alleged covert CIA operative against the grand jury's putative need for the reporters' testimony as articulated by the Special Counsel. How might such a balancing test impact the motivations of a prospective confidential source to impart information at the newsgathering stage? Does such a test effectively reconcile competing tensions between the "rule of law and free speech," *id.* at 1003, or does it encroach on the discretion inherent in independent editorial functioning?

5. In order to prove a violation of the Intelligence Identities Protection Act of 1982, Pub. L. No. 97-200, 1982 U.S.C.C.A.N. (96 Stat. 122) 145 (codified at 50 U.S.C. §§ 421-26), the government must show, among other things, that the United States was taking affirmative measures to conceal a covert agent's intelligence relationship to the United States, the covert agent whose identity was disclosed has been an employee of an intelligence agency and has a relationship with such agency that is classified, the person disclosing the identity knows that the government is taking affirmative measures to conceal the relationship, and the disclosure is intentional. What sort of independent evaluation should the court undertake to determine that the government will satisfy this showing before compelling the disclosure of confidential sources? In addition, how may a reporter reasonably contest the government's showing if the proffer is made *in camera?*

6. By early 2005, legislation had been introduced to create a federal statutory shield law. *See, e.g.,* S. 340, H.R. 581 (109th Congress, 1st Sess.). Known as the "Free Flow of Information Act of 2005," the bill would codify an absolute privilege against disclosure of confidential sources and a qualified privilege against the production of documents.

* * * * *

"The Press" and Internet Publications

substitute the following for the last sentence of the second paragraph on page 60 of Law of Internet Speech:

On appeal, the Utah Supreme Court conceded that "[q]uite obviously, the plain language of Utah's statute[, Utah Code Ann. §§ 76-9-501-503,] does not comport with the requirements laid down by the United States Supreme Court [since the statute's enactment]." *In re I. M. L., a minor v. State of Utah,* No. 20010159 at ¶ 18 (Utah Sup. Ct. Nov. 15, 2002), *available at* <http://courtlink.utcourts.gov/opinions/supopin/iml.htm>. The statute is constitutionally infirm because it punishes statements even when they are about public figures and were made without actual malice and provides no immunity for truthful statements. *Id.* at ¶¶ 18-30. The charges against the teenager subsequently were dismissed at the request of the County Attorney and a civil libel suit brought by the school principal reportedly was settled on undisclosed terms. *See* Associated Press, *Utah High Court Tosses Criminal-Libel Law* (Nov. 18, 2002), *available at* <http://www.freedomforum.org/templates/document.asp?document ID=17264>. Are the statements made by the teenager tantamount to a journalistic publication? Were the state statute constitutional, would he have been subject to the same standards as any other "member of the press"?

* * * * *

insert the following before the last full paragraph on page 61 of Law of Internet Speech:

In December 2004, Apple Computer, Inc. filed suit in Santa Clara County, California against unnamed individuals, alleging that they had leaked specific, trade secret information about new Apple products to news web-sites, including AppleInsider and PowerPage. *See Apple Computer, Inc. v. Doe 1, an unknown individual, and Does 2-25, inclusive,* No.: 1-04-CV-032178, at 2 (Cal. Super. Ct. Mar. 11, 2005), *available at* <http://www. eff.org/Censorship/Apple_v_Does/20050311_apple_decision.pdf>. Apple maintained that the information the movants published constituted trade secrets under California law, the Uniform Trade Secrets Act, Civil Code §§ 3426, *et seq.,* and section 499c ofthe California Penal Code, and sought the identities of the source(s) of the information and subpoenaed Nfox.com for e-mail messages that might identify the source(s). *See Apple Computer, Inc. v. Doe 1, an unknown individual, and Does 2-25, inclusive,* No.: 1-04-CV-032178, at 3-4, *available at* <http://www.eff.org/Censorship/Apple_v_Does/20050311_ apple_decision.pdf>. The movants sought a protective order blocking the subpoena on the ground that they were privileged from disclosing their sources under California's shield law, Cal. Evid. Code §§ 1070(a)- (b). *See Apple Computer, Inc. v. Doe 1, an unknown individual, and Does 2-25, inclusive,* No.: 1-04-CV-032178, at 3, *available at* <http://www.eff.org/Censorship/Apple_ v_Does/20050311_apple_decision.pdf>.

The court concluded that the trade secrets statute "support[s] the compelling interest of disclosure which may, in the proper civil case, outweigh First Amendment rights. ....[T]he United States and California Supreme Courts have underscored that trade secret laws apply to everyone regardless of their status, title or chosen profession. The California Legislature has not carved out any exception to these statutes for journalists, bloggers or anyone else." *Id.* at 6. The court acknowledged that "[d]efining what is a 'journalist' has become more complicated as the variety of media has expanded." *Id.* at 8. Nevertheless, even if the movants were characterized as journalists, the court concluded that they are not entitled to "the equivalent of a free pass. The journalist's privilege is not absolute." *Id.* at 8-9. Ultimately, the court did not reach the question of whether one individual qualified for relief from the subpoena under California's shield law to be immune from being adjudged in contempt because "there is no license conferred on anyone to violate criminal laws." *Id.* at 11 (citations omitted).

Should the court be influenced by any proffer of evidence that the posters were former employees of Apple Computer and owed a duty of confidentiality? *Compare Dendrite Int'l, Inc. v. Doe No. 3, et al.,* 342 N.J. Super. 134, 775 A.2d 756 (N.J. App. Div. 2001) (upholding the denial of the plaintiff's requests to conduct limited discovery aimed at disclosing the identity of an unnamed defendant notwithstanding that the plaintiff's defamation claims would survive a traditional motion to dismiss for failure to state a cause of action) *with Immunomedics, Inc. v. Doe,* 342 N.J. Super. 160, 167, 775 A.2d 773, 777 (N.J. App. Div. 2001) (countenancing a subpoena seeking the identity of an anonymous poster in light of evidence that the poster was an employee of the plaintiff, that employees execute confidentiality agreements, and that the content of messages in issue indicated a possible breach of such agreements); *see generally Virologic, Inc. v. Doe,* Nos. A101571, A102811,

2004 Cal. App. Unpub. LEXIS 8070, 32 Media L. Rep. 2219 (Cal. Ct. App. Sept. 1, 2004) (unpublished).

* * * * *

insert the following at the end of Notes and Questions # 3 on page 77 of Law of Internet Speech:

On appeal, the U.S. Court of Appeals for the Sixth Circuit considered the plaintiffs' facial challenges to the defendants' policy; the plaintiffs argued that a policy allowing links exclusively to web-sites that promoted the economic welfare, commerce, tourism, and industry of the local area was void for vagueness under the due process clause of the Fourteenth Amendment and unconstitutionally overbroad under the First Amendment. *See Putnam Pit, Inc. v. City of Cookeville,* 76 Fed. Appx. 607, 2003 U.S. App. LEXIS 17775 (6th Cir. Aug. 20, 2003) (unpublished). The appellate court declined to rule on the challenges, however, on the ground that the issues had not been properly raised in the proceedings below. *See id.* at 614-15.

* * * * *

insert the following before Notes and Questions on page 82 of Law of Internet Speech:

A "blog," sometimes referred to as a "Weblog" or a "Web log," is an "online diary; a personal chronological log of thoughts published on a Web page." <http://www.dictionary.reference.co/search?q=blog>. As the Pew Internet & American Life Project observed, "[a] blog is basically a web site consisting of a collection of entries in reverse chronological order. It is more personal and informal than institutional web sites, more accessible to web roamers and searchers than email, more spontaneous than advertisements, and more open to discussion than video, audio, textual, and statistical files. At the same time, a blog can be linked to all these other internet forms." Michael Cornefield, *et al.,* Pew Internet & American Life Project, *Buzz, Blogs, and Beyond: The Internet and the National Discourse in the Fall of 2004* (May 16, 2005), at 4, *available at* <http://www. pewinternet.org/ppt/BUZZ_ BLOGS_BEYOND_Final05-16-05.pdf>. A network of blogs may be called a "blogosphere," and blogs may contain features that "interlac[e] it with other blogs.... These connective features include a 'blogroll' of favorite blogs, a 'permalink' identifying a blog entry, or post, for ready reference elsewhere, a 'track back' capacity whereby outsiders who link to the entry are listed and given a reciprocal link, and 'RSS feed' capability to deliver an entry automatically to those who have requested its type." *Id.*

According to the Pew Internet and American Life Project in early 2005, 27 percent of adults who went on-line in the United States read blogs. *See* Anick Jesdanun, *Influence of Bloggers Raises Concerns About Ethical Standards,* Marin Independent Journal (Jan. 24, 2005), *available at* <http://www.marinij.com/cda/article/print/0,1674,234%7E26641% 7E2670931,00.html>. Two studies conducted in early 2005 indicated that 16 percent of adults in the United States, or 32 million people, were blog readers. Michael Cornefield, Jonathan Carson, Alison Kalis, and Emily Simon, *Buzz, Blogs, and Beyond: The Internet and the National Discourse in the Fall of 2004,* Pew Internet & American Life Project (May 16, 2005) at 3, *available at* <http://www.pewinternet.org/ppt/BUZZ_BLOGS_BEYOND_ Final05-16-05.pdf>. The same report of the studies stated that six percent of the entire U.S. population has created a blog; this is the equivalent of 11 million people or one out of every 17 American citizens. *Id.* (citing Memorandum from Lee Rainie, Pew Internet & American Life Project, *The State of Blogging,* (Jan. 2, 2005), *available at* <http://www.pewinternet.

org/pdfs/PIP_blogging_data.pdf>; Press Release, Pew Internet & American Life Project, *New Data on Blogs and Blogging* (May 2, 2005), *available at* <http://www.pewinternet. org/press_release.asp?r=104)>.

A "wiki" is a collaborative web-site that is continuously comprised of the work of multiple contributors. Whereas typically a blog is authored by one individual who is the only one that can modify or delete the content, a wiki permits participants to edit, delete, or modify content that has been posted on the web-site by using a browser interface. *See generally* Webopedia, *available at* <http://www.webopedia.com/TERM/w/wiki.html>.

Wikinews, for example, is a collaborative blog of sorts, designed as an open-source site that "allows anyone to create entries or edit and correct other people's work, so long as each change is recorded." *See generally* Joanna Glasner, *All the News That's Fit to Wiki*, Wired News.com (Apr. 22, 2005), *available at* <http://www.wired.com/news/ebiz/0,1272, 67286,00.html?tw=wn_tophead_1>. Although Wikinews evolved from Wikipedia, it shares certain challenges with other media entities; both have "fac[ed such] pressures ... as ferreting out fake posts, incorporating original sources and updating coverage to reflect rapidly changing current events." *Id.*

One commentator asked pointedly, "Are blogs journalism?" and concluded, "How could the answer be anything but an emphatic 'sometimes!'" Graham Webster, *Forget Blogs*, Editor & Publisher (Apr. 21, 2005), *available at* <http://www.editorandpublisher.com/eandp/ columns/shoptalk_display.jsp?vnu_content_id=1000892803>. Blogs do not necessarily prioritize the significance of the content that is delivered; nor are they invariably "ranked by an editorial filter we trust." *Id.* Blogs may owe much of their popularity to the fact that they are inexpensive, easy to use, and offer a customized substantive experience. *See generally id.*

Should there be journalistic or other ethical guidelines for bloggers? One blogger, a research fellow at Harvard's Berkman Center for Internet and Society, observed that "[b]logging is more like a conversation, and 'you can't develop a code of ethics for conversations.'" *See* Anick Jesdanun, *Influence of Bloggers Raises Concerns About Ethical Standards*, Marin Independent Journal (Jan. 24, 2005), *available at* <http://www. marinij.com/cda/article/print/0,1674,234%7E26641%7E2670931,00.html> (quoting David Weinberger). A managing producer at MSNBC.com and publisher of Cyberjournalist.net modified the Society of Professional Journalists' code of ethics and urged its adoption by fellow bloggers. *See id.* (citing Jonathan Dube).

* * * * *

Analytical Frameworks for Internet Speech

insert the following at the top of page 101 of Law of Internet Speech:

One commentator opined, "As legal conflicts in cyberspace proliferate, analysts argue over which institution – the legislature, the courts or the market – should be used to resolve them. Yet more often than not, such arguments are motivated by strategic positions rather than impartial analysis." Susan Freiwald, *Comparative Institutional Analysis in Cyberspace: The Case of Intermediary Liability for Defamation*, 14 Harv. J. Law & Tech. 569, 571 (2001) (footnotes omitted). As a general matter, is there a more appropriate arena for the resolution of conflicts relating to Internet communications? Arguably the legislature has the means to ferret out factual findings and come to a conclusion based on democratic preference; the judiciary is positioned to reflect on legal principles based on evidence garnered through the adversarial process; and the market can evolve based on consumer demand. Is it possible to consider objectively the best possible means for resolution irrespective of a specific issue or dispute?

To what extent should the efficiency of pursuit of redress for a wrong help shape the contours of a cause of action or affect its cognizability? In the P2P file sharing context, for example, Judge Richard Posner, writing for the U.S. Court of Appeals for the Seventh Circuit, observed:

> The [music] swappers, who are ignorant or more commonly disdainful of copyright and in any event discount the likelihood of being sued or prosecuted for copyright infringement, are the direct infringers. But firms that facilitate their infringement, even if they are not themselves infringers because they are not making copies of the music that is shared, may be liable to the copyright owners as contributory infringers. Recognizing the impracticability or futility of a copyright owner's suing a multitude of individual infringers ("chasing individual consumers is time consuming and is a teaspoon solution to an ocean problem," the law allows a copyright holder to sue a contributor to the infringement instead, in effect as an aider and abettor. Another analogy is to the tort of intentional interference with contract, that is, inducing a breach of contract. If a breach of contract (and a copyright license is just a type of contract) can be prevented most effectively by actions taken by a third party, it makes sense to have a legal mechanism for placing liability for the consequences of the breach on him as well as on the party that broke the contract.

In re Aimster Copyright Litig., 334 F.3d 643, 645-46 (7th Cir. 2004) (quoting Randal C. Picker, *Copyright as Entry Policy: The Case of Digital Distribution,* 47 Antitrust Bull. 423, 442 (2002)) (citing *Sufrin v. Hosier,* 128 F.3d 594, 587 (7th Cir. 1997)); *see* Supplement *infra* at 345, 391, *cert. denied,* 540 U.S. 1107 (2004). Such theories of secondary liability ameliorate the cumbersome and tedious process of individual suits against direct copyright infringers. Does the efficiency of contributory and vicarious copyright infringement actions buttress their analytical cognizability or merely suggest countenancing such claims for pragmatic reasons?

Consider as well options by one who is aggrieved by spam e-mail messages. In *Intel v. Hamidi,* 30 Cal. 4th 1342, 71 P.3d 296, 1 Cal. Rptr. 3d 32 (Cal. 2003), the majority court pointed out that the plaintiff, an entity aggrieved by spam sent by the defendant, had alternative avenues for legal relief. Rather than pursuing a trespass to chattels claim, the plaintiff might have had viable causes of action sounding in interference with prospective economic relations, interference with contract, intentional infliction of emotional distress, or defamation. *Id.,* 30 Cal. 4th at 1347-48, 71 P.2d at 300, 1 Cal. Rptr. at 37. Judge Mosk, dissenting, acknowledged that other causes of action may under certain circumstances also apply to the defendant's conduct, but characterized the remedy based on trespass to chattels as "the most efficient and appropriate. It simply requires [the defendant] to stop the unauthorized use of property without regard to the content of the transmissions. Unlike trespass to chattels, the other potential causes of action suggested by the majority and Hamidi would require an evaluation of the transmissions' content and, in the case of a nuisance action, for example, would involve questions of degree and value judgments based on competing interests." *Id.*, 30 Cal. 4th at 1392, 71 P.2d at 330, 1 Cal. Rptr. 3d at 72 (Mosk, J., dissenting).

* * * * *

Jurisdiction as an Illustration

insert the following before Notes and Questions on page 120 of Law of Internet Speech:

STANLEY K. YOUNG, Plaintiff-Appellee
v.
NEW HAVEN ADVOCATE, et al., Defendants
ADVANCE PUBLICATIONS, INCORPORATED, et al., Amici Supporting Appellants

United States Court of Appeals for the Fourth Circuit

No. 01-2340, 315 F.3d 256

December 13, 2002

The question in this appeal is whether two Connecticut newspapers and certain of their staff (sometimes, the "newspaper defendants") subjected themselves to personal jurisdiction in Virginia by posting on the Internet news articles that, in the context of discussing the State of Connecticut's policy of housing its prisoners in Virginia institutions, allegedly defamed the warden of a Virginia prison. Our recent decision in *ALS Scan, Inc. v. Digital Service Consultants, Inc.*, 293 F.3d 707 (4th Cir. 2002), supplies the standard for determining a court's authority to exercise personal jurisdiction over an out-of-state person who places information on the Internet. Applying that standard, we hold that a court in Virginia cannot constitutionally exercise jurisdiction over the Connecticut-based newspaper defendants because they did not manifest an intent to aim their websites or the posted articles at a Virginia audience. Accordingly, we reverse the district court's order denying the defendants' motion to dismiss for lack of personal jurisdiction.

I.

Sometime in the late 1990s the State of Connecticut was faced with substantial overcrowding in its maximum security prisons. To alleviate the problem, Connecticut contracted with the Commonwealth of Virginia to house Connecticut prisoners in Virginia's correctional facilities. Beginning in late 1999 Connecticut transferred about 500 prisoners, mostly African-American and Hispanic, to the Wallens Ridge State Prison, a "supermax" facility in Big Stone Gap, Virginia. The plaintiff, Stanley Young, is the warden at Wallens Ridge. Connecticut's arrangement to incarcerate a sizeable number of its offenders in Virginia prisons provoked considerable public debate in Connecticut. Several Connecticut legislators openly criticized the policy, and there were demonstrations against it at the state capitol in Hartford.

Connecticut newspapers, including defendants the *New Haven Advocate* (the *Advocate*) and the *Hartford Courant* (the *Courant*), began reporting on the controversy. On March 30, 2000, the *Advocate* published a news article, written by one of its reporters, defendant

Camille Jackson, about the transfer of Connecticut inmates to Wallens Ridge. The article discussed the allegedly harsh conditions at the Virginia prison and pointed out that the long trip to southwestern Virginia made visits by prisoners' families difficult or impossible. In the middle of her lengthy article, Jackson mentioned a class action that inmates transferred from Connecticut had filed against Warden Young and the Connecticut Commissioner of Corrections. The inmates alleged a lack of proper hygiene and medical care and the denial of religious privileges at Wallens Ridge. Finally, a paragraph at the end of the article reported that a Connecticut state senator had expressed concern about the presence of Confederate Civil War memorabilia in Warden Young's office. At about the same time the *Courant* published three columns, written by defendant-reporter Amy Pagnozzi, questioning the practice of relocating Connecticut inmates to Virginia prisons. The columns reported on letters written home by inmates who alleged cruelty by prison guards. In one column Pagnozzi called Wallens Ridge a "cut-rate gulag." Warden Young was not mentioned in any of the Pagnozzi columns.

On May 12, 2000, Warden Young sued the two newspapers, their editors (Gail Thompson and Brian Toolan), and the two reporters for libel in a diversity action filed in the Western District of Virginia. He claimed that the newspapers' articles imply that he "is a racist who advocates racism" and that he "encourages abuse of inmates by the guards" at Wallens Ridge. Young alleged that the newspapers circulated the allegedly defamatory articles throughout the world by posting them on their Internet websites.

The newspaper defendants filed motions to dismiss the complaint under Federal Rule of Civil Procedure 12(b)(2) on the ground that the district court lacked personal jurisdiction over them. In support of the motions the editor and reporter from each newspaper provided declarations establishing the following undisputed facts. The *Advocate* is a free newspaper published once a week in New Haven, Connecticut. It is distributed in New Haven and the surrounding area, and some of its content is published on the Internet. The *Advocate* has a small number of subscribers, and none of them are in Virginia. The *Courant* is published daily in Hartford, Connecticut. The newspaper is distributed in and around Hartford, and some of its content is published on the Internet. When the articles in question were published, the *Courant* had eight mail subscribers in Virginia. Neither newspaper solicits subscriptions from Virginia residents. No one from either newspaper, not even the reporters, traveled to Virginia to work on the articles about Connecticut's prisoner transfer policy. The two reporters, Jackson of the *Advocate* and Pagnozzi of the *Courant,* made a few telephone calls into Virginia to gather some information for the articles. Both interviewed by telephone a spokesman for the Virginia Department of Corrections. All other interviews were done with people located in Connecticut. The two reporters wrote their articles in Connecticut. The individual defendants (the reporters and editors) do not have any traditional contacts with the Commonwealth of Virginia. They do not live in Virginia, solicit any business there, or have any assets or business relationships there. The newspapers do not have offices or employees in Virginia, and they do not regularly solicit or do business in Virginia. Finally, the newspapers do not derive any substantial revenue from goods used or services rendered in Virginia.

In responding to the declarations of the editors and reporters, Warden Young pointed out that the newspapers posted the allegedly defamatory articles on Internet websites that were accessible to Virginia residents. In addition, Young provided copies of assorted printouts from the newspapers' websites. For the *Advocate*, Young submitted eleven pages from newhavenadvocate.com and newmassmedia.com for January 26, 2001. The two pages from newhavenadvocate.com are the *Advocate*'s homepage, which includes links to articles about the "Best of New Haven" and New Haven's park police. The nine pages from newmassmedia.com, a website maintained by the publishers of the *Advocate*, consist of classified advertising from that week's newspapers and instructions on how to submit a classified ad. The listings include advertisements for real estate rentals in New Haven and Guilford, Connecticut, for roommates wanted and tattoo services offered in Hamden, Connecticut, and for a bassist needed by a band in West Haven, Connecticut. For the *Courant,* Young provided nine pages from hartfordcourant.com and ctnow.com for January 26, 2001. The hartfordcourant.com homepage characterizes the website as a "source of news and entertainment in and about Connecticut." A page soliciting advertising in the *Courant* refers to "exposure for your message in this market" in the "best medium in the state to deliver your advertising message." The pages from ctnow.com, a website produced by the *Courant,* provide news stories from that day's edition of the *Courant,* weather reports for Hartford and New Haven, Connecticut, and links to sites for the University of Connecticut and Connecticut state government. The website promotes its online advertising as a "source for jobs in Connecticut." The website printouts provided for January 26, 2001, do not have any content with a connection to readers in Virginia. ...

II.

  A.

A federal court may exercise personal jurisdiction over a defendant in the manner provided by state law. *See ESAB Group, Inc. v. Centricut, Inc.*, 126 F.3d 617, 622 (4th Cir. 1997); Fed. R. Civ. P. 4(k)(1)(A). Because Virginia's long-arm statute extends personal jurisdiction to the extent permitted by the Due Process Clause, *see English & Smith v. Metzger*, 901 F.2d 36, 38 (4th Cir. 1990), "the statutory inquiry necessarily merges with the constitutional inquiry, and the two inquiries essentially become one." *Stover v. O'Connell Assocs., Inc.*, 84 F.3d 132, 135-36 (4th Cir. 1996). The question, then, is whether the defendant has sufficient "minimum contacts with [the forum] such that the maintenance of the suit does not offend 'traditional notions of fair play and substantial justice.'" *Int'l Shoe Co. v. Washington*, 326 U.S. 310, 316, 90 L.Ed. 95, 66 S. Ct. 154 (1945) (quoting *Milliken v. Meyer*, 311 U.S. 457, 463, 85 L.Ed. 278, 61 S. Ct. 339 (1940)). A court may assume power over an out of-state defendant either by a proper "finding [of] specific jurisdiction based on conduct connected to the suit or by [a proper] finding [of] general jurisdiction." *ALS Scan, Inc. v. Digital Serv. Consultants, Inc.*, 293 F.3d 707, 711 (4th Cir. 2002). Warden Young argues only for specific jurisdiction, so we limit our discussion accordingly. When a defendant's contacts with the forum state "are also the basis for the suit, those contacts may establish specific jurisdiction." *Id.* at 712. In determining whether specific jurisdiction exists, we traditionally ask (1) whether the defendant purposefully availed itself of the privileges of conducting activities in the forum state, (2) whether the plaintiff's claim arises out of the defendant's forum-related activities, and (3) "whether the exercise of personal jurisdiction over the defendant would be constitutionally reasonable." *Id.* at 712. *See also Christian Sci. Bd.*, 259 F.3d at 216. The plaintiff, of course, has the burden to establish that personal jurisdiction exists over the out-of-state defendant. *Young v. FDIC*, 103 F.3d 1180, 1191 (4th Cir. 1997).

B.

We turn to whether the district court can exercise specific jurisdiction over the newspaper defendants, namely, the two newspapers, the two editors, and the two reporters. To begin with, we can put aside the few Virginia contacts that are not Internet based because Warden Young does not rely on them. Thus, Young does not claim that the reporters' few telephone calls into Virginia or the *Courant*'s eight Virginia subscribers are sufficient to establish personal jurisdiction over those defendants. Nor did the district court rely on these traditional contacts.

Warden Young argues that the district court has specific personal jurisdiction over the newspaper defendants (hereafter, the "newspapers") because of the following contacts between them and Virginia: (1) the newspapers, knowing that Young was a Virginia resident, intentionally discussed and defamed him in their articles, (2) the newspapers posted the articles on their websites, which were accessible in Virginia, and (3) the primary effects of the defamatory statements on Young's reputation were felt in Virginia. Young emphasizes that he is not arguing that jurisdiction is proper in any location where defamatory Internet content can be accessed, which would be anywhere in the world. Rather, Young argues that personal jurisdiction is proper in Virginia because the newspapers understood that their defamatory articles, which were available to Virginia residents on the Internet, would expose Young to public hatred, contempt, and ridicule in Virginia, where he lived and worked. As the district court put it, "the defendants were all well aware of the fact that the plaintiff was employed as a warden within the Virginia correctional system and resided in Virginia," and they "also should have been aware that any harm suffered by Young from the circulation of these articles on the Internet would primarily occur in Virginia."

Young frames his argument in a way that makes one thing clear: if the newspapers' contacts with Virginia were sufficient to establish personal jurisdiction, those contacts arose solely from the newspapers' Internet-based activities. Recently, in *ALS Scan* we discussed the challenges presented in applying traditional jurisdictional principles to decide when "an out-of-state citizen, through electronic contacts, has conceptually 'entered' the State via the Internet for jurisdictional purposes." *ALS Scan*, 293 F.3d at 713. There, we held that "specific jurisdiction in the Internet context may be based only on an out-of-state person's Internet activity directed at [the forum state] and causing injury that gives rise to a potential claim cognizable in [that state]." *Id.* at 714. We noted that this standard for determining specific jurisdiction based on Internet contacts is consistent with the one used by the Supreme Court in *Calder v. Jones*, 465 U.S. 783, 79 L.Ed.2d 804, 104 S. Ct. 1482 (1984). *ALS Scan*, 293 F.3d at 714. *Calder*, though not an Internet case, has particular relevance here because it deals with personal jurisdiction in the context of a libel suit. In *Calder* a California actress brought suit there against, among others, two Floridians, a reporter and an editor who wrote and edited in Florida a *National Enquirer* article claiming that the actress had a problem with alcohol. The Supreme Court held that California had jurisdiction over the Florida residents because "California [was] the focal point both of the story and of the harm suffered." *Calder*, 465 U.S. at 789. The writers' "actions were expressly aimed at California," the Court said, "and they knew that the brunt of [the potentially devastating] injury would be felt by [the actress] in the State in which she lives and works and in which the *National Enquirer* has its largest circulation," 600,000 copies. *Calder*, 465 U.S. at 789-90.

Warden Young argues that *Calder* requires a finding of jurisdiction in this case simply because the newspapers posted articles on their Internet websites that discussed the warden and his Virginia prison, and he would feel the effects of any libel in Virginia, where he lives and works. *Calder* does not sweep that broadly, as we have recognized. For example, in *ESAB Group, Inc. v. Centricut, Inc.*, 126 F.3d 617, 625-26 (4th Cir. 1997), we emphasized how important it is in light of *Calder* to look at whether the defendant has expressly aimed or directed its conduct toward the forum state. We said that "although the place that the plaintiff feels the alleged injury is plainly relevant to the [jurisdictional] inquiry, it must ultimately be accompanied by the defendant's own [sufficient minimum] contacts with the state if jurisdiction ... is to be upheld." *Id.* at 626. We thus had no trouble in concluding in *ALS Scan* that application of *Calder* in the Internet context requires proof that the out-of-state defendant's Internet activity is expressly targeted at or directed to the forum state. *ALS Scan*, 293 F.3d at 714. In *ALS Scan* we went on to adapt the traditional standard for establishing specific jurisdiction so that it makes sense in the Internet context. We "concluded that a State may, consistent with due process, exercise judicial power over a person outside of the State when that person (1) directs electronic activity into the State, (2) with the manifested intent of engaging in business or other interactions within the State, and (3) that activity creates, in a person within the State, a potential cause of action cognizable in the State's courts." *ALS Scan*, 293 F.3d at 714.

When the Internet activity is, as here, the posting of news articles on a website, the *ALS Scan* test works more smoothly when parts one and two of the test are considered together. We thus ask whether the newspapers manifested an intent to direct their website content -- which included certain articles discussing conditions in a Virginia prison -- to a Virginia audience. As we recognized in *ALS Scan*, "a person's act of placing information on the Internet" is not sufficient by itself to "subject[ ] that person to personal jurisdiction in each State in which the information is accessed." *Id.* at 712. Otherwise, a "person placing information on the Internet would be subject to personal jurisdiction in every State," and the traditional due process principles governing a State's jurisdiction over persons outside of its borders would be subverted. *Id. See also GTE New Media Servs. Inc. v. Bellsouth Corp.*, 339 U.S. App. D.C. 332, 199 F.3d 1343, 1350 (D.C. Cir. 2000). Thus, the fact that the newspapers' websites could be accessed anywhere, including Virginia, does not by itself demonstrate that the newspapers were intentionally directing their website content to a Virginia audience. Something more than posting and accessibility is needed to "indicate that the [newspapers] purposefully (albeit electronically) directed [their] activity in a substantial way to the forum state," Virginia. *Panavision Int'l, L.P. v. Toeppen*, 141 F.3d 1316, 1321 (9th Cir. 1998) (quotation omitted). The newspapers must, through the Internet postings, manifest an intent to target and focus on Virginia readers.

We therefore turn to the pages from the newspapers' websites that Warden Young placed in the record, and we examine their general thrust and content. The overall content of both websites is decidedly local, and neither newspaper's website contains advertisements aimed at a Virginia audience. For example, the website that distributes the *Courant*, ctnow.com, provides access to local (Connecticut) weather and traffic information and links to websites for the University of Connecticut and Connecticut state government. The *Advocate*'s website features stories focusing on New Haven, such as one entitled "The Best of New Haven." In sum, it appears that these newspapers maintain their websites to serve local readers in Connecticut, to expand the reach of their papers within their local markets, and to provide their local markets with a place for classified ads. The websites are not designed to attract or serve a Virginia audience.

We also examine the specific articles Young complains about to determine whether they were posted on the Internet with the intent to target a Virginia audience. The articles included discussions about the allegedly harsh conditions at the Wallens Ridge prison, where Young was warden. One article mentioned Young by name and quoted a Connecticut state senator who reported that Young had Confederate Civil War memorabilia in his office. The focus of the articles, however, was the Connecticut prisoner transfer policy and its impact on the transferred prisoners and their families back home in Connecticut. The articles reported on and encouraged a public debate in Connecticut about whether the transfer policy was sound or practical for that state and its citizens. Connecticut, not Virginia, was the focal point of the articles. *Cf. Griffis v. Luban*, 646 N.W.2d 527, 536 (Minn. 2002) ("The mere fact that [the defendant, who posted allegedly defamatory statements about the plaintiff on the Internet] knew that [the plaintiff] resided and worked in Alabama is not sufficient to extend personal jurisdiction over [the defendant] in Alabama, because that knowledge does not demonstrate targeting of Alabama as the focal point of the ... statements.").

The facts in this case establish that the newspapers' websites, as well as the articles in question, were aimed at a Connecticut audience. The newspapers did not post materials on the Internet with the manifest intent of targeting Virginia readers. Accordingly, the newspapers could not have "reasonably anticipated being haled into court [in Virginia] to answer for the truth of the statements made in their articles." *Calder*, 465 U.S. at 790 (quotation omitted). In sum, the newspapers do not have sufficient Internet contacts with Virginia to permit the district court to exercise specific jurisdiction over them.[*]

We reverse the order of the district court denying the motions to dismiss for lack of personal jurisdiction made by the New Haven *Advocate*, Gail Thompson (its editor), and Camille Jackson (its reporter) and by the Hartford *Courant*, Brian Toolan (its editor), and Amy Pagnozzi (its reporter).

REVERSED.

* * * * *

Notes and Questions

1. Would the conclusion reached by the U.S. Court of Appeals for the Fourth Circuit have been different if the *Advocate* and the *Courant* had extensively marketed their newspapers in a national advertising campaign? Suppose the newspapers had held themselves out to the public as "covering national and international events of interest to all." Would it matter if any such marketing efforts had been unsuccessful?

Note the Fourth Circuit's reference to *Griffis v. Luban*, which stated, "The mere fact that [the defendant, who posted allegedly defamatory statements about the plaintiff on the Internet] knew that [the plaintiff] resided and worked in Alabama is not sufficient to extend personal jurisdiction over [the defendant] in Alabama, because that knowledge does not demonstrate targeting of Alabama as the focal point of the ... statements." 646 N.W.2d 527, 536 (Minn. 2002). How does this compare with the reasoning by the Australian court in *Dow*

---

[*] Because the newspapers did not intentionally direct Internet activity to Virginia, and jurisdiction fails on that ground, we have no need to explore the last part of the *ALS Scan* inquiry, that is, whether the challenged conduct created a cause of action in Virginia. *See ALS Scan*, 293 F.3d at 714.

Jones & Co. v. Gutnick, [2002] HCA 56, *see Law of Internet Speech* at 122 and Supplement, *infra* at 95.

2. After the Fourth Circuit issued its decision in *Young v. New Haven Advocate,* 315 F.3d 256 (4th Cir. 2002); *see* Supplement *supra* at 80, the same court affirmed the dismissal of a trademark infringement action for lack of personal jurisdiction. The court held that the plaintiff, a Maryland corporation, could not satisfy its burden to establish jurisdiction in Maryland over the defendant, an Illinois corporation. The plaintiff argued that the defendant had a "semi-interactive website" that was accessible in Maryland, as well as a business relationship with a Maryland-based Web hosting company. *Carefirst of Md., Inc. v. Carefirst Pregnancy Ctrs.,* 334 F.3d 390, 398 (4th Cir. 2003). The court deemed it "pertinent that the overall content of [the defendant's] website has a strongly local character, emphasizing that [defendant's] mission is to assist *Chicago-area* women in pregnancy crises." *Id.* at 401 (emphasis in original).

A New York federal district court similarly declined to exercise jurisdiction over the defendants, including the *Philippine Daily Inquirer* and an Internet news service whose content was prepared in the Philippines and was maintained on computer network servers in the Philippines. *Pompeyo Roa Realuyo v. Carolos Villa Abrille, et al.,* No. 01 Civ. 10158, 2003 U.S. Dist. LEXIS 11529 (S.D.N.Y. July 8, 2003), *aff'd sub nom Realuyo v. Abrille,* 93 Fed. Appx. 297, 2004 U.S. App. LEXIS 5771 (2d Cir. 2004) (concluding that the district court had not abused its discretion by denying discovery or evidentiary hearings on jurisdictional issues). The plaintiff, a New Jersey resident who practiced law in New York, challenged an article published and posted by defendants that allegedly defamed him. Specifically as to the Internet news service, the court concluded that electronic publication by itself was an insufficient basis on which to exercise jurisdiction because there was "no *prima facie* showing that the [defendant's] posting was directed towards the potential New York audience so as to defame the plaintiff in the forum state." No. 01 Civ. 10158, 2003 U.S. Dist. LEXIS 11529 at *31.

* * * * *

OLIVER "BUCK" REVELL, Plaintiff-Appellant

v.

HART G.W. LIDOV, an individual; BOARD OF TRUSTEES OF
COLUMBIA UNIVERSITY IN THE CITY OF NEW YORK, a
foreign corporation (Columbia University); COLUMBIA
UNIVERSITY SCHOOL OF JOURNALISM, an agency and/or
Department of Columbia University in the City of New York,
Defendants-Appellees

United States Court of Appeals for the Fifth Circuit

No. 01-10521, 317 F.3d 467

December 31, 2002

Oliver "Buck" Revell sued Hart G.W. Lidov and Columbia University for defamation arising out of Lidov's authorship of an article that he posted on an internet bulletin board hosted by Columbia. The district court dismissed Revell's claims for lack of personal jurisdiction over both Lidov and Columbia. We affirm.

I.

Hart G.W. Lidov, an Assistant Professor of Pathology and Neurology at the Harvard Medical School and Children's Hospital, wrote a lengthy article on the subject of the terrorist bombing of Pan Am Flight 103, which exploded over Lockerbie, Scotland in 1988. The article alleges that a broad politically motivated conspiracy among senior members of the Reagan Administration lay behind their willful failure to stop the bombing despite clear advance warnings. Further, Lidov charged that the government proceeded to cover up its receipt of advance warning and repeatedly misled the public about the facts. Specifically, the article singles out Oliver "Buck" Revell, then Associate Deputy Director of the FBI, for severe criticism, accusing him of complicity in the conspiracy and cover-up. The article further charges that Revell, knowing about the imminent terrorist attack, made certain his son, previously booked on Pan Am 103, took a different flight. At the time he wrote the article, Lidov had never been to Texas, except possibly to change planes, or conducted business there, and was apparently unaware that Revell then resided in Texas.

Lidov has also never been a student or faculty member of Columbia University, but he posted his article on a website maintained by its School of Journalism. In a bulletin board section of the website, users could post their own works and read the works of others. As a result, the article could be viewed by members of the public over the internet.

Revell, a resident of Texas, sued the Board of Trustees of Columbia University, whose principal offices are in New York City, and Lidov, who is a Massachusetts resident, in the Northern District of Texas. Revell claimed damage to his professional reputation in Texas and emotional distress arising out of the alleged defamation of the defendants, and sought several million dollars in damages. Both defendants moved to dismiss for lack of personal jurisdiction under Federal Rule of Civil Procedure 12(b)(2). The district court granted the defendants' motions, and Revell now appeals.

II.

A.

Our question is whether the district court could properly exercise personal jurisdiction over Hart Lidov and Columbia University, an issue of law we review *de novo*. The plaintiff bears the burden of establishing jurisdiction, but need only present *prima facie* evidence. ...

A federal district court sitting in diversity may exercise personal jurisdiction over a foreign defendant if (1) the long-arm statute of the forum state creates personal jurisdiction over the defendant; and (2) the exercise of personal jurisdiction is consistent with the due process guarantees of the United States Constitution. Because Texas's long-arm statute reaches to the constitutional limits, we ask, therefore, if exercising personal jurisdiction over Lidov and Columbia would offend due process.

The Due Process Clause of the Fourteenth Amendment permits a court to exercise personal jurisdiction over a foreign defendant when (1) "that defendant has purposefully availed himself of the benefits and protections of the forum state by establishing 'minimum contacts' with the forum state; and (2) the exercise of jurisdiction over that defendant does not offend 'traditional notions of fair play and substantial justice.'"[7] Sufficient minimum

---

[7] *Mink v. AAAA Dev. LLC*, 190 F.3d 333, 336 (5th Cir. 1999) (quoting *Int'l Shoe Co. v. Washington*, 326 U.S. 310, 316, 90 L. Ed. 95, 66 S. Ct. 154 (1945)).

contacts will give rise to either specific or general jurisdiction.[8] "General jurisdiction exists when a defendant's contacts with the forum state are unrelated to the cause of action but are 'continuous and systematic.'"[9] Specific jurisdiction arises when the defendant's contacts with the forum "arise from, or are directly related to, the cause of action."[10]

B.

Answering the question of personal jurisdiction in this case brings these settled and familiar formulations to a new mode of communication across state lines. Revell first urges that the district court may assert general jurisdiction over Columbia because its website provides internet users the opportunity to subscribe to the *Columbia Journalism Review*, purchase advertising on the website or in the journal, and submit electronic applications for admission.

This circuit has drawn upon the approach of *Zippo Manufacturing Co. v. Zippo Dot Com, Inc.*[12] in determining whether the operation of an internet site can support the minimum contacts necessary for the exercise of personal jurisdiction.[13] *Zippo* used a "sliding scale" to measure an internet site's connections to a forum state.[14] A "passive" website, one that merely allows the owner to post information on the internet, is at one end of the scale.[15] It will not be sufficient to establish personal jurisdiction.[16] At the other end are sites whose owners engage in repeated online contacts with forum residents over the internet, and in these cases personal jurisdiction may be proper.[17] In between are those sites with some interactive elements, through which a site allows for bilateral information exchange with its visitors. Here, we find more familiar terrain, requiring that we examine the extent of the interactivity and nature of the forum contacts.[18]

While we deployed this sliding scale in *Mink v. AAAA Development LLC*, it is not well adapted to the general jurisdiction inquiry, because even repeated contacts with forum residents by a foreign defendant may not constitute the requisite substantial, continuous and

---

[8] *Wilson v. Belin*, 20 F.3d 644, 647 (5th Cir. 1994).

[9] *Mink*, 190 F.3d at 336.

[10] *Lewis v. Fresne*, 252 F.3d 352, 358 (5th Cir. 2001) (internal quotation marks omitted).

[12] 952 F. Supp. 1119 (W.D. Pa. 1997).

[13] *Mink*, 190 F.3d at 336.

[14] *Zippo*, 952 F. Supp. 1119, 1124.

[15] *Id.*

[16] *Id.*

[17] *Id.*

[18] *Id.*

systematic contacts required for a finding of general jurisdiction -- in other words, while it may be doing business *with* Texas, it is not doing business *in* Texas.[19]

Irrespective of the sliding scale, the question of general jurisdiction is not difficult here. Though the maintenance of a website is, in a sense, a continuous presence everywhere in the world, the cited contacts of Columbia with Texas are not in any way "substantial."[20]

Columbia's contacts with Texas are in stark contrast to the facts of the Supreme Court's seminal case on general jurisdiction, *Perkins v. Benguet Consolidated Mining Co.*[21] In *Perkins*, a Philippine corporation temporarily relocated to Ohio.[22] The corporation's president resided in Ohio, the records of the corporation were kept in Ohio, director's meetings were held in Ohio, accounts were held in Ohio banks, and all key business decisions were made there. Columbia's internet presence in Texas quite obviously falls far short of this standard.

Our conclusion also comports with the recent decision in *Bird v. Parsons*,[24] where the Sixth Circuit found Ohio courts lacked general jurisdiction over a non-resident business that registered domain names despite the fact that: (1) the defendant maintained a website open for commerce with Ohio residents and (2) over 4000 Ohio residents had in fact registered domain names with the defendant.[25] By contrast, Columbia, since it began keeping records, never received more than twenty internet subscriptions to the *Columbia Journalism Review* from Texas residents.

C.

Turning to the issue of specific jurisdiction, the question is whether Revell has made out his *prima facie* case with respect to the defendants' contacts with Texas. *Zippo*'s scale does more work with specific jurisdiction -- the context in which it was originally conceived.[27]

Revell urges that, given the uniqueness of defamation claims and their inherent ability to inflict injury in far-flung jurisdictions, we should abandon the imagery of *Zippo*. It is a bold

---

[19] *Access Telecom, Inc. v. MCI Telecomm. Corp.*, 197 F.3d 694, 717 (5th Cir. 1999); *see also Bancroft & Masters, Inc. v. Augusta Nat'l Inc.*, 223 F.3d 1082, 1086 (9th Cir. 2000) ("Engaging in commerce with residents of the forum state is not in and of itself the kind of activity that approximates physical presence within the state's borders.").

[20] *See Wilson v. Belin*, 20 F.3d 644, 650-51 (5th Cir. 1994) (finding no personal jurisdiction over individual defamation defendants where the defendants did not conduct regular business in Texas and did not make a substantial part of their business decisions in Texas).

[21] 342 U.S. 437, 438, 96 L. Ed. 485, 72 S. Ct. 413, 63 Ohio Law Abs. 146 (1952).

[22] *Id.* at 447-48.

[24] 289 F.3d 865 (6th Cir. 2002).

[25] *Id.* at 873-74.

[27] *Zippo Mfg. Co. v. Zippo Dot Com, Inc.*, 952 F. Supp. 1119, 1122 (W.D. Pa. 1997) (noting that the plaintiff conceded that only specific jurisdiction was at issue in the case).

but ultimately unpersuasive argument. Defamation has its unique features, but shares relevant characteristics with various business torts.[28] Nor is the *Zippo* scale, as has been suggested, in tension with the "effects" test of *Calder v. Jones*[29] for intentional torts....

For specific jurisdiction we look only to the contact out of which the cause of action arises[31] -- in this case the maintenance of the internet bulletin board. Since this defamation action does not arise out of the solicitation of subscriptions or applications by Columbia, those portions of the website need not be considered.

The district court concluded that the bulletin board was *"Zippo*-passive" and therefore could not create specific jurisdiction. The defendants insist that Columbia's bulletin board is indistinguishable from the website in *Mink*. In that case, we found the website would not support a finding of minimum contacts because it only solicited customers, provided a toll-free number to call, and an e-mail address.[32] It did not allow visitors to place orders online. But in this case, any user of the internet can post material to the bulletin board. This means that individuals *send* information to be posted, and *receive* information that others have posted. In *Mink* and *Zippo*, a visitor was limited to expressing an interest in a commercial product. Here the visitor may participate in an open forum hosted by the website.[34] Columbia's bulletin board is thus interactive, and we must evaluate the extent of this interactivity as well as Revell's arguments with respect to *Calder*.

D.

1. In *Calder*, an editor and a writer for the *National Enquirer*, both residents of Florida, were sued in California for libel arising out of an article published in the *Enquirer* about Shirley Jones, an actress. The Supreme Court upheld the exercise of personal jurisdiction over the two defendants because they had "expressly aimed" their conduct towards California.

> The allegedly libelous story concerned the California activities of a California resident. It impugned the professionalism of an entertainer whose television career was centered in California. The article was drawn from California sources, and the brunt of the harm, in terms both of respondent's emotional distress and the injury to her professional reputation, was suffered in California. *In sum, California is the focal point both of the story and of the harm suffered.*[37]

---

[28] *See Indianapolis Colts v. Metro. Balt. Football Club Ltd. P'ship*, 34 F.3d 410, 411-12 (7th Cir. 1994).

[29] 465 U.S. 783, 79 L. Ed. 2d 804, 104 S. Ct. 1482 (1984).

[31] *Lewis v. Fresne*, 252 F.3d 352, 358 (5th Cir. 2001).

[32] *Mink v. AAAA Dev. LLC*, 190 F.3d 333, 336-37 (5th Cir. 1999).

[34] *See, e.g., Barrett v. Catacombs Press*, 44 F. Supp. 2d 717, 728 (E.D. Pa. 1999) (finding interactive internet newsgroups where defendant posted messages in common cyberspace accessible to all but ultimately holding personal jurisdiction could not be obtained).

[37] [*Calder*,] 465 U.S. 783 at 788-89 (emphasis added).

The Court also relied upon the fact that the *Enquirer* had its largest circulation -- over 600,000 copies -- in California, indicating that the defendants knew the harm of their allegedly tortious activity would be felt there.[38]

2. Revell urges that, measured by the "effects" test of *Calder*, he has presented his *prima facie* case for the defendants' minimum contacts with Texas. At the outset we emphasize that the "effects" test is but one facet of the ordinary minimum contacts analysis, to be considered as part of the full range of the defendant's contacts with the forum.[39]

We find several distinctions between this case and *Calder* -- insurmountable hurdles to the exercise of personal jurisdiction by Texas courts. First, the article written by Lidov about Revell contains no reference to Texas, nor does it refer to the Texas activities of Revell, and it was not directed at Texas readers as distinguished from readers in other states. Texas was not the focal point of the article or the harm suffered, unlike *Calder*, in which the article contained descriptions of the California activities of the plaintiff, drew upon California sources, and found its largest audience in California. This conclusion fits well with our decisions in other intentional tort cases where the plaintiff relied upon *Calder*. In those cases we stated that the plaintiff's residence in the forum, and suffering of harm there, will not alone support jurisdiction under *Calder*.[41] We also find instructive the defamation decisions of the Sixth, Third, and Fourth Circuits in *Reynolds v. International Amateur Athletic Federation*,[42] *Remick v. Manfredy*,[43] and *Young v. New Haven Advocate*,[44] respectively.

---

[38] *Id.* 465 U.S. 783 at 789-90 ("And they knew that the brunt of that injury would be felt by respondent in the State in which she lives and works and in which the *National Enquirer* has its largest circulation.").

[39] *Panda Brandywine Corp. v. Potomac Elec. Power Co.*, 253 F.3d 865, 869 (5th Cir. 2001).

[41] *See Panda Brandywine*, 253 F.3d at 870 ("If we were to accept Appellants' arguments, a nonresident defendant would be subject to jurisdiction in Texas for an intentional tort simply because the plaintiff's complaint alleged injury in Texas to Texas residents regardless of the defendant's contacts...."); *Southmark Corp. v. Life Investors, Inc.*, 851 F.2d 763, 772-73 (5th Cir. 1988) (rejecting application of *Calder* and describing the plaintiff's decision to maintain its principal place of business in the forum state as "a mere fortuity" that could not support personal jurisdiction). *But see Janmark, Inc. v. Reidy*, 132 F.3d 1200, 1202 (7th Cir. 1997) (finding personal jurisdiction over a California business proper under *Calder* on the basis that the defendant's alleged threatening of one of the plaintiff's customers in New Jersey injured the plaintiff, an Illinois business, in Illinois); *IMO Indus., Inc. v. Kiekert AG*, 155 F.3d 254, 263-65 (3d Cir. 1998) (recognizing circuit split between *Janmark* and views of the First, Fourth, Fifth, Eighth, Ninth and Tenth Circuits and adopting the majority view). We do not suggest that the analysis for defamation claims under *Calder* should differ from that utilized in our other cases, but merely provide further explication because this case is factually more similar to *Calder*.

[42] 23 F.3d 1110 (6th Cir. 1994).

[43] 238 F.3d 248 (3d Cir. 2001).

[44] __ F.3d __, 315 F.3d 256, 2002 U.S. App. LEXIS 25535, No. 01-2340, 2002 WL 31780988, at *1 (4th Cir. Dec. 13, 2002).

In *Reynolds* a London-based association published a press release regarding the plaintiff's disqualification from international track competition for two years following his failure of a drug test.[45] The plaintiff, an Ohio resident, claimed that the alleged defamation had cost him endorsement contracts in Ohio and cited *Calder* in support of his argument that personal jurisdiction over the defendant in Ohio was proper. The court found *Calder* inapposite because, *inter alia*, the allegedly defamatory press release dealt with the plaintiff's activities in Monaco, not Ohio; the source of the report was a urine sample taken in Monaco and analyzed in Paris; and the "focal point" of the release was not Ohio. We agree with the *Reynolds* court that the sources relied upon and activities described in an allegedly defamatory publication should in some way connect with the forum if *Calder* is to be invoked. Lidov's article, insofar as it relates to Revell, deals exclusively with his actions as Associate Deputy Director of the FBI -- just as the offending press release in *Reynolds* dealt only with a failed drug test in Monaco. It signifies that there is no reference to Texas in the article or any reliance on Texas sources. These facts weigh heavily against finding the requisite minimum contacts in this case. ...

As with *Remick* and *Young*, the post to the bulletin board here was presumably directed at the entire world, or perhaps just concerned U.S. citizens. But certainly it was not directed specifically at Texas, which has no especial relationship to the Pan Am 103 incident. Furthermore, here there is nothing to compare to the targeting of California readers represented by approximately 600,000 copies of the *Enquirer* the *Calder* defendants knew would be distributed in California, the *Enquirer*'s largest market.[59]

3. As these cases aptly demonstrate, one cannot purposefully avail oneself of "some forum someplace;" rather, as the Supreme Court has stated, due process requires that "the defendant's conduct and connection with the forum State are such that he should reasonably anticipate being haled into court there."[60] Lidov's affidavit, uncontroverted by the record, states that he did not even know that Revell was a resident of Texas when he posted his article. Knowledge of the particular forum in which a potential plaintiff will bear the brunt of the harm forms an essential part of the *Calder* test.[61] The defendant must be chargeable with knowledge of the forum at which his conduct is directed in order to reasonably anticipate being haled into court in that forum, as *Calder* itself and numerous cases from other circuits applying *Calder* confirm. Demanding knowledge of a particular forum to which conduct is directed, in defamation cases, is not altogether distinct from the requirement that the forum be the focal point of the tortious activity because satisfaction of the latter will ofttimes provide sufficient evidence of the former. Lidov must have known that the harm of the article would hit home wherever Revell resided. But that is the case with virtually any defamation. A more direct aim is required than we have here. In short, this was not about Texas. If the article had a geographic focus it was Washington, D.C.

---

[45] 23 F.3d at 1112.

[59] *Calder v. Jones*, 465 U.S. 783 at 785 n.2, 79 L. Ed. 2d 804, 104 S. Ct. 1482 (1984).

[60] *Burger King Corp. v. Rudzewicz*, 471 U.S. 462, 474, 85 L. Ed. 2d 528, 105 S. Ct. 2174 (1985).

[61] Further evidence that the *Calder* defendants knew that the harm of their conduct would be felt in California came from their knowledge that the *Enquirer* enjoyed its largest circulation there. 465 U.S. at 789.

III.

Our ultimate inquiry is rooted in the limits imposed on states by the Due Process Clause of the Fourteenth Amendment. It is fairness judged by the reasonableness of Texas exercising its power over residents of Massachusetts and New York. This inquiry into fairness captures the reasonableness of hauling a defendant from his home state before the court of a sister state; in the main a pragmatic account of reasonable expectations -- if you are going to pick a fight in Texas, it is reasonable to expect that it be settled there. It is not fairness calibrated by the likelihood of success on the merits or relative fault. Rather, we look to the geographic focus of the article, not the bite of the defamation, the blackness of the calumny, or who provoked the fight. ...

IV.

In sum, Revell has failed to make out a *prima facie* case of personal jurisdiction over either defendant. General jurisdiction cannot be obtained over Columbia. Considering both the "effects" test of *Calder* and the low-level of interactivity of the internet bulletin board, we find the contacts with Texas insufficient to establish the jurisdiction of its courts, and hence the federal district court in Texas, over Columbia and Lidov. We AFFIRM the dismissal for lack of personal jurisdiction as to both defendants.

AFFIRMED.

* * * * *

In *The Cadel Co. v. Jan. R. Schlichtmann, et al.,* No. 04-3145, 123 Fed. Appx. 675, 2005 U.S. App. LEXIS 2097 (6th Cir. Feb. 8, 2005) (unpublished), the U.S. Court of Appeals for the Sixth Circuit ruled that when the defendant's alleged contact with the forum state occurs via the Internet, "the plaintiff faces an initial hurdle in showing *where* this internet conduct took place for jurisdictional purposes. We have held that the operation of 'a website that is accessible to anyone over the Internet is insufficient to justify general jurisdiction,' even where the website enables the defendant to do business with residents of the forum state, because such activity does not "approximate[ ] physical presence within the state's borders." *Id.,* 123 Fed. Appx. at 677, 2005 U.S. LEXIS 2097 at *6 (citation omitted). The court opined that the operation of a web-site may justify the exercise of specific jurisdiction if: the defendant's operation of the web-site constitutes purposeful availment, the web-site is the basis of the cause of action against the defendant, and jurisdiction over the defendant is generally reasonable. *See id,* 123 Fed. Appx. at 678, 2005 U.S. App. LEXIS 2097 at *6.

With respect to the web-site in issue, the appellate court noted that the defendant had created the site to inform people about the plaintiff's allegedly illegal activities in Massachusetts, as well as details about the actions taken by the Massachusetts Attorney General and the Banking Division against the plaintiff. *See id.,* 123 Fed. Appx. at 678, 2005 U.S. App. LEXIS 2097 at *8. The site also linked to an interactive Web page that solicited others to join the defendant against the plaintiff. However, there was no evidence that the defendant's site linked to a class action complaint form and the plaintiff did not allege that any Ohio resident used the form. *See id.,* 123 Fed. Appx. at 678, 2005 U.S. App. LEXIS 2097 at *9.

The Sixth Circuit concluded that the defendant's web-site "probably falls between being interactive and passive, particularly because the website provides contact information, and arguably solicits support for the campaign against [the plaintiff's] activities. If the website is 'semi-interactive,' 'the exercise of jurisdiction is determined by examining the level of interactivity and commercial nature of the exchange of information that occurs.' Because [the plaintiff] has not alleged that any interaction or exchange of information occurred between [the defendant] and Ohio residents via the website, personal jurisdiction over [the defendant] does not exist based on the nature of the website." *Id.* (citing *Zippo Mfg. Co. v. Zippo Dot Com, Inc.,* 952 F. Supp. 1119, 1124 (W.D. Pa. 1997)). The court then turned to a jurisdictional analysis under *Calder v. Jones,* 465 U.S. 783 (1984), to determine whether the defendant's publication or dissemination of information could give rise to specific jurisdiction. The Sixth Circuit concluded that the challenged site did not demonstrate purposeful availment in Ohio because it specifically referred to the plaintiff's activities in Massachusetts and was not directed to Ohio readers. *See The Cadel Co. v. Jan. R. Schlichtmann, et al.,* No. 04-3145, 123 Fed. Appx. at 679-80, 2005 U.S. App. LEXIS at *10.

＊ ＊ ＊ ＊ ＊

substitute the following for the second full paragraph of Notes and Questions # 6 on page 121 of Law of Internet Speech:

Yahoo!'s motion for a declaratory judgment was successful in the U.S. District Court for the Northern District of California; the French court's ruling, requiring Yahoo! Inc. to prohibit access by Web surfers in France to sales of Nazi-related memorabilia, was deemed to have violated First Amendment principles. *See Yahoo! Inc. v. La Ligue Contre Le Racisme et L'Antisemitisme,* 169 F. Supp. 2d 1181, 1184 (N.D. Cal. 2001). Thereafter, however, the Ninth Circuit determined that the action had been premature, stating:

> France is within its rights as a sovereign nation to enact hate speech laws against the distribution of Nazi propaganda in response to its terrible experience with Nazi forces during World War II. Similarly, [La Ligue Contre Le Racisme Et L'Antisemitisme ("LICRA") and L'Union Des Etudiants Juifs De France ("UEJF")] are within their rights to bring suit in France against Yahoo! for violation of French speech law. The only adverse consequence experienced by Yahoo! as a result of the acts with which we are concerned is that Yahoo! must wait for LICRA and UEJF to come to the United States to enforce the French judgment before it is able to raise its First Amendment claim. However, it was not wrongful for the French organizations to place Yahoo! in this position.

> … Yahoo! obtains commercial advantage from the fact that users located in France are able to access its website; in fact the company displays advertising banners in French to those users whom it identifies as French. Yahoo! cannot expect both to benefit from the fact that its content may be viewed around the world and to be shielded from the resulting costs – one of which is that, if Yahoo! violates the speech laws of another nation, it must wait for the foreign litigants to come to the United States to enforce the judgment before its First Amendment claim may be heard by a U.S. court.

> LICRA and UEJF took action to enforce their legal rights under French law. Yahoo! makes no allegation that could lead a court to conclude that there was anything wrongful in the organizations' conduct. As a result, the District Court did not properly exercise

personal jurisdiction over LICRA and UEJF. Because the District Court had no personal jurisdiction over the French parties, we do not review whether Yahoo!'s action for declaratory relief was ripe for adjudication or whether the District Court properly refused to abstain from hearing this case.

Yahoo! Inc. v. La Ligue Contre Le Racisme Et L'Antisemitisme, 379 F.3d 1120, 1126-27 (9th Cir. 2004) (footnotes omitted), *reh'g en banc granted by* 399 F.3d 1010 (9th Cir. 2005); *see also Law of Internet Speech* at 84, 121, 163.

* * * * *

insert the following at the end of Notes and Questions # 9 on page 122 of Law of Internet Speech:

In December 2002, Australia's highest court unanimously held that Dow Jones could be sued in Victoria and that Australian law would govern the plaintiff's libel claim. *Dow Jones & Co., Inc. v. Gutnick* [2002] HCA 56. The High Court stated that it was bound by the traditional Commonwealth notion that each publication of a defamatory article is a separate tort that can give rise to a separate action, concluding that "those who make information accessible by a particular method do so knowing of the reach that their information may have. In particular, those who post information on the World Wide Web do so knowing that the information they make available is available to all and sundry without any geographic restriction." *Id.*

How does this approach compare with that of the Fourth Circuit in *Young v. New Haven Advocate*, 315 F.3d 256 (4th Cir. 2002), *cert. denied*, 538 U.S. 1035 (2003); *see* Supplement *supra* at 80?

Stuart Karle, in-house counsel at Dow Jones, commented that "the hegemony permitted by th[e *Gutnick*] decision is that of Victorian libel law over a communication that beyond dispute was by and large published in America by an American magazine that is directed at Americans and that is concerned exclusively with issues of concern to American investors. Publication may for the Australian High Court be a local issue, but the problems left by this decision are global." Stuart Karle, *Australian High Court: Publishers Should Keep Their Assets, If Not Their Articles, in the United States*, LDRC MediaLawLetter (Dec. 2002) at 5, 10.

Dow Jones and Company Inc. reportedly settled *Gutnick v. Dow Jones* without a payment of monetary damages but with a payment of approximately US$150,000 of plaintiff's legal fees. In addition, *Barron's* magazine published a clarification in its "Corrections & Amplifications" section stating that there was no intention to criminally link the plaintiff to a convicted money launderer who was mentioned in the article that gave rise to the suit. *See generally Gutnick v. Dow Jones Internet Libel Case Settled*, MLRC MediaLawLetter (Oct. 2004) at 40.

Other international courts have reached conclusions similar to that of Australia's High Court. The Ontario Superior Court of Justice, for example, held that an American company whose press releases allegedly defamed the plaintiff was subject to jurisdiction on the ground that the press releases had been made available on-line in Canada. *See Barrick Gold Corp. v. Blanchard & Co.*, 03-CV-244956CM3, [2003] O.J. No. 5817, 2003 ON.C. LEXIS 4993 (O.S.C.J. Dec. 9, 2003). The court observed that a libel judgment rendered under Canadian law might be inconsistent with American legal principles and thus would not be enforceable in the United States. Nevertheless, the court concluded, the Canadian ruling "may be a real value" to the plaintiff because "the vindication of one's reputation is as important as any monetary award of damages that might be obtained. For its purposes, [the plaintiff] may be quite content with a declaration by a court in Ontario that the statements made by the defendants are untrue even if it cannot recover any damages that might be awarded to it as a consequence." *Id.* at *20.

In *Bangoura v. Washington Post,* 235 D.L.R.4th 564 (O.S.C.J. 2004), *available at* <http://www.canlii.org/on/cas/onsc/2004onsc10181.html>, the plaintiff sued in the Ontario Superior Court of Justice, claiming that he had been defamed by three articles in the *Washington Post* concerning the plaintiff's work at the United Nations. When the articles were published, the plaintiff was an International Public Servant working in Kenya. There had been no wholesale distribution of the *Washington Post* in Ontario or elsewhere in Canada and there were only seven paid *Washington Post* subscribers in Ontario. The articles' reporters were all residents of the United States. Although the plaintiff was a resident of Ontario at the time of the decision, he had been a resident for only two years and had not been in Ontario when the articles were published.

Nevertheless, the court ruled that the requisite "real and substantial connection" existed between the plaintiff and the tribunal, and exercised jurisdiction. Characterizing the plaintiff as "an international public servant, who has found a home and work in Ontario where the damages to his reputation would have the greatest impact," jurisdiction was assumed, particularly in light of the "international profile" of the *Washington Post* whose influence reached "throughout the English speaking world." *Id.* at 572. The court also noted that the *Washington Post* had knowingly posted the articles on-line without restricting access geographically, and thus could have "reasonably foreseen that the story would follow the plaintiff wherever he resided" as "few well-informed North Americans (including Canadians) do not encounter, at least indirectly, the views expressed in the Post," which is "often spoken of in the same breath as the New York Times and the London Telegraph." *Id.*

How might a publisher of content on the Internet minimize its exposure to potential liability? Absent the existence and exploitation of technological means designed to confine the dissemination of content geographically, what options are available for publishers? Are publishers' risks minimized if they know more or know less about the persons and entities that are the subjects of the statements they post?

* * * * *

John Wagner, Plaintiff and Appellee

v.

Glenda Miskin, Defendant and Appellant

Supreme Court of North Dakota

No. 20020200, 2003 ND 69; 660 N.W.2d 593

May 6, 2003

Glenda Miskin appealed from a judgment entered on a jury verdict which awarded John Wagner $3,000,000 in damages for libel, slander, and intentional interference with a business relationship. We affirm.

I.

In the fall of 1998, Miskin enrolled in a University of North Dakota ("UND") physics class taught by Professor John Wagner. Wagner and Miskin give very different descriptions of their relationship and the nature of their communications. Wagner asserted, for example, Miskin sent him harassing and sexually explicit email messages and conveyed false statements about him professionally and personally. Miskin contended her oral, written, and electronic communications with Wagner were consensual and reciprocal. Furthermore, she asserted her communications regarding Wagner were privileged.

In April 1999, the UND Student Relations Committee ("Committee") held a hearing to consider Miskin's possible violations of UND's student code. The Committee found she had violated student policies by stalking and harassing Wagner; disrupting the physics department and other campus offices; and misusing the computer system by using it to stalk and harass. This decision, upheld in UND's appeal process, resulted in Miskin's indefinite suspension from UND beginning with the fall 1999 semester and required her to leave campus housing.

In June 2000, Wagner filed a complaint against Miskin in district court alleging intentional infliction of emotional distress, libel, slander, and intentional interference with a business relationship. The court granted Wagner's motion for summary judgment, but later vacated the judgment due to concerns Miskin did not receive the summary judgment papers. Wagner amended his complaint in June 2001 to include Miskin's conduct which occurred after the original complaint was filed, particularly her publication of defamatory statements about him on the Internet. The amended complaint sought damages for libel, slander, and intentional interference with a business relationship. The court dismissed Miskin's cross-complaint against UND and multiple UND employees.

In April 2002, a jury found Miskin had libeled and slandered Wagner and intentionally interfered with his business relationships; he was awarded $3,000,000 in damages. ...

B.

[Among Miskin's contentions is her assertion that] ... the court and North Dakota "have no jurisdiction over the Internet." She has also stated the court lacked "area and subject matter jurisdiction," but she has not specifically argued the court lacked personal jurisdiction. Many courts have examined jurisdictional issues involving the Internet, and the cases focus on how electronic contacts affect the exercise of personal jurisdiction. *See generally* Richard E. Kaye, *Annotation, Internet Web Site Activities of Nonresident Person or Corporation as Conferring Personal Jurisdiction Under Long-Arm Statutes and Due Process Clause*, 81 A.L.R.5th 41 (2003). Some courts apply a "sliding scale" test in Internet cases to determine whether they have personal jurisdiction over a nonresident defendant, examining the active versus passive nature of the website at issue. *See, e.g., Zippo Mfg. Co. v. Zippo Dot Com, Inc.*, 952 F. Supp. 1119, 1124 (W.D. Pa. 1997) (utilizing a "sliding scale" test for jurisdiction which considers a website's level of interactivity and the nature of commercial activities conducted over the Internet).

Other courts apply the "effects test" derived from *Calder v. Jones*, 465 U.S. 783, 79 L. Ed. 2d 804, 104 S. Ct. 1482 (1984), in which a California resident sued Florida residents, the author and editor of a National Enquirer article, for libel. *See, e.g., Young v. New Haven Advocate,* 315 F.3d 256, 262-63 (4th Cir. 2002), *petition for cert. filed* (analogizing *Calder* and stating "application of Calder in the Internet context requires proof that the out-of-state defendant's Internet activity is expressly targeted at or directed to the forum state"). In *Calder,* the United States Supreme Court held the exercise of jurisdiction was proper because of the foreseeable "effects" in California of the non-resident defendants' activities. *Calder,* at 789, 791 (stating the article concerned the California activities of a California resident and the alleged harm, injury to reputation and career and emotional distress, would occur in California).

This Court has not previously had occasion to consider an Internet jurisdiction case. The present case, lacking a complete transcript of the district court proceedings, does not provide us with a sufficient record to undertake such an analysis.

Nevertheless, the record before us clearly contradicts Miskin's assertion that her Internet communications were "not directed uniquely toward the State of North Dakota." *Cf. Revell v. Lidov,* 317 F.3d 467, 473 (5th Cir. 2002) (holding Texas could not exercise jurisdiction over nonresident defendants who posted an article about plaintiff on the Internet because the article did not refer to Texas and was not specifically directed at Texas readers, and defendants did not know plaintiff was a Texas resident); *Rodenburg v. Fargo-Moorhead YMCA,* 2001 ND 139, P19, 632 N.W.2d 407 (stating North Dakota courts may be justified in exercising personal jurisdiction over nonresidents who intentionally direct their activities towards the State); *Auction Effertz, Ltd. v. Schecher,* 2000 ND 109, PP7-8, 611 N.W.2d 173 (recognizing courts have considered a nonresident's initiation of a telephone or electronic business transaction with the forum state sufficient to exercise personal jurisdiction over the nonresident). Printed copies of Miskin's website indicate its Internet address is "www.undnews.com." On the website, the subjects of linked articles relate to UND issues and staff, demonstrating a North Dakota university was the focus of her website. Articles about Wagner, his trial attorney, and the litigation were the primary topics. Contrary to her assertion, we conclude from the record available to us that Miskin did particularly and directly target North Dakota with her website, specifically North Dakota resident John Wagner.

However, we note this case does not depend solely on Internet communications, either for jurisdictional purposes or defamation liability. Wagner's amended complaint alleged Miskin defamed him through several different mediums, not just over the Internet. Although she is currently a Minnesota resident, the record reflects Miskin was a North Dakota resident, attending a North Dakota university and living in campus housing, when many of the communications and incidents alleged in Wagner's amended complaint occurred. She also used a North Dakota University System email account to send messages to Wagner.

After considering the record before this Court, the district court did not err in exercising jurisdiction over Miskin.

IV.

Absent a complete transcript of the district court proceedings, we are unable to conduct a meaningful and intelligent review of the other errors alleged by Miskin. We affirm the judgment awarding John Wagner $3,000,000 in damages for libel, slander, and intentional interference with a business relationship.

CHAPTER II

REGULATION OF INTERNET CONTENT

Hate Speech and Speech That Promotes Harm

insert the following in the second full paragraph after the citation to Planned Parenthood of Columbia/Willamette Inc. v. American Coalition of Life on page 133 of Law of Internet Speech:

aff'd in part, vacated in part, remanded in part, 290 F.3d 1058 (9th Cir. 2002), *cert. denied,* 123 S. Ct. 2367 (2003); *see* Supplement *infra* at 99.

* * * * *

insert the following before United States of America v. Abraham Jacob Alkhabaz, also known as Jake Baker, on page 141 of Law of Internet Speech:

PLANNED PARENTHOOD OF THE
COLUMBIA/WILLAMETTE, INC.; PORTLAND FEMINIST
WOMEN'S HEALTH CENTER; ROBERT CRIST, M.D.;
WARREN M. HERN, M.D.; ELIZABETH NEWHALL, M.D.;
JAMES NEWHALL, M.D., Plaintiffs-Appellees
and KAREN SWEIGERT, M.D., Plaintiff
v.
AMERICAN COALITION OF LIFE ACTIVISTS, *et al.,*
Defendants-Appellants

United States Court of Appeals for the Ninth Circuit

No. 99-35320, No. 99-35325, No. 99-35327, No. 99-35331, No.
99-35333, No. 99-35405, 290 F.3d 1058

May 16, 2002

For the first time we construe what the Freedom of Access to Clinics Entrances Act (FACE), 18 U.S.C. § 248, means by "threat of force." FACE gives aggrieved persons a right of action against whoever by "threat of force ... intentionally ... intimidates ... any person because that person is or has been ... providing reproductive health services." 18 U.S.C. § 248(a)(1) and (c)(1)(A). This requires that we define "threat of force" in a way that comports with the First Amendment, and it raises the question whether the conduct that occurred here falls within the category of unprotected speech.

Four physicians, Dr. Robert Crist, Dr. Warren M. Hern, Dr. Elizabeth Newhall, and Dr. James Newhall, and two health clinics that provide medical services to women including abortions, Planned Parenthood of the Columbia/Willamette, Inc. (PPCW) and the Portland Feminist Women's Health Center (PFWHC), brought suit under FACE claiming that they were targeted with threats by the American Coalition of Life Activists (ACLA), Advocates for Life Ministries (ALM), and numerous individuals. Three threats remain at issue: the

Deadly Dozen "GUILTY" poster which identifies Hern and the Newhalls among ten others; the Crist "GUILTY" poster with Crist's name, addresses and photograph; and the "Nuremberg Files," which is a compilation about those whom the ACLA anticipated one day might be put on trial for crimes against humanity. The "GUILTY" posters identifying specific physicians were circulated in the wake of a series of "WANTED" and "unWANTED" posters that had identified other doctors who performed abortions before they were murdered.

Although the posters do not contain a threat on their face, the district court held that context could be considered. It defined a threat under FACE in accordance with our "true threat" jurisprudence, as a statement made when "a reasonable person would foresee that the statement would be interpreted by those to whom the maker communicates the statement as a serious expression of intent to harm." Applying this definition, the court denied ACLA's motion for summary judgment in a published opinion. The jury returned a verdict in physicians' favor, and the court enjoined ACLA from publishing the posters or providing other materials with the specific intent to threaten Crist, Hern, Elizabeth Newhall, James Newhall, PPCW, or the Health Center. ...

A panel of this court reversed. In its view, the standard adopted by the district court allowed the jury to find ACLA liable for putting the doctors in harm's way by singling them out for the attention of unrelated but violent third parties, conduct which is protected by the First Amendment, rather than for authorizing or directly threatening harm itself, which is not. The panel decided that it should evaluate the record independently to determine whether ACLA's statements could reasonably be construed as saying that ACLA, or its agents, would physically harm doctors who did not stop performing abortions. Having done so, the panel found that the jury's verdict could not stand.

We reheard the case *en banc* because these issues are obviously important. We now conclude that it was proper for the district court to adopt our long-standing law on "true threats" to define a "threat" for purposes of FACE. FACE itself requires that the threat of force be made with the intent to intimidate. Thus, the jury must have found that ACLA made statements to intimidate the physicians, reasonably foreseeing that physicians would interpret the statements as a serious expression of ACLA's intent to harm them because they provided reproductive health services. Construing the facts in the light most favorable to physicians, the verdict is supported by substantial evidence. ACLA was aware that a "wanted"-type poster would likely be interpreted as a serious threat of death or bodily harm by a doctor in the reproductive health services community who was identified on one, given the previous pattern of "WANTED" posters identifying a specific physician followed by that physician's murder. The same is true of the posting about these physicians on that part of the "Nuremberg Files" where lines were drawn through the names of doctors who provided abortion services and who had been killed or wounded. We are independently satisfied that to this limited extent, ACLA's conduct amounted to a true threat and is not protected speech.

As we see no reversible error on liability or in the equitable relief that was granted, we affirm. However, we remand for consideration of whether the punitive damages award comports with due process.

... III.

ACLA argues that the First Amendment requires reversal because liability was based on political speech that constituted neither an incitement to imminent lawless action nor a true threat. It suggests that the key question for us to consider is whether these posters can be considered "true threats" when, in fact, the posters on their face contain no explicitly threatening language. Further, ACLA submits that classic political speech cannot be converted into non-protected speech by a context of violence that includes the independent action of others.

Physicians counter that this threats case must be analyzed under the settled threats law of this circuit. Following precedent, it was proper for the jury to take context into account. They point out that the district court limited evidence of antiabortion violence to evidence tending to show knowledge of a particular defendant, and maintain that the objective standard on which the jury was instructed comports both with Ninth Circuit law and congressional intent. As the First Amendment does not protect true threats of force, physicians conclude, ACLA's speech was not protected.

A.

We start with the statute under which this action arises. Section 248(c)(1)(A) gives a private right of action to any person aggrieved by reason of the conduct prohibited by subsection (a). Subsection (a)(1) provides:

> (a) ... Whoever--
>
> (1) by force or threat of force or by physical obstruction, intentionally injures, intimidates or interferes with or attempts to injure, intimidate or interfere with any person because that person is or has been, or in order to intimidate such person or any other person or any class of persons from, obtaining or providing reproductive health services ...
>
> shall be subject to the ... civil remedies provided in subsection (c)....

18 U.S.C. § 248(a)(1). The statute also provides that "nothing in this section shall be construed ... to prohibit any expressive conduct (including peaceful picketing or other peaceful demonstration) protected from legal prohibition by the First Amendment to the Constitution." 18 U.S.C. § 248(d)(1).

FACE does not define "threat," although it does provide that "the term 'intimidate' means to place a person in reasonable apprehension of bodily harm to him- or herself or to another." 18 U.S.C. § 248(e)(3). Thus, the first task is to define "threat" for purposes of the Act. This requires a definition that comports with the First Amendment, that is, a "true threat."

The Supreme Court has provided benchmarks, but no definition.

Brandenburg v. Ohio, 395 U.S. 444, 447, 23 L.Ed.2d 430, 89 S. Ct. 1827, 48 Ohio Op. 2d 320 (1969), makes it clear that the First Amendment protects speech that advocates violence, so long as the speech is not directed to inciting or producing imminent lawless action and is not likely to incite or produce such action. So do *Hess v. Indiana*, 414 U.S. 105, 38 L.Ed.2d 303, 94 S. Ct. 326 (1973) (overturning disorderly conduct conviction of antiwar protestor who yelled "We'll take the fucking street later (or again)"), and *NAACP v. Claiborne Hardware Co.*, 458 U.S. 886, 73 L.Ed.2d 1215, 102 S. Ct. 3409 (1982). If ACLA had merely endorsed or encouraged the violent actions of others, its speech would be protected.

However, while advocating violence is protected, threatening a person with violence is not. In *Watts v. United States*, 394 U.S. 705 (1969), the Court explicitly distinguished between political hyperbole, which is protected, and true threats, which are not. Considering how to construe a statute which prohibited "knowingly and willfully ... (making) any threat to take the life of or to inflict bodily harm upon the President," the Court admonished that any statute which criminalizes a form of pure speech "must be interpreted with the commands of the First Amendment clearly in mind. What is a threat must be distinguished from what is constitutionally protected speech." *Id.* at 705, 707. In that case, an 18-year old war protester told a discussion group of other young people at a public rally on the Washington Monument grounds: "They always holler at us to get an education. And now I have already received my draft classification as 1-A and I have got to report for my physical this Monday coming. I am not going. If they ever make me carry a rifle the first man I want to get in my sights is L.B.J." *Id.* at 706. His audience laughed. Taken in context, and given the conditional nature of the statement and the reaction of the listeners, the Court concluded that the speech could not be interpreted other than as "a kind of very crude offensive method of stating a political opposition to the President." *Id.* at 708. Accordingly, it ordered judgment entered for Watts.

ACLA's position is that the posters, including the Nuremberg Files, are protected political speech under *Watts*, and cannot lose this character by context. But this is not correct. The Court itself considered context and determined that Watts's statement was political hyperbole instead of a true threat because of context. *Id.* at 708. Beyond this, ACLA points out that the posters contain no language that is a threat. We agree that this is literally true. Therefore, ACLA submits, this case is really an incitement case in disguise. So viewed, the posters are protected speech under *Brandenburg* and *Claiborne*, which ACLA suggests is the closest analogue. We disagree that *Claiborne* is closely analogous.

In March 1966 black citizens in Claiborne County made a list of demands for racial equality and integration. Unsatisfied by the response, several hundred black persons at a meeting of the local National Association for the Advancement of Colored People (NAACP) voted to place a boycott on white merchants in the area. The boycott continued until October 1969. During this period, stores were watched and the names of persons who violated the boycott were read at meetings of the NAACP at the First Baptist Church, and published in a local paper called "Black-Times." These persons were branded as traitors to the black cause, were called demeaning names, and were socially ostracized. A few incidents of violence occurred. Birdshot was fired at the houses of two boycott violators; a brick was thrown through a windshield; and a flower garden was damaged. None of the victims ceased trading with white merchants. Six other incidents of arguably unlawful conduct occurred. White business owners brought suit against the NAACP and Charles Evers, its field secretary, along with other individuals who had participated in the boycott, for violating Mississippi state laws on malicious interference with a business, antitrust, and illegal boycott. Plaintiffs pursued several theories of liability: participating in management of the boycott; serving as an "enforcer" or monitor; committing or threatening acts of violence, which showed that the perpetrator wanted the boycott to succeed by coercion when it could not succeed by persuasion; and as to Evers, threatening violence against boycott breakers, and as to the NAACP because he was its field secretary when he committed tortious and constitutionally unprotected acts. Damages for business losses during the boycott and injunctive relief were awarded.

The Court held that there could be no recovery based on intimidation by threats of social ostracism, because offensive and coercive speech is protected by the First Amendment. "The use of speeches, marches, and threats of social ostracism cannot provide the basis for a damages award. But violent conduct is beyond the pale of constitutional protection." 458 U.S. at 933. There was some evidence of violence, but the violence was not pervasive as it had been in *Milk Wagon Drivers Union Local 753 v. Meadowmoor Dairies, Inc.*, 312 U.S. 287, 85 L.Ed. 836, 61 S. Ct. 552 (1941). Accordingly, the Court made clear that only losses proximately caused by unlawful conduct could be recovered. Further, civil liability could not be imposed consistent with the First Amendment solely on account of an individual's association with others who have committed acts of violence; he must have incited or authorized them himself.

For the same reasons the Court held that liability could not be imposed on Evers for his participation in the boycott itself, or for his threats of vilification or ostracism. However, the merchants also sought damages from Evers for his speeches. He gave one in April 1966, and two others in April 1969. In the first, he told his audience that they would be watched and that blacks who traded with white merchants would be answerable to him; he also said that any "uncle toms" who broke the boycott would "have their necks broken" by their own people. In his April 19, 1969 speech, Evers stated that boycott violators would be "disciplined" by their own people and warned that the Sheriff could not sleep with boycott violators at night. And on April 21, Evers gave another speech to several hundred people calling for a total boycott of white-owned businesses and saying: "If we catch any of you going in any of them racist stores, we're gonna break your damn neck." The Court concluded that the "emotionally charged rhetoric" of Evers's speeches was within the bounds of *Brandenberg*. It was not followed by violence, and there was no evidence -- apart from the speeches themselves -- that Evers authorized, ratified, or directly threatened violence. "If there were other evidence of his authorization of wrongful conduct, the references to discipline in the speeches could be used to corroborate that evidence." *Claiborne*, 458 U.S. at 929. As there was not, the findings were constitutionally inadequate to support the damages judgment against him and, in turn, the NAACP.

Claiborne, of course, did not arise under a threats statute. The Court had no need to consider whether Evers's statements were true threats of force within the meaning of a threats statute; it held only that his speeches did not incite illegal activity, thus could not have caused business losses and could not be the basis for liability to white merchants. As the opinion points out, there was no context to give the speeches (including the expression "break your neck") the implication of authorizing or directly threatening unlawful conduct. To the extent there was any intimidating overtone, Evers's rhetoric was extemporaneous, surrounded by statements supporting non-violent action, and primarily of the social ostracism sort. No specific individuals were targeted. For all that appears, "the break your neck" comments were hyperbolic vernacular. Certainly there was no history that Evers or anyone else associated with the NAACP had broken anyone's neck who did not participate in, or opposed, this boycott or any others. Nor is there any indication that Evers's listeners took his statement that boycott breakers' "necks would be broken" as a serious threat that their necks would be broken; they kept on shopping at boycotted stores.

Thus, *Watts* was the only Supreme Court case that discussed the First Amendment in relation to true threats before we first confronted the issue. Apart from holding that Watts's crack about L.B.J. was not a true threat, the Court set out no standard for determining when a statement is a true threat that is unprotected speech under the First Amendment. Shortly after *Watts* was rendered, we had to decide in *Roy v. United States*, 416 F.2d 874 (9th Cir. 1969), whether a Marine Corps private made a true threat for purposes of 18 U.S.C. § 871 against the President, who was coming to his base the next day, by saying: "I am going to get him." We adopted a "reasonable speaker" test. As it has come to be articulated, the test is:

> Whether a particular statement may properly be considered to be a threat is governed by an objective standard -- whether a reasonable person would foresee that the statement would be interpreted by those to whom the maker communicates the statement as a serious expression of intent to harm or assault.

United States v. Orozco-Santillan, 903 F.2d 1262, 1265 (9th Cir. 1990).

We have applied this test to threats statutes that are similar to FACE, *see, e.g., United States v. Gilbert (Gilbert II)*, 884 F.2d 454, 457 (9th Cir. 1989) (Fair Housing Act banning threat of force to intimidate person based on race and housing practices, 42 U.S.C. § 3631); *United States v. Mitchell*, 812 F.2d 1250, 1255 (9th Cir. 1987) (threats against the President, 18 U.S.C. § 871); *Merrill*, 746 F.2d at 462-63 (same); *United States v. Gordon*, 974 F.2d 1110, 1117 (9th Cir. 1992) (threat to kill a former President, 18 U.S.C. § 879); *Orozco-Santillan*, 903 F.2d at 1265 (threats to assault a law enforcement officer with intent to intimidate, 18 U.S.C. § 115); *Melugin*, 38 F.3d at 1483-84 (threat to influence judicial proceeding under Alaska state law*)*; *McCalden v. California Library Ass'n*, 955 F.2d 1214, 1222 (9th Cir. 1990) (threat to disrupt conference under California's Unruh Act); and *Lovell*, 90 F.3d at 371 (9th Cir. 1996) (§ 1983 action involving threat to shoot teacher). Other circuits have, too. We see no reason not to apply the same test to FACE.

Under our cases, a threat is "an expression of an intention to inflict evil, injury, or damage on another." *Gilbert II*, 884 F.2d at 457; *Orozco-Santillan*, 903 F.2d at 1265. "Alleged threats should be considered in light of their entire factual context, including the surrounding events and reaction of the listeners." [*Id.*] at 1265; *see also Mitchell*, 812 F.2d at 1255 (citing *Watts*, 394 U.S. at 708; *Merrill*, 746 F.2d at 462; *Roy*, 416 F.2d at 876). "'The fact that a threat is subtle does not make it less of a threat.'" *Orozco-Santillan*, 903 F.2d at 1265 (quoting *Gilbert II*, 884 F.2d at 457). A true threat, that is one "where a reasonable person would foresee that the listener will believe he will be subjected to physical violence upon his person, is unprotected by the first amendment." *Id.* (citing *Merrill*, 746 F.2d at 462).

It is not necessary that the defendant intend to, or be able to carry out his threat; the only intent requirement for a true threat is that the defendant intentionally or knowingly communicate the threat. *Orozco-Santillan*, 903 F.2d at 1265 n.3; *Gilbert II*, 884 F.2d at 456-57; *Mitchell*, 812 F.2d at 1256 (upholding § 871 conviction of defendant with no capacity to carry out threat); *Roy*, 416 F.2d at 877. Other circuits are in accord. ... [The FACE statute requires that] the threat of force be made with the intent to intimidate. The "requirement of intent to intimidate serves to insulate the statute from unconstitutional application to protected speech." *Gilbert I*, 813 F.2d at 1529 (construing the Fair Housing Act's threat provision, 42 U.S.C. § 3631, which is essentially the same as FACE's). No reason appears to engraft another intent requirement onto the statute, because whether or not the maker of the threat has an actual intention to carry it out, "an apparently serious threat may cause the mischief or evil toward which the statute was in part directed." *Gilbert II*, 884 F.2d at 458 (quoting *Roy*, 416 F.2d at 877).

....[We do not] agree that threatening speech made in public is entitled to heightened constitutional protection just because it is communicated publicly rather than privately. As

Madsen indicates, threats are unprotected by the First Amendment "however communicated." *Madsen,* 512 U.S. at 753.

Therefore, we hold that "threat of force" in FACE means what our settled threats law says a true threat is: a statement which, in the entire context and under all the circumstances, a reasonable person would foresee would be interpreted by those to whom the statement is communicated as a serious expression of intent to inflict bodily harm upon that person. So defined, a threatening statement that violates FACE is unprotected under the First Amendment.

B.

Although ACLA does not believe we should reach this point, if we do it submits that no claim was made out even under "true threats" cases. First, it argues that other threats cases were criminal actions against someone who made a real threat directly to others, not political speech as is the case here. It contrasts what it calls "a threat plus context" present in *United States v. Dinwiddie*, 76 F.3d 913 (8th Cir. 1996), and in other out-of-circuit cases, with the absence of a direct threat in this case. However, our cases do not require that the maker of the threat personally cause physical harm to the listener. In *Orozco-Santillan,* we made it clear that the speaker did not need to be able to carry out the threat. Likewise in *Mitchell*, the speaker could not possibly have done so. In *Gilbert*, the threatening letter mentions neither the intended victim nor who would carry out the threat. No case to our knowledge has imposed such a requirement, and we decline to now. It is the making of the threat with intent to intimidate -- not the implementation of it -- that violates FACE. ...

....[C]ontext is critical in a true threats case and history can give meaning to the medium. Use of Ryder trucks -- which the Eighth Circuit found to be a true threat in *United States v. Hart*, 212 F.3d 1067 (8th Cir. 2000) -- is an example that is strikingly similar to the use of "wanted"-type posters in this case. Hart, who was a known anti-abortion activist, parked two Ryder trucks in the driveways of an abortion clinic. He was prosecuted and convicted of violating FACE. The court held that Hart had threatened the clinic to intimidate it by using Ryder trucks, because a Ryder truck had been used in the Oklahoma City bombing of the Murrah Federal Building. Hart knew the clinicians knew this and would fear for their lives. Thus, use of the Ryder truck was a true threat. Like the poster format here, the Ryder truck in Hart was a symbol of something beyond the vehicle: there, a devastating bomb; in this case, murder.

... Nor does consideration of context amount to viewpoint discrimination, as ACLA contends. ACLA's theory appears to be that because the posters did not contain any threat on their face, the views of abortion foes are chilled more than the views of abortion-right proponents because of the random acts of violence committed by some people against abortion providers. However, FACE itself is viewpoint neutral. *See, e.g., United States v. Weslin*, 156 F.3d 292, 296-97 (2d Cir. 1998); *United States v. Wilson*, 154 F.3d 658, 663 (7th Cir. 1998) ("The Act punishes anyone who engages in the prohibited conduct, irrespective of the person's viewpoint and does not target any message based on content. 'The Access Act thus does not play favorites: it protects from violent or obstructive activity not only abortion clinics, but facilities providing pre-pregnancy and pregnancy counseling services, as well as facilities counseling alternatives to abortion.'") (quoting *Terry v. Reno*, 101 F.3d 1412, 1419 (D.C. Cir. 1996)). Moreover, ACLA could not be liable under FACE unless it made a true threat with the intent to intimidate physicians. Thus it is making a threat to intimidate that makes ACLA's conduct unlawful, not its viewpoint.

Because of context, we conclude that the Crist and Deadly Dozen posters are not just a political statement. Even if the Gunn poster, which was the first "WANTED" poster, was a purely political message when originally issued, and even if the Britton poster were too, by the time of the Crist poster, the poster format itself had acquired currency as a death threat for abortion providers. Gunn was killed after his poster was released; Britton was killed after his poster was released; and Patterson was killed after his poster was released. Knowing this, and knowing the fear generated among those in the reproductive health services community who were singled out for identification on a "wanted"-type poster, ACLA deliberately identified Crist on a "GUILTY" poster and intentionally put the names of Hern and the Newhalls on the Deadly Dozen "GUILTY" poster to intimidate them. This goes well beyond the political message (regardless of what one thinks of it) that abortionists are killers who deserve death too.

The Nuremberg Files are somewhat different. Although they name individuals, they name hundreds of them. The avowed intent is "collecting dossiers on abortionists in anticipation that one day we may be able to hold them on trial for crimes against humanity." The web page states: "One of the great tragedies of the Nuremberg trials of Nazis after WWII was that complete information and documented evidence had not been collected so many war criminals went free or were only found guilty of minor crimes. We do not want the same thing to happen when the day comes to charge abortionists with their crimes. We anticipate the day when these people will be charged in PERFECTLY LEGAL COURTS once the tide of this nation's opinion turns against child-killing (as it surely will)." However offensive or disturbing this might be to those listed in the Files, being offensive and provocative is protected under the First Amendment. But, in two critical respects, the Files go further. In addition to listing judges, politicians and law enforcement personnel, the Files separately categorize "Abortionists" and list the names of individuals who provide abortion services, including, specifically, Crist, Hern, and both Newhalls. Also, names of abortion providers who have been murdered because of their activities are lined through in black, while names of those who have been wounded are highlighted in grey. As a result, we cannot say that it is clear as a matter of law that listing Crist, Hern, and the Newhalls on both the Nuremberg Files and the GUILTY posters is purely protected, political expression.

Accordingly, whether the Crist Poster, the Deadly Dozen poster, and the identification of Crist, Hern, Dr. Elizabeth Newhall and Dr. James Newhall in the Nuremburg Files as well as on "wanted"-type posters, constituted true threats was properly for the jury to decide.

C.

ACLA next argues that the true threat instructions require reversal because they permitted consideration of motive, history of violence including the violent actions of others, and the defendants' subjective motives as part of context. We have already explained why it is proper for the whole factual context and all the circumstances bearing on a threat to be considered. The court also instructed the jury to consider evidence presented by the defense of non-violence and permissive exercise of free speech. That the contextual facts may have included the violent actions of others does not infect the instruction, because the issue is whether a reasonable person should have foreseen that the Crist Guilty Poster, the Deadly Dozen Poster, and the Nuremberg Files, would be interpreted as a serious threat of harm by doctors who provide abortions and were identified on them.

ACLA also contends that the district court employed the wrong standard of intent, allowing the jury to find in physicians' favor regardless of ACLA's subjective intent. The court instructed: "A statement is a 'true threat' when a reasonable person making the statement would foresee that the statement would be interpreted by those to whom it is communicated as a serious expression of an intent to bodily harm or assault." This language is taken from *Orozco-Santillan*, 903 F.2d at 1265, is an accurate statement of our law, and is faithful to the objective standard we use for determining whether a statement is a true threat. For reasons we have already explained, we decline to read into FACE (or the Hobbs Act) a specific intent to threaten violence or to commit unlawful acts in addition to the intent to intimidate which the statute itself requires. ...

Finally, we note that the jury was instructed that "even speech that is coercive may be protected if the speaker refrains from violence or from making a true threat. Moreover, the mere abstract teaching of the moral propriety or even moral necessity for resort to force and violence is protected speech under the First Amendment." It was reminded that "plaintiffs' claims are based only on the three statements I have listed for you," and that it should determine the case as to each defendant and each claim separately. Accordingly, the court did not abuse its discretion in formulating the instructions, nor was the jury incorrectly instructed as a matter of law on true threats or the elements of FACE.

... F.

Having concluded that "threat of force" was properly defined and that no trial error requires reversal, we consider whether the core constitutional fact -- a true threat -- exists such that the Crist and Deadly Dozen Posters, and the Nuremberg Files as to Crist, Hern, and the Newhalls, are without First Amendment protection. The task in this case does not seem dramatically different from determining that the issue should have gone to the jury and that the jury was properly instructed under FACE. Nevertheless, we review the evidence on true threats independently.

The true threats analysis turns on the poster pattern. Neither the Crist poster nor the Deadly Dozen poster contains any language that is overtly threatening. Both differ from prior posters in that the prior posters were captioned "WANTED" while these are captioned "GUILTY." The text also differs somewhat, but differences in caption or words are immaterial because the language itself is not what is threatening. Rather, it is use of the "wanted"-type format in the context of the poster pattern -- poster followed by murder -- that constitutes the threat. Because of the pattern, a "wanted"-type poster naming a specific doctor who provides abortions was perceived by physicians, who are providers of reproductive health services, as a serious threat of death or bodily harm. After a "WANTED" poster on Dr. David Gunn appeared, he was shot and killed. After a "WANTED" poster on Dr. George Patterson appeared, he was shot and killed. After a "WANTED" poster on Dr. John Britton appeared, he was shot and killed. None of these "WANTED" posters contained threatening language, either. Neither did they identify who would pull the trigger. But knowing this pattern, knowing that unlawful action had followed "WANTED" posters on Gunn, Patterson and Britton, and knowing that "wanted"-type posters were intimidating and caused fear of serious harm to those named on them, ACLA published a "GUILTY" poster in essentially the same format on Dr. Crist and a Deadly Dozen "GUILTY" poster in similar format naming Dr. Hern, Dr. Elizabeth Newhall and Dr. James Newhall because they perform abortions. Physicians could well believe that ACLA would make good on the threat. One of the other doctors on the Deadly Dozen poster had in fact been shot before the poster was published. This is not political hyperbole. Nor is it merely "vituperative, abusive, and inexact." *Watts*, 394 U.S. at 708 (comparing language used in political arena to language used in labor disputes). In the context of the poster pattern, the posters were precise in their meaning to those in the relevant community of reproductive health service providers. They were a true threat.

The posters are a true threat because, like Ryder trucks or burning crosses, they connote something they do not literally say, yet both the actor and the recipient get the message. To the doctor who performs abortions, these posters meant "You're Wanted or You're Guilty; You'll be shot or killed." This was reinforced by the scorecard in the Nuremberg Files. The communication was not conditional or casual. It was specifically targeted. Crist, Hern, and the Newhalls, who performed abortions, were not amused. *Cf. Watts*, 394 U.S. at 708 (no true threat in political speech that was conditional, extemporaneous, and met with laughter); *Claiborne*, 458 U.S. at 928 (spontaneous and emotional appeal in extemporaneous speech protected when lawless action not incited).

The "GUILTY" posters were publicly distributed, but personally targeted. While a privately communicated threat is generally more likely to be taken seriously than a diffuse public one, this cannot be said of a threat that is made publicly but is about a specifically identified doctor and is in the same format that had previously resulted in the death of three doctors who had also been publicly, yet specifically, targeted. There were no individualized threats in *Brandenberg, Watts* or *Claiborne*. However, no one putting Crist, Hern, and the Newhalls on a "wanted"-type poster, or participating in selecting these particular abortion providers for such a poster or publishing it, could possibly believe anything other than that each would be seriously worried about being next in line to be shot and killed. And they were seriously worried.

As a direct result of having a "GUILTY" poster out on them, physicians wore bullet-proof vests and took other extraordinary security measures to protect themselves and their families. ACLA had every reason to foresee that its expression of intent to harm (the "GUILTY" poster identifying Crist, Hern, Elizabeth Newhall and James Newhall by name and putting them in the File that tracks hits and misses) would elicit this reaction. Physicians' fear did not simply happen; ACLA intended to intimidate them from doing what they do.

This is the point of the statute and is conduct that we are satisfied lacks any protection under the First Amendment.

Violence is not a protected value. Nor is a true threat of violence with intent to intimidate. ACLA may have been staking out a position for debate when it merely advocated violence as in *Bray's A Time to Kill,* or applauded it, as in the Defense Action petitions. Likewise, when it created the Nuremberg Files in the abstract, because the First Amendment does not preclude calling people demeaning or inflammatory names, or threatening social ostracism or vilification to advocate a political position. *Claiborne*, 458 U.S. at 903, 909-12. But, after being on "wanted"-type posters, Dr. Gunn, Dr. Patterson, and Dr. Britton can no longer participate in the debate. By replicating the poster pattern that preceded the elimination of Gunn, Patterson and Britton, and by putting Crist, Hern, and the Newhalls in an abortionists' File that scores fatalities, ACLA was not staking out a position of debate but of threatened demise. This turns the First Amendment on its head.

Like "fighting words," true threats are proscribable. We therefore conclude that the judgment of liability in physicians' favor is constitutionally permissible.

... V.

After trial, the district court found that each defendant used intimidation as a means of interfering with the provision of reproductive health services and acted with malice and with specific intent in threatening physicians. It found that physicians remain threatened by ACLA's threats, and have no adequate remedy at law. The court concluded that physicians had proved by clear and convincing evidence that each defendant acting independently and as a co-conspirator prepared and published the Deadly Dozen Poster, the Crist Poster, and the Nuremberg Files with specific intent to make true threats to kill or do bodily harm to physicians, and to intimidate them from engaging in legal medical practices. ... The court also ordered ACLA to turn over possession of materials that are not in compliance with the injunction.

ACLA complains principally about the restraint on possessing the posters. Pointing to *Stanley v. Georgia,* 394 U.S. 557, 567, 22 L.Ed.2d 542, 89 S. Ct. 1243 (1969), where the Court observed that "the State may no more prohibit mere possession of obscene matter on the ground that it may lead to antisocial conduct than it may prohibit possession of chemistry books on the ground that they may lead to the manufacture of homemade spirits," ACLA contends that the injunction treats the posters worse than obscenity. However, the posters in this case are quite different from a book; the "wanted"-type posters themselves -- not their ideological content -- are the tool for threatening physicians. In this sense the posters' status is more like conduct than speech. *Cf. United States v. O'Brien,* 391 U.S. 367, 376, 20 L.Ed.2d 672, 88 S. Ct. 1673-82 (1968) (explaining distinction between speech and conduct, and holding that expressive aspect of conduct does not exempt it from warranted regulation). The First Amendment interest in retaining possession of the threatening posters is *de minimis,* while ACLA's continued possession of them constitutes part of the threat. The court heard all the evidence, which included testimony that some defendants obstructed justice and ignored injunctions. Accordingly, we cannot say that the turn-over order was broader than necessary to assure that this particular threat will not be used again.

ACLA also suggests that the injunction is an improper prior restraint on speech because it prohibits dissemination of the posters. It is not. The Supreme Court has rejected the notion that all injunctions which incidentally affect expression are prior restraints. *Madsen,* 512 U.S. at 764 n.2; *Schenck v. Pro-Choice Network of Western New York,* 519 U.S. 357, 374 n.6 (1997). Like *Madsen* and *Schenck,* the injunction here was not issued because of the content of ACLA's expression, but because of prior unlawful conduct.

The terms of the injunction are finely tuned and exceedingly narrow. Only threats or use of the posters or their equivalent with the specific intent to threaten Crist, Hern, either Newhall, PPCW or PFWHC are prohibited. Only personal information about these particular persons may not be used in the Nuremberg Files with the specific intent to threaten them. This leaves huge room for ACLA to express its views.

CONCLUSION

A "threat of force" for purposes of FACE is properly defined in accordance with our long-standing test on "true threats," as "whether a reasonable person would foresee that the statement would be interpreted by those to whom the maker communicates the statement as a serious expression of intent to harm or assault." This, coupled with the statute's requirement of intent to intimidate, comports with the First Amendment.

We have reviewed the record and are satisfied that use of the Crist Poster, the Deadly Dozen Poster, and the individual plaintiffs' listing in the Nuremberg Files constitute a true threat. In three prior incidents, a "wanted"-type poster identifying a specific doctor who provided abortion services was circulated, and the doctor named on the poster was killed. ACLA and physicians knew of this, and both understood the significance of the particular posters specifically identifying each of them. ACLA realized that "wanted" or "guilty" posters had a threatening meaning that physicians would take seriously. In conjunction with the "guilty" posters, being listed on a Nuremberg Files scorecard for abortion providers impliedly threatened physicians with being next on a hit list. To this extent only, the Files are also a true threat. However, the Nuremberg Files are protected speech.

There is substantial evidence that these posters were prepared and disseminated to intimidate physicians from providing reproductive health services. Thus, ACLA was appropriately found liable for a true threat to intimidate under FACE.

Holding ACLA accountable for this conduct does not impinge on legitimate protest or advocacy. Restraining it from continuing to threaten these physicians burdens speech no more than necessary.

Therefore, we affirm the judgment in all respects but for punitive damages, as to which we remand.

AFFIRMED IN PART; VACATED AND REMANDED IN PART.

KOZINSKI, Circuit Judge, with whom Circuit Judges REINHARDT, O'SCANNLAIN, KLEINFELD and BERZON join, dissenting:

The majority writes a lengthy opinion in a vain effort to justify a crushing monetary judgment and a strict injunction against speech protected by the First Amendment. The apparent thoroughness of the opinion, addressing a variety of issues that are not in serious dispute, masks the fact that the majority utterly fails to apply its own definition of a threat, and affirms the verdict and injunction when the evidence in the record does not support a finding that defendants threatened plaintiffs.

After meticulously canvassing the caselaw, the majority correctly distills the following definition of a true threat: "a statement which, in the entire context and under all the circumstances, a reasonable person would foresee would be interpreted by those to whom the statement is communicated as a serious expression of intent to inflict bodily harm upon that person." Th[is] ... language is crucial, because it is not illegal -- and cannot be made so -- merely to say things that would frighten or intimidate the listener. For example, when a doctor says, "You have cancer and will die within six months," it is not a threat, even though you almost certainly will be frightened. Similarly, "Get out of the way of that bus" is not a threat, even though it is said in order to scare you into changing your behavior. By contrast, "If you don't stop performing abortions, I'll kill you" is a true threat and surely illegal.

The difference between a true threat and protected expression is this: A true threat warns of violence or other harm that the speaker controls. Thus, when a doctor tells a patient, "Stop smoking or you'll die of lung cancer," that is not a threat because the doctor obviously can't cause the harm to come about. Similarly, "If you walk in that neighborhood late at night, you're going to get mugged" is not a threat, unless it is clear that the speaker himself (or one of his associates) will be doing the mugging.

In this case, none of the statements on which liability was premised were overtly threatening. On the contrary, the two posters and the web page, by their explicit terms, foreswore the use of violence and advocated lawful means of persuading plaintiffs to stop performing abortions or punishing them for continuing to do so. Nevertheless, because context matters, the statements could reasonably be interpreted as an effort to intimidate plaintiffs into ceasing their abortion-related activities. If that were enough to strip the speech of First Amendment protection, there would be nothing left to decide. But the Supreme Court has told us that "speech does not lose its protected character ... simply because it may embarrass others or coerce them into action." *NAACP v. Claiborne Hardware Co.*, 458 U.S. 886, 910 (1982). In other words, some forms of intimidation enjoy constitutional protection.

Only a year after *Claiborne Hardware*, we incorporated this principle into our circuit's true threat jurisprudence. Striking down as overbroad a Montana statute that made it a crime to communicate to another "a threat to ... commit a criminal offense," we stated: "The mere fact that communication induces or 'coerces' action in others does not remove it from first amendment protection." *Wurtz v. Risley,* 719 F.2d 1438, 1441 (9th Cir. 1983) (quoting *Claiborne Hardware*, 458 U.S. at 911). We noted -- referring to *Claiborne Hardware* again -- that the statute criminalized pure speech designed to alter someone else's conduct, so that a "civil rights activist who states to a restaurant owner, 'if you don't desegregate this restaurant I am going to organize a boycott' could be punished for the mere statement, even if no action followed." 719 F.2d at 1442. *Claiborne Hardware* and *Wurtz* hold that statements that are intimidating, even coercive, are protected by the First Amendment, so long as the speaker does not threaten that he, or someone acting in concert with him, will resort to violence if the warning is not heeded.

The majority recognizes that this is the standard it must apply, yet when it undertakes the critical task of canvassing the record for evidence that defendants made a true threat -- a task the majority acknowledges we must perform *de novo* -- its opinion fails to come up with any proof that defendants communicated an intent to inflict bodily harm upon plaintiffs.

Buried deep within the long opinion is a single paragraph that cites evidence supporting the finding that the two wanted posters prepared by defendants constituted a true threat. The majority does not point to any statement by defendants that they intended to inflict bodily harm on plaintiffs, nor is there any evidence that defendants took any steps whatsoever to plan or carry out physical violence against anyone. Rather, the majority relies on the fact that "the poster format itself had acquired currency as a death threat for abortion providers. Gunn was killed after his poster was released; Britton was killed after his poster was released; and Patterson was killed after his poster was released." But neither Dr. Gunn nor Dr. Patterson was killed by anyone connected with the posters bearing their names. *Planned Parenthood of the Columbia/Willamette, Inc. v. Am. Coalition of Life Activists*, 41 F. Supp. 2d 1130, 1134-35 (D. Or. 1999). In fact, Dr. Patterson's murder may have been unrelated to abortion: He was killed in what may have been a robbery attempt five months after his poster was issued; the crime is unsolved and plaintiffs' counsel conceded that no evidence ties his murderer to any anti-abortion group.

The record reveals one instance where an individual -- Paul Hill, who is not a defendant in this case -- participated in the preparation of the poster depicting a physician, Dr. Britton, and then murdered him some seven months later. All others who helped to make that poster, as well as those who prepared the other posters, did not resort to violence. And for years, hundreds of other posters circulated, condemning particular doctors with no violence ensuing. There is therefore no pattern showing that people who prepare wanted-type posters then engage in physical violence. To the extent the posters indicate a pattern, it is that almost all people engaged in poster-making were non-violent.

The majority tries to fill this gaping hole in the record by noting that defendants "knew the fear generated among those in the reproductive health services community who were singled out for identification on a 'wanted'-type poster." But a statement does not become a true threat because it instills fear in the listener; as noted above, many statements generate fear in the listener, yet are not true threats and therefore may not be punished or enjoined consistent with the First Amendment. In order for the statement to be a threat, it must send the message that the speakers themselves -- or individuals acting in concert with them -- will engage in physical violence. The majority's own definition of true threat makes this clear. Yet the opinion points to no evidence that defendants who prepared the posters would have been understood by a reasonable listener as saying that they will cause the harm.

Plaintiffs themselves explained that the fear they felt came, not from defendants, but from being singled out for attention by abortion protesters across the country. For example, plaintiff Dr. Elizabeth Newhall testified, "I feel like my risk comes from being identified as a target. And ... all the John Salvis in the world know who I am, and that's my concern." *Planned Parenthood of the Columbia/Willamette, Inc. v. Am. Coalition of Life Activists,* No. CV-95-01671-JO, at 302 (D. Or. Jan. 8, 1999); *see also id.* at 290 ("Up until January of '95, I felt relatively diluted by the -- you know, in the pool of providers of abortion services. I didn't feel particularly visible to the people who were -- you know, to the John Salvis of the world, you know. I sort of felt one of a big, big group."). Likewise, Dr. Warren Martin Hern, another plaintiff, testified that when he heard he was on the list, "I was terrified. It's hard to describe the feeling that -- that you are on a list of people to -- who have been brought to public attention in this way. I felt that this was a -- a list of doctors to be killed." *Planned Parenthood,* No. CV-95-01671-JO, at 625 (Jan. 11, 1999).

From the point of view of the victims, it makes little difference whether the violence against them will come from the makers of the posters or from unrelated third parties; bullets kill their victims regardless of who pulls the trigger. But it makes a difference for the purpose of the First Amendment. Speech -- especially political speech, as this clearly was -- may not be punished or enjoined unless it falls into one of the narrow categories of unprotected speech recognized by the Supreme Court: true threat, *Watts v. United States,* 394 U.S. 705, 707 (1969), incitement, *Brandenburg v. Ohio,* 395 U.S. 444, 447 (1969), conspiracy to commit criminal acts, *Scales v. United States,* 367 U.S. 203, 229, 6 L.Ed.2d 782, 81 S. Ct. 1469 (1961), fighting words, *Chaplinsky v. New Hampshire,* 315 U.S. 568, 572, 86 L.Ed. 1031, 62 S. Ct. 766-73 (1942), etc.

Even assuming that one could somehow distill a true threat from the posters themselves, the majority opinion is still fatally defective because it contradicts the central holding of *Claiborne Hardware*: Where the speaker is engaged in public political speech, the public statements themselves cannot be the sole proof that they were true threats, unless the speech directly threatens actual injury to identifiable individuals. Absent such an unmistakable, specific threat, there must be evidence aside from the political statements themselves showing that the public speaker would himself or in conspiracy with others inflict unlawful harm. 458 U.S. at 932-34. The majority cites not a scintilla of evidence -- other than the posters themselves -- that plaintiffs or someone associated with them would carry out the threatened harm.

Given this lack of evidence, the posters can be viewed, at most, as a call to arms for other abortion protesters to harm plaintiffs. However, the Supreme Court made it clear that under *Brandenburg,* encouragement or even advocacy of violence is protected by the First Amendment: "Mere advocacy of the use of force or violence does not remove speech from the protection of the First Amendment." *Claiborne Hardware,* 458 U.S. at 927 (citing *Brandenburg,* 395 U.S. at 447) (emphasis in the original). *Claiborne Hardware* in fact goes much farther; it cautions that where liability is premised on "politically motivated" activities, we must" examine critically the basis on which liability was imposed." 458 U.S. at 915. As the Court explained, "Since respondents would impose liability on the basis of a public address -- which predominantly contained highly charged political rhetoric lying at the core of the First Amendment -- we approach this suggested basis for liability with extreme care." 458 U.S. at 926-27. This is precisely what the majority does not do; were it to do so, it would have no choice but to reverse.

The activities for which the district court held defendants liable were unquestionably of a political nature. There is no allegation that any of the posters in this case disclosed private information improperly obtained. We must therefore assume that the information in the posters was obtained from public sources. All defendants did was reproduce this public information in a format designed to convey a political viewpoint and to achieve political goals. The "Deadly Dozen" posters and the "Nuremberg Files" dossiers were unveiled at political rallies staged for the purpose of protesting *Roe v. Wade,* 410 U.S. 113, 35 L.Ed.2d 147, 93 S. Ct. 705 (1973). Similarly, defendants presented the poster of Dr. Crist at a rally held on the steps of the St. Louis federal courthouse, where the *Dred Scott* decision was handed down, in order to draw a parallel between "blacks being declared property and unborn children being denied their right to live." *Planned Parenthood,* CV-95-01671-JO, at 2677 (Jan. 22, 1999). The Nuremberg Files website is clearly an expression of a political point of view. The posters and the website are designed both to rally political support for the views espoused by defendants, and to intimidate plaintiffs and others like them into desisting abortion-related activities. This political agenda may not be to the liking of many people -- political dissidents are often unpopular -- but the speech, including the intimidating message, does not constitute a direct threat because there is no evidence other than the speech itself that the speakers intend to resort to physical violence if their threat is not heeded.

In determining whether the record here supports a finding of true threats, not only the reasoning but also the facts of *Claiborne Hardware* are highly relevant. *Claiborne Hardware* arose out of a seven-year effort (1966 to 1972) to obtain racial justice in Claiborne County, Mississippi. *Claiborne Hardware,* 458 U.S. at 898. The campaign employed a variety of tactics, one among them being the boycotting of white merchants. *Id.* at 900. The boycott and other concerted activities were organized by the NAACP, in the person of its Mississippi field secretary Charles Evers, as well as by other black organizations and leaders. *Id.* at 898-900.

In order to persuade or coerce recalcitrant blacks to join the boycott, the organizers resorted to a variety of enforcement mechanisms. These included the posting of store watchers outside the boycotted stores. These watchers, also known as "Black Hats" or "Deacons," would "identify those who traded with the merchants." *Id.* at 903. The names were collected and "read aloud at meetings at the First Baptist Church and published in a local black newspaper." *Id.* at 909. Evers made several speeches containing threats -- including those of physical violence -- against the boycott violators. *Id.* at 900 n.28, 902, 926-27. In addition, a number of violent acts -- including shots fired at individuals' homes -- were committed against the boycott breakers. *Id.* at 904-06.

The lawsuit that culminated in the *Claiborne Hardware* opinion was brought against scores of individuals and several organizations, including the NAACP. The state trial court found defendants liable in damages and entered "a broad permanent injunction," which prohibited the defendants from engaging in virtually all activities associated with the boycott, including picketing and using store watchers. *Id.* at 893. The Mississippi Supreme Court affirmed, finding liability based on a variety of state law theories, some of which had as their gravamen the use of force or threat of force by those engaged in the boycott. *Id.* at 894-95.

... While set in a different time and place, and involving a very different political cause, *Claiborne Hardware* bears remarkable similarities to our case:

> ~ Like *Claiborne Hardware*, this case involves a concerted effort by a variety of groups and individuals in pursuit of a common political cause. Some of the activities were lawful, others were not. In both cases, there was evidence that the various players communicated with each other and, at times, engaged in concerted action. The Supreme Court, however, held that mere association with groups or individuals who pursue unlawful conduct is an insufficient basis for the imposition of liability, unless it is shown that the defendants actually participated in or authorized the illegal conduct.

> ~ Both here and in *Claiborne Hardware*, there were instances of actual violence that followed heated rhetoric. The Court made clear, however, that unless the violence follows promptly after the speeches, thus meeting the stringent *Brandenburg* standard for incitement, no liability could be imposed on account of the speech.

> ~ The statements on which liability was premised in both cases were made during the course of political rallies and had a coercive effect on the intended targets. Yet the Supreme Court held in *Claiborne Hardware* that coercion alone could not serve as the basis for liability, because it had not been shown -- by evidence aside from the political speeches themselves -- that defendants or their agents were involved in or authorized actual violence.

> ~ In *Claiborne Hardware*, the boycott organizers gathered facts -- the identity of those who violated the boycott--and publicized them to the community by way of speeches and a newspaper. As in our case, this ostentatious gathering of information, and publication thereof, were intended to put pressure on those whose names were publicized, and perhaps put them in fear that they will become objects of violence by members of the community. Yet the Supreme Court held that this could not form the basis for liability.

To the extent *Claiborne Hardware* differs from our case, the difference makes ours a far weaker case for the imposition of liability. To begin with, Charles Evers's speeches in *Claiborne Hardware* explicitly threatened physical violence. Referring to the boycott violators, Evers repeatedly went so far as to say that "we," presumably including himself, would "break your damn neck." 458 U.S. at 902. In our case, the defendants never called for violence at all, and certainly said nothing suggesting that they personally would be involved in any violence against the plaintiffs.

Another difference between the two cases is that the record in *Claiborne Hardware* showed a concerted action between the boycott organizers, all of whom operated within close physical proximity in a small Mississippi county. By contrast, there is virtually no evidence that defendants had engaged in any concerted action with any of the other individuals who prepared "wanted" posters in the past.

The most striking difference between the two cases is that one of Evers's speeches in *Claiborne Hardware*, which expressly threatened violence against the boycott violators, was in fact followed by violence; he then made additional speeches, again referring to violence against boycott breakers. 458 U.S. at 900 (April 1966 speech), 902 (April 1969 speeches). By contrast, the record here contains no evidence that violence was committed against any doctor after his name appeared on defendants' posters or web page.

The opinion's effort to distinguish *Claiborne Hardware* does not bear scrutiny. The majority claims that in *Claiborne Hardware*, "there was no context to give the speeches (including the expression 'break your neck') the implication of ... directly threatening unlawful conduct." As explained above, the majority is quite wrong on this point, but it doesn't matter anyway: Evers's statements were threatening on their face. Not only did he speak of breaking necks and inflicting "discipline," he used the first person plural "we" to indicate that he himself and those associated with him would be doing the neck-breaking, 458 U.S. at 902, and he said that "blacks who traded with white merchants would be answerable to him," *Id.* at 900 n.28.

… The majority also relies on the fact that the posters here "were publicly distributed, but personally targeted." But the threats in *Claiborne Hardware* were also individually targeted. Store watchers carefully noted the names of blacks who entered the boycotted stores, and those names were published in a newspaper and read out loud at the First Baptist Church, where Evers delivered his speeches. 458 U.S. at 903-04. When speaking of broken necks and other discipline, Evers was quite obviously referring to those individuals who had been identified as defying the boycott; in fact, he stated explicitly that he knew their identity and that they would be answerable to him. *Id.* at 900 n.28. The majority's opinion simply cannot be squared with *Claiborne Hardware.*

Claiborne Hardware ultimately stands for the proposition that those who would punish or deter protected speech must make a very substantial showing that the speech stands outside the umbrella of the First Amendment. This message was reinforced recently by the Supreme Court in *Ashcroft v. Free Speech Coalition,* 152 L.Ed.2d 403, 122 S. Ct. 1389, 2002 WL 552476 (U.S. Apr. 16, 2002), where the government sought to prohibit simulated child pornography without satisfying the stringent requirements of *Miller v. California,* 413 U.S. 15, 37 L.Ed.2d 419, 93 S. Ct. 2607 (1973). The Court rejected this effort, even though the government had earnestly argued that suppression of the speech would advance vital legitimate governmental interests, such as avoiding the exploitation of real children and punishing producers of real child pornography. *See* 152 L.Ed.2d 403, *id.* at *11-*13; *see also* 152 L.Ed.2d 403, *id.* at *16 (Thomas, J., concurring in the judgment); 152 L.Ed.2d 403, *id.* at *17-*18 (O'Connor, J., concurring in the judgment in part and dissenting in part); 152 L.Ed.2d 403, *id.* at *21 (Rehnquist, C. J., dissenting). The Court held that the connection between the protected speech and the harms in question is simply too "contingent and indirect" to warrant suppression. 152 L.Ed.2d 403, *id.* at *10; *see also* 152 L.Ed.2d 403, *id.* at *12 ("The Government has shown no more than a remote connection between speech that might encourage thoughts or impulses and any resulting child abuse."). …

Finally, a word about the remedy. The majority affirms a crushing liability verdict, including the award of punitive damages, in addition to the injunction. An injunction against political speech is bad enough, but the liability verdict will have a far more chilling effect.

Defendants will be destroyed financially by a huge debt that is almost certainly not dischargeable in bankruptcy; it will haunt them for the rest of their lives and prevent them from ever again becoming financially self-sufficient. The Supreme Court long ago recognized that the fear of financial ruin can have a seriously chilling effect on all manner of speech, and will surely cause other speakers to hesitate, lest they find themselves at the mercy of a local jury. *See N.Y. Times Co. v. Sullivan*, 376 U.S. 254, 277-79, 11 L.Ed.2d 686, 84 S. Ct. 710 (1964). The lesson of what a local jury has done to defendants here will not be lost on others who would engage in heated political rhetoric in a wide variety of causes.

In that regard, a retrospective liability verdict is far more damaging than an injunction; the latter at least gives notice of what is prohibited and what is not. The fear of liability for damages, and especially punitive damages, puts the speaker at risk as to what a jury might later decide is a true threat, and how vindictive it might feel towards the speaker and his cause. In this case, defendants said nothing remotely threatening, yet they find themselves crucified financially. Who knows what other neutral statements a jury might imbue with a menacing meaning based on the activities of unrelated parties. In such circumstances, it is especially important for an appellate court to perform its constitutional function of reviewing the record to ensure that the speech in question clearly falls into one of the narrow categories that is unprotected by the First Amendment. The majority fails to do this.

While today it is abortion protesters who are singled out for punitive treatment, the precedent set by this court -- the broad and uncritical deference to the judgment of a jury -- will haunt dissidents of all political stripes for many years to come. Because this is contrary to the principles of the First Amendment as explicated by the Supreme Court in *Claiborne Hardware* and its long-standing jurisprudence stemming from *Brandenburg v. Ohio*, I respectfully dissent.

* * * * *

Notes and Questions

1. This was to be the judiciary's final word. A petition for a writ of *certiorari* was denied in 2003. 539 U.S. 958 (2003).

2. Is it reasonable to evaluate the speech posted on a web-site by the same standards by which other media's publications are assessed? "[Could] ... a newspaper speaking to the public at large be seen as making such a threat? A newspaper speaks to all readers and not to named individuals." James C. Goodale, *Planned Parenthood and ACLU Lose Bid to Silence Media*, N.Y.L.J., Apr. 6, 2001, at 3. Does this presuppose the absence of targeting of comments to specific individuals?

3. How might an electronic posting affect a prosecutor's burden to prove that the threat in fact was received? According to Salon.com, a computer expert admitted that he posted offers to kill others. While a jury found him guilty on charges of threatening to kill, he nonetheless was acquitted of solicitation and attempt to solicit murder; prosecutors failed to prove that anyone other than the putative victims could have located the web-sites. *See Man Acquitted of Internet Murder Plot*, Salon.com (Dec. 12, 2000), *available at* <http://www.salon.com/tech/ wire/2000/1212/web_murder/index.html>.

4. The U.S. District Court for the District of Massachusetts denied a motion to dismiss brought by the North American Man Boy Love Association after the family of a murder victim claimed that the entity should be liable for postings on its web-site. *See Curley v. North Am. Man Boy Love Ass'n, et al.,* Civ. Action No. 00-CV-10956-GAO, 2001 U.S. Dist. LEXIS 18305 (D. Mass. Sept. 27, 2001), *dismissed in part by* Civ. Action No. 00-CV-10956 GAO, 2002 U.S. Dist. LEXIS 3090 (D. Mass. Feb. 22, 2002), *motion to dismiss granted by* Civ. Action No. 00-CV-10956-GAO, 2002 U.S. Dist. LEXIS 3090 (D. Mass. Feb. 22, 2002) (dismissing the plaintiffs claim pursuant to 42 U.S.C. § 1985(3)). The family claimed that immediately before committing the crime, the alleged killer accessed the web-site that allegedly encouraged members to rape male children. *See* Civ. Action No. 00-CV-10956-GAO, 2001 U.S. Dist. LEXIS 18305 at *3 n.1 (citing amended complaint). The lower court noted that speech consisting of mere advocacy is not subject to sanction, but denied the motion on the ground that it was not clear that, depending upon the factual record to be elicited, liability would be foreclosed. *See id.* at *4-8.

* * * * *

Internet Speech Relating to Violence

insert the following before R.A.V. v. City of St. Paul, Minnesota on page 145 of Law of Internet Speech:

One commentator observed that "[w]hen one witnesses the anti-Semitic, racist, homophobic, and Holocaust-denying Web sites that are proliferating, and … hate mongers … who capitalize on the Internet as a tool to spread their messages, a natural response is 'There ought to be a law!' But the promulgation of new legal rules and further criminal penalties is not necessarily what is called for. … Technology, education, and guidance are other relevant tools." Christopher Wolf, *Regulating Hate Speech Qua Speech is Not the Solution to the Epidemic of Hate on the Internet – Part II,* Metropolitan Corporate Couns. (Sept. 2004) at 21, *available at* <http://www.metrocorpcounsel.com/pdf/2004/September/21.pdf>.

Another commentator observed that "[e]xtremists … tend to host their sites in jurisdictions geographically out of reach of the authorities of countries that might want to shut them down. For example, several hundred German neo-Nazi websites, aimed at German-only audiences, are hosted in the US because of the freedom of speech laws. In addition, various offshore and island nations have also provided a haven for extremists wishing to host sites and services beyond the reach of law enforcement." Nick Ryan, *Fear and Loathing,* Guardian Unlimited (Aug. 12, 2004), *available at* <http://www.guardian.co.uk/online/story/0,3605,1280992,00.html>.

On balance, how do American First Amendment principles enhance libertarian values and deter hatemongering? What is the impact of other approaches on speech in the United States?

* * * * *

insert the following at the end of page 150 of Law of Internet Speech:

Virginia, Petitioner

v.

Barry Elton Black, Richard J. Elliott, and Jonathan O'Mara

Supreme Court of the United States

No. 01-1107, 538 U.S. 343

April 7, 2003

Justice O'Connor announced the judgment of the Court and delivered the opinion of the Court with respect to Parts I, II, and III, and an opinion with respect to Parts IV and V, in which The Chief Justice, Justice Stevens, and Justice Breyer join.

[Respondents were separately convicted of violating a Virginia statute that makes it a felony "for any person ..., with the intent of intimidating any person or group ..., to burn ... a cross on the property of another, a highway or other public place," and specifies that "[a]ny such burning ... shall be *prima facie* evidence of an intent to intimidate a person or group." Va. Code § 18.2-423 (1996). When respondent Black objected on First Amendment grounds to his trial court's jury instruction that cross burning by itself is sufficient evidence from which the required "intent to intimidate" could be inferred, the prosecutor responded that the instruction incorporated the Virginia Model Instructions. Respondent O'Mara pleaded guilty to charges of violating the statute, but reserved the right to challenge its constitutionality. At respondent Elliott's trial, the judge instructed the jury as to what the Commonwealth was required to prove, but did not give an instruction on the meaning of the word "intimidate" or on the statute's *prima facie* evidence provision.

The Virginia Supreme Court consolidated the three cases and held that the cross-burning statute was unconstitutional on its face; was analytically indistinguishable from the ordinance found unconstitutional in *R. A. V. v. St. Paul,* 505 U.S. 377; discriminated on the basis of content and viewpoint because it selectively criminalized cross burning in light of its distinctive message; and the *prima facie* evidence provision rendered the statute overbroad because the increased probability of prosecution under the statute chills the expression of protected speech.]

... In this case we consider whether the Commonwealth of Virginia's statute banning cross burning with "an intent to intimidate a person or group of persons" violates the First Amendment. Va. Code Ann. § 18.2-423 (1996). We conclude that while a State, consistent with the First Amendment, may ban cross burning carried out with the intent to intimidate, the provision in the Virginia statute treating any cross burning as *prima facie* evidence of intent to intimidate renders the statute unconstitutional in its current form.

... II.

Cross burning originated in the 14th century as a means for Scottish tribes to signal each other. *See* M. Newton & J. Newton, *The Ku Klux Klan: An Encyclopedia* 145 (1991). ... Cross burning in this country, however, long ago became unmoored from its Scottish ancestry. Burning a cross in the United States is inextricably intertwined with the history of the Ku Klux Klan.

The first Ku Klux Klan began in Pulaski, Tennessee, in the spring of 1866. Although the Ku Klux Klan started as a social club, it soon changed into something far different. The Klan fought Reconstruction and the corresponding drive to allow freed blacks to participate in the political process. Soon the Klan imposed "a veritable reign of terror" throughout the South. S. Kennedy, *Southern Exposure* 31 (1991) (hereinafter Kennedy). The Klan employed tactics such as whipping, threatening to burn people at the stake, and murder. W. Wade, *The Fiery Cross: The Ku Klux Klan in America* 48-49 (1987) (hereinafter Wade). The Klan's victims included blacks, southern whites who disagreed with the Klan, and "carpetbagger" northern whites.

The activities of the Ku Klux Klan prompted legislative action at the national level. ... [Although b]y the end of Reconstruction in 1877, the first Klan no longer existed[, a] second Klan began in 1905, with the publication of Thomas Dixon's *The Clansmen: An Historical Romance of the Ku Klux Klan*. Dixon's book was a sympathetic portrait of the first Klan, depicting the Klan as a group of heroes "saving" the South from blacks and the "horrors" of Reconstruction. Although the first Klan never actually practiced cross burning, Dixon's book depicted the Klan burning crosses to celebrate the execution of former slaves. *Id.* at 324-326; *see also Capitol Square Review and Advisory Bd. v. Pinette,* 515 U.S. 753, 770-771 (1995) (Thomas, J., concurring). Cross burning thereby became associated with the first Ku Klux Klan. When D. W. Griffith turned Dixon's book into the movie *The Birth of a Nation* in 1915, the association between cross burning and the Klan became indelible. In addition to the cross burnings in the movie, a poster advertising the film displayed a hooded Klansman riding a hooded horse, with his left hand holding the reins of the horse and his right hand holding a burning cross above his head. Wade 127. Soon thereafter, in November 1915, the second Klan began.

From the inception of the second Klan, cross burnings have been used to communicate both threats of violence and messages of shared ideology. ...

Often, the Klan used cross burnings as a tool of intimidation and a threat of impending violence. For example, in 1939 and 1940, the Klan burned crosses in front of synagogues and churches. *See* Kennedy 175. ...

The Klan continued to use cross burnings to intimidate after World War II. In one incident, an African-American "school teacher who recently moved his family into a block formerly occupied only by whites asked the protection of city police ... after the burning of a cross in his front yard." *Richmond News Leader,* Jan. 21, 1949, p. 19. ...

The decision of this Court in *Brown v. Board of Education,* 347 U.S. 483 (1954), along with the civil rights movement of the 1950's and 1960's, sparked another outbreak of Klan violence. These acts of violence included bombings, beatings, shootings, stabbings, and mutilations. *See, e.g.,* Chalmers 349-350; Wade 302-303. Members of the Klan burned crosses on the lawns of those associated with the civil rights movement, assaulted the Freedom Riders, bombed churches, and murdered blacks as well as whites whom the Klan viewed as sympathetic toward the civil rights movement.

Throughout the history of the Klan, cross burnings have also remained potent symbols of shared group identity and ideology. The burning cross became a symbol of the Klan itself and a central feature of Klan gatherings. According to the Klan constitution (called the kloran), the "fiery cross" was the "emblem of that sincere, unselfish devotedness of all klansmen to the sacred purpose and principles we have espoused." The Ku Klux Klan Hearings before the House Committee on Rules, 67th Cong., 1st Sess., 114, Exh. G (1921); *see also* Wade 419. And the Klan has often published its newsletters and magazines under the name *The Fiery Cross. See* Wade 226, 489.

At Klan gatherings across the country, cross burning became the climax of the rally or the initiation. ... Throughout the Klan's history, the Klan continued to use the burning cross in their ritual ceremonies.

For its own members, the cross was a sign of celebration and ceremony. During a joint Nazi-Klan rally in 1940, the proceeding concluded with the wedding of two Klan members who "were married in full Klan regalia beneath a blazing cross." *Id.* at 271. In response to antimasking bills introduced in state legislatures after World War II, the Klan burned crosses in protest. *See* Chalmers 340. On March 26, 1960, the Klan engaged in rallies and cross burnings throughout the South in an attempt to recruit 10 million members. *See* Wade 305. Later in 1960, the Klan became an issue in the third debate between Richard Nixon and John Kennedy, with both candidates renouncing the Klan. After this debate, the Klan reiterated its support for Nixon by burning crosses. *See id.* at 309. And cross burnings featured prominently in Klan rallies when the Klan attempted to move toward more nonviolent tactics to stop integration. *See id.* at 323; *cf.* Chalmers 368-369, 371-372, 380, 384. In short, a burning cross has remained a symbol of Klan ideology and of Klan unity.

To this day, regardless of whether the message is a political one or whether the message is also meant to intimidate, the burning of a cross is a "symbol of hate." *Capitol Square Review and Advisory Bd.* v. *Pinette,* 515 U.S., at 771 (Thomas, J., concurring). And while cross burning sometimes carries no intimidating message, at other times the intimidating message is the *only* message conveyed. For example, when a cross burning is directed at a particular person not affiliated with the Klan, the burning cross often serves as a message of intimidation, designed to inspire in the victim a fear of bodily harm. Moreover, the history of violence associated with the Klan shows that the possibility of injury or death is not just hypothetical. The person who burns a cross directed at a particular person often is making a serious threat, meant to coerce the victim to comply with the Klan's wishes unless the victim is willing to risk the wrath of the Klan. Indeed, as the cases of respondents Elliott and O'Mara indicate, individuals without Klan affiliation who wish to threaten or menace another person sometimes use cross burning because of this association between a burning cross and violence.

In sum, while a burning cross does not inevitably convey a message of intimidation, often the cross burner intends that the recipients of the message fear for their lives. And when a cross burning is used to intimidate, few if any messages are more powerful.

III.

    A.

    ... The hallmark of [First Amendment] ... protection of free speech is to allow "free trade in ideas" -- even ideas that the overwhelming majority of people might find distasteful or discomforting. *Abrams v. United States,* 250 U.S. 616, 630 (1919) (Holmes, J., dissenting); *see also Texas v. Johnson,* 491 U.S. 397, 414 (1989) ("If there is a bedrock principle underlying the First Amendment, it is that the government may not prohibit the expression of an idea simply because society finds the idea itself offensive or disagreeable"). Thus, the First Amendment "ordinarily" denies a State "the power to prohibit dissemination of social, economic and political doctrine which a vast majority of its citizens believes to be false and fraught with evil consequence." *Whitney v. California,* 274 U.S. 357, 374 (1927) (Brandeis, J., dissenting). The First Amendment affords protection to symbolic or expressive conduct as well as to actual speech. *See, e.g., R. A. V. v. City of St. Paul,* 505 U.S., at 382; *Texas v. Johnson, supra,* at 405-406; *United States v. O'Brien,* 391 U.S. 367, 376-377 (1968); *Tinker v. Des Moines Independent Community School Dist.,* 393 U.S. 503, 505 (1969).

    The protections afforded by the First Amendment, however, are not absolute, and we have long recognized that the government may regulate certain categories of expression consistent with the Constitution. *See, e.g., Chaplinsky v. New Hampshire,* 315 U.S. 568, 571-572 (1942) ("There are certain well-defined and narrowly limited classes of speech, the prevention and punishment of which has never been thought to raise any Constitutional problem"). The First Amendment permits "restrictions upon the content of speech in a few limited areas, which are 'of such slight social value as a step to truth that any benefit that may be derived from them is clearly outweighed by the social interest in order and morality.'" *R. A. V. v. City of St. Paul, supra,* at 382-383 (quoting *Chaplinsky v. New Hampshire, supra,* at 572).

    Thus, for example, a State may punish those words "which by their very utterance inflict injury or tend to incite an immediate breach of the peace." *Chaplinsky v. New Hampshire, supra,* at 572; *see also R. A. V. v. City of St. Paul, supra,* at 383 (listing limited areas where the First Amendment permits restrictions on the content of speech). We have consequently held that fighting words -- "those personally abusive epithets which, when addressed to the ordinary citizen, are, as a matter of common knowledge, inherently likely to provoke violent reaction" -- are generally proscribable under the First Amendment. *Cohen v. California,* 403 U.S. 15, 20 (1971); *see also Chaplinsky v. New Hampshire, supra,* at 572. Furthermore, "the constitutional guarantees of free speech and free press do not permit a State to forbid or proscribe advocacy of the use of force or of law violation except where such advocacy is directed to inciting or producing imminent lawless action and is likely to incite or produce such action." *Brandenburg v. Ohio,* 395 U.S. 444, 447 (1969) *(per curiam).* And the First Amendment also permits a State to ban a "true threat." *Watts v. United States,* 394 U.S. 705, 708 (1969) *(per curiam)* (internal quotation marks omitted); *accord, R. A. V. v. City of St. Paul, supra,* at 388 ("[T]hreats of violence are outside the First Amendment"); *Madsen v. Women's Health Center, Inc.,* 512 U.S. 753, 774 (1994); *Schenck v. Pro-Choice Network of Western N. Y.,* 519 U.S. 357, 373 (1997).

"True threats" encompass those statements where the speaker means to communicate a serious expression of an intent to commit an act of unlawful violence to a particular individual or group of individuals. *See Watts v. United States, supra*, at 708 ("political hyperbole" is not a true threat); *R. A. V. v. City of St. Paul*, 505 U.S., at 388. The speaker need not actually intend to carry out the threat. Rather, a prohibition on true threats "protect[s] individuals from the fear of violence" and "from the disruption that fear engenders," in addition to protecting people "from the possibility that the threatened violence will occur." *Ibid.* Intimidation in the constitutionally proscribable sense of the word is a type of true threat, where a speaker directs a threat to a person or group of persons with the intent of placing the victim in fear of bodily harm or death. Respondents do not contest that some cross burnings fit within this meaning of intimidating speech, and rightly so. As noted in Part II, *supra*, the history of cross burning in this country shows that cross burning is often intimidating, intended to create a pervasive fear in victims that they are a target of violence.

B.

The Supreme Court of Virginia ruled that in light of *R. A. V. v. City of St. Paul, supra*, even if it is constitutional to ban cross burning in a content-neutral manner, the Virginia cross-burning statute is unconstitutional because it discriminates on the basis of content and viewpoint. 262 Va., at 771-776, 553 S. E. 2d, at 742-745. It is true, as the Supreme Court of Virginia held, that the burning of a cross is symbolic expression. The reason why the Klan burns a cross at its rallies, or individuals place a burning cross on someone else's lawn, is that the burning cross represents the message that the speaker wishes to communicate. Individuals burn crosses as opposed to other means of communication because cross burning carries a message in an effective and dramatic manner.

The fact that cross burning is symbolic expression, however, does not resolve the constitutional question. The Supreme Court of Virginia relied upon *R. A. V. v. City of St. Paul, supra,* to conclude that once a statute discriminates on the basis of this type of content, the law is unconstitutional. We disagree.

....[W]e noted that it would be constitutional to ban only a particular type of threat: "[T]he Federal Government can criminalize only those threats of violence that are directed against the President ... since the reasons why threats of violence are outside the First Amendment ... have special force when applied to the person of the President." [*Id.* at 388.] And a State may "choose to prohibit only that obscenity which is the most patently offensive *in its prurience -- i.e.,* that which involves the most lascivious displays of sexual activity." *Ibid.* (emphasis in original). Consequently, while the holding of *R. A. V.* does not permit a State to ban only obscenity based on "offensive *political* messages," *ibid.* or "only those threats against the President that mention his policy on aid to inner cities," *ibid.* the First Amendment permits content discrimination "based on the very reasons why the particular class of speech at issue ... is proscribable," *id.* at 393.

Similarly, Virginia's statute does not run afoul of the First Amendment insofar as it bans cross burning with intent to intimidate. Unlike the statute at issue in *R. A. V.*, the Virginia statute does not single out for opprobrium only that speech directed toward "one of the specified disfavored topics." *Id.* at 391. It does not matter whether an individual burns a cross with intent to intimidate because of the victim's race, gender, or religion, or because of the victim's "political affiliation, union membership, or homosexuality." *Ibid.* Moreover, as a factual matter it is not true that cross burners direct their intimidating conduct solely to racial or religious minorities. *See, e.g., supra,* at 8 (noting the instances of cross burnings directed at union members); *State v. Miller,* 6 Kan. App. 2d 432, 629 P. 2d 748 (1981) (describing the case of a defendant who burned a cross in the yard of the lawyer who had previously represented him and who was currently prosecuting him). Indeed, in the case of Elliott and O'Mara, it is at least unclear whether the respondents burned a cross due to racial animus. *See* 262 Va., at 791, 553 S.E.2d, at 753 (Hassell, J., dissenting) (noting that "these defendants burned a cross because they were angry that their neighbor had complained about the presence of a firearm shooting range in the Elliott's yard, not because of any racial animus").

The First Amendment permits Virginia to outlaw cross burnings done with the intent to intimidate because burning a cross is a particularly virulent form of intimidation. Instead of prohibiting all intimidating messages, Virginia may choose to regulate this subset of intimidating messages in light of cross burning's long and pernicious history as a signal of impending violence. Thus, just as a State may regulate only that obscenity which is the most obscene due to its prurient content, so too may a State choose to prohibit only those forms of intimidation that are most likely to inspire fear of bodily harm. A ban on cross burning carried out with the intent to intimidate is fully consistent with our holding in *R. A. V.* and is proscribable under the First Amendment.

IV.

The Supreme Court of Virginia ruled in the alternative that Virginia's cross-burning statute was unconstitutionally overbroad due to its provision stating that "[a]ny such burning of a cross shall be *prima facie* evidence of an intent to intimidate a person or group of persons." Va. Code Ann. § 18.2-423 (1996). The Commonwealth added the *prima facie* provision to the statute in 1968. The court below did not reach whether this provision is severable from the rest of the cross-burning statute under Virginia law. *See* §1-17.1 ("The provisions of all statutes are severable unless ... it is apparent that two or more statutes or provisions must operate in accord with one another"). In this Court, as in the Supreme Court of Virginia, respondents do not argue that the *prima facie* evidence provision is unconstitutional as applied to any one of them. Rather, they contend that the provision is unconstitutional on its face.

The Supreme Court of Virginia has not ruled on the meaning of the *prima facie* evidence provision. It has, however, stated that "the act of burning a cross alone, with no evidence of intent to intimidate, will nonetheless suffice for arrest and prosecution and will insulate the Commonwealth from a motion to strike the evidence at the end of its case-in-chief." 262 Va., at 778, 553 S. E.2d, at 746. The jury in the case of Richard Elliott did not receive any instruction on the *prima facie* evidence provision, and the provision was not an issue in the case of Jonathan O'Mara because he pleaded guilty. The court in Barry Black's case, however, instructed the jury that the provision means: "The burning of a cross, by itself, is sufficient evidence from which you may infer the required intent." This jury instruction is the same as the Model Jury Instruction in the Commonwealth of Virginia. *See* Virginia Model Jury Instructions, Criminal, Instruction No. 10.250 (1998 and Supp. 2001).

123

The *prima facie* evidence provision, as interpreted by the jury instruction, renders the statute unconstitutional. Because this jury instruction is the Model Jury Instruction, and because the Supreme Court of Virginia had the opportunity to expressly disavow the jury instruction, the jury instruction's construction of the *prima facie* provision "is a ruling on a question of state law that is as binding on us as though the precise words had been written into" the statute. *E.g., Terminiello v. Chicago,* 337 U.S. 1, 4 (1949) (striking down an ambiguous statute on facial grounds based upon the instruction given to the jury).... As construed by the jury instruction, the *prima facie* provision strips away the very reason why a State may ban cross burning with the intent to intimidate. The *prima facie* evidence provision permits a jury to convict in every cross-burning case in which defendants exercise their constitutional right not to put on a defense. And even where a defendant like Black presents a defense, the *prima facie* evidence provision makes it more likely that the jury will find an intent to intimidate regardless of the particular facts of the case. The provision permits the Commonwealth to arrest, prosecute, and convict a person based solely on the fact of cross burning itself.

It is apparent that the provision as so interpreted "'would create an unacceptable risk of the suppression of ideas.'" *Secretary of State of Md. v. Joseph H. Munson Co., supra*, at 965, n.13 (quoting *Members of City Council of Los Angeles v. Taxpayers for Vincent*, 466 U.S. 789, 797 (1984)). The act of burning a cross may mean that a person is engaging in constitutionally proscribable intimidation. But that same act may mean only that the person is engaged in core political speech. The *prima facie* evidence provision in this statute blurs the line between these two meanings of a burning cross. As interpreted by the jury instruction, the provision chills constitutionally protected political speech because of the possibility that a State will prosecute -- and potentially convict -- somebody engaging only in lawful political speech at the core of what the First Amendment is designed to protect.

As the history of cross burning indicates, a burning cross is not always intended to intimidate. Rather, sometimes the cross burning is a statement of ideology, a symbol of group solidarity. It is a ritual used at Klan gatherings, and it is used to represent the Klan itself. Thus, "[b]urning a cross at a political rally would almost certainly be protected expression." *R. A. V. v. St. Paul*, 505 U.S., at 402, n.4 (White, J., concurring in judgment) (citing *Brandenburg v. Ohio*, 395 U.S., at 445). *Cf. National Socialist Party of America v. Skokie*, 432 U.S. 43 (1977) *(per curiam)*. Indeed, occasionally a person who burns a cross does not intend to express either a statement of ideology or intimidation. Cross burnings have appeared in movies such as Mississippi Burning, and in plays such as the stage adaptation of Sir Walter Scott's *The Lady of the Lake*.

The *prima facie* provision makes no effort to distinguish among these different types of cross burnings. It does not distinguish between a cross burning done with the purpose of creating anger or resentment and a cross burning done with the purpose of threatening or intimidating a victim. It does not distinguish between a cross burning at a public rally or a cross burning on a neighbor's lawn. It does not treat the cross burning directed at an individual differently from the cross burning directed at a group of like-minded believers. It allows a jury to treat a cross burning on the property of another with the owner's acquiescence in the same manner as a cross burning on the property of another without the owner's permission. To this extent I agree with Justice Souter that the *prima facie* evidence provision can "skew jury deliberations toward conviction in cases where the evidence of intent to intimidate is relatively weak and arguably consistent with a solely ideological reason for burning." (opinion concurring in judgment and dissenting in part).

It may be true that a cross burning, even at a political rally, arouses a sense of anger or hatred among the vast majority of citizens who see a burning cross. But this sense of anger or hatred is not sufficient to ban all cross burnings. As Gerald Gunther has stated, "The lesson I have drawn from my childhood in Nazi Germany and my happier adult life in this country is the need to walk the sometimes difficult path of denouncing the bigot's hateful ideas with all my power, yet at the same time challenging any community's attempt to suppress hateful ideas by force of law." Casper, Gerry, 55 Stan. L. Rev. 647, 649 (2002) (internal quotation marks omitted). The *prima facie* evidence provision in this case ignores all of the contextual factors that are necessary to decide whether a particular cross burning is intended to intimidate. The First Amendment does not permit such a shortcut.

For these reasons, the *prima facie* evidence provision, as interpreted through the jury instruction and as applied in Barry Black's case, is unconstitutional on its face. We recognize that the Supreme Court of Virginia has not authoritatively interpreted the meaning of the *prima facie* evidence provision. Unlike Justice Scalia, we refuse to speculate on whether *any* interpretation of the *prima facie* evidence provision would satisfy the First Amendment. Rather, all we hold is that because of the interpretation of the *prima facie* evidence provision given by the jury instruction, the provision makes the statute facially invalid at this point. We also recognize the theoretical possibility that the court, on remand, could interpret the provision in a manner different from that so far set forth in order to avoid the constitutional objections we have described. We leave open that possibility. We also leave open the possibility that the provision is severable, and if so, whether Elliott and O'Mara could be retried under § 18.2-423.

V.

With respect to Barry Black, we agree with the Supreme Court of Virginia that his conviction cannot stand, and we affirm the judgment of the Supreme Court of Virginia. With respect to Elliott and O'Mara, we vacate the judgment of the Supreme Court of Virginia, and remand the case for further proceedings.

Justice Thomas, dissenting.

In every culture, certain things acquire meaning well beyond what outsiders can comprehend. That goes for both the sacred, *see Texas v. Johnson*, 491 U.S. 397, 422-429 (1989) (Rehnquist, C.J., dissenting) (describing the unique position of the American flag in our Nation's 200 years of history), and the profane. I believe that cross burning is the paradigmatic example of the latter.

I.

Although I agree with the majority's conclusion that it is constitutionally permissible to "ban ... cross burning carried out with intent to intimidate," I believe that the majority errs in imputing an expressive component to the activity in question (relying on one of the exceptions to the First Amendment's prohibition on content-based discrimination outlined in *R. A. V. v. St. Paul,* 505 U.S. 377 (1992)). In my view, whatever expressive value cross burning has, the legislature simply wrote it out by banning only intimidating conduct undertaken by a particular means. A conclusion that the statute prohibiting cross burning with intent to intimidate sweeps beyond a prohibition on certain conduct into the zone of expression overlooks not only the words of the statute but also reality.

A.

"In holding [the ban on cross burning with intent to intimidate] unconstitutional, the Court ignores Justice Holmes' familiar aphorism that 'a page of history is worth a volume of logic.'" *Texas v. Johnson, supra,* at 421 (*Rehnquist,* C. J., dissenting) (quoting *New York Trust Co. v. Eisner,* 256 U.S. 345, 349 (1921)).

> The world's oldest, most persistent terrorist organization is not European or even Middle Eastern in origin. Fifty years before the Irish Republican Army was organized, a century before Al Fatah declared its holy war on Israel, the Ku Klux Klan was actively harassing, torturing and murdering in the United States. Today ... its members remain fanatically committed to a course of violent opposition to social progress and racial equality in the United States.

M. Newton & J. Newton, *The Ku Klux Klan: An Encyclopedia* vii (1991).

To me, the majority's brief history of the Ku Klux Klan only reinforces this common understanding of the Klan as a terrorist organization, which, in its endeavor to intimidate, or even eliminate those its dislikes, uses the most brutal of methods.

Such methods typically include cross burning -- "a tool for the intimidation and harassment of racial minorities, Catholics, Jews, Communists, and any other groups hated by the Klan." *Capitol Square Review and Advisory Bd. v. Pinette,* 515 U.S. 753, 770 (1995) (Thomas, J., concurring). For those not easily frightened, cross burning has been followed by more extreme measures, such as beatings and murder. Juan Williams, *Eyes on the Prize: America's Civil Rights Years 1954-1965,* at 39 (1965). As the Solicitor General points out, the association between acts of intimidating cross burning and violence is well documented in recent American history. Indeed, the connection between cross burning and violence is well ingrained, and lower courts have so recognized:

> After the mother saw the burning cross, she was crying on her knees in the living room. [She] felt feelings of frustration and intimidation and feared for her husband's life. She testified what the burning cross symbolized to her as a black American: "murder, hanging, rape, lynching. Just about anything bad that you can name. It is the worst thing that can happen to a person." Mr. Heisser told the probation officer that at the time of the occurrence, if the family did not leave, he believed someone would return to commit murder. ... *Seven months*

after the incident, the family still lived in fear.... This is a reaction reasonably to be anticipated from this criminal conduct.

United States v. Skillman, 922 F.2d 1370, 1378 (CA9 1991) (emphasis added).

But the perception that a burning cross is a threat and a precursor of worse things to come is not limited to blacks. Because the modern Klan expanded the list of its enemies beyond blacks and "radical[s]," to include Catholics, Jews, most immigrants, and labor unions, Newton & Newton, *supra*, at ix, a burning cross is now widely viewed as a signal of impending terror and lawlessness. I wholeheartedly agree with the observation made by the Commonwealth of Virginia that

> A white, conservative, middle-class Protestant, waking up at night to find a burning cross outside his home, will reasonably understand that someone is threatening him. His reaction is likely to be very different than if he were to find, say, a burning circle or square. In the latter case, he may call the fire department. In the former, he will probably call the police.

In our culture, cross burning has almost invariably meant lawlessness and understandably instills in its victims well-grounded fear of physical violence.

B.

Virginia's experience has been no exception. ...

Most of the crosses were burned on the lawns of black families, who either were business owners or lived in predominantly white neighborhoods. *See Police Aid Requested by Teacher: Cross is Burned in Negro's Yard,* Richmond News Leader, Jan. 21, 1949, at 19; *Cross Fired Near Suffolk Stirs Probe: Burning Second in Past Week,* Richmond Times-Dispatch, Jan. 23, 1949, § 2, at 1; *Cross is Burned at Reedville Home,* Richmond News Leader, Apr. 14, 1951, at 1. At least one of the cross burnings was accompanied by a shooting. *Cross Burned at Manakin; Third in Area,* Richmond Times-Dispatch, Feb. 26, 1951, at 4. ...

That in the early 1950s the people of Virginia viewed cross burning as creating an intolerable atmosphere of terror is not surprising: Although the cross took on some religious significance in the 1920's when the Klan became connected with certain southern white clergy, by the postwar period it had reverted to its original function "as an instrument of intimidation." W. Wade, *The Fiery Cross: The Ku Klux Klan in America* 185, 279 (1987).

Strengthening Delegate Godwin's explanation, as well as my conclusion, that the legislature sought to criminalize terrorizing *conduct* is the fact that at the time the statute was enacted, racial segregation was not only the prevailing practice, but also the law in Virginia. And, just two years after the enactment of this statute, Virginia's General Assembly embarked on a campaign of "massive resistance" in response to *Brown v. Board of Education,* 347 U.S. 483 (1954). *See generally, Griffin v. County School Board,* 377 U.S. 218, 221 (1964); *Harrison v. Day,* 106 S.E.2d 636 (Va. 1959) (describing "massive resistance" as legislatively mandated attempt to close public schools rather than desegregate). …

It strains credulity to suggest that a state legislature that adopted a litany of segregationist laws self-contradictorily intended to squelch the segregationist message. Even for segregationists, violent and terroristic conduct, the Siamese twin of cross burning, was intolerable. The ban on cross burning with intent to intimidate demonstrates that even segregationists understood the difference between intimidating and terroristic conduct and racist expression. It is simply beyond belief that, in passing the statute now under review, the Virginia legislature was concerned with anything but penalizing conduct it must have viewed as particularly vicious.

Accordingly, this statute prohibits only conduct, not expression. And, just as one cannot burn down someone's house to make a political point and then seek refuge in the First Amendment, those who hate cannot terrorize and intimidate to make their point. In light of my conclusion that the statute here addresses only conduct, there is no need to analyze it under any of our First Amendment tests.

II.

Even assuming that the statute implicates the First Amendment, in my view, the fact that the statute permits a jury to draw an inference of intent to intimidate from the cross burning itself presents no constitutional problems. Therein lies my primary disagreement with the plurality. …

The legislature finds the behavior so reprehensible that the intent is satisfied by the mere act committed by a perpetrator. Considering the horrific effect cross burning has on its victims, it is also reasonable to presume intent to intimidate from the act itself. ….

Because the *prima facie* clause here is an inference, not an irrebuttable presumption, there is all the more basis under our Due Process precedents to sustain this statute.

  B.

The plurality, however, is troubled by the presumption because this is a First Amendment case. The plurality laments the fate of an innocent cross-burner who burns a cross, but does so without an intent to intimidate. The plurality fears the chill on expression because, according to the plurality, the inference permits "the Commonwealth to arrest, prosecute and convict a person based solely on the fact of cross burning itself." First, it is, at the very least, unclear that the inference comes into play during arrest and initiation of a prosecution, that is, prior to the instructions stage of an actual trial. Second, as I explained above, the inference is rebuttable and, as the jury instructions given in this case demonstrate, Virginia law still requires the jury to find the existence of each element, including intent to intimidate, beyond a reasonable doubt.

Moreover, even in the First Amendment context, the Court has upheld such regulations where conduct that initially appears culpable, ultimately results in dismissed charges. A regulation of pornography is one such example. While possession of child pornography is

128

illegal, *Ferber v. New York*, 458 U.S. 747, 764 (1982), possession of adult pornography, as long as it is not obscene, is allowed, *Miller v. California*, 413 U.S. 15 (1973). As a result, those pornographers trafficking in images of adults who look like minors, may be not only deterred but also arrested and prosecuted for possessing what a jury might find to be legal materials. This "chilling" effect has not, however, been a cause for grave concern with respect to overbreadth of such statutes among the members of this Court.

That the First Amendment gives way to other interests is not a remarkable proposition. What is remarkable is that, under the plurality's analysis, the determination of whether an interest is sufficiently compelling depends not on the harm a regulation in question seeks to prevent, but on the area of society at which it aims. For instance, in *Hill v. Colorado*, 530 U.S. 703 (2000), the Court upheld a restriction on protests near abortion clinics, explaining that the State had a legitimate interest, which was sufficiently narrowly tailored, in protecting those seeking services of such establishments "from unwanted advice" and "unwanted communication," *id.* at 708; *id.* at 716; *id.* at 717; *id.* at 729. In so concluding, the Court placed heavy reliance on the "vulnerable physical and emotional conditions" of patients. *Id.* at 729. Thus, when it came to the rights of those seeking abortions, the Court deemed restrictions on "unwanted advice," which, notably, can be given only from a distance of at least 8 feet from a prospective patient, justified by the countervailing interest in obtaining abortion. Yet, here, the plurality strikes down the statute because one day an individual might wish to burn a cross, but might do so without an intent to intimidate anyone. That cross burning subjects its targets, and, sometimes, an unintended audience, *see* 262 Va., at 782, to extreme emotional distress, and is virtually never viewed merely as "unwanted communication," but rather, as a physical threat, is of no concern to the plurality. Henceforth, under the plurality's view, physical safety will be valued less than the right to be free from unwanted communications.

III.

Because I would uphold the validity of this statute, I respectfully dissent.

* * * * *

On remand, the Virginia Supreme Court upheld the constitutionality of the state statute that criminalized the burning of a cross with intent to intimidate, but unanimously struck down the statute's provision that made the act of burning a cross *prima facie* evidence of an intent to intimidate. The convictions of two men charged under the statute were affirmed. *See Elliott v. Commonwealth of Va.*, 267 Va. 464, 593 S.E.2d 263 (Va. 2004).

Two commentators opined that the Virginia Supreme Court "appear[ed] to have misapprehended both the basis of the Supreme Court's ruling in *Black v. Commonwealth* and the doctrinal underpinnings of *Brandenburg* [*v. Ohio,* 395 U.S. 444 (1969) (*per curiam*)]. *Brandenburg* established those circumstances in which speech that incites a third party to commit imminent lawless action can be proscribed or punished, while the issue in the Virginia cases ... was whether the cross burnings constituted unprotected 'true threats.' Incitement concerns speech that is alleged to cause others to act and seeks to protect against the resulting violence or other lawless action. The threats doctrine, by contrast, is concerned primarily about the fear that a listener experiences upon receiving a threat." Seth D. Berlin and Audrey Critchley, *Virginia Supreme Court Rules on Constitutionality of Cross Burning Statute,* MLRC MediaLawLetter (Mar. 2004) at 41, 42.

* * * * *

insert the following after Notes and Questions # 6 on page 163 of Law of Internet Speech:

7. The U.S. Court of Appeals for the Ninth Circuit upheld the issuance of an injunction under a federal statute that permits injunctions against the organization, marketing, and promotion of tax evasion schemes. *See United States v. Schiff*, 379 F.3d 621 (9th Cir. 2004). The order required the defendants to post the injunction on the web-site that promoted the sale of fraudulent tax advice. *See id.* The court concluded that the injunction did not violate the First Amendment rights of the defendants, who were characterized as persistent, albeit unsuccessful, protesters of tax laws. The defendants' speech was deemed to be commercial speech that deserved lesser constitutional protection than were the speech purely political. *See id.* at 630. The court also concluded that requiring the posting of the injunction on the defendants' web-site did not violate the First Amendment because the injunction constituted factual commercial information, and the posting of the injunction would alert potential customers to the possibility of exposure to criminal liability for tax evasion. *See id.* at 631.

8. Would Paladin Press have a viable copyright claim against mirror sites that contained the entire *Hit Man* work? Would there be equitable or other bases on which such a copyright claim would be defeated?

9. *New York Times* columnist Nicholas D. Kristof opined that notwithstanding his support of civil liberties generally, he would "like to see a tougher approach [taken with respect to] ... 'cookbooks' to make anthrax, sarin and other chemical, biological or nuclear weapons. ... They have as little free-speech value as child pornography, and they are more dangerous." Nicholas D. Kristof, *May I See Your ID?*, N.Y. Times, Mar. 17, 2004 at A25.

* * * * *

TERRY L. STEWART, Director, ARIZONA DEPARTMENT OF
CORRECTIONS, *et al.*
v.
JERRY DEAN MCCOY

Supreme Court of the United States

No. 02-20, 537 U.S. 993

October 21, 2002

The motion of respondent for leave to proceed *in forma pauperis* is granted. The petition for writ of *certiorari* to the United States Court of Appeals for the Ninth Circuit is denied.

Statement of JUSTICE STEVENS respecting the denial of the petition for writ of *certiorari*:

An Arizona jury found respondent guilty of participating in a criminal syndicate, and the trial court sentenced him to a term of 15 years' imprisonment. After his conviction was affirmed by the Arizona Court of Appeals, the Federal District Court granted his petition for a writ of habeas corpus, and the Court of Appeals for the Ninth Circuit affirmed the order releasing him from custody. The harsh sentence for a relatively minor offense provides a permissible justification for this Court's discretionary decision to deny the warden's petition for *certiorari*. Nevertheless, the issue raised by her petition has sufficient importance to merit comment.

The specific crime committed by respondent was giving advice to members of a street gang. In the words of the relevant Arizona statute, he was guilty of: "Furnishing advice or direction in the conduct, financing or management of a criminal syndicate's affairs with the intent to promote or further the criminal objectives of a criminal syndicate."[1] The evidence showed that he had been a member of a street gang in California before moving to Arizona, and that at two social gatherings he gave several members of a Tucson gang specific advice on how to operate their gang.[2] The state appellate court concluded that the evidence was sufficient to prove his knowledge of the Tucson gang's criminal activities and his intent to promote those activities. It also rejected respondent's contention that the statute violated the First Amendment because it prohibited constitutionally protected speech.

The federal courts both concluded, however, that respondent's speech was protected by that Amendment. Relying primarily on *Brandenburg v. Ohio,* 395 U.S. 444, 23 L. Ed. 2d 430, 89 S. Ct. 1827, 48 Ohio Op. 2d 320 (1969) *(per curiam),* and *Hess v. Indiana,* 414 U.S. 105, 38 L. Ed. 2d 303, 94 S. Ct. 326 (1973) *(per curiam),* the Court of Appeals held that respondent's speech "was mere abstract advocacy" that was not constitutionally proscribable because it did not incite "imminent" lawless action. Given the specific character of respondent's advisory comments, that holding is surely debatable. But whether right or wrong, it raises a most important issue concerning the scope of our holding in *Brandenburg,* for our opinion expressly encompassed nothing more than "mere advocacy," *Brandenburg,* 395 U.S. at 449.

The principle identified in our *Brandenburg* opinion is that "the constitutional guarantees of free speech and free press do not permit a State to forbid or proscribe advocacy of the use of force or of law violation except where such advocacy is directed to inciting or producing imminent lawless action and is likely to incite or produce such action." *Brandenburg,* 395 U.S. at 447. While the requirement that the consequence be "imminent" is justified with respect to mere advocacy, the same justification does not necessarily adhere to some speech that performs a teaching function. As our cases have long identified, the First Amendment does not prevent restrictions on speech that have "clear support in public danger." *Thomas v. Collins,* 323 U.S. 516, 530, 89 L. Ed. 430, 65 S. Ct. 315 (1945). Long range planning of

---

[1] Ariz. Rev. Stat. Ann. § 13-2308(A)(3) (West 2001).

[2] "Appellant moved to Tucson from California, where he had been a member of a gang since the 1980s. In Tucson, he became acquainted with his girlfriend's son and a number of his friends who belonged to a gang called the 'Bratz.' Several Bratz members testified that appellant was present at a barbecue at the son's house attended by a number of Bratz members and that he spoke to them about his experiences in the California gang. He advised them to formalize their gang by electing officers, collecting money to establish a bail fund for members, and spray painting more gang graffiti to make their presence known in their territory. He also advised them to 'jump in' more loyal members and 'jump out' those who were not loyal. There was testimony explaining that 'jumping' or 'courting' meant initiating a new member or removing a current member by means of a group beating in which a number of members participated in beating or kicking the person 'jumped' or 'courted.' Finally, he advised them to establish friendly relations with other gangs who would support them." *State* v. *McCoy,* 187 Ariz. 223, 224, 928 P.2d 647, 648 (App. 1996).

criminal enterprises -- which may include oral advice, training exercises, and perhaps the preparation of written materials -- involves speech that should not be glibly characterized as mere "advocacy" and certainly may create significant public danger. Our cases have not yet considered whether, and if so to what extent, the First Amendment protects such instructional speech. Our denial of *certiorari* in this case should not be taken as an endorsement of the reasoning of the Court of Appeals.

* * * * *

insert the following after the second full paragraph on page 166 of Law of Internet Speech:

Thereafter, the Ninth Circuit determined that the action had been premature. *See Yahoo! Inc. v. La Ligue Contre Le Racisme Et L'Antisemitisme,* 379 F.3d 1120 (9th Cir. 2004), *reh'g en banc granted by* 399 F.3d 1010 (9th Cir. 2005); *see* Supplement *supra* at 94.

* * * * *

Auction Web-Sites of Nazi Memorabilia: The *Yahoo* Decisions

insert the following before Speech Relating to Matters of National Security on page 166 of Law of Internet Speech:

How might the courts have been influenced by the availability of geo-tracking technology programs? In 2002, for example, Quova Inc. announced that it had developed an upgrade to its Internet-mapping technology that was capable of identifying the geographic location of web-site visitors as specifically as the country, state, and city level. *See, e.g.,* Stefanie Olsen, *Quova Upgrade Pins Down AOL Users,* CNetNews.com (Feb. 13, 2002), *available at* <http://news.com.com/Quova+upgrade+pins+down+AOL+users/2100-1023_3-36138.html>.

How accurately should a court expect geographic tracking technology to be before expecting its use? What sort of costs or inconveniences might be reasonably expected? Should the court's analysis change if users were able to re-configure their computers to evade the tracking?

* * * * *

Speech Relating to Matters of National Security

insert the following at the end of Notes and Questions # 7 on page 193 of Law of Internet Speech:

A laptop purchased in Kabul by a *Wall Street Journal* reporter apparently contained secret documents relating to Al-Quaeda. *See* David Usborne, *Has an Old Computer Revealed that Reid Toured World Searching Out New Targets for Al-Qa'ida?,* Independent (Jan. 17, 2003), *available at* <http://www.independent.co.uk/story.jsp?story=114885>.

* * * * *

insert the following after Notes and Questions # 11 on page 194 of Law of Internet Speech:

12. Some Internet experts and scholars observed that the "[g]overnment will be forced to become increasingly transparent, accessible over the Net, and almost impenetrable if you're not on the Net." Pew Internet & American Life Project, *The Future of the Internet* (Jan. 9, 2005) at iii, *available at* <http://www.pewinternet.org/pdfs/PIP_Future_of_Internet.pdf>.

* * * * *

Various governmental agencies have requested data about customers from the private sector. When identifiable information such as names, addresses, credit card numbers, and travel itineraries of passengers is systematically furnished by an airline to a governmental agency without prior consent from or even notice to the passengers, do the passengers have recourse in civil actions against the airline?

In *Dyer v. Northwest Airlines Corps.*, 334 F. Supp. 2d 1196, 1197 (D.N.D. 2004), customers objected to the disclosure by Northwest Airlines of personal information for a three-month period to the National Aeronautical and Space Administration ("NASA"). In addition to asserting a breach of contract claim, the plaintiffs alleged that the unauthorized disclosure violated the Electronic Communications Privacy Act ("ECPA"), 18 U.S.C. §§ 2702(a)(1), (a)(3), *see Law of Internet Speech* at 473. The North Dakota federal court rejected both claims; as to the ECPA claim, the court determined that Northwest Airlines was beyond the scope of the statute because it is not an electronic communications service provider. *See Dyer v. Northwest Airline Corps.*, 334 F. Supp. 2d at 1199-1200. "Instead, Northwest Airlines sells its products and services over the internet as opposed to access over the internet itself. ....[B]usinesses offering their traditional products and services online through a website are not providing an 'electronic communication service.'" *Id.* at 1199.

In *In re Northwest Airlines Privacy Litig.*, Civ. File No. 04-126 (PAM/JSM), 2004 U.S. Dist. LEXIS 10580 (D. Minn. June 6, 2004), consolidated putative class actions were brought against Northwest Airlines, asserting, among other claims, a violation of ECPA. The Minnesota federal court similarly ruled that the airline was not an Internet service provider and therefore is not subject to section 2702 of ECPA. *See id.* at *6-*7. Nor did the court agree with the plaintiffs that Northwest's disclosure violated section 2701 of ECPA, because that clause "does not prohibit improper disclosure of information. Rather, this section prohibits improper access to an electronic communications service provider or the information contained on that service provider. There is no dispute that Northwest obtained Plaintiff's personal information properly, in the ordinary course of business." *Id.* at *7.

Other airlines, including Delta, Continental, America West, JetBlue, and Frontier, also reportedly have released passenger information to governmental authorities. *See, e.g.,* Ryan Singel, *More False Information from TSA,* Wired News (June 23, 2004), *available at* <http://wired-vig.wired.com/news/politics/0,1283,63958,00.html>. A U.S. Department of Homeland Security report concluded that although the Transportation Security Administration did not violate the Privacy Act of 1974, it did transgress the spirit of the statute when it asked JetBlue Airlines to furnish its customer database to a defense contractor. *See* Department of Homeland Security Privacy Office, *Report to the Public on Events Surrounding JetBlue Data Transfer: Findings and Recommendations* (Feb. 20, 2004) at 8-10, *available at* <http://www.cdt.org/privacy/20040220dhsreport.pdf>. The report included recommendations for comprehensive privacy training and the formation of guidelines relating to data sharing between the private sector and the federal government. *See id.* at 9-10. *But compare The Electronic Privacy Information Center v. Northwest Airlines, Inc.,* No. OST-2004-16939-10, 2004 DOT Av. LEXIS 894 (U.S. Dep't of Transp. Sept. 10, 2004), *available at* <http://www.epic.org/privacy/airtravel/nasa/dot_order.pdf> (concluding that the airline privacy policy in issue did not unambiguously preclude the sharing of customer data with a government agency, and in any event, such a limitation would be unenforceable as against public policy); *and* Ryan Singel, *Army: JetBlue Data Use was Legal,* Wired News.com (Aug. 23, 2004), *available at* <http://www.wired.com/news/politics/0,1283,64647,00.html> (reporting on conclusion by the Army Inspector General that a data-mining project by the Army that included review of JetBlue's passenger records did not violate federal privacy law). In 2004, the Transportation Security Administration announced that it planned to order airlines to turn over passenger information so authorities could cross-check names against watch lists maintained by the FBI's Terrorist Screening Center as part of a new screening system called "Secure Flight." *See, e.g., Government Will Order Airlines to Turn Over Passenger Data to Test Screening System,* Mercury News.com (Sept. 21, 2004), *available at* <http://www.siliconvalley.com/mld/siliconvalley/news/editorial/9723490.htm>.

* * * * *

insert the following at the end of the first sentence in the second full paragraph on page 195 of Law of Internet Speech:

on remand at 116 Cal. App. 4th 241, 255-56, 10 Cal. Rptr. 3d 185, 196 (Cal. App. Ct. Feb. 27, 2004); *see* Supplement *infra* at 341.

* * * * *

National Security and Internet Speech

Anti-Terrorism Legislation

insert the following after Notes and Questions # 3 on page 201 of Law of Internet Speech:

4. Paradoxically, the USA PATRIOT Act was designed to facilitate investigation into and procurement of documents relating to illicit terrorist activity, but because many are troubled by the expanded governmental powers to seize records, they have shortened their document retention policies. Some booksellers, for example, purged customer records upon request and disposed of records reflecting the particular titles purchased by readers' clubs. *See, e.g., Librarians Chafe Under Federal Patriot Act Restrictions,* CNN.com (July 31, 2003), *available at* <http://www.cnn.com/2003/LAW/07/31/libraries.patriotact.ap/index.html> (discussing weekly, rather than monthly, purges of patrons' records at a Boulder, Colorado library); *Bookseller Purges Files to Avoid Potential "Patriot Act" Searches,* CNN.com (Feb. 20, 2003), *available at* <http://cnn.usnews.printthis.clickability.com/pt/cpt?expire=03%2F21%2F2003&fb=Y&urlI> (Feb. 20, 2003).

5. In May 2005, the Bush administration and Senate Republican leaders endorsed a proposal to expand significantly the FBI's power to demand business records in investigations of terrorism without first obtaining approval from a judge. The plan would allow federal investigators to subpoena records from businesses and other institutions without a judge's approval if the investigators declared that the information was needed as part of a foreign

intelligence investigation. *See, e.g.,* Eric Lichtblau, *Plan Would Broaden F.B.I.'s Terror Role,* N.Y. Times, May 19, 2005 at A20.

One critic observed:

> Nearly 400 communities, includ[ing] seven states, have passed resolutions calling on lawmakers to bring the Patriot Act in line with the Constitution. Instead of addressing these legitimate concerns, and reviewing the act in daylight, some in Congress would rather hide behind closed doors away from public scrutiny. The Patriot Act has been the subject of heated debates in recent months – in Congress, in the media, and in households around the country. There is no good reason for the mark-up and vote on this public law to be kept secret from the public.

American Civil Liberties Union, *Senate Committee to Review Controversial Patriot Act Legislation in Secret; Draft Legislation Hidden from Public* (May 17, 2005), *available at* <http://www.aclu.org/SafeandFree/SafeandFree.cfm?ID=18256&c=206> (quoting Anthony D. Romero, Executive Director of ACLU).

6. The U.S. Department of Justice stated in a report declassified in April 2005 that it had relied on section 215 of the USA PATRIOT Act 35 times since late 2003 to gather information about apartment leasing, driver's licenses, financial records, and other data in the course of intelligence investigations. The Justice Department emphasized that it had not exercised its authority to demand records from libraries or bookstores. *See* Eric Lichtblau, *Plan Would Broaden F.B.I.'s Terror Role,* N.Y. Times, May 19, 2005 at A20. How does the existence of the authority even without its exercise affect individuals' privacy interests?

7. The American Civil Liberties Union challenged the FBI's authority to issue National Security Letters ordering certain kinds of businesses to turn over sensitive customer records, and also challenged the USA PATRIOT Act's gap provision, which prohibits a recipient of a National Security Letter from disclosing even the fact of his receipt. Because of the gag provision, the ACLU filed its suit under seal; "it was three weeks before the ACLU could announce that it had challenged the law." American Civil Liberties Union, *ACLU Challenge to "National Security Letter" Authority, available at* <http://www.aclu.org/SafeandFree/SafeandFree.cfm?ID=15543&c=262>.

* * * * *

insert the following after Notes and Questions on page 201 of Law of Internet Speech:

In November 2002, the Homeland Security Act of 2002, Pub. L. No. 107-296, 116 Stat 2135 (codified at 6 U.S.C. § 101-907 (2002)) ("HSA"), was signed into law by President George W. Bush. Among other things, the HSA gives the Homeland Security Department considerable authority to gather information, notably with respect to information on "critical infrastructure." This includes both physical and virtual systems and assets whose "incapacity or destruction ... would have a debilitating impact on security, national economic security, [or] national public health or safety." *Id.,* §§ 2, 211-15; *see also* 42 U.S.C. § 5195c(e) (defining "critical infrastructure").

The HSA contemplates the gathering of information not only from public sectors, but from private sectors as well. The statute encourages private entities to voluntarily submit information regarding possible systems securities breaches and insulates the voluntary submission of certain information pertaining to critical infrastructures from Freedom of Information Act disclosures. *See* 6 U.S.C. § 133. The USA PATRIOT Act defines critical infrastructure as "systems and assets, whether physical or virtual, so vital to the United States that the incapacity or destruction of such systems and assets would have a debilitating impact on security, national economic security, national public health or safety, or any combination of those matters." Pub. L. No. 107-56, § 1016(e), 115 Stat 272 § 1016(e) (codified at 42 U.S.C. § 272 (codified at 42 U.S.C. § 5195c(e)). Information gathered from the private sector is significant because an estimated 90 percent of all critical infrastructure in the United States is controlled by the private sector. *See* Joseph Summerill, *Is it Safe For Your Client to Provide the Government With Homeland Security Data?*, 50-Jan Fed. Law. 24, 25 (Jan. 2003), *cited by* Karen E. Jones, *The Effect of the Homeland Security Act on Online Privacy and the Freedom of Information Act,* 72 U. Cin. L. Rev. 787, 800 & n.100 (2003).

One commentator described the tensions inherent in this statutory provision:

> Groups supporting this exemption argue that ... with no absolute protection from disclosure, the entities' interests in protecting their businesses will triumph over their interests in assisting the government. No business will risk informing the government of problems with their systems if the end result is negative publicity.

> On the other hand, groups such as the American Civil Liberties Union (ACLU) are concerned that keeping information secret will ultimately be detrimental to public security and are also upset that "officials who blow the whistle on threats to public health (uranium stockpiling or tainted blood)" will be subject to criminal penalties. In addition, information submitted in good faith as part of the critical infrastructure cannot be used in a civil case against the submitter under the Homeland Security Act. As one author has stated, this infringes upon basic principles of a democracy, since "[t]he ability of citizens and the press to seek redress in court is a pillar of an open society, and this exemption knocks down that pillar."

Id. at 804-05 & n.141 (quoting People for the America Way, *Homeland Security Act Poses Threat to Government Oversight, Civil Rights and Liberties,* (Nov. 19, 2002), *available at* <http://www.pfaw.org/pfaw/general/default.aspx?oid=7020>) (footnotes omitted)).

Senator Patrick Leahy introduced legislation to override this provision, observing:

> We do not keep America safer by chilling federal officials from warning the public about threats to their health and safety. We do not ensure our nation's security by refusing to tell the American people whether or not their federal agencies are doing their jobs or their government is spending their hard earned tax dollars wisely. We do not encourage real two-way cooperation by giving companies protection from civil liability when they break the law. We do not respect the

spirit of our democracy when we cloak in secrecy the workings of our government from the public we are elected to serve.

149 Cong Rec S3631-35 (daily ed. Mar. 12, 2003) (statement of Sen. Leahy), *available at* <http://leahy.senate.gov/press/200303/031203e.html>.

The HSA also encompasses the Cyber Security Enhancement Act, which broadens the exemption from liability under the Electronic Communications Privacy Act of 1986 tit. 2, 18 U.S.C. §§ 2701-10, for service providers that voluntarily furnish information concerning subscribers to governmental authorities. The exception insulates Internet service providers that believe, "in good faith, ... that an emergency involving danger of death or serious physical injury to any person requires disclosure without delay...." HSA § 225 (codified at 18 U.S.C. § 2702(b)(7)).

The reaction to this provision was described by one commentator who stated:

> Supporters hailed the changes to the disclosure laws as a means of encouraging ISP providers to cooperate with government authorities in the war against terrorism. By eliminating the requirement that the danger had to be immediate and the suspicion had to be reasonable, the Homeland Security Act removed much of the uncertainty faced by ISPs in trying to determine whether a communication could be disclosed to government officials with no adverse consequences.

> Critics ... are concerned that disclosure to government agencies of communications of ISP subscribers may be exceedingly and unacceptably easy to obtain due to the relaxed standard of disclosure. Given that the disclosure is not only to law enforcement, but also to any government agency, and the belief no longer needs to be reasonable but only in "good faith," arguably an unreasonable good-faith belief, regardless of whether the belief was formed carelessly, that there was some sort of danger or emergency would shield the ISP of any liability. The unfortunate outcome of this low standard is that there will no longer be an "opportunity for objective scrutiny" in many, if not most, situations where the government desires to acquire contents of the communications of an online user.

Karen E. Jones, *The Effect of the Homeland Security Act on Online Privacy and the Freedom of Information Act,* 72 U. Cin. L. Rev. at 809-10 & n.179 (quoting Center for Democracy & Technology, *The New Homeland Security Department-Challenge, Potential and Risk-Privacy Guidelines, Careful Oversight Required* (Dec. 10, 2002), *available at* <http://www.cdt.org/security/homelandsecuritydept/021210cdt.shtml>) (footnotes omitted).

The efficacy of the allocation of resources by the U.S. Department of Homeland Security has been questioned as well. For example, Homeland Security has been criticized for failing to develop a contingency plan to restore Internet functionality compromised by such threats as bot networks, criminal gangs, foreign intelligence services, spammers, spyware authors, and terrorists. Federal auditors expressed concern that the Department is unprepared for such emergencies. *See, e.g.,* Declan McCullagh, *Homeland Security Flunks Cybersecurity Prep*

Test, CNet News.com (May 26, 2005), *available at* <http://news.com.com/2102-7348_3-5722227.html>.

* * * * *

HUMANITARIAN LAW PROJECT, *et al.*, Plaintiffs

v.

JOHN ASHCROFT, *et al.*, Defendants

United States District Court for the Central District of California

NO.: CV 03-6107 ABC (MCx), 309 F. Supp. 2d 1185

March 17, 2004

AMENDED ORDER RE: PLAINTIFFS' MOTION FOR SUMMARY JUDGMENT AND DEFENDANTS' MOTION TO DISMISS

This action involves a challenge to the constitutionality of § 805(a)(2)(B) of the Uniting and Strengthening America by Providing Appropriate Tools Required to Intercept and Obstruct Terrorism Act ("USA PATRIOT Act") and §§ 302 and 303 of the Antiterrorism and Effective Death Penalty Act (the "AEDPA") which prohibit the provision of material support, including "expert advice or assistance," to designated foreign terrorist organizations. *See* § 805(a)(2)(B), 18 U.S.C. §§ 2339A(a) and 2339B(a). Plaintiffs seek to provide support for the lawful activities of two organizations that have been designated as "foreign terrorist organizations." Plaintiffs seek summary judgment and an injunction to prohibit Defendants from enforcing the criminal prohibition on providing "expert advice or assistance" to such organizations on the ground that, like the prohibitions on providing "training" and "personnel," which the Court previously enjoined, the prohibition is unconstitutionally vague and overbroad. *See Humanitarian Law Project v. Reno,* 9 F. Supp. 2d 1176 (C.D. Cal. 1998) (granting Plaintiffs' motion for preliminary injunction), *aff'd,* 205 F.3d 1130 (9th Cir. 2000) and *Humanitarian Law Project v. Reno,* No CV 98-1971 ABC (BQRx), 2001 U.S. Dist. LEXIS 16729 (C.D. Cal. 2001) (granting in part and denying in part Plaintiffs' motion for summary judgment and denying Defendants' motion to dismiss), *aff'd in part and rev'd in part,* 352 F.3d 382 (9th Cir. 2003) (hereinafter referred to as *HLP I*).

... I. FACTUAL BACKGROUND

... 2. The Regulatory Scheme

On October 26, 2001, Congress enacted the USA PATRIOT Act, which broadened the AEDPA's definition of "material support or resources" to add as a proscribed act the provision of "expert advice or assistance." ....[T]he AEDPA permits the Secretary of State, in consultation with the Secretary of the Treasury and the Attorney General, to designate an organization as a foreign terrorist organization after making certain findings as to the organization's involvement in terrorist activity. *See* 8 U.S.C. § 1189(a)(1). "Terrorist activity" is defined as "an act which the actor knows, or reasonably should know, affords material support to any individual, organization, or government in conducting a terrorist activity at any time." 8 U.S.C. § 1182(a)(3)(B)(iii).

Section 303 of the AEDPA, as modified by Section 810 of the USA PATRIOT Act, provides: "Whoever, within the United States or subject to the jurisdiction of the United

States, knowingly provides material support or resources to a foreign terrorist organization, or attempts or conspires to do so, shall be fined under this title or imprisoned not more than 15 years, or both, and, if the death of any person results, shall be imprisoned for any term of years or for life." 18 U.S.C. § 2339B(a). "Material support or resources" is defined as "currency or monetary instruments or financial securities, financial services, lodging, training, expert advice or assistance, safehouses, false documentation or identification, communications equipment, facilities, weapons, lethal substances, explosives, personnel, transportation, and other physical assets, except medicine or religious materials." *Id.* § 2339A(b).

B. The Secretary's Designation

On October 8, 1997, then Secretary of State Madeline Albright designated 30 organizations as "foreign terrorist organizations" under the AEDPA. *See* 62 Fed. Reg. 52,650-51. The designated organizations included the Kurdistan Workers' Party, a.k.a. Partiya Karkeran Kurdistan, a.k.a. PKK ("PKK") and the Liberation Tigers of Tamil Eelam, a.k.a. LTTE, a.k.a. Tamil Tigers, a.k.a. Ellalan Force ("LTTE").

C. The Plaintiffs

Plaintiffs are five organizations and two United States citizens. Plaintiffs seek to provide support to the lawful, nonviolent activities of the PKK and the LTTE. Since October 8, 1997, the date on which the Secretary designated the PKK and the LTTE as foreign terrorist organizations, Plaintiffs, their members and individuals associated with the organizational Plaintiffs have not provided such support, fearing criminal investigation, prosecution and conviction. ...

2. The PKK and the Plaintiffs that Support It

The PKK, the leading political organization representing the interests of the Kurds in Turkey, was formed approximately 25 years ago with the goal of achieving self-determination for the Kurds in Southeastern Turkey. It is comprised primarily of Turkish Kurds. Plaintiffs allege that for more than 75 years, the Turkish government has subjected the Kurds to human rights abuses and discrimination. The PKK's efforts on behalf of the Kurds include political organizing and advocacy both inside and outside Turkey, providing social services and humanitarian aid to Kurdish refugees and engaging in military combat with Turkish armed forces in accordance with the Geneva Convention and Protocols.

Two Plaintiffs, Humanitarian Law Project ("HLP") and Administrative Judge Ralph Fertig, HLP's President, seek to support the PKK's peaceful and non-violent activities. The HLP, a not-for-profit organization headquartered in Los Angeles, is dedicated to furthering international compliance with humanitarian law and human rights law and the peaceful resolution of armed conflicts.

The HLP has consultative status to the United Nations ("UN") as a non-governmental organization and regularly participates in meetings of the UN Commission on Human Rights in Geneva, Switzerland. The HLP conducts fact-finding missions, writes and publishes reports, and works for the peaceful resolution of armed conflicts around the world.

Judge Fertig has a career of over 50 years in human rights work. He has been a member of the HLP's Board of Directors since 1989, serving as President from 1993 to 1995 and from 1997 to the present. He has participated in HLP delegations that have investigated alleged human rights violations in Turkey, Mexico, and El Salvador, has written reports for the HLP, and has trained others in the use of international human rights law and other lawful means for the peaceful resolution of disputes.

Since 1991, the HLP and Judge Fertig have devoted substantial time and resources advocating on behalf of the Kurds living in Turkey and working with and providing training, expert advice and other forms of support to the PKK. Judge Fertig and other individuals associated with the HLP have conducted fact-finding investigations on the Kurds in Turkey and have published reports and articles presenting their findings, which are supportive of the PKK and the struggle for Kurdish liberation. They assert that the Turkish government has committed extensive human rights violations against the Kurds, including the summary execution of more than 18,000 Kurds, the widespread use of arbitrary detentions and torture against persons who speak out for equal rights for Kurds or are suspected of sympathizing with those who do, and the wholesale destruction of some 2,400 Kurdish villages. Applying international law principles, they have concluded that the PKK is a party to an armed conflict governed by Geneva Conventions and Protocols and, therefore, is not a terrorist organization under international law.

To further peaceful resolutions of the armed conflict in Turkey and protect the human rights of the Kurds, the HLP, Judge Fertig, and other individuals associated with the HLP have worked with and supported the PKK in numerous ways. They have petitioned members of Congress to support Kurdish human rights and to encourage negotiations between the PKK and the Turkish government. They have argued for the release of Leyla Zana, Hatip Dicle, Orhan Dogan, and Selim Sadak, four Kurds who were elected to the Turkish Parliament in 1991, but sentenced to 15 years in prison by the Turkish courts for being members or supporters of the PKK. In addition, the HLP, Judge Fertig, and other individuals associated with the HLP have provided training to some PKK members and other Kurds in using humanitarian law and international human rights law and in seeking a peaceful resolution of the conflict in Turkey. Both the HLP and Judge Fertig only support the PKK in its non-violent and lawful activities.

Since the Secretary designated the PKK as a foreign terrorist organization, the HLP and Judge Fertig have been deterred from continuing to assist the PKK to improve conditions for the Kurds living in Turkey. But for the AEDPA and the USA PATRIOT Act, they would continue to provide the type of support which they provided in the past, as well as additional support. However, they fear that doing so would subject them to criminal prosecution.

The HLP, Judge Fertig, and individuals associated with the HLP would specifically like to, but are afraid to, provide support to the PKK in the following ways:

> (1) engage in political advocacy on behalf of the PKK and the Kurds before the U.N. Commission on Human Rights and the United States Congress;

> (2) provide the PKK and the Kurds with training and written publications on how to engage in political advocacy on their own behalf and on how to use international law to seek redress for human rights violations;

> (3) write and distribute publications supportive of the PKK and the cause of Kurdish liberation;

(4) advocate for the freedom of Turkish political prisoners, including Leyla Zana, Hatip Dicle, Orhan Dogan, and Selim Sadak; and

(5) assist PKK members at peace conferences and other meetings designed to support a peaceful resolution of the Turkish conflict.

HLP and Judge Fertig are committed to providing the above-mentioned support. However, they are afraid that the conduct in which they have engaged and in which they wish to continue to engage may come within the scope of "expert advice or assistance." Since the enactment of the USA PATRIOT ACT and the amendment of the term "material support" to include "expert advice or assistance," the HLP and Judge Fertig have refrained from providing this advice and assistance for fear that they may be subjected to criminal prosecution. ...

2. The LTTE and the Plaintiffs that Support It

The LTTE was formed in 1976 with the goal of achieving self-determination for the Tamil residents of Tamil Eelam, in the Northern and Eastern provinces of Sri Lanka. Plaintiffs allege that the Tamils constitute an ethnic group that has for decades been subjected to human rights abuses and discriminatory treatment by the Sinhalese, who have governed Sri Lanka since the nation gained its independence from Great Britain in 1948. The Sinhalese constitute a numerical majority of Sri Lanka's population.

Plaintiffs allege that the LTTE, to further its goal of self-determination for the Tamils, engages in: (1) political organizing and advocacy; (2) diplomatic activity; (3) the provision of social services and humanitarian aid; (4) the establishment of a quasi-governmental structure in Tamil Eelam; (5) economic development; (6) defense of the Tamil people from human rights abuses; and (7) military struggle against the government of Sri Lanka.

Five Plaintiffs – four membership organizations and an individual-seek to provide support to the LTTE. These Plaintiffs are committed to the human rights and well-being of the Tamils in Sri Lanka. Many members of these organizations and the individual Plaintiff, Dr. Nagalingam Jeyalingam, are Tamils born in Sri Lanka. Although they now reside in the United States and many are United States citizens, they still have close friends and family members living in Sri Lanka, many of whom have been the victims of alleged abuses by the Sri Lankan government.

... IV. DISCUSSION

... B. Plaintiffs' Motion for Summary Judgment.

Plaintiffs bring their motion for summary judgment on several grounds. First, they argue that the prohibition on providing expert advice and assistance is both impermissibly vague and substantially overbroad. Second, they contend that prohibition violates the First and Fifth Amendments by criminalizing associational speech without proof of intent to incite imminent violence or to support a group's illegal ends. ...

... 1. Plaintiffs Have Demonstrated that the Prohibition is Impermissibly Vague But Have Failed to Demonstrate that the Prohibition is Substantially Overbroad

... a. Plaintiffs Have Demonstrated that the Prohibition is Impermissibly Vague

A challenge to a statute based on vagueness grounds requires the Court to consider whether the statute is sufficiently clear so as not to cause persons "'of common intelligence ...

necessarily [to] guess at its meaning and [to] differ as to its application.'" *United States v. Wunsch,* 84 F.3d 1110, 1119 (9th Cir. 1996) (quoting *Connally v. General Constr. Co.,* 269 U.S. 385, 391, 70 L. Ed. 322, 46 S. Ct. 126 (1926)). Vague statutes are void for three reasons: "(1) to avoid punishing people for behavior that they could not have known was illegal; (2) to avoid subjective enforcement of the laws based on 'arbitrary and discriminatory enforcement' by government officers; and (3) to avoid any chilling effect on the exercise of First Amendment freedoms." *Foti v. City of Menlo Park,* 146 F.3d 629, 638 (9th Cir. 1998) (citing *Grayned v. City of Rockford,* 408 U.S. 104, 108-09, 33 L. Ed. 2d 222, 92 S. Ct. 2294 (1972)).

"Perhaps the most important factor affecting the clarity that the Constitution demands of a law is whether it threatens to inhibit the exercise of constitutionally protected rights. If, for example, the law interferes with the right of free speech or of association, a more stringent vagueness test should apply." *Village of Hoffman Estates v. Flipside, Hoffman Estates, Inc.,* 455 U.S. 489, 499, 71 L. Ed. 2d 362, 102 S. Ct. 1186 (1982). "The requirement of clarity is enhanced when criminal sanctions are at issue or when the statute abuts upon sensitive areas of basic First Amendment freedoms." *Information Providers' Coalition for the Defense of the First Amendment v. FCC,* 928 F.2d 866, 874 (9th Cir. 1991) (quotation omitted). Thus, under the Due Process Clause, a criminal statute is void for vagueness if it "fails to give a person of ordinary intelligence fair notice that his contemplated conduct is forbidden by the statute." *United States v Harriss,* 347 U.S. 612, 618, 98 L. Ed. 989, 74 S. Ct. 808 (1954).

The determinative issue is thus whether the USA PATRIOT Act sufficiently identifies the prohibited conduct. ....[T]he Court concludes that the term "expert advice or assistance," like the terms "training" and "personnel," is not "sufficiently clear so as to allow persons of 'ordinary intelligence a reasonable opportunity to know what is prohibited.'" *Foti,* 146 F.3d at [638] (quoting *Grayned,* 408 U.S. at 108). Defendants have failed to adequately distinguish the provision of "expert advice or assistance" from the provision of "training" or "personnel" in a way that allows the Court to reconcile its prior finding that the terms "training" and "personnel" are impermissibly vague, with a finding that the term "expert advice or assistance" is not.

Furthermore, Defendants' contradictory arguments on the scope of the prohibition underscore the vagueness of the prohibition. The "expert advice or assistance" Plaintiffs seek to offer includes advocacy and associational activities protected by the First Amendment, which Defendants concede are not prohibited under the USA PATRIOT Act. Despite this, the USA PATRIOT Act places no limitation on the type of expert advice and assistance which is prohibited, and instead bans the provision of all expert advice and assistance regardless of its nature. Thus, like the terms "personnel" and "training," "expert advice or assistance" "could be construed to include unequivocally pure speech and advocacy protected by the First Amendment" or to "encompass First Amendment protected activities." 2003 U.S. App. LEXIS 24305 at *60-61 (9th Cir. Dec. 3, 2003).

Based on the foregoing, the Court finds that Plaintiffs have satisfied their burden on their claim that the term "expert advice or assistance" is impermissibly vague, and concludes that Plaintiffs are entitled to injunctive relief.

2. Plaintiffs Have Failed to Demonstrate that the Prohibition is Substantially Overbroad

"The First Amendment doctrine of overbreadth is an exception to [the] normal rule regarding the standards for facial challenges." *Virginia v. Hicks,* 539 U.S. 113, 123 S. Ct.

2191, 2196, 156 L. Ed. 2d 148 (2003). Under the overbreadth doctrine, a "showing that a law punishes a 'substantial' amount of protected free speech judged in relation to the statute's plainly legitimate sweep ... suffices to invalidate *all* enforcement of that law, until and unless a limiting construction or partial invalidation so narrows it as to remove the seeming threat or deterrence to constitutionally protected expression." *Id.* (internal citations and quotations omitted.)

Despite the foregoing, the Supreme Court has recognized that "there comes a point at which the chilling effect of an overbroad law, significant though it may be, cannot justify prohibiting all enforcement of that law-particularly a law that reflects legitimate state interests in maintaining comprehensive controls over harmful, constitutionally unprotected conduct." *Id.* at 2197. "To ensure that [the substantial social costs created by the overbreadth doctrine] do not swallow the social benefits of declaring a law 'overbroad,'" the Supreme Court requires that the "law's application to protected speech be 'substantial,' not only in an absolute sense, but also relative to the scope of the law's plainly legitimate applications before applying the 'strong medicine' of the overbreadth invalidation." *Id.*

[The question before the court is whether the term "expert advice or assistance" is substantially overbroad on the ground that it prohibits a substantial amount of speech activity which is clearly protected by the First Amendment, such as training in human rights advocacy, giving advice on how to improve medical care and education, and distributing human rights literature.] ... The Court agrees with Defendants that Plaintiffs have failed to meet their burden in establishing that the prohibition on the provision of "expert advice or assistance" is substantially overbroad, thereby warranting an injunction of its enforcement. Although Plaintiffs have provided examples of some protected speech which may be prohibited by the application of the ban, this is not sufficient to meet the burden imposed by *Virginia v. Hicks*. The USA PATRIOT Act's prohibition of the provision of "expert advice or assistance" is aimed at furthering a legitimate state interest: curbing support for designated foreign terrorist organizations' activities, which unquestionably constitute "harmful, constitutionally unprotected conduct." *Virginia v. Hicks*, 123 S. Ct. at 2197. Plaintiffs have failed to demonstrate that the USA PATRIOT Act's application to protected speech is "substantial" both in an absolute sense and relative to the scope of the law's plainly legitimate applications. The Court therefore declines to apply the "strong medicine" of the overbreadth doctrine, finding instead that as-applied litigation will provide a sufficient safeguard for any potential First Amendment violation.

3. Plaintiffs Have Failed to Demonstrate that the Prohibition on the Provision of "Expert Advice or Assistance" Criminalizes Associational Speech

[In addition to agreeing with] ... Defendants that Plaintiffs' attempt to relitigate this issue is improper[, the Court notes that] ... the Ninth Circuit recently clarified that the knowledge required by the statute is of a group's designation as a terrorist organization, or its participation in unlawful activities that caused it to be so designated. There is thus no risk of the prosecution of "moral innocents" under the law, contrary to Plaintiffs' assertion. The Court therefore DENIES Plaintiffs' motion for summary judgment on this basis.

... V. CONCLUSION

For the reasons set forth above, Defendants' Motion to Dismiss is DENIED.

Plaintiffs' Motion for Summary Judgment is GRANTED IN PART and DENIED IN PART as follows:

1. Plaintiffs' motion is GRANTED to the extent the Court finds that the term "expert advice or assistance" is impermissibly vague; and

2. Plaintiffs' motion is DENIED with respect to the remaining arguments raised.

Accordingly, Defendants, their officers, agents, employees, and successors are ENJOINED from enforcing the USA PATRIOT Act's prohibition on providing "expert advice or assistance" to either the Kurdistan Workers' Party, a.k.a. Partiya Karkeran Kurdistan, a.k.a. PKK, a.k.a. the Kurdistan Freedom and Democracy Congress, a.k.a. KADEK, a.k.a. Freedom and Democracy Congress of Kurdistan, a.k.a. the People's Defense Force, a.k.a. Halu Mesru Savunma Kuvveti (HSK); or the Liberation Tigers of Tamil Eelam, a.k.a. LTTE, a.k.a. Tamil Tigers, a.k.a. Ellalan Force against any of the named Plaintiffs or their members. The Court declines to grant a nationwide injunction.

* * * * * *

Obscenity and Indecency

insert the following before Application of "Community Standards" to Internet Speech on page 215 of Law of Internet Speech:

JOHN ASHCROFT, ATTORNEY GENERAL
v.
AMERICAN CIVIL LIBERTIES UNION, et al.

Supreme Court of the United States

No. 99-1324, 535 U.S. 194

May 13, 2002

JUSTICE THOMAS announced the judgment of the Court and delivered the opinion of the Court with respect to Parts I, II, and IV, an opinion with respect to Parts III-A, III-C, and III-D, in which THE CHIEF JUSTICE and JUSTICE SCALIA join, and an opinion with respect to Part III-B, in which THE CHIEF JUSTICE, JUSTICE O'CONNOR, and JUSTICE SCALIA join.

This case presents the narrow question whether the Child Online Protection Act's (COPA or Act) use of "community standards" to identify "material that is harmful to minors" violates the First Amendment. We hold that this aspect of COPA does not render the statute facially unconstitutional. ...

Congress first attempted to protect children from exposure to pornographic material on the Internet by enacting the Communications Decency Act of 1996 (CDA), 110 Stat: 133. The CDA prohibited the knowing transmission over the Internet of obscene or indecent messages to any recipient under 18 years of age. *See* 47 U.S.C. § 223 (a). It also forbade any individual from knowingly sending over or displaying on the Internet certain "patently offensive" material in a manner available to persons under 18 years of age. *See* § 223(d). The prohibition specifically extended to "any comment, request, suggestion, proposal, image, or other communication that, in context, depicted or described, in terms patently offensive as measured by contemporary community standards, sexual or excretory activities or organs." § 223(d)(1).

The CDA provided two affirmative defenses to those prosecuted under the statute. The first protected individuals who took "good faith, reasonable, effective, and appropriate actions" to restrict minors from accessing obscene, indecent, and patently offensive material over the Internet. *See* § 223(e)(5)(A). The second shielded those who restricted minors from accessing such material "by requiring use of a verified credit card, debit account, adult access code, or adult personal identification number." § 223(e)(5)(B).

Notwithstanding these affirmative defenses, in *Reno v. American Civil Liberties Union,* we held that the CDA's regulation of indecent transmissions, *see* § 223(a), and the display of patently offensive material, *see* § 223(d), ran afoul of the First Amendment. We concluded that "the CDA lacked the precision that the First Amendment requires when a statute regulates the content of speech" because, "in order to deny minors access to potentially harmful speech, the CDA effectively suppressed a large amount of speech that adults had a constitutional right to receive and to address to one another." 521 U.S. at 874.

Our holding was based on three crucial considerations. First, "existing technology did not include any effective method for a sender to prevent minors from obtaining access to its communications on the Internet without also denying access to adults." *Id.* at 876. Second, "the breadth of the CDA's coverage [was] wholly unprecedented." *Id.* at 877. "Its open-ended prohibitions embraced," not only commercial speech or commercial entities, but also "all nonprofit entities and individuals posting indecent messages or displaying them on their own computers in the presence of minors." *Ibid.* In addition, because the CDA did not define the terms "indecent" and "patently offensive," the statute "covered large amounts of nonpornographic material with serious educational or other value." *Ibid.* As a result, regulated subject matter under the CDA extended to "discussions about prison rape or safe sexual practices, artistic images that include nude subjects, and arguably the card catalog of the Carnegie Library." *Id.* at 878. Third, we found that neither affirmative defense set forth in the CDA "constituted the sort of 'narrow tailoring' that [would] save an otherwise patently invalid unconstitutional provision." *Id.* at 882. Consequently, only the CDA's ban on the knowing transmission of obscene messages survived scrutiny because obscene speech enjoys no First Amendment protection. *See id.* at 883.

After our decision in *Reno v. American Civil Liberties Union,* Congress explored other avenues for restricting minors' access to pornographic material on the Internet. In particular, Congress passed and the President signed into law the Child Online Protection Act, 112 Stat. 2681-736 (codified in 47 U.S.C. § 231 (1994 ed., Supp. V)). COPA prohibits any person from "knowingly and with knowledge of the character of the material, in interstate or foreign commerce by means of the World Wide Web, making any communication for commercial purposes that is available to any minor and that includes any material that is harmful to minors." 47 U.S.C. § 231 (a)(1).

Apparently responding to our objections to the breadth of the CDA's coverage, Congress limited the scope of COPA's coverage in at least three ways. First, while the CDA applied to communications over the Internet as a whole, including, for example, e-mail messages, COPA applies only to material displayed on the World Wide Web. Second, unlike the CDA,

COPA covers only communications made "for commercial purposes."[3] *Ibid.* And third, while the CDA prohibited "indecent" and "patently offensive" communications, COPA restricts only the narrower category of "material that is harmful to minors." *Ibid.*

Drawing on the three-part test for obscenity set forth in *Miller v. California*, 413 U.S. 15, 37 L.Ed.2d 419, 93 S. Ct. 2607 (1973), COPA defines "material that is harmful to minors" as

> any communication, picture, image, graphic image file, article, recording, writing, or other matter of any kind that is obscene or that--
>
> (A) the average person, applying contemporary community standards, would find, taking the material as a whole and with respect to minors, is designed to appeal to, or is designed to pander to, the prurient interest;
>
> (B) depicts, describes, or represents, in a manner patently offensive with respect to minors, an actual or simulated sexual act or sexual contact, an actual or simulated normal or perverted sexual act, or a lewd exhibition of the genitals or post-pubescent female breast; and
>
> (C) taken as a whole, lacks serious literary, artistic, political, or scientific value for minors.

47 U.S.C. § 231 (e)(6).

Like the CDA, COPA also provides affirmative defenses to those subject to prosecution under the statute. An individual may qualify for a defense if he, "in good faith, has restricted access by minors to material that is harmful to minors -- (A) by requiring the use of a credit card, debit account, adult access code, or adult personal identification number; (B) by accepting a digital certificate that verifies age; or (C) by any other reasonable measures that are feasible under available technology." § 231(c)(1). Persons violating COPA are subject to both civil and criminal sanctions. A civil penalty of up to $50,000 may be imposed for each violation of the statute. Criminal penalties consist of up to six months in prison and/or a maximum fine of $50,000. An additional fine of $50,000 may be imposed for any intentional violation of the statute. § 231(a).

---

[3] The statute provides that "[a] person shall be considered to make a communication for commercial purposes only if such person is engaged in the business of making such communications." 47 U.S.C. § 231 (e)(2)(A) (1994 ed., Supp. V). COPA then defines the term "engaged in the business" to mean a person:

> who makes a communication, or offers to make a communication, by means of the World Wide Web, that includes any material that is harmful to minors, devotes time, attention, or labor to such activities, as a regular course of such person's trade or business, with the objective of earning a profit as a result of such activities (although it is not necessary that the person make a profit or that the making or offering to make such communications be the person's sole or principal business or source of income).

§ 231(e)(2)(B).

... II.

The First Amendment states that "Congress shall make no law ... abridging the freedom of speech." This provision embodies "our profound national commitment to the free exchange of ideas." *Harte-Hanks Communications, Inc.* v. *Connaughton*, 491 U.S. 657, 686, 105 L.Ed.2d 562, 109 S. Ct. 2678 (1989). "As a general matter, 'the First Amendment means that government has no power to restrict expression because of its message, its ideas, its subject matter, or its content.'" *Bolger* v. *Youngs Drug Products Corp.*, 463 U.S. 60, 65, 77 L.Ed.2d 469, 103 S. Ct. 2875 (1983) (quoting *Police Dept. of Chicago* v. *Mosley*, 408 U.S. 92, 95, 33 L.Ed.2d 212, 92 S. Ct. 2286 (1972)). However, this principle, like other First Amendment principles, is not absolute. *Cf. Hustler Magazine, Inc.* v. *Falwell*, 485 U.S. 46, 56, 99 L.Ed.2d 41, 108 S. Ct. 876 (1988).

Obscene speech, for example, has long been held to fall outside the purview of the First Amendment. *See, e.g., Roth* v. *United States*, 354 U.S. 476, 484-485, 1 L.Ed.2d 1498, 77 S. Ct. 1304 (1957). But this Court struggled in the past to define obscenity in a manner that did not impose an impermissible burden on protected speech. *See Interstate Circuit, Inc.* v. *Dallas*, 390 U.S. 676, 704, 20 L.Ed.2d 225, 88 S. Ct. 1298 (1968) (Harlan, J., concurring in part and dissenting in part) (referring to the "intractable obscenity problem"); *see also Miller* v. *California*, 413 U.S. at 20-23 (reviewing "the somewhat tortured history of this Court's obscenity decisions"). The difficulty resulted from the belief that "in the area of freedom of speech and press the courts must always remain sensitive to any infringement on genuinely serious literary, artistic, political, or scientific expression." *Id.* at 22-23.

Ending over a decade of turmoil, this Court in *Miller* set forth the governing three-part test for assessing whether material is obscene and thus unprotected by the First Amendment: "(a) Whether 'the average person, *applying contemporary community standards*' would find that the work, taken as a whole, appeals to the prurient interest; (b) whether the work depicts or describes, in a patently offensive way, sexual conduct specifically defined by the applicable state law; and (c) whether the work, taken as a whole, lacks serious literary, artistic, political, or scientific value." *Id.* at 24 (internal citations omitted; emphasis added).

Miller adopted the use of "community standards" from *Roth,* which repudiated an earlier approach for assessing objectionable material. Beginning in the 19th century, English courts and some American courts allowed material to be evaluated from the perspective of particularly sensitive persons. *See, e.g., Queen v. Hicklin* [1868] L.R. 3 Q.B. 360; *see also Roth*, 354 U.S. at 488-489, and n.25 (listing relevant cases). But in *Roth,* this Court held that this sensitive person standard was "unconstitutionally restrictive of the freedoms of speech and press" and approved a standard requiring that material be judged from the perspective of "the average person, applying contemporary community standards." *Id.* at 489. The Court preserved the use of community standards in formulating the *Miller* test, explaining that they furnish a valuable First Amendment safeguard: "The primary concern ... is to be certain that ... [material] will be judged by its impact on an average person, rather than a particularly susceptible or sensitive person -- or indeed a totally insensitive one." *Miller*, 413 U.S. at 33 (internal quotation marks omitted); *see also Hamling* v. *United States*, 418 U.S. 87, 107, 41 L.Ed.2d 590, 94 S. Ct. 2887 (1974) (emphasizing that the principal purpose of the community standards criterion "is to assure that the material is judged neither on the basis of each juror's personal opinion, nor by its effect on a particularly sensitive or insensitive person or group").

III.

The Court of Appeals, however, concluded that this Court's prior community standards jurisprudence "has no applicability to the Internet and the Web" because "Web publishers are currently without the ability to control the geographic scope of the recipients of their communications." 217 F.3d at 180. We therefore must decide whether this technological limitation renders COPA's reliance on community standards constitutionally infirm.

A.

In addressing this question, the parties first dispute the nature of the community standards that jurors will be instructed to apply when assessing, in prosecutions under COPA, whether works appeal to the prurient interest of minors and are patently offensive with respect to minors. Respondents contend that jurors will evaluate material using "local community standards," while petitioner maintains that jurors will not consider the community standards of any particular geographic area, but rather will be "instructed to consider the standards of the adult community as a whole, without geographic specification."

In the context of this case, which involves a facial challenge to a statute that has never been enforced, we do not think it prudent to engage in speculation as to whether certain hypothetical jury instructions would or would not be consistent with COPA, and deciding this case does not require us to do so. It is sufficient to note that community standards need not be defined by reference to a precise geographic area. *See Jenkins v. Georgia*, 418 U.S. 153, 157, 41 L.Ed.2d 642, 94 S. Ct. 2750 (1974) ("A State may choose to define an obscenity offense in terms of 'contemporary community standards' as defined in *Miller* without further specification ... or it may choose to define the standards in more precise geographic terms, as was done by California in *Miller*"). Absent geographic specification, a juror applying community standards will inevitably draw upon personal "knowledge of the community or vicinage from which he comes." *Hamling, supra,* at 105. Petitioner concedes the latter point, and admits that, even if jurors were instructed under COPA to apply the standards of the adult population as a whole, the variance in community standards across the country could still cause juries in different locations to reach inconsistent conclusions as to whether a particular work is "harmful to minors."

B.

Because juries would apply different standards across the country, and Web publishers currently lack the ability to limit access to their sites on a geographic basis, the Court of Appeals feared that COPA's "community standards" component would effectively force all speakers on the Web to abide by the "most puritan" community's standards. 217 F.3d at 175. And such a requirement, the Court of Appeals concluded, "imposes an overreaching burden and restriction on constitutionally protected speech." *Id.* at 177.

In evaluating the constitutionality of the CDA, this Court expressed a similar concern over that statute's use of community standards to identify patently offensive material on the Internet. We noted that "the 'community standards' criterion as applied to the Internet means that any communication available to a nationwide audience will be judged by the standards of the community most likely to be offended by the message." *Reno,* 521 U.S. at 877-878. The Court of Appeals below relied heavily on this observation, stating that it was "not persuaded that the Supreme Court's concern with respect to the 'community standards' criterion has been sufficiently remedied by Congress in COPA." 217 F.3d at 174.

The CDA's use of community standards to identify patently offensive material, however, was particularly problematic in light of that statute's unprecedented breadth and vagueness. The statute covered communications depicting or describing "sexual or excretory activities or organs" that were "patently offensive as measured by contemporary community standards" -- a standard somewhat similar to the second prong of *Miller's* three-prong test. But the CDA did not include any limiting terms resembling *Miller's* additional two prongs. *See Reno,* 521 U.S. at 873. It neither contained any requirement that restricted material appeal to the prurient interest nor excluded from the scope of its coverage works with serious literary, artistic, political, or scientific value. *Ibid.* The tremendous breadth of the CDA magnified the impact caused by differences in community standards across the country, restricting Web publishers from openly displaying a significant amount of material that would have constituted protected speech in some communities across the country but run afoul of community standards in others.

COPA, by contrast, does not appear to suffer from the same flaw because it applies to significantly less material than did the CDA and defines the harmful-to-minors material restricted by the statute in a manner parallel to the *Miller* definition of obscenity. *See supra,* at 5-6, 10. To fall within the scope of COPA, works must not only "depict, describe, or represent, in a manner patently offensive with respect to minors," particular sexual acts or parts of the anatomy, they must also be designed to appeal to the prurient interest of minors and "taken as a whole, lack serious literary, artistic, political, or scientific value for minors." 47 U.S.C. § 231 (e)(6).

These additional two restrictions substantially limit the amount of material covered by the statute. Material appeals to the prurient interest, for instance, only if it is in some sense erotic. *Cf. Erznoznik v. Jacksonville,* 422 U.S. 205, 213, 45 L.Ed.2d 125, 95 S. Ct. 2268, and n.10 (1975). Of even more significance, however, is COPA's exclusion of material with serious value for minors. *See* 47 U.S.C. § 231(e)(6)(C). In *Reno,* we emphasized that the serious value "requirement is particularly important because, unlike the 'patently offensive' and 'prurient interest' criteria, it is not judged by contemporary community standards." 521 U.S. at 873 (citing *Pope v. Illinois,* 481 U.S. 497, 500, 95 L.Ed.2d 439, 107 S. Ct. 1918 (1987)). This is because "the value of [a] work [does not] vary from community to community based on the degree of local acceptance it has won." *Id.* at 500. Rather, the relevant question is "whether a reasonable person would find ... value in the material, taken as a whole." *Id.* at 501. Thus, the serious value requirement "allows appellate courts to impose some limitations and regularity on the definition by setting, *as a matter of law,* a national floor for socially redeeming value." *Reno, supra,* at 873 (emphasis added), a safeguard nowhere present in the CDA.

C.

When the scope of an obscenity statute's coverage is sufficiently narrowed by a "serious value" prong and a "prurient interest" prong, we have held that requiring a speaker disseminating material to a national audience to observe varying community standards does not violate the First Amendment. In *Hamling v. United States,* 418 U.S. 87, 41 L.Ed.2d 590, 94 S. Ct. 2887 (1974), this Court considered the constitutionality of applying community standards to the determination of whether material is obscene under 18 U.S.C. § 1461, the federal statute prohibiting the mailing of obscene material. Although this statute does not define obscenity, the petitioners in *Hamling* were tried and convicted under the definition of obscenity set forth in *Book Named "John Cleland's Memoirs of a Woman of Pleasure" v. Attorney General of Mass.,* 383 U.S. 413, 16 L.Ed.2d 1, 86 S. Ct. 975 (1966), which included both a "prurient interest" requirement and a requirement that prohibited material be "'utterly without redeeming social value.'" *Hamling, supra*, at 99 (quoting *Memoirs, supra,* at 418).

... "The fact that distributors of allegedly obscene materials may be subjected to varying community standards in the various federal judicial districts into which they transmit the materials does not render a federal statute unconstitutional." *Id.* at 106.

Fifteen years later, *Hamling's* holding was reaffirmed in *Sable Communications of Cal., Inc.* v. *FCC*, 492 U.S. 115, 106 L.Ed.2d 93, 109 S. Ct. 2829 (1989). *Sable* addressed the constitutionality of 47 U.S.C. § 223 (b) (1982 ed., Supp. V), a statutory provision prohibiting the use of telephones to make obscene or indecent communications for commercial purposes. The petitioner in that case, a "dial-a-porn" operator, challenged, in part, that portion of the statute banning obscene phone messages. Like respondents here, the "dial-a-porn" operator argued that reliance on community standards to identify obscene material impermissibly compelled "message senders ... to tailor all their messages to the least tolerant community." 492 U.S. at 124. Relying on *Hamling,* however, this Court once again rebuffed this attack on the use of community standards in a federal statute of national scope: "There is no constitutional barrier under *Miller* to prohibiting communications that are obscene in some communities under local standards even though they are not obscene in others. *If Sable's audience is comprised of different communities with different local standards, Sable ultimately bears the burden of complying with the prohibition on obscene messages.*" 492 U.S. at 125-126 (emphasis added). ...

... If a publisher chooses to send its material into a particular community, this Court's jurisprudence teaches that it is the publisher's responsibility to abide by that community's standards. The publisher's burden does not change simply because it decides to distribute its material to every community in the Nation. *See Sable, supra,* at 125-126. Nor does it change because the publisher may wish to speak only to those in a "community where *avant garde* culture is the norm" (KENNEDY, J., concurring in judgment), but nonetheless utilizes a medium that transmits its speech from coast to coast. If a publisher wishes for its material to be judged only by the standards of particular communities, then it need only take the simple step of utilizing a medium that enables it to target the release of its material into those communities.

Respondents offer no other grounds upon which to distinguish this case from *Hamling* and *Sable*. While those cases involved obscenity rather than material that is harmful to minors, we have no reason to believe that the practical effect of varying community standards under COPA, given the statute's definition of "material that is harmful to minors," is significantly greater than the practical effect of varying community standards under federal obscenity statutes. It is noteworthy, for example, that respondents fail to point out even a single exhibit in the record as to which coverage under COPA would depend upon which community in the country evaluated the material. As a result, if we were to hold COPA unconstitutional *because of* its use of community standards, federal obscenity statutes would likely also be unconstitutional as applied to the Web, a result in substantial tension with our prior suggestion that the application of the CDA to obscene speech was constitutional. *See Reno*, 521 U.S. at 877, n.44, 882-883.

D.

Respondents argue that COPA is "unconstitutionally overbroad" because it will require Web publishers to shield some material behind age verification screens that could be displayed openly in many communities across the Nation if Web speakers were able to limit access to their sites on a geographic basis. "To prevail in a facial challenge," however, "it is not enough for a plaintiff to show 'some' overbreadth." *Reno, supra,* at 896 (O'CONNOR, J., concurring in judgment in part and dissenting in part). Rather, "the overbreadth of a statute must not only be real, but substantial as well." *Broadrick v. Oklahoma,* 413 U.S. 601, 615, 37 L.Ed.2d 830, 93 S. Ct. 2908 (1973). At this stage of the litigation, respondents have failed to satisfy this burden, at least solely as a result of COPA's reliance on community standards. Because Congress has narrowed the range of content restricted by COPA in a manner analogous to *Miller's* definition of obscenity, we conclude, consistent with our holdings in *Hamling* and *Sable,* that any variance caused by the statute's reliance on community standards is not substantial enough to violate the First Amendment.

IV.

The scope of our decision today is quite limited. We hold only that COPA's reliance on community standards to identify "material that is harmful to minors" does not *by itself* render the statute substantially overbroad for purposes of the First Amendment. We do not express any view as to whether COPA suffers from substantial overbreadth for other reasons, whether the statute is unconstitutionally vague, or whether the District Court correctly concluded that the statute likely will not survive strict scrutiny analysis once adjudication of the case is completed below. While respondents urge us to resolve these questions at this time, prudence dictates allowing the Court of Appeals to first examine these difficult issues.

Petitioner does not ask us to vacate the preliminary injunction entered by the District Court, and in any event, we could not do so without addressing matters yet to be considered by the Court of Appeals. As a result, the Government remains enjoined from enforcing COPA absent further action by the Court of Appeals or the District Court.

For the foregoing reasons, we vacate the judgment of the Court of Appeals and remand the case for further proceedings.

JUSTICE STEVENS, dissenting.

Appeals to prurient interests are commonplace on the Internet, as in older media. Many of those appeals lack serious value for minors as well as adults. Some are offensive to certain viewers but welcomed by others. For decades, our cases have recognized that the standards for judging their acceptability vary from viewer to viewer and from community to community. Those cases developed the requirement that communications should be protected if they do not violate contemporary community standards. In its original form, the community standard provided a shield for communications that are offensive only to the least tolerant members of society. Thus, the Court "has emphasized on more than one occasion that a principal concern in requiring that a judgment be made on the basis of 'contemporary community standards' is to assure that the material is judged neither on the basis of each juror's personal opinion, nor by its effect on a particularly sensitive or insensitive person or group." *Hamling v. United States,* 418 U.S. 87, 107, 41 L.Ed.2d 590, 94 S. Ct. 2887 (1974). In the context of the Internet, however, community standards become a sword, rather than a shield. If a prurient appeal is offensive in a puritan village, it may be a crime to post it on the World Wide Web.

The Child Online Protection Act (COPA) restricts access by adults as well as children to materials that are "harmful to minors." 47 U.S.C. § 231 (a)(1) (1994 ed., Supp. V). COPA is a substantial improvement over its predecessor, the Communications Decency Act of 1996 (CDA), which we held unconstitutional five years ago in *Reno v. American Civil Liberties Union,* 521 U.S. 844 (1997) *(ACLU I).* Congress has thoughtfully addressed several of the First Amendment problems that we identified in that case. Nevertheless, COPA preserves the use of contemporary community standards to define which materials are harmful to minors. As we explained in *ACLU I,* 521 U.S. at 877-878, "the 'community standards' criterion as applied to the Internet means that any communication available to a nationwide audience will be judged by the standards of the community most likely to be offended by the message."

We have recognized that the State has a compelling interest in protecting minors from harmful speech, *Sable Communications of Cal., Inc.* v. *FCC,* 492 U.S. 115, 126, 106 L.Ed.2d 93, 109 S. Ct. 2829 (1989), and on one occasion we upheld a restriction on indecent speech that was made available to the general public, because it could be accessed by minors, *FCC v. Pacifica Foundation,* 438 U.S. 726, 57 L.Ed.2d 1073, 98 S. Ct. 3026 (1978). Our decision in that case was influenced by the distinctive characteristics of the broadcast medium, as well as the expertise of the agency, and the narrow scope of its order. *Id.* at 748-750; *see also, ACLU I,* 521 U.S. at 867. On the other hand, we have repeatedly rejected the position that the free speech rights of adults can be limited to what is acceptable for children. *See id.* at 875 (quoting *Bolger v. Youngs Drug Products Corp.,* 463 U.S. 60, 74-75, 77 L.Ed.2d 469, 103 S. Ct. 2875 (1983) ("Regardless of the strength of the government's interest" in protecting children, "the level of discourse reaching a mailbox simply cannot be limited to that which would be suitable for a sandbox") (quotation marks omitted)); *Sable,* 492 U.S. at 128; *Butler v. Michigan,* 352 U.S. 380, 383, 1 L.Ed.2d 412, 77 S. Ct. 524 (1957).

Petitioner relies on our decision in *Ginsberg v. New York,* 390 U.S. 629, 20 L.Ed.2d 195, 88 S. Ct. 1274 (1968), for the proposition that Congress can prohibit the *display* of materials that are harmful to minors. But the statute upheld in *Ginsberg* prohibited *selling* indecent materials directly to children, *id.* at 633 (describing N.Y. Penal Law § 484-h, making it unlawful "'knowingly to sell ... to a minor...'"), whereas the speech implicated here is simply posted on a medium that is accessible to both adults and children, 47 U.S.C. § 231(a)(1) (prohibiting anyone from "knowingly ... making any communication for commercial purposes that is available to any minor...."). Like the restriction on indecent "dial-a-porn" numbers invalidated in *Sable,* the prohibition against mailing advertisements for contraceptives invalidated in *Bolger,* and the ban against selling adult books found impermissible in *Butler,* COPA seeks to limit protected speech that is not targeted at children, simply because it can be obtained by them while surfing the Web. In evaluating the overbreadth of such a statute, we should be mindful of Justice Frankfurter's admonition not to "burn the house to roast the pig," *Butler,* 352 U.S. at 383.

COPA not only restricts speech that is made available to the general public, it also covers a medium in which speech cannot be segregated to avoid communities where it is likely to be considered harmful to minors. The Internet presents a unique forum for communication because information, once posted, is accessible everywhere on the network at once. The speaker cannot control access based on the location of the listener, nor can it choose the pathways through which its speech is transmitted. By approving the use of community standards in this context, JUSTICE THOMAS endorses a construction of COPA that has "the intolerable consequence of denying some sections of the country access to material, there deemed acceptable, which in others might be considered offensive to prevailing community standards of decency." *Manual Enterprises, Inc. v. Day*, 370 U.S. 478, 488, 8 L.Ed.2d 639, 82 S. Ct. 1432 (1962).

If the material were forwarded through the mails, as in *Hamling*, or over the telephone, as in *Sable,* the sender could avoid destinations with the most restrictive standards. Indeed, in *Sable,* we upheld the application of community standards to a nationwide medium because the speaker was "free to tailor its messages ... to the communities it *chooses* to serve," by either "hiring operators to determine the source of the calls ... [or] arranging for the screening and blocking of out-of-area calls." 492 U.S. at 125 (emphasis added). Our conclusion that it was permissible for the speaker to bear the ultimate burden of compliance, *id.* at 126, assumed that such compliance was at least possible without requiring the speaker to choose another medium or to limit its speech to what all would find acceptable. Given the undisputed fact that a provider who posts material on the Internet cannot prevent it from entering any geographic community, a law that criminalizes a particular communication in just a handful of destinations effectively prohibits transmission of that message to all of the 176.5 million Americans that have access to the Internet. In light of this fundamental difference in technologies, the rules applicable to the mass mailing of an obscene montage or to obscene dial-a-porn should not be used to judge the legality of messages on the World Wide Web.[2]

In his attempt to fit this case within the framework of *Hamling* and *Sable,* JUSTICE THOMAS overlooks the more obvious comparison -- namely, the CDA invalidated in *ACLU I.* When we confronted a similar attempt by Congress to limit speech on the Internet based on community standards, we explained that because Web publishers cannot control who accesses their Web sites, using community standards to regulate speech on the Internet creates an overbreadth problem. "The 'community standards' criterion as applied to the Internet means that any communication available to a nationwide audience will be judged by the standards of the community most likely to be offended by the message." 521 U.S. at 877-878. Although our holding in *ACLU I* did not turn on that factor alone, we did not adopt the position relied on by JUSTICE THOMAS -- that applying community standards to the Internet is constitutional based on *Hamling* and *Sable.* ...

Petitioner's argument that the "serious value" prong minimizes the statute's overbreadth is also unpersuasive. Although we have recognized that the serious value determination in obscenity cases should be based on an objective, reasonable person standard, *Pope v. Illinois,* 481 U.S. 497, 500, 95 L.Ed.2d 439, 107 S. Ct. 1918 (1987), this criterion is inadequate to cure COPA's overbreadth because COPA adds an important qualifying phrase to the standard *Miller v. California*, 413 U.S. 15, 37 L.Ed.2d 419, 93 S. Ct. 2607 (1973), formulation of the serious value prong. The question for the jury is not whether a reasonable person would conclude that the materials have serious value; instead, the jury must determine whether the materials have serious value *for minors.* Congress reasonably concluded that a substantial number of works, which have serious value for adults, do not have serious value for minors.

---

[2] It is hardly a solution to say, as JUSTICE THOMAS suggests, that a speaker need only choose a different medium in order to avoid having its speech judged by the least tolerant community. Our overbreadth doctrine would quickly become a toothless protection if we were to hold that substituting a more limited forum for expression is an acceptable price to pay. Since a content-based restriction is presumptively invalid, I would place the burden on parents to "take the simple step of utilizing a medium that enables," them to avoid this material before requiring the speaker to find another forum.

Cf. ACLU I, 521 U.S. at 896 (O'CONNOR, J., concurring in judgment in part and dissenting in part) ("While discussions about prison rape or nude art ... may have some redeeming educational value for *adults,* they do not necessarily have any such value for *minors*"). Thus, even though the serious value prong limits the total amount of speech covered by the statute, it remains true that there is a significant amount of protected speech within the category of materials that have no serious value for minors. That speech is effectively prohibited whenever the least tolerant communities find it harmful to minors. While the objective nature of the inquiry may eliminate any worry that the serious value determination will be made by the least tolerant community, it does not change the fact that, within the subset of images deemed to have no serious value for minors, the decision whether minors and adults throughout the country will have access to that speech will still be made by the most restrictive community. ...

Even if most, if not all, of these works would be excluded from COPA's coverage by the serious value prong, they illustrate the diversity of public opinion on the underlying themes depicted. This diversity of views surely extends to whether materials with the same themes, that do not have serious value for minors, appeal to their prurient interests and are patently offensive. There is no reason to think the differences between communities' standards will disappear once the image or description is no longer within the context of a work that has serious value for minors. Because communities differ widely in their attitudes toward sex, particularly when minors are concerned, the Court of Appeals was correct to conclude that, regardless of how COPA's other provisions are construed, applying community standards to the Internet will restrict a substantial amount of protected speech that would not be considered harmful to minors in many communities.

Whether that consequence is appropriate depends, of course, on the content of the message. The kind of hard-core pornography involved in *Hamling,* which I assume would be obscene under any community's standard, does not belong on the Internet. Perhaps "teasers" that serve no function except to invite viewers to examine hardcore materials, or the hidden terms written into a Web site's "metatags" in order to dupe unwitting Web surfers into visiting pornographic sites, deserve the same fate. But COPA extends to a wide range of prurient appeals in advertisements, online magazines, Web-based bulletin boards and chat rooms, stock photo galleries, Web diaries, and a variety of illustrations encompassing a vast number of messages that are unobjectionable in most of the country and yet provide no "serious value" for minors. It is quite wrong to allow the standards of a minority consisting of the least tolerant communities to regulate access to relatively harmless messages in this burgeoning market.

In the context of most other media, using community standards to differentiate between permissible and impermissible speech has two virtues. As mentioned above, community standards originally served as a shield to protect speakers from the least tolerant members of society. By aggregating values at the community level, the *Miller* test eliminated the outliers at both ends of the spectrum and provided some predictability as to what constitutes obscene speech. But community standards also serve as a shield to protect audience members, by allowing people to self-sort based on their preferences. Those who abhor and those who tolerate sexually explicit speech can seek out like-minded people and settle in communities that share their views on what is acceptable for themselves and their children. This sorting mechanism, however, does not exist in cyberspace; the audience cannot self-segregate. As a result, in the context of the Internet this shield also becomes a sword, because the community that wishes to live without certain material not only rids itself, but the entire Internet of the offending speech.

In sum, I would affirm the judgment of the Court of Appeals and therefore respectfully dissent.

* * * * *

AMERICAN CIVIL LIBERTIES UNION, *et al,*
v.
JOHN ASHCROFT

United States Court of Appeals for the Third Circuit

No. 99-1324, 322 F.3d 240

March 6, 2003

This case comes before us on *vacatur* and remand from the Supreme Court's decision in *Ashcroft v. ACLU,* 535 U.S. 564, 152 L.Ed.2d 771, 122 S. Ct. 1700 (2002), in which the Court held that our decision affirming the District Court's grant of a preliminary injunction against the enforcement of the Child Online Protection Act ("COPA") could not be sustained because "COPA's reliance on community standards to identify 'material that is harmful to minors' does not *by* itself render the statute substantially overbroad for purposes of the First Amendment." *Id. at* 1713 (emphasis in original). Pursuant to the Supreme Court's instructions in *Ashcroft,* we have revisited the question of COPA's constitutionality in light of the concerns expressed by the Supreme Court.

Our present review of the District Court's decision and the analysis on which that decision was based does not change the result that we originally had reached, albeit on a ground neither decided nor discussed by the District Court. *See ACLU v. Reno,* 217 F.3d 162 (3d Cir. 2000) (*"Reno III"*), *vacated and remanded,* 535 U.S. 564, 152 L.Ed.2d 771, 122 S. Ct. 1700 (2002). We had affirmed the District Court's judgment granting the plaintiffs a preliminary injunction against the enforcement of COPA because we had determined that COPA's reliance on "community standards" to identify material "harmful to minors" could not meet the exacting standards of the First Amendment. On remand from the Supreme Court, with that Court's instruction to consider the other aspects of the District Court's analysis, we once again will affirm.

I.

COPA, Pub. L. No. 105-277, 112 Stat. 2681 (1998) (codified at 47 U.S.C. § 231), is Congress's second attempt to regulate pornography on the Internet. The Supreme Court struck down Congress's first endeavor, the Communications Decency Act, ("CDA"), on First Amendment grounds. *See Reno v. ACLU,* 521 U.S. 844, 138 L.Ed.2d 874, 117 S. Ct. 2329 (1997) (*"Reno I"*). To place our COPA discussion in context, it is helpful to understand its predecessor, the CDA, and the opinion of the Supreme Court which held it to be unconstitutional.

A.

In *Reno I,* the Supreme Court analyzed the CDA, which prohibited *any* person from posting material on the *Internet* that would be considered either *indecent* or obscene. *See*

155

Reno I, 521 U.S. at 859. Like COPA, the CDA provided two affirmative defenses to prosecution: (1) the use of a credit card or other age verification system, and (2) any good faith effort to restrict access by minors. *See id.* at 860.

The Court, in a 7-2 decision, and speaking through Justice Stevens, held that the CDA violated many different facets of the First Amendment. The Court held that the use of the term "indecent," without definition, to describe prohibited content was too vague to withstand constitutional scrutiny. Justice Stevens further determined that "[u]nlike the regulations upheld in *Ginsberg* and *Pacifica*, the scope of the CDA is not limited to commercial speech or commercial entities.... [Rather, i]ts open-ended prohibitions embrace all nonprofit entities and individuals posting indecent messages or displaying them on their own computers." *Id.* at 877.

In holding that "the breadth of the CDA's coverage is wholly unprecedented," the Court continued by noting that "the 'community standards' criterion as applied to the Internet means that any communication available to a nationwide audience will be judged by the standards of the community most likely to be offended by the message." *Id.* at 877-78.

The Court also discussed the constitutional propriety of the credit card/age verification defenses authorized by the CDA. Utilizing the District Court's findings, the Court held that such defenses would not be feasible for most noncommercial Web publishers, and that even with respect to commercial publishers, the technology had yet to be proven effective in shielding minors from harmful material. *See id.* at 881. As a result, the Court determined that the CDA was not narrowly tailored to the Government's purported interest, and "lacks the precision that the First Amendment requires when a statute regulates the content of speech." *Id.* at 874.

B.

COPA, by contrast, represents an attempt by Congress, having been informed by the concerns expressed by the Supreme Court in *Reno I*, to cure the problems identified by the Court when it had invalidated the CDA. Thus, COPA is somewhat narrower in scope than the CDA. COPA provides for civil and criminal penalties for an individual who, or entity that,

> knowingly and with *knowledge* of the character of the material, in interstate or foreign commerce by means of the *World Wide Web*, makes any communication *for commercial purposes* that is available to any minor and that includes any *material that is harmful to minors*.

47 U.S.C. § 231(a)(1) (emphasis added).

Unfortunately, the recited standard for liability in COPA still contains a number of provisions that are constitutionally infirm. True, COPA, in an effort to circumvent the fate of the CDA, expressly defines most of these key terms. For instance, the phrase "by means of the World Wide Web" is defined as the "placement of material in a computer server-based file archive so that it is publicly accessible, over the Internet, using hypertext transfer protocol or any successor protocol." *Id.* § 231(e)(1). As a result, and as is detailed below, COPA does not target *all* of the other methods of online communication, such as e-mail, newsgroups, etc. that make up what is colloquially known as the "Internet." *See ACLU v. Reno*, 31 F. Supp. 2d 473, 482-83 (Finding of Fact ¶ 7) (E.D. Pa. 1999) ("*Reno II*").

1.

Further, only "commercial" publishers of content on the World Wide Web can be found liable under COPA. The statute defines "commercial purposes" as those individuals or entities that are "engaged in the business of making such communications." 47 U.S.C. § 231(e)(2)(A). In turn, a person is "engaged in the business" under COPA if that person

> who makes a communication, or offers to make a communication, by means of the World Wide Web, that includes any material that is harmful to minors, devotes time, attention, or labor to such activities, as a regular course of such person's trade or business, with the *objective* of earning a profit as a result of such activities (although it is not necessary that the person *make* a profit or that the making or offering to make such communications be the person's sole or principal business or source of income).

Id. § 231(e)(2)(B) (emphasis added). Individuals or entities therefore can be found liable under COPA if they seek to make a profit from publishing material on the World Wide Web -- thus, individuals who place such material on the World Wide Web *solely* as a hobby, or for fun, or for other than commercial profiteering are not in danger of either criminal or civil liability.

2.

Furthermore, and of greater importance, is the manner in which the statute defines the content of prohibited material; that is, what type of material is considered "harmful to minors." The House Committee Report that accompanied COPA explains that the statute's definition of the "harmful to minors" test constitutes an attempt to fuse the standards upheld by the Supreme Court in *Ginsberg v. New York*, 390 U.S. 629, 20 L.Ed.2d 195, 88 S. Ct. 1274 (1968), and *Miller v. California*, 413 U.S. 15, 37 L.Ed.2d 419, 93 S. Ct. 2607 (1973). *See* H.R. REP. NO. 105-775, at 12-13 (1998).

In particular, whether material published on the World Wide Web is "harmful to minors" is governed by a three-part test, *each* prong of which must be satisfied before one can be found liable under COPA:

> (A) the average person, applying contemporary community standards, would find, taking the material as a whole and with respect to minors, is designed to appeal to, or is designed to pander to, the prurient interest;

> (B) depicts, describes, or represents, in a manner patently offensive with respect to minors, an actual or simulated sexual act or sexual contact, an actual or simulated normal or perverted sexual act, or a lewd exhibition of the genitals or post-pubescent female breast; and

> (C) taken as a whole, lacks serious literary, artistic, political, or scientific value for minors.

47 U.S.C. § 231(e)(6).

157

COPA, as earlier noted, also provides a putative defendant with affirmative defenses. If an individual or entity "has restricted access by minors to material that is harmful to minors" through the use of a "credit card, debit account, adult access code, or adult personal identification number ... a digital certificate that verifies age ... or by any other reasonable measures that are feasible under available technology," the individual will not be liable if a minor should access this restricted material. *Id.* § 231(c)(1). The defense also applies if an individual or entity attempts "in good faith to implement a defense" listed above. *Id.* § 231(c)(2).

... E.

....[O]n remand, we must again review the District Court's grant of a preliminary injunction in favor of the plaintiffs. This time, however, we must do so in light of the Supreme Court's mandate that the community standards language is not *by itself* a sufficient ground for holding COPA constitutionally overbroad. This direction requires an independent analysis of the issues addressed by the District Court in its original opinion. To assist us in this task, we asked the parties for additional submissions addressed to the opinion of the Supreme Court and to authorities filed subsequent to that opinion and since we last addressed COPA in *Reno III*.

II.

... We hold that the District Court did not abuse its discretion in granting the preliminary injunction, nor did it err in ruling that the plaintiffs had a probability of prevailing on the merits of their claim inasmuch as COPA cannot survive strict scrutiny. By sustaining that holding, as we do, we would not then be obliged to answer the question of whether COPA is overly broad or vague. However, in order to "touch all bases" on this remand, we will nevertheless address the overbreadth doctrine with respect to COPA and the related doctrine of vagueness. In doing so, we hold that COPA is similarly deficient in that aspect as well.

A. Strict Scrutiny

We turn first, however, to the question of whether COPA may withstand strict scrutiny. Strict scrutiny requires that a statute (1) serve a compelling governmental interest; (2) be narrowly tailored to achieve that interest; and (3) be the least restrictive means of advancing that interest. *Sable*, 492 U.S. at 126.

1. Compelling Interest

The Supreme Court has held that "there is a compelling interest in protecting the physical and psychological well-being of minors." *Id.* (citing *Ginsberg*, 390 U.S. at 639-40). The parties agree that the Government's stated interest in protecting minors from harmful material online is compelling. This being so, we proceed to the next question of whether COPA is narrowly tailored to meet that interest.

2. Narrowly Tailored

We hold that the following provisions of COPA are not narrowly tailored to achieve the Government's compelling interest in protecting minors from harmful material and therefore fail the strict scrutiny test: (a) the definition of "material that is harmful to minors," which includes the concept of taking "*as a whole*" material designed to appeal to the "prurient interest" of minors; and material which (when judged as a whole) lacks "serious literary" or other "value" *for minors*; (b) the definition of "commercial purposes," which limits the reach of the statute to persons "*engaged in the business*" (broadly defined) of making communications of material that is harmful to minors; and (c) the *"affirmative defenses"* available to publishers, which require the technological screening of users for the purpose of age verification.

(a) "Material Harmful to Minors"

We address first the provision defining "material harmful to minors." Because COPA's definition of harmful material is explicitly focused on minors, it automatically impacts non-obscene, sexually suggestive speech that is otherwise protected for adults. The remaining constitutional question, then, is whether the definition's subsets of "prurient interest" and lacking "serious ... value for minors" are sufficiently narrowly tailored to satisfy strict scrutiny in light of the statute's stated purpose. We address each of these subsets.

COPA limits its targeted material to that which is designed to appeal to the "prurient interest" of minors. It leaves that judgment, however, to "the average person, applying contemporary community standards" and "taking the material as a whole."

As discussed in our initial opinion on the matter, when contemporary community standards are applied to the Internet, which does not permit speakers or exhibitors to limit their speech or exhibits geographically, the statute effectively limits the range of permissible material under the statute to that which is deemed acceptable only by the most puritanical communities. This limitation by definition burdens speech otherwise protected under the First Amendment for adults as well as for minors living in more tolerant settings. *See Reno III*, 217 F.3d at 173-80.

This burden becomes even more troublesome when those evaluating questionable material consider it "as a whole" in judging its appeal to minors' prurient interests. As Justice Kennedy suggested in his concurring opinion, it is "essential to answer the vexing question of what it means to evaluate Internet material 'as a whole,' when everything on the Web is connected to everything else." *Ashcroft*, 122 S. Ct. at 1721 (internal citation omitted). We agree with Justice Kennedy's suggestion, and consider this issue here.

While COPA does not define what is intended to be judged "as a whole," the plain language of COPA's "harmful material" definition describes such material as "*any* communication, picture, image file, article, recording, writing, or other matter of any kind" that satisfies the three prongs of the "material harmful to minors" test: prurient interest, patently offensive, and serious value. 47 U.S.C. § 231(e)(6) (emphasis added). In light of the particularity and specificity of Congress's language, Congress had to mean that each individual communication, picture, image, exhibit, etc. be deemed "a whole" by itself in determining whether it appeals to the prurient interests of minors, because that is the unmistakable manner in which the statute is drawn.

The taken "as a whole" language is crucial because the First Amendment requires the consideration of context. As Justice Kennedy observed in his concurring opinion in *Ashcroft*, the application of the constitutional taken "as a whole" requirement is complicated in the Internet context: "It is unclear whether what is to be judged as a whole is a single image on a Web page, a whole Web page, an entire multipage Web site, or an interlocking set of Web sites." *Ashcroft*, 122 S. Ct. at 1717. As the Supreme Court has recently noted:

> [It is] an essential First Amendment rule that the artistic merit of a work does not depend on the presence of a single explicit scene.... Under *Miller*, the First Amendment requires that redeeming value be judged

by considering the work as a whole. Where the scene is part of the narrative, the work itself does not for this reason become obscene, even though the scene in isolation might be offensive.

Ashcroft v. Free Speech Coalition, 535 U.S. 234, 122 S. Ct. 1389, 1401, 152 L.Ed.2d 403 (2002) (citation omitted).

Yet, here the plain meaning of COPA's text mandates evaluation of an exhibit on the Internet in isolation, rather than in context. As such, COPA's taken "as a whole" definition surely fails to meet the strictures of the First Amendment.

By limiting the material to individual expressions, rather than to an expanded context, we would be hard-pressed to hold that COPA was narrowly tailored to achieve its designed purpose. For example, one sexual image, which COPA may proscribe as harmful material, might not be deemed to appeal to the prurient interest of minors if it were to be viewed in the context of an entire collection of Renaissance artwork. However, evaluating just that one image or picture or writing by itself rules out a context which may have alleviated its prurient appeal. As a result, individual communications that may be a integral part of an entirely non-prurient presentation may be held to violate COPA, despite the fact that a completely different result would obtain if the entire context in which the picture or communication was evaluated "as a whole."

Because we view such a statute, construed as its own text unquestionably requires, as pertaining only to single individual exhibits, COPA endangers a wide range of communications, exhibits, and speakers whose messages do not comport with the type of harmful materials legitimately targeted under COPA, i.e., material that is obscene as to minors. *See Ginsberg*, 390 U.S. at 639-43. Accordingly, while COPA penalizes publishers for making available improper material for minors, at the same time it impermissibly burdens a wide range of speech and exhibits otherwise protected for adults. Thus, in our opinion, the Act, which proscribes publication of material harmful to minors, is not narrowly tailored to serve the Government's stated purpose in protecting minors from such material.

Lastly, COPA's definition of "material that is harmful to minors" only permits regulation of speech that when "taken as a whole, lacks serious literary, artistic, political, or scientific value *for minors*." 47 U.S.C. § 231(e)(6)(C) (emphasis added). COPA defines the term minor as "any person under 17 [seventeen] years of age." *Id.* § 231(e)(7). The statute does not limit the term minor in any way, and indeed, in its briefing, the Government, in complete disregard of the text, contends that minor means a "normal, older adolescent."

We need not suggest how the statute's targeted population could be more narrowly defined, because even the Government does not argue, as it could not, that materials that have "serious literary, artistic, political or scientific value" for a sixteen-year-old would have the same value for a minor who is three years old. Nor does any party argue, despite Congress's having targeted and included *all* minors seventeen or under, that *pre-adolescent minors* (i.e., ages two, three, four, etc.) could be patently offended by a "normal or perverted sexual act" or have their "prurient interest" aroused by a "post-pubescent female breast," or by being exposed to whatever other material may be designed to appeal to prurient interests.

The term "minor," as Congress has drafted it, thus applies in a literal sense to an infant, a five-year old, or a person just shy of age seventeen. In abiding by this definition, Web publishers who seek to determine whether their Web sites will run afoul of COPA cannot tell which of these "minors" should be considered in deciding the particular content of their

Internet postings. Instead, they must guess at which minor should be considered in determining whether the content of their Web site has "serious ... value for [those] minors." 47 U.S.C. § 231(e)(6)(C). Likewise, if they try to comply with COPA's "harmful to minors" definition, they must guess at the potential audience of minors and their ages so that the publishers can refrain from posting material that will trigger the prurient interest, or be patently offensive with respect to those minors who may be deemed to have such interests.

The Government has argued that "minors" should be read to apply only to normal, older adolescents. We realize as a pragmatic matter that some *pre*-adolescent minors may, by definition, be incapable of possessing a prurient interest. It is not clear, however, that the Government's proffered definition meets Congress's intended meaning for the term "minor" with respect to the "patently offensive" and "serious value" prongs. Furthermore, Congress has identified as objects of its concern children who cannot be described as "older" adolescents:

> Moreover, because of sophisticated, yet easy to use navigating software, minors who can read and type are capable of conducting Web searches as easily as operating a television remote. While a *four-year old may not be as capable as a thirteen year old*, given the right tools (e.g., a child trackball and browser software) each has the ability to "surf" the Net and will likely be exposed to harmful material.

H.R. REP. NO. 105-775, at 9-10 (emphasis added). Moreover, the statute, if meant to pertain only to normal, older adolescents (as the Government claims it does), does not by its own definition restrict its application to older adolescents, although we assume that Congress could have defined that universe in that manner.

Because the plain meaning of the statute's text is evident, we decline to rewrite Congress's definition of "minor." We would note, however, that even if we accepted the Government's argument, the term "minors" would not be tailored narrowly enough to satisfy strict scrutiny.

Regardless of what the lower end of the range of relevant minors is, Web publishers would face great uncertainty in deciding what minor could be exposed to its publication, so that a publisher could predict, and guard against, potential liability. Even if the statutory meaning of "minor" were limited to minors between the ages of thirteen and seventeen, Web publishers would still face too much uncertitude as to the nature of material that COPA proscribes.

We do not suggest how Congress could have tailored its statute -- that is not our function. We do no more than conclude that the use of the term "minors" in all three prongs of the statute's definition of "material harmful to minors" is not narrowly drawn to achieve the statute's purpose -- it is not defended by the Government in the exact terms of the statute, and does not lend itself to a commonsense meaning when consideration is given to the fact that minors range in age from infants to seventeen years. Therefore, even if we were to accept the narrowing construction that the Government proposes -- and we do not -- COPA's definition of the term "minor," viewed in conjunction with the "material harmful to minors" test, is not tailored narrowly enough to satisfy the First Amendment's requirements.

(b) "Commercial Purposes"

COPA's purported limitation of liability to persons making communications "for commercial purposes" does not narrow the reach of COPA sufficiently. Instead, COPA's definitions subject too wide a range of Web publishers to potential liability. As the District Court observed, "There is nothing in the text of COPA ... that limits its applicability to so-called commercial pornographers only." *Reno II*, 31 F. Supp. 2d at 480. Indeed, as we read COPA, it extends to any Web publisher who makes any communication "for commercial purposes." 47 U.S.C. § 231(a)(1).

The statute includes within "commercial purposes" any Web publisher who meets COPA's broad definition of being "engaged in the business" of making such communications. *Id.* § 231(e)(2)(A). The definition of "engaged in the business" applies to any person whose communication "includes *any material* that is harmful to minors" and who "devotes time ... to such activities, as a *regular* course of such person's trade or business, with the objective of earning a profit," if that person "knowingly causes [or solicits] the material that is harmful to minors to be posted on the World Wide Web." *Id.* § 231(e)(2)(B) (emphasis added).

Based on this broad definition of "engaged in the business," we read COPA to apply to Web publishers who have posted *any* material that is "harmful to minors" on their Web sites, even if they do not make a profit from such material itself or do not post such material as the principal part of their business. Under the plain language of COPA, a Web publisher will be subjected to liability if even a small part of his or her Web site displays material "harmful to minors."

Moreover, the definition of "commercial purposes" further expands COPA's reach beyond those enterprises that sell services or goods to consumers, including those persons who sell advertising space on their otherwise non-commercial Web sites. *See Reno II*, 31 F. Supp. 2d at 487 (Finding of Fact ¶ 33). Thus, the "engaged in the business" definition would encompass both the commercial pornographer who profits from his or her online traffic, as well as the Web publisher who provides free content on his or her Web site and seeks advertising revenue, perhaps only to defray the cost of maintaining the Web site. *See also Ashcroft*, 122 S. Ct. at 1721 (Kennedy, J., concurring) ("Indeed, the plain text of the Act does not limit its scope to pornography that is offered for sale; it seems to apply even to speech provided for free, so long as the speaker merely hopes to profit as an indirect result."). The latter model is a common phenomenon on the Internet. *See Reno II*, 31 F. Supp. 2d at 484 (Findings of Fact ¶¶ 23, 30). This expansive definition of "engaged in the business" therefore includes a large number of Web publishers. Indeed, the District Court in its findings of fact cited to testimony that approximately one-third of the 3.5 million global Web sites (existing at that time) are "commercial," or "intend[ed] to make a profit." *Id. at* 486 (Finding of Fact ¶ 27).

... In sum, while the "commercial purposes" limitation makes the reach of COPA less broad than its predecessor, inasmuch as the Communications Decency Act (CDA) was not limited to commercial entities, *see Reno I*, 521 U.S. at 877, COPA's definition of "commercial purposes" nevertheless imposes content restrictions on a substantial number of "commercial," non-obscene speakers in violation of the First Amendment. We are satisfied that COPA is not narrowly tailored to proscribe commercial pornographers and their ilk, as the Government contends, but instead prohibits a wide range of protected expression.

(c) Affirmative Defenses

The Government argues that COPA's burdens are limited and reasonable, and points to COPA's affirmative defenses in support of the statute's constitutionality. We examine whether the affirmative defenses in COPA serve to tailor the statute narrowly, as the Government asserts.

COPA's affirmative defenses shield Web publishers from liability under the statute if they, in good faith, restrict access to material deemed harmful to minors. COPA provides as follows:

> It is an affirmative defense to prosecution under this section that the defendant, in good faith, has restricted access by minors to material that is harmful to minors --
>
> (A) by requiring use of a credit card, debit account, adult access code, or adult personal identification number;
>
> (B) by accepting a digital certificate that verifies age; or
>
> (C) by any other reasonable measures that are feasible under available technology.

47 U.S.C. § 231(c)(1). ...

The Government maintains that the District Court overstated the burdens on protected speech created by utilization of COPA's affirmative defenses. The record and our own limited standard of review, however, belie that claim.

First, the actual effect on users as a result of COPA's affirmative defenses, which the Government minimizes, was determined by the District Court in its factual findings, after hearing testimony from both parties. Both the expert offered by the plaintiffs and one of the experts proffered by the Government testified that users could be deterred from accessing the plaintiffs' Web sites as a result of COPA's affirmative defenses. The plaintiffs' expert went on to testify that "economic harm ... would result from loss of traffic." *Id.* at 491 (Finding of Fact ¶ 61).

Although the Government presented its own expert who testified that "COPA would not impose an unreasonable economic burden ... on the seven Web sites of the plaintiffs," the District Court, in exercising its fact-finding function, determined that "plaintiffs have shown that they are likely to convince the Court that implementing the affirmative defenses in COPA will cause most Web sites to lose some adult users to the portions of the sites that are behind screens." *Id.* at 492 (Findings of Fact ¶¶ 61-62). We cannot say, nor has the Government claimed, that the District Court's factual determination is clearly erroneous.

COPA's restrictions on speech, as the District Court has found and as we agree, are not, as the Government has argued, analogous to the incidental restrictions caused by slow response times, broken links, or poor site design that "already inhibit a user's ... experience." Requiring a user to pay a fee for use of an adult verification service or to enter personal information prior to accessing certain material constitutes a much more severe burden on speech than any technical difficulties, which are often repairable and cause only minor delays.

We agree with the District Court's determination that COPA will likely deter many adults from accessing restricted content, because many Web users are simply unwilling to provide identification information in order to gain access to content, especially where the information they wish to access is sensitive or controversial. People may fear to transmit their personal information, and may also fear that their personal, identifying information will be collected and stored in the records of various Web sites or providers of adult identification numbers.

The Supreme Court has disapproved of content-based restrictions that require recipients to identify themselves affirmatively before being granted access to disfavored speech, because such restrictions can have an impermissible chilling effect on those would-be recipients.

Second, the affirmative defenses do not provide the Web publishers with assurances of freedom from prosecution. As the Supreme Court noted in *Free Speech Coalition*, "The Government raises serious constitutional difficulties by seeking to impose on the defendant the burden of proving his speech is not unlawful." *Free Speech Coalition*, 122 S. Ct. at 1404. Although the criminal penalties under the federal statute concerning virtual child pornography, at issue in *Free Speech Coalition,* were more severe than the penalties under COPA, the logic is applicable: "An affirmative defense applies only after prosecution has begun, and the speaker must himself prove ... that his conduct falls within the affirmative defense." *Id.*

Lastly, none of the display-restriction cases relied on by the Government are apposite here, as each involved the use of blinder racks to shield minors from viewing harmful material on display. The use of "blinder racks," or some analogous device, does not create the same deterrent effect on adults as would COPA's credit card or adult verification screens. Blinder racks do not require adults to compromise their anonymity in their viewing of material harmful to minors, nor do they create any financial burden on the user. Moreover, they do not burden the speech contained in the targeted publications any more than is absolutely necessary to shield minors from its content. We cannot say the same with respect to COPA's affirmative defenses.

The effect of the affirmative defenses, as they burden "material harmful to minors" which is constitutionally protected for adults, is to drive this protected speech from the marketplace of ideas on the Internet. This type of regulation is prohibited under the First Amendment. As the Supreme Court has recently said, "[S]peech within the rights of adults to hear may not be silenced completely in an attempt to shield children from it." *Free Speech Coalition*, 122 S. Ct. at 1402 (citation omitted). COPA, though less broad than the CDA, "effectively resembles [a] ban," on adults' access to protected speech; the chilling effect occasioned by the affirmative defenses results in the "unnecessarily broad suppression of speech addressed to adults." *Reno I*, 521 U.S. at 875.

3. Least Restrictive Means

As we have just explained, COPA is not narrowly tailored and as such fails strict scrutiny. We are also satisfied that COPA does not employ the "least restrictive means" to effect the Government's compelling interest in protecting minors.

The Supreme Court has stated that "[i]f a less restrictive alternative would serve the Government's purpose, the legislature must use that alternative." *United States v. Playboy*

Entertainment Group, 529 U.S. 803, 813, 146 L.Ed.2d 865, 120 S. Ct. 1878 (2000); *see also Reno I*, 521 U.S. at 874 ("[The CDA's Internet indecency provisions'] burden on adult speech is unacceptable if less restrictive alternatives would be at least as effective in achieving the legitimate purpose that the statute was enacted to serve"); *Sable*, 492 U.S. at 126.

The District Court determined, based on its findings of fact, that COPA would be of limited effectiveness in achieving its aim. *See Reno II*, 31 F. Supp. 2d at 496 (COPA has "problems ... with efficaciously meeting its goal.") To reach that conclusion, the District Court relied on its findings that (1) under COPA children may still be able to access material deemed harmful to them on "foreign Web sites, non-commercial sites, and ... via protocols other than http," *id.* at 496; *see also id.* at 482-84, 492 (Findings of Fact ¶¶ 7-8, 19-20, 66); and (2) that children may be able to obtain credit cards -- either their parents' or their own -- legitimately and so circumvent the screening contemplated by COPA's affirmative defenses. *See id. at* 489 (Finding of Fact ¶ 48).

....[F]iltering software is a less restrictive alternative that can allow parents some measure of control over their children's access to speech that parents consider inappropriate.

We agree with the District Court that the various blocking and filtering techniques which that Court discussed may be substantially less restrictive than COPA in achieving COPA's objective of preventing a minor's access to harmful material. We are influenced further in this conclusion by our reading of the Report of the House Committee on Commerce, which had advocated the enactment of COPA. *See* H.R. REP. NO. 105-775 (1998). That Report described a number of techniques and/or alternatives to be used in conjunction with blocking and filtering software, although the techniques were not adopted at that time. In each instance, these techniques would appear to constitute a less restrictive alternative than COPA's prescriptions. Moreover, we are at least four years beyond the technology then considered by the Committee, and as we had initially observed, "in light of rapidly developing technological advances, what may now be impossible to regulate constitutionally may, in the not-too-distant future, become feasible." *Reno III*, 217 F.3d at 166.

Because the techniques and/or alternatives considered by the Committee (i.e., "tagging," "domain name zoning," etc., *see* H.R. REP. NO. 105-775, at 16-20), were not addressed either by the parties or the District Court, we do not rely upon them here. We do no more than draw attention to the fact that other possibly less restrictive alternatives existed when COPA was enacted and more undoubtedly will be available in the future -- many of which might well be a less restrictive alternative to COPA.

The existence of less restrictive alternatives renders COPA unconstitutional under strict scrutiny. As the Supreme Court has said:

> "Precision of regulation must be the touchstone in an area so closely touching our most precious freedoms." If the State has open to it a less drastic way of satisfying its legitimate interests, it may not choose a legislative scheme that broadly stifles the exercise of fundamental personal liberties ... and the benefit gained must outweigh the loss of constitutionally protected rights.

Elrod v. Burns, 427 U.S. 347, 363, 49 L.Ed.2d 547, 96 S. Ct. 2673 (1976) (quoting *Kusper v. Pontikes*, 414 U.S. 51, 59, 38 L.Ed.2d 260, 94 S. Ct. 303 (1973)).

In sum, the District Court did not abuse its discretion in granting the plaintiffs a preliminary injunction on the grounds that COPA, in failing to satisfy strict scrutiny, had no probability of success on the merits. COPA is clearly a content-based restriction on speech. Although it does purport to serve a compelling governmental interest, it is not narrowly tailored, and thus fails strict scrutiny. COPA also fails strict scrutiny because it does not use the least restrictive means to achieve its ends. The breadth of the "harmful to minors" and "commercial purposes" text of COPA, especially in light of applying community standards to a global medium and the burdens on speech created by the statute's affirmative defenses, as well as the fact that Congress could have, but failed to employ the least restrictive means to accomplish its legitimate goal, persuade us that the District Court did not abuse its discretion in preliminarily enjoining the enforcement of COPA.

B. Overbreadth

Though the Supreme Court held in *Ashcroft* that COPA's reliance on community standards did not alone render the statute overbroad, the Court specifically declined to "express any view as to whether COPA suffers from substantial overbreadth for other reasons [or] whether the statute is unconstitutionally vague," instead explaining that "prudence dictates allowing the Court of Appeals to first examine these difficult issues." *Ashcroft*, 122 S. Ct. at 1713. ....[W]e ... hold that ... [COPA] is overbroad.

In *Broadrick v. Oklahoma*, 413 U.S. 601, 37 L.Ed.2d 830, 93 S. Ct. 2908 (1973), the Supreme Court ruled that a statute that burdens otherwise protected speech is facially invalid if that burden is not only real, but "substantial as well, judged in relation to the statute's plainly legitimate sweep." *Id. at* 615. As the Court has recently stated, "The overbreadth doctrine prohibits the Government from banning unprotected speech if a substantial amount of protected speech is prohibited or chilled in the process." *Free Speech Coalition*, 122 S. Ct. at 1404.

Our analysis of whether COPA is overbroad is akin to the portion of the strict scrutiny analysis we have conducted in which we concluded that COPA is not narrowly tailored. Overbreadth analysis -- like the question whether a statute is narrowly tailored to serve a compelling governmental interest -- examines whether a statute encroaches upon speech in a constitutionally overinclusive manner.

We conclude that the statute is substantially overbroad in that it places significant burdens on Web publishers' communication of speech that is constitutionally protected as to adults and adults' ability to access such speech. In so doing, COPA encroaches upon a significant amount of protected speech beyond that which the Government may target constitutionally in preventing children's exposure to material that is obscene for minors. *See Ginsberg*, 390 U.S. at 639-43; *see also, e.g.*, *Sable*, 492 U.S. at 126; *Erznoznik v. City of Jacksonville*, 422 U.S. 205, 212-14, 45 L.Ed.2d 125, 95 S. Ct. 2268 (1975).

1. "Material Harmful to Minors"

First, COPA's definition of "material harmful to minors" impermissibly places at risk a wide spectrum of speech that is constitutionally protected. As we have discussed in our strict scrutiny analysis, two of the three prongs of the "harmful to minors" test -- the "serious value" and "prurient interest" prongs -- contain requirements that material be "taken as a whole." *See* 47 U.S.C. § 231(e)(6)(C). We have earlier explained that the First Amendment requires the consideration of context. COPA's text, however, as we have interpreted it, calls for evaluation of "any material" on the Web *in isolation*. Such evaluation *in isolation* results in significant overinclusiveness. Thus, an isolated item located somewhere on a Web site that meets the "harmful to minors" definition can subject the publisher of the site to liability under COPA, even though the entire Web page (or Web site) that provides the context for the item would be constitutionally protected for adults (and indeed, may be protected as to minors).

An examination of the claims of certain *amici curiae* that COPA threatens their speech illustrates this problem. For example, *amicus* California Museum of Photography/University of California at Riverside, maintains a Web site that, among other things, displays artwork from the museum's collection. The Web site contains a page that introduces the "photographers" section of the Web site. *See* California Museum of Photography/University of California at Riverside, *UCR/CMP Photographers*, *at* http://www.cmp.ucr.edu/ photos/photographers.html (last visited Feb. 6, 2003). This Web page contains several photographs, each which serves as a link to that museum's on-line exhibit on a particular photographer. One of these photographs on the introductory page, by Lucien Clergue, links to the museum's exhibit of his work. This photograph is of a naked woman whose "post-pubescent female breast," 47 U.S.C. § 231(e)(6)(B), is exposed.

Viewing this photograph "as a whole," but without reference to the surrounding context, as per COPA's definition of "material," the photograph arguably meets the definition of "harmful to minors." Yet, this same photograph, when treated in context as a component of the entire Web page, cannot be said to be "harmful to minors." In the context of the Web page, which displays several art exhibits, none of which are even arguably "harmful to minors," the Clergue photograph and its surroundings would have "serious [artistic] value." Of course, it would also be protected speech as to adults. ...

As th[is] example[ ] illustrate[s,] ... the burden that COPA would impose on harmless material accompanying such single images causes COPA to be substantially overinclusive.

2. "Minor"

As we have earlier explained, the term "minor" appears in all three prongs of the statute's modified-for-minors *Miller* test. COPA's definition of a "minor" as any person under the age of seventeen serves to place at risk too wide a range of speech that is protected for adults. The type of material that might be considered harmful to a younger minor is vastly different -- and encompasses a much greater universe of speech -- than material that is harmful to a minor just shy of seventeen years old.

Thus, for example, sex education materials may have "serious value" for, and not be "patently offensive" as to, sixteen-year-olds. The same material, however, might well be considered "patently offensive" as to, and without "serious value" for, children aged, say, ten to thirteen, and thus meet COPA's standard for material harmful to minors.

Because COPA's definition of "minor" therefore broadens the reach of "material that is harmful to minors" under the statute to encompass a vast array of speech that is clearly protected for adults -- and indeed, may not be obscene as to older minors -- the definition renders COPA significantly overinclusive.

3. "Commercial Purposes"

COPA's purported limitation of liability to persons making communications "for commercial purposes" does not narrow the sweep of COPA sufficiently. Instead, the definition subjects too wide a range of Web publishers to potential liability. As we have explained, under the plain language of COPA, a Web publisher will be subjected to liability due to the fact that even a small part of his or her Web site has material "harmful to minors." Furthermore, because the statute does not require that a Web publisher seek profit as a sole or primary objective, COPA can reach otherwise non-commercial Web sites that obtain revenue through advertising. We have explored this subject in greater detail in the strict scrutiny section of this opinion. The conclusion we reach there is every bit as relevant here.

4. Affirmative Defenses

The affirmative defenses do not save the statute from sweeping too broadly. First, the affirmative defenses, if employed by Web publishers, will result in a chilling effect upon adults who seek to view, and have a right to access, constitutionally protected speech. Compliance with COPA's affirmative defenses requires that Web publishers place obstacles in the way of adults seeking to obtain material that may be considered harmful to minors under the statute. As the District Court found, these barriers, which would require adults to identify themselves as a precondition to accessing disfavored speech, are likely to deter many adults from accessing that speech.

Second, the affirmative defenses impose a burden on Web publishers, and as such, do not alleviate the chilling effect that COPA has on their speech. Web publishers will be forced to take into account the chilling effect that COPA's affirmative defenses have on adult Web users. Consequently, COPA will cause Web publishers to recoil from engaging in such expression at all, rather than availing themselves of the affirmative defenses. Additionally, the financial costs of implementing the barriers necessary for compliance with COPA may further deter some Web publishers from posting protected speech on their Web sites.

Moreover, because the affirmative defenses are not included as elements of the statute, Web publishers are saddled with the substantial burden of proving that their "conduct falls within the affirmative defense." *Free Speech Coalition*, 122 S. Ct. at 1404.

Thus, the affirmative defenses do not cure nor diminish the broad sweep of COPA sufficiently.

5. "Community Standards"

As the Supreme Court has now explained, community standards by itself did not suffice to render COPA substantially overbroad. Justice Kennedy's concurring opinion, however, explained that community standards, in conjunction with other provisions of the statute, might render the statute substantially overbroad. *See Ashcroft*, 122 S. Ct. at 1720 (Kennedy, J., concurring) ("We cannot know whether variation in community standards renders the Act substantially overbroad without first assessing the extent of the speech covered and the variations in community standards with respect to that speech.").

As we have just discussed earlier, the expansive definitions of "material harmful to minors" and "for commercial purposes," as well as the burdensome affirmative defenses, likely render the statute substantially overbroad. COPA's application of "community standards" exacerbates these constitutional problems in that it further widens the spectrum of protected speech that COPA affects. As we said in our original decision, "COPA essentially requires that every Web publisher subject to the statute abide by the most restrictive and conservative state's community standards in order to avoid criminal liability." *Reno III*, 217 F.3d at 166; *see also Ashcroft*, 122 S. Ct. at 1719 (Kennedy, J., concurring) ("if an eavesdropper in a more traditional, rural community chooses to listen in, there is nothing the publisher can do. As a practical matter, COPA makes the eavesdropper the arbiter of propriety on the Web.").

The "community standards" requirement, when viewed *in conjunction with* the other provisions of the statute -- the "material harmful to minors" provision and the "commercial purposes" provisions, as well as the affirmative defenses -- adds to the already wide range of speech swept in by COPA. Because the community standards inquiry further broadens the scope of speech covered by the statute, the limitations that COPA purports to place on its own reach are that much more ineffective.

6. Unavailability of Narrowing Construction

Before concluding that a statute is overbroad, we are required to assess whether it is subject to "a narrowing construction that would make it constitutional." *Virginia v. American Booksellers Ass'n*, 484 U.S. 383, 397, 98 L.Ed.2d 782, 108 S. Ct. 636 (1988). We may impose such a narrowing construction, however, "only if it is readily susceptible to such a construction," *Reno I*, 521 U.S. at 884, because courts "will not rewrite a ... law to conform it to constitutional requirements." *American Booksellers*, 484 U.S. at 397. As the Supreme Court once noted, "It would certainly be dangerous if the legislature could set a net large enough to catch all possible offenders, and leave it to the courts to step inside and say who could be rightfully detained, and who should be set at large. This would, to some extent, substitute the judicial for the legislative department of the government." *United States v. Reese*, 92 U.S. 214, 221, 23 L.Ed. 563 (1875).

We originally declined to redraw COPA when we held that the "contemporary community standards" rendered the statute overbroad; we certainly decline to perform even more radical surgery here. In order to satisfy the constitutional prerequisites consistent with our holding today, we would be required, *inter alia*, to redraw the text of "commercial purposes" and redraw the meaning of "minors" and what is "harmful to minors," including the reach of "contemporary community standards." We would also be required to redraw a new set of affirmative defenses. Any attempt to resuscitate this statute would constitute a "serious invasion of the legislative domain." *United States v. National Treasury Employees Union*, 513 U.S. 454, 479 n.26, 130 L.Ed.2d 964, 115 S. Ct. 1003 (1995).

Accordingly, we hold that the plaintiffs will more probably prove at trial that COPA is substantially overbroad, and therefore, we will affirm the District Court on this independent ground as well.

III.

This appeal concerns the issuance of a preliminary injunction pending the resolution of the merits of the case. Because the ACLU will likely succeed on the merits in establishing that COPA is unconstitutional because it fails strict scrutiny and is overbroad, we will affirm the issuance of a preliminary injunction.

* * * * *

Notes and Questions

1. The terms "blocking" and "filtering" are commonly used synonymously to describe technologies that prevent access to certain on-line content. "Inclusion filters" allow access to specified web-sites deemed acceptable and block access to the balance of content available on the Internet; "exclusion filtering" is designed to develop blocking lists, sometimes referred

to as "blacklists," and allow access to content unless it has been classified as unacceptable; and "content filtering" examines certain keywords or graphic images in Web pages to determine acceptability. Some commercial filtering products may use a combination of techniques.

2. Among the deficiencies cited by opponents of Internet blocking technology are under- and over-blocking, the use of subjective and vague criteria to determine the content to be blocked, errors resulting from automated processing, and inadequate means to rectify or contest inappropriate blocking. *See, e.g.,* Electronic Frontier Foundation, *Internet Blocking & Censorware (Online Content/Filtering/Labeling/Rating), Why Blocking Technology Can't Work, available at* <http://www.eff.org/Censorship/Censorware/>.

* * * * *

JOHN D. ASHCROFT, ATTORNEY GENERAL, Petitioner

v.

AMERICAN CIVIL LIBERTIES UNION *et al.*

Supreme Court of the United States

No. 03-218, 542 U.S. 656

June 29, 2004

Justice Kennedy delivered the opinion of the Court.

This case presents a challenge to a statute enacted by Congress to protect minors from exposure to sexually explicit materials on the Internet, the Child Online Protection Act (COPA). 112 Stat. 2681-736, codified at 47 U. S. C. § 231. We must decide whether the Court of Appeals was correct to affirm a ruling by the District Court that enforcement of COPA should be enjoined because the statute likely violates the First Amendment.

In enacting COPA, Congress gave consideration to our earlier decisions on this subject, in particular the decision in *Reno* v. *American Civil Liberties Union*, 521 U.S. 844 (1997). For that reason, "the Judiciary must proceed with caution and ... with care before invalidating the Act." *Ashcroft* v. *American Civil Liberties Union*, 535 U.S. 564, 592 (*Ashcroft I*) (Kennedy, J., concurring in judgment). The imperative of according respect to the Congress, however, does not permit us to depart from well-established First Amendment principles. Instead, we must hold the Government to its constitutional burden of proof.

Content-based prohibitions, enforced by severe criminal penalties, have the constant potential to be a repressive force in the lives and thoughts of a free people. To guard against that threat the Constitution demands that content-based restrictions on speech be presumed invalid, *R. A.V.* v. *St. Paul*, 505 U.S. 377, 382 (1992), and that the Government bear the burden of showing their constitutionality. *United States v. Playboy Entertainment Group,*

Inc., 529 U.S. 803, 817 (2000). This is true even when Congress twice has attempted to find a constitutional means to restrict, and punish, the speech in question.

This case comes to the Court on *certiorari* review of an appeal from the decision of the District Court granting a preliminary injunction. The Court of Appeals reviewed the decision of the District Court for abuse of discretion. Under that standard, the Court of Appeals was correct to conclude that the District Court did not abuse its discretion in granting the preliminary injunction. The Government has failed, at this point, to rebut the plaintiffs' contention that there are plausible less restrictive alternatives to the statute. Substantial practical considerations, furthermore, argue in favor of upholding the injunction and allowing the case to proceed to trial. For those reasons, we affirm the decision of the Court of Appeals upholding the preliminary injunction, and we remand the case so that it may be returned to the District Court for trial on the issues presented.

… II.

A.

When plaintiffs challenge a content-based speech restriction, the burden is on the Government to prove that the proposed alternatives will not be as effective as the challenged statute. [*Reno* v. *American Civil Liberties Union*, 521 U.S. at 874].

In considering this question, a court assumes that certain protected speech may be regulated, and then asks what is the least restrictive alternative that can be used to achieve that goal. The purpose of the test is not to consider whether the challenged restriction has some effect in achieving Congress' goal, regardless of the restriction it imposes. The purpose of the test is to ensure that speech is restricted no further than necessary to achieve the goal, for it is important to assure that legitimate speech is not chilled or punished. For that reason, the test does not begin with the status quo of existing regulations, then ask whether the challenged restriction has some additional ability to achieve Congress' legitimate interest. Any restriction on speech could be justified under that analysis. Instead, the court should ask whether the challenged regulation is the least restrictive means among available, effective alternatives. …

Filters are less restrictive than COPA. They impose selective restrictions on speech at the receiving end, not universal restrictions at the source. Under a filtering regime, adults without children may gain access to speech they have a right to see without having to identify themselves or provide their credit card information. Even adults with children may obtain access to the same speech on the same terms simply by turning off the filter on their home computers. Above all, promoting the use of filters does not condemn as criminal any category of speech, and so the potential chilling effect is eliminated, or at least much diminished. All of these things are true, moreover, regardless of how broadly or narrowly the definitions in COPA are construed.

Filters also may well be more effective than COPA. First, a filter can prevent minors from seeing all pornography, not just pornography posted to the Web from America. The District Court noted in its factfindings that one witness estimated that 40% of harmful-to-minors content comes from overseas. *Id.* at 484. COPA does not prevent minors from having access to those foreign harmful materials. That alone makes it possible that filtering software might be more effective in serving Congress' goals. Effectiveness is likely to diminish even further if COPA is upheld, because the providers of the materials that would be covered by the statute simply can move their operations overseas. It is not an answer to say that COPA reaches some amount of materials that are harmful to minors; the question is whether it would reach more of them than less restrictive alternatives. In addition, the District Court found that verification systems may be subject to evasion and circumvention, for example by minors who have their own credit cards. *See id.* at 484, 496-497. Finally, filters also may be more effective because they can be applied to all forms of Internet communication, including e-mail, not just communications available via the World Wide Web.

That filtering software may well be more effective than COPA is confirmed by the findings of the Commission on Child Online Protection, a blue-ribbon commission created by Congress in COPA itself. Congress directed the Commission to evaluate the relative merits of different means of restricting minors' ability to gain access to harmful materials on the Internet. Note following 47 U. S. C. § 231. It unambiguously found that filters are more effective than age-verification requirements. *See* Commission on Child Online Protection (COPA), Report to Congress, at 19-21, 23-25, 27 (Oct. 20, 2000) (assigning a score for "Effectiveness" of 7.4 for server-based filters and 6.5 for client-based filters, as compared to 5.9 for independent adult-id verification, and 5.5 for credit card verification). Thus, not only has the Government failed to carry its burden of showing the District Court that the proposed alternative is less effective, but also a Government Commission appointed to consider the question has concluded just the opposite. That finding supports our conclusion that the District Court did not abuse its discretion in enjoining the statute.

Filtering software, of course, is not a perfect solution to the problem of children gaining access to harmful-to-minors materials. It may block some materials that are not harmful to minors and fail to catch some that are. *See* 31 F. Supp. 2d at 492. Whatever the deficiencies of filters, however, the Government failed to introduce specific evidence proving that existing technologies are less effective than the restrictions in COPA. The District Court made a specific factfinding that "[n]o evidence was presented to the Court as to the percentage of time that blocking and filtering technology is over- or underinclusive." *Ibid.* In the absence of a showing as to the relative effectiveness of COPA and the alternatives proposed by respondents, it was not an abuse of discretion for the District Court to grant the preliminary injunction. The Government's burden is not merely to show that a proposed less restrictive alternative has some flaws; its burden is to show that it is less effective. *Reno*, 521 U. S. at 874. It is not enough for the Government to show that COPA has some effect. Nor do respondents bear a burden to introduce, or offer to introduce, evidence that their proposed alternatives are more effective. The Government has the burden to show they are less so. The Government having failed to carry its burden, it was not an abuse of discretion for the District Court to grant the preliminary injunction.

One argument to the contrary is worth mentioning -- the argument that filtering software is not an available alternative because Congress may not require it to be used. That argument carries little weight, because Congress undoubtedly may act to encourage the use of filters. We have held that Congress can give strong incentives to schools and libraries to use them. *United States* v. *American Library Assn., Inc.*, 539 U.S. 194 (2003). It could also take steps to promote their development by industry, and their use by parents. It is incorrect, for that reason, to say that filters are part of the current regulatory status quo. The need for parental cooperation does not automatically disqualify a proposed less restrictive alternative. *Playboy Entertainment Group*, 529 U.S. at 824. ("A court should not assume a plausible, less restrictive alternative would be ineffective; and a court should not presume parents, given full information, will fail to act"). In enacting COPA, Congress said its goal was to prevent the "widespread availability of the Internet" from providing "opportunities for minors to access materials through the World Wide Web in a manner that can frustrate parental supervision or control." Congressional Findings, note following 47 U. S. C. § 231 (quoting Pub. L. 105-277, Tit. XIV, § 1402(1), 112 Stat. 2681-736). COPA presumes that parents lack the ability, not the will, to monitor what their children see. By enacting programs to promote use of filtering software, Congress could give parents that ability without subjecting protected speech to severe penalties.

    ... B

    There are also important practical reasons to let the injunction stand pending a full trial on the merits. First, the potential harms from reversing the injunction outweigh those of leaving it in place by mistake. Where a prosecution is a likely possibility, yet only an affirmative defense is available, speakers may self-censor rather than risk the perils of trial. There is a potential for extraordinary harm and a serious chill upon protected speech. *Cf. id.* at 817 ("Error in marking that line exacts an extraordinary cost"). The harm done from letting the injunction stand pending a trial on the merits, in contrast, will not be extensive. No prosecutions have yet been undertaken under the law, so none will be disrupted if the injunction stands. Further, if the injunction is upheld, the Government in the interim can enforce obscenity laws already on the books.

    Second, there are substantial factual disputes remaining in the case. As mentioned above, there is a serious gap in the evidence as to the effectiveness of filtering software. For us to assume, without proof, that filters are less effective than COPA would usurp the District Court's factfinding role. By allowing the preliminary injunction to stand and remanding for trial, we require the Government to shoulder its full constitutional burden of proof respecting the less restrictive alternative argument, rather than excuse it from doing so.

    Third, and on a related point, the factual record does not reflect current technological reality -- a serious flaw in any case involving the Internet. The technology of the Internet evolves at a rapid pace. Yet the factfindings of the District Court were entered in February 1999, over five years ago. Since then, certain facts about the Internet are known to have changed. *Compare, e.g.,* 31 F. Supp. 2d at 481 (36.7 million Internet hosts as of July 1998) *with* Internet Systems Consortium, *Internet Domain Survey,* Jan. 2004, http://www.isc.org/index.pl?/ops/ds (as visited June 22, 2004, and *available in* the Clerk of Court's case file) (233.1 million hosts as of Jan. 2004). It is reasonable to assume that other technological developments important to the First Amendment analysis have also occurred during that time. More and better filtering alternatives may exist than when the District Court entered its findings. Indeed, we know that after the District Court entered its factfindings, a congressionally appointed commission issued a report that found that filters are more effective than verification screens.

    Delay between the time that a district court makes factfindings and the time that a case reaches this Court is inevitable, with the necessary consequence that there will be some discrepancy between the facts as found and the facts at the time the appellate court takes up the question. *See, e.g.,* Benjamin, *Stepping into the Same River Twice: Rapidly Changing Facts and the Appellate Process,* 78 Texas L. Rev. 269, 290-296 (1999) (noting the problems presented for appellate courts by changing facts in the context of cases involving the Internet, and giving as a specific example the Court's decision in *Reno,* 521 U.S. 844). We do not mean, therefore, to set up an insuperable obstacle to fair review. Here, however, the usual gap has doubled because the case has been through the Court of Appeals twice. The additional two years might make a difference. By affirming the preliminary injunction and remanding for trial, we allow the parties to update and supplement the factual record to reflect current technological realities.

Remand will also permit the District Court to take account of a changed legal landscape. Since the District Court made its factfindings, Congress has passed at least two further statutes that might qualify as less restrictive alternatives to COPA -- a prohibition on misleading domain names, and a statute creating a minors-safe "Dot Kids" domain. Remanding for trial will allow the District Court to take into account those additional potential alternatives.

On a final point, it is important to note that this opinion does not hold that Congress is incapable of enacting any regulation of the Internet designed to prevent minors from gaining access to harmful materials. The parties, because of the conclusion of the Court of Appeals that the statute's definitions rendered it unconstitutional, did not devote their attention to the question whether further evidence might be introduced on the relative restrictiveness and effectiveness of alternatives to the statute. On remand, however, the parties will be able to introduce further evidence on this point. This opinion does not foreclose the District Court from concluding, upon a proper showing by the Government that meets the Government's constitutional burden as defined in this opinion, that COPA is the least restrictive alternative available to accomplish Congress' goal.

... On this record, the Government has not shown that the less restrictive alternatives proposed by respondents should be disregarded. Those alternatives, indeed, may be more effective than the provisions of COPA. The District Court did not abuse its discretion when it entered the preliminary injunction. The judgment of the Court of Appeals is affirmed, and the case is remanded for proceedings consistent with this opinion.

* * * * *

Applications of "Community Standards" to Internet Speech

insert the following after Notes and Questions # 7 on page 219 of Law of Internet Speech:

8. According to a children's charity, NCH (formerly National Children's Homes), evidence exists that the demand for child pornography on the Internet has led to an increase in sex abuse cases. The charity said that there had been a 1,500 percent increase in child pornography cases from 1988 to 1991, which would be reflected in more children being abused to produce pornographic pictures. *See Internet Porn "Increasing Child Abuse,"* Guardian Unlimited (Jan. 12, 2004), *available at* <http://www.guardian.co.uk/online/news/0,12597,1121316,00.html>. Does this statistic alone suggest the need for additional regulations and harsher penalties for on-line child pornography? Is more information needed

before inferences may be drawn between an increase in child pornography cases and the availability of pornographic content on the Internet? Is it possible that the availability of such content has enhanced the detection and apprehension of sex offenders?

* * * * *

Virtual Child Pornography

insert the following after Notes and Questions # 4 on page 239 of Law of Internet Speech:

JOHN D. ASHCROFT, ATTORNEY GENERAL, et al.,
PETITIONERS
v.
THE FREE SPEECH COALITION, et al.

Supreme Court of the United States

No. 00-795, 535 U.S. 234

April 16, 2002

JUSTICE KENNEDY delivered the opinion of the Court.

We consider in this case whether the Child Pornography Prevention Act of 1996 (CPPA), 18 U.S.C. § 2251, *et seq.,* abridges the freedom of speech. The CPPA extends the federal prohibition against child pornography to sexually explicit images that appear to depict minors but were produced without using any real children. The statute prohibits, in specific circumstances, possessing or distributing these images, which may be created by using adults who look like minors or by using computer imaging. The new technology, according to Congress, makes it possible to create realistic images of children who do not exist. *See* Congressional Findings, notes following 18 U.S.C. § 2251.

By prohibiting child pornography that does not depict an actual child, the statute goes beyond *New York* v. *Ferber*, 458 U.S. 747, 73 L.Ed.2d 1113, 102 S. Ct. 3348 (1982), which distinguished child pornography from other sexually explicit speech because of the State's interest in protecting the children exploited by the production process. *See id.* at 758. As a general rule, pornography can be banned only if obscene, but under *Ferber*, pornography showing minors can be proscribed whether or not the images are obscene under the definition set forth in *Miller* v. *California*, 413 U.S. 15, 37 L.Ed.2d 419, 93 S. Ct. 2607 (1973). *Ferber* recognized that "the *Miller* standard, like all general definitions of what may be banned as obscene, does not reflect the State's particular and more compelling interest in prosecuting those who promote the sexual exploitation of children." 458 U.S. at 761.

While we have not had occasion to consider the question, we may assume that the apparent age of persons engaged in sexual conduct is relevant to whether a depiction offends community standards. Pictures of young children engaged in certain acts might be obscene where similar depictions of adults, or perhaps even older adolescents, would not. The CPPA, however, is not directed at speech that is obscene; Congress has proscribed those materials through a separate statute. 18 U.S.C. §§ 1460-1466. Like the law in *Ferber*, the CPPA seeks to reach beyond obscenity, and it makes no attempt to conform to the *Miller* standard. For

175

instance, the statute would reach visual depictions, such as movies, even if they have redeeming social value.

The principal question to be resolved, then, is whether the CPPA is constitutional where it proscribes a significant universe of speech that is neither obscene under *Miller* nor child pornography under *Ferber*.

I.

Before 1996, Congress defined child pornography as the type of depictions at issue in *Ferber*, images made using actual minors. 18 U.S.C. § 2252 (1994 ed.). The CPPA retains that prohibition at 18 U.S.C. § 2256(8)(A) and adds three other prohibited categories of speech, of which the first, § 2256(8)(B), and the third, § 2256(8)(D), are at issue in this case. Section 2256(8)(B) prohibits "any visual depiction, including any photograph, film, video, picture, or computer or computer-generated image or picture" that "is, or appears to be, of a minor engaging in sexually explicit conduct." The prohibition on "any visual depiction" does not depend at all on how the image is produced. The section captures a range of depictions, sometimes called "virtual child pornography," which include computer-generated images, as well as images produced by more traditional means. For instance, the literal terms of the statute embrace a Renaissance painting depicting a scene from classical mythology, a "picture" that "appears to be, of a minor engaging in sexually explicit conduct." The statute also prohibits Hollywood movies, filmed without any child actors, if a jury believes an actor "appears to be" a minor engaging in "actual or simulated ... sexual intercourse." § 2256(2).

These images do not involve, let alone harm, any children in the production process; but Congress decided the materials threaten children in other, less direct, ways. Pedophiles might use the materials to encourage children to participate in sexual activity. "[A] child who is reluctant to engage in sexual activity with an adult, or to pose for sexually explicit photographs, can sometimes be convinced by viewing depictions of other children 'having fun' participating in such activity." Congressional Findings, note (3) following § 2251. Furthermore, pedophiles might "whet their own sexual appetites" with the pornographic images, "thereby increasing the creation and distribution of child pornography and the sexual abuse and exploitation of actual children." *Id.* notes (4), (10)(B). Under these rationales, harm flows from the content of the images, not from the means of their production. In addition, Congress identified another problem created by computer-generated images: Their existence can make it harder to prosecute pornographers who do use real minors. *See id.* note (6)(A). As imaging technology improves, Congress found, it becomes more difficult to prove that a particular picture was produced using actual children. To ensure that defendants possessing child pornography using real minors cannot evade prosecution, Congress extended the ban to virtual child pornography.

Section 2256(8)(C) prohibits a more common and lower tech means of creating virtual images, known as computer morphing. Rather than creating original images, pornographers can alter innocent pictures of real children so that the children appear to be engaged in sexual activity. Although morphed images may fall within the definition of virtual child pornography, they implicate the interests of real children and are in that sense closer to the images in *Ferber*. Respondents do not challenge this provision, and we do not consider it.

Respondents do challenge § 2256(8)(D). Like the text of the "appears to be" provision, the sweep of this provision is quite broad. Section 2256(8)(D) defines child pornography to include any sexually explicit image that was "advertised, promoted, presented, described, or distributed in such a manner that conveys the impression" it depicts "a minor engaging in sexually explicit conduct." One Committee Report identified the provision as directed at sexually explicit images pandered as child pornography. *See* S. Rep. No. 104-358, p. 22 (1996) ("This provision prevents child pornographers and pedophiles from exploiting prurient interests in child sexuality and sexual activity through the production or distribution of pornographic material which is intentionally pandered as child pornography"). The statute is not so limited in its reach, however, as it punishes even those possessors who took no part in pandering. Once a work has been described as child pornography, the taint remains on the speech in the hands of subsequent possessors, making possession unlawful even though the content otherwise would not be objectionable. ...

II.

The First Amendment commands, "Congress shall make no law ... abridging the freedom of speech." The government may violate this mandate in many ways, ... but a law imposing criminal penalties on protected speech is a stark example of speech suppression. The CPPA's penalties are indeed severe. A first offender may be imprisoned for 15 years. § 2252A(b)(1). A repeat offender faces a prison sentence of not less than 5 years and not more than 30 years in prison. *Ibid.* While even minor punishments can chill protected speech, *see Wooley v. Maynard,* 430 U.S. 705, 51 L.Ed.2d 752, 97 S. Ct. 1428 (1977), this case provides a textbook example of why we permit facial challenges to statutes that burden expression. With these severe penalties in force, few legitimate movie producers or book publishers, or few other speakers in any capacity, would risk distributing images in or near the uncertain reach of this law. The Constitution gives significant protection from overbroad laws that chill speech within the First Amendment's vast and privileged sphere. Under this principle, the CPPA is unconstitutional on its face if it prohibits a substantial amount of protected expression. *See Broadrick v. Oklahoma,* 413 U.S. 601, 612, 37 L.Ed.2d 830, 93 S. Ct. 2908 (1973).

The sexual abuse of a child is a most serious crime and an act repugnant to the moral instincts of a decent people. In its legislative findings, Congress recognized that there are subcultures of persons who harbor illicit desires for children and commit criminal acts to gratify the impulses. *See* Congressional Findings, notes following § 2251; *see also* U.S. Dept. of Health and Human Services, Administration on Children, Youth and Families, Child Maltreatment 1999 (estimating that 93,000 children were victims of sexual abuse in 1999). Congress also found that surrounding the serious offenders are those who flirt with these impulses and trade pictures and written accounts of sexual activity with young children.

Congress may pass valid laws to protect children from abuse, and it has. *E.g.,* 18 U.S.C. §§ 2241, 2251. The prospect of crime, however, by itself does not justify laws suppressing protected speech. *See Kingsley Int'l Pictures Corp. v. Regents of Univ. of N.Y.,* 360 U.S. 684, 689, 3 L.Ed.2d 1512, 79 S. Ct. 1362 (1959) ("Among free men, the deterrents ordinarily to be applied to prevent crime are education and punishment for violations of the law, not abridgment of the rights of free speech") (internal quotation marks and citation omitted)). It is also well established that speech may not be prohibited because it concerns subjects offending our sensibilities. *See FCC v. Pacifica Foundation,* 438 U.S. 726, 745, 57 L.Ed.2d 1073, 98 S. Ct. 3026 (1978) ("The fact that society may find speech offensive is not a sufficient reason for suppressing it"); *see also Reno v. American Civil Liberties Union,* 521 U.S. 844, 874, 117 S. Ct. 2329, 138 L.Ed.2d 874 (1997) ("In evaluating the free speech rights of adults, we have made it perfectly clear that 'sexual expression which is indecent but not obscene is protected by the First Amendment'") (quoting *Sable Communications of Cal., Inc.*

v. *FCC,* 492 U.S. 115, 126, 106 L.Ed.2d 93, 109 S. Ct. 2829 (1989); *Carey v. Population Services Int'l,* 431 U.S. 678, 701, 52 L.Ed.2d 675, 97 S. Ct. 2010 (1977) ("The fact that protected speech may be offensive to some does not justify its suppression").

As a general principle, the First Amendment bars the government from dictating what we see or read or speak or hear. The freedom of speech has its limits; it does not embrace certain categories of speech, including defamation, incitement, obscenity, and pornography produced with real children. *See Simon & Schuster, Inc.* v. *Members of N.Y. State Crime Victims Bd.,* 502 U.S. 105, 127, 116 L.Ed.2d 476, 112 S. Ct. 501 (1991) (KENNEDY, J., concurring). While these categories may be prohibited without violating the First Amendment, none of them includes the speech prohibited by the CPPA. In his dissent from the opinion of the Court of Appeals, Judge Ferguson recognized this to be the law and proposed that virtual child pornography should be regarded as an additional category of unprotected speech. *See* 198 F.3d at 1101. It would be necessary for us to take this step to uphold the statute.

As we have noted, the CPPA is much more than a supplement to the existing federal prohibition on obscenity. Under *Miller* v. *California,* 413 U.S. 15, 37 L.Ed.2d 419, 93 S. Ct. 2607 (1973), the Government must prove that the work, taken as a whole, appeals to the prurient interest, is patently offensive in light of community standards, and lacks serious literary, artistic, political, or scientific value. *Id.* at 24. The CPPA, however, extends to images that appear to depict a minor engaging in sexually explicit activity without regard to the *Miller* requirements. The materials need not appeal to the prurient interest. Any depiction of sexually explicit activity, no matter how it is presented, is proscribed. The CPPA applies to a picture in a psychology manual, as well as a movie depicting the horrors of sexual abuse. It is not necessary, moreover, that the image be patently offensive. Pictures of what appear to be 17-year-olds engaging in sexually explicit activity do not in every case contravene community standards.

The CPPA prohibits speech despite its serious literary, artistic, political, or scientific value. The statute proscribes the visual depiction of an idea -- that of teenagers engaging in sexual activity -- that is a fact of modern society and has been a theme in art and literature throughout the ages. Under the CPPA, images are prohibited so long as the persons appear to be under 18 years of age. 18 U.S.C. § 2256(1). This is higher than the legal age for marriage in many States, as well as the age at which persons may consent to sexual relations. *See* § 2243(a) (age of consent in the federal maritime and territorial jurisdiction is 16); *U.S. National Survey of State Laws* 384-388 (R. Leiter ed., 3d ed. 1999) (48 States permit 16-year-olds to marry with parental consent); W. Eskridge & N. Hunter, *Sexuality, Gender, and the Law* 1021-1022 (1997) (in 39 States and the District of Columbia, the age of consent is 16 or younger). It is, of course, undeniable that some youths engage in sexual activity before the legal age, either on their own inclination or because they are victims of sexual abuse.

Both themes -- teenage sexual activity and the sexual abuse of children -- have inspired countless literary works. William Shakespeare created the most famous pair of teenage lovers, one of whom is just 13 years of age. *See Romeo and Juliet*, act I, sc. 2, l. 9 ("She hath not seen the change of fourteen years"). In the drama, Shakespeare portrays the relationship as something splendid and innocent, but not juvenile. The work has inspired no less than 40 motion pictures, some of which suggest that the teenagers consummated their relationship. *E.g., Romeo and Juliet* (B. Luhrmann director, 1996). Shakespeare may not have written sexually explicit scenes for the Elizabethan audience, but were modern directors to adopt a less conventional approach, that fact alone would not compel the conclusion that the work was obscene.

Contemporary movies pursue similar themes. Last year's Academy Awards featured the movie *Traffic,* which was nominated for Best Picture. *See Predictable and Less So, the Academy Award Contenders,* N.Y. Times, Feb. 14, 2001, p. E11. The film portrays a teenager, identified as a 16-year-old, who becomes addicted to drugs. The viewer sees the degradation of her addiction, which in the end leads her to a filthy room to trade sex for drugs. The year before, *American Beauty* won the Academy Award for Best Picture. *See "American Beauty" Tops the Oscars,* N.Y. Times, Mar. 27, 2000, p. E1. In the course of the movie, a teenage girl engages in sexual relations with her teenage boyfriend, and another yields herself to the gratification of a middle-aged man. The film also contains a scene where, although the movie audience understands the act is not taking place, one character believes he is watching a teenage boy performing a sexual act on an older man.

Our society, like other cultures, has empathy and enduring fascination with the lives and destinies of the young. Art and literature express the vital interest we all have in the formative years we ourselves once knew, when wounds can be so grievous, disappointment so profound, and mistaken choices so tragic, but when moral acts and self-fulfillment are still in reach. Whether or not the films we mention violate the CPPA, they explore themes within the wide sweep of the statute's prohibitions. If these films, or hundreds of others of lesser note that explore those subjects, contain a single graphic depiction of sexual activity within the statutory definition, the possessor of the film would be subject to severe punishment without inquiry into the work's redeeming value. This is inconsistent with an essential First Amendment rule: The artistic merit of a work does not depend on the presence of a single explicit scene. *See Book Named "John Cleland's Memoirs of a Woman of Pleasure" v. Attorney General of Mass.,* 383 U.S. 413, 419, 16 L.Ed.2d 1, 86 S. Ct. 975 (1966) (plurality opinion) ("The social value of the book can neither be weighed against nor canceled by its prurient appeal or patent offensiveness"). Under *Miller,* the First Amendment requires that redeeming value be judged by considering the work as a whole. Where the scene is part of the narrative, the work itself does not for this reason become obscene, even though the scene in isolation might be offensive. *See Kois v. Wisconsin,* 408 U.S. 229, 231, 33 L.Ed.2d 312, 92 S. Ct. 2245 (1972) *(per curiam).* For this reason, and the others we have noted, the CPPA cannot be read to prohibit obscenity, because it lacks the required link between its prohibitions and the affront to community standards prohibited by the definition of obscenity.

The Government seeks to address this deficiency by arguing that speech prohibited by the CPPA is virtually indistinguishable from child pornography, which may be banned without regard to whether it depicts works of value. *See New York v. Ferber,* 458 U.S. at 761. Where the images are themselves the product of child sexual abuse, *Ferber* recognized that the State had an interest in stamping it out without regard to any judgment about its content. *Id.* at 761, n.12; *see also id.* at 775 (O'CONNOR, J., concurring) ("As drafted, New York's statute does not attempt to suppress the communication of particular ideas"). The production of the work, not its content, was the target of the statute. The fact that a work contained serious literary, artistic, or other value did not excuse the harm it caused to its child participants. It was simply "unrealistic to equate a community's toleration for sexually oriented materials with the permissible scope of legislation aimed at protecting children from sexual exploitation." *Id.* at 761, n.12.

Ferber upheld a prohibition on the distribution and sale of child pornography, as well as its production, because these acts were "intrinsically related" to the sexual abuse of children in two ways. *Id.* at 759. First, as a permanent record of a child's abuse, the continued circulation itself would harm the child who had participated. Like a defamatory statement, each new publication of the speech would cause new injury to the child's reputation and emotional well-being. *See id.* at 759, and n.10. Second, because the traffic in child pornography was an economic motive for its production, the State had an interest in closing the distribution network. "The most expeditious if not the only practical method of law enforcement may be to dry up the market for this material by imposing severe criminal penalties on persons selling, advertising, or otherwise promoting the product." *Id.* at 760. Under either rationale, the speech had what the Court in effect held was a proximate link to the crime from which it came.

Later, in *Osborne* v. *Ohio*, 495 U.S. 103, 109 L.Ed.2d 98, 110 S. Ct. 1691 (1990), the Court ruled that these same interests justified a ban on the possession of pornography produced by using children. ... *Osborne* also noted the State's interest in preventing child pornography from being used as an aid in the solicitation of minors. *Id.* at 111. The Court, however, anchored its holding in the concern for the participants, those whom it called the "victims of child pornography." *Id.* at 110. It did not suggest that, absent this concern, other governmental interests would suffice.

In contrast to the speech in *Ferber*, speech that itself is the record of sexual abuse, the CPPA prohibits speech that records no crime and creates no victims by its production. Virtual child pornography is not "intrinsically related" to the sexual abuse of children, as were the materials in *Ferber*. 458 U.S. at 759. While the Government asserts that the images can lead to actual instances of child abuse, the causal link is contingent and indirect. The harm does not necessarily follow from the speech, but depends upon some unquantified potential for subsequent criminal acts.

The Government says these indirect harms are sufficient because, as *Ferber* acknowledged, child pornography rarely can be valuable speech. *See* 458 U.S. at 762 ("The value of permitting live performances and photographic reproductions of children engaged in lewd sexual conduct is exceedingly modest, if not *de minimis*"). This argument, however, suffers from two flaws. First, *Ferber's* judgment about child pornography was based upon how it was made, not on what it communicated. The case reaffirmed that where the speech is neither obscene nor the product of sexual abuse, it does not fall outside the protection of the First Amendment. *See id.* at 764-765 ("The distribution of descriptions or other depictions of sexual conduct, not otherwise obscene, which do not involve live performance or photographic or other visual reproduction of live performances, retains First Amendment protection").

The second flaw in the Government's position is that *Ferber* did not hold that child pornography is by definition without value. On the contrary, the Court recognized some works in this category might have significant value, *see id.* at 761, but relied on virtual images -- the very images prohibited by the CPPA -- as an alternative and permissible means of expression: "If it were necessary for literary or artistic value, a person over the statutory age who perhaps looked younger could be utilized. Simulation outside of the prohibition of the statute could provide another alternative." *Id.* at 763. *Ferber,* then, not only referred to the distinction between actual and virtual child pornography, it relied on it as a reason supporting its holding. *Ferber* provides no support for a statute that eliminates the distinction and makes the alternative mode criminal as well.

III.

The CPPA, for reasons we have explored, is inconsistent with *Miller* and finds no support in *Ferber*. The Government seeks to justify its prohibitions in other ways. It argues that the CPPA is necessary because pedophiles may use virtual child pornography to seduce children. There are many things innocent in themselves, however, such as cartoons, video games, and candy, that might be used for immoral purposes, yet we would not expect those to be prohibited because they can be misused. The Government, of course, may punish adults who provide unsuitable materials to children, *see Ginsberg* v. *New York*, 390 U.S. 629, 20 L.Ed.2d 195, 88 S. Ct. 1274 (1968), and it may enforce criminal penalties for unlawful solicitation. The precedents establish, however, that speech within the rights of adults to hear may not be silenced completely in an attempt to shield children from it. *See Sable Communications of Cal., Inc.* v. *FCC,* 492 U.S. 115, 106 L.Ed.2d 93, 109 S. Ct. 2829 (1989). In *Butler* v. *Michigan*, 352 U.S. 380, 381, 1 L.Ed.2d 412, 77 S. Ct. 524 (1957), the Court invalidated a statute prohibiting distribution of an indecent publication because of its tendency to "incite minors to violent or depraved or immoral acts." A unanimous Court agreed upon the important First Amendment principle that the State could not "reduce the adult population ... to reading only what is fit for children." *Id.* at 383. We have reaffirmed this holding. *See United States* v. *Playboy Entertainment Group, Inc.,* 529 U.S. 803, 814, 146 L.Ed.2d 865, 120 S. Ct. 1878 (2000) ("The objective of shielding children does not suffice to support a blanket ban if the protection can be accomplished by a less restrictive alternative"); *Reno* v. *American Civil Liberties Union,* 521 U.S. at 875 (The "governmental interest in protecting children from harmful materials ... does not justify an unnecessarily broad suppression of speech addressed to adults"); *Sable Communications* v. *FCC,* 492 U.S. at 130-131 (striking down a ban on "dial-a-porn" messages that had "the invalid effect of limiting the content of adult telephone conversations to that which is suitable for children to hear").

Here, the Government wants to keep speech from children not to protect them from its content but to protect them from those who would commit other crimes. The principle, however, remains the same: The Government cannot ban speech fit for adults simply because it may fall into the hands of children. The evil in question depends upon the actor's unlawful conduct, conduct defined as criminal quite apart from any link to the speech in question. This establishes that the speech ban is not narrowly drawn. The objective is to prohibit illegal conduct, but this restriction goes well beyond that interest by restricting the speech available to law-abiding adults.

The Government submits further that virtual child pornography whets the appetites of pedophiles and encourages them to engage in illegal conduct. This rationale cannot sustain the provision in question. The mere tendency of speech to encourage unlawful acts is not a sufficient reason for banning it. The government "cannot constitutionally premise legislation on the desirability of controlling a person's private thoughts." *Stanley* v. *Georgia*, 394 U.S. 557, 566, 22 L.Ed.2d 542, 89 S. Ct. 1243 (1969). First Amendment freedoms are most in danger when the government seeks to control thought or to justify its laws for that impermissible end. The right to think is the beginning of freedom, and speech must be protected from the government because speech is the beginning of thought.

To preserve these freedoms, and to protect speech for its own sake, the Court's First Amendment cases draw vital distinctions between words and deeds, between ideas and conduct. *See Kingsley Int'l Pictures Corp.*, 360 U.S. at 689; *see also Bartnicki* v. *Vopper*, 532 U.S. 514, 529, 149 L.Ed.2d 787, 121 S. Ct. 1753 (2001) ("The normal method of deterring unlawful conduct is to impose an appropriate punishment on the person who engages in it"). The government may not prohibit speech because it increases the chance an unlawful act will be committed "at some indefinite future time." *Hess v. Indiana,* 414 U.S. 105, 108, 38 L.Ed.2d 303, 94 S. Ct. 326 (1973) *(per curiam)*. The government may suppress speech for advocating the use of force or a violation of law only if "such advocacy is directed to inciting or producing imminent lawless action and is likely to incite or produce such action." *Brandenburg v. Ohio,* 395 U.S. 444, 447, 23 L.Ed.2d 430, 89 S. Ct. 1827 (1969) *(per curiam)*. There is here no attempt, incitement, solicitation, or conspiracy. The Government has shown no more than a remote connection between speech that might encourage thoughts or impulses and any resulting child abuse. Without a significantly stronger, more direct connection, the Government may not prohibit speech on the ground that it may encourage pedophiles to engage in illegal conduct.

The Government next argues that its objective of eliminating the market for pornography produced using real children necessitates a prohibition on virtual images as well. Virtual images, the Government contends, are indistinguishable from real ones; they are part of the same market and are often exchanged. In this way, it is said, virtual images promote the trafficking in works produced through the exploitation of real children. The hypothesis is somewhat implausible. If virtual images were identical to illegal child pornography, the illegal images would be driven from the market by the indistinguishable substitutes. Few pornographers would risk prosecution by abusing real children if fictional, computerized images would suffice.

In the case of the material covered by *Ferber*, the creation of the speech is itself the crime of child abuse; the prohibition deters the crime by removing the profit motive. *See Osborne*, 495 U.S. at 109-110. Even where there is an underlying crime, however, the Court has not allowed the suppression of speech in all cases. *E.g., Bartnicki, supra*, at 529 (market deterrence would not justify law prohibiting a radio commentator from distributing speech that had been unlawfully intercepted). We need not consider where to strike the balance in this case, because here, there is no underlying crime at all. Even if the Government's market deterrence theory were persuasive in some contexts, it would not justify this statute.

Finally, the Government says that the possibility of producing images by using computer imaging makes it very difficult for it to prosecute those who produce pornography by using real children. Experts, we are told, may have difficulty in saying whether the pictures were made by using real children or by using computer imaging. The necessary solution, the argument runs, is to prohibit both kinds of images. The argument, in essence, is that protected speech may be banned as a means to ban unprotected speech. This analysis turns the First Amendment upside down.

The Government may not suppress lawful speech as the means to suppress unlawful speech. Protected speech does not become unprotected merely because it resembles the latter. The Constitution requires the reverse. "The possible harm to society in permitting some unprotected speech to go unpunished is outweighed by the possibility that protected speech of others may be muted...." *Broadrick v. Oklahoma,* 413 U.S. at 612. The overbreadth doctrine prohibits the Government from banning unprotected speech if a substantial amount of protected speech is prohibited or chilled in the process.

To avoid the force of this objection, the Government would have us read the CPPA not as a measure suppressing speech but as a law shifting the burden to the accused to prove the speech is lawful. In this connection, the Government relies on an affirmative defense under the statute, which allows a defendant to avoid conviction for nonpossession offenses by showing that the materials were produced using only adults and were not otherwise distributed in a manner conveying the impression that they depicted real children. *See* 18 U.S.C. § 2252A(c).

The Government raises serious constitutional difficulties by seeking to impose on the defendant the burden of proving his speech is not unlawful. An affirmative defense applies only after prosecution has begun, and the speaker must himself prove, on pain of a felony conviction, that his conduct falls within the affirmative defense. In cases under the CPPA, the evidentiary burden is not trivial. Where the defendant is not the producer of the work, he may have no way of establishing the identity, or even the existence, of the actors. If the evidentiary issue is a serious problem for the Government, as it asserts, it will be at least as difficult for the innocent possessor. The statute, moreover, applies to work created before 1996, and the producers themselves may not have preserved the records necessary to meet the burden of proof. Failure to establish the defense can lead to a felony conviction.

We need not decide, however, whether the Government could impose this burden on a speaker. Even if an affirmative defense can save a statute from First Amendment challenge, here the defense is incomplete and insufficient, even on its own terms. It allows persons to be convicted in some instances where they can prove children were not exploited in the production. A defendant charged with possessing, as opposed to distributing, proscribed works may not defend on the ground that the film depicts only adult actors. *See ibid.* So while the affirmative defense may protect a movie producer from prosecution for the act of distribution, that same producer, and all other persons in the subsequent distribution chain, could be liable for possessing the prohibited work. Furthermore, the affirmative defense provides no protection to persons who produce speech by using computer imaging, or through other means that do not involve the use of adult actors who appear to be minors. *See ibid.* In these cases, the defendant can demonstrate no children were harmed in producing the images, yet the affirmative defense would not bar the prosecution. For this reason, the affirmative defense cannot save the statute, for it leaves unprotected a substantial amount of speech not tied to the Government's interest in distinguishing images produced using real children from virtual ones.

In sum, § 2256(8)(B) covers materials beyond the categories recognized in *Ferber* and *Miller*, and the reasons the Government offers in support of limiting the freedom of speech have no justification in our precedents or in the law of the First Amendment. The provision abridges the freedom to engage in a substantial amount of lawful speech. For this reason, it is overbroad and unconstitutional. ...

V.

For the reasons we have set forth, the prohibition[ ] of ... § 2256(8)(B)[a] ... overbroad and unconstitutional. Having reached this conclusion, we need not address respondents' further contention that the provision[ ] is ... unconstitutional because of vague statutory language.

The judgment of the Court of Appeals is affirmed.

CHIEF JUSTICE REHNQUIST, with whom JUSTICE SCALIA joins in part, dissenting.

... Congress has a compelling interest in ensuring the ability to enforce prohibitions of actual child pornography, and we should defer to its findings that rapidly advancing technology soon will make it all but impossible to do so. *Turner Broadcasting System, Inc. v. FCC,* 520 U.S. 180, 195, 137 L.Ed.2d 369, 117 S. Ct. 1174 (1997) (we "accord substantial deference to the predictive judgment of Congress" in First Amendment cases).

I also agree with JUSTICE O'CONNOR that serious First Amendment concerns would arise were the Government ever to prosecute someone for simple distribution or possession of a film with literary or artistic value, such as "*Traffic*" or "*American Beauty*." I write separately, however, because the Child Pornography Prevention Act of 1996 (CPPA), 18 U.S.C. § 2251, *et seq.,* need not be construed to reach such materials.

We normally do not strike down a statute on First Amendment grounds "when a limiting instruction has been or could be placed on the challenged statute." *Broadrick v. Oklahoma,* 413 U.S. 601, 613, 37 L.Ed.2d 830, 93 S. Ct. 2908 (1973). *See, e.g., New York v. Ferber,* 458 U.S. 747, 769, 73 L.Ed.2d 1113, 102 S. Ct. 3348 (1982) (appreciating "the wide-reaching effects of striking down a statute on its face"); *Parker* v. *Levy,* 417 U.S. 733, 760, 41 L.Ed.2d 439, 94 S. Ct. 2547 (1974) ("This Court has ... repeatedly expressed its reluctance to strike down a statute on its face where there were a substantial number of situations to which it might be validly applied"). This case should be treated no differently.

Other than computer generated images that are virtually indistinguishable from real children engaged in sexually explicitly conduct, the CPPA can be limited so as not to reach any material that was not already unprotected before the CPPA. The CPPA's definition of "sexually explicit conduct" is quite explicit in this regard. It makes clear that the statute only reaches "visual depictions" of:

> Actual or simulated ... sexual intercourse, including genital-genital, oral-genital, anal-genital, or oral-anal, whether between persons of the same or opposite sex; ... bestiality; ... masturbation; ... sadistic or masochistic abuse; ... or lascivious exhibition of the genitals or pubic area of any person.

18 U.S.C. § 2256(2).

The Court and JUSTICE O'CONNOR suggest that this very graphic definition reaches the depiction of youthful looking adult actors engaged in suggestive sexual activity, presumably because the definition extends to "simulated" intercourse. (majority opinion); (opinion concurring in judgment in part and dissenting in part). Read as a whole, however, I think the definition reaches only the sort of "hard core of child pornography" that we found without protection in *Ferber,* 485 U.S. at 773-774. So construed, the CPPA bans visual depictions of youthful looking adult actors engaged in *actual* sexual activity; mere *suggestions* of sexual activity, such as youthful looking adult actors squirming under a blanket, are more akin to written descriptions than visual depictions, and thus fall outside the purview of the statute.

The reference to "simulated" has been part of the definition of "sexually explicit conduct" since the statute was first passed. *See* Protection of Children Against Sexual Exploitation Act of 1977, Pub. L. 92-225, 92 Stat. 8. But the inclusion of "simulated" conduct, alongside "actual" conduct, does not change the "hard core" nature of the image banned. The reference to "simulated" conduct simply brings within the statute's reach depictions of hard core pornography that are "made to look genuine," *Webster's Ninth New Collegiate Dictionary* 1099 (1983) -- including the main target of the CPPA, computer generated images virtually indistinguishable from real children engaged in sexually explicit conduct. Neither actual conduct nor simulated conduct, however, is properly construed to reach depictions such as those in a film portrayal of *Romeo and Juliet*, which are far removed from the hard core pornographic depictions that Congress intended to reach.

Indeed, we should be loath to construe a statute as banning film portrayals of Shakespearian tragedies, without some indication -- from text or legislative history -- that such a result was intended. In fact, Congress explicitly instructed that such a reading of the CPPA would be wholly unwarranted. ...

This narrow reading of "sexually explicit conduct" not only accords with the text of the CPPA and the intentions of Congress; it is exactly how the phrase was understood prior to the broadening gloss the Court gives it today. Indeed, had "sexually explicit conduct" been thought to reach the sort of material the Court says it does, then films such as *"Traffic"* and *"American Beauty"* would not have been made the way they were. *"Traffic"* won its Academy Award in 2001. *"American Beauty"* won its Academy Award in 2000. But the CPPA has been on the books, and has been enforced, since 1996. The chill felt by the Court ("Few legitimate movie producers ... would risk distributing images in or near the uncertain reach of this law") has apparently never been felt by those who actually make movies.

To the extent the CPPA prohibits possession or distribution of materials that "convey the impression" of a child engaged in sexually explicit conduct, that prohibition can and should be limited to reach "the sordid business of pandering" which lies outside the bounds of First Amendment protection. *Ginzburg v. United States*, 383 U.S. 463, 467, 16 L.Ed.2d 31, 86 S. Ct. 942 (1966); *e.g., id.* at 472 (conduct that "deliberately emphasized the sexually provocative aspects of the work, in order to catch the salaciously disposed" may lose First Amendment protection); *United States v. Playboy Entertainment Group, Inc.*, 529 U.S. 803, 831-832, 146 L.Ed.2d 865, 120 S. Ct. 1878 (2000) (SCALIA, J., dissenting) (collecting cases). This is how the Government asks us to construe the statute, and it is the most plausible reading of the text, which prohibits only materials *"advertised, promoted, presented, described, or distributed in such a manner* that conveys the impression that the material is or contains a visual depiction of a minor engaging in sexually explicit conduct." 18 U.S.C. § 2256(8)(D) (emphasis added).

The First Amendment may protect the video shop owner or film distributor who promotes material as "entertaining" or "acclaimed" regardless of whether the material contains depictions of youthful looking adult actors engaged in nonobscene but sexually suggestive conduct. The First Amendment does not, however, protect the panderer. Thus, materials promoted as conveying the impression that they depict actual minors engaged in sexually explicit conduct do not escape regulation merely because they might warrant First Amendment protection if promoted in a different manner. *See Ginzburg*, 383 U.S. at 474-476; *cf. Jacobellis v. Ohio*, 378 U.S. 184, 201, 12 L.Ed.2d 793, 84 S. Ct. 1676 (1964) (Warren, C.J., dissenting) ("In my opinion, the use to which various materials are put -- not just the words and pictures themselves -- must be considered in determining whether or not the materials are obscene"). I would construe "conveys the impression" as limited to the panderer, which makes the statute entirely consistent with *Ginzburg* and other cases.

The Court says that "conveys the impression" goes well beyond *Ginzburg* to "prohibit [the] possession of material described, or pandered, as child pornography by someone earlier in the distribution chain." The Court's concern is that an individual who merely possesses protected materials (such as videocassettes of "*Traffic*" or "*American Beauty*") might offend the CPPA regardless of whether the individual actually intended to possess materials containing unprotected images.

This concern is a legitimate one, but there is, again, no need or reason to construe the statute this way. In *X-Citement Video, supra*, we faced a provision of the Protection of Children Against Sexual Exploitation Act of 1977, the precursor to the CPPA, which lent itself much less than the present statute to attributing a "knowingly" requirement to the contents of the possessed visual depictions. We held that such a requirement nonetheless applied, so that the Government would have to prove that a person charged with possessing child pornography actually knew that the materials contained depictions of real minors engaged in sexually explicit conduct. 513 U.S. at 77-78. In light of this holding, and consistent with the narrow class of images the CPPA is intended to prohibit, the CPPA can be construed to prohibit only the knowing possession of materials actually containing visual depictions of real minors engaged in sexually explicit conduct, or computer generated images virtually indistinguishable from real minors engaged in sexually explicit conduct. The mere possession of materials containing only suggestive depictions of youthful looking adult actors need not be so included.

In sum, while potentially impermissible applications of the CPPA may exist, I doubt that they would be "substantial ... in relation to the statute's plainly legitimate sweep." *Broadrick*, 413 U.S. at 615. The aim of ensuring the enforceability of our Nation's child pornography laws is a compelling one. The CPPA is targeted to this aim by extending the definition of child pornography to reach computer-generated images that are virtually indistinguishable from real children engaged in sexually explicit conduct. The statute need not be read to do any more than precisely this, which is not offensive to the First Amendment.

For these reasons, I would construe the CPPA in a manner consistent with the First Amendment, reverse the Court of Appeals' judgment, and uphold the statute in its entirety.

* * * * *

add the following at the end of the first paragraph of Notes and Questions # 2 on page 267 of Law of Internet Speech:

With respect to the U.S. Supreme Court's ruling regarding the constitutionality of the Children's Internet Protection Act; *see* Supplement *infra* at 187.

* * * * *

Filtering Devices

substitute the following for the first paragraph of Notes and Questions # 2 on page 267 of Law of Internet Speech:

UNITED STATES, *et al.*, APPELLANTS

v.

AMERICAN LIBRARY ASSOCIATION, INC., *et al.*.

Supreme Court of the United States

No. 02-361, 539 U.S. 194

June 23, 2003

CHIEF JUSTICE REHNQUIST announced the judgment of the Court and delivered an opinion, in which JUSTICE O'CONNOR, JUSTICE SCALIA, and JUSTICE THOMAS joined.

To address the problems associated with the availability of Internet pornography in public libraries, Congress enacted the Children's Internet Protection Act (CIPA), 114 Stat. 2763A-335. Under CIPA, a public library may not receive federal assistance to provide Internet access unless it installs software to block images that constitute obscenity or child pornography, and to prevent minors from obtaining access to material that is harmful to them. The District Court held these provisions facially invalid on the ground that they induce public libraries to violate patrons' First Amendment rights. We now reverse.

To help public libraries provide their patrons with Internet access, Congress offers two forms of federal assistance. First, the E-rate program established by the Telecommunications Act of 1996 entitles qualifying libraries to buy Internet access at a discount. 110 Stat. 71, 47 U.S.C. § 254(h)(1)(B). In the year ending June 30, 2002, libraries received $58.5 million in such discounts. Second, pursuant to the Library Services and Technology Act (LSTA), 110 Stat. 3009-295, as amended, 20 U.S.C. § 9101, *et seq.*, the Institute of Museum and Library Services makes grants to state library administrative agencies to "electronically link libraries with educational, social, or information services," "assist libraries in accessing information through electronic networks," and "pay costs for libraries to acquire or share computer systems and telecommunications technologies." §§ 9141(a)(1)(B), (C), (E). In fiscal year 2002, Congress appropriated more than $149 million in LSTA grants. These programs have succeeded greatly in bringing Internet access to public libraries: By 2000, 95% of the Nation's libraries provided public Internet access.

By connecting to the Internet, public libraries provide patrons with a vast amount of valuable information. But there is also an enormous amount of pornography on the Internet, much of which is easily obtained. The accessibility of this material has created serious problems for libraries, which have found that patrons of all ages, including minors, regularly search for online pornography. Some patrons also expose others to pornographic images by leaving them displayed on Internet terminals or printed at library printers.

Upon discovering these problems, Congress became concerned that the E-rate and LSTA programs were facilitating access to illegal and harmful pornography. S. Rep. No. 105-226,

p. 5 (1998). Congress learned that adults "use library computers to access pornography that is then exposed to staff, passersby, and children," and that "minors access child and adult pornography in libraries."[1]

But Congress also learned that filtering software that blocks access to pornographic Web sites could provide a reasonably effective way to prevent such uses of library resources. *Id.* at 20-26. By 2000, before Congress enacted CIPA, almost 17% of public libraries used such software on at least some of their Internet terminals, and 7% had filters on all of them. Library Research Center of U. Ill., *Survey of Internet Access Management in Public Libraries* 8, http://alexia.lis.uiuc.edu/gslis/research/internet.pdf. A library can set such software to block categories of material, such as "Pornography" or "Violence." When a patron tries to view a site that falls within such a category, a screen appears indicating that the site is blocked. But a filter set to block pornography may sometimes block other sites that present neither obscene nor pornographic material, but that nevertheless trigger the filter. To minimize this problem, a library can set its software to prevent the blocking of material that falls into categories like "Education," "History," and "Medical." A library may also add or delete specific sites from a blocking category, and anyone can ask companies that furnish filtering software to unblock particular sites.

Responding to this information, Congress enacted CIPA. It provides that a library may not receive E-rate or LSTA assistance unless it has "a policy of Internet safety for minors that includes the operation of a technology protection measure ... that protects against access" by all persons to "visual depictions" that constitute "obscenity" or "child pornography," and that protects against access by minors to "visual depictions" that are "harmful to minors." 20 U.S.C. §§ 134(f)(1)(A)(i) and (B)(i); 47 U.S.C. §§ 254(h)(6)(B)(i) and (C)(i). The statute defines a "technology protection measure" as "a specific technology that blocks or filters Internet access to material covered by" CIPA. § 254(h)(7)(I). CIPA also permits the library to "disable" the filter "to enable access for *bona fide* research or other lawful purposes." 20 U.S.C. § 9134(f)(3); 47 U.S.C. § 254(h)(6)(D). Under the E-rate program, disabling is permitted "during use by an adult." § 254(h)(6)(D). Under the LSTA program, disabling is permitted during use by any person. 20 U.S.C. § 9134(f)(3).

Appellees are a group of libraries, library associations, library patrons, and Web site publishers, including the American Library Association (ALA) and the Multnomah County Public Library in Portland, Oregon (Multnomah). They sued the United States and the Government agencies and officials responsible for administering the E-rate and LSTA programs in District Court, challenging the constitutionality of CIPA's filtering provisions. ...

---

[1] The Children's Internet Protection Act: Hearing on S. 97 before the Senate Committee on Commerce, Science, and Transportation, 106th Cong., 1st Sess., 49 (1999) (prepared statement of Bruce Taylor, President and Chief Counsel, National Law Center for Children and Families). *See also Obscene Material Available Via The Internet: Hearing before the Subcommittee on Telecommunications,* Trade, and Consumer Protection of the House Committee on Commerce, 106th Cong., 2d Sess. 1, 27 (2000) (citing D. Burt, *Dangerous Access, 2000 Edition: Uncovering Internet Pornography in America's Libraries* (2000)) (noting more than 2,000 incidents of patrons, both adults and minors, using library computers to view online pornography, including obscenity and child pornography).

Congress has wide latitude to attach conditions to the receipt of federal assistance in order to further its policy objectives. *South Dakota v. Dole,* 483 U.S. 203, 206, 97 L.Ed.2d 171, 107 S. Ct. 2793 (1987). But Congress may not "induce" the recipient "to engage in activities that would themselves be unconstitutional." *Id.* at 210. To determine whether libraries would violate the First Amendment by employing the filtering software that CIPA requires, we must first examine the role of libraries in our society. ...

We have held in two analogous contexts that the government has broad discretion to make content-based judgments in deciding what private speech to make available to the public. In *Arkansas Ed. Television Comm'n v. Forbes,* 523 U.S. 666, 672-673, 140 L.Ed. 2d 875, 118 S. Ct. 1633 (1998), we held that public forum principles do not generally apply to a public television station's editorial judgments regarding the private speech it presents to its viewers. "Broad rights of access for outside speakers would be antithetical, as a general rule, to the discretion that stations and their editorial staff must exercise to fulfill their journalistic purpose and statutory obligations." *Id.* at 673. Recognizing a broad right of public access "would [also] risk implicating the courts in judgments that should be left to the exercise of journalistic discretion." *Id.* at 674.

Similarly, in *National Endowment for Arts v. Finley,* 524 U.S. 569, 141 L.Ed.2d 500, 118 S. Ct. 2168 (1998), we upheld an art funding program that required the National Endowment for the Arts (NEA) to use content-based criteria in making funding decisions. We explained that "any content-based considerations that may be taken into account in the grant-making process are a consequence of the nature of arts funding." *Id.* at 585. In particular, "the very assumption of the NEA is that grants will be awarded according to the 'artistic worth of competing applicants,' and absolute neutrality is simply inconceivable." *Ibid.* (some internal quotation marks omitted). We expressly declined to apply forum analysis, reasoning that it would conflict with "NEA's mandate ... to make esthetic judgments, and the inherently content-based 'excellence' threshold for NEA support." *Id.* at 586.

The principles underlying *Forbes* and *Finley* also apply to a public library's exercise of judgment in selecting the material it provides to its patrons. Just as forum analysis and heightened judicial scrutiny are incompatible with the role of public television stations and the role of the NEA, they are also incompatible with the discretion that public libraries must have to fulfill their traditional missions. Public library staffs necessarily consider content in making collection decisions and enjoy broad discretion in making them.

... Internet access in public libraries is neither a "traditional" nor a "designated" public forum. *See Cornelius v. NAACP Legal Defense & Ed. Fund, Inc.,* 473 U.S. 788, 802, 87 L.Ed.2d 567, 105 S. Ct. 3439 (1985) (describing types of forums). First, this resource -- which did not exist until quite recently -- has not "immemorially been held in trust for the use of the public and, time out of mind, ... been used for purposes of assembly, communication of thoughts between citizens, and discussing public questions." *International Soc. for Krishna Consciousness, Inc.* v. *Lee,* 505 U.S. 672, 679 (1992) (internal quotation marks omitted). We have "rejected the view that traditional public forum status extends beyond its historic confines." *Forbes, supra,* at 678. The doctrines surrounding traditional public forums may not be extended to situations where such history is lacking.

Nor does Internet access in a public library satisfy our definition of a "designated public forum." To create such a forum, the government must make an affirmative choice to open up its property for use as a public forum. *Cornelius, supra,* at 802-803; *Perry Ed. Assn.* v. *Perry Local Educators' Assn.,* 460 U.S. 37, 45 (1983). "The government does not create a public forum by inaction or by permitting limited discourse, but only by intentionally opening a non-traditional forum for public discourse." *Cornelius, supra*, at 802. ... A public library does not acquire Internet terminals in order to create a public forum for Web publishers to express themselves, any more than it collects books in order to provide a public forum for the authors of books to speak. It provides Internet access, not to "encourage a diversity of views from private speakers," *Rosenberger* [*v. Rector and Visitors of Univ. of Va.*, 515 U.S. 819, 834 (1995)], but for the same reasons it offers other library resources: to facilitate research, learning, and recreational pursuits by furnishing materials of requisite and appropriate quality. *See Cornelius, supra,* at 805 (noting, in upholding limits on participation in the Combined Federal Campaign (CFC), that "the Government did not create the CFC for purposes of providing a forum for expressive activity"). As Congress recognized, "the Internet is simply another method for making information available in a school or library." S. Rep. No. 106-141, p. 7 (1999). It is "no more than a technological extension of the book stack." *Ibid.*

A library's failure to make quality-based judgments about all the material it furnishes from the Web does not somehow taint the judgments it does make. A library's need to exercise judgment in making collection decisions depends on its traditional role in identifying suitable and worthwhile material; it is no less entitled to play that role when it collects material from the Internet than when it collects material from any other source. Most libraries already exclude pornography from their print collections because they deem it inappropriate for inclusion. We do not subject these decisions to heightened scrutiny; it would make little sense to treat libraries' judgments to block online pornography any differently, when these judgments are made for just the same reason.

Moreover, because of the vast quantity of material on the Internet and the rapid pace at which it changes, libraries cannot possibly segregate, item by item, all the Internet material that is appropriate for inclusion from all that is not. While a library could limit its Internet collection to just those sites it found worthwhile, it could do so only at the cost of excluding an enormous amount of valuable information that it lacks the capacity to review. Given that tradeoff, it is entirely reasonable for public libraries to reject that approach and instead exclude certain categories of content, without making individualized judgments that everything they do make available has requisite and appropriate quality.

Like the District Court, the dissents fault the tendency of filtering software to "overblock" -- that is, to erroneously block access to constitutionally protected speech that falls outside the categories that software users intend to block. Due to the software's limitations, "many erroneously blocked [Web] pages contain content that is completely innocuous for both adults and minors, and that no rational person could conclude matches the filtering companies' category definitions, such as 'pornography' or 'sex.'" Assuming that such erroneous blocking presents constitutional difficulties, any such concerns are dispelled by the ease with which patrons may have the filtering software disabled. When a patron encounters a blocked site, he need only ask a librarian to unblock it or (at least in the case of adults) disable the filter. As the District Court found, libraries have the capacity to permanently unblock any erroneously blocked site, and the Solicitor General stated at oral argument that a "library may ... eliminate the filtering with respect to specific sites ... at the request of a patron." With respect to adults, CIPA also expressly authorizes library officials to "disable" a filter altogether "to enable access for *bona fide* research or other lawful purposes." 20 U.S.C. § 9134(f)(3) (disabling permitted for both adults and minors); 47 U.S.C. § 254(h)(6)(D) (disabling permitted for adults). The Solicitor General confirmed that a "librarian can, in response to a request from a patron, unblock the filtering mechanism altogether," and further explained that a patron would not "have to explain ... why he was asking a site to be unblocked or the filtering to be disabled." The District Court viewed unblocking and disabling as inadequate because some patrons may be too embarrassed to request them. But the Constitution does not guarantee the right to acquire information at a public library without any risk of embarrassment. ...

JUSTICE STEVENS asserts the premise that "[a] federal statute penalizing a library for failing to install filtering software on every one of its Internet-accessible computers would unquestionably violate [the First] Amendment." But -- assuming again that public libraries have First Amendment rights -- CIPA does not "penalize" libraries that choose not to install such software, or deny them the right to provide their patrons with unfiltered Internet access. Rather, CIPA simply reflects Congress' decision not to subsidize their doing so. To the extent that libraries wish to offer unfiltered access, they are free to do so without federal assistance. "'A refusal to fund protected activity, without more, cannot be equated with the imposition of a 'penalty' on that activity.'" *Rust, supra*, at 193 (quoting *Harris v. McRae*, 448 U.S. 297, 317, n.19, 65 L.Ed. 2d 784, 100 S. Ct. 2671 (1980)). "'[A] legislature's decision not to subsidize the exercise of a fundamental right does not infringe the right.'" *Rust, supra*, at 193 (quoting *Regan v. Taxation With Representation of Wash.*, 461 U.S. 540, 549, 76 L.Ed. 2d 129, 103 S. Ct. 1997 (1983)). ...

Because public libraries' use of Internet filtering software does not violate their patrons' First Amendment rights, CIPA does not induce libraries to violate the Constitution, and is a valid exercise of Congress' spending power. Nor does CIPA impose an unconstitutional condition on public libraries. Therefore, the judgment of the District Court for the Eastern District of Pennsylvania is

Reversed.

JUSTICE STEVENS, dissenting.

"To fulfill their traditional missions, public libraries must have broad discretion to decide what material to provide their patrons." Accordingly, I agree with the plurality that it is neither inappropriate nor unconstitutional for a local library to experiment with filtering software as a means of curtailing children's access to Internet Web sites displaying sexually explicit images. I also agree with the plurality that the 7% of public libraries that decided to use such software on *all* of their Internet terminals in 2000 did not act unlawfully. Whether it is constitutional for the Congress of the United States to impose that requirement on the other 93%, however, raises a vastly different question. Rather than allowing local decisionmakers to tailor their responses to local problems, the Children's Internet Protection Act (CIPA) operates as a blunt nationwide restraint on adult access to "an enormous amount of valuable information" that individual librarians cannot possibly review. Most of that information is constitutionally protected speech. In my view, this restraint is unconstitutional.

I.

The unchallenged findings of fact made by the District Court reveal fundamental defects in the filtering software that is now available or that will be available in the foreseeable future. Because the software relies on key words or phrases to block undesirable sites, it does not have the capacity to exclude a precisely defined category of images. ...

Given the quantity and ever-changing character of Web sites offering free sexually explicit material,[1] it is inevitable that a substantial amount of such material will never be blocked. Because of this "underblocking," the statute will provide parents with a false sense of security without really solving the problem that motivated its enactment. Conversely, the software's reliance on words to identify undesirable sites necessarily results in the blocking of thousands of pages that "contain content that is completely innocuous for both adults and minors, and that no rational person could conclude matches the filtering companies' category definitions, such as 'pornography' or 'sex.'" *Id.* at 449. In my judgment, a statutory blunderbuss that mandates this vast amount of "overblocking" abridges the freedom of speech protected by the First Amendment.

The effect of the overblocking is the functional equivalent of a host of individual decisions excluding hundreds of thousands of individual constitutionally protected messages from Internet terminals located in public libraries throughout the Nation. Neither the interest in suppressing unlawful speech nor the interest in protecting children from access to harmful materials justifies this overly broad restriction on adult access to protected speech. "The Government may not suppress lawful speech as the means to suppress unlawful speech." *Ashcroft v. Free Speech Coalition,* 535 U.S. 234, 255, 152 L.Ed.2d 403, 122 S. Ct. 1389 (2002).

Although CIPA does not permit any experimentation, the District Court expressly found that a variety of alternatives less restrictive are available at the local level:

> Less restrictive alternatives exist that further the government's legitimate interest in preventing the dissemination of obscenity, child pornography, and material harmful to minors, and in preventing patrons from being unwillingly exposed to patently offensive, sexually explicit content. To prevent patrons from accessing visual depictions that are obscene and child pornography, public libraries may enforce Internet use policies that make clear to patrons that the library's Internet terminals may not be used to access illegal speech. Libraries may then impose penalties on patrons who violate these policies, ranging from a warning to notification of law enforcement, in the appropriate case. Less restrictive alternatives to filtering that further libraries' interest in preventing minors from exposure to visual depictions that are harmful to minors include requiring parental consent to or presence during unfiltered access, or restricting minors' unfiltered access to terminals within view of library staff. Finally, optional filtering, privacy screens, recessed monitors, and placement of unfiltered Internet terminals outside of sight-lines provide less restrictive alternatives for libraries to prevent patrons from being unwillingly exposed to sexually explicit content on the Internet.

201 F. Supp. 2d at 410.

---

[1] "The percentage of Web pages on the indexed Web containing sexually explicit content is relatively small. Recent estimates indicate that no more than 1-2% of the content on the Web is pornographic or sexually explicit. However, the absolute number of Web sites offering free sexually explicit material is extremely large, approximately 100,000 sites." 201 F. Supp. 2d. 401, 419 (E.D. Pa. 2002).

Those findings are consistent with scholarly comment on the issue arguing that local decisions tailored to local circumstances are more appropriate than a mandate from Congress. The plurality does not reject any of those findings. Instead, "assuming that such erroneous blocking presents constitutional difficulties," it relies on the Solicitor General's assurance that the statute permits individual librarians to disable filtering mechanisms whenever a patron so requests. In my judgment, that assurance does not cure the constitutional infirmity in the statute.

Until a blocked site or group of sites is unblocked, a patron is unlikely to know what is being hidden and therefore whether there is any point in asking for the filter to be removed. It is as though the statute required a significant part of every library's reading materials to be kept in unmarked, locked rooms or cabinets, which could be opened only in response to specific requests. Some curious readers would in time obtain access to the hidden materials, but many would not. Inevitably, the interest of the authors of those works in reaching the widest possible audience would be abridged. Moreover, because the procedures that different libraries are likely to adopt to respond to unblocking requests will no doubt vary, it is impossible to measure the aggregate effect of the statute on patrons' access to blocked sites. Unless we assume that the statute is a mere symbolic gesture, we must conclude that it will create a significant prior restraint on adult access to protected speech. A law that prohibits reading without official consent, like a law that prohibits speaking without consent, "constitutes a dramatic departure from our national heritage and constitutional tradition." *Watchtower Bible & Tract Soc. of N.Y., Inc.* v. *Village of Stratton,* 536 U.S. 150, 166, 153 L.Ed.2d 205, 122 S. Ct. 2080 (2002).

II.

The plurality incorrectly argues that the statute does not impose "an unconstitutional condition on public libraries." On the contrary, it impermissibly conditions the receipt of Government funding on the restriction of significant First Amendment rights.

The plurality explains the "worthy missions" of the public library in facilitating "learning and cultural enrichment." It then asserts that in order to fulfill these missions, "libraries must have broad discretion to decide what material to provide to their patrons." Thus the selection decision is the province of the librarians, a province into which we have hesitated to enter....

As the plurality recognizes, we have always assumed that libraries have discretion when making decisions regarding what to include in, and exclude from, their collections. That discretion is comparable to the "'business of a university ... to determine for itself on academic grounds who may teach, what may be taught, how it shall be taught, and who may be admitted to study.'" *Sweezy* v. *New Hampshire,* 354 U.S. 234, 263, 1 L.Ed.2d 1311, 77 S. Ct. 1203 (1957) (Frankfurter, J., concurring in result) (citation omitted). As the District Court found, one of the central purposes of a library is to provide information for educational purposes: "'Books and other library resources should be provided for the interest, information, and enlightenment of all people of the community the library serves.'" 201 F. Supp. 2d at 420 (quoting the American Library Association's Library Bill of Rights). Given our Nation's deep commitment "to safeguarding academic freedom" and to the "robust exchange of ideas," *Keyishian* v. *Board of Regents of Univ. of State of N.Y.,* 385 U.S. 589, 603, 17 L.Ed.2d 629, 87 S. Ct. 675 (1967), a library's exercise of judgment with respect to its collection is entitled to First Amendment protection.

A federal statute penalizing a library for failing to install filtering software on every one of its Internet-accessible computers would unquestionably violate that Amendment. *Cf. Reno*

v. *American Civil Liberties Union*, 521 U.S. 844 (1997). I think it equally clear that the First Amendment protects libraries from being denied funds for refusing to comply with an identical rule. An abridgment of speech by means of a threatened denial of benefits can be just as pernicious as an abridgment by means of a threatened penalty.

Our cases holding that government employment may not be conditioned on the surrender of rights protected by the First Amendment illustrate the point. It has long been settled that "Congress could not 'enact a regulation providing that no Republican, Jew or Negro shall be appointed to federal office, or that no federal employee shall attend Mass or take any active part in missionary work.'" *Wieman v. Updegraff*, 344 U.S. 183, 191-192, 97 L.Ed. 216, 73 S. Ct. 215 (1952). Neither discharges, as in *Elrod v. Burns*, 427 U.S. 347, 350-351, 49 L.Ed.2d 547, 96 S. Ct. 2673 (1976), nor refusals to hire or promote, as in *Rutan v. Republican Party of Ill.*, 497 U.S. 62, 66-67, 111 L.Ed.2d 52, 110 S. Ct. 2729 (1990), are immune from First Amendment scrutiny. Our precedents firmly rejecting "Justice Holmes' famous dictum, that a policeman 'may have a constitutional right to talk politics, but he has no constitutional right to be a policeman,'" *Board of Comm'rs, Wabaunsee Cty.* v. *Umbehr*, 518 U.S. 668, 674, 135 L.Ed.2d 843, 116 S. Ct. 2342 (1996), draw no distinction between the penalty of discharge from one's job and the withholding of the benefit of a new job. The abridgment of First Amendment rights is equally unconstitutional in either context. *See Sherbert* v. *Verner*, 374 U.S. 398, 404, 10 L.Ed.2d 965, 83 S. Ct. 1790 (1963) ("Governmental imposition of such a choice puts the same kind of burden upon the free exercise of religion as would a fine.... It is too late in the day to doubt that the liberties of religion and expression may be infringed by the denial of or placing of conditions upon a benefit or privilege").

The issue in this case does not involve governmental attempts to control the speech or views of its employees. It involves the use of its treasury to impose controls on an important medium of expression. In an analogous situation, we specifically held that when "the Government seeks to use an existing medium of expression and to control it, in a class of cases, in ways which distort its usual functioning," the distorting restriction must be struck down under the First Amendment. *Legal Services Corporation v. Velazquez*, 531 U.S. 533, 543, 149 L.Ed.2d 63, 121 S. Ct. 1043 (2001). The question, then, is whether requiring the filtering software on all Internet-accessible computers distorts that medium. As I have discussed above, the over- and underblocking of the software does just that. ...

This Court should not permit federal funds to be used to enforce this kind of broad restriction of First Amendment rights, particularly when such a restriction is unnecessary to accomplish Congress' stated goal. The abridgment of speech is equally obnoxious whether a rule like this one is enforced by a threat of penalties or by a threat to withhold a benefit.

I would affirm the judgment of the District Court.

JUSTICE SOUTER, with whom JUSTICE GINSBURG joins, dissenting.

I agree in the main with JUSTICE STEVENS (dissenting opinion) that the blocking requirements of the Children's Internet Protection Act, 20 U.S.C. §§ 9134(f)(1) (A)(i) and (B)(i); 47 U.S.C. §§ 254(h)(6)(B)(i) and (C)(i), impose an unconstitutional condition on the Government's subsidies to local libraries for providing access to the Internet. I also agree with the library appellees on a further reason to hold the blocking rule invalid in the exercise of the spending power under Article I, § 8: the rule mandates action by recipient libraries that would violate the First Amendment's guarantee of free speech if the libraries took that action entirely on their own. I respectfully dissent on this further ground.

I.

Like the other Members of the Court, I have no doubt about the legitimacy of governmental efforts to put a barrier between child patrons of public libraries and the raw offerings on the Internet otherwise available to them there, and if the only First Amendment interests raised here were those of children, I would uphold application of the Act. We have said that the governmental interest in "shielding" children from exposure to indecent material is "compelling," *Reno v. American Civil Liberties Union,* 521 U.S. 844, 869-870 (1997), and I do not think that the awkwardness a child might feel on asking for an unblocked terminal is any such burden as to affect constitutionality.

Nor would I dissent if I agreed with the majority of my colleagues (plurality opinion); (BREYER, J., concurring in judgment); (KENNEDY, J., concurring in judgment), that an adult library patron could, consistently with the Act, obtain an unblocked terminal simply for the asking. I realize the Solicitor General represented this to be the Government's policy, and if that policy were communicated to every affected library as unequivocally as it was stated to us at argument, local librarians might be able to indulge the unblocking requests of adult patrons to the point of taking the curse off the statute for all practical purposes. But the Federal Communications Commission, in its order implementing the Act, pointedly declined to set a federal policy on when unblocking by local libraries would be appropriate under the statute. *See In re Federal-State Joint Board on Universal Service: Children's Internet Protection Act,* 16 FCC Rcd. 8182, 8204, P53 (2001) ("Federally-imposed rules directing school and library staff when to disable technology protection measures would likely be overbroad and imprecise, potentially chilling speech, or otherwise confusing schools and libraries about the requirements of the statute. We leave such determinations to the local communities, whom we believe to be most knowledgeable about the varying circumstances of schools or libraries within those communities"). Moreover, the District Court expressly found that "unblocking may take days, and may be unavailable, especially in branch libraries, which are often less well staffed than main libraries." 201 F. Supp. 2d 401, 411 (E.D. Pa. 2002); *see id.* at 487-488 (same).

In any event, we are here to review a statute, and the unblocking provisions simply cannot be construed, even for constitutional avoidance purposes, to say that a library must unblock upon adult request, no conditions imposed and no questions asked. First, the statute says only that a library "may" unblock, not that it must. 20 U.S.C. § 9134(f)(3); *see* 47 U.S.C. § 254(h)(6)(D). In addition, it allows unblocking only for a "*bona fide* research or other lawful purposes," 20 U.S.C. § 134(f)(3); *see* 47 U.S.C. § 254(h)(6)(D), and if the "lawful purposes" criterion means anything that would not subsume and render the "*bona fide* research" criterion superfluous, it must impose some limit on eligibility for unblocking, *see, e.g., Connecticut Nat. Bank v. Germain,* 503 U.S. 249, 253, 117 L.Ed.2d 391, 112 S. Ct. 1146 (1992) ("Courts should disfavor interpretations of statutes that render language superfluous"). There is therefore necessarily some restriction, which is surely made more onerous by the uncertainty of its terms and the generosity of its discretion to library staffs in deciding who gets complete Internet access and who does not. *Cf. Forsyth County v. Nationalist Movement,* 505 U.S. 123, 130, 120 L.Ed.2d 101, 112 S. Ct. 2395 (1992) (noting that the First Amendment bars licensing schemes that grant unduly broad discretion to licensing officials, given the potential for such discretion to "become a means of suppressing a particular point of view" (internal quotation marks omitted)).

We therefore have to take the statute on the understanding that adults will be denied access to a substantial amount of nonobscene material harmful to children but lawful for adult examination, and a substantial quantity of text and pictures harmful to no one. As the plurality concedes, this is the inevitable consequence of the indiscriminate behavior of current filtering mechanisms, which screen out material to an extent known only by the manufacturers of the blocking software.

We likewise have to examine the statute on the understanding that the restrictions on adult Internet access have no justification in the object of protecting children. Children could be restricted to blocked terminals, leaving other unblocked terminals in areas restricted to adults and screened from casual glances. And of course the statute could simply have provided for unblocking at adult request, with no questions asked. The statute could, in other words, have protected children without blocking access for adults or subjecting adults to anything more than minimal inconvenience, just the way (the record shows) many librarians had been dealing with obscenity and indecency before imposition of the federal conditions. *See id.* at 422-427. Instead, the Government's funding conditions engage in overkill to a degree illustrated by their refusal to trust even a library's staff with an unblocked terminal, one to which the adult public itself has no access. *See id.* at 413 (quoting 16 FCC Rcd., at 8196, ¶ 30).

The question for me, then, is whether a local library could itself constitutionally impose these restrictions on the content otherwise available to an adult patron through an Internet connection, at a library terminal provided for public use. The answer is no. A library that chose to block an adult's Internet access to material harmful to children (and whatever else the undiscriminating filter might interrupt) would be imposing a content-based restriction on communication of material in the library's control that an adult could otherwise lawfully see. This would simply be censorship. True, the censorship would not necessarily extend to every adult, for an intending Internet user might convince a librarian that he was a true researcher or had a "lawful purpose" to obtain everything the library's terminal could provide. But as to those who did not qualify for discretionary unblocking, the censorship would be complete and, like all censorship by an agency of the Government, presumptively invalid owing to strict scrutiny in implementing the Free Speech Clause of the First Amendment. "The policy of the First Amendment favors dissemination of information and opinion, and the guarantees of freedom of speech and press were not designed to prevent the censorship of the press merely, but any action of the government by means of which it might prevent such free and general discussion of public matters as seems absolutely essential." *Bigelow v. Virginia,* 421 U.S. 809, 829, 44 L.Ed.2d 600, 95 S. Ct. 2222 (1975) (internal quotation marks and brackets omitted).

II.

The Court's plurality does not treat blocking affecting adults as censorship, but chooses to describe a library's act in filtering content as simply an instance of the kind of selection from available material that every library (save, perhaps, the Library of Congress) must perform. But this position does not hold up.

A.

Public libraries are indeed selective in what they acquire to place in their stacks, as they must be. There is only so much money and so much shelf space, and the necessity to choose some material and reject the rest justifies the effort to be selective with an eye to demand, quality, and the object of maintaining the library as a place of civilized enquiry by widely different sorts of people. Selectivity is thus necessary and complex, and these two characteristics explain why review of a library's selection decisions must be limited: the decisions are made all the time, and only in extreme cases could one expect particular choices to reveal impermissible reasons (reasons even the plurality would consider to be illegitimate), like excluding books because their authors are Democrats or their critiques of organized Christianity are unsympathetic. *See Board of Ed., Island Trees Union Free School Dist. No. 26 v. Pico,* 457 U.S. 853, 870-871, 73 L.Ed.2d 435, 102 S. Ct. 2799 (1982) (plurality opinion). Review for rational basis is probably the most that any court could conduct, owing to the myriad particular selections that might be attacked by someone, and the difficulty of untangling the play of factors behind a particular decision.

At every significant point, however, the Internet blocking here defies comparison to the process of acquisition. Whereas traditional scarcity of money and space require a library to make choices about what to acquire, and the choice to be made is whether or not to spend the money to acquire something, blocking is the subject of a choice made after the money for Internet access has been spent or committed. Since it makes no difference to the cost of Internet access whether an adult calls up material harmful for children or the Articles of Confederation, blocking (on facts like these) is not necessitated by scarcity of either money or space. In the instance of the Internet, what the library acquires is electronic access, and the choice to block is a choice to limit access that has already been acquired. Thus, deciding against buying a book means there is no book (unless a loan can be obtained), but blocking the Internet is merely blocking access purchased in its entirety and subject to unblocking if the librarian agrees. The proper analogy therefore is not to passing up a book that might have been bought; it is either to buying a book and then keeping it from adults lacking an acceptable "purpose," or to buying an encyclopedia and then cutting out pages with anything thought to be unsuitable for all adults.

B.

The plurality claims to find support for its conclusions in the "traditional mission" of the public library. The plurality thus argues, in effect, that the traditional responsibility of public libraries has called for denying adult access to certain books, or bowdlerizing the content of what the libraries let adults see. But, in fact, the plurality's conception of a public library's mission has been rejected by the libraries themselves. And no library that chose to block adult access in the way mandated by the Act could claim that the history of public library practice in this country furnished an implicit gloss on First Amendment standards, allowing for blocking out anything unsuitable for adults.

Institutional history of public libraries in America discloses an evolution toward a general rule, now firmly rooted, that any adult entitled to use the library has access to any of its holdings. To be sure, this freedom of choice was apparently not within the inspiration for the mid-19th century development of public libraries, *see* J. Shera, *Foundations of the Public Library: The Origins of the Public Library Movement in New England,* 1629-1855, p. 107 (1949), and in the infancy of their development a "moral censorship" of reading material was assumed, E. Geller, *Forbidden Books in American Public Libraries,* 1876-1939, p. 12 (1984).

But even in the early 20th century, the legitimacy of the librarian's authority as moral arbiter was coming into question. *See, e.g.,* Belden, *President's Address: Looking Forward,* 20 Bull. Am. Libr. Assn. 273, 274 (1926) ("The true public library must stand for the intellectual freedom of access to the printed word"). And the practices of European fascism fueled the reaction against library censorship. *See* M. Harris, *History of Libraries in the Western World* 248 (4th ed. 1995). The upshot was a growing understanding that a librarian's job was to guarantee that "all people had access to all ideas," Geller, *supra,* at 156, and by the end of the 1930s, librarians' "basic position in opposition to censorship [had] emerged," Krug & Harvey, *ALA and Intellectual Freedom: A Historical Overview, in Intellectual Freedom Manual,* pp. xi, xv (American Library Association 1974) (hereinafter *Intellectual Freedom Manual*); *see also* Darling, *Access, Intellectual Freedom and Libraries,* 27 Library Trends 315-316 (1979).

By the time McCarthyism began its assaults, appellee American Library Association had developed a Library Bill of Rights against censorship, Library Bill of Rights, in *Intellectual Freedom Manual,* pt. 1, p. 7, and an Intellectual Freedom Committee to maintain the position that beyond enforcing existing laws against obscenity, "there is no place in our society for extra-legal efforts to coerce the taste of others, to confine adults to the reading matter deemed suitable for adolescents, or to inhibit the efforts of writers to achieve artistic expression." Freedom to Read, in *Id.,* pt. 2, p. 8; *see also* Krug & Harvey, in *id.,* at xv. So far as I have been able to tell, this statement expressed the prevailing ideal in public library administration after World War II, and it seems fair to say as a general rule that libraries by then had ceased to deny requesting adults access to any materials in their collections. The adult might, indeed, have had to make a specific request, for the literature and published surveys from the period show a variety of restrictions on the circulation of library holdings, including placement of materials apart from open stacks, and availability only upon specific request. But aside from the isolated suggestion, *see, e.g.,* Born, *Public Libraries and Intellectual Freedom,* in *id.,* pt. 3, pp. 4, 9, I have not been able to find from this period any record of a library barring access to materials in its collection on a basis other than a reader's age. It seems to have been out of the question for a library to refuse a book in its collection to a requesting adult patron, or to presume to evaluate the basis for a particular request.

This take on the postwar years is confirmed by evidence of the dog that did not bark. During the second half of the 20th century, the ALA issued a series of policy statements, since dubbed Interpretations of the Library Bill of Rights, *see id.,* pt. 1, p. 13, commenting on library administration and pointing to particular practices the ALA opposed. ....[T]he ALA even adopted a statement against any restriction on access to library materials by minors. It acknowledged that age restrictions were common across the Nation in "a variety of forms, including, among others, restricted reading rooms for adult use only, library cards limiting circulation of some materials to adults only, closed collections for adult use only, and interlibrary loan for adult use only." *Id.,* pt. 1, p. 16. Nevertheless, the ALA opposed all such limitations, saying that "only the parent ... may restrict his children -- and only *his* children -- from access to library materials and services." *Id.,* pt. 1, p. 17.

And in 1973, the ALA adopted a policy opposing the practice already mentioned, of keeping certain books off the open shelves, available only on specific request. *See id.,* pt. 1, p. 42. ...

Amidst these and other ALA statements from the latter half of the 20th century, however, one subject is missing. There is not a word about barring requesting adults from any materials in a library's collection, or about limiting an adult's access based on evaluation of his purposes in seeking materials. If such a practice had survived into the latter half of the 20th century, one would surely find a statement about it from the ALA, which had become the nemesis of anything sounding like censorship of library holdings, as shown by the history just sampled. The silence bespeaks an American public library that gives any adult patron any material at hand, and a history without support for the plurality's reading of the First Amendment as tolerating a public library's censorship of its collection against adult enquiry.

C.

Thus, there is no preacquisition scarcity rationale to save library Internet blocking from treatment as censorship, and no support for it in the historical development of library practice. To these two reasons to treat blocking differently from a decision declining to buy a book, a third must be added. Quite simply, we can smell a rat when a library blocks material already in its control, just as we do when a library removes books from its shelves for reasons having nothing to do with wear and tear, obsolescence, or lack of demand. Content-based blocking and removal tell us something that mere absence from the shelves does not.

I have already spoken about two features of acquisition decisions that make them poor candidates for effective judicial review. The first is their complexity, the number of legitimate considerations that may go into them, not all pointing one way, providing cover for any illegitimate reason that managed to sneak in. A librarian should consider likely demand, scholarly or esthetic quality, alternative purchases, relative cost, and so on. The second reason the judiciary must by shy about reviewing acquisition decisions is the sheer volume of them, and thus the number that might draw fire. Courts cannot review the administration of every library with a constituent disgruntled that the library fails to buy exactly what he wants to read.

After a library has acquired material in the first place, however, the variety of possible reasons that might legitimately support an initial rejection are no longer in play. Removal of books or selective blocking by controversial subject matter is not a function of limited resources and less likely than a selection decision to reflect an assessment of esthetic or scholarly merit. Removal (and blocking) decisions being so often obviously correlated with content, they tend to show up for just what they are, and because such decisions tend to be few, courts can examine them without facing a deluge. The difference between choices to keep out and choices to throw out is thus enormous, a perception that underlay the good sense of the plurality's conclusion in *Board of Ed., Island Trees Union Free School Dist. No. 26 v. Pico,* 457 U.S. 853, 73 L.Ed.2d 435, 102 S. Ct. 2799 (1982), that removing classics from a school library in response to pressure from parents and school board members violates the Speech Clause.

III.

There is no good reason, then, to treat blocking of adult enquiry as anything different from the censorship it presumptively is. For this reason, I would hold in accordance with conventional strict scrutiny that a library's practice of blocking would violate an adult patron's First and Fourteenth Amendment right to be free of Internet censorship, when unjustified (as here) by any legitimate interest in screening children from harmful material. On that ground, the Act's blocking requirement in its current breadth calls for unconstitutional action by a library recipient, and is itself unconstitutional.

* * * * *

insert the following after Notes and Questions # 4 on page 268 of Law of Internet Speech:

5. Should it be mandatory to disclose the use of filters?

6. Does the use of a comprehensive rating system assuage concerns about filters? What speech issues are raised by the use of rating systems?

7. If a library patron must request of a librarian that the filter be disabled, how are the patron's privacy interests implicated?

CHAPTER III

DEFAMATION

Publication

Publication By Conduits

The Common Law Privilege and the *Lunney v. Prodigy Servs. Co.* Decision

insert the following after the citation to Anderson v. New York Telephone Co. at the end of the first full paragraph on page 297 of Law of Internet Speech:

Cf. CCH Canadian Ltd. v. Law Society of Upper Canada, [2004] 1 S.C.R. 339, *available at* <http://www.canlii.org/ca/cas/scc/2004/2004scc13.html> (stating that the mere provision of photocopiers for use by library patrons does not constitute a breach of Canadian copyright law; there was no evidence that the photocopiers had been used in violation of copyright law, the library had posted a notice over the copiers stating that it was not responsible for infringing copies made by users, and the library did not have sufficient control over its patrons to permit the conclusion that it had sanctioned, approved, or countenanced the infringement).

* * * * *

insert the following at the end of Notes and Questions # 5 on page 299 of Law of Internet Speech:

6. Dicta by the U.S. Court of Appeals for the Ninth Circuit noted that because an ISP could not be held liable for posting a defamatory message, the ISP may have little incentive to remove such material even after notice that the content is defamatory. *See Batzel v. Smith*, 333 F.3d 1018, 1031 n.19 (9th Cir. 2003), *cert. denied*, 541 U.S. 1085 (2004); *see* Supplement *infra* at 207. The court mused that section 230 of the Communications Decency Act could be amended to incorporate notice, take-down, and put-back procedures similar to those imposed by the DMCA, *see* 17 U.S.C. §§ 512(c), (g). 333 F.3d at 1031, n.19. Is such an analogous approach to copyright infringement claims reasonable in the context of libelous (or allegedly libelous) speech?

7. Section 230 of the Communications Decency Act was applied to a police officers' union that had publicly campaigned against its police chief. Anonymous e-mail messages were posted on the defendant's web-site, but the court concluded that the union was acting as an interactive service provider and had not controlled the messages in issue. *See Roskowski v. Corvallis Police Officers' Association*, No. 03-474-AS (D. Or. Mar. 9, 2005) (Magistrate's Recommendation).

8. One commentator opined that the "legal rule of total immunity for intermediaries rather than distributor liability represents a failure of public policy and the poor resolution of legal

conflict." Susan Freiwald, *Comparative Institutional Analysis in Cyberspace: The Case of Intermediary Liability for Defamation,* 14 Harv. J. Law & Tech. 569, 654 (2001). Were the law otherwise, what likely ramifications would there be to the diversity of speech and the immediacy, reach, and cost of its dissemination?

* * * * *

Characterizing Content Providers

insert the following before John Does 1 through 30 inclusive, and Unknown Illinois State University Football Players v. Franco Productions, Dan Franco, individually and d/b/a Franco Productions, et al. on page 301 of Law of Internet Speech:

According to a Texas federal court, the operator of a consumer complaint web-site was deemed an "information content provider" because it had added allegedly defamatory report titles and headings to materials that consumers had posted on the site. *See MCW, Inc., d/b/a Bernard Haldane Associates v. Badbusinessbureau.com, L.L.C.,* Civ. Action No. 3:02-CV-2727-G, 2004 U.S. Dist. LEXIS 6678 (N.D. Tex. Apr. 19, 2004). The court observed that the plaintiff was "not seeking to hold the defendants liable for merely publishing information provided by a third party. Rather, [the plaintiff was] seeking relief because the defendants themselves create[d], develop[ed], and post[ed] original, defamatory information concerning [the plaintiff]." *Id.* at *32. The defendants did not dispute the plaintiff's allegations that the defendants' personnel had created titles and headings, but maintained that the plaintiff's trademark infringement and defamation claims were based on the content of reports from third-party consumers and not on the titles or headings of the reports. *See id.*

The court determined, however, that the claims in fact were based on disparaging titles, headings, and editorial messages that the plaintiff claimed the defendants had created. The court also observed that the defendants were alleged to have actively encouraged a consumer to take certain photographs that were included on the web-sites. "The defendants cannot disclaim responsibility for disparaging material that they actively solicit," the court concluded. "Furthermore, actively encouraging and instructing a consumer to gather specific detailed information is an activity that goes substantially beyond the traditional publisher's editorial role. The defendants are clearly doing more than making minor alterations to a consumer's message. They are participating in the process of developing information. Therefore, the defendants have not only incurred responsibility for the information developed and created by consumers, but have also gone beyond the publisher's role and developed some of the defamatory information posted on the websites." *Id.* at 34-35.

* * * * *

insert the following before Lori Sabbato v. James Hardy on page 304 of Law of Internet Speech:

Thereafter, the athletes were awarded $11,000,000, of which $10,000,000 constituted punitive damages. Defendants also were ordered to pay court costs and attorney's fees, making the aggregate award more than $500,000,000, although it was not clear that the judgment would be fully satisfied. In addition, the defendants were ordered to surrender the videotapes in question and to permanently refrain from distributing the tapes. *See* Jere Longman, *Videotaped Athletes Victorious in Court,* N.Y. Times, Dec. 5, 2002, § D at 8.

* * * * *

insert the following before Other Applications of Section 230 of the Communications Decency Act on page 306 of Law of Internet Speech:

* * * * *

GREG LLOYD SMITH, *et al.*
v.
INTERCOSMOS MEDIA GROUP, INC., *et al.*

United States District Court for the Eastern District of Louisiana

CIVIL ACTION NO. 02-1964 SECTION "C," 2002 U.S. Dist. LEXIS 24251

December 17, 2002

This matter comes before the Court on motion for summary judgment filed by the defendant, Intercosmos Media Group, Inc. d/b/a directNIC.com ("Intercosmos"). Having considered the record, the memoranda of counsel and the law, the Court has determined that summary judgment is appropriate for the following reasons.

The plaintiffs, Greg Lloyd Smith and Kestel Trading Corporation, sue Intercosmos in diversity for defamation and libel. Specifically, the plaintiffs claim that Intercosmos, an interactive internet service provider, is liable for the actions of one of its customers who registered three second-level domain ("SLD") names with Intercosmos. The plaintiffs claim that this Intercosmos customer used various domains or universal resource locators ("URLs") to defame the plaintiffs. The plaintiffs claim to have determined that the name of the registrants for the domains were fictitious and so advised Intercosmos, which has nonetheless failed to permanently "block" the websites and has not revoked the registrations for the domain names.

The defendant argues that the plaintiffs' claims for defamation and libel and for damages and injunctive relief are preempted by the 1996 Communications Decency Act, 47 U.S.C. § 230 ("CDA"), and that the CDA provides immunity for all claims made by the plaintiffs. The plaintiffs in their opposition maintain that they have viable claims for (a) negligent performance of duties of a domain-name registrar under La. Civ. Code art 2315; and (b) injunctive-relief claim for defamation.

… *Does the CDA Immunize the Defendant from State Law Claims?*

In their opposition, the plaintiffs contend that Intercosmos can be held liable for "the negligent performance of defendant's duties as a domain name registrar." The crux of this claim is that the defendant's negligence allowed the defamation to continue. The defendant claims this is not a valid cause of action because the CDA immunizes them from liability for such actions.

For purposes of the CDA immunity, the party claiming the immunity must be, first, a provider or user of an interactive computer service. Second, the alleged defamatory statement must be made by a third party. Third, the defamation claim the party seeks immunity from must treat the interactive computer service as the publisher or speaker of the alleged defamatory statement.

Intercosmos is an Interactive Service Provider

The CDA defines interactive computer service as "any information service, system, or access software that provides access to the internet and such systems operated or services offered by libraries or educational institutions." 47 U.S.C. § 230(f)(2).

The purpose of the CDA and case law present a clear picture of the type of activities a service provider must perform to qualify for CDA immunity. The purpose of the CDA is "to promote the continued development of the internet" by allowing it to expand "unfettered by federal or state regulation." 47 U.S.C. § 230. "Courts have broadly construed the ISP [internet service provider] immunity broadly, in the spirit of the CDA's stated purpose of promoting rather than impeding technology and Internet use." Sewali K. Patel, *Immunizing Internet Service Providers From Third Party Internet Defamation Claims: How Far Should the Courts Go?*, Vanderbilt Law Review, March, 2002, 55 Vand. L. Rev. 647, at 661.

Case law shows that the type of activities alleged to have been performed by the defendant here are similar and in some aspects identical to the functions performed by other defendant internet access providers that have been granted immunity by the CDA. Specifically, the defendant's role as information service providers and web-hosting service providers describes an internet service provider for purposes of CDA immunity. *Schneider v. Amazon.com, Inc.,* 108 Wn. App. 454, 31 P.3d 37 (Wn. App. 2001); *Does 1-30 v. Franco Productions*, 2000 U.S. Dist. LEXIS 8645, 2000 WL 816779, *1 (N.D .Ill.). For purposes of CDA immunity, the defendant is an interactive computer service provider.

Statements Were Made by a Third Party

In the complaint, the plaintiffs refer to the source of the alleged defamatory statements at issue here as "an as yet unknown and unnamed individual." In the motion for summary judgment, the defendant states "In the present case, nowhere in the complaint is it alleged or suggested that Intercosmos authored or created the alleged defamatory statements made against the plaintiffs."

The plaintiffs and the defendant concede that the alleged defamatory statements were made by a third party.

The Complaint Treats the Defendant as the Publisher of the Alleged Defamatory Statements

For CDA immunity from state and federal claims, the defendant must be treated as the publisher of the alleged defamatory statements. In the opposition, the plaintiffs claim that the defendant "allowed the defamation to continue." In so doing, they are treating the defendant as publisher of the alleged defamatory statements. The Restatement (Second) of Tort § 577 defines publication:

> (1)   Publication of defamatory matter is its communication intentionally or by a negligent act to one other then the person defamed.

> One who intentionally and unreasonably fails to remove defamatory matter that he knows to be exhibited on land or chattels in his possession or under his control is subject to liability for its continued publication.

Thus, "the law also treats as a publisher or speaker one who fails to take reasonable steps to remove defamatory statements from property under her control." *Zeran v. America Online, Inc.,* 958 F. Supp. 1124, 1132.

The basis of the plaintiffs' claim is that the defendant allowed the defamation to continue by failing to take reasonable steps to remove the alleged defamatory statements. The law treats such a party as a publisher.

The defendant is immunized from liability for this state claim of negligence because the defendant meets the three requirements of the CDA immunity. First, the defendant qualifies as an interactive service provider. Second, the defendant is not the source of the alleged defamatory statements. Third, the claim against the defendant treats the defendant as publisher of the alleged defamatory statements.

Injunctive Relief

The plaintiffs also maintain that their claims for injunctive relief are not precluded under the CDA, apparently relying on cases cited by the Intercosmos in its motion, *Does 1-30 v. Franco Productions,* 2000 U.S. Dist. LEXIS 8645, 2000 WL 816779 (N.D. Ill.), and *Mainstream Loudoun v. Board of Trustees of the Loudoun County Library,* 24 F. Supp. 2d 552, 561 (E.D. Va. 1998). A reading of the *Does* case indicates no discussion of the issue at all, only a citation to the *Loudoun* case. The cited *Loudoun* case, however, is merely a denial of reconsideration of the original decision on the issue, at 2 F. Supp. 2d 783, 790. The defendant in *Loudoun* was a local library and the plaintiffs brought a First Amendment action under 42 U.S.C. § 1983 for the defendant's regulation of content on library computers with the use of site-blocking software. Noting that the CDA defines "interactive computer service" to include "a service or system that provides access to the Internet offered by libraries or educational institutions," the original *Loudoun* decision distinguished between private and governmental defendants.

> Thus, as its name implies, § 230 was enacted to minimize state regulation of Internet speech by encouraging *private* content providers to self-regulate against offensive material; § 230 was not enacted to insulate government regulation of Internet speech from judicial review. Even if § 230 were construed to apply to public libraries, defendants cite no authority to suggest that the "tort-based" immunity to "civil liability" described by § 230 would bar the instant action, which is for declaratory and injunctive relief."

Loudoun, 2 F. Supp. 2d at 790 (emphasis original). It is important to note that the immunity sought by the defendant in *Loudoun* was under § 230(c)(2), which is not applicable in this matter at all.

Furthermore, *Loudoun* has been challenged even [as to] its distinction between private and governmental agency. In *Kathleen R. v. City of Livermore,* 87 Cal. App. 4th 684, 104 Cal. Rptr. 2d 772 (Cal. App. 1st Dist. 2001), the plaintiffs sought injunctive relief against a governmental defendant under a number of state law claims as well as Section 1983. With regard to the state law claims, that court found that the *Loudoun* discussion of § 230(c)(2) immunity "cannot be stretched to deprive governmental entities of immunity under section 230(c)(1)." *Livermore*, 87 Cal. App. 4th at 693.

> Thus, any suggestion in *Loudoun I* that section 230 could never be applied to public libraries would have been dicta. In any event, there can be no doubt that the Loudoun court thought that public libraries could claim immunity under section 230(c)(1) because the court ventured in *Loudoun II* that this immunity should alleviate any concern the library might have had with potential criminal liability.

Id., 87 Cal App. 4th at 693-694. The *Livermore* court directly addressed the plaintiffs' arguments that immunity can not apply to claims for injunctive relief:

> We reject these arguments and hold that the respondent is immune from all of appellant's state law claims. *Loudoun I* is distinguishable, again, because it involved immunity under section 230(c)(2), not section 230(c)(1). Whereas section 230(c)(2) prohibits interactive computer service providers from being "held liable for specified conduct, and that language may arguably refer only to damage claims, no such limiting language appears in section 230(c)(1).

Id., 87 Cal. App. 4th at 697-698. It continued:

> Section 230 provides broadly that no cause of action may be brought *and* no liability may be imposed under any State or local law that is inconsistent with this section. ... Thus, even if for purposes of section 230 "liability" means only an award of damages ... the statute by its terms also precludes other causes of action for other forms of relief.

Id., 87 Cal. App. 4th at 698. *See also Ben Ezra, Weinstein & Co., Inc. v. America Online, Inc.*, 1999 U.S. Dist. LEXIS 23095, 1999 WL 727402 (D.N.M. 1999), *aff'd,* 206 F.3d 980 (10th Cir. 2000).

This Court adopts the sound reasoning of the court in *Livermore*, and concludes that any claim made by the plaintiffs for damages or injunctive relief with regard to either defamation and libel, or negligence and fault under Article 2315, are precluded by the immunity afforded by Section 230(c)(1), and subject to dismissal.

Accordingly,

IT IS ORDERED that the motion for summary judgment filed by the defendant, Intercosmos Media Group, Inc. d/b/a directNIC.com is GRANTED.

* * * * *

ELLEN L. BATZEL, a citizen of the State of California, Plaintiff-Appellee

v.

ROBERT SMITH, a citizen of the State of North Carolina, *et al.,* Defendants

and, TON CREMERS, a citizen or subject of the Netherlands, Defendant-Appellant

United States Court of Appeals for the Ninth Circuit

No. 01-56380, No. 01-56556, 333 F.3d 1018

June 24, 2003

There is no reason inherent in the technological features of cyberspace why First Amendment and defamation law should apply differently in cyberspace than in the brick and mortar world. Congress, however, has chosen for policy reasons to immunize from liability for defamatory or obscene speech "providers and users of interactive computer services" when the defamatory or obscene material is "provided" by someone else. This case presents the question whether and, if so, under what circumstances a moderator of a listserv and operator of a website who posts an allegedly defamatory e-mail authored by a third party can be held liable for doing so. ...

I.

In the summer of 1999, sometime-handyman Robert Smith was working for Ellen Batzel, an attorney licensed to practice in California and North Carolina, at Batzel's house in the North Carolina mountains. Smith recounted that while he was repairing Batzel's truck, Batzel told him that she was "the granddaughter of one of Adolf Hitler's right-hand men." Smith also maintained that as he was painting the walls of Batzel's sitting room he overheard Batzel tell her roommate that she was related to Nazi politician Heinrich Himmler. According to Smith, Batzel told him on another occasion that some of the paintings hanging in her house were inherited. To Smith, these paintings looked old and European.

After assembling these clues, Smith used a computer to look for websites concerning stolen artwork and was directed by a search engine to the Museum Security Network ("the Network") website. He thereupon sent the following e-mail message to the Network:

> From: Bob Smith [e-mail address omitted]
>
> To: securma@museum-security.org [the Network][1]
>
> Subject: Stolen Art
>
> Hi there,
>
> I am a building contractor in Asheville, North Carolina, USA. A month ago, I did a remodeling job for a woman, Ellen L. Batzel who

---

[1] We are including this e-mail address because the precise e-mail address used is relevant to our later discussion.

bragged to me about being the grand daughter [sic] of "one of Adolph Hitler's right-hand men." At the time, I was concentrating on performing my tasks, but upon reflection, I believe she said she was the descendant of Heinrich Himmler.

Ellen Batzel has hundreds of older European paintings on her walls, all with heavy carved wooden frames. She told me she inherited them.

I believe these paintings were looted during WWII and are the rightful legacy of the Jewish people. Her address is [omitted].

I also believe that the descendants of criminals should not be persecuted for the crimes of the [sic] fathers, nor should they benefit. I do not know who to contact about this, so I start with your organization. Please contact me via email [...] if you would like to discuss this matter.

Bob.

Ton Cremers, then-Director of Security at Amsterdam's famous Rijksmuseum and (in his spare time) sole operator of the Museum Security Network ("the Network"), received Smith's e-mail message. The nonprofit Network maintains both a website and an electronic e-mailed newsletter about museum security and stolen art. Cremers periodically puts together an electronic document containing: e-mails sent to him, primarily from Network subscribers; comments by himself as the moderator of an on-line discussion; and excerpts from news articles related to stolen works of art. He exercises some editorial discretion in choosing which of the e-mails he receives are included in the listserv mailing, omitting e-mails unrelated to stolen art and eliminating other material that he decides does not merit distribution to his subscribers. The remaining amalgamation of material is then posted on the Network's website and sent to subscribers automatically via a listserv. The Network's website and listserv mailings are read by hundreds of museum security officials, insurance investigators, and law enforcement personnel around the world, who use the information in the Network posting to track down stolen art.

After receiving it, Cremers published Smith's e-mail message to the Network, with some minor wording changes, on the Network listserv. He also posted that listserv, with Smith's message included, on the Network's website. Cremers later included it on the Network listserv and posted a "moderator's message" stating that "the FBI has been informed of the contents of [Smith's] original message."

After the posting, Bob Smith e-mailed a subscriber to the listserv, Jonathan Sazonoff, explaining that he had had no idea that his e-mail would be posted to the listserv or put on the web. Smith told Sazanoff:

> I [was] trying to figure out how in blazes I could have posted me [sic] email to [the Network] bulletin board. I came into MSN through the back door, directed by a search engine, and never got the big picture. I don't remember reading anything about a message board either so I am a bit confused over how it could happen. Every message board to which I have ever subscribed required application, a pass-word, and/or registration, and the instructions explained this is necessary to keep out the advertisers, cranks, and bumbling idiots like me.

Batzel discovered the message several months after its initial posting and complained to Cremers about the message. Cremers then contacted Smith via e-mail to request additional information about Smith's allegations. Smith continued to insist on the truth of his statements. He also told Cremers that if he had thought his e-mail "message would be posted on an international message board [he] never would have sent it in the first place."

Upon discovering that Smith had not intended to post his message, Cremers apologized for the confusion. He told Smith in an e-mail that "[y]ou were not a subscriber to the list and I believe that you did not realize your message would be forwarded to the mailinglist [sic]." Apparently, subscribers send messages for inclusion in the listserv to securma@x54all.nl, a different address from that to which Smith had sent his e-mail contacting the Network. Cremers further explained that he "receive[s] many e-mails each day some of which contain queries [he thinks] interesting enough to for-ward to the list. [Smith's] was one of those."

Batzel disputes Smith's account of their conversations. She says she is not, and never said she is, a descendant of a Nazi official, and that she did not inherit any art. Smith, she charges, defamed her not because he believed her artwork stolen but out of pique, because Batzel refused to show Hollywood contacts a screenplay he had written.

Batzel claims further that because of Cremers's actions she lost several prominent clients in California and was investigated by the North Carolina Bar Association. Also, she represents that her social reputation suffered.

... III

A. *California's Anti-SLAPP Statute*

California law provides for pre-trial dismissal of "SLAPPs": "Strategic Lawsuits against Public Participation." Cal. Civ. Proc. Code § 425.16. These are lawsuits that "masquerade as ordinary lawsuits" but are brought to deter common citizens from exercising their political or legal rights or to punish them for doing so. *Wilcox v. Superior Court*, 27 Cal. App. 4th 809, 816, 33 Cal. Rptr. 2d 446 (1994), *overruled on other grounds by Equilon Enter. v. Consumer Cause, Inc.*, 29 Cal. 4th 53, 124 Cal. Rptr. 2d 507, 52 P.3d 685 (2002) (citations omitted). "The anti-SLAPP statute was enacted to allow for early dismissal of meritless first amendment cases aimed at chilling expression through costly, time-consuming litigation." *Metabolife Int'l, Inc. v. Wornick*, 264 F.3d 832, 839 (9th Cir. 2001).

If the defendant files an anti-SLAPP motion to strike, all discovery proceedings are stayed. *See* § 425.16(g). A court may, however, permit specified discovery "on noticed motion and for good cause shown." *Id.* In order to prevail on an anti-SLAPP motion, the defendant is required to make a *prima facie* showing that the plaintiff's suit arises from an act by the defendant made in connection with a public issue in furtherance of the defendant's right to free speech under the United States or California Constitution. *See United States ex rel. Newsham v. Lockheed Missiles & Space Co.*, 190 F.3d 963, 971 (9th Cir. 1999); *see also* § 425.16(e) (defining "act in furtherance of a person's right of ... free speech.").

The burden then shifts to the plaintiff to establish a reasonable probability that the plaintiff will prevail on his or her defamation claim. *See Lockheed*, 190 F.3d at 971. "[T]he plaintiff must demonstrate that 'the complaint is legally sufficient and supported by a *prima facie* showing of facts to sustain a favorable judgment if the evidence submitted by plaintiff is [sic] credited.'" *Metabolife*, 264 F.3d at 840 (quoting *Wilcox v. Superior Court*, 27 Cal. App. 4th 809, 33 Cal. Rptr. 2d 446, 454).

If the court denies an anti-SLAPP motion to strike, the parties continue with discovery. *See* § 425.16(g). Once the plaintiff's case has survived the motion, the anti-SLAPP statute no longer applies and the parties proceed to litigate the merits of the action.

... C. *Probability of Success*

To resist a motion to strike pursuant to California's anti-SLAPP law, Batzel must demonstrate a probability that she will prevail on the merits of her complaint. Cal. Civ. Proc. Code § 425.16. The district court held that Batzel had made such a showing, and absent 47 U.S.C. § 230, we would be inclined to agree.

Section 230(c)(1) [of 47 U.S.C.] specifies that "[n]o provider or user of an interactive computer service shall be treated as the publisher or speaker of any information provided by another information content provider." The provision thereby set limitations on liability under state law for postings on the Internet and other computer networks. The district court declined to extend the legislative grant of immunity pursuant to § 230(c) to Cremers and the Network, holding that the Network is not "an internet service provider" and therefore is not covered by the statute. We do not agree with the district court's reading of § 230.

1. *Section 230(c)*

We begin with a brief survey of the background of § 230(c), as that background is useful in construing the statutory terms here at issue.

Title V of the Telecommunications Act of 1996, Pub. L. No. 104-104, is known as the "Communications Decency Act of 1996" [the "CDA" or "the Act"]. The primary goal of the Act was to control the exposure of minors to indecent material. *See* Pub. L. No. 104-104, Title V (1996); *see also* H.R. Rep. No. 104-458, at 81-91 (1996); S. Rep. No. 104-230, at 187-193 (1996); S. Rep. No. 104-23, at 9 (1995).

... The specific provision at issue here, § 230(c)(1), overrides the traditional treatment of publishers, distributors, and speakers under statutory and common law. As a matter of policy, "Congress decided not to treat providers of interactive computer services like other information providers such as newspapers, magazines or television and radio stations, all of which may be held liable for publishing or distributing obscene or defamatory material written or prepared by others." *Blumenthal v. Drudge*, 992 F. Supp.44, 49 (D.D.C. 1998). ...

Congress made this legislative choice for two primary reasons. First, Congress wanted to encourage the unfettered and unregulated development of free speech on the Internet, and to promote the development of e-commerce. ...

Consistent with these provisions, courts construing § 230 have recognized as critical in applying the statute the concern that lawsuits could threaten the "freedom of speech in the new and burgeoning Internet medium." *Zeran v. America Online, Inc.*, 129 F.3d 327, 330 (4th Cir. 1997). ... Making interactive computer services and their users liable for the speech of third parties would severely restrict the information available on the Internet. Section 230 therefore sought to prevent lawsuits from shutting down websites and other services on the Internet.

The second reason for enacting § 230(c) was to encourage interactive computer services and users of such services to self-police the Internet for obscenity and other offensive material, so as to aid parents in limiting their children's access to such material. *See* §

230(b)(4); *see also* 141 Cong. Rec. H8469-70 (Statements of Representatives Cox, Wyden, and Barton); *Zeran*, 129 F.3d at 331; *Blumenthal*, 992 F. Supp. at 52.

We recognize that there is an apparent tension between Congress's goals of promoting free speech while at the same time giving parents the tools to limit the material their children can access over the Internet. ... [But] laws often have more than one goal in mind, and that it is not uncommon for these purposes to look in opposite directions. The need to balance competing values is a primary impetus for enacting legislation. Tension within statutes is often not a defect but an indication that the legislature was doing its job. *See, e.g., United States v. Kalustian*, 529 F.2d 585, 588 (9th Cir. 1975) (describing dual and some-what competing purposes of the Federal wiretap statute of both protecting individual privacy and combating crime).

So, even though the CDA overall may have had the purpose of restricting content, there is little doubt that the Cox-Wyden amendment, which added what ultimately became § 230 to the Act, sought to further First Amendment and e-commerce interests on the Internet while also promoting the protection of minors. *See* 141 Cong. Rec. H8469-72 (Statements of Representatives Cox, Wyden, Lofgren, and Goodlatte). Fostering the two ostensibly competing purposes here works because parents best can control the material accessed by their children with the cooperation and assistance of Inter-net service providers ("ISPs") and other providers and users of services on the Internet. Section 230(b)(4) describes this goal: "It is the policy of the United States ... to remove disincentives for the development and utilization of blocking and filtering technologies that empower parents to restrict their children's access to objectionable or inappropriate online material." § 230(b)(4). Some blocking and filtering programs depend on the cooperation of website operators and access providers who label material that appears on their services.

Without the immunity provided in Section 230(c), users and providers of interactive computer services who review material could be found liable for the statements of third parties, yet providers and users that disavow any responsibility would be free from liability. ...

2. *Application to Cremers and the Museum Security Network*

To benefit from § 230(c) immunity, Cremers must first demonstrate that his Network website and listserv qualify as "provider[s] or user[s] of an *interactive computer service*." § 230(c)(1)(emphasis added). An "interactive computer service" is defined as "any information service, system, or access software provider that provides or enables computer access by multiple users to a computer server, including specifically a service or system that provides access to the Internet and such systems operated or services offered by libraries or educational institutions." § 230(f)(2).

The district court concluded that only services that provide access to the Internet as a whole are covered by this definition. But the definition of "interactive computer service" on its face covers "*any*" information services or other systems, as long as the service or system allows "multiple users" to access "a computer server." Further, the statute repeatedly refers to "the Internet and *other* interactive computer services," (emphasis added), making clear that the statutory immunity extends beyond the Internet itself. §§ 230(a)(3), (a)(4), (b)(1), (b)(2), and (f)(3). Also, the definition of "inter-active computer service" after the broad definition language, states that the definition "*includ[es]* specifically a service or system that provides access to the Internet," § 230(f)(2) (emphasis added), thereby confirming that services providing access to the Internet as a whole are only a subset of the services to which the statutory immunity applies.[15]

There is, however, no need here to decide whether a listserv or website itself fits the broad statutory definition of "interactive computer service," because the language of § 230(c)(1) confers immunity not just on "providers" of such services, but also on "users" of such services.[16] § 230(c)(1). There is no dispute that the Network uses interactive computer services to distribute its on-line mailing and to post the listserv on its website. Indeed, to make its website available and to mail out the listserv, the Network *must* access the Inter-net through some form of "interactive computer service." Thus, both the Network website and the listserv are potentially immune under § 230.

Critically, however, § 230 limits immunity to information "provided by another information content provider." § 230(c)(1). An "information content provider" is defined by the statute to mean "any person or entity that is responsible, in whole or in part, for the creation or development of information provided through the Internet or any other interactive computer service." § 230(f)(3). The reference to "*another* information content provider" (emphasis added) distinguishes the circumstance in which the interactive computer service itself meets the definition of "information content provider" with respect to the information in question. The pertinent question therefore becomes whether Smith was the sole content provider of his e-mail, or whether Cremers can also be considered to have "creat[ed]" or "develop[ed]" Smith's e-mail message forwarded to the listserv.

Obviously, Cremers did not create Smith's e-mail. Smith composed the e-mail entirely on his own. Nor do Cremers's minor alterations of Smith's e-mail prior to its posting or his choice to publish the e-mail (while rejecting other e-mails for inclusion in the listserv) rise to the level of "development." As we have seen, a central purpose of the Act was to protect from liability service providers and users who take some affirmative steps to edit the material posted. Also, the exclusion of "publisher" liability necessarily precludes liability for exercising the usual prerogative of publishers to choose among proffered material and to edit the material published while retaining its basic form and message.

---

[15] Other courts construing § 230(f)(2) have recognized that the definition includes a wide range of cyberspace services, not only internet service providers. *See, e.g., Gentry v. eBay, Inc.*, 99 Cal. App. 4th 816, 831, 121 Cal. Rptr. 2d 703 & n.7 (2002) (on-line auction website is an "interactive computer service"); *Schneider v. Amazon.com*, 108 Wn. App. 454, 31 P.3d 37, 40-41 (Wash Ct. App. 2001) (on-line bookstore Amazon.com is an "interactive computer service"); *Barrett v. Clark*, 2001 WL 881259 at *9 (Cal. Sup. Ct. 2001) (newsgroup considered an "interactive computer service"); *see also Ben Ezra[, Weinstein, & Co. v. America Online, Inc.*, 206 F.3d 980, 985 (10th Cir. 2000)] (parties conceded that AOL was an interactive computer service when it published an on-line stock quotation service); *Zeran*, 129 F.3d at 330 (AOL assumed to be interactive computer service when it operated bulletin board service for subscribers); *Blumenthal*, 992 F. Supp. at 49-50 (parties conceded that AOL was an "interactive computer service" even when it functioned as the publisher of an on-line gossip column).

[16] We note that several courts to reach the issue have decided that a web-site is an "interactive computer service." *See, e.g., Carafano v. Metrosplash.com, Inc.*, 207 F. Supp. 2d 1055, 1065-66 (C.D. Cal. 2002); *Gentry*, 99 Cal. App. 4th at 831 (holding that website is an interactive computer service); *Schneider*, 31 P.3d at 40-41 (same).

The "development of information" therefore means something more substantial than merely editing portions of an e-mail and selecting material for publication.[18] Because Cremers did no more than select and make minor alterations to Smith's e-mail, Cremers cannot be considered the content provider of Smith's e-mail for purposes of § 230.

The partial dissent does not register any disagreement with this interpretation of the definition of "information content provider" or with the observation that immunity for "publisher[s]" indicates a recognition that the immunity will extend to the selection of material supplied by others. It nonetheless simultaneously maintains that 1) a defendant who takes an active role in selecting information for publication is not immune; and 2) interactive computer service users and providers who screen the material submitted and remove offensive content are immune. These two positions simply cannot logically coexist.

Such a distinction between deciding to publish only some of the material submitted and deciding *not* to publish some of the material submitted is not a viable one. The scope of the immunity cannot turn on whether the publisher approaches the selection process as one of inclusion or removal, as the difference is one of method or degree, not substance.

A distinction between removing an item once it has appeared on the Internet and screening before publication cannot fly either. For one thing, there is no basis for believing that Congress intended a one-bite-at-the-apple form of immunity. Also, Congress could not have meant to favor removal of offending material over more advanced software that screens out the material before it ever appears. If anything, the goal of encouraging assistance to parents seeking to control children's access to offensive material would suggest a preference for a system in which the offensive material is not available even temporarily. The upshot is that the partial dissent's posit concerning the limitations of § 230(c) immunity simply cannot be squared with the statute's language and purposes, whatever merit it, or a variant of it, might have as a policy matter.

In most cases our conclusion that Cremers cannot be considered a content provider would end matters, but this case presents one twist on the usual § 230 analysis: Smith maintains that he never "imagined [his] message would be posted on an international message board or [he] never would have sent it in the first place." The question thus becomes whether Smith can be said to have "provided" his e-mail in the sense intended by § 230(c). If the defamatory information is not "*provided* by another information content provider," then § 230(c) does not confer immunity on the publisher of the information.

"[P]rovided" suggests, at least, some active role by the "provider" in supplying the material to a "provider or user of an interactive computer service." One would not say, for example, that the author of a magazine article "provided" it to an interactive computer service provider or user by allowing the article to be published in hard copy off-line. Although such

---

[18] Other courts have agreed that the "exercise of a publisher's traditional editorial functions -- such as deciding whether to publish, withdraw, post-pone or alter content" do not transform an individual into a "content provider" within the meaning of § 230. *Zeran*, 129 F.3d at 330; *see also Ben Ezra*, 206 F.3d at 985-86 (defendant not "information content provider" although it edited and altered stock quotations provided by third party); *Blumenthal*, 992 F. Supp. at 49-53 (defendant not "information content provider" although it had editorial control over content in gossip column); *Schneider*, 31 P.3d at 39-43 (website not "information content provider" although it had strict posting guidelines and could edit and republish posted material).

an article is available to anyone with access to a library or a newsstand, it is not "provided" for use on the Internet.

The result in the foregoing example should not change if the interactive computer service provider or user has a subscription to the magazine. In that instance, the material in question is "provided" to the "provider or user of an interactive computer service," but not in its role as a provider or user of a computer service. The structure and purpose of § 230(c)(1) indicate that the immunity applies only with regard to third-party information provided *for use on the Internet* or another interactive computer service. As we have seen, the section is concerned with providing special immunity for individuals who would otherwise be publishers or speakers, because of Congress's concern with assuring a free market in ideas and information on the Internet. If information is provided to those individuals in a capacity unrelated to their function as a provider or user of interactive computer services, then there is no reason to protect them with the special statutory immunity.

So, if, for example, an individual who happens to operate a website receives a defamatory "snail mail" letter from an old friend, the website operator cannot be said to have been "provided" the information in his capacity as a website service. Section 230(c)(1) supplies immunity for only individuals or entities acting as "provider[s]" or "user[s]" of an "interactive computer service," and therefore does not apply when it is not "provided" to such persons in their roles as providers or users.

The situation here is somewhat more complicated than our letter example, because Smith did provide his e-mail over the Internet and transmitted it to the Network, an operator of a website that is an user of an interactive computer service. Nevertheless, Smith contends that he did not intend his e-mail to be placed on an interactive computer service for public viewing.

Smith's confusion, even if legitimate, does not matter, Cremers maintains, because the § 230(c)(1) immunity should be available simply because Smith was the author of the e-mail, without more.

We disagree. Under Cremers's broad interpretation of § 230(c), users and providers of interactive computer services could with impunity intentionally post material they knew was never meant to be put on the Internet. At the same time, the creator or developer of the information presumably could not be held liable for unforeseeable publication of his material to huge numbers of people with whom he had no intention to communicate. The result would be nearly limitless immunity for speech never meant to be broadcast over the Internet.

Supplying a "provider or user of an interactive computer service" with immunity in such circumstances is not consistent with Congress's expressly stated purposes in adopting § 230. Free speech and the development of the Internet are not "promote[d]" by affording immunity when providers and users of "interactive computer service[s]" knew or had reason to know that the information provided was not intended for publication on the Internet. Quite the contrary: Users of the Internet are likely to be discouraged from sending e-mails for fear that their e-mails may be published on the web without their permission.

Such a scenario is very different from the bulletin boards that Congress had in mind when passing § 230. When a user sends a message to a bulletin board, it is obvious that by doing so, he or she will be publicly posting the message. Here, by contrast, Smith claims that he had no idea that the Network even had a listserv. His expectation, he says, was that he was simply sending a private e-mail to an organization informing it of his concern about Batzel's artwork, and, he insists, he would not have sent the message had he known it would be sent on through the listserv. Absent an incentive for service providers and users to evaluate whether the content they receive is meant to be posted, speech over the Internet will be chilled rather than encouraged. Immunizing providers and users of "interactive computer service[s]" for publishing material when they have reason to know that the material is not intended for publication therefore contravenes the Congressional purpose of encouraging the "development of the Internet."

Immunizing individuals and entities in such situations also interferes with Congress's objective of providing incentives for providers and users of interactive computer services to remove offensive material, especially obscene and defamatory speech. Far from encouraging such actions, immunizing a publisher or distributor for including content not intended for Internet publication increases the likelihood that obscene and defamatory material will be widely available. Not only will on-line publishers be able to distribute such material obtained from "hard copy" sources with impunity, but, because the content provider him or herself never intended publication, there is a greater likelihood that the distributed material will in fact be defamatory or obscene. A person is much more likely to exercise care in choosing his words when he knows that those words will be widely read. This is true not only for altruistic reasons but also because liability for defamation attaches only upon publication. In the current case, Smith claimed exactly that: He told Cremers that if he had known his e-mail would be posted, he never would have sent it. The congressional objectives in passing § 230 therefore are not furthered by providing immunity in instances where posted material was clearly not meant for publication.

At the same time, Congress's purpose in enacting § 230(c)(1) suggests that we must take great care in determining whether another's information was "provided" to a "provider or user of an interactive computer service" for publication. Otherwise, posting of information on the Internet and other interactive computer services would be chilled, as the service provider or user could not tell whether posting was contemplated. To preclude this possibility, the focus should be not on the information provider's intentions or knowledge when transmitting content but, instead, on the service provider's or user's reasonable perception of those intentions or knowledge. We therefore hold that a service provider or user is immune from liability under § 230(c)(1) when a third person or entity that created or developed the information in question furnished it to the provider or user under circumstances in which a reasonable person in the position of the service provider or user would conclude that the information was provided for publication on the Internet or other "interactive computer service."

It is not entirely clear from the record whether Smith "provided" the e-mail for publication on the Internet under this standard. There are facts that could have led Cremers reasonably to conclude that Smith sent him the information because he operated an Internet service. On the other hand, Smith was not a subscriber to the listserv and apparently sent the information to a different e-mail account from the one at which Cremers usually received information for publication. More development of the record may be necessary to determine whether, under all the circumstances, a reasonable person in Cremers' position would conclude that the information was sent for internet publication, or whether a triable issue of fact is presented on that issue.

We therefore vacate the district court's order denying Cremers's anti-SLAPP motion and remand to the district court for further proceedings to develop the facts under this newly announced standard and to evaluate what Cremers should have reasonably concluded at the time he received Smith's e-mail. If Cremers should have reasonably concluded, for example, that because Smith's e-mail arrived via a different e-mail address it was not provided to him for possible posting on the listserv, then Cremers cannot take advantage of the § 230(c) immunities. Under that circumstance, the posted information was not "provided" by another "information con-tent provider" within the meaning of § 230. After making such an inquiry, the district court must then evaluate whether Batzel adequately has demonstrated a probability that she will prevail on the merits of her complaint under California's anti-SLAPP statute.

... VACATED IN PART, AFFIRMED IN PART, AND REMANDED

Gould, J., concurring in part, dissenting in part:

I respectfully dissent from the majority's analysis of the statutory immunity from libel suits created by § 230 of the Communications Decency Act (CDA).[1] The majority gives the phrase "information provided by another" an incorrect and unworkable meaning that extends CDA immunity far beyond what Congress intended. Under the majority's interpretation of § 230, many persons who intentionally spread vicious falsehoods on the Internet will be immune from suit. This sweeping preemption of valid state libel laws is not necessary to promote Internet use and is not what Congress had in mind.

... The majority and I agree on the importance of the CDA and on the proper interpretation of the first and second elements. We disagree only over the third element.

The majority holds that information is "provided by another" when "a third person or entity that created or developed the information in question furnished it to the provider or user under circumstances in which a reasonable person in the position of the service provider or user would conclude that the information was provided for publication on the Internet or other 'interactive computer service.'" In other words, whether information is "provided" depends on the *defendant's perception* of the *author's intention*. Nothing in the statutory language suggests that "provided" should be interpreted in this convoluted and unworkable fashion.

Under the majority's rule, a court determining whether to extend CDA immunity to a defendant must determine whether the author of allegedly defamatory information -- a person who often will be beyond reach of the court's process or, worse, unknown -- intended that the information be distributed on the Internet. In many cases, the author's intention may not be discernable from the face of the defamatory communication. Even people who want an e-mail message widely disseminated may not preface the message with words such as "Please pass it on." Moreover, the fact-intensive question of the author's intent is particularly unsuited for a judge's determination before trial, when the immunity question will most often arise.

The majority's rule will be incomprehensible to most citizens, who will be unable to plan their own conduct mindful of the law's requirements. Laypersons may not grasp that their tort liability depends on whether they reasonably should have known that the author of a particular communication intended that it be distributed on the Internet. Laypersons certainly will not grasp *why* this should be the case, as a matter of justice, morality, or politics. Those who receive a potentially libelous e-mail message from another person would seldom

---

[1] ... I dissent only from Part III.C of the opinion.

wonder, when deciding whether to forward the message to others, "Did *the author* of this defamatory information intend that it be distributed on the Internet?" However, those who receive a potentially libelous e-mail almost certainly would wonder, "Is it appropriate *for me* to spread this defamatory message?" By shifting its inquiry away from the defendant's conduct, the majority has crafted a rule that encourages the casual spread of harmful lies. The majority has improvidently crafted a rule that is foreign to the statutory text and foreign to human experience.

The majority rule licenses professional rumor-mongers and gossip-hounds to spread false and hurtful information with impunity. So long as the defamatory information was written by a person who wanted the information to be spread on the Internet (in other words, a person with an axe to grind), the rumormonger's injurious conduct is beyond legal redress. Nothing in the CDA's text or legislative history suggests that Congress intended CDA immunity to extend so far. Nothing in the text, legislative history, or human experience would lead me to accept the notion that Congress in § 230 intended to immunize users or providers of interactive computer services who, by their discretionary decisions to spread particular communications, cause trickles of defamation to swell into rivers of harm.

The problems caused by the majority's rule all would vanish if we focused our inquiry not on the *author's intent*, but on the *defendant's acts*, as I believe Congress intended. We should hold that the CDA immunizes a defendant only when the defendant took no active role in selecting the questionable information for publication. If the defendant took an active role in selecting information for publication, the information is no longer "information provided by another" within the meaning of § 230. We should draw this conclusion from the statute's text and purposes.

A person's decision to select particular information for distribution on the Internet changes that information in a subtle but important way: it adds the person's imprimatur to it. The recipient of information that has been selected by another person for distribution understands that the information has been deemed worthy of dissemination by the sender. Information that bears such an implicit endorsement[5] is no longer merely the "information provided by" the original sender. 47 U.S.C. § 230(c)(1). It is information transformed. It is information bolstered, strengthened to do more harm if it is wrongful. A defendant who has actively selected libelous information for distribution thus should not be entitled to CDA immunity for disseminating "information provided by another."

My interpretation of § 230 is consistent with the CDA's legislative history. Congress understood that entities that facilitate communication on the Internet -- particularly entities that operate e-mail networks, "chat rooms," "bulletin boards," and "listservs" -- have special needs. The amount of information communicated through such services is staggering. Millions of communications are sent daily. It would be impossible to screen all such communications for libelous or offensive content. Faced with potential liability for each message republished by their services, interactive computer service users and providers might choose to restrict severely the number and type of messages posted. The threat of tort

---

[5] By "endorsement," I do not mean that the person who selects information for distribution agrees with the content of that information. Rather, I mean that the person has endorsed the information insofar as he or she has deemed it appropriate for distribution to others. That adds enough to the information to remove it from CDA immunity.

liability in an area of such prolific speech would have an obvious chilling effect on free speech and would hamper the new medium.

These policy concerns have force when a potential defendant uses or provides technology that enables others to disseminate information directly without intervening human action. These policy concerns lack force when a potential defendant does not offer users this power of direct transmission. If a potential defendant employs a person to screen communications to select some of them for dissemination, it is not impossible (or even difficult) for that person to screen communications for defamatory content. Immunizing that person or the person's employer from liability would not advance Congress's goal of protecting those in need of protection.

If a person is charged with screening all communications to select some for dissemination, that person can decide not to disseminate a potentially offensive communication. Or that person can undertake some reasonable investigation. Such a process would be relatively inexpensive and would reduce the serious social costs caused by the spread of offensive and defamatory communications.

Under my interpretation of § 230, a company that operates an e-mail network would be immune from libel suits arising out of e-mail messages transmitted automatically across its network. Similarly, the owner, operator, organizer, or moderator of an Internet bulletin board, chat room, or listserv would be immune from libel suits arising out of messages distributed using that technology, provided that the person does not actively select particular messages for publication.

On the other hand, a person who receives a libelous communication and makes the decision to disseminate that message to others -- whether via e-mail, a bulletin board, a chat room, or a listserv -- would not be immune.

My approach also would further Congress's goal of encouraging "self-policing" on the Internet. Congress decided to immunize from liability those who publish material on the Internet, so long as they do not actively select defamatory or offensive material for distribution. As a result, those who *remove* all or part of an offensive information posted on (for example) an Internet bulletin board are immune from suit. Those who employ blocking or filtering technologies that allow readers to avoid obscene or offensive materials also are immune from suit.

On the other hand, Congress decided not to immunize those who actively select defamatory or offensive information for distribution on the Internet. Congress thereby ensured that users and providers of interactive computer services would have an incentive not to spread harmful gossip and lies intentionally.

Congress wanted to ensure that excessive government regulation did not slow America's expansion into the exciting new frontier of the Internet. But Congress did not want this new frontier to be like the Old West: a lawless zone governed by retribution and mob justice. The CDA does not license anarchy. A person's decision to disseminate the rankest rumor or most blatant falsehood should not escape legal redress merely because the person chose to disseminate it through the Internet rather than through some other medium. A proper analysis of § 230, which makes a human being's decision to disseminate a particular communication the touchstone of CDA immunity, reconciles Congress's intent to deregulate the Internet with Congress's recognition that certain beneficial technologies, which promote efficient global communication and advance values enshrined in our First Amendment, are unique to the Internet and need special protection. Congress wanted to preserve the Internet and aid its growth, but not at all costs. Congress did not want to remove incentives for people armed with the power of the Internet to act with reasonable care to avoid unnecessary harm to others.

In this case, I would hold that Cremers is *not* entitled to CDA immunity because Cremers actively selected Smith's e-mail message for publication. Whether Cremers's Museum Security Network is characterized as a "moderated listserv," an "e-mail newsletter," or otherwise, it is certain that the Network did not permit users to disseminate information to other users directly without intervening human action. According to Cremers, "To post a response or to provide new information, the subscriber merely replies to the listserv mailing and *the message is sent directly to Cremers, who includes it* in the listserv with the subsequent distribution." (emphasis added).

This procedure was followed with respect to Smith's e-mail message accusing Batzel of owning art stolen by a Nazi ancestor. Smith transmitted the message to one e-mail account, from which Cremers received it. Cremers forwarded the message to a second e-mail account. He pasted the message into a new edition of the Museum Security Network newsletter. He then sent that newsletter to his subscribers and posted it on the Network's website. Cremers's decision to select Smith's e-mail message for publication effectively altered the message's meaning, adding to the message the unstated suggestion that Cremers deemed the message worthy of readers' attention. Cremers therefore did not merely distribute "information provided by another," and he is not entitled to CDA immunity.

From the record before us, we have no reason to think that Cremers is not well-meaning or that his concerns about stolen artwork are not genuine. Nor on this appeal do we decide whether his communications were defamatory or harmful in fact. We deal only with immunity. And, in my view, there is no immunity under the CDA if Cremers made a discretionary decision to distribute on the Internet defamatory information about another person, without any investigation whatsoever. If Cremers made a mistake, we should not hold that he may escape all accountability just because he made that mistake on the Internet.

I respectfully dissent.

* * * * *

Ellen L. BATZEL, a citizen of the State of California, Plaintiff-Appellee

v.

Robert SMITH, a citizen of the State of North Carolina;
Netherlands Museums Association, an entity of unknown form; Mosler, Inc., a
Delaware corporation with its principal place of business in Ohio, Defendants

and

Ton Cremers, a citizen or subject of the Netherlands, Defendant-Appellant.

United States Court of Appeals for the Ninth Circuit

Nos. 01-56380, 01-56556

December 3, 2003

ORDER

The majority of the panel has voted to deny appellee's petition for rehearing. Judge Berzon has voted to deny the petition for rehearing *en banc* and Judge Canby so recommends. Judge Gould has voted to grant the petition for rehearing and petition for rehearing *en banc*. ...

GOULD, Circuit Judge, with whom Circuit Judges TALLMAN and CALLAHAN join, dissenting from denial of rehearing *en banc*.

I dissent from the denial of *en banc* review of this case. I remain convinced that the panel majority's interpretation of the statutory immunity found in 47 U.S.C. § 230(c) is wrong in light of Congress's intent, and will needlessly harm persons defamed on the Internet. Section 230(c) states: "[n]o provider or user of an interactive computer service shall be treated as the publisher or speaker of any information provided by another information content provider." Immunity thus requires, *inter alia,* that the communication must have been "information provided by another information content provider." "[I]nformation content provider," in turn, is defined as "any person or entity that is responsible, in whole or in part, for the creation or development of information provided through the Internet or any other interactive computer service." 47 U.S.C. § 230(e)(3).

The panel agreed that if a person who posted defamatory material on the Internet "develop[ed]" that material, that person would become the information content provider of the material and lose § 230(c) immunity. The panel majority held that Cremers did not "develop[ ]" the information by "merely editing portions of [Smith's] e-mail and selecting [it] for publication." *Batzel v. Smith,* 333 F.3d 1018, 1031 (9th Cir. 2003).

The panel majority's conclusion that pre-publication selection and editing is not "development" is not supported by the text, history, or precedent surrounding § 230(c). Initially, any entity that "creat[es]" *or* "develop[s]" information is an "information content provider." 47 U.S.C. § 230(e)(3). To avoid rendering "creation" superfluous, "development" must mean adding to or improving the information initially created by another "information content provider."

Development is defined as "a change in the course of action or events or in conditions; a state of advancement; an addition; an elaboration." *The New Shorter Oxford English Dictionary* 654 (Thumb Index ed.1993). *See also www.m-w.com* (definition of "develop" includes "1b: to make visible or manifest" and "3b(1): to make available or usable"). The ordinary usage of a "development" of information suggests change in, addition to, or novel presentation of, the information.

There should be little doubt, given ordinary usage that Congress presumably intended, that a publisher's affirmative choice to select certain information for publication for the first time on the Internet "develops" that information. To put the point more concretely, imagine a defamatory e-mail sent to both an on-line bulletin board for appellate litigation and to a popular appellate litigation blog. Let us say, for example, that the e-mail falsely stated that Judge X of the Y Circuit was paid by Z to render decisions in Z's favor. If the blogger decides to publish the e-mail, there is something qualitatively different about the e-mail as published on the appellate blog, as contrasted with the one posted on the bulletin board. The blogger's conscious decision to publish an e-mail would add, by virtue of his or her reputation and that of the blog, a layer of credibility and endorsement that would be lacking from the e-mail merely posted to the bulletin board. And being the first person to post the defamatory material on the Internet would be a novel presentation of the defamatory material.

The panel majority agrees that if Cremers "developed" the defamatory content, he would lose § 230(c) immunity. The question is whether Cremers' actions are a development of the information. Similar to the blog hypothetical above, Cremers' actions constituted a change in, addition to, and novel presentation of, the information. Cremers changed Smith's e-mail (by deleting the key word "some" describing the inherited artwork) and provided a novel presentation thereof by formatting it for Cremers' e-mail newsletter. Moreover, Cremers added what credibility he and his organization may have had to Smith's bare allegations when Cremers selected and published Smith's e-mail. And posting the message on the Internet, as Cremers did, is a novel presentation of the information because Smith, as original sender, had not posted it. Cremers' decision to select, edit, and publish Smith's e-mail in an edition of the Museum Security Network's newsletter was a change in, an addition to, and a novel presentation of what Smith had already written.

To bolster the incorrect theory that "development" does not include editing information or selecting that information for publication, the panel majority points to Congress's "exclusion of 'publisher' liability," *Batzel,* 333 F.3d at 1031, and argues that "development" does not include the exercise of traditional editorial functions. *Id.* However, this reading omits a key qualification within § 230(c); namely that immunity is provided for claims that "treat[ ]" the defendant as a publisher. This method of using the word "publisher" does not at all imply that Congress intended to immunize all of the functions exercised by a "publisher" as asserted by the panel majority, but that the only immunity Congress intended to provide was immunity from defamation-type claims. *Cf. Zeran v. America Online, Inc.,* 129 F.3d 327, 332 (4th Cir.1997) ("the terms 'publisher' and 'distributor'" in § 230(c) "derive their legal significance from the context of defamation law."). In the defamation context, "publisher" has a broad meaning that includes any person who automatically republishes or distributes the defamatory material. *See, e.g.,* W. Page Keeton *et al., Prosser and Keeton on the Law of Torts* § 113 (5th ed.1984). "Publisher" in the context of § 230(c) must be read to encompass the broad meaning of "publisher" in defamation law. Thus, "publisher" was meant to define the type of *claim* that § 230(c) would immunize -- e.g., a claim alleging defamation must prove the element of "publication" -- not to define the meaning of "development" as found in § 230(e)(3). All claims that require proof of publishing or speaking (traditionally, libel and slander) would be immunized because the plaintiff could not "treat[ ]" the defendant as "publisher or speaker." On the other hand, claims that do not require proof of publication are not, and should not be, immunized. Because Congress limited immunity only to claims that require proof of the defendant being a publisher or a speaker, it is incorrect to hold that Congress intended that the word "publisher" in § 230(c) be used to shed light on when information content is sufficiently "developed" by the publisher to prevent it from being "information provided by another information content provider."[6]

Further, it is not as if the panel reached this result by simply following the holdings of other circuits. Make no mistake: the panel majority coldly goes where no circuit court has gone before, reaching further and providing broader automatic immunity of the most callous and damaging defamation that anyone might maliciously post on the Internet. The majority cites four out-of-circuit cases for the proposition that "development" does not include the exercise of traditional editorial functions. *Batzel,* 333 F.3d at 1031 n.18. These cases have no persuasive force in assessing Batzel's claim against Cremers. None of these cases dealt with similar facts, and none address the question of whether the pre-publication selecting and editing of another entity's information is a "development" of information, which would place the selector or editor outside the statutory immunity declared by Congress. Each of the four cases involved the actual or potential editing or removing of posted information after the information had already been posted on the Internet. No federal court of appeals, save the panel majority in *Batzel,* has ever held that statutory immunity should be given for the pre-publication selection and posting of harshly defamatory material.

It is one thing to say, as all of the cited cases have said, that Congress wanted to preserve the ability of a website operator to edit something posted by another, thereby diminishing harm to the public when defamation or harmful material are excised. It is quite another, and

---

[6] If Congress wanted to use this more specialized meaning of the word "development," as opposed to the ordinary meaning as previously described, it could have done so in the § 230(3) "[d]efinitions" section. Congress's deliberate silence on the definition of "development" should lead us to conclude that Congress intended for us to employ an ordinary meaning of development. *See Will v. Michigan Dep't of State Police,* 491 U.S. 58, 64, 109 S. Ct. 2304, 105 L.Ed.2d 45 (1989) (courts should follow ordinary usage of terms unless Congress gives them a specified or technical meaning); *Pittston Coal Group v. Sebben,* 488 U.S. 105, 113, 109 S. Ct. 414, 102 L.Ed.2d 408 (1988) (courts should follow the dictionary definition of terms, unless Congress has provided a specific definition). These principles, of course, should lead us to reject the majority's explanation that (1) Congress intended a definition of "development" that excluded traditional editorial functions and (2) Congress chose to demonstrate this intent by using the word "publisher" in § 230(c) rather than, less deviously, defining "development" in § 230(e). The panel majority's theory makes sense if Congress routinely played "hide the ball," but observers of the legislative process in the United States know that legislators and Congressional committees do all that they can to explicate the meaning and extent of what they legislate. We should not tread the majority's path, because here there is no reason not to abide the plain meaning of the statutory text. *See, e.g., United States v. Providence Journal Co.,* 485 U.S. 693, 700-01, 108 S. Ct. 1502, 99 L.Ed.2d 785 (1988).

diametrically opposed to what Congress had in mind, to hold, as the panel majority mistakenly held, that Congress intended to immunize someone like Cremers who first places on the Internet a patently defamatory missive that the sender had not even aimed for Internet publication.

Finally, the panel majority argues that there is no functional difference between a selection and a screening approach, rendering the addition of Cremers' credibility moot. *Batzel,* 333 F.3d at 1032. But Congress recognized this difference when it granted immunity for good faith actions to "restrict availability" of objectionable material. Congress knew the difference between screening (or "restricting availability") and selecting (or providing availability). Moreover, the panel majority's argument is flawed by the fact that a screening approach leads to the inclusion on the Internet of more material than a selection approach, and less of an endorsement. This demonstrates the difference between selection and screening that Congress recognized: Screeners of matters posted by others get immunity; those who select what is posted do not. Section 230 demonstrates a clear Congressional intent to immunize screening and post-publication removal, but shows no corresponding Congressional intent to immunize pre-publication selection and editing. This line, drawn by Congress, is sensible, easy to defend, and easy to apply. By contrast, the line drawn by the majority is not sensible, cannot be defended, and will be difficult to define in proceedings related to what a recipient "reasonably" understood a sender to want, especially since immunity questions arise at the beginning of litigation. Congress provided immunity for web site operators who edit or remove what another has placed on the Internet. But Congress did not provide for immunity for web site operators who place, for the first time, defamatory information on the Internet.

Not only is the majority's interpretation unfaithful to the statutory text, it opens the door for any Internet publisher to amplify the defamatory words of any person who communicates, or reasonably seems to communicate, a desire that their defamatory missive be published. It can only be imagined that a malicious sender of defamatory material will *want* the publisher to post the information. Thus, in the worst cases of malicious defamation, the defamer will only be too happy to ask expressly for publication to spread damaging lies and accomplish an illicit purpose. In such a case, under the majority's non-test, the publisher surely would reasonably think that publication was intended, and immunity would surely and automatically follow, no matter how false and defamatory the content.

The most blatant and malicious defamers doubtless would request publication of their poisoned words on a blog or other publication with a large audience. History, as well as this case, tells us that such persons exist and that they will seek an audience for defamation. And if immunity automatically follows, why would any Internet publisher refuse to publish anything that might draw eyes to the website? Doubtless some would decline out of virtue, but others will almost certainly publish what brings profit.[12] None of this would do any good

---

[12] Although defamation might be bad enough amplified by blogs and newsletters, imagine the damage if it were amplified by the Internet portal of a major news organization, e.g., www.cnn.com, www.msnbc.com, or www.foxnews.com. We might hope that these organizations would be responsible and not amplify the defamatory message to a world-wide audience. But, apart from the protections mandated by the First Amendment, *see, e.g., New York Times v. Sullivan,* 376 U.S. 254, 84 S. Ct. 710, 11 L.Ed.2d 686 (1964), the panel majority has demolished any remaining legal and

for the person defamed within the lawless territory that the majority would make of the Internet.

I do not believe that Congress intended to make, or ever would consciously make, the policy choice made by the panel majority. Human reputations, built on good conduct over decades, should be not so easily tarnished and lost in a second of global Internet defamation. Under the panel majority's rule, there might be a remedy against the initial sender, but there is no remedy against the person who willingly chooses, with no exercise of care, to amplify a malicious defamation by lodging it on the Internet for all persons and for all time. Unless this result were commanded by Congress, we should not create such a system.

The panel majority's decision is not faithful to Congressional intent, will have a broad and potentially harmful impact in cases of misuse of the Internet, and should have been reconsidered by our entire court. I respectfully dissent from our decision not to do so.

* * * * *

SpamCop is an interactive, Internet-based service that operates a spammer blacklist and forwards complaints to ISPs to encourage them to sanction spammers, including by terminating spammers' bandwidth. *See Optinrealbig.com, LLC v. Ironport Sys., Inc.,* 323 F. Supp. 2d 1037, 1040 (N.D. Cal. 2004). In a suit brought in California federal court, the plaintiff contended that SpamCop had sent multiple copies of the same reports to ISPs, which inflated the number of complaints against the plaintiff, leading ISPs to curtail the bandwith they allowed the plaintiff. SpamCop maintained that it was not responsible for the actions of the ISPs against the plaintiff, which, in turn, denied that it was a spammer. *See id.* at 1042, 1043.

One question before the California federal court was whether SpamCop was insulated from liability by section 230 of the Communications Decency Act. In order to analyze this, the court considered whether SpamCop had contributed to the reports in issue. The court ruled in favor of SpamCop; it did "not alter, shape, or even edit the content." *Id.* at 1047.

But can the defendant's immunity be jeopardized by the extent of his dissemination of content, even if the the defendant didn't alter the content in question? The plaintiff also complained that by sending out numerous reports, SpamCop had affected the impact of the reports. *See id.* at 1046. But the court determined that while "it may be true that SpamCop is aggressive in mailing the reports to any and all ISPs that it can identify in the mailing header of the purported spam," the plaintiff had failed to show "that SpamCop sends multiple copies of the same report to the same recipient in order to inflate its impact ... [and in any event the court was] not persuaded that multiple mailings would amount to an alteration in the content found within each report." *Id.* at 1047. Thus the court ruled that SpamCopy was immune from liability and denied the plaintiff's motion for a preliminary injunction.

* * * * *

---

financial incentive for these major news outlets to be responsible with what they publish on their Internet portals.

CHRISTIANNE CARAFANO, a/k/a Chase Masterson, Plaintiff-Appellant

v.

METROSPLASH.COM, INC., a Delaware corporation; LYCOS, INC., a Delaware corporation; MATCHMAKER.COM, INC., a Texas corporation, Defendants-Appellees

United States Court of Appeals for the Ninth Circuit

No. 02-55658, 339 F.3d 1119

August 13, 2003

This is a case involving a cruel and sadistic identity theft. In this appeal, we consider to what extent a computer match-making service may be legally responsible for false content in a dating profile provided by someone posing as another person. Under the circumstances presented by this case, we conclude that the service is statutorily immune pursuant to 47 U.S.C. § 230(c)(1).

I.

Matchmaker.com is a commercial Internet dating service. For a fee, members of Matchmaker post anonymous profiles and may then view profiles of other members in their area, contacting them via electronic mail sent through the Matchmaker server. A typical profile contains one or more pictures of the subject, descriptive information such as age, appearance and interests, and answers to a variety of questions designed to evoke the subject's personality and reason for joining the service.

Members are required to complete a detailed questionnaire containing both multiple-choice and essay questions. In the initial portion of the questionnaire, members select answers to more than fifty questions from menus providing between four and nineteen options. Some of the potential multiple choice answers are innocuous; some are sexually suggestive. In the subsequent essay section, participants answer up to eighteen additional questions, including "anything that the questionnaire didn't cover." Matchmaker policies prohibit members from posting last names, addresses, phone numbers or e-mail addresses within a profile. Matchmaker reviews photos for impropriety before posting them but does not review the profiles themselves, relying instead upon participants to adhere to the service guidelines.

On October 23, 1999, an unknown person using a computer in Berlin posted a "trial" personal profile of Christianne Carafano in the Los Angeles section of Matchmaker. (New members were permitted to post "trial" profiles for a few weeks without paying.) The posting was without the knowledge, consent or permission of Carafano. The profile was listed under the identifier "Chase529."

Carafano is a popular actress. Under the stage name of Chase Masterson, Carafano has appeared in numerous films and television shows, such as "Star Trek: Deep Space Nine," and "General Hospital." Pictures of the actress are widely available on the Internet, and the false Matchmaker profile "Chase529" contained several of these pictures. Along with fairly innocuous responses to questions about interests and appearance, the person posting the profile selected "Playboy/ Playgirl" for "main source of current events" and "looking for a one-night stand" for "why did you call." In addition, the open-ended essay responses indicated that "Chase529" was looking for a "hard and dominant" man with "a strong sexual appetite" and that she "liked sort of being controlled by a man, in and out of bed." The profile text did not include a last name for "Chase" or indicate Carafano's real name, but it listed two of her movies (and, as mentioned, included pictures of the actress).

In response to a question about the "part of the LA area" in which she lived, the profile provided Carafano's home address. The profile included a contact e-mail address, cmla2000@yahoo.com, which, when contacted, produced an automatic e-mail reply stating, "You think you are the right one? Proof it!!" [sic], and providing Carafano's home address and telephone number.

Unaware of the improper posting, Carafano soon began to receive messages responding to the profile. Although she was traveling at the time, she checked her voicemail on October 31 and heard two sexually explicit messages. When she returned to her home on November 4, she found a highly threatening and sexually explicit fax that also threatened her son. Alarmed, she contacted the police the following day. As a result of the profile, she also received numerous phone calls, voicemail messages, written correspondence, and e-mail from fans through her professional e-mail account. Several men expressed concern that she had given out her address and phone number (but simultaneously expressed an interest in meeting her). Carafano felt unsafe in her home, and she and her son stayed in hotels or away from Los Angeles for several months.

Sometime around Saturday, November 6, Siouxzan Perry, who handled Carafano's professional website and much of her e-mail correspondence, first learned of the false profile through a message from "Jeff." Perry exchanged e-mails with Jeff, visited the Matchmaker site, and relayed information about the profile to Carafano. Acting on Carafano's instructions, Perry contacted Matchmaker and demanded that the profile be removed immediately. The Matchmaker employee indicated that she could not remove the profile immediately because Perry herself had not posted it, but the company blocked the profile from public view on Monday morning, November 8. At 4:00 AM the following morning, Matchmaker deleted the profile. …

II.

The dispositive question in this appeal is whether Carafano's claims are barred by 47 U.S.C. § 230(c)(1), which states that "[n]o provider or user of an interactive computer service shall be treated as the publisher or speaker of any information provided by another information content provider." Through this provision, Congress granted most Internet services immunity from liability for publishing false or defamatory material so long as the information was provided by another party. As a result, Internet publishers are treated differently from corresponding publishers in print, television and radio. *See Batzel v. Smith*, 333 F.3d 1018, 1026-27 (9th Cir. 2003).

Congress enacted this provision as part of the Communications Decency Act of 1996 for two basic policy reasons: to promote the free exchange of information and ideas over the Internet and to encourage voluntary monitoring for offensive or obscene material. *See id.* at 1026-30 (recounting the legislative history and purposes of this section). Congress incorporated these ideas into the text of § 230 itself, expressly noting that "interactive computer services have flourished, to the benefit of all Americans, with a minimum of government regulation," and that "[i]ncreasingly Americans are relying on interactive media for a variety of political, educational, cultural, and entertainment services." 47 U.S.C. §

230(a)(4), (5). Congress declared it the "policy of the United States" to "promote the continued development of the Internet and other interactive computer services," "to preserve the vibrant and competitive free market that presently exists for the Internet and other interactive computer services," and to "remove disincentives for the development and utilization of blocking and filtering technologies." 47 U.S.C. § 230(b)(1), (2), (4).

In light of these concerns, reviewing courts have treated § 230(c) immunity as quite robust, adopting a relatively expansive definition of "interactive computer service" and a relatively restrictive definition of "information content provider." Under the statutory scheme, an "interactive computer service" qualifies for immunity so long as it does not also function as an "information content provider" for the portion of the statement or publication at issue. …

The fact that some of the content was formulated in response to Matchmaker's questionnaire does not alter [our] … conclusion. Doubtless, the questionnaire facilitated the expression of information by individual users. However, the selection of the content was left exclusively to the user. The actual profile "information" consisted of the particular options chosen and the additional essay answers provided. Matchmaker was not responsible, even in part, for associating certain multiple choice responses with a set of physical characteristics, a group of essay answers, and a photograph. Matchmaker cannot be considered an "information content provider" under the statute because no profile has any content until a user actively creates it.

As such, Matchmaker's role is similar to that of the customer rating system at issue in *Gentry v. eBay, Inc.*, 99 Cal. App. 4th 816, 121 Cal. Rptr. 2d 703 (Cal. Ct. App. 2002). In that case, the plaintiffs alleged that eBay "was an information content provider in that it was responsible for the creation of information, or development of information, for the online auction it provided through the Internet." *Id.* at 717. Specifically, the plaintiffs noted that eBay created a highly structured Feedback Forum, which categorized each response as a "Positive Feedback," a "Negative Feedback," or a "Neutral Feedback." *Id.* In addition, eBay provided a color coded star symbol next to the user name of a seller who had achieved certain levels of "Positive Feedback" and offered a separate "Power Sellers" endorsement based on sales volume and Positive Feedback ratings. *Id.* The court concluded that § 230 barred the claims:

> Appellants' negligence claim is based on the assertion that the information is false or misleading because it has been manipulated by the individual defendants or other co-conspiring parties. Based on these allegations, enforcing appellants' negligence claim would place liability on eBay for simply compiling false and/or misleading content created by the individual defendants and other coconspirators. We do not see such activities transforming eBay into an information content provider with respect to the representations targeted by appellants as it did not create or develop the underlying misinformation.

Id. at 717-18. Similarly, the fact that Matchmaker classifies user characteristics into discrete categories and collects responses to specific essay questions does not transform Matchmaker into a "developer" of the "underlying misinformation."

We also note that, as with eBay, Matchmaker's decision to structure the information provided by users allows the company to offer additional features, such as "matching" profiles with similar characteristics or highly structured searches based on combinations of multiple choice questions. Without standardized, easily encoded answers, Matchmaker might not be able to offer these services and certainly not to the same degree. Arguably, this promotes the expressed Congressional policy "to promote the continued development of the Internet and other interactive computer services." 47 U.S.C. § 230(b)(1).

Carafano responds that Matchmaker contributes much more structure and content than eBay by asking 62 detailed questions and providing a menu of "pre-prepared responses." However, this is a distinction of degree rather than of kind, and Matchmaker still lacks responsibility for the "underlying misinformation."

Further, even assuming Matchmaker could be considered an information content provider, the statute precludes treatment as a publisher or speaker for "*any* information provided by *another* information content provider." 47 U.S.C. § 230(c)(1) (emphasis added). The statute would still bar Carafano's claims unless Matchmaker created or developed the particular information at issue. As the *Gentry* court noted,

> [T]he fact appellants allege eBay is an information content provider is irrelevant if eBay did not itself create or develop the content for which appellants seek to hold it liable. It is not inconsistent for eBay to be an interactive service provider and also an information content provider; the categories are not mutually exclusive. The critical issue is whether eBay acted as an information content provider with respect to the information that appellants claim is false or misleading.

121 Cal. Rptr. 2d at 717 n.11.

In this case, critical information about Carafano's home address, movie credits, and the e-mail address that revealed her phone number were transmitted unaltered to profile viewers. Similarly, the profile directly reproduced the most sexually suggestive comments in the essay section, none of which bore more than a tenuous relationship to the actual questions asked. Thus Matchmaker did not play a significant role in creating, developing or "transforming" the relevant information.

Thus, despite the serious and utterly deplorable consequences that occurred in this case, we conclude that Congress intended that service providers such as Matchmaker be afforded immunity from suit. Thus, we affirm the judgment of the district court, albeit on other grounds.

AFFIRMED.

* * * * *

A subscriber to an Internet "match service" was deemed to lack standing to assert a claim against the service under New York's Dating Services Law, N.Y. General Business Law § 394-c, because the subscriber had not alleged any "actual harm" arising from the service's failure to comply with the law's requirements. *See Grossman v. MatchNet PLC,* 782 N.Y.S.2d 246 (N.Y. Sup. Ct. App. Div., 1st Dep't Sept. 30, 2004), *available at* <http:// www.courts.state.ny.us/reporter/3dseries/2004/2004_06826.htm>.

A Ukrainian woman sued an Internet match-making service, alleging that the man who they arranged for her abused her and that the service failed to screen its clients or tell her about a law that helps foreign nationals escape abusive relationships without fear of automatic deportation. She was awarded as much as $434,000. *See Internet Matchmaker Sued for Abuse,* KATC.com (Nov. 21, 2004), a*vailable at* <http://www.katc.com/Global/story.asp?S=2595724&nav=EyAzTNXj>. Some have questioned whether on-line dating services should verify subscribers through criminal background screening. *See generally* Declan McCullagh, *True Love With a Criminal-Background Check,* CNet News.com (Feb. 28, 2005), *available at* <http://news.com.com/2010-1071_3-5591000.html> As of early 2005, legislatures in California, Michigan, Texas, and Virginia were considering bills that would require dating services to post warnings to participants that felony-conviction searches had not been conducted. *See id.*

Could liability be imposed on Internet service providers if such legislation were enacted and on-line dating services web-sites failed to make such disclosures?

* * * * *

insert the following before Other Applications of Section 230 of the Communications Decency Act on page 306 of Law of Internet Speech:

What constitutes "information" under section 230 of the Communications Decency Act? In *Green v. AOL,* 318 F.3d 465 (3d Cir. 2003), *cert. denied,* 540 U.S. 877, the Third Circuit deemed an electronic signal known as a "punter" that allegedly had been sent through an AOL chatroom for the purpose of disrupting a subscriber's computer constituted "information" within the meaning of section 230 of the Communications Decency Act. In so ruling, the court rejected the appellant's argument that the term "information" as used in the statute was limited to "'communication or reception of knowledge or intelligence, and not an unseen signal that halts someone's computer.'" 318 F.3d at 471 (quoting plaintiff-appellant). The Third Circuit endorsed the district court's conclusion that "the narrow interpretation offered by [the plaintiff-appellant] to hold AOL liable for [the plaintiff's] reception of the punter signal or program would run afoul of the intention of section 230." *Id.* (citation omitted).

* * * * *

ROGER M. GRACE, Plaintiff and Appellant

v.

EBAY INC., Defendant and Respondent

Court of Appeal of California,
Second Appellate District, Division Three

B168765, 120 Cal. App. 4th 984; 16 Cal. Rptr. 3d 192

July 22, 2004

Roger M. Grace appeals a judgment of dismissal after the court sustained a demurrer to his complaint against eBay Inc. (eBay). The superior court concluded that title 47 United States Code section 230 (section 230), part of the Communications Decency Act of 1996 (Pub. L. No. 104-104, §§ 501, 509 (Feb. 8, 1996) 110 Stat. 133, 137), immunizes eBay against liability for libel and violation of the unfair competition law (Bus. & Prof. Code, §

17200 *et seq.*) as a publisher of information provided by another person. Grace challenges that conclusion.

Section 230 states that federal policy is to promote the continued development of the Internet and other interactive computer services, to encourage the development of technologies that enable user control over information received through the Internet, and to remove disincentives to the development and use of technologies that restrict children's access to objectionable Internet content. (47 U.S.C. § 230(b).) Section 230 provides immunity against civil liability for certain conduct in furtherance of those policies. (47 U.S.C. § 230(c)(1), (2).)

We conclude that section 230 provides no immunity against liability for a distributor of information who knew or had reason to know that the information was defamatory. We conclude further, however, that the written release in eBay's User Agreement relieves eBay of the liability alleged in the complaint. We therefore affirm the judgment.

FACTUAL AND PROCEDURAL BACKGROUND

eBay maintains an Internet website that describes goods for sale by third party sellers. Potential buyers bid on the goods by sending e-mail to eBay. After a sale is consummated, the buyer and seller may provide comments on each other and the transaction, or "feedback," which is displayed on the website. The website displays a "feedback profile" on each user, including the comments and a numerical rating. eBay discourages inflammatory language and libel and requires buyers and sellers to agree to a User Agreement that prohibits defamation, but eBay's stated policy is not to remove objectionable comments. ...

Grace purchased several items from another individual and then posted negative comments on the seller pertaining to some of the transactions. The seller responded by commenting on Grace as to each transaction, "Complaint: SHOULD BE BANNED FROM EBAY!!!! DISHONEST ALL THE WAY!!!!" Grace notified eBay that the seller's comments were defamatory, but eBay refused to remove them.

Grace sued eBay and the seller, alleging counts against eBay for libel, specific performance of eBay's User Agreement with the seller, and violation of the unfair competition law. Grace withdrew the second count after eBay removed the challenged comments from its website. ...

CONTENTIONS

Grace contends (1) eBay as the proprietor of an Internet website is not a "provider or user of an interactive computer service" within the meaning of section 230; (2) even if eBay were a "provider or user," section 230 does not immunize against liability for libel as a distributor of information if the defendant knew or had reason to know that the information was defamatory; (3) the release in the User Agreement does not relieve eBay of liability for failure to remove defamatory material after receiving notice that the material is defamatory; and (4) the denial of leave to amend the complaint was error. Grace challenges the demurrer on the unfair competition count only insofar as that count is based on the alleged libel.

DISCUSSION

... 2. *eBay Is a User of an Interactive Computer Service*

Section 230 states that federal policy is to promote the continued development of the Internet and other interactive computer services, to encourage the development of technologies that enable user control over information received through the Internet, and to remove disincentives to the development and use of technologies that block and filter access to objectionable Internet content. (47 U.S.C. § 230(b).)

Section 230 states that no provider or user of an interactive computer service can be held liable for an action taken in good faith to restrict access to material that the provider or user considers obscene or otherwise objectionable, or for an action taken to enable or make available the technical means to restrict access to such material. (47 U.S.C. § 230(c)(2).)

Section 230 also states, "No provider or user of an interactive computer service shall be treated as the publisher or speaker of any information provided by another information content provider." (47 U.S.C. § 230(c)(1).)

"Interactive computer service" is defined as, "any information service, system, or access software provider that provides or enables computer access by multiple users to a computer server, including specifically a service or system that provides access to the Internet and such systems operated or services offered by libraries or educational institutions." (47 U.S.C. § 230(f)(2).)

"Information content provider" is defined as, "any person or entity that is responsible, in whole or in part, for the creation or development of information provided through the Internet or any other interactive computer service." (47 U.S.C. § 230(f)(3).)

Section 230 states further, "No cause of action may be brought and no liability may be imposed under any State or local law that is inconsistent with this section." (47 U.S.C. § 230(e)(3).)

"Internet service provider" or "ISP" is the term commonly used to describe a company that provides computer users access to the Internet. An ISP is a "provider" of an interactive computer service within the meaning of section 230(c)(1) because the service provided is, in the language of section 230(f)(2), "a service or system that provides access to the Internet." eBay is not an ISP.

Some courts have held or stated that the operator of a website is a provider of an interactive computer service under section 230(c)(1). (*Gentry v. eBay, Inc.* (2002) 99 Cal. App. 4th 816, 831, fn.7 [121 Cal. Rptr. 2d 703]; *Carafano v. Metrosplash.com, Inc.* (C.D. Cal. 2002) 207 F. Supp. 2d 1055, 1066, *affd. on other grounds* (2003) 339 F.3d 1119; *Schneider v. Amazon.com, Inc.* (2001) 108 Wn. App. 454 [31 P.3d 37, 40-41].)

We need not decide that question because section 230(c)(1) also expressly applies to a "user" of an interactive computer service. We conclude based on the plain meaning of the statutory language that the term "user" as used in the statute encompasses all persons who gain access to the Internet through an ISP or other service or system (*see* 47 U.S.C. § 230(f)(2)), including both individual computer users and website operators. (*Batzel v. Smith* (9th Cir. 2003) 333 F.3d 1018, 1030-1031 [held that an operator of an online newsletter was a "user" of an interactive computer service].)

3. *Section 230(c)(1) Provides No Immunity Against Liability for Libel as a Distributor*

a. *Construction of Section 230(c)(1) in Light of the Common Law Background*

Section 230(c)(1) states that a provider or user of an interactive computer service may not "be treated as the publisher or speaker" of information provided by another person. To understand the intended effect of this provision on the common law of libel requires an understanding of the common law of libel. We presume that Congress was aware of common law principles and intended those principles to apply absent some indication to the contrary. (*Astoria Fed. Sav. & Loan Ass'n v. Solimino* (1991) 501 U.S. 104, 108 [115 L. Ed. 2d 96, 111 S. Ct. 2166].) "It is a well-established principle of statutory construction that '[t]he common law ... ought not to be deemed to be repealed, unless the language of a statute be clear and explicit for this purpose.' [Citation.]" (*Norfolk Redev. & Housing Auth. v. C. & P. Tel.* (1983) 464 U.S. 30, 35 [78 L. Ed. 2d 29, 104 S. Ct. 304].) "'[S]tatutes which invade the common law ... are to be read with a presumption favoring the retention of long-established and familiar principles, except when a statutory purpose to the contrary is evident.' [Citations.] In such cases, Congress does not write upon a clean slate. [Citation.] In order to abrogate a common-law principle, the statute must 'speak directly' to the question addressed by the common law. [Citations.]" (*United States v. Texas* (1993) 507 U.S. 529, 534 [123 L. Ed. 2d 245, 113 S. Ct. 1631].)

The common law of libel distinguishes between liability as a primary publisher and liability as a distributor. A primary publisher, such as an author or a publishing company, is presumed to know the content of the published material, has the ability to control the content of the publication, and therefore generally is held liable for a defamatory statement, provided that constitutional requirements imposed by the First Amendment are satisfied. (Rest.2d *Torts*, § 581, subd. (1), com. c, p. 232; Prosser & Keeton, *Torts* (5th ed. 1984) § 113, p. 810; Smolla, *The Law of Defamation* (2d ed. 1999) §§ 4:87, pp. 4-136.3 to 4-136.4, 4:92, pp. 4-140 to 4-140.1.) A distributor, such as a book seller, news vendor, or library, may or may not know the content of the published matter and therefore can be held liable only if the distributor knew or had reason to know that the material was defamatory. (Rest.2d *Torts*, § 581, subd. (1), coms. b, c, d & e, pp. 232-234; Prosser & Keeton, *Torts*, *supra*, § 113, pp. 810-811; 2 Harper *et al.*, *The Law of Torts* (2d ed. 1986) Defamation, § 5.18, pp. 144-145; Smolla, *The Law of Defamation, supra*, § 4:92, pp. 4-140 to 4-140.1.) The Restatement Second of Torts distinguishes the liability of "one who only delivers or transmits defamatory matter published by a third person" (*id.*, § 581, subd. (1), p. 231), such as a book seller, news dealer, or library (*id.*, § 581, coms. b, d & e, pp. 232-234), from the liability of the "original publisher," such as an author or publishing company (*id.*, §§ 578, com. b, p. 212, 581, com. c, p. 232). Similarly, Prosser and Keeton distinguish "secondary publishers or disseminators" from "primary publishers" and explain, "those who have commonly been regarded as disseminators or transmitters of defamatory matter who simply assist primary publishers in distributing information" are afforded greater protection from liability. (Prosser & Keeton, *Torts*, *supra*, § 113, pp. 803, 811.)

Thus, although a distributor can be held liable for libel in certain circumstances, a distributor is subject to a different standard of liability from that of a primary publisher, and liability as a distributor ordinarily requires a greater showing of culpability. Section 230(c)(1) does not state that a provider or user of an interactive computer service may not be treated as a "distributor" or "transmitter" of information provided by another person, but only that a provider or user may not "be treated as the publisher or speaker." In light of the common law distinction between liability as a primary publisher and liability as a distributor, we conclude that section 230(c)(1) does not clearly and directly address distributor liability and therefore does not preclude distributor liability.

b. *Legislative History of Section 230(c)(1)*

The legislative history of section 230 supports our conclusion. The conference committee report on the Telecommunications Act of 1996, of which the Communications Decency Act of 1996 is a part (Pub.L. No. 104-104, §§ 1, 501 (Feb. 8, 1996) 110 Stat. 56, 133), stated of section 230:

> This section provides "Good Samaritan" protections from civil liability for providers or users of an interactive computer service for actions to restrict or to enable restriction of access to objectionable online material. One of the specific purposes of this section is to overrule *Stratton-Oakmont v. Prodigy* and any other similar decisions which have treated such providers and users as publishers or speakers of content that is not their own because they have restricted access to objectionable material. The conferees believe that such decisions create serious obstacles to the important federal policy of empowering parents to determine the content of communications their children receive through interactive computer services.

(H.R.Rep. No.104-458, 2d Sess., p.194 (1996).)

The conference committee report stated that one of the specific purposes of section 230 was to overrule *Stratton Oakmont, Inc. v. Prodigy Services Co.*, [*Stratton Oakmont, Inc. v. Prodigy Services Co.* (N.Y. Sup. Ct., May 24, 1995) 1995 WL 323710 at *3 (citations omitted) (stating that Prodigy could be held liable for libel only if it was a "publisher ... because one who repeats or otherwise republishes a libel is subject to liability as if he had originally published it.")] and any other decisions that treated providers and users of interactive computer services "as publishers or speakers" of information provided by another person "because they have restricted access to objectionable material." (H.R. Rep. No. 104-458, 2d Sess., p.194.) This statement reflects a legislative intent to repudiate the holding in *Stratton Oakmont* that an operator of a computer bulletin board, or other provider or user of an interactive computer service, can be held liable for libel without regard to whether the operator knew or had reason to know that the matter was defamatory (i.e., liable as a primary publisher rather than a distributor) because of the operator's efforts to control content (i.e., act as a "Good Samaritan"). There is no indication, however, that Congress intended to preclude liability where the provider or user knew or had reason to know that the matter was defamatory, that is, common law distributor liability.

c. *Conclusion*

We conclude that section 230 provides no immunity against liability as a distributor. (*See Doe v. America Online, Inc.* (Fla. 2001) 783 So. 2d 1010, 1018 (dis. opn. of Lewis, J.).) We decline to follow *Zeran v. America Online, Inc.* (4th Cir. 1997) 129 F.3d 327 and its progeny, including *Gentry v. eBay, Inc., supra*, 99 Cal. App. 4th at page 833, footnote 10, and *Kathleen R. v. City of Livermore* (2001) 87 Cal. App. 4th 684, 695, footnote 3 [104 Cal. Rptr. 2d 772]. For the reasons we have stated, we disagree with the *Zeran* court's conclusion that because the term "publication" can encompass any repetition of a defamatory statement, use of the term "publisher" in section 230(c)(1) indicates a clear legislative intention to abrogate common law distributor liability. (*Zeran, supra*, 129 F.3d at pp. 332-334.) In light of the well-established common law distinction between liability as a primary publisher and liability as a distributor and Congress's expressed intention to overrule an opinion that held the operator of a computer bulletin board liable as a primary publisher rather than a distributor (*Stratton Oakmont, Inc. v. Prodigy Services Co., supra*, 1995 WL 323710), we cannot conclude that use of the term "publisher" in section 230(c)(1) discloses a clear legislative intention to abrogate distributor liability.

We also disagree with the *Zeran* court's conclusion that for providers and users of interactive computer services to be subject to distributor liability would defeat the purposes of the statute and therefore could not be what Congress intended. (*Zeran v. America Online, Inc., supra*, 129 F.3d at pp. 333-334.) The *Zeran* court opined that the threat of distributor liability would encourage providers and users to remove potentially offensive material upon notice that the material is potentially offensive rather than risk liability for failure to do so. (*Id.* at p. 333.) The *Zeran* court opined further that a provider or user who undertakes efforts to block and filter objectionable material is more likely to know or have reason to know of potentially defamatory material and therefore more likely to be held liable as a distributor, so the threat of distributor liability would discourage undertaking those efforts. (*Ibid.*) The broad immunity provided under *Zeran*, however, would eliminate potential liability for providers and users even if they made no effort to control objectionable content, and therefore would neither promote the development of technologies to accomplish that task nor remove disincentives to that development as Congress intended (47 U.S.C. § 230(b)). Rather, the total elimination of distributor liability under *Zeran* would eliminate a potential incentive to the development of those technologies, that incentive being the threat of distributor liability. (*See* Note, *Immunizing Internet Service Providers from Third-Party Internet Defamation Claims: How Far Should Courts Go?* (2002) 55 Vand. L.Rev. 647, 683-685; Freiwald, *Comparative Institutional Analysis in Cyberspace: The Case of Intermediary Liability for Defamation* (2001) 14 Harv. J.L. & Tech. 569, 616-623.) We conclude that Congress reasonably could have concluded that the threat of distributor liability together with the immunity provided for efforts to restrict access to objectionable material (47 U.S.C. § 230(c)(2)) would encourage the development and application of technologies to block and filter access to objectionable material, consistent with the expressed legislative purposes.

d. *Other Interpretive Arguments*

eBay and the *amici curiae* cite a congressional committee report pertaining to the Dot Kids Implementation and Efficiency Act of 2002 (Pub. L. No. 107-317 (Dec. 4, 2002) 116 Stat. 2766). The act enacted a new statute (47 U.S.C. § 941) that provides for the creation of an Internet domain limited to material appropriate for children. The statute states that the registry that operates the new domain, entities that contract with the registry to ensure that the material on the domain complies with the content restrictions, and registrars for the registry "are deemed to be interactive computer services for purposes of section 230(c) of the Communications Act of 1934 (47 U.S.C. 230(c))." The committee report stated that the new provision "is intended to shield the '.kids.us' registry, registrars, and parties who contract with the registry, from liability based on self-policing efforts to intercept and take down material that is not 'suitable for minors' or is 'harmful to minors.' The Committee notes that ISPs have successfully defended many lawsuits using section 230(c). The courts have correctly interpreted section 230(c), which was aimed at protecting against liability for such claims as negligence (*See, e.g., Doe v. America Online*, 783 So. 2d 1010 (Fla. 2001)) and defamation

(*Ben Ezra, Weinstein, and Co. v. America Online*, 206 F.3d 980 (2000); *Zeran v. America Online*, 129 F.3d 327 (1997)). The Committee intends these interpretations of section 230(c) to be equally applicable to those entities covered by H.R. 3833." (H.R. Rep. No. 107-449, 2d Sess., p. 13 (2002), *reprinted in* 2002 U.S. Code Cong. & Admin. News, p. 1749.)

To the extent the House committee may have endorsed the specific holding of *Zeran v. America Online, Inc., supra*, 129 F.3d 327 and its progeny that is at issue here, the committee report does not affect our construction of section 230.

A statement in a legislative committee report as to the meaning of an existing statute is not a reliable indication of the intent of a prior Congress. (*United States v. Texas, supra*, 507 U.S. at p. 535, fn. 4 ["subsequent legislative history is a 'hazardous basis for inferring the intent of an earlier' Congress"], quoting *Pension Benefit Guaranty Corp. v. The LTV Corp.* (1990) 496 U.S. 633, 650 [110 L. Ed. 2d 579, 110 S. Ct. 2668]; *Consumer Product Safety Comm'n v. GTE Sylvania* (1980) 447 U.S. 102, 118, fn. 13 [64 L. Ed. 2d 766, 100 S. Ct. 2051].) The language of section 230 and its legislative history discussed *ante* are far more illuminating as to the legislative intent of the statute.

We also reject the argument that Congress's failure to amend section 230(c)(1) when it added a new section 230(d) to the statute (Pub. L. No. 105-277, § 1404(a) (Oct. 21, 1998) 112 Stat. 2681-739) indicates congressional approval of consistent judicial interpretation of the statute. "[W]hen, as here, Congress has not comprehensively revised a statutory scheme but has made only isolated amendments. ... 'It is "impossible to assert with any degree of assurance that congressional failure to act represents" affirmative congressional approval of the Court's statutory interpretation.' [Citation.]" (*Alexander v. Sandoval* (2001) 532 U.S. 275, 292 [149 L. Ed. 2d 517, 121 S. Ct. 1511].)

… [The release relieves eBay of liability, however. Grace's argument that the language of the release is "not sufficiently precise" to encompass a claim against eBay based on defamatory information provided by a third party is rejected. T]he plain meaning of the release encompasses Grace's claim for libel and his claim or demand for injunctive relief in connection with the alleged libel. No greater specificity is required of the release.

… DISPOSITION

The judgment is affirmed. eBay is entitled to costs on appeal.

* * * * *

Respondent's petition for review was granted. The Supreme Court of California limited the issue to be briefed and argued to whether the Communications Decency Act, 47 U.S.C. § 230, confers immunity on interactive computer services, such as eBay, from liability for publishing or distributing defamatory statements posted by third parties. *Grace v. eBay Inc.*, 99 P.3d 2, 19 Cal. Rptr. 3d 824 (Cal. 2004).

* * * * *

VINCENT DONATO and GINA A. CALOGERO, Plaintiffs-
Appellants
and ERIC OBERNAUER and LAWRENCE R. CAMPAGNA,
Plaintiffs
v.
STEPHEN MOLDOW, Defendant/Third-Party Plaintiff-
Respondent
and JOHN DOES 1-40 and JANE DOES 1-20, Defendants
v.
KENNETH HOFFMAN, Third-Party Defendant

Superior Court of New Jersey, Appellate Division

No. A-5942-02T1, 374 N.J. Super. 475, 865 A.2d 711

January 31, 2005

We consider in this case the potential liability of the operator of an electronic community bulletin board website based on allegedly actionable messages posted anonymously by others. Appellants, Vincent Donato and Gina A. Calogero, elected members of the Emerson Borough Council, sued the website operator, defendant Stephen Moldow, and numerous fictitious parties, identifying them by the pseudonyms they used when posting their messages. The primary thrust of the complaint against Moldow was that the messages constituted defamation, harassment and intentional infliction of emotional distress, and that Moldow was liable for damages because he was the publisher. The trial judge found that Moldow was immune from liability under a provision in the Communications Decency Act of 1996, 47 U.S.C.A. § 230, and granted Moldow's motion to dismiss the complaint against him for failure to state a claim upon which relief can be granted. We affirm.

I.

Moldow established the website, known as "Eye on Emerson," in late 1999. He posted information about local government activities, including, for example, minutes of meetings of the borough council, planning board and board of education. Public opinion polls were conducted on the site, which included approval ratings of local elected officials. The site included a discussion forum, in which any user could post messages, either with attribution or anonymously.

Initially, appellants favored the Eye on Emerson website, believing it provided a good source of community information and citizen participation. But, beginning in early 2001, many negative messages about appellants were posted. Some concerned the discharge of their official duties. Others were personal. Many were vile and derogatory in their language and tone. We give a few examples, taken directly from the complaint:

> A false message from "my window is not a peep show" posted July 4, 2001 falsely claiming that Donato climbed a ladder to the author's bedroom window and was videotaping him or her with a camera while he/she was dressing;

False statements by "Doctor in the House" that plaintiff Donato was emotionally and mentally unstable and in need of psychiatric help, ready to explode and should be on medication;

... A false statement by "Concerned Resident" on or about June 13, 2001 claiming that [] and Calogero "do drugs;" ...

Various false statements including a message from "Investigator" falsely claiming that Donato and Calogero "use police reports against the residents" and claiming that Donato and Calogero abused their authority over the Emerson Police Department and violated Department Rules and Regulations and/or state laws;

Messages from "RM," "Insider Investigator" and "Ron" on various dates falsely accusing Donato and Calogero of stealing files and other public records from borough hall and accusing Calogero of violating police department policies;

... Messages from "Voter," "Resident Informed," "Duped Again," "Tommy Boy" and others calling Donato a "slippery slimy fish," "hate mongering political boob," "slime of a thing," "Hitler reborn," an "evil bitter old man," "sneak and a liar," "sleeze." "vermin," "a-hole;"

... Messages from "Jackie" and others calling Calogero a "piece of sh--," "this Bitch," "corrupt influence," "Queen of Hate," "witch," "fashion violation," "nut case," claiming that she "hasn't told the truth since she was sworn into office" and other harsh and offensive comments.

The complaint alleged that Moldow and the fictitiously-named anonymous posters published the statements knowing they were false, with actual malice, and with intent to injure and cause emotional distress to appellants, who sought damages for loss of esteem in the community, damage to their reputation, and physical and mental pain and suffering. We recognize that some of the statements may be non-actionable, consisting merely of unpleasant name-calling and expressions of opinions, particularly when directed at public figures. For purposes of our analysis, we assume that some of the statements are actionable, particularly under the extremely deferential standard applicable to motions to dismiss on the pleadings. *See Printing Mart-Morristown v. Sharp Electronics Corp.,* 116 N.J. 739, 766-67, 563 A.2d 31 (1989). We will refer to them generically as "defamatory statements."

Of course the authors of the defamatory statements would be liable to appellants upon proof of all elements of the cause of action. Their potential liability is not before us. Appellants took steps in the trial court to ascertain the identity of the fictitious parties. Immediately upon filing the action they issued a subpoena *duces tecum* to FreeTools.com, trading as VantageNet, Inc., which was the electronic host of the Eye on Emerson bulletin board, seeking the Internet Protocol (IP) address of each anonymous poster.

The fictitious parties, without divulging their identities, engaged counsel, who moved to quash the subpoena. ...

....[A]ppellants' contention on appeal is limited to their position that Moldow should be potentially liable because he published defamatory statements made by third parties.

Appellants premise their appeal arguments on the assertion that the trial judge in effect converted the motion to dismiss into a motion for summary judgment because he considered matters outside the pleadings. Appellants then argue (1) because discovery was incomplete the matter was not ripe for summary judgment and (2) because material fact issues existed regarding Moldow's conduct, his status as an information content provider, and whether he exercised good faith in editing, the court erred in finding immunity under § 230 and granting dismissal or summary judgment.

... II.

Appellants' overriding allegation against Moldow is that he is liable as a publisher of the defamatory statements made by others. They further allege that Moldow was more than passive in his role as publisher, and "has actively participated in selective editing, deletion and re-writing of anonymously posted messages on the Eye on Emerson website and, as such, is entirely responsible for the content of the messages." Appellants elaborate with these factual allegations, by which they argue that Moldow shaped the discussion and thus participated in developing the defamatory statements:

> 24. The technology is available to require users to register with the webmaster prior to using the discussion forum message board and to identify themselves by name, address and e-mail address; however, Moldow designed the Eye on Emerson website and its discussion forum to allow all users to post messages anonymously.

> 25. The format of the discussion forum encourages the use of harassing, defamatory, obscene and annoying messages because users may state their innermost thoughts and vicious statements free from civil recourse by their victims.

> 26. Defendant Moldow controls the content of the discussion forum by various methods, including selectively deleting messages he deems offensive, banning users whose messages he finds "disruptive" to the forum and posting messages to the users who violate his rules of usage. While Moldow is quick to remove any negative message about himself or people he associates with, he allows offensive messages against the plaintiffs and their supporters to remain.

> 27. Moldow actively participates in the editing of messages. By way of example and not limitation, Moldow deleted a message from "the Saint" but not until after several other users complained; he deleted the messages from "Destroyer", "the Champ" and others after Donato and Obernauer threatened litigation; after two days of complaints, he deleted messages from "Football Parent" accusing a former football coach of having sex with female students. Moldow has also deleted messages from "Pee in My Pool" and other users. On May 8, 2001, Moldow said he deleted the post of "Resident Informed" because of profanity but he re-posted an edited version of the message with the profanity partially redacted, thus instructing participants in how to convey offensive language without encountering censorship.

> 28. Moldow knows the identities of users of the website. On July 15, 2001, he posted a message explaining that "The posts from the author

'Ouch,' 'Amazed,' 'spiderman,' and 'Web Master' were removed. All of these messages appear to be from the same person. By the nature of the messages and attempting to impersonate the web master you obviously intended to disrupt the message board. This is not welcome here."

29. On separate occasion in or around April of 2001, plaintiffs Donato and Obernauer met with Moldow individually. Donato and Obernauer showed him downloaded copies of some of the more offensive messages about them and requested three things: (a) the identity of the individuals who posted the offensive, harassing and/or defamatory messages, (b) that Moldow remove the messages and post a disclaimer and (c) that Moldow change the format of the discussion forum to require registration of users so as to discourage any future harassment and defamation.

30. Although Moldow did post a retraction regarding Obernauer and he deleted two offending messages, Moldow stated to Obernauer and Donato that he had no intention of changing the existing format.

In the context of traditional media, such as newspapers and magazines, the publisher of defamatory statements might well be exposed to liability for conduct such as that alleged against Moldow. *See, e.g., Kotlikoff v. The Community News,* 89 N.J. 62, 65-66, 444 A.2d 1086 (1982). In the context of cyberspace, however, Congress has chosen a different course. It granted a broad immunity to providers or users of interactive computer services with the enactment of § 230. ...

Section 230 provides that "no provider or user of an interactive computer service shall be treated as the publisher or speaker of any information provided by another information content provider." 47 U.S.C.A. § 230(c)(1). This general grant of immunity is then supplemented by the so-called "good samaritan" provision that no provider or user of an interactive computer service shall be held liable on account of "any action voluntarily taken in good faith to restrict access to or availability of material that the provider or user considers to be obscene, lewd, lascivious, filthy, excessively violent, harassing, or otherwise objectionable, whether or not such material is constitutionally protected." 47 U.S.C.A. § 230(c)(2)(A).

An "interactive computer service" is defined as "any information service, system, or access software provider that provides or enables computer access by multiple users to a computer server, including specifically a service or system that provides access to the Internet...." 47 U.S.C.A. § 230(f)(2). An "information content provider" is "any person or entity that is responsible, in whole or in part, for the creation or development of information provided through the Internet or any other interactive computer service." 47 U.S.C.A. § 230(f)(3).

In a clear exercise of its Commerce power, Congress preempted any contrary state law provisions: "No cause of action may be brought and no liability may be imposed under any State or local law that is inconsistent with this section." 47 U.S.C.A. § 230(e)(3). *See Zeran v. America Online, Inc.,* 129 F.3d 327, 334 (4th Cir. 1997), *cert. denied,* 524 U.S. 937, 118 S. Ct. 2341, 141 L. Ed. 2d 712 (1998). Because of this provision and Congress' expressed desire to promote unfettered speech on the Internet, the sweep of § 230's preemption includes common law causes of action. *Ibid.*

III.

The dispositive issues on appeal, then, are (1) whether Moldow was a provider or user of an interactive computer service and thus covered by § 230's general immunity provision; (2) whether, by his conduct, Moldow was not also an information content provider with respect to the anonymously-posted defamatory statements; and (3) whether, as a matter of law, Moldow's conduct as described in the complaint did not constitute bad faith within the meaning of § 230's good samaritan provision. Resolution of all three issues in the affirmative results in immunity and renders appellants' claim against Moldow one for which relief cannot be granted.

Section 230 has not been the subject of any reported New Jersey decisions. We look to decisions from other jurisdictions for guidance. Particularly instructive are federal court decisions, to which state courts should give due regard in interpreting a federal statute. *Glukowsky v. Equity One, Inc.*, 180 N.J. 49, 64, 848 A.2d 747 (2004) (citing *Dewey v. R.J. Reynolds Tobacco Co.*, 121 N.J. 69, 80, 577 A.2d 1239 (1990)).

A.

By the plain language of § 230 it is clear that Moldow fits the definition of a "provider or user of an interactive computer service." This is so under either of two rationales. He is the provider of a website, Eye on Emerson, which is an information service or system that provides or enables computer access by multiple users to a computer server. Alternatively, he is the user of a service or system, VantageNet, the website's electronic host, that provides or enables access by multiple users to a computer server; he is also, of necessity, the user of an Internet service provider (ISP), which provides him access to the Internet. Our conclusion is supported by the case law interpreting the statutory provisions.

There is no dispute that large, commercial ISPs fit the "interactive computer service" definition. *See Ben Ezra, Weinstein, and Co., Inc. v. America Online, Inc.*, 206 F.3d 980, 985 (10th Cir.), *cert. denied*, 531 U.S. 824, 121 S. Ct. 69, 148 L. Ed. 2d 33 (2000); *Zeran, supra*, 129 F.3d at 330 n.2. Website operators are also included. *See Carfano v. Metrosplash.com, Inc.*, 339 F.3d 1119, 1124 (9th Cir. 2003) (subscription-based dating website); *Gentry v. eBay, Inc.*, 99 Cal. App. 4th 816, 121 Cal. Rptr.2d 703, 714-15 (Ct. App. 2002) (online auction website); *Schneider v. Amazon.com, Inc.*, 108 Wn. App. 454, 31 P.3d 37, 40-41 (Wash. App. 2001) (online bookstore website).

It is not relevant to immunity status that the website is not commercially operated or is directed at a relatively limited user base. In *Batzel v. Smith*, 333 F.3d 1018, 1021 (9th Cir. 2003), *cert. denied*, __ U.S. __, 124 S. Ct. 2812, 159 L. Ed. 2d 246 (2004), for example, the nonprofit website operator operated in his spare time the website, which provided information about stolen art. The website and listserv mailings generated by the network in *Batzel* were read by "hundreds" of museum officials, insurance investigators, and law enforcement personnel around the world who were interested in locating stolen art. *Id.* at 1021-22.

In *Schneider*, the court succinctly explained how a website operator comes within § 230's immunity provision as a "provider" of an interactive computer service:

But Amazon's web site postings appear indistinguishable from AOL's message board for § 230 purposes. Schneider points out that web site operators do not provide access to the Internet, but this is irrelevant. Under the statutory definition, access providers are only a subclass of the broader definition of interactive service providers entitled to immunity ("provides or enables computer access by multiple users to a computer server, including specifically a service ... that provides access"). [47 U.S.C.A. § 230(f)(2).] According to Schneider's complaint, Amazon's web site enables visitors to the site to comment about authors and their work, thus providing an information service that necessarily enables access by multiple users to a server. This brings Amazon squarely within the definition.

> [*Schneider, supra*, 31 P.3d at 40.]

We agree with this analysis, and it applies to the Eye on Emerson website with the same result.

In *Batzel,* the court engaged in a similar analysis regarding "provider" status, but then chose to predicate the museum security and stolen art website's immunity on "user" status:

> There is, however, no need here to decide whether a listserv or website itself fits the broad statutory definition of "interactive computer service," because the language of § 230(c)(1) confers immunity not just on "providers" of such services, but also on "users" of such services. § 230(c)(1).

> There is no dispute that the Network uses interactive computer services to distribute its on-line mailing and to post the listserv on its website. Indeed, to make its website available and to mail out the listserv, the Network must access the Internet through some form of "interactive computer service." Thus, both the Network website and the listserv are potentially immune under § 230.

> [*Batzel, supra*, 333 F.3d at 1030-31 (footnote omitted).]

This reasoning, with which we agree, supports our conclusion that Moldow qualifies as a user, as well as a provider, of an interactive computer service. On either basis, he is covered by the general immunity provision of § 230.

B.

This brings us to the second issue. Appellants contend that by the manner in which Moldow conducted the website he was also an information content provider with respect to the defamatory messages. This would make him an author, for which § 230 does not provide immunity, rather than as a publisher, for which it does. The complaint alleges that Moldow "actively participated in selective editing, deletion and re-writing of anonymously posted messages." Thus, according to appellants, Moldow controls the "content of the discussion." He accomplishes this by posting messages of his own, commenting favorably or unfavorably on messages posted by others, selectively deleting some messages while allowing others to remain, and selectively banning users whose messages he deems disruptive to the forum. He designed the website to allow the posting of messages anonymously without first requiring users to register with him. He edited a message to remove profanity, but then reposted it in redacted form "thus instructing participants in how to convey offensive language without encountering censorship." In this way, according to appellants, Moldow shaped the content provided by others, encouraging and facilitating unfavorable and defamatory statements about them.

In essence, appellants contend that because an "information content provider" includes any person "that is responsible, in whole or in part, for the creation or development of information provided," 47 U.S.C.A. § 230(f)(3), Moldow is included because he is responsible in part for the development of the defamatory statements. We do not agree.

First of all, with respect to any messages posted by Moldow, using his own name or the appellation "Webmaster," he was a content provider. However, appellants have not alleged that any of the statements posted by Moldow were themselves defamatory or otherwise actionable. There is nothing inconsistent or unusual about a website operator being both an interactive computer service provider or user and an information content provider. The two are not mutually exclusive. *See, e.g., Batzel, supra,* 333 F.3d at 1022 (website operator posted a "moderator's message" commenting on the allegedly defamatory message of a third party). The dual status is irrelevant to immunity, which applies to "any information provided by another information content provider." 47 U.S.C.A. § 230(c)(1) (emphasis added).

Whether Moldow's conduct in "shaping" the content of the discussion forum can be equated with responsibility for the "development" of the defamatory messages requires consideration of Congress' purposes in enacting § 230. ....[T]he good samaritan provision ...grants immunity for voluntary good faith action by a service provider or user "to restrict access to or availability of material that the provider or user considers to be obscene, lewd, lascivious, filthy, excessively violent, harassing, or otherwise objectionable, whether or not such material is constitutionally protected." 47 U.S.C.A. § 230(c)(2)(A). This section was added by Congress to encourage self-regulation and to remove disincentives for self-regulation. ...

In *Ben Ezra,* [for instance,] the plaintiff, a publicly traded corporation, sought to impose liability against AOL because it published incorrect information about the plaintiff's stock price and share volume. *Ben Ezra, supra,* 206 F.3d at 983. The plaintiff contended AOL failed to exercise reasonable care in the manipulation, alteration, and change in the stock information that was submitted to it by two other entities for publication. *Ibid.* The plaintiff argued that because AOL engaged in ongoing communications with content providers and from time to time deleted inaccurate information about it, AOL's conduct constituted "creation or development" of information and transformed AOL into an information content provider. *Id.* at 985-86. The Tenth Circuit held that by deleting inaccurate information, AOL "simply made the data unavailable and did not develop or create the stock quotation information displayed," and "was simply engaging in the editorial functions Congress sought to protect." *Id.* at 986. AOL's communications with the two content providers when errors came to AOL's attention did not "constitute the development or creation of the stock quotation information." *Id.* at 985. AOL's conduct was within the scope of editorial functions protected by § 230. *Id.* at 986.

Applying similar reasoning, the Court of Appeals of Washington reached the same result in Schneider, *supra,* 31 P.3d 37. The court refused to impose liability on Amazon.com because of allegedly defamatory postings by "visitors" to the website about Schneider and his books. *Id.* at 38. One posting alleged Schneider was a felon. *Ibid.* When Schneider complained, Amazon acknowledged some of the postings were improper and in violation of its guidelines and agreed to remove them within one or two days, but did not do so. *Id.* at 38-39. The court held that any failure by Amazon to remove the comments constituted an exercise of editorial discretion immunized by § 230. *Id.* at 42. The court rejected Schneider's argument that, although Amazon did not create the information about him, because it had the right to edit it and claimed licensing rights in the posted materials, "Amazon in effect became the content provider." *Ibid.* The court noted that if, as in *Ben Ezra,* "actual editing does not create liability, the mere right to edit can hardly do so." *Id.* at 43. Thus, in *Schneider,* immunity was not defeated by allowing admittedly improper (and potentially actionable) material to remain posted after notice from the offended party and an agreement to remove it.

The Third Circuit followed the same approach in *Green v. America Online,* 318 F.3d 465 (3d Cir. 2003). Green attempted to hold AOL liable for negligently failing to address allegedly defamatory and other harmful conduct directed at him by others in a "chat room" hosted by AOL. *Id.* at 468-69, 471. The court reasoned that Green was attempting "to hold AOL liable for decisions relating to the monitoring, screening, and deletion of content from its network -- actions quintessentially related to a publisher's role. Section 230 'specifically proscribes liability' in such circumstances." *Id.* at 471 (quoting *Zeran, supra,* 129 F.3d at 332-33). Addressing Green's contention that the good Samaritan provision violates the First Amendment because it allows a service provider to restrict material deemed inappropriate by the provider "whether or not such material is constitutionally protected," the court found no merit to the contention and stated: "Section 230(c)(2) does not require AOL to restrict speech; rather it allows AOL to establish standards of decency without risking liability for doing so." *Id.* at 472.

In *Batzel, supra,* 333 F.3d 1018, the Ninth Circuit expressed its strong agreement with the *Zeran* approach in construing and applying § 230. The court noted the two-fold purpose of § 230: (1) "to encourage the unfettered and unregulated development of free speech on the Internet, and to promote the development of e-commerce," and, more to the point in the litigation context, "to prevent lawsuits from shutting down websites and other services on the Internet;" and (2) "to encourage interactive computer services and users of such services to self-police the Internet for obscenity and other offensive material...." *Id.* at 1027-28. The court pointed out the anomaly that would result if the general grant of immunity did not include the good samaritan provision, namely that "if efforts to review and omit third-party defamatory, obscene or inappropriate material make a computer service provider or user liable for posted speech, then website operators and Internet service providers are likely to abandon efforts to eliminate such material from their site." *Id.* at 1029 (citing legislative history and other authorities).

Factually in *Batzel,* a third party, Robert Smith, was the content provider of a message accusing Batzel of being a descendant of a high-ranking Nazi official and possessing numerous paintings looted by the Nazis during World War II. *Id.* at 1021. The operator of the Museum Security Network posted the message, with some minor wording changes, accompanied by a "moderator's message" that "the FBI has been informed of the contents of [Smith's] original message." *Id.* at 1022. Batzel learned of the posting several months later and complained to the website operator. *Ibid.* Batzel denied the allegations and contended the defamatory statement caused her harm. *Ibid.*

The court rejected Batzel's contention that, by his conduct, the website operator in effect was jointly responsible with Smith for creating or developing the message. *Id.* at 1031. Smith composed the message and thus "created" it, and the website operator's "minor alterations ... or his choice to publish the e-mail" while rejecting others did not "rise to the level of 'development.'" *Ibid.* Providers and users of interactive computer services who "take some affirmative steps to edit the material posted" are protected by § 230, which precludes liability "for exercising the usual prerogative of publishers to choose among proffered material and to edit the material published while retaining its basic form and message." *Ibid.* The court concluded that "the 'development of information' therefore means something more substantial than merely editing portions of an e-mail and selecting material for publication." *Ibid.*

... Our canvass of the decisions interpreting and applying § 230 reveals a common thread. The provision has received a narrow, textual construction, not one that has welcomed creative theories or exhibited judicial creativity. Following this approach and applying these principles to the case before us, we are satisfied that Moldow, by virtue of his conduct, cannot be deemed an information content provider with respect to the anonymously-posted defamatory statements. His status as a provider or user of an interactive computer service garners for him the broad general immunity of § 230(c)(1). That he allows users to post messages anonymously or that he knows the identity of users of the website are simply not relevant to the terms of Congress' grant of immunity. The allegation that the anonymous format encourages defamatory and otherwise objectionable messages "because users may state their innermost thoughts and vicious statements free from civil recourse by their victims" does not pierce the immunity for two reasons: (1) the allegation is an unfounded conclusory statement, not a statement of fact; and (2) the allegation misstates the law; the anonymous posters are not immune from liability, and procedures are available, upon a proper showing, to ascertain their identities. *See Dendrite, supra,* 342 N.J. Super. at 141-42.

That Moldow posts messages of his own and participates in the discussion does make him an information content provider with respect to his postings. But no posting of his is alleged to be actionable. The source of potential liability is messages posted by others, and § 230(c)(1) grants him immunity for the content of information provided by "another." *Green, supra,* 318 F.3d at 470-71.

Appellants claim that Moldow controlled the content of the discussion forum, thus shaping it, as a result of which he was transformed into an information content provider. He accomplished this, according to appellants, by selectively choosing which messages to delete and which to leave posted. These activities, however, are nothing more than the exercise of a publisher's traditional editorial functions, namely, whether to publish, withdraw, postpone or alter content provided by others. *Zeran, supra,* 129 F.3d at 330. This is the very conduct Congress chose to immunize by § 230. Granting immunity furthers the legislative purpose of encouraging self-regulation to eliminate access to obscene or otherwise offensive materials while at the same time advancing the purpose of promoting free speech on the Internet, without fear of liability. *Id.* at 335. As stated in *Schneider, supra,* 108 Wn. App. at 467, the immunity continues to apply even if the self-policing effort is unsuccessful or not even attempted.

Notice from the offended party that the material is false or otherwise improper does not defeat the immunity. In *Zeran,* in the days following the Oklahoma City federal building bombing, postings by an unidentified third party on an AOL bulletin board advertised the sale of T-shirts and other items containing offensive and tasteless slogans related to the bombing, directing interested parties to Zeran and listing his home phone number. *Zeran, supra*, 129 F.3d at 329. Zeran immediately began receiving angry and threatening phone calls. He reported to AOL the falsity of the first message, and when additional similar messages appeared, he continued to complain. *Ibid.* The court found AOL immune from liability for allegedly delaying in removing the messages, failing to issue retractions, and failing to screen for similar additional postings after being placed on notice that the messages were false and defamatory. *Id.* at 328-34.

Receipt of such notice thrusts the service provider into the role of a traditional publisher, a role Congress chose to immunize. *Id.* at 332-33. Allowing liability upon notice would undermine the dual purposes of § 230 and would provide an incentive, rather than disincentive, for the provider to restrict free speech and abstain from self-regulation. *Id.* at 333. If notice could defeat immunity, anyone in any way "displeased" with posted materials could utilize notice as a "no-cost" means to create the basis for future lawsuits. *Ibid.* The specter of potential litigation, with its attendant cost and effort, would likely result in shutting down many websites, a result not intended by Congress. *Ibid.*

Therefore, we are unpersuaded by appellants' contention that Moldow's conduct in removing some messages after receiving complaints, but not removing others, transforms him into an information content provider. Nor does his act of deleting profanity from a posted message and then reposting it in redacted form. This is the very kind of self-regulation envisioned by the good samaritan provision in § 230. Moldow should not be exposed to the risk of liability because he has established his own standards of decency; nor is he potentially liable because of the degree of success he achieved or the effort he exerted to enforce them. *See Schneider, supra,* 108 Wn. App. at 467.

Whether Moldow's conduct facilitated the posting of the defamatory messages has no bearing on his immunity status. *See Carafano* [*v. Metrosplash.com, Inc.,* 339 F.3d 1119, 1124-25 (9th Cir. 2003)]. Nor does it matter that Moldow praised some comments favorable to him and ridiculed some comments favorable to appellants, and vice versa. *See Gentry, supra,* 121 Cal. Rptr.2d at 717. The fact remains that the "essential published content," the defamatory statements, were provided by third parties. *Carafano, supra,* 339 F.3d at 1124.

It cannot be said that, by the totality of his conduct, as alleged in the complaint, Moldow was responsible, in part, for the creation or development of the defamatory messages. They were created by their authors. Development requires material substantive contribution to the information that is ultimately published. Deleting profanity, selectively deleting or allowing to remain certain postings, and commenting favorably or unfavorably on some postings, without changing the substance of the message authored by another, does not constitute "development" within the meaning of § 230(f)(3).

C.

Finally, we address appellants' contention that the "good faith" requirement of the good samaritan provision has not been established as a matter of law, which would preclude dismissal on the pleadings under Rule 4:6-2(e). The complaint alleges that Moldow admitted "that he had a long-standing resentment against Donato, implying that Donato deserved the treatment he was receiving on the Eye on Emerson website." The complaint also alleges that Moldow posted the defamatory messages with actual malice. Appellants contend that these facts negate good faith on Moldow's part and are sufficient to withstand a Rule 4:6-2(e) dismissal. Appellants point out that none of the reported decisions address the good faith issue, and none dealt with a service provider who knew the plaintiffs and had ill will toward them.

In our view, appellants' argument rests on a misconception about the purpose of the good samaritan provision. It was inserted not to diminish the broad general immunity provided by § 230(c)(1), but to assure that it not be diminished by the exercise of traditional publisher functions. If the conduct falls within the scope of the traditional publisher's functions, it cannot constitute, within the context of § 230(c)(2)(A), bad faith. This principle, although not articulated in the cases we have discussed, is implicit in them. The service provider's conduct in some of the cases could, in a general sense, be characterized as bad faith. *E.g., Schneider, supra*, 31 P.3d at 38-39 (provider of interactive computer service agreed that one or more postings violated guidelines and should be removed, and promised to take steps to remove the postings within one to two business days, but failed to do so); *Zeran, supra*, 129 F.3d at 329 (provider of interactive computer service failed to immediately remove an allegedly defamatory posting on its bulletin board after being notified of its existence). But in each case the conduct was found to fall within the scope of the traditional publisher's function, and was therefore subject to immunity.

Nothing more is alleged here. Whether Moldow knew and disliked appellants is not relevant to the immunity terms of § 230. Selective editing and commenting are activities within the scope of the traditional publisher's function. The conclusory allegation that Moldow published the defamatory statements with actual malice is not sufficient to withstand a motion to dismiss on the pleadings. *See Printing Mart, supra*, 116 N.J. at 767-69.

We recognize, of course, the basic tenet of statutory construction that the legislature intended the words of a statute to have a meaning that is not superfluous or irrelevant. *Phillips v. Curiale*, 128 N.J. 608, 618, 608 A.2d 895 (1992). Thus, "good faith" must be ascribed some meaning. In light of the allegations here, however, we need not say any more on the subject. To raise an issue of an absence of good faith, an allegation of conduct outside the scope of the traditional publisher's function would be required. Our review of the complaint reveals no such allegation, and we have no occasion in this case to explore the outer boundary of "good faith" in the good samaritan provision. We conclude that, as a matter of law, Moldow's conduct did not constitute bad faith within the meaning of § 230(c)(2)(A). *See Printing Mart, supra*, 116 N.J. at 766-67.

Affirmed.

* * * * *

Other Applications of Section 230 of the Communications Decency Act

insert the following before Archived Materials on page 307 of Law of Internet Speech:

A California federal court relied on section 230 of the Communications Decency Act when it granted summary judgment to a web-site operator that had been sued by two local fair housing councils for allegedly violating federal and state housing laws. The court concluded that the plaintiffs' claims were barred by the CDA because they were based on web-site users' postings that suggested discriminatory preferences for roommates. The court did not reach the separate argument that the claims should be defeated based on the First Amendment on the ground that the users' postings implicated a right of intimate association.

See Fair Hous. Council of San Fernando Valley v. Roommate.com, LLC, No. CV-03-09386 PA (RZx), 2004 U.S. Dist. LEXIS 27987 (C.D. Cal. Sept. 30, 2004).

Not all claims are immune from the imposition of liability, however. Because section 230 of the CDA does not "limit or expand any law pertaining to intellectual property," 47 U.S.C. § 230(e)(2), allegations of wrongful use of a registered trademark have not been insulated from liability. *See Perfect 10, Inc. v. CCBill, LLC,* 340 F. Supp. 2d 1077, 1107-08 (C.D. Cal. 2004). The U.S. District Court for the Central District of California considered claims for unfair competition arising from a defendant's alleged infringement of a trademark under the state's Business and Professions Code, Cal. Bus. & Prof. Code § 17200. The court held that the mere fact that violations of intellectual property laws may create the underlying unfair or unlawful act giving rise to the unfair competition claim does not transform the statute into an intellectual property law within the CDA's exemption. Accordingly, CDA immunity was rejected for a California unfair competition claim. *See Perfect 10, Inc. v. CCBill, LLC,* 340 F. Supp. 2d at 1108.

Does CDA immunity apply to a right of publicity claim pursuant to section 3344 of the California Civil Code and common law rights of publicity? Noting that the California Supreme Court had characterized the right of publicity as a form of intellectual property, the California federal district court ruled that such claims asserted under California law are excluded from immunity under the CDA. *See Perfect 10, Inc. v. CCBill, LLC,* 340 F. Supp. 2d at 1108-09. The court distinguished false advertising claims asserted pursuant to section 17500 of California's Business and Professions Code and common law. Characterizing such as claims as ones "not pertain[ing] to intellectual property rights," the court determined that CDA immunity may be available. *See Perfect 10, Inc. v. CCBill, LLC,* 340 F. Supp. 2d at 1109-10.

* * * * *

SAAD NOAH, Plaintiff
v.
AOL TIME WARNER INC. and AMERICA ONLINE, INC., Defendants

United States District Court for the Eastern District of Virginia, Alexandria Division

Civil Action No. 02-1316-A, 261 F. Supp. 2d 532

May 15, 2003

MEMORANDUM OPINION

Plaintiff, on behalf of himself and a class of those similarly situated, sues his Internet service provider (ISP) for damages and injunctive relief, claiming that the ISP wrongfully refused to prevent participants in an online chat room from posting or submitting harassing comments that blasphemed and defamed plaintiff's Islamic religion and his co-religionists. Specifically, plaintiff claims his ISP's failure to prevent chat room participants from using the ISP's chat room to publish the harassing and defamatory comments constitutes a breach of the ISP's customer agreement with plaintiff and a violation of Title II of the Civil Rights Act of 1964, 42 U.S.C. § 2000a, *et seq.*

At issue on a threshold dismissal motion are[, *inter alia,*] the now familiar and well-litigated question whether a claim, like plaintiff's, which seeks to hold an ISP civilly liable as a publisher of third party statements is barred by the immunity granted ISP's by the Communications Decency Act of 1996, 47 U.S.C. § 230, [and] the less familiar, indeed novel question whether an online chat room is a "place of public accommodation" under Title II....

For the reasons that follow, plaintiff's claims do not survive threshold inspection and must therefore be dismissed.

I.

Plaintiff Saad Noah, a Muslim, is a resident of Illinois and was a subscriber of defendant America Online, Inc. ("AOL")'s Internet service until he cancelled the service in July of 2000. AOL, which is located in the Eastern District of Virginia, is, according to the complaint, the world's largest Internet service provider, with more than 30 million subscribers, or "members," worldwide. Defendant AOL Time Warner Inc. is the parent company of AOL.

Among the many services AOL provides its members are what are popularly known as "chat rooms." These occur where, as AOL does here, an ISP allows its participants to use its facilities to engage in real-time electronic conversations. Chat room participants type in their comments or observations, which are then read by other chat room participants, who may then type in their responses. Conversations in a chat room unfold in real time; the submitted comments appear transiently on participants' screens and then scroll off the screen as the conversation progresses. AOL chat rooms are typically set up for the discussion of a particular topic or area of interest, and any AOL member who wishes to join a conversation in a public chat room may do so.

Two AOL chat rooms are the focus of plaintiff's claims: the "Beliefs Islam" chat room and the "Koran" chat room. It is in these chat rooms that plaintiff alleges that he and other Muslims have been harassed, insulted, threatened, ridiculed and slandered by other AOL members due to their religious beliefs. The complaint lists dozens of harassing statements made by other AOL members in these chat rooms on specified dates, all of which plaintiff alleges he brought to AOL's attention together with requests that AOL take action to enforce its member guidelines and halt promulgation of the harassing statements. The statements span a period of two and one-half years, from January 10, 1998 to July 1, 2000, and are attributable to various AOL chat room participants only by virtue of a screen name. A representative sample of the reported offensive comments follows:

> ... (ii) On April 26, 1998, "Twotoneleg" wrote "I HATE MUSLIMS," "THE KORAN SUCKS," etc., and "BOSS30269" wrote "I LIKE SHOOTING MUSLIMS," "I WILL BOMB THE MIDDLE EAST," and "FUCK ISLAM."
>
> (iii) On November 4, 1998, "Hefedehefe" wrote "SMELLY TOWEL HEADS" and "MUSLIM TOWEL HEADS."
>
> (iv) On July 11, 1999, "Jzingher" wrote "The Koran and Islam are creations of Satan to distract people from the true faith which is Judaism. Mohammed was merely a huckster who found a simple people he could manipulate." ...

Plaintiff understandably complained about these offensive, obnoxious, and indecent statements, initially through the channels provided by AOL for such complaints and eventually through emails sent directly to AOL's CEO Steve Case. Plaintiff alleges that although he reported every one of the alleged violations to AOL, AOL refused to exercise its power to eliminate the harassment in the "Beliefs Islam" and "Koran" chat rooms. Moreover, plaintiff contends that AOL gave a "green light" to the harassment of Muslims in these forums, claiming that such harassment was not tolerated in chat rooms dealing with other subjects and faiths. In protest, plaintiff cancelled his AOL account in July 2000. Plaintiff further alleges that other Muslim members of AOL have also complained to AOL about similar harassing statements.

The relationship between AOL and each of its subscribing members is governed by the Terms of Service ("TOS"), which include a Member Agreement and the Community Guidelines. The Member Agreement is a "legal document that details [a member's] rights and obligations as an AOL member," and it requires, *inter alia,* that AOL members adhere to AOL's standards for online speech, as set forth in the Community Guidelines. These Guidelines state, in pertinent part, that

> ... You will be considered in violation of the Terms of Service if you (or others using your account) do any of the following: ...
>
> ~ Harass, threaten, embarrass, or do anything else to another member that is unwanted. This means: ... don't attack their race, heritage, etc. ...
>
> ~ Transmit or facilitate distribution of content that is harmful, abusive, racially or ethnically offensive, vulgar, sexually explicit, or in a reasonable person's view, objectionable. Community standards may vary, but there is no place on the service where hate speech is tolerated.
>
> ~ Disrupt the flow of chat in chat rooms with vulgar language, abusiveness, ...

The Member Agreement states that AOL has the right to enforce these Community Guidelines "in its sole discretion." In response to a violation, "AOL may take action against your account," ranging from "issuance of a warning about a violation to termination of your account." AOL's Community Action Team is responsible for enforcing the content and conduct standards and members are encouraged to notify AOL of violations they observe online. Importantly, however, the Member Agreement states that AOL members "....also understand and agree that the AOL Community Guidelines and the AOL Privacy Policy, including AOL's enforcement of those policies, are not intended to confer, and do not confer, any rights or remedies upon any person." ...

In addition to ... [other] claims raised in the complaint, plaintiff seems to assert a ... claim against defendants in his response to the motion to dismiss, where he alleges new facts concerning several incidents involving disciplinary actions taken by AOL against plaintiff and other, unnamed Muslim AOL members. Although the nature of the incidents is not entirely clear, plaintiff alleges that AOL discriminated against plaintiff and other Muslim AOL members by issuing false warnings against them and terminating their accounts in an effort to silence their pro-Islam speech. Plaintiff alleges his own AOL account was briefly terminated by AOL and subsequently reinstated, but his past messages were not restored. Relying on these incidents, plaintiff belatedly claims a violation of his First Amendment rights and of the First Amendment rights of similarly situated Muslims. Although not properly pled in the complaint, given plaintiff's *pro se* status this claim will nonetheless be considered on this motion to dismiss as if it had been raised in the original complaint. ...

IV.

Plaintiff's Title II claim fails for two alternate and independent reasons. First, plaintiff's claim against AOL is barred because of the immunity granted AOL, as an interactive computer service provider, by the Communications Decency Act of 1996, 47 U.S.C. § 230. Second, plaintiff's claim fails because a chat room is not a "place of public accommodation" as defined by Title II, 42 U.S.C. § 2000a(b). Each dismissal ground is separately addressed.

A.

The question presented at the threshold is whether AOL has been granted statutory immunity against plaintiff's Title II claim. Section 230 states, in relevant part, that "no provider or user of an interactive computer service shall be treated as the publisher or speaker of any information provided by another information content provider." 47 U.S.C. § 230(c)(1). Thus, the "plain language" of § 230 "creates a federal immunity to any cause of action that would make service providers liable for information originating with a third-party user of the service." *Zeran v. American Online, Inc.,* 129 F.3d 327, 330 (4th Cir. 1997), *cert denied,* 524 U.S. 937, 141 L.Ed.2d 712, 118 S. Ct. 2341 (1998). In other words, "§ 230 precludes courts from entertaining claims that would place a computer service provider in a publisher's role," and "lawsuits seeking to hold a service provider liable for its exercise of a publisher's traditional editorial functions -- such as deciding whether to publish, withdraw, postpone, or alter content -- are barred." *Id.* By specific statutory exclusion, certain causes of action are not barred by § 230; namely, causes of action based on (i) federal criminal statutes, (ii) intellectual property law, (iii) state law "that is consistent with this section," and (iv) the Electronic Communications Privacy Act of 1986. 47 U.S.C. §§ 230(e)(1)-(4).

Congress's purpose in providing such immunity is evident. As the Fourth Circuit noted in *Zeran,* -- ISPs such as AOL have millions of users who generate a "staggering" amount of content or information; thus it is "impossible for service providers to screen each of their millions of postings for possible problems." 129 F.3d at 331. If ISPs faced tort liability for information posted through their services by third parties, they might be forced to restrict access to their public forums. *Id.* Such a result would be counter to the statutory purpose of ensuring that the Internet remain a "forum for true diversity of political discourse, unique opportunities for cultural development, and myriad avenues for intellectual activity." *Id. at* 330; 47 U.S.C. § 230(a)(3). Thus, while parties that post information in Internet forums remain accountable under all applicable federal and state laws, they cannot be reached indirectly through the imposition of liability on the ISPs that serve as intermediaries in posting the information. *See Zeran,* 129 F.3d at 330.

Here, there is no question that § 230 bars plaintiff's Title II claim. First, the parties agree, as they must, that AOL is an "interactive computer service provider" as defined by § 230. AOL is clearly an "information service" that "provides ... access by multiple users to a computer server" and "provides access to the Internet." 47 U.S.C. § 230(f)(2). Second, all of the reported chat room statements are "information provided by another information content provider." 47 U.S.C. 230(c)(1). Individual AOL members, not AOL itself, created the content of the reported chat room statements. *See, e.g., Green v. America Online, Inc.*, 318 F.3d 465, 470 (3d Cir. 2003) (holding that chat room messages written by an AOL member are information "provided by another information content provider"). Finally, it is also clear that plaintiff's Title II claim "treats" AOL as the "publisher" of information provided by another.

Yet, relying on the fact that his claim is brought under Title II, not state defamation or negligence law, plaintiff contends that the claim treats AOL as the owner of a place of public accommodation, not a "publisher." This argument, though novel, is unpersuasive. An examination of the injury claimed by plaintiff and the remedy he seeks clearly indicates that his Title II claim seeks to "place" AOL "in a publisher's role," in violation of § 230. *Zeran*, 128 F.3d at 330. Thus, plaintiff contends that AOL is liable for its refusal to intervene and stop the allegedly harassing statements, and requests an injunction requiring AOL to adopt "affirmative measures" to stop such harassment, presumably by screening out the offensive statements and banning the members responsible for them. These allegations make clear that plaintiff seeks to hold AOL liable for its failure to exercise "a publisher's traditional editorial functions -- such as deciding whether to publish, withdraw, postpone or alter content." *Id.* As such, they are barred by § 230, for as the Fourth Circuit made clear in *Zeran*, all suits seeking to place a service provider in a publisher's role in this manner are barred under § 230. *Id.; see also Green*, 318 F.3d at 470 (holding that "holding AOL liable for its alleged negligent failure to properly police its network for content transmitted by its users ... would 'treat' AOL 'as the publisher or speaker' of that content").

Plaintiff's further attempts to argue that his Title II claim is beyond the reach of § 230 are similarly unavailing. First, plaintiff argues that § 230 immunity does not apply to claims brought under federal civil rights statutes. Yet, this argument runs counter to § 230's expansive language, which plainly reaches such claims. Significantly, this expansive language grants a broad immunity limited only by specific statutory exclusions, none of which is applicable here. Only four classes of claims are excluded: claims involving a "Federal criminal statute," "any law pertaining to intellectual property," "any State law that is consistent with this section," and "the Electronic Communications Privacy Act." 47 U.S.C. § 230(e)(1)-(4). Plaintiff's claim fits into none of these exclusions.

Nor can it be plausibly argued that § 230 is limited to immunity from state law claims for negligence or defamation. Such a limitation is flatly contradicted by § 230's exclusion of some specific federal claims. Those exclusions would be superfluous were § 230 immunity applicable only to certain state claims. Moreover, the exclusion of federal *criminal* claims, but not federal civil rights claims, clearly indicates, under the canon of *expressio unius est exclusio alterius,* that Congress did not intend to place federal civil rights claims outside the scope of § 230 immunity. In short, Congress's decision to exclude certain claims but not federal civil rights claims as a group, or Title II specifically, must be respected. *See TRW, Inc. v. Andrews,* 534 U.S. 19, 28, 151 L.Ed.2d 339, 122 S. Ct. 441 (2001) (noting that "where Congress explicitly enumerates certain exceptions to a general prohibition, additional exceptions are not to be implied, in the absence of evidence of a contrary legislative intent").

Second, plaintiff argues, unpersuasively, that § 230 does not apply to claims for injunctive relief, relying on *Mainstream Loudon v. Board of Trustees of the Loudon Cty. Library,* 2 F. Supp. 2d 783, 790 (E.D. Va. 1998). This reliance is misplaced. *Loudon* held that "the 'tort-based' immunity to 'civil liability'" described by § 230 did not apply to the action in that case for "declaratory and injunctive relief." *Id.* (citing *Zeran,* 129 F.3d at 330). Yet, *Loudon* is not only readily distinguishable from the instant case, its continuing authority is questionable. Subsequent courts have not followed *Loudon* in limiting § 230 immunity to claims for liability only, but have found § 230 applicable to claims seeking injunctive relief as well. *See Ben Ezra,* 206 F.3d at 983-986 (applying § 230 to claims for injunctive relief); *Smith v. Intercosmos Media Group, Inc.,* 2002 U.S. Dist. LEXIS 24251, 2002 WL 31844907 (E.D. La. Dec. 17, 2002) (holding that § 230 provides immunity from claims for injunctive relief); *Kathleen R.,* 87 Cal. App. 4th 684, 104 Cal. Rptr. 2d 772, 781 (same). Indeed, given that the purpose of § 230 is to shield service providers from legal responsibility for the statements of third parties, § 230 should not be read to permit claims that request only injunctive relief. After all, in some circumstances injunctive relief will be at least as burdensome to the service provider as damages, and is typically more intrusive.

In sum, § 230 bars plaintiff's claim under Title II because it seeks to treat AOL as the publisher of the allegedly harassing statements of other AOL members. To be sure, the offensive statements plaintiff complains of are a far cry from the "diversity of political discourse, unique opportunities for cultural development, and myriad avenues for intellectual activity" that § 230 is intended to promote and protect. 47 U.S.C. § 230(a). Indeed, the statements reported by plaintiff suggest a darker side of what has been called the "robust nature of Internet communication." *Zeran,* 129 F.3d at 330. Nonetheless, § 230 reflects Congress's judgment that imposing liability on service providers for the harmful speech of others would likely do more harm than good, by exposing service providers to unmanageable liability and potentially leading to the closure or restriction of such open forums as AOL's chat rooms. *Id.* at 331. Accordingly, under § 230, plaintiff may not seek recourse against AOL as publisher of the offending statements; instead, plaintiff must pursue his rights, if any, against the offending AOL members themselves.

B.

Even assuming, *arguendo,* that plaintiff's Title II claim is not barred by § 230, it must nonetheless be dismissed for failure to state a claim because AOL's chat rooms and other online services do not constitute a "place of public accommodation" under Title II. ....[I]t is clear that the logic of the statute and the weight of authority indicate that "places of entertainment" must be actual physical facilities. With this principle firmly established, it is clear that AOL's online chat rooms cannot be construed as "places of public accommodation" under Title II. An online chat room may arguably be a "place of entertainment, "but it is not a physical structure to which a member of the public may be granted or denied access, and as such is fundamentally different from a "motion picture house, theater, concert hall, sports arena, [or] stadium." 42 U.S.C. § 2000a(b)(3). Although a chat room may serve as a *virtual* forum through which AOL members can meet and converse in cyberspace, it is not an "establishment," under the plain meaning of that term as defined by the statute. Unlike a theater, concert hall, arena, or any of the other "places of entertainment" specifically listed in § 2000a(b), a chat room does not exist in a particular physical location, indeed it can be accessed almost anywhere, including from homes, schools, cybercafes and libraries. In sum, although a chat room or other online forum might be referred to metaphorically as a "location" or "place," it lacks the physical presence necessary to constitute a place of public accommodation under Title II. ...

E.

Finally, plaintiff's belatedly-raised First Amendment claim is easily disposed of at this stage. In essence, plaintiff claims that AOL violated his First Amendment rights by issuing him warnings and briefly terminating his account, allegedly in response to his pro-Islamic

252

statements. Yet, even assuming the truth of plaintiff's allegations, the First Amendment is of no avail to him in these circumstances; it does not protect against actions taken by private entities, rather it is "a guarantee only against abridgment by government, federal or state." *Hudgens v. NLRB,* 424 U.S. 507, 513, 47 L.Ed.2d 196, 96 S. Ct. 1029 (1976). Plaintiff does not argue that AOL is a state actor, nor is there any evident basis for such an argument. *See Green,* 318 F.3d at 472 (noting that AOL is a "private, for profit company" and rejecting the argument that AOL should be treated as a state actor); *Cyber Promotions Inc. v. American Online, Inc.,* 948 F. Supp.436, 441-44 (E.D. Pa. 1996) (rejecting the argument that AOL is a state actor). Accordingly, because AOL is not a state actor, plaintiff's First Amendment claim must be dismissed.

*   *   *   *   *

Archived Materials

insert the following before the reference to Simon v. Arizona Bd. of Regents in the first full paragraph on page 308 of Law of Internet Speech:

The New York Court of Appeals agreed. Policy considerations amply supported the ruling; "[i]n addition to increasing the exposure of publishers to stale claims, applying the multiple publication rule to a communication distributed via mass media would permit a multiplicity of actions, leading to potential harassment and excessive liability, and draining of judicial resources. ... [A] multiple publication rule would implicate an even greater potential for endless retriggering of the statute of limitations, multiplicity of suits and harassment of defendants. Inevitably, there would be a serious inhibitory effect on the open, pervasive dissemination of information and ideas over the Internet, which is, of course, its greatest beneficial promise." 98 N.Y.2d 365, 369-70, 747 N.Y.S.2d 69, 71-72, 775 N.E.2d 463, 465-66 (N.Y. 2002) (citations omitted).

Nor was the court persuaded by the plaintiff's argument that the web-site had added new content within the applicable statute of limitations period. The modification to the site consisted of material that was unrelated to the allegedly defamatory content and so did not defeat the application of the re-publication rule to the site. Critical to the court's determination was that the modifications to the web-site did not give rise to allegations of defamation.

Moreover, "it is not reasonably inferable that the addition [to the web-site] was made either with the intent or the result of communicating the earlier and separate defamatory information to a new audience. We observe that many Web sites are in a constant state of change, with information posted sequentially on a frequent basis. For example, this Court has a Web site which includes its decisions, to which it continually adds its slip opinions as they are handed down. Similarly, Web sites are used by news organizations to provide readily accessible records of newsworthy events as they occur and are reported." *Id.,* 98 N.Y.2d at 371, 747 N.Y.S.2d at 72-73, 775 N.E.2d at 466-67.

The New York Court of Appeals specifically identified the underlying policy considerations; to apply the re-publication exception in these circumstances "would either discourage the placement of information on the Internet or slow the exchange of such information, reducing the Internet's unique advantages. In order not to retrigger the statute of limitations, a publisher would be forced either to avoid posting on a Web site or use a separate site for each new piece of information. These policy concerns militate against a holding that any modification to a Web site constitutes a republication of the defamatory communication itself." *Id., * 98 N.Y.2d at 372, 747 N.Y.S.2d at 73, 775 N.E.2d at 467 (citations omitted).

* * * * *

insert the following after the reference to Van Buskirk v. New York Times Co. in the first full paragraph on page 308 of Law of Internet Speech:

On appeal, the U.S. Court of Appeals for the Second Circuit echoed the rationales explicated in *Firth v. State,* and also emphasized that the single publication rule benefits both parties. It "implements a public policy of avoiding the exposure of publishers to 'a multiplicity of actions, leading to potential harassment and excessive liability, and draining of judicial resources,' as well as 'reduc[ing] the possibility of hardship to plaintiffs by allowing the collection of damages in one case commenced in a single jurisdiction.'" *Van Buskirk v. New York Times Co.,* 325 F.3d 87, 89 (2d Cir. 2003) (citations omitted).

Other courts likewise have applied the single publication rule to allegedly defamatory statements disseminated on-line. In *Mitan v. Davis,* 243 F. Supp. 2d 719 (W.D. Ky. 2003), for example, libel claims based on statements posted on the Internet more than one year before suit was initiated were deemed barred by the Kentucky statute of limitations. The court applied the single publication rule, analogizing the statement located on a server that is called up whenever a Web page is accessed to a statement on a page in a book that is accessed whenever the book is taken off the shelf and opened. *Id.* at 724; *see also McCandliss v. Cox Enters, Inc.,* 265 Ga. App. 377; 593 S.E.2d 856 (Ga. Ct. App. 2004) (applying the single publication rule in a *pro se* action regarding the publication of allegedly libelous material on an Internet web-site), *cert. denied,* No. S04C1008, 2004 Ga. LEXIS 438 (Ga. May 24, 2004).

Similarly, in *Abate v. Maine Antique Digest,* 17 Mass. L. Rep. 288 (Mass. Super. Ct. 2004), the plaintiff complained that he was defamed by an article that had been continuously posted since it first appeared several years earlier. The Massachusetts court applied the single publication rule, stating that treating Internet publications differently from print publications "would result in the endless retriggering of the statute of limitations, thus exposing those who 'publish' information on the internet to a multiplicity of lawsuits and thereby inhibiting the open dissemination of information and ideas." *Id.* at 288 (citation omitted).

A California appellate court likewise recognized that "the need to protect Web publishers from almost perpetual liability for statements they make available to the hundreds of millions of people who have access to the Internet is greater even than the need to protect the publishers of conventional hard copy newspapers, magazines and books." *The Traditional Cat Ass'n v. Gilbreath,* 118 Cal. App. 4th 392, 404, 13 Cal. Rptr. 3d 353, 362 (Cal. Ct. App. 2004) (applying the single publication rule to allegedly defamatory statements posted on a web-site). The court thereby recognized a greater need for application of the single publication rule in the context of on-line communications, where dissemination of content is potentially exponentially increased.

* * * * *

Of and Concerning the Plaintiff

The "Other Side" of Of and Concerning: Identifying the Creator of On-Line Content

insert the following after the second paragraph on page 311 of Law of Internet Speech:

A religious organization sought to enjoin a village in Ohio from enforcing an ordinance that required those who canvassed, solicited, peddled, or hawked in private residences to register with the mayor's office. *Watchtower Bible and Tract Soc'y of N.Y., Inc. v. Village of Stratton,* 240 F.3d 553 (6th Cir. 2001), *rev'd,* 536 U.S. 150 (2002). Registration requirements included specification of the reasons for canvassing, the residences to be canvassed, the length of time the participants intended to canvass, and other information "as may be reasonably necessary to accurately describe the nature of the privilege desired." 240 F.3d at 558. The plaintiffs objected, pointing out that the registration requirements precluded anonymity. *See id.* at 563.

The Sixth Circuit rejected the argument, concluding that "[i]ndividuals going door-to-door to engage in political speech are not anonymous by virtue of the fact that they reveal a portion of their identities – their physical identities – to the residents they canvass. In other words, the ordinance does not require canvassers going door-to-door to reveal their identities; instead, the very act of going door-to-door requires the canvassers to reveal a portion of their identities." *Id.*

But is one able to meaningfully withhold his identity simply because he can distribute leaflets without specifying one's name and withholding one's identity, in light of the fact that the individual revealed his physical self by offering the pamphlet? On appeal, the U.S. Supreme Court concluded that the interests the ordinance ostensibly served, namely, the prevention of fraud and crime and the protection of residents' privacy, are important. Accordingly, the village may endeavor to safeguard them through some form of regulation of solicitation activity. However, the ordinance was not narrowly tailored to those interests. The pernicious effect of the permit's requirement necessarily resulted in a surrender of protected anonymity. 536 U.S. 150.

* * * * *

insert the following before Efforts to Compel Disclosure of the Putative Defendant's Identity on page 316 of Law of Internet Speech:

JOHN DOE, Plaintiff

v.

2THEMART.COM INC., Defendant

United States District Court for the Western District of Washington

No. C01-453Z, 140 F. Supp. 2d 1088

April 27, 2001

ORDER

This matter comes before the Court on the motion of J. Doe (Doe) to proceed under a pseudonym and to quash a subpoena issued by 2TheMart.com (TMRT) to a local internet service provider, Silicon Investor/InfoSpace, Inc. (InfoSpace). The motion raises important First Amendment issues regarding Doe's right to speak anonymously on the Internet and to proceed in this Court using a pseudonym in order to protect that right. ...

FACTUAL BACKGROUND

There is a federal court lawsuit pending in the Central District of California in which the shareholders of TMRT have brought a shareholder derivative class action against the company and its officers and directors alleging fraud on the market. In that litigation, the defendants have asserted as an affirmative defense that no act or omission by the defendants caused the plaintiffs' injury. By subpoena, TMRT seeks to obtain the identity of twenty-three speakers who have participated anonymously on Internet message boards operated by InfoSpace. That subpoena is the subject of the present motion to quash.

InfoSpace is a Seattle based Internet company that operates a website called "Silicon Investor." The Silicon Investor site contains a series of electronic bulletin boards, and some of these bulletin boards are devoted to specific publicly traded companies. InfoSpace users can freely post and exchange messages on these boards. Many do so using Internet pseudonyms, the often fanciful names that people choose for themselves when interacting on the Internet. By using a pseudonym, a person who posts or responds to a message on an Internet bulletin board maintains anonymity.

One of the Internet bulletin boards on the Silicon Investor website is specifically devoted to TMRT. According to the brief filed on behalf of J. Doe, "to date, almost 1500 messages have been posted on the TMRT board, covering an enormous variety of topics and posters. Investors and members of the public discuss the latest news about the company, what new businesses it may develop, the strengths and weaknesses of the company's operations, and what its managers and its employees might do better." Past messages posted on the site are archived, so any new user can read and print copies of prior postings.

Some of the messages posted on the TMRT site have been less than flattering to the company. In fact, some have been downright nasty. For example, a user calling himself "Truthseeker" posted a message stating "TMRT is a Ponzi scam that Charles Ponzi would be proud of.... The company's CEO, Magliarditi, has defrauded employees in the past. The company's other large shareholder, Rebeil, defrauded customers in the past." Another poster named "Cuemaster" indicated that "they were dumped by their accountants ... these guys are friggin liars ... why haven't they told the public this yet??? Liars and criminals!!!!!" Another user, not identified in the exhibits, wrote "Lying, cheating, thieving, stealing, lowlife criminals!!!!" Other postings advised TMRT investors to sell their stock. "Look out below!!!! This stock has had it ... get short or sell your position now while you still can." "They [TMRT] are not building anything, except extensions on their homes...bail out now."

TMRT, the defendant in the California lawsuit, issued the present subpoena to InfoSpace pursuant to Fed. R. Civ. P. 45(a)(2). The subpoena seeks, among other things, "all identifying information and documents, including, but not limited to, computerized or computer stored records and logs, electronic mail (E-mail), and postings on your online message boards," concerning a list of twenty-three InfoSpace users, including Truthseeker, Cuemaster, and the current J. Doe, who used the pseudonym NoGuano. These users have posted messages on the TMRT bulletin board or have communicated via the Internet with users who have posted such messages. The subpoena would require InfoSpace to disclose the subscriber information for these twenty-three users, thereby stripping them of their Internet anonymity.

InfoSpace notified these users by e-mail that it had received the subpoena, and gave them time to file a motion to quash. One such user who used the Internet pseudonym NoGuano now seeks to quash the subpoena[, making the motion anonymously].

NoGuano alleges that enforcement of the subpoena would violate his or her First Amendment right to speak anonymously. ...

DISCUSSION

The Internet represents a revolutionary advance in communication technology. It has been suggested that the Internet may be the "greatest innovation in speech since the invention of the printing press[.]" *See* Raymond Shih Ray Ku, *Open Internet Access and Freedom of Speech: A First Amendment Catch-22*, 75 Tul. L. Rev. 87, 88 (2000). It allows people from all over the world to exchange ideas and information freely and in "real-time." Through the use of the Internet, "any person with a phone line can become a town crier with a voice that resonates farther than it could from any soapbox." *Reno v. ACLU*, 521 U.S. 844, 870, 138 L. Ed. 2d 874, 117 S. Ct. 2329 (1997).

The rapid growth of Internet communication and Internet commerce has raised novel and complex legal issues and has challenged existing legal doctrine in many areas. This motion raises important and challenging questions of: (1) what is the scope of an individual's First Amendment right to speak anonymously on the Internet, and (2) what showing must be made by a private party seeking to discover the identity of anonymous Internet users through the enforcement of a civil subpoena?

A. The anonymity of Internet speech is protected by the First Amendment.

The right to the freedom of speech is enshrined in the First Amendment to the United States Constitution, which provides that "Congress shall make no law ... abridging the freedom of speech, or of the press[.]" U.S. Const. amend. I. This limitation on governmental interference with free speech applies directly to the federal government, and has been imposed on the states via the Fourteenth Amendment. *See, e.g., First Nat'l Bank v. Bellotti,* 435 U.S. 765, 779-80, 55 L. Ed. 2d 707, 98 S. Ct. 1407 (1978).

A court order, even when issued at the request of a private party in a civil lawsuit, constitutes state action and as such is subject to constitutional limitations. *See, e.g., New York Times Co. v. Sullivan,* 376 U.S. 254, 265, 11 L. Ed. 2d 686, 84 S. Ct. 710 (1964); *Shelley v. Kraemer,* 334 U.S. 1, 92 L. Ed. 1161, 68 S. Ct. 836 (1948). For this reason, numerous cases have discussed the limitations on the subpoena power when that power is invoked in such a manner that it impacts First Amendment rights. *See, e.g., NAACP v. Alabama ex rel. Patterson,* 357 U.S. 449, 461, 2 L. Ed. 2d 1488, 78 S. Ct. 1163 (1958) (discussing the First Amendment implications of a civil subpoena to disclose the membership list for the NAACP); *Los Angeles Memorial Coliseum Comm'n v. Nat'l Football League,* 89 F.R.D. 489 (C.D. Cal. 1981) (discussing the First Amendment implications of a civil subpoena to disclose the names of confidential journalistic sources); *Snedigar v. Hoddersen,* 114 Wn.2d 153, 786 P.2d 781 (1990) (discussing the First Amendment implications of a civil subpoena to disclose the meeting minutes of a political association).

First Amendment protections extend to speech via the Internet. "Through the use of web pages, mail exploders and newsgroups, [any person] can become a pamphleteer." *Reno,* 521 U.S. at 870. A component of the First Amendment is the right to speak with anonymity. This component of free speech is well established. *See, e.g., Buckley v. American Constitutional Law Found.,* 525 U.S. 182, 200, 142 L. Ed. 2d 599, 119 S. Ct. 636 (1999) (invalidating, on First Amendment grounds, a Colorado statute that required initiative petition circulators to wear identification badges); *McIntyre v. Ohio Elections Comm'n,* 514 U.S. 334, 357, 131 L. Ed. 2d 426, 115 S. Ct. 1511 (1995) (overturning an Ohio law that prohibited the distribution of campaign literature that did not contain the name and address of the person issuing the literature, holding that "under our Constitution, anonymous pamphleteering is not a pernicious, fraudulent practice, but an honorable tradition of advocacy and dissent. Anonymity is a shield from the tyranny of the majority."); *Talley v. California,* 362 U.S. 60, 65, 4 L. Ed. 2d 559, 80 S. Ct. 536 (1960) (invalidating a California statute prohibiting the distribution of "any handbill in any place under any circumstances" that did not contain the name and address of the person who prepared it, holding that identification and fear of reprisal might deter "perfectly peaceful discussions of public matters of importance.")

The right to speak anonymously was of fundamental importance to the establishment of our Constitution. Throughout the revolutionary and early federal period in American history, anonymous speech and the use of pseudonyms were powerful tools of political debate. The Federalist Papers (authored by Madison, Hamilton, and Jay) were written anonymously under the name "Publius." The anti-federalists responded with anonymous articles of their own, authored by "Cato" and "Brutus," among others. *See generally McIntyre,* 514 U.S. at 341-42. Anonymous speech is a great tradition that is woven into the fabric of this nation's history.

The right to speak anonymously extends to speech via the Internet. Internet anonymity facilitates the rich, diverse, and far ranging exchange of ideas. The "ability to speak one's mind" on the Internet "without the burden of the other party knowing all the facts about one's identity can foster open communication and robust debate." *Columbia Ins. Co. v. Seescandy.com,* 185 F.R.D. 573, 578 (N.D. Cal. 1999). People who have committed no wrongdoing should be free to participate in online forums without fear that their identity will be exposed under the authority of the court. *Id.*

When speech touches on matters of public political life, such as debate over the qualifications of candidates, discussion of governmental or political affairs, discussion of political campaigns, and advocacy of controversial points of view, such speech has been described as the "core" or "essence" of the First Amendment. *See McIntyre*, 514 U.S. at 346-47. Governmental restrictions on such speech are entitled to "exacting scrutiny," and are upheld only where they are "narrowly tailored to serve an overriding state interest." *Id.* at 347. However, even non-core speech is entitled to First Amendment protection. "First Amendment protections are not confined to 'the exposition of ideas[.]'" *Id.* at 346, citing *Winters v. New York*, 333 U.S. 507, 510, 92 L. Ed. 840, 68 S. Ct. 665 (1948). Unlike the speech at issue in *Buckley, McIntyre* and *Talley,* the speech here is not entitled to "exacting scrutiny," but to normal strict scrutiny analysis.

In support of its subpoena request, TMRT argues that the right to speak anonymously does not create any corresponding right to remain anonymous after speech. In support of this contention, TMRT cites only to *Buckley*. TMRT argues that in *Buckley*, while the Court struck down a requirement that petition circulators wear identification badges when soliciting signatures, the Court upheld a provision of the same statute that required circulators to execute an identifying affidavit when they submitted the collected signatures to the state for counting. However, the Court's reasoning in *Buckley* does not support the contention that there is no First Amendment right to remain anonymous. It merely establishes that in the context of the submission of initiative petitions to the State, the State's enforcement interest outweighs the circulator's First Amendment protections. *Buckley*, 525 U.S. at 200, quoting *McIntyre*, 514 U.S. at 523 (Ginsberg, J., concurring) ("We recognize that a State's enforcement interest might justify a more limited identification requirement.") The right to speak anonymously is therefore not absolute. However, this right would be of little practical value if, as TMRT urges, there was no concomitant right to remain anonymous after the speech is concluded.

B. Applicable legal standard.

The free exchange of ideas on the Internet is driven in large part by the ability of Internet users to communicate anonymously. If Internet users could be stripped of that anonymity by a civil subpoena enforced under the liberal rules of civil discovery, this would have a significant chilling effect on Internet communications and thus on basic First Amendment rights. Therefore, discovery requests seeking to identify anonymous Internet users must be subjected to careful scrutiny by the courts.

As InfoSpace has urged, "unmeritorious attempts to unmask the identities of online speakers ... have a chilling effect on" Internet speech. The "potential chilling effect imposed by the unmasking of anonymous speakers would diminish if litigants first were required to make a showing in court of their need for the identifying information." "Requiring litigants to make such a showing would allow [the Internet] to thrive as a forum for speakers to express their views on topics of public concern." InfoSpace and NoGuano have accordingly urged this Court to "adopt a balancing test requiring litigants to demonstrate ... that their need for identity information outweighs anonymous online speakers' First Amendment rights[.]" *Id.*

In the context of a civil subpoena issued pursuant to Fed. R. Civ. P. 45, this Court must determine when and under what circumstances a civil litigant will be permitted to obtain the identity of persons who have exercised their First Amendment right to speak anonymously. ... When the anonymous Internet user is not a party to the case, the litigation can go forward without the disclosure of their identity. Therefore, non-party disclosure is only appropriate in the exceptional case where the compelling need for the discovery sought outweighs the First Amendment rights of the anonymous speaker.

Accordingly, this Court adopts the following standard for evaluating a civil subpoena that seeks the identity of an anonymous Internet user who is not a party to the underlying litigation. The Court will consider four factors in determining whether the subpoena should issue. These are whether: (1) the subpoena seeking the information was issued in good faith and not for any improper purpose, (2) the information sought relates to a core claim or defense, (3) the identifying information is directly and materially relevant to that claim or defense, and (4) information sufficient to establish or to disprove that claim or defense is unavailable from any other source.[5]

This test provides a flexible framework for balancing the First Amendment rights of anonymous speakers with the right of civil litigants to protect their interests through the litigation discovery process. The Court shall give weight to each of these factors as the court determines is appropriate under the circumstances of each case. This Court is mindful that it is imposing a high burden. "But the First Amendment requires us to be vigilant in making [these] judgments, to guard against undue hindrances to political conversations and the exchange of ideas." *Buckley*, 525 U.S. at 192.

C. Analysis of the present motion.

In the present case, TMRT seeks information it says will validate its defense that "changes in [TMRT] stock prices were *not* caused by the Defendants but by the illegal actions of individuals who manipulated the [TMRT] stock price using the Silicon Investor message boards." This Court must evaluate TMRT's stated need for the information in light of the four factors outlined above.

1. Was the subpoena brought in good faith?

This Court does not conclude that this subpoena was brought in bad faith or for an improper purpose. TMRT and its officers and directors are defending against a shareholder derivative class action lawsuit. They have asserted numerous affirmative defenses, one of which alleges that defendants did not cause the drop in TMRT's stock value. TMRT could reasonably believe that the posted messages are relevant to this defense.

However, as originally issued the subpoena seeking the identity information was extremely broad. The subpoena would have required the disclosure of personal e-mails and other personal information that has no relevance to the issues raised in the lawsuit. This apparent disregard for the privacy and the First Amendment rights of the online users, while not demonstrating bad faith *per se*, weighs against TMRT in balancing the interests here.

---

[5] This Court is aware that many civil subpoenas seeking the identifying information of Internet users may be complied with, and the identifying information disclosed, without notice to the Internet users themselves. This is because some Internet service providers do not notify their users when such a civil subpoena is received. The standard set forth in this Order may guide Internet service providers in determining whether to challenge a specific subpoena on behalf of their users. However, this will provide little solace to Internet users whose Internet service company does not provide them notice when a subpoena is received.

2. Does the information sought relate to a core claim or defense?

Only when the identifying information is needed to advance core claims or defenses can it be sufficiently material to compromise First Amendment rights. *See Silkwood v. Kerr-McGee Corp.*, 563 F.2d 433, 438 (10th Cir. 1977) (in order to overcome the journalistic privilege of maintaining confidential sources, a party seeking to identify those sources must demonstrate, *inter alia,* that the "information goes to the heart of the matter[.]") If the information relates only to a secondary claim or to one of numerous affirmative defenses, then the primary substance of the case can go forward without disturbing the First Amendment rights of the anonymous Internet users.

The information sought by TMRT does not relate to a core defense. Here, the information relates to only one of twenty-seven affirmative defenses raised by the defendant, the defense that "no act or omission of any of the Defendants was the cause in fact or the proximate cause of any injury or damage to the plaintiffs." This is a generalized assertion of the lack of causation. Defendants have asserted numerous other affirmative defenses that go more "to the heart of the matter," such as the lack of material misstatements by the defendants, actual disclosure of material facts by the defendants, and the business judgment defense. Therefore, this factor also weighs in favor of quashing the subpoena.

3. Is the identifying information directly and materially relevant to a core claim or defense?

Even when the claim or defense for which the information is sought is deemed core to the case, the identity of the Internet users must also be materially relevant to that claim or defense. Under the Federal Rules of Civil Procedure discovery is normally very broad, requiring disclosure of any relevant information that "appears reasonably calculated to lead to the discovery of admissible evidence." Fed. R. Civ. P. 26(b)(1). But when First Amendment rights are at stake, a higher threshold of relevancy must be imposed. Only when the information sought is directly and materially relevant to a core claim or defense can the need for the information outweigh the First Amendment right to speak anonymously. *See Los Angeles Memorial Coliseum Comm'n,* 89 F.R.D. at 494 (holding that a party seeking to enforce a subpoena to disclose non-party journalistic sources must demonstrate that the information is of "certain relevance.")

TMRT has failed to demonstrate that the identity of the Internet users is directly and materially relevant to a core defense. These Internet users are not parties to the case and have not been named as defendants as to any claim, cross-claim or third-party claim. Therefore, … their identity is not needed to allow the litigation to proceed.

According to the pleadings, the Internet user known as NoGuano has never posted messages on Silicon Investor's TMRT message board. At oral argument, TMRT's counsel conceded this point but stated that NoGuano's information was sought because he had "communicated" via the Internet with Silicon Investor posters such as Truthseeker. Given that NoGuano admittedly posted no public statements on the TMRT site, there is no basis to conclude that the identity of NoGuano and others similarly situated is directly and materially relevant to TMRT's defense.

As to the Internet users such as Truthseeker and Cuemaster who posted messages on the TMRT bulletin board, TMRT has failed to demonstrate that their identities are directly and materially relevant to a core defense. TMRT argues that the Internet postings caused a drop in TMRT's stock price. However, what was said in these postings is a matter of public record, and the identity of the anonymous posters had no effect on investors. If these messages did influence the stock price, they did so without *anyone* knowing the identity of the speakers.

TMRT speculates that the users of the InfoSpace website may have been engaged in stock manipulation in violation of federal securities law. TMRT indicates that it intends to compare the names of the InfoSpace users with the names of individuals who traded TMRT stock during the same period to determine whether any illegal stock manipulation occurred. However, TMRT's innuendos of stock manipulation do not suffice to overcome the First Amendment rights of the Internet users. Those rights cannot be nullified by an unsupported allegation of wrongdoing raised by the party seeking the information.

> 4. Is information sufficient to establish TMRT's defense available from any other source?

TMRT has failed to demonstrate that the information it needs to establish its defense is unavailable from any other source. The chat room messages are archived and are available to anyone to read and print. TMRT obtained copies of some of these messages and submitted them to this Court. TMRT can therefore demonstrate what was said, when it was said, and can compare the timing of those statements with information on fluctuations in the TMRT stock price. The messages are available for use at trial, and TMRT can factually support its defense without encroaching on the First Amendment rights of the Internet users.

CONCLUSION

The Internet is a truly democratic forum for communication. It allows for the free exchange of ideas at an unprecedented speed and scale. For this reason, the constitutional rights of Internet users, including the First Amendment right to speak anonymously, must be carefully safeguarded.

Courts should impose a high threshold on subpoena requests that encroach on this right. In order to enforce a civil subpoena seeking the identifying information of a non-party individual who has communicated anonymously over the Internet, the party seeking the information must demonstrate, by a clear showing on the record, that four requirements are met: (1) the subpoena seeking the information was issued in good faith and not for any improper purpose, (2) the information sought relates to a core claim or defense, (3) the identifying information is directly and materially relevant to that claim or defense, and (4) information sufficient to establish or to disprove that claim or defense is unavailable from any other source.

The Court has weighed these factors in light of the present facts. TMRT has failed to demonstrate that the identity of these Internet users is directly and materially relevant to a core defense in the underlying securities litigation. Accordingly, Doe's motion to quash the subpoena is GRANTED.

* * * * *

Efforts to Compel Disclosure of the Putative Defendant's Identity

insert the following after the second paragraph on page 317 of Law of Internet Speech:

Thereafter, the Pennsylvania Supreme Court granted the ACLU's petition for allowance of appeal and, in November 2003, sent the case back to the Superior Court for consideration on the merits. *See Melvin v. Doe,* 836 A.2d 42 (Pa. 2003). The state Supreme Court characterized the lower court's order to reveal Doe's identity as a collateral order because it was not impermissibly intertwined with the resolution of the underlying defamation action, and because the trial court's discovery order affected a right that would be lost were review postponed until trial concluded. The court noted that "the court-ordered disclosure of [Does' identities] presents a significant possibility of trespass upon their First Amendment rights," and concluded that "[t]here is no question that generally, the constitutional right to anonymous free speech is a right deeply rooted in public policy that goes beyond this particular litigation, and that it falls within the class of rights that are too important to be denied review." *Id.* at 47. Moreover, it was clear to the court that once the identities were disclosed, the Does' First Amendment claim would be "irreparably lost as there are no means by which to later cure such disclosure." *Id.* at 50 (footnote omitted). Accordingly, the court vacated the Superior Court's order quashing the appeal and remanded the case for consideration of the constitutional question; namely, whether the First Amendment requires a public official defamation plaintiff to establish a *prima facie* case of actual economic harm prior to discovering an anonymous defamation defendant's identity. *See id.* Thereafter, however, Judge Joan Orie Melvin asked the court to dismiss her suit; her reason for declining to pursue the action was not apparent. *See Judge Drops Internet Defamation Suit,* NewsMax.com (Apr. 5, 2005), *available at* <http://www.newsmax.com/archives/articles/2004/4/4/142559.shtml>.

* * * * *

Compelling Disclosure of Identity and Pursuit of Extra-Judicial Relief

insert the following after Notes and Questions # 11 on page 326 of Law of Internet Speech:

12. The identities of thousands of anonymous posters of book reviews on on-line retail bookseller Amazon.com were revealed. Amy Harmon, *Amazon Glitch Unmasks War of Reviewers,* N.Y. Times, Feb. 14, 2004 at A1. Do anonymous reviews bolster or detract from the reviewers' credibility?

13. Should the identity of alleged copyright infringers be compelled? Verizon Internet Services, Inc., an Internet service provider, moved to quash a subpoena served by the Recording Industry Association of America (the "RIAA") pursuant to the Digital Millennium Copyright Act of 1998 ("DMCA"), 17 U.S.C. § 512. *In re: Verizon Internet Servs., Inc.,* 257 F. Supp. 2d 244 (D.D.C. 2003), *cert. denied sub nom. Verizon Internet Servs. v. Recording Indus. Ass'n of America, Inc.,* 125 S. Ct. 347 (2004); *see generally Law of Internet Speech* at 583. On behalf of copyright owners, the RIAA sought the identity of an anonymous user of the conduit functions of Verizon's Internet service who allegedly infringed copyrights by offering hundreds of songs for downloading over the Internet. *In re: Verizon Internet Servs., Inc.,* 257 F. Supp. 2d at 246.

In an earlier action, the court had rejected Verizon's statutory challenges to a similar subpoena, holding that Verizon's conduit functions were within the scope of the subpoena authority of section 512(h) of the DMCA. *See In re: Verizon Internet Servs., Inc., Subpoena Enforcement Matter,* 240 F. Supp. 2d 24 (D.D.C. 2003). In the latter proceeding, Verizon claimed, *inter alia,* that section 512(h) violated the First Amendment rights of Internet users "by piercing their anonymity -- both because it does not provide sufficient procedural protection for expressive and associational rights and because it is overbroad and sweeps in protected expression." *See In re: Verizon Internet Servs.,* 257 F. Supp. 2d at 246-47, 257.

The court rejected the argument, holding that the subpoena power authorized by section 512(h) of the DMCA does not abridge Internet users' free speech rights. The court determined that the DMCA

> does not directly impact core political speech, and thus may not warrant the type of "exacting scrutiny" reserved for that context. Section 512(h) deals strictly with copyright infringement. Verizon concedes, as it must, that there is no First Amendment defense to copyright violations. ... [T]he DMCA neither authorizes governmental censorship nor involves prior restraint of potentially protected expression. Section 512(h) merely allows a private copyright owner to obtain the identity of an alleged copyright infringer in order to protect constitutionally-recognized rights in creative works; it does not even directly seek or restrain the underlying expression (the sharing of copyrighted material). Thus, the DMCA does not regulate protected expression or otherwise permit prior restraint of protected speech. It only requires production of the identity of one who has engaged in unprotected conduct -- sharing copyrighted material on the Internet.

Id. at 260-61.

Verizon asserted that, under the DMCA, a copyright owner does not have to show that the allegation of copyright infringement could withstand a motion to dismiss. The court rejected this argument, too, stating that in order to obtain a subpoena, the copyright owner must, in effect, plead a *prima facie* case of copyright infringement, including ownership of a valid copyright and the copying of constituent elements of the work that are original. *Id.* at 263 (citations omitted). Under section 512 of the DMCA, one must assert ownership of an exclusive copyright, *see* § 512(c)(3)(A)(i), and a good faith belief that the use of copyrighted material is not authorized, *see* § 512(c)(3)(A)(v). "In other words," concluded the court, "the subpoena notification must establish ownership and unauthorized use -- a *prima facie* case of copyright infringement." *Id.* at 263. Disparities between the standard for obtaining a section 512(h) subpoena and through the Federal Rules of Civil Procedure were not deemed to be "substantial." *Id.* at 263 n.21.

* * * * *

Defamatory Import

Allegedly Defamatory Statements About Internet Users

insert the following after the first full paragraph on page 341 of Law of Internet Speech:

The Second Circuit affirmed the district court's decision regarding a claim based on the Electronic Communications Privacy Act, 18 U.S.C. § 2511(1)(a), against EarthLink. The subscriber asserted that the ISP had illegally intercepted his e-mail communications, but the court ruled that EarthLink's conduct did not constitute an interception. *See Hall v. EarthLink Network, Inc.,* 396 F.3d 500 (2d Cir. 2005). The federal appellate court explained that the action had been appropriately dismissed as EarthLink's continued reception of the e-mails in question was not an "interception" because the ISP had acted in the "ordinary course" of its business and thus came within an exception to ECPA, *see* 18 U.S.C. § 2510(5)(a). *See Hall v. EarthLink Network, Inc.,* 396 F.3d at 504-05; *see generally Law of Internet Speech* at 473.

How might legislation proscribing certain spam practices; *see* Supplement *infra* at 318, affect the determination that falsely characterizing one as a "spammer" may affect his reputation?

* * * * *

Falsity

Opinion

insert the following after the third full paragraph on page 345 of Law of Internet Speech:

In *Hammer v. Trendl,* for example, the plaintiff premised a defamation claim on allegedly unfavorable reviews of books he had authored. CV 02-2462, 2003 U.S. Dist. LEXIS 623 at *1-*2 (E.D.N.Y. Jan. 18, 2003). The federal court noted that the defendant's statements, posted on Amazon.com, appeared in the context of a book review and were labeled as such, and thus "the average person understands that such reviews are the reviewer's interpretation and not 'objectively verifiable' false statements of facts." *Id.* at *9 (quoting *Levin v. McPhee,* 119 F.3d 189, 195 (2d Cir. 1997)). Because the statements were "merely his personal opinion about the plaintiff's books, the Court [found] that the plaintiff fail[ed] to prove a likelihood of success on the merits with respect to his defamation claim." *Id.*

Statements may be opinions even when they are not expressly denoted as such, however. When the PageRank system of Google Technology, Inc. was challenged by an entity that claimed it suffered devaluation because Google decreased its rank, Google asserted, among other defenses, that its ranking system was speech protected by the First Amendment. *See Search King, Inc. v. Google Technology, Inc.,* No. CIV-02-1457-M (W.D. Okla. Jan. 13, 2003), *available at* <http://news.findlaw.com/hdocs/docs/google/skgoogle101702cmp.pdf>. The PageRank system is a component of a mathematical algorithm that represents the significance of individual Web pages as they correspond to each search query. Such rankings have value, notwithstanding that they are not available for sale, because highly-ranked web-sites generally can charge a premium for advertising space. The U.S. District Court for the Western District of Oklahoma concluded that PageRank

> is an opinion – an opinion of the significance of a particular web site as it corresponds to a search query. Other search engines express different opinions, as each search engine's method of determining relative significance is unique. There is no question that the opinion relates to a matter of public concern. [The plaintiff] points out that 150 million searches occur every day on Google's search engine alone. Finally, the PageRanks do not contain provably false factual connotations. While Google's decision to intentionally deviate from its mathematical algorithm in decreasing [the plaintiff's] PageRank may raise questions about the "truth" of the PageRank system, there is no conceivable way to prove that the relative significance assigned to a given web site is false. A statement of relative significance, as represented by the PageRank, is inherently subjective in nature. Accordingly, the Court concludes that Google's Page Ranks are entitled to First Amendment protection.

Id. at 9.

* * * * *

insert the following before The Requisite Degree of Fault on page 350 of Law of Internet Speech:

BRYAN FRANKLIN *et al.*, Plaintiffs and Appellants
v.
DYNAMIC DETAILS, INC., *et al.,* Defendants and Respondents

Court of Appeal of California, Fourth Appellate District, Division Three

G031625, 116 Cal. App. 4th 375, 10 Cal. Rptr. 3d 429

March 2, 2004

Introduction

Bryan Franklin and Franklin-Choi Corporation (FCC) sued Dynamic Details, Inc. (Ddi), and Jim Axton, contending[, *inter alia,* that] three e-mail messages that Axton prepared and sent to companies with which Franklin and FCC did business were defamatory....

With respect to the causes of action for libel and trade libel, the dispositive issue is … whether the e-mails were actionable as libel; more specifically, whether the e-mails contained opinions based upon fully disclosed, provably true facts. (*See Milkovich v. Lorain Journal Co.* (1990) 497 U.S. 1, 19 [111 L. Ed. 2d 1, 110 S. Ct. 2695] (*Milkovich*); *Standing Committee v. Yagman* (9th Cir. 1995) 55 F.3d 1430, 1438-1439 (*Standing Committee*).) …

We hold two of Axton's e-mails were not actionable as libel or trade libel because they expressed Axton's opinions and fully disclosed provably true facts on which the opinions were based. Axton's e-mails contained statements that would be defamatory *per se* if actionable. The statements in Axton's e-mails expressed Axton's opinions because they purported to apply copyright and contract law to facts to reach the conclusion Franklin and FCC were acting unlawfully. The e-mails disclosed the facts upon which the opinions were based by directing the reader to the FCC Web site and (via a Web link on the FCC Web site) to another company's Web site. The Web sites were provably true because their existence, content, and layout were not in dispute in any material way. A reader of the e-mails could view those Web sites and was free to accept or reject Axton's opinions based on his or her own independent evaluation. Our conclusion is the result of an application of the principles of *Milkovich* and *Standing Committee* and, in our view, strikes the proper balance between constitutional guarantees of free speech and the interest in preventing attacks on reputation. The third e-mail was not actionable because the statements were true or vague.

… Facts

Franklin formed FCC in 1995 and has been its sole shareholder since late 1998. FCC serves as a sales representative for vendors of electronic testing products and equipment, including USA MicroCraft, Inc. (MicroCraft), and Test-X Fixture Products (Test-X). FCC was MicroCraft's exclusive sales representative in the western United States, and MicroCraft was FCC's largest source of business.

Ddi provides design and manufacturing services to the electronics manufacturing industry. Axton is Ddi's corporate director of test. MicroCraft sold Ddi several moving contact probers for high speed precise testing of printed circuit boards. Franklin testified in his deposition this was an "important" relationship and both Ddi and MicroCraft "needed each other."

On May 7, 2001, Franklin sent an advisory e-mail to all of his electronic sales contacts, including Axton, stating: "Test-X has made its' [*sic*] site more interactive. Now you can get a decent picture of a part before you order it. Go here: http://4FCC.com/return.cfm?remote=http://www.test-x.com. Please reply with REMOVE to be deleted from our list."

The Internet address in Franklin's May 7 e-mail led the viewer to FCC's Web site; from there, the Test-X Web site could be accessed by a Web link. The FCC Web site displayed logos of FCC's principal vendors. When the Web user clicked on a logo with the browser, the Web user would be led to that vendor's Web site via a Web link. The FCC Web site acted as the host or frame for Web sites accessed via the Web link. "Framing refers to the process whereby one Web site can be visited while remaining in a previous Web site." (*Digital Equipment Corp. v. AltaVista Technology, Inc.* (D. Mass. 1997) 960 F. Supp. 456, 461, fn.12.)

After receiving Franklin's May 7 e-mail, Axton visited the Test-X Web site by first visiting the FCC Web site and clicking on the Test-X logo. At the Test-X Web site, Axton viewed a catalog of Test-X products. He noticed part of the catalog included parts and part number schemes he believed had been copied from two other companies, Giese International (Giese) and Test Connections, Inc. (TCI). He saw the Giese logo in the catalog on the Test-X Web site.

On May 7, 2001, Axton contacted Ed Shea, TCI's general manager, concerning the FCC Web site. Shea told Axton that "Franklin and Test-X did not have permission to copy TCI's materials onto their website." Shea also told Axton that Franklin initially had refused to sign a domestic representative agreement with TCI because the agreement included a trade secret clause, and that Franklin had told Shea he "'didn't believe there were such things as trade secrets.'" Shea visited FCC's Web site and concluded FCC was representing products for Test-X that competed with TCI, in violation of the written contract between FCC and TCI. TCI terminated FCC as its sales representative. An attorney for TCI contacted Test-X's president and demanded Test-X cease posting TCI "proprietary materials."

Axton spoke with Larry Cannedy of Giese. When Cannedy told Axton that Test-X did not represent Giese, Axton responded, "[t]hen I think it is in your best interests to go to this web site and take a look at this." Axton forwarded Franklin's May 7 e-mail to Cannedy. Soon thereafter, FCC received a letter from an attorney representing Giese stating, "Giese International is extremely unhappy about the test-x.com site carrying unauthorized copies of its product pages without ever having obtained or even requested permission to do so." The letter continued, "[e]ach page is an original work of Giese International with content which is new, original, and well exceeds the content threshold necessary for copyright protection."

After viewing the Test-X Web site via the FCC Web site, Axton sent the three e-mails forming the basis for this lawsuit.

The first e-mail. Axton's first e-mail was sent to Yorio Hidehira, MicroCraft's chief executive officer, on May 15, 2001, and read: "I thought you might find this e-mail from Brian [*sic*] Franklin very disturbing. Please follow the path. FCC & Test-X stole copyrighted materials from Giese International & Test Connections and placed this data on their websites as their own. Please review the music wire 2.50 inch crimped prints. [T]hey still have Giese's title block on the documents. It's bad enough that FCC & Test-X violated US copyright laws when they took this data and tried to make it look like their own. FCC took Test Connections['] copyrighted materials and plagiarized the data. FCC had a legal contract with Test Connections (TCI) and pretended to act as sales agent. Unfortunately, FCC represents USA MicroCraft in the US market. What makes you believe that he would honor your intellectual properties? DDI has non-disclosure agreements on file with Giese, TCI, MicroCraft, and FCC. We take our customers['] and vendors['] intellectual properties very seriously. Now, DDI has been compromised by MicroCraft's US sales agent. DDI does not condone this type of unlawful practices and as such FCC will not be able to participate in any DDI business activity. I am concerned as we are giving MicroCraft, our customer data ... and FCC has access to this data. Also when this incident becomes public in the next few days, MicroCraft's relationship with FCC could be misconstrued by DDI's customers and vendors. This is not good and FCC is not a [*sic*] honorable company."

Axton's e-mail prompted an exchange of e-mails between Axton and Hidehira. Hidehira responded to Axton's first e-mail with an e-mail thanking Axton for the information and stating in part: "We take intellectual properties rights very seriously. However currently, I do not know or understand what Bryan Franklin is doing on the website. Please understand that FCC does represent MicroCraft in the West Coast, however not for DDI account. ... I will make sure that we keep all information between MicroCraft and DDI."

The second e-mail. On May 16, 2001, Axton responded to Hidehira's e-mail by sending him the second e-mail, which read: "Apparently, you misunderstand my intent. Ddi's customers (and competitors) are being led to believe that FCC has an active role in the Ddi/MicroCraft relationship. FCC's profound lack of respect for intellectual properties will reflect poorly on MicroCraft & Ddi. FCC is clearly involved in this Test-X web site and this constitutes a breach of the Ddi/FCC non-discl[o]sure agreement. DDI will not be conducting business with FCC & Test-X. Mr. Franklin has made comments to myself and others as to his belief that trade secrets are bogus. His words. We respect your position in regards to this issue. Please understand our situation, FCC has seriously undermined DDI's ability to protect our (& our clients['] and vendors[']) intellectual property. Therefore, we will not be forwarding any data to MicroCraft and any ongoing evaluations of MicroCraft products and/or services will be immediately discontinued."

Hidehira responded with an e-mail to Axton announcing, in essence, MicroCraft would end its relationship with FCC. The e-mail stated, in part: "[W]e don't have enough time to investigate all issues, contracts with FCC and legal issues. However I can issue this immediate letter to FCC. 1. As of May 12, 2001 FCC will stop all communications, interactions, and sales activities between DDI and MicroCraft regarding MicroCraft issues. 2. As of May 12, 2001 FCC will not receive any compensation with any sales on MicroCraft Products. 3. FCC will remove the MicroCraft Link from its website immediately. 4. FCC will not communicate, ask questions, or inquire any information from any MicroCraft employee. I am prepared to write a letter like this to Bryan Franklin of FCC. This will insure that all DDI customers' information will be safe with MicroCraft." The record contains no evidence such a letter was ever prepared or sent.

The third e-mail. On June 4, 2001, Axton received an e-mail from Dave Runyon of FastFixtures, one of FCC's principal vendors, requesting that Ddi consider purchasing a new technology that FastFixtures had developed. In response, Axton sent Runyon the third e-mail stating, in part: "Unfortunately, your product has not been evaluated at this time due to your relationship with FCC. FCC is not in good standing with DDI due to their intolerance of intellectual properties, copyrights, and trade secrets." Runyon responded with an e-mail to Axton stating, in part: "I do not understand your situation with FCC and neither myself, nor my product should be disqualified on that basis. I will indeed refrain from any further references to DDI. In fact, I request that you withdraw my product from consideration in any of your facilities. Your hostile response to my harmless letter has left me with no desire to develop[ ] a relationship."

Axton did not seek legal advice before sending any of the e-mails. Axton contends that before he sent the first e-mail he called Franklin and left a message saying, "Bryan, you need to call me. I am very concerned about this link." Franklin denied ever receiving this message or any communication from Axton.

After June 11, 2001, Franklin made no effort to sell MicroCraft products, having placed the relationship between MicroCraft and FCC "on hold," despite a request by Adelino Sousa, MicroCraft's president, that Franklin continue sales efforts. Sousa expressed concern that Franklin intended to sue Ddi, a MicroCraft customer. On July 8, 2001, Franklin sent an e-mail to Sousa stating: "Please begin your search for a Rep in So. Cal. This is not a resignation however, I may resign due to circumstances." Sousa responded with an e-mail to Franklin stating, in part: "I can no longer keep waiting for FCC's response. I am requesting th[at] you send me a Formal Resignation by Tomorrow Afternoon (6[*sic*]/17/2001). It is not our intent to look for a new rep at this time. MicroCraft will wait approximately 90 days and then review our sales strategy. We can then discuss a new contract if you wish." Franklin responded to Sousa's e-mail with an e-mail of July 16, 2001, stating: "You know the exact date that I put FCC and MicroCraft on hold. I suggest you wait until DDI responds before you or I decide what we do. The choice is yours. ... If you choose not to wait and terminate please be my guest."

Franklin resigned from his position as sales representative for MicroCraft, stating in an e-mail dated July 17, 2001, "[t]he relationship that we've had for the last 8+ years has been severed and I find I can no longer work under the current environment/condition."

... Discussion

I. *Libel Per Se and Trade Libel Causes of Action*

In the first cause of action, Franklin and FCC alleged Axton's three e-mails were libelous on their face. In the second cause of action, Franklin and FCC alleged Axton's three e-mails disparaged Franklin and FCC's services. The relevant law is the same as to libel and trade libel, and the same conditional privileges apply to both causes of action. (*ComputerXpress, Inc. v. Jackson* (2001) 93 Cal. App. 4th 993, 1010-1011 [113 Cal. Rptr. 2d 625]; 5 Witkin, *Summary of Cal. Law* (9th ed. 1988) Torts, § 576, p. 671.)

"Libel is a false and unprivileged publication by writing ... which exposes any person to hatred, contempt, ridicule, or obloquy, or which causes him to be shunned or avoided, or which has a tendency to injure him in his occupation." (Civ. Code, § 45.) "Trade libel is the publication of matter disparaging the quality of another's property, which the publisher should recognize is likely to cause pecuniary loss to the owner." (*ComputerXpress, Inc. v. Jackson, supra,* 93 Cal. App. 4th at p. 1010.) "The *sine qua non* of recovery for defamation ... is the existence of falsehood." (*Letter Carriers v. Austin* (1974) 418 U.S. 264, 283 [41 L. Ed. 2d 745, 94 S. Ct. 2770].) A statement is libel on its face if it "is defamatory of the plaintiff without the necessity of explanatory matter, such as an inducement, innuendo or other extrinsic fact." (Civ. Code, § 45a.)

… Our analysis starts with *Baker v. Los Angeles Herald Examiner* (1986) 42 Cal.3d 254, 260 [228 Cal. Rptr. 206, 721 P.2d 87], in which the California Supreme Court strictly distinguished between statements of fact and statements of opinion for purposes of defamation liability. In *Baker*, the court concluded statements of fact may be actionable as libel; statements of opinion are constitutionally protected. (*Ibid.*) However, "[t]his categorical exemption of opinions from the reach of defamation law rested on a passage from *Gertz v. Robert Welch, Inc.* (1974) 418 U.S. 323, 339-340 [41 L. Ed. 2d 789, 94 S. Ct. 2997]," and "[t]he viability of this categorical 'opinion rule' was considered in *Milkovich*[, supra, 497 U.S. 1, 18-19]." (*Kahn v. Bower* (1991) 232 Cal. App. 3d 1599, 1606 [284 Cal. Rptr. 244].)

In *Milkovich, supra*, 497 U.S. 1, the United States Supreme Court rejected the contention that statements of opinion enjoy blanket constitutional protection. The Supreme Court reasoned that "[s]imply couching such statements in terms of opinion does not dispel these [false, defamatory] implications" (*id.* at p. 19) because a speaker may still imply "a knowledge of facts which lead to the [defamatory] conclusion" (*id.* at p. 18). The court explained that expressions of opinion may imply an assertion of objective fact. For example, "[i]f a speaker says, 'In my opinion John Jones is a liar,' he implies a knowledge of facts which lead to the conclusion that Jones told an untruth. Even if the speaker states the facts upon which he bases his opinion, if those facts are either incorrect or incomplete, or if his assessment of them is erroneous, the statement may still imply a false assertion of fact." (*Id.* at pp. 18-19.) Statements of opinion that imply a false assertion of fact are actionable. (*Id.* at p. 19.)

Thus, after *Milkovich*, the question is not strictly whether the published statement is fact or opinion. Rather, the dispositive question is whether a reasonable fact finder could conclude the published statement declares or implies a provably false assertion of fact. (*Milkovich, supra*, 497 U.S. at p. 19; *see also Standing Committee, supra*, 55 F.3d 1430, 1438-1439; *Eisenberg v. Alameda Newspapers, Inc.* (1999) 74 Cal. App. 4th 1359, 1383 [88 Cal. Rptr. 2d 802]; *Kahn v. Bower, supra*, 232 Cal. App. 3d at p. 1607; *Moyer v. Amador Valley J. Union High School Dist.* (1990) 225 Cal. App. 3d 720, 724 [275 Cal. Rptr. 494].) *Milkovich* did not change the rule that satirical, hyperbolic, imaginative, or figurative statements are protected because "the context and tenor of the statements negate the impression that the author seriously is maintaining an assertion of actual fact." (*Weller v. American Broadcasting Companies, Inc.* (1991) 232 Cal. App. 3d 991, 1000-1001 [283 Cal. Rptr. 644].)

Whether a statement declares or implies a provably false assertion of fact is a question of law for the court to decide (*Eisenberg v. Alameda Newspapers, Inc., supra*, 74 Cal. App. 4th at p. 1382; *Copp v. Paxton* (1996) 45 Cal. App. 4th 29, 837 [52 Cal. Rptr. 2d 831]), unless the statement is susceptible of both an innocent and a libelous meaning, in which case the jury must decide how the statement was understood (*Kahn v. Bower, supra*, 232 Cal. App. 3d at p. 1608; *Weller v. American Broadcasting Companies, Inc., supra*, 232 Cal. App. 3d at p. 1001, fn.8).

In determining whether a statement is actionable fact or nonactionable opinion, *Baker* instructed courts to use a "'totality of the circumstances'" test. (*Baker v. Los Angeles Herald Examiner, supra*, 42 Cal.3d at p. 260.) After *Milkovich*, the same totality of the circumstances test is used to determine whether the statement in question communicates or implies a provably false statement of fact. (*Kahn v. Bower, supra,* 232 Cal. App. 3d at p. 1608.) Under the totality of the circumstances test, "[f]irst, the language of the statement is examined. For words to be defamatory, they must be understood in a defamatory sense .... Next, the context in which the statement was made must be considered." (*Baker v. Los Angeles Herald Examiner, supra,* 42 Cal.3d at pp. 260-261.) "*Milkovich* did not substantially change these principles." (*Moyer v. Amador Valley J. Union High School Dist., supra,* 225 Cal. App. 3d at p. 724.)

Applying the totality of the circumstances test, we conclude Axton's first and second e-mails are best characterized as Axton's protected opinions that Franklin and FCC stole copyrighted material, plagiarized data, breached a nondisclosure agreement with Ddi, compromised Ddi, and were dishonorable. In reaching this conclusion, we are persuaded by the analysis of *Coastal Abstract Service, Inc. v. First American Title Ins. Co.* (9th Cir. 1999) 173 F.3d 725 (*Coastal Abstract*) and *Standing Committee, supra,* 55 F.3d 1430.

... The Ninth Circuit, using examples from section 566 of the Restatement Second of Torts, contrasted opinion statements based upon expressly stated facts with opinion statements based on implied, undisclosed facts. (*Standing Committee, supra,* 55 F.3d at p. 1439.) "The statement, 'I think Jones is an alcoholic,' for example, is an expression of opinion based on implied facts, [citation], because the statement 'gives rise to the inference that there are undisclosed facts that justify the forming of the opinion,' [citation]. Readers of this statement will reasonably understand the author to be implying he knows facts supporting his view -- *e.g.,* that Jones stops at a bar every night after work and has three martinis. If the speaker has no such factual basis for his assertion, the statement is actionable, even though phrased in terms of the author's personal belief." (*Ibid.*)

The Ninth Circuit provided this example from section 566 of the Restatement Second of Torts of an opinion based on expressly stated facts: "'[Jones] moved in six months ago. He works downtown, and I have seen him during that time only twice, in his backyard around 5:30 seated in a deck chair ... with a drink in his hand. I think he must be an alcoholic.' [Citation.]" (*Standing Committee, supra,* 55 F.3d at p. 1439.) This opinion disclosed all the facts on which it was based and did not imply there are other, unstated facts supporting the belief Jones is an alcoholic. The opinion that Jones "'must be an alcoholic'" is actionable only if the disclosed facts are false and defamatory. "A statement of opinion based on fully disclosed facts can be punished only if the stated facts are themselves false and demeaning." (*Ibid.*) The rationale for this rule is that "[w]hen the facts underlying a statement of opinion are disclosed, readers will understand they are getting the author's interpretation of the facts presented; they are therefore unlikely to construe the statement as insinuating the existence of additional, undisclosed facts." (*Ibid.*) When the facts supporting an opinion are disclosed, "readers are free to accept or reject the author's opinion based on their own independent evaluation of the facts." (*Ibid.*; *see also Partington v. Bugliosi* (9th Cir. 1995) 56 F.3d 1147, 1156-1157 ["when an author outlines the facts available to him, thus making it clear that the challenged statements represent his own interpretation of those facts and leaving the reader free to draw his own conclusions, those statements are generally protected by the First Amendment"]; *Chapin v. Knight-Ridder, Inc.* (4th Cir. 1992) 993 F.2d 1087, 1093 ["[b]ecause the bases for the ... conclusion are fully disclosed, no reasonable reader would consider the term anything but the opinion of the author drawn from the circumstances related"]; *Phantom Touring, Inc. v. Affiliated Publications* (1st Cir. 1992) 953 F.2d 724, 730 [if author discloses basis for statement, it can only be read as the author's "personal conclusion about the information presented, not as a statement of fact"].)

Axton's statements in the first and second e-mails that FCC stole copyrighted material and plagiarized data are similar to the comment in *Coastal Abstract, supra*, 173 F.3d 725 that Coastal was operating illegally without a license. Axton's statements purported to interpret copyright law and contract law and apply that law to fully disclosed facts — the FCC Web site and its link to the Test-X Web site — to conclude Franklin and FCC engaged in unlawful conduct. Axton's comments similarly are opinion even if construed as accusing Franklin of criminal activity. "Accusations of criminal activity, like other statements, are not actionable if the underlying facts are disclosed." (*Nicosia v. De Rooy* (N.D. Cal. 1999) 72 F. Supp. 2d 1093, 1103.)

The first and second e-mails disclosed the facts on which Axton's opinions were based and did not imply the existence of any other facts on which the opinions were based. The first e-mail enclosed Franklin's e-mail and invited the reader to "follow the path" leading to the FCC and Test-X Web sites. The first e-mail then invited the reader to "review the music wire 2.50 inch crimped prints" and described the prints as having Giese's "title block" on them. The first e-mail thus disclosed Franklin's e-mail, the FCC Web site, the Test-X Web site, and the prints found on the Test-X Web site as the bases for the opinions stated.

Franklin and FCC argue in their reply letter brief the average reader of the first e-mail would not understand the e-mail fully disclosed the basis for Axton's opinions. A reasonable reader, Franklin and FCC argue, "would not be able to discern that the link [from] the FCC website to the Test-X website was the basis for the defamatory statements in Axton's e-mails to MicroCraft." We disagree. The first e-mail identified the link to the FCC Web site and the link to the Test-X Web site and neither the first e-mail nor the second e-mail expressed or implied any other factual for the opinions. Although the process of accessing the factual bases for the opinions involved clicking onto each Web site, the dispositive point is those factual bases were disclosed and were accessible to the reader.

The facts upon which Axton's opinions were based were provably true because the existence, content, and layout of the Web sites were not in dispute in any material way. Because we are not determining the truth or reasonableness of Axton's opinions, the issue in determining whether the Web sites were provably true is not whether the Web sites made truthful assertions of fact, but whether the Web sites in fact existed and made the assertions claimed. Franklin's e-mail, the FCC Web site, and the Test-X Web site existed, and the parties agree on their layout and content. Although the parties dispute the type size of the Giese logo on the Test-X Web site, they do not in any other respect dispute the layout or content of the Web sites or of Franklin's e-mail. It is undeniable the FCC Web site frames the Test-X Web site when the Web site links are used.

The first two e-mails expressed Axton's opinions about the Web sites. The reader, Hidehira, was invited to view the Web sites. He was "free to accept or reject the author's opinion based on [his] own independent evaluation of the facts" (*Standing Committee, supra,* 55 F.3d at p. 1439) and "'free to form another, perhaps contradictory opinion from the same facts'" (*id.* at p. 1440). Finally, the statement in the first e-mail that FCC is not an "honorable company" and the statement in the second e-mail that FCC displayed a "profound lack of respect for intellectual properties" are classic assertions of subjective judgment.

In determining whether the first two e-mails implied a provably false factual assertion, we must also consider the context in which the e-mails were made. (*Baker v. Los Angeles*

Herald Examiner, supra, 42 Cal. 3d at pp. 260-261; *Moyer v. Amador Valley J. Union High School Dist., supra,* 225 Cal. App. 3d at pp. 724-725.) "This contextual analysis demands that the courts look at the nature and full content of the communication and to the knowledge and understanding of the audience to whom the publication was directed." (*Baker v. Los Angeles Herald Examiner, supra,* 42 Cal. 3d at p. 261.) The circumstances in which the e-mails were prepared, sent, and understood support our conclusion the e-mails contained protected statements. Axton received Franklin's e-mail, reviewed the FCC Web site, and formed the opinions expressed in the e-mails. These circumstances support the conclusion Axton's opinions in the first and second e-mails were based only upon the Web sites.

Axton is not, and did not purport to be, an attorney. The average reader therefore would not have assumed the statements in the first and second e-mails had the weight of a legal opinion. Although Axton did not temper his opinions with words of transparency, neither did he present his opinions as legal truths framed in legal verbiage. Indeed, his statements that Franklin "stole" copyrighted material, "compromised" Ddi, and "plagiarized" data appear in context as rhetorical hyperbole. (*Moyer v. Amador Valley J. Union High School Dist., supra,* 225 Cal. App. 3d at p. 726; *see also Letter Carriers v. Austin, supra,* 418 U.S. at p. 283 ["'traitor[s]'" understood to mean that plaintiffs' actions were reprehensible, not that plaintiffs had committed treason]; *Greenbelt Coop. Pub. Assn. v. Bresler* (1970) 398 U.S. 6, 13-14 [26 L. Ed. 2d 6, 90 S. Ct. 1537] ["'blackmail'" a vigorous epithet used to describe unreasonable negotiations]; *Rosenaur v. Scherer* (2001) 88 Cal. App. 4th 260, 278-279, 105 Cal. Rptr. 2d 674 [calling plaintiff "thief" and "liar" during political campaign was hyperbole]; *Morningstar, Inc. v. Superior Court* (1994) 23 Cal. App. 4th 676, 687-694 [29 Cal. Rptr. 2d 547] [title stating "'Lies, Damn Lies, and Fund Advertisements'" held not to imply money management fund actually lied].)

As Franklin and FCC point out, Hidehira was a Japanese national and professed to a lack of understanding of American law, but those facts do not suggest the first two e-mails implied a provably false factual assertion. The specific understanding of Hidehira — the only and therefore "average reader" of the two e-mails to MicroCraft — supports the conclusion the e-mails adequately disclosed the factual basis for the opinions expressed. Hidehira, given his position, understood Internet matters, including such concepts as framing and Web links, and could navigate the path to the FCC Web site and the Test-X Web site.

The third e-mail, to Dave Runyon of FastFixtures, is an easier call. The e-mail was not actionable. Axton's statements "your product has not been evaluated at this time due to your relationship with FCC" and "FCC is not in good standing with DDI" were true. Axton's statement that FCC was "intoleran[t] of intellectual properties, copyrights, and trade secrets" was too vague to be actionable. (*Moyer v. Amador Valley J. Union High School Dist., supra,* 225 Cal. App. 3d at pp. 725-726; *see also Chapin v. Knight-Ridder, Inc., supra,* 993 F.2d at p. 1093 [" 'Hefty' is just too subjective a word to be proved false"].)

Our conclusion that Axton's e-mails conveyed protected statements properly balances, we believe, the First Amendment guarantee of free speech and society's "'pervasive and strong interest in preventing and redressing attacks upon reputation.'" (*Milkovich, supra,* 497 U.S. at p. 22.) Franklin's natural and compensable interest in his and FCC's reputation was protected because the first and second e-mails disclosed the factual basis for Axton's opinions. The reader could access the FCC Web site and link to the Test-X Web site, and based upon those Web sites could decide whether to accept or reject Axton's opinions.

Because we conclude the three e-mails sent by Axton were not actionable as libel or trade libel, we do not reach the issue whether the e-mails were privileged under Civil Code section 47, subdivision (c). …

* * * * *

Matters of Public Concern

insert the following at the end of page 376 of Law of Internet Speech:

When Apple Computer, Inc. sought to ascertain the identity of persons who were alleged to have leaked trade secret information to on-line news sites, the California state court stated that the movants who sought to quash the subpoenas missed the point. *See Apple Computer, Inc. v. Doe 1, an unknown individual, and Does 2-25, inclusive,* No.: 1-04-CV-032178 (Cal. Super. Ct. Mar. 11, 2005), *available at* <http://www.eff.org/Censorship/Apple_v_Does/ 20050311_apple_decision.pdf>. The court drew a distinction between "*an interested public*" and "the *public interest.*" *Id.* at 12 (emphasis in original). "Of course the public is interested in Apple," declared the court.

> It is a company which has achieved iconic status. … [T]he public has had, and continues to have a profound interest in gossip about Apple. … At the hearing the Court specifically asked what public interest was served by publishing private, proprietary product information that was ostensibly stolen and turned over to those with no business reason for getting it. Movants' response was to again reiterate the self-evident interest of the public in Apple, rather than justifying why citizens have a right to know the private and secret information of a business entity, bet it Apple, H-P, a law firm, a newspaper, Coca-Cola, a restaurant, or anyone else. Unlike the whistleblower who discloses a health, safety, or welfare hazard affecting all, or the government employee who reveals mismanagement or worse by our public officials, the movants are doing nothing more than feeding the public's insatiable desire for information.

Id.

* * * * *

insert the following after Notes and Questions # 3 on page 379 of Law of Internet Speech:

4. A California jury awarded $775,000 in damages to a biotechnology company that brought a defamation claim against former employees in connection with statements the defendants posted on various Internet message boards about the company and its executives. *Varian Medical Sys. v. Delfino,* No. CV 780187 (Cal. Super. Ct. jury verdict Dec. 18, 2001). The judge issued an injunction barring the defendants from posting additional messages but an appellate court stayed contempt proceedings when the defendants were found to have violated the injunction. *Varian Medical Sys. v. Delfino,* No. H024214 (Cal. Super. Ct. Mar. 26, 2002), *see generally Update: Contempt Proceedings for Internet Posters,* LDRC MediaLawLetter (Apr. 2002) at 16; *see also Internet Posters Found Liable and Enjoined From Future Postings,* LDRC LibelLetter (Jan. 2002) at 13. Even assuming that the verdict of liability were upheld on appeal, could the injunction prohibiting additional electronic postings withstand constitutional scrutiny?

On appeal in *Varian Medical Sys., Inc. v. Delfino*, 35 Cal. 4th 180, 25 Cal. Rptr. 3d 298 (Cal. 2005), the California Supreme Court considered only the question of whether an appeal from the denial of a special motion to strike under the state's anti-SLAPP statute, Cal. Civ. Proc. Code § 425.16, affects an automatic stay of the trial court proceedings. The court concluded that because granting a motion to strike under section 425.16 results in the dismissal of a cause of action on the merits, an appellate reversal of an order denying such a motion similarly may result in a dismissal. "Such an appellate outcome is irreconcilable with a judgment for the plaintiff on that cause of action following a proceeding on the merits. Moreover, such a proceeding is inherently inconsistent with the appeal because the appeal seeks to avoid that very proceeding." Noting that "'[t]he point of the anti-SLAPP statute is that you have a right *not* to be dragged through the courts because you exercised your constitutional rights,' an appeal from the denial of an anti-SLAPP motion is no different than an appeal from the denial of a motion to compel arbitration." *Id.*, 35 Cal. 4th at 193 (citations omitted) (emphasis in original). The court reversed and remanded, ruling that the trial court lacked subject matter jurisdiction over the matters on trial and voided the ensuing judgment. *See id.* at 196.

5. As of the end of 2004, approximately two dozen states had anti-SLAPP statutes. *See, e.g.*, Cal. Civ. Pro. Code §§ 425.16, 425.17; Del. Code Ann. §§ 8136-38, Fla. Stat. §§ 720.304(4), 768.295; Ga. Code Ann. § 9-11-11.1; Haw. Rev. Stat. §§ 634F-1-634F-4; Ind. Code § 34-7-7-1; La. Code Civ. Pro. Ann. Art. 971; Me. Rev. Stat. Ann. tit. 14 § 556; Md. Code Ann. § 5-807; Mass. Gen. Laws ch. 231 § 59H; Minn. Stat. §§ 554.01-.05; Neb. Rev. Stat. §§ 25-21,241-46; Nev. Rev. Stat. §§ 41.635-70; N.M. Stat. Ann. §§ 38-2-9.1, 9.2; N.Y. Civ. Rights Law §§ 70-a, 76-a; N.Y. C.P.L.R. 3211(g), 3212(h); R.I. Gen. Laws Title 9, Ch. 33, §§ 9-33-1-4; R.I. Gen. Laws § 45-24-67; Tenn. Code §§ 4-21-1001-04; Utah Code Ann. §§ 78-58-101-05; Wash. Rev. Code §§ 4.24.500-20; *see also* 7 Guam Code, §§ 17101-09. Such statutes, known by their acronym for "strategic lawsuits against public participation," generally provide for the dismissal of claims at an early stage in the proceedings when the claims are brought against the right of petition and/or the right of free speech.

* * * * *

insert the following before Retractions and Clarifications on page 381 of Law of Internet Speech:

According to the *San Francisco Chronicle,* some of the 14 boxes of FBI surveillance files about anti-war activities in the 1970s that Gerald Nicosia had worked for more than a decade to obtain were filched from Nicosia's home in March 2004. *See* Stephanie Salter, *Stolen Files Recount John Kerry's Anti-War Days: FBI Files Were Swiped From the Home of Bay Area Beat Author Gerald Nicosia,* S.F. Chron. (Apr. 11, 2004), *available at* <http://www.sfgate.com/cgi-bin/article.cgi?f=/c/a/2004/04/11/LVGHM61CCB1.DTL>.

* * * * *

Retractions and Clarifications

insert the following after the first full paragraph on page 382 of Law of Internet Speech:

The Georgia Supreme Court held that the state's libel retraction statute, Ga. Stat. Ann. § 51-5-11, applies to on-line postings. *Mathis v. Cannon*, 276 Ga. 16, 573 S.E.2d 376 (Ga. 2002). The statute provides that a plaintiff in a libel action shall not be entitled to an award of punitive damages if the defendant corrects and retracts the libelous statement "in a regular issue of the newspaper or other publication in question" after receiving a written demand. Ga. Stat. Ann. § 51-5-11(b)(1)(A). A similar statute, Ga. Stat. Ann. § 51-5-12, applies to retractions of defamatory statements made in a visual or sound broadcast. The court concluded based on its review of the language of the statute and the relevant legislative history that the statute was intended to apply to more than "newspaper libel" and that a distinction between media and non-media defendants would be difficult to apply and make little sense in connection with speech about matters of public concern. Nor would such a distinction properly "accommodate changes in communications and the publishing industry due to the computer and the Internet. For example, [such a distinction would mean that] the retraction statute would not apply to a story that appears only on the on-line version of a newspaper or an advocacy group's monthly electronic newsletter to its members reporting on congressional voting." *Mathis v. Cannon*, 276 Ga. at 27, 573 S.E.2d at 385.

Additional policy rationales supported the court's decision. Construing the retraction statute to apply to electronic communication treats a publication for purposes of seeking a retraction the same way as a publication for purposes of imposing liability. Thus, "[i]t encourages defamation victims to seek self-help, their first remedy, by using available opportunities to contradict the lie or correct the error and thereby minimize its adverse impact on reputation.'" *Id.*, 276 Ga. at 28, 573 S.E.2d at 385 (quoting *Gertz v. Robert Welch, Inc.*, 418 U.S. 323, 344 (1974)). Furthermore, the court deemed a retraction posted on an Internet bulletin board as likely to reach the same people who read the original message as a retraction printed in a newspaper or published in a broadcast. *Id.*, 276 Ga. at 26, 573 S.E.2d at 385. Note, too, that the court regarded its interpretation as "support[ing] free speech by extending the same protection to the private individual who speaks on matters of public concern as newspapers and other members of the press now enjoy." *Id.*, 276 Ga. at 29, 573 S.E.2d at 385.

* * * * *

Privilege

insert the following at the end of page 387 of Law of Internet Speech:

In *Amway Corp. v. Procter & Gamble Co.*, 346 F.3d 180 (6th Cir. 2003), the court ruled that under Michigan law, the fair reporting privilege shielded the defendant from the imposition of damages in a libel claim based on its publication on the Internet of pleadings, such as a complaint filed in court. The Sixth Circuit affirmed the district court's grant of summary judgment dismissing the libel claim based on publication of such complaints on a third-party web-site. *See id.* The appellate court observed, "Assuming that any allegations in the [complaints] … were libelous, the libel was included in the actual complaint and the Appellees did not add any statements, let alone false statements, when they supposedly published the complaint on the internet. Accordingly, we find that Michigan's fair reporting privilege applies to the publication of the entire complaints on [the defendant's] website, and no exception to the privilege applies to the Appellees' conduct complained of here." *Id.* at 187.

* * * * *

CHRISTOPHER WIEST, Plaintiff

v.

E-FENSE, INC., *et al.,* Defendants

United States District Court for the Eastern District of Virginia
Alexandria Division

CIVIL ACTION NO. 04-1201, 356 F. Supp. 2d 604

February 9, 2005

ORDER

This matter is before the Court on Defendants E-Fense, Inc., *et al.*'s Motion to Dismiss pursuant to Federal Rule of Civil Procedure 12(b)(6). Plaintiff Mr. Christopher Wiest ("Plaintiff," "Mr. Wiest"), formerly an Air Force Academy cadet whose conviction by a military trial judge was overturned by the United States Court of Appeals for the Armed Forces, alleges claims of libel and invasion of privacy against the defendants for publishing allegedly false and defamatory information on their corporate website. The question[ ] before the Court [is, *inter alia,*] ...whether Mr. Wiest states a claim for defamation when he alleges that Defendants published on their website allegedly incomplete information regarding his court martial and allegedly false information regarding his conduct.... The Court holds that Mr. Wiest states a claim for defamation under Virginia law because the statements made about him on the E-Fense website are allegedly false, and as to his interactions with military justice, they are not a fair and accurate description of the public record. ...

I. BACKGROUND

Plaintiff Christopher Wiest ("Wiest," "Plaintiff"), a cadet at the Air Force Academy, was convicted of one specification of Article 134, Uniform Code of Military Justice [hereinafter "UCMJ"] 10 U.S.C. § 934 (2000), in violation of 18 U.S.C. § 1030(a)(5)(B) (2000), and acquitted of three specifications of Article 134, in violation of 18 U.S.C. § 1030(A)(5)(A). He was sentenced to dismissal and partial forfeitures, and the Air Force Court of Criminal Appeals affirmed the findings and sentence. *United States v. Wiest,* No. ACM33964, 2002 WL 31235026 (A.F.C.M.R. Sept. 24, 2002). After finding that the military trial judge abused his discretion in denying a continuance request made for the purpose of obtaining civilian counsel, the United States Court of Appeals for the Armed Forces reversed the findings, set aside the sentence and returned the record of trial to the Judge Advocate General for further disposition not inconsistent with its opinion. *United States v. Wiest,* 59 M.J. 276 (C.A.A.F. 2004).

Plaintiff alleges that on and after October 31, 2003, Defendants E-Fense, Inc., Andrew Fahey, an officer and employee of E-Fense, Inc., and John Doe Employees, 1 through 20, employees of E-Fense, Inc. located in Virginia, Colorado or Texas (collectively, "Defendants"), published on their website "false assertions ... that he was convicted of a federal felony and engaged in acts that constituted a federal felony." Furthermore, Plaintiff alleges that Defendants falsely asserted that he was dishonorably discharged, engaged in illegal "hacking," and was tried and convicted of several sections of the UCMJ and discharged from service as a result. Plaintiff attaches to his complaint the August 17, 2004 version of the website stating:

> In 1996, the United States Air Force Academy blocked the use of direct Internet relay chatting (IRC) from its cadets. A few months later, around July 1997, Air Force Academy Cadet Christopher Wiest received an email from a friend he used to chat with online, questioning why he hadn't been using IRC. Wiest explained the Academy's new regulations regarding Internet chat, and the friend suggested he attempt telneting in order to get onto IRC.
>
> With that suggestion, and support from his friend, Wiest began to develop his skills as a hacker -- breaking into commercial servers to develop artificial accounts and IRC servers. Soon after, the Air Force Office of Special Investigations, having reason to suspect Wiest of his activities, searched his room, seized his PC, and took a written statement from the cadet. Tried for several sections of the UCMJ, Wiest was eventually dishonorably discharged from service.

Plaintiff alleges that Defendants published information they knew to be false "by asserting that he was convicted of a federal felony and engaged in acts that constituted a federal felony" and stating that he was "dishonorably discharged from service." Plaintiff alleges that his reputation was damaged by this erroneous information.

On September 14, 2004, Plaintiff sent a letter to Defendants, also attached to his complaint, stating that Mr. Andrew Fahey, an E-Fense, Inc. employee, had "botched the investigation of ... [his] case by failing to follow up material leads, failing to log on with the information given him following my interview to ascertain and establish key facts" and other actions. The letter further states that the Court of Appeals for the Armed Forces set aside his court martial on March 16, 2004 and points the reader to a website with the appellate opinion. In addition, Mr. Wiest writes, "I point this information out in light of the fact that you might not have been aware of this information prior to this letter, or prior to publishing or continuing to publish your website," and demands that any and all language concerning him be removed from the website.

On September 20, 2004, a new version of the information under the section entitled "Case History" was published on the E-Fense website. The September 20, 2004 version of the website states:

> In 1996, the United States Air Force Academy blocked the use of direct Internet relay chatting (IRC) from its cadets. A few months later, around July 1997, An [sic] Air Force Academy Cadet received an email from a friend he used to chat with online, questioning why he hadn't been using IRC. The cadet explained the Academy's new regulations regarding Internet chat, and the friend suggested he attempt telneting in order to get onto IRC.
>
> With that suggestion, and support from his friend, Wiest began to develop his skills as a hacker -- breaking into commercial servers to develop artificial accounts and IRC servers. Soon after, the Air Force Office of Special Investigations, having reason to suspect the cadet of his activities, searched his room, seized his PC, and took a written

statement from the cadet. Tried for several sections of the UCMJ, the cadet was eventually discharged from service.

Plaintiff alleges that this revised publication, which continues to contain his name and allegedly incorrect information regarding his conduct, status as a member of the military, and how many sections of the UCMJ he was tried for, was also defamatory and "damages his reputation."

... II. DISCUSSION

... C. Analysis

Causes of Action No. 1 and No. 2: Libel and Slander, Libel and Slander Per Se, Violation of Insulting Words Statute

The Court denies Defendants' Motion to Dismiss Causes of Action Numbers One and Two because Plaintiff alleges that the statements at issue were false, and the Court finds that the statements do not represent a fair and accurate description of the court martial proceeding. Although slander is defined as defamation by speech, while libel is defamation by published writing, Virginia makes no distinction between actions for libel and slander. 12A MICHIE'S JUR. Libel and Slander §§ 1 - 3 (2004). Furthermore, actions under the insulting words statute, Va. Code Ann. § 8.01-45 (Michie 2005), are "virtually coextensive with the common-law action for defamation," with the exception that the insulting words statute does not require publication of the defamatory statement to a third party. *Potomac Valve & Fitting v. Crawford Fitting Co.,* 829 F.2d 1280, 1284 (4th Cir. 1987). The elements of defamation under Virginia law are "(1) publication of (2) an actionable statement with (3) the requisite intent." *Chapin v. Knight-Ridder, Inc.,* 993 F.2d 1087, 1092 (4th Cir. 1993) (citations omitted).

Despite Defendants' assertions to the contrary, the E-Fense website statements constitute "actionable statements" because they are allegedly false and do not accurately reflect the public record. An "actionable statement" is one that is both false and defamatory, meaning it must "tend [so] to harm the reputation of another as to lower him in the estimation of the community or to deter third persons from associating or dealing with him." *Id.* (citing RESTATEMENT (SECOND) TORTS § 559). Whether a statement is actionable must be determined by the Court, as it is a matter of law. *Id.* (citing *Chaves v. Johnson,* 230 Va. 112, 335 S.E.2d 97 (Va. 1985)); *see also WJLA-TV v. Levin,* 264 Va. 140, 564 S.E.2d 383, 390 (Va. 2002) (citing *Yeagle v. Collegiate Times,* 255 Va. 293, 497 S.E.2d 136, 138 (Va. 1998)). On a motion to dismiss a libel suit for lack of an actionable statement, a court must "credit the plaintiff's allegation of the factual falsity of a statement." *Chapin,* 993 F.2d at 1092 (citing *Conley v. Gibson,* 355 U.S. 41, 2 L. Ed. 2d 80, 78 S. Ct. 99 (1957)). Defendants may shield themselves from liability for defamation if they rely upon a public record, so long as their publication is a "fair and substantially correct" restatement of the public record. *See Alexandria Gazette v. West,* 198 Va. 154, 93 S.E.2d 274 (Va. 1956); *see also Bull,* 323 F. Supp. 115, 135 (E.D. Va. 1971) (stating that allegations, when filed, become "public record, and therefore privileged. The privilege requires that the article by [*sic*] a fair and accurate account of the record").

Plaintiff alleges the falsity of the allegedly defamatory statements. As to the August 2004 version of the website, Plaintiff alleges that Defendants published information they knew to be false "by asserting that he was convicted of a federal felony and engaged in acts that constituted a federal felony" and stating that he was "dishonorably discharged from service." As to the September 2004 version of the website, he alleges the presence of incorrect information regarding his conduct, status as a member of the military, and the number of violations of the UCMJ he faced. Defendants wrote one statement that referenced the court martial as evidenced by the August 2004 version of the website, and then slightly altered it for the September 2004 version. The August 2004 version states: "Tried for several sections of the UCMJ, Wiest was eventually dishonorably discharged from service." The September version states: "Tried for several sections of the UCMJ, the cadet was eventually discharged from service." Both statements assert that Plaintiff was "discharged," although the first one says that he was "dishonorably" discharged. Also, both statements assert that Mr. Wiest engaged in conduct that was illegal under the UCMJ. Because Mr. Wiest alleges that the statements regarding his conduct are false, and the Court must view the complaint in the light most favorable to him and credit the alleged falsity, the Court denies Defendants' motion to dismiss the complaint as to Counts 1 and 2. *See Chapin*, 993 F.2d at 1092.

Furthermore, the fact that Defendants relied on a public record does not shield them from liability since their depiction of the record is not a "fair and accurate" representation. In *Alexandria Gazette*, the Virginia Supreme Court held that "the publication of public records to which everyone has a right of access is privileged, if the publication is a fair and substantially correct statement of the transcript of the record." *Id.* at 279 (citations omitted) (noting that while the publication does not have to be verbatim, it must be "substantially correct"). When allegations are filed, they become "public record, and therefore privileged. The privilege requires that the article by [*sic*] a fair and accurate account of the record." *Bull*, 323 F. Supp. 115, 135 (E.D. Va. 1971) (holding that Plaintiff's press release stating that he had filed suit against two defendants for "conspiracy to defraud" was a "fair and accurate" account of the issues in the suit and "no action lies from such publication"). Defendants' description of events relating to the public record or Mr. Wiest's interaction with military justice, however, is not fair and accurate.

Both versions of the website state that Mr. Wiest was tried for "several sections of the UCMJ" and that he was "eventually discharged" or "eventually dishonorably discharged" from service. Mr. Wiest was tried for one specification of Article 134 of the UCMJ in violation of 18 U.S.C. § 1030(A)(5)(B) (2000) and for three specifications of Article 134 in violation of 18 U.S.C. § 1030(a)(5)(A) (2000). *See Wiest*, No. ACM33964, 2002 WL 31235026, at *1. Consequently, it is arguably substantially correct to assert that he was tried for violation of "several sections" of the UCMJ. It is, however, incorrect to assert that Mr. Wiest was "discharged" or "dishonorably discharged" from service, since the United States Court of Appeals for the Armed Services reversed the conviction and set aside the sentence, which included dismissal. Furthermore, the obvious implication generated by the statement that he was tried for violation of "several sections" of the UCMJ and "eventually … discharged" is that he was convicted of these violations. It is a misleading half-truth to say that a person was convicted of a violation of the UCMJ without including the fact that his conviction was overturned on appeal. *See James v. Powell*, 154 Va. 96, 152 S.E. 539 (Va. 1930) (holding a newspaper liable for libel when it erroneously stated that the plaintiff was charged with both murder and robbery when he was charged only with murder). Consequently, Mr. Wiest does state a claim for defamation, since he alleges the falsity of the statements on E-Fense's website, and the defendants cannot shield themselves from liability because they did not provide a fair and accurate description of the public record.

... III. CONCLUSION

The Court holds that Plaintiff Mr. Wiest states claims as to Counts One (Libel/Slander) and Two (Insulting Words) of his Complaint because he properly alleges the falsity of the statements on Defendants' website, and the statements on Defendants' website were not a fair and accurate depiction of the public record. ... For the foregoing reasons, it is hereby

ORDERED that Defendants' motion to dismiss is GRANTED IN PART and DENIED IN PART. Defendants' motion to dismiss is GRANTED as to Cause of Action Number Four. ...

CHAPTER IV

PRIVACY INTERESTS

Fundamental Principles of Privacy

insert the following before Common Law Invasion of Privacy Claims on page 391 of Law of Internet Speech:

When an individual's interest in privacy is transgressed, what is the appropriate remedy?

In *Doe v. Chao,* 540 U.S. 614 (2004), the plaintiff claimed that when he filed a claim for black lung benefits with the U.S. Department of Labor, the agency used his Social Security number to identify his claim on official agency documents in violation of the Privacy Act of 1974, 5 U.S.C. § 552a. The Act specifies how agencies are to manage their records and provides for various types of relief when the government fails to comply with the requirements. For example, there is a civil action for agency misconduct relating to deficient management of records, *see* 5 U.S.C. § 552a(g)(1)(A), and for an agency's failure to maintain adequate records about an individual when the result is a determination "adverse" to the individual, *see* 5 U.S.C. § 552a(g)(1)(D). The plaintiff had not proffered evidence of actual damages but argued, *inter alia,* that the statutory entitlement to recovery of a minimum award of $1000 should be satisfied by demonstrating an intentional or willful violation of the Act producing some adverse effect. The U.S. Supreme Court disagreed, relying on a textual analysis of the statute. *See Doe v. Chao,* 540 U.S. at 620-27.

If privacy interests are encroached without the imposition of liability, how effective are privacy regulatory schemes? Noted privacy specialist Joel R. Reidenberg opine:

> The *misuse* of personal information is both a personal wrong to individuals and a public wrong to society. Harm comes through the transgression of fair information practices and does not depend on additional consequences from the wrong. Some argue, however, that privacy redress should only occur if there is a monetary harm. ... Under this "monetary" harm approach, wrongful disclosure is not considered "actual" harm. This approach either misses the point of data privacy or is a disingenuous answer to the privacy wrongs. The very breach of a recognized fair information practice standard inherently wrongs the individual. Such "unfair" information practices are autonomous wrongful acts that do not depend on financial consequences for their harm. The wrongful disclosure in and of itself is an "actual harm" to the individual. More broadly, the corrosive effect of information trafficking on society does not depend on the monetary damages potentially caused to particular victims.

Joel R. Reidenberg, *Privacy Wrongs in Search of Remedies,* 54 Hastings L.J. 877, 896 (2003).

Should there be more latitude for the press to transgress privacy rights because of the important role the press plays in the democratic process? Should there be less latitude for the press to encroach on such rights because of the likely increased dissemination and receipt of infringing material? Would similar arguments apply to those who post infringing content on freely accessible web-sites?

* * * * *

Common Law Invasion of Privacy Claims

False Light

insert the following after Notes and Questions # 4 on page 396 of Law of Internet Speech:

In September 2003, the Oklahoma trial court considered claims against The Oklahoma Publishing Company, publisher of *The Oklahoman* newspaper, and Griffin Television OKC, L.L.C. (KWTV), based on a posting of their joint web-site, NewsOK. The site had posted information about registered sex offenders maintained by the Oklahoma Department of Corrections, which supplied the information electronically to the site to upload onto its server. NewsOK did not modify the data it was supplied, unless directed to do so by the Oklahoma Department of Corrections.

The plaintiff, Dennis Stewart, advanced claims grounded in false light invasion of privacy and defamation, complaining that a man listed as a sex offender in the database included a reference to Stewart's address. The address in issue had belonged to the offender's sister when he registered but he subsequently sold the property to the plaintiff and his wife. The Department of Corrections evidently was not notified of the change of address by the offender and did not revise its records until it completed its annual verification process some time later. *See Stewart v. The Oklahoma Publishing Co., et al.* No. 100,099 (Okla. Ct. Civ. App. Apr. 1, 2005); *see generally* Jon Epstein and Robert D. Nelon, *$3.7 Million Libel and False Light Verdict Reversed: News Website Published Sex Offender Records,* MDRC MediaLawLetter (April 2005) at 13.

The trial court rejected the defendants' requested jury instructions on privilege defenses, *see generally Law of Internet Speech* at 384, and based on section 230 of the Communications Decency Act, 47 U.S.C. § 230, *see generally Law of Internet Speech* at 281; *see also* Jon Epstein and Robert D. Nelon, *$3.7 Million Libel and False Light Verdict Reversed: News Website Published Sex Offender Records,* MDRC MediaLawLetter (April 2005) at 14. The jury awarded Stewart $200,000 in compensatory damages and $3.5 million in punitive damages. *See Stewart v. Oklahoma Publishing Co., et al.,* No. CJ-02-490 (Dist. Ct., Creek Cty. Okla. Sept. 18, 2003).

The Oklahoma Court of Civil Appeals reversed the verdict in April 2005. *See Stewart v. The Oklahoma Publishing Co., et al.* No. 100,099 (Okla. Ct. Civ. App. Apr. 1, 2005); *see generally* Jon Epstein and Robert D. Nelon, *$3.7 Million Libel and False Light Verdict Reversed: News Website Published Sex Offender Records,* MDRC MediaLawLetter (April 2005) at 13. The appellate court ruled that NewsOK "merely republished a public government document and that 'such a publication is privileged and immune from liability.'" *Id.* (quoting appellate court). The appellate court applied the Communications Decency Act as an alternative ground, holding that in any event the defendants were immunized from liability because NewsOK satisfied the definition of "interactive computer service" under section 230(f)(2) of the Act and because the Oklahoma Department of Corrections had created or developed the information in issue. *See id.*

* * * * *

Misappropriation and Right of Publicity

insert the following before Public Disclosure of Private Facts on page 405 of Law of Internet Speech:

* * * * *

CHRISTOPHER WIEST, Plaintiff

v.

E-FENSE, INC., *et al.,* Defendants

United States District Court for the Eastern District of Virginia
Alexandria Division

CIVIL ACTION NO. 04-1201, 356 F. Supp. 2d 604

February 9, 2005

ORDER

[For the background of this case, *see* Supplement *supra* at 277.]

... Another ...question[ ] before the Court [is] whether Mr. Wiest states a claim for statutory invasion of privacy when his name and information about his trial proceedings were placed on Defendants' website, and for common law invasion of privacy under Virginia law... The Court holds that Mr. Wiest ... states a claim for statutory invasion of privacy under Virginia law because the allegations in the complaint meet the requirements of Va. Code Ann. § 8.01-40 (Michie 2004). Mr. Wiest fails to state a claim for common law invasion of privacy because no such cause of action exists in Virginia. ...

Cause of Action No. 3: Statutory Invasion of Privacy

The Court denies Defendants' motion to dismiss as to Mr. Wiest's statutory invasion of privacy claim because Mr. Wiest's allegations satisfy the requirements of Va. Code Ann. § 8.01-40 (Michie 2004) and fall under none of its exceptions. Under the relevant portions of this Code provision, a person whose name is used for "advertising purposes or for the purposes of trade" without first obtaining the person's consent may sue for an injunction preventing use of his name and for damages for injuries, as well as exemplary damages if "the defendant shall have knowingly used" the name in a forbidden manner. Va. Code Ann. § 8.01-40; *see also Town & Country Properties, Inc. v. Riggins,* 249 Va. 387, 457 S.E.2d 356, 362 (Va. 1995) (holding the statute constitutional). Use for "advertising purposes" occurs when "'it appears in a publication which, taken in its entirety, was distributed for use in, or as part of, an advertisement or solicitation for patronage of a particular product or services.'" *Riggins,* 457 S.E. 2d at 362 (citing *Beverley v. Choices Women's Medical Center,*

Inc., 78 N.Y.2d 745, 587 N.E.2d 275, 278, 579 N.Y.S.2d 637 (N.Y. 1991)[5]). If a name or likeness is used without consent in connection with matters that are "newsworthy" or of "public interest," the statute does not apply. *Williams v. Newsweek, Inc.,* 63 F. Supp. 2d 734 (E.D. Va. 1999), *aff'd,* 202 F.3d 262 (4th Cir. 1999). Similarly, uses of names or images that are merely incidental to the main purpose of the work are not actionable. *See id.* (holding that the incidental appearance of a person's image in a photograph from a book that was published in a *Newsweek* profile of the book was not actionable under the statute).

The use of Mr. Wiest's name and "facts" about his conduct and legal troubles is actionable because Mr. Wiest properly alleges it was used as an advertisement to solicit business for Defendant E-Fense. In *Riggins,* the Virginia Supreme Court held that a flyer prominently displaying a famous Washington Redskins NFL running back's name as a selling point for purchasing his former home was an "advertisement" and violated the privacy statute. *See Riggins,* 457 S.E. 2d at 362. Similarly, the New York Court of Appeals held that a non-profit medical center performing abortions whose promotional calendar included an image of the plaintiff without her consent was liable under the New York statute because the calendar constituted an "advertisement." *Beverley,* 587 N.E.2d at 278. The quoted sections regarding Mr. Wiest appear on a page entitled "Case Histories" on E-Fense Inc.'s website. E-Fense is not a news organization, but rather a private organization that provides services to clients. The top of the page states:

> Hackers with the right tools and experience can threaten the integrity of any system -- public or private. As former Air Force Office of Special Investigations agents specializing in digital forensics and cyber intrusion investigations, members of our team have served as case agents in some of the biggest hacking investigations to date. Highlights of their experience involve contributions to the following renowned cases....

....Mr. Wiest's properly alleges that E-Fense, Inc. used his name and statements concerning him to solicit customers for business. Because Mr. Wiest properly alleges that Defendants used Mr. Wiest's name and statements concerning him to profile and sell their services to other customers, Mr. Wiest states a claim for violation of Va. Code. Ann. § 8.01-40.

Furthermore, despite Defendants' argument to the contrary, publication of these statements is not protected because the trial was a matter of public record. In *Riggins,* the defendant similarly attempted to rely on *Cox Broadcasting Corp.,* [420 U.S. at 494,] arguing that real estate records were matters in the public record and therefore information gleaned from them could be used without fear of violating the plaintiff's privacy rights. 457 S.E.2d at 364. The Virginia Supreme Court rejected this argument, holding that the defendant's reliance on *Cox Broadcasting Corp.* was "misplaced" because of the United States Supreme Court's qualification that "we do not have at issue here an action for the invasion of privacy involving the appropriation of one's name." *Id.* (citing *Cox Broadcasting Corp.,* 420 U.S. at 489) (internal quotations omitted). As in *Riggins* and unlike *Cox Broadcasting Corp.,* the

---

[5] Because this code provision is substantially similar to New York's corresponding statute, Virginia courts look to New York courts for guidance in analyzing the statute. *Falwell v. Flynt,* 797 F.2d 1270, 1278 (4th Cir. 1986), *rev'd on other grounds,* 485 U.S. 46, 99 L. Ed. 2d 41, 108 S. Ct. 876 (1988).

very issue in this case *is* invasion of privacy. Consequently, because Mr. Wiest properly alleges the elements of a violation of Va. Code Ann. § 8.01-40 and because Defendants are not protected from liability just because his trial was a matter of public record, the Court denies Defendants' motion to dismiss Plaintiff's statutory invasion of privacy claim.

Cause of Action No. 4: Common Law Invasion of Privacy

The Court dismisses Plaintiff's claim for common law invasion of privacy because no such cause of action exists under Virginia law. Va. Code. Ann. § 8.01-40 "provides the only remedy under Virginia law for a claim of invasion of privacy." *See, e.g., Williams,* 63 F. Supp.2d at 736 (citations omitted); *see also Levin,* 564 S.E.2d at 395 n.5 (stating that the General Assembly's decision to codify only misappropriation of name or likeness for commercial purposes as an actionable invasion of privacy tort "implicitly excluded" invasion of privacy torts recognized in other jurisdictions). Consequently, the Court dismisses Count 4 of Plaintiff's Complaint.

... II. CONCLUSION

....[T]he Court holds that Plaintiff Mr. Wiest states a claim for statutory invasion of privacy, Va. Code Ann. § 8.01-40, but not for common law invasion since no such cause of action exists in Virginia. ...

ORDERED that Defendants' motion to dismiss is GRANTED IN PART and DENIED IN PART. ....Defendants' motion to dismiss is DENIED as to Causes of Action Numbers One through Three. ...

* * * * *

Public Disclosure of Private Facts

insert the following after the first full paragraph on page 406 of Law of Internet Speech:

One commentator noted that "[u]ntil recently, it was potentially risky business in California for the media to identify an individual as having a not-so-recent criminal past, even though this information was documented in public records." Robert S. Gutierrez, *California Appellate Court Rejects Claim for Publication of Old Crime Information: Concludes Briscoe No Longer the Law,* MLRC MediaLawLetter (Mar. 2003) at 29. In *Gates v. Discovery Communications, Inc.,* 131 Cal. Rptr. 2d 534, 106 Cal. App. 4th 677, 693 (Cal. App. 4th 2003), *aff'd,* 34 Cal. 4th 679, 101 P.3d 552, 21 Cal. Rptr. 3d 663 (Cal. 2004), the court considered a program produced by New Dominion Pictures and broadcast on the Discovery Channel that re-enacted crimes and chronicled the investigation and prosecution of the perpetrators. One episode disclosed that a man had been convicted of being an accessory after the fact to a murder for hire. Facts pertaining to the conviction were accessible to the public in court records relating to a judicial proceeding. Nevertheless, the plaintiff alleged his privacy had been invaded by the disclosure in the program. 131 Cal. Rptr. 2d at 536-37, 106 Cal. App. 4th at 680.

The California appellate court concluded that "insofar as *Briscoe* held that criminal or civil penalties could result from the publication of the public record of a judicial proceeding, it was overruled by [the U.S. Supreme Court's decision in] *Cox [Broadcasting Corp. v. Cohn,* 420 U.S. 469 (1975)]." 131 Cal. Rptr. 2d at 545, 106 Cal. App. 4th at 680. In *Cox,* the U.S. Supreme Court had ruled that "[i]n preserving [our] form of government the First and

Fourteenth Amendments command nothing less than that the States may not impose sanctions on the publication of truthful information contained in official records open to public inspection." 420 U.S. at 495. The California court noted that "no suggestion in *Cox* that the fact the public record of [a] criminal proceeding is one or two or ten years old affects the absolute right of the press or a documentarian or a historian to report it fully." *Gates v. Discovery Communications, Inc.,* 131 Cal. Rptr. 2d at 545, 106 Cal. App. 4th at 692.

The California Supreme Court agreed, concluding that "courts are not freed, by the mere passage of time, to impose sanctions on the publication of truthful information that is obtained from public official court records." 34 Cal. 4th at 694, 101 P.3d at 561, 21 Cal. Rptr. 3d at 673 (citation omitted). At bottom, "an invasion of privacy claim based on allegations of harm caused by a media defendant's publication of facts obtained from public official records of a criminal proceeding is barred by the First Amendment to the United States Constitution." *Id.,* 34 Cal. 4th at 696, 101 P.3d at 562, 21 Cal. Rptr. 3d at 675 (citations omitted).

Likewise, in *Uranga v. Federated Publ'ns, Inc.,* 67 P.3d 29 (Idaho 2003), *cert. denied,* 540 U.S. 940 (2003), the plaintiff complained that *The Idaho Statesman* published an article in 1995 concerning events that had occurred in 1955 and 1956 surrounding an investigation into allegations that adult homosexual men were propositioning teenage boys. The newspaper reported that one man stated he had a sexual encounter with another, claiming that he was forced to do so at gunpoint. The allegations of force were denied in a handwritten statement that described "gay affairs that [the man alleging that force had been used] had had with [a classmate] and his cousin[, the plaintiff]." 67 P.3d at 31. The newspaper printed a photographic representation of the statement and referred to "a cousin" but did not mention the plaintiff's name in the text of the article.

The plaintiff complained that the newspaper's publication concerned a criminal prosecution that had occurred almost forty years earlier. The Idaho Supreme Court found the protestations unavailing. "There is no indication that the First Amendment provides less protection to historians than to those reporting current events," said the court. *Id.* at 35. The court also concluded that

> although the circumstances surrounding the publication in question certainly evoke sympathy for [the plaintiff], this case cannot be distinguished from [*Cox Broadcasting Corp. v. Cohn,* 420 U.S. 469 (1975),] based upon the age of the court record and the lack of significance in having [the plaintiff's] name appear in the story. Furthermore, [the plaintiff] has not offered any standard by which to determine when a court record is too old or a particular fact in such record too insignificant for its publication to merit First Amendment protection. Absent such a standard, there would be no way to judge in advance whether or not a publication would enjoy First Amendment protection.

Id.

* * * * *

insert the following before Are There Privacy Interests in Social Security Numbers? on page 411 of Law of Internet Speech:

Thereafter, with respect to the invasion of privacy by public disclosure of private facts claim, the California federal court considered whether the facts published in the broadcast by "Hard Copy" disclosed private facts. The court distinguished the broadcast from dissemination over the Internet on the ground that the former was a past use. Although the excerpts broadcast were "blurry, and in some places the video image was manipulated to make body parts unrecognizable[,] … the Court conclude[d] that a reasonable jury could find that the excerpts depict private facts regarding the plaintiffs in this action." *Michaels v. Internet Entertainment Group, Inc.,* No. CV 98-0583 DDP (CWx), 1998 U.S. Dist. LEXIS 20786 at *21 (C.D. Cal. Sept. 14, 1998). Despite the contention that "the public has already seen [Pamela Anderson] Lee naked and having sex," and thus the facts disclosed in the broadcast were no longer private, the court reiterated its earlier determination that "publication of pictures of Lee having sex on one occasion with one partner does not waive her privacy interest in future sex acts with other partners." *Id.* at *21-23. Although the court ruled that a genuine issue of fact existed as to whether the broadcast depicted private facts, *id.* at *24, summary judgment for the defendant was granted based on the newsworthiness privilege. While the social value of the facts published arguably was low, California courts previously had held that romantic interests of celebrities are matters of legitimate public concern. In this case, Lee was a voluntary public figure, and the allegedly private matters broadcast bore a substantial nexus to a matter of public interest; "[t]here is no genuine issue of fact as to the reason for Lee's fame. She is famous as a sex symbol." *Id.* at *26, *29. Because the plaintiff was a voluntary public figure, the depth of intrusion standard was applied with even greater deference to the public interest in unfettered news reporting. *See id.* at *28.

* * * * *

Are There Privacy Interests in Social Security Numbers?

Notes and Questions

1. According to the FTC, there were 9.9 million cases of identity theft in the United States in 2003. *See* Eric J. Sinrod, *Steal Your Face: The Dangers of Identity Theft,* USA Today.com (Nov. 10, 2004), *available at* <http://www.usatoday.com/tech/columnist/ericjsinrod/2004-11-10-sinrod_x.htm>.

2. According to a survey conducted by the Ponemon Institute, more than 70 percent of consumers share such personal information as name, address, postal code, telephone number, or account number, or will answer security questions in response to unsolicited calls or e-mails and 61 percent of consumers do not change their passwords periodically. *See id.* (citing Identity Management Survey conducted by the Ponemon Institute, "a think tank dedicated to advancing responsible information management practices for business and government").

* * * * *

insert the following before Intrusion on Seclusion on page 413 of Law of Internet Speech:

HELEN REMSBURG,
ADMINISTRATRIX OF THE ESTATE OF AMY LYNN BOYER

v.

DOCUSEARCH, INC., d/b/a DOCUSEARCH.COM *& a*

Supreme Court of New Hampshire

U.S. District Court No. 2002-255, 149 N.H. 148, 816 A.2d 1001

February 18, 2003

Pursuant to Supreme Court Rule 34, the United States District Court for the District of New Hampshire (Barbadoro, C.J.) certified to us the following questions of law:

1. Under the common law of New Hampshire and in light of the undisputed facts presented by this case, does a private investigator or information broker who sells information to a client pertaining to a third party have a cognizable legal duty to that third party with respect to the sale of the information?

2. If a private investigator or information broker obtains a person's social security number from a credit reporting agency as a part of a credit header without the person's knowledge or permission and sells the social security number to a client, does the individual whose social security number was sold have a cause of action for intrusion upon her seclusion against the private investigator or information broker for damages caused by the sale of the information?

3. When a private investigator or information broker obtains a person's work address by means of a pretextual telephone call and sells the work address to a client, does the individual whose work address was deceitfully obtained have a cause of action for intrusion upon her seclusion against the private investigator or information broker for damages caused by the sale of the information?

4. If a private investigator or information broker obtains a social security number from a credit reporting agency as a part of a credit header, or a work address by means of a pretextual telephone call, and then sells the information, does the individual whose social security number or work address was sold have a cause of action for commercial appropriation against the private investigator or information broker for damages caused by the sale of the information? …

For the reasons expressed below, we respond to the first, second and fifth questions in the affirmative, and the third and fourth questions in the negative.

I. Facts

We adopt the district court's recitation of the facts. Docusearch, Inc. and Wing and a Prayer, Inc. (WAAP) jointly own and operate an Internet-based investigation and information service known as Docusearch.com. Daniel Cohn and Kenneth Zeiss each own 50% of each company's stock. Cohn serves as president of both companies and Zeiss serves as a director of WAAP. Cohn is licensed as a private investigator by both the State of Florida and Palm Beach County, Florida.

On July 29, 1999, New Hampshire resident Liam Youens contacted Docusearch through its Internet website and requested the date of birth for Amy Lynn Boyer, another New Hampshire resident. Youens provided Docusearch his name, New Hampshire address, and a contact telephone number. He paid the $20 fee by credit card. Zeiss placed a telephone call to Youens in New Hampshire on the same day. Zeiss cannot recall the reason for the phone call, but speculates that it was to verify the order. The next day, July 30, 1999, Docusearch provided Youens with the birth dates for several Amy Boyers, but none was for the Amy Boyer sought by Youens. In response, Youens e-mailed Docusearch inquiring whether it would be possible to get better results using Boyer's home address, which he provided. Youens gave Docusearch a different contact phone number.

Later that same day, Youens again contacted Docusearch and placed an order for Boyer's social security number (SSN), paying the $45 fee by credit card. On August 2, 1999, Docusearch obtained Boyer's social security number from a credit reporting agency as a part of a "credit header" and provided it to Youens. A "credit header" is typically provided at the top of a credit report and includes a person's name, address and social security number. The next day, Youens placed an order with Docusearch for Boyer's employment information, paying the $109 fee by credit card, and giving Docusearch the same phone number he had provided originally. Docusearch phone records indicate that Zeiss placed a phone call to Youens on August 6, 1999. The phone number used was the one Youens had provided with his follow-up inquiry regarding Boyer's birth date. The phone call lasted for less than one minute, and no record exists concerning its topic or whether Zeiss was able to speak with Youens. On August 20, 1999, having received no response to his latest request, Youens placed a second request for Boyer's employment information, again paying the $109 fee by credit card. On September 1, 1999, Docusearch refunded Youens' first payment of $109 because its efforts to fulfill his first request for Boyer's employment information had failed.

With his second request for Boyer's employment information pending, Youens placed yet another order for information with Docusearch on September 6, 1999. This time, he requested a "locate by social security number" search for Boyer. Youens paid the $30 fee by credit card, and received the results of the search – Boyer's home address – on September 7, 1999.

On September 8, 1999, Docusearch informed Youens of Boyer's employment address. Docusearch acquired this address through a subcontractor, Michele Gambino, who had obtained the information by placing a "pretext" telephone call to Boyer in New Hampshire. Gambino lied about who she was and the purpose of her call in order to convince Boyer to reveal her employment information. Gambino had no contact with Youens, nor did she know why Youens was requesting the information.

On October 15, 1999, Youens drove to Boyer's workplace and fatally shot her as she left work. Youens then shot and killed himself. A subsequent police investigation revealed that Youens kept firearms and ammunition in his bedroom, and maintained a website containing references to stalking and killing Boyer as well as other information and statements related to violence and killing.

II. Question 1

All persons have a duty to exercise reasonable care not to subject others to an unreasonable risk of harm. *See Walls v. Oxford Management Co.,* 137 N.H. 653, 656 (1993). Whether a defendant's conduct creates a risk of harm to others sufficiently foreseeable to charge the defendant with a duty to avoid such conduct is a question of law, *Iannelli v. Burger King Corp.,* 145 N.H. 190, 193 (2000), because "the existence of a duty does not arise solely from the relationship between the parties, but also from the need for protection against reasonably foreseeable harm." *Hungerford v. Jones,* 143 N.H. 208, 211 (1998) (quotation omitted). Thus, in some cases, a party's actions give rise to a duty. *Walls,* 137 N.H. at 656. Parties owe a duty to those third parties foreseeably endangered by their conduct with respect to those risks whose likelihood and magnitude make the conduct unreasonably dangerous. *Hungerford,* 143 N.H. at 211.

In situations in which the harm is caused by criminal misconduct, however, determining whether a duty exists is complicated by the competing rule "that a private citizen has no general duty to protect others from the criminal attacks of third parties." *Dupont v. Aavid Thermal Technologies,* 147 N.H. 706, 709 (2002). This rule is grounded in the fundamental unfairness of holding private citizens responsible for the unanticipated criminal acts of third parties, because "[u]nder all ordinary and normal circumstances, in the absence of any reason to expect the contrary, the actor may reasonably proceed upon the assumption that others will obey the law." *Walls,* 137 N.H. at 657-58 (quotation omitted).

In certain limited circumstances, however, we have recognized that there are exceptions to the general rule where a duty to exercise reasonable care will arise. *See Dupont,* 147 N.H. at 709. We have held that such a duty may arise because: (1) a special relationship exists; (2) special circumstances exist; or (3) the duty has been voluntarily assumed. *Id.* The special circumstances exception includes situations where there is "an especial temptation and opportunity for criminal misconduct brought about by the defendant." *Walls,* 137 N.H. at 658 (quotation omitted). This exception follows from the rule that a party who realizes or should realize that his conduct has created a condition which involves an unreasonable risk of harm to another has a duty to exercise reasonable care to prevent the risk from occurring. *Id.* The exact occurrence or precise injuries need not have been foreseeable. *Iannelli,* 145 N.H. at 194. Rather, where the defendant's conduct has created an unreasonable risk of criminal misconduct, a duty is owed to those foreseeably endangered. *See id.*

Thus, if a private investigator or information broker's (hereinafter "investigator" collectively) disclosure of information to a client creates a foreseeable risk of criminal misconduct against the third person whose information was disclosed, the investigator owes a duty to exercise reasonable care not to subject the third person to an unreasonable risk of harm.   In determining whether the risk of criminal misconduct is foreseeable to an investigator, we examine two risks of information disclosure implicated by this case: stalking and identity theft.

It is undisputed that stalkers, in seeking to locate and track a victim, sometimes use an investigator to obtain personal information about the victims.   ...   Public concern about stalking has compelled all fifty States to pass some form of legislation criminalizing stalking. Approximately one million women and 371,000 men are stalked annually in the United States.   P. Tjaden & N. Thoennes, Nat'l Inst. of Justice Ctr. for Disease Control and Prevention, *Stalking in America: Findings from the National Violence Against Women Survey*, Apr. 1998, at 2.   Stalking is a crime that causes serious psychological harm to the victims, and often results in the victim experiencing post-traumatic stress disorder, anxiety, sleeplessness, and sometimes, suicidal ideations.   *See* Mullen & Pathe, *Stalking*, 29 Crime & Just. 273, 296-97 (2002).   Not only is stalking itself a crime, but it can lead to more violent crimes, including assault, rape or homicide.   *See, e.g., Brunner v. State*, 683 So. 2d 1129, 1130 (Fla. Dist. Ct. App. 1996); *People v. Sowewimo*, 657 N.E.2d 1047, 1049 (Ill. App. Ct. 1995); *Com. v. Cruz*, 675 N.E.2d 764, 765 (Mass. 1997).

Identity theft, i.e., the use of one person's identity by another, is an increasingly common risk associated with the disclosure of personal information, such as a SSN. ...   A person's SSN has attained the status of a quasi-universal personal identification number.   At the same time, however, a person's privacy interest in his or her SSN is recognized by state and federal statutes, including RSA 260:14, IV-a (Supp. 2002) which prohibits the release of SSNs contained within drivers' license records.   *See also* Financial Services Modernization Act of 1999, 15 U.S.C. §§ 6801-6809 (2000); Privacy Act of 1974, 5 U.S.C. § 552a (2000). "[A]rmed with one's SSN, an unscrupulous individual could obtain a person's welfare benefits or Social Security benefits, order new checks at a new address on that person's checking account, obtain credit cards, or even obtain the person's paycheck." *Greidinger v. Davis*, 988 F.2d 1344, 1353 (4th Cir. 1993).

Like the consequences of stalking, the consequences of identity theft can be severe. ... Victims of identity theft risk the destruction of their good credit histories.   This often destroys a victim's ability to obtain credit from any source and may, in some cases, render the victim unemployable or even cause the victim to be incarcerated.

The threats posed by stalking and identity theft lead us to conclude that the risk of criminal misconduct is sufficiently foreseeable so that an investigator has a duty to exercise reasonable care in disclosing a third person's personal information to a client.   And we so hold.   This is especially true when, as in this case, the investigator does not know the client or the client's purpose in seeking the information.

III. Questions 2 and 3

A tort action based upon an intrusion upon seclusion must relate to something secret, secluded or private pertaining to the plaintiff. *Fischer v. Hooper*, 143 N.H. 585, 590 (1999). Moreover, liability exists only if the defendant's conduct was such that the defendant should have realized that it would be offensive to persons of ordinary sensibilities. *Id.* "It is only where the intrusion has gone beyond the limits of decency that liability accrues." *Hamberger v. Eastman*, 106 N.H. 107, 111 (1964) (quotation omitted); *see Restatement (Second) of Torts* § 652B comment *d* at 380 (1977).

In addressing whether a person's SSN is something secret, secluded or private, we must determine whether a person has a reasonable expectation of privacy in the number. *See Fischer*, 143 N.H. at 589-90. SSNs are available in a wide variety of contexts. *Bodah v. Lakeville Motor Express Inc.*, 649 N.W.2d 859, 863 (Minn. Ct. App. 2002). SSNs are used to identify people to track social security benefits, as well as when taxes and credit applications are filed. *See Greidinger*, 988 F.2d at 1352-53. In fact, "the widespread use of SSNs as universal identifiers in the public and private sectors is one of the most serious manifestations of privacy concerns in the Nation." *Id.* at 1353 (quotation omitted). ...

....[W]hile a SSN must be disclosed in certain circumstances, a person may reasonably expect that the number will remain private.

Whether the intrusion would be offensive to persons of ordinary sensibilities is ordinarily a question for the fact-finder and only becomes a question of law if reasonable persons can draw only one conclusion from the evidence. *See Swarthout v. Mutual Service Life Ins. Co.*, 632 N.W.2d 741, 745 (Minn. Ct. App. 2001). The evidence underlying the certified question is insufficient to draw any such conclusion here, and we therefore must leave this question to the fact-finder. In making this determination, the fact-finder should consider "the degree of intrusion, the context, conduct and circumstances surrounding the intrusion as well as the intruder's motives and objectives, the setting into which he intrudes, and the expectations of those whose privacy is invaded." *Bauer v. Ford Motor Credit C*o., 149 F. Supp. 2d 1106, 1109 (D. Minn. 2001). Accordingly, a person whose SSN is obtained by an investigator from a credit reporting agency without the person's knowledge or permission may have a cause of action for intrusion upon seclusion for damages caused by the sale of the SSN, but must prove that the intrusion was such that it would have been offensive to a person of ordinary sensibilities.

We next address whether a person has a cause of action for intrusion upon seclusion where an investigator obtains the person's work address by using a pretextual phone call. We must first establish whether a work address is something secret, secluded or private about the plaintiff. *See Fischer*, 143 N.H. at 590.

In most cases, a person works in a public place. "On the public street, or in any other public place, [a person] has no legal right to be alone." W. Page Keeton *et al., Prosser and Keeton on the Law of Torts* § 117, at 855 (5th ed. 1984).

> A person's employment, where he lives, and where he works are exposures which we all must suffer. We have no reasonable expectation of privacy as to our identity or as to where we live or work. Our commuting to and from where we live and work is not done clandestinely and each place provides a facet of our total identity.

Webb v. City of Shreveport, 371 So. 2d 316, 319 (La. Ct. App. 1979). Thus, where a person's work address is readily observable by members of the public, the address cannot be private and no intrusion upon seclusion action can be maintained.

IV. Question 4

"One who appropriates to his own use or benefit the name or likeness of another is subject to liability to the other for invasion of his privacy." *Restatement (Second) of Torts* § 652C at 380. ... We now hold that New Hampshire recognizes the tort of invasion of privacy by appropriation of an individual's name or likeness, and adopt the *Restatement* view. "The interest protected by the rule ... is the interest of the individual in the exclusive use of his own identity, in so far as it is represented by his name or likeness, and in so far as the use may be of benefit to him or to others." *Restatement (Second) of Torts* § 652C comment a at 381.

> ....[I]n order that there may be liability under the rule stated in this Section, the defendant must have appropriated to his own use or benefit the reputation, prestige, social or commercial standing, public interest or other values of the plaintiff's name or likeness. The misappropriation tort does not protect one's name *per se*; rather it protects the value associated with that name.

Matthews v. Wozencraft, 15 F.3d 432, 437 (5th Cir. 1994) (citation, brackets and quotation omitted). Appropriation is not actionable if the person's name or likeness is published for "purposes other than taking advantage of [the person's] reputation, prestige or other value" associated with the person. *Restatement (Second) of Torts* § 652C comment d at 382-83. ...

An investigator who sells personal information sells the information for the value of the information itself, not to take advantage of the person's reputation or prestige. The investigator does not capitalize upon the goodwill value associated with the information but rather upon the client's willingness to pay for the information. In other words, the benefit derived from the sale in no way relates to the social or commercial standing of the person whose information is sold. Thus, a person whose personal information is sold does not have a cause of action for appropriation against the investigator who sold the information. ...

Remanded.

* * * * *

Intrusion on Seclusion

insert the following after Notes and Question # 4 on page 415 of Law of Internet Speech:

5. Should liability for an unlawful disclosure of social security numbers be triggered by a showing of specific monetary damages or by a showing of some other adverse effect on the holders of the numbers?

* * * * *

Trespass to Chattels Claims

insert the following before Register.com, Inc. v. Verio, Inc. on page 417 of Law of Internet Speech:

Notes and Questions

1. Nearly 25 percent of e-mail has been estimated to constitute spam, according to a sampling conducted in January 2003 by MessageLabs, a United Kingdom e-mail security provider. *See Spam Comprises Nearly Quarter of Email,* SMH.com.au (Feb. 11, 2003), *available at* <http://www.smh.com.au/articles/2003/02/11/1044725778765.html>. As of the Fall 2002, the Federal Trade Commission received approximately 70,000 forwarded spam messages each day, as compared with an estimated 100 missives received each *year* in 1998. *See* Michelle Delio, *FTC: Where Spam Goes to Die,* Wired News (Nov. 5, 2002), *available at* <http://www.wired.com/news/politics/0,1283,55972,00.html>.

2. Techniques used by spam programmers to evade deletion before reading the message's content and circumvent filtering devices include:

    ~ forging identifying headers;

    ~ including plausible subject lines;

    ~ suggesting that the message is in response to a query the recipient initiated;

    ~ inserting the recipient's name in the subject line

    ~ ironically, even suggesting that the message can assist the recipient in filtering future spam

For business entities, spam is costly because it impacts worker productivity and can affect network operability if there is inadequate capacity to accommodate the volume of messages. In addition, companies may incur technical support costs to conduct security investigations, may need to modify sexual harassment policies to address unwanted access to pornographic messages, and invariably need to regularly explore effective marketing means of distributing legitimate advertising messages without running afoul of spam legislation, *see* Supplement *infra* at 318. Internet service providers are affected, too. They experience increased strain on their servers from the dissemination and receipt of massive quantities of e-mail messages in concentrated time periods, bounced messages resulting from spam sent to non-existent addresses, and customer complaints about the inconvenience of receiving unwanted messages.

3. Among the pragmatic challenges of addressing spam is that the cost is borne by the recipient, rather than by the programmer. "Spam is at bottom caused by an economic or pricing problem; ISP pricing structures – pay a flat rate, send and receive all the email you want – disperse the costs of spam onto all users, rather than those actually using bandwidth sending mass emails. And the other costs of becoming a spammer, the software and email address lists, are low." Hanah Metchis and Solveig Singleton, *Spam, That Ill O' The ISP: A Reality Check for Legislators* (Competitive Enterprise Institute) at 7. Note the disparate

allocation of costs as between the sender and the recipient in the context of postal mail; in the latter case, the sender bears the costs associated with the transmission.

4. Access by the public to governmental agencies has been impaired by technology designed to filter spam. *See, e.g.,* Declan McCullagh, *Public Access to FTC Hurt by Spam Lists*, CNet News.com (Nov. 26, 2002), *available at* <http://news.com.com/2100-1023-975473.html> (describing an incident in which an e-mail message to the FTC was bounced back because the blacklisting service to which the agency subscribes precluded access by the author's Internet service provider). Does such a practice violate the right to petition the government?

5. The origin of the first spam messages has been attributed to a salesperson who, in 1978, manually typed several hundred addresses of scientists and researchers on the Arpanet to distribute an announcement of a product presentation. *See* James Gleick, *Tangled Up in Spam,* N.Y. Times, Feb. 9, 2003, § 6 at 42 (citing Brad Templeton, an "online pioneer," as the person who believes he identified the first spam).

* * * * *

insert the following before Intel Corporation v. Kourosh Kenneth Hamidi on page 422 of Law of Internet Speech:

REGISTER.COM, INC., Plaintiff-Appellee
v.
VERIO, INC., Defendant-Appellant

United States Court of Appeals for the Second Circuit

No. 00-9596, 356 F.3d 393

January 23, 2004

Defendant, Verio, Inc. ("Verio") appeals from an order of the United States District Court for the Southern District of New York (Barbara S. Jones, J.) granting the motion of plaintiff Register.com, Inc. ("Register") for a preliminary injunction. The court's order enjoined Verio from (1) using Register's trademarks; (2) representing or otherwise suggesting to third parties that Verio's services have the sponsorship, endorsement, or approval of Register; (3) accessing Register's computers by use of automated software programs performing multiple successive queries; and (4) using data obtained from Register's database of contact information of registrants of Internet domain names to solicit the registrants for the sale of web site development services by electronic mail, telephone calls, or direct mail. We affirm.

BACKGROUND

This plaintiff Register is one of over fifty companies serving as registrars for the issuance of domain names on the world wide web. As a registrar, Register issues domain names to persons and entities preparing to establish web sites on the Internet. Web sites are identified and accessed by reference to their domain names.

Register was appointed a registrar of domain names by the Internet Corporation for Assigned Names and Numbers, known by the acronym "ICANN." ICANN is a private, non-profit public benefit corporation which was established by agencies of the U.S. government to administer the Internet domain name system. To become a registrar of domain names, Register was required to enter into a standard form agreement with ICANN, designated as the

ICANN Registrar Accreditation Agreement, November 1999 version (referred to herein as the "ICANN Agreement").

Applicants to register a domain name submit to the registrar contact information, including at a minimum, the applicant's name, postal address, telephone number, and electronic mail address. The ICANN Agreement, referring to this registrant contact information under the rubric "WHOIS information," requires the registrar, under terms discussed in greater detail below, to preserve it, update it daily, and provide for free public access to it through the Internet as well as through an independent access port, called port 43.

... In addition to performing the function of a registrar of domain names, Register also engages in the business of selling web-related services to entities that maintain web sites. These services cover various aspects of web site development. In order to solicit business for the services it offers, Register sends out marketing communications. Among the entities it solicits for the sale of such services are entities whose domain names it registered. However, during the registration process, Register offers registrants the opportunity to elect whether or not they will receive marketing communications from it.

The defendant Verio, against whom the preliminary injunction was issued, is engaged in the business of selling a variety of web site design, development and operation services. In the sale of such services, Verio competes with Register's web site development business. To facilitate its pursuit of customers, Verio undertook to obtain daily updates of the WHOIS information relating to newly registered domain names. To achieve this, Verio devised an automated software program, or robot, which each day would submit multiple successive WHOIS queries through the port 43 accesses of various registrars. Upon acquiring the WHOIS information of new registrants, Verio would send them marketing solicitations by email, telemarketing and direct mail. To the extent that Verio's solicitations were sent by email, the practice was inconsistent with the terms of the restrictive legend Register attached to its responses to Verio's queries.

... On December 8, 2000, the district court entered a preliminary injunction. The injunction barred Verio from[, *inter alia,*] the following activities:

> ... 3. Accessing Register.com's computers and computer networks in any manner, including, but not limited to, by software programs performing multiple, automated, successive queries, provided that nothing in this Order shall prohibit Verio from accessing Register.com's WHOIS database in accordance with the terms and conditions thereof; and

> 4. Using any data currently in Verio's possession, custody or control, that using its best efforts, Verio can identify as having been obtained from Register.com's computers and computer networks to enable the transmission of unsolicited commercial electronic mail, telephone calls, or direct mail to the individuals listed in said data, provided that nothing in this Order shall prohibit Verio from (i) communicating with any of its existing customers, (ii) responding to communications received from any Register.com customer initially contacted before August 4, 2000, or (iii) communicating with any Register.com customer whose contact

information is obtained by Verio from any source other than Register.com's computers and computer networks.

Register.com, Inc. v. Verio, Inc., 126 F. Supp. 2d 238, 255 (S.D.N.Y. 2000). Verio appeals from that order.

DISCUSSION

... (d) Trespass to chattels

Verio ... attacks the grant of the preliminary injunction against its accessing Register's computers by automated software programs performing multiple successive queries. This prong of the injunction was premised on Register's claim of trespass to chattels. Verio contends the ruling was in error because Register failed to establish that Verio's conduct resulted in harm to Register's servers and because Verio's robot access to the WHOIS database through Register was "not unauthorized." We believe the district court's findings were within the range of its permissible discretion.

"A trespass to a chattel may be committed by intentionally ... using or intermeddling with a chattel in the possession of another," Restatement (Second) of Torts § 217(b) (1965), where "the chattel is impaired as to its condition, quality, or value," *id.* § 218(b); *see also City of Amsterdam v. Goldreyer Ltd.*, 882 F. Supp. 1273, 1281 (E.D.N.Y. 1995) (citing the Restatement definition as New York law).

The district court found that Verio's use of search robots, consisting of software programs performing multiple automated successive queries, consumed a significant portion of the capacity of Register's computer systems. While Verio's robots alone would not incapacitate Register's systems, the court found that if Verio were permitted to continue to access Register's computers through such robots, it was "highly probable" that other Internet service providers would devise similar programs to access Register's data, and that the system would be overtaxed and would crash. We cannot say these findings were unreasonable.

Nor is there merit to Verio's contention that it cannot be engaged in trespass when Register had never instructed it not to use its robot programs. As the district court noted, Register's complaint sufficiently advised Verio that its use of robots was not authorized and, according to Register's contentions, would cause harm to Register's systems.

... CONCLUSION

The ruling of the district court is hereby AFFIRMED, with the exception that the court is directed to delete the reference to "first step on the web" from paragraph one of its order.

* * * * *

insert the following before Data Mining and Data Protection Directives, Policies, and Legislation on page 431 of Law of Internet Speech:

INTEL CORPORATION, Plaintiff and Respondent

v.

KOUROSH KENNETH HAMIDI, Defendant and Appellant

Supreme Court of California

No. S103781, 30 Cal. 4th 1342, 71 P.3d 296, 1 Cal. Rptr. 3d 32

June 30, 2003

Intel Corporation (Intel) maintains an electronic mail system, connected to the Internet, through which messages between employees and those outside the company can be sent and received, and permits its employees to make reasonable nonbusiness use of this system. On six occasions over almost two years, Kourosh Kenneth Hamidi, a former Intel employee, sent e-mails criticizing Intel's employment practices to numerous current employees on Intel's electronic mail system. Hamidi breached no computer security barriers in order to communicate with Intel employees. He offered to, and did, remove from his mailing list any recipient who so wished. Hamidi's communications to individual Intel employees caused neither physical damage nor functional disruption to the company's computers, nor did they at any time deprive Intel of the use of its computers. The contents of the messages, however, caused discussion among employees and managers.

On these facts, Intel brought suit, claiming that by communicating with its employees over the company's e-mail system Hamidi committed the tort of Hamidi from any further mailings. A divided Court of Appeal affirmed.

After reviewing the decisions analyzing unauthorized electronic contact with computer systems as potential trespasses to chattels, we conclude that under California law the tort does not encompass, and should not be extended to encompass, an electronic communication that neither damages the recipient computer system nor impairs its functioning. Such an electronic communication does not constitute an actionable trespass to personal property, i.e., the computer system, because it does not interfere with the possessor's use or possession of, or any other legally protected interest in, the personal property itself. (*See Zaslow v. Kroenert* (1946) 29 Cal.2d 541, 551, [176 P.2d 1]; *Ticketmaster Corp. v. Tickets.com, Inc.* (C.D. Cal., Aug. 10, 2000, No. 99CV7654) 2000 U.S. Dist. LEXIS 12987 at *17, 2000 WL 1887522, p. *4; Rest.2d *Torts*, § 218.) The consequential economic damage Intel claims to have suffered, i.e., loss of productivity caused by employees reading and reacting to Hamidi's messages and company efforts to block the messages, is not an injury to the company's interest in its computers -- which worked as intended and were unharmed by the communications -- any more than the personal distress caused by reading an unpleasant letter would be an injury to the recipient's mailbox, or the loss of privacy caused by an intrusive telephone call would be an injury to the recipient's telephone equipment.

Our conclusion does not rest on any special immunity for communications by electronic mail; we do not hold that messages transmitted through the Internet are exempt from the ordinary rules of tort liability. To the contrary, e-mail, like other forms of communication, may in some circumstances cause legally cognizable injury to the recipient or to third parties and may be actionable under various common law or statutory theories. Indeed, on facts somewhat similar to those here, a company or its employees might be able to plead causes of action for interference with prospective economic relations (*see Guillory v. Godfrey* (1955) 134 Cal. App. 2d 628, 630-632, [286 P.2d 474] [defendant berated customers and prospective customers of plaintiffs' cafe with disparaging and racist comments]), interference with contract (*see Blender v. Superior Court* (1942) 55 Cal. App. 2d 24, 25-27, [130 P.2d 179] [defendant made false statements about plaintiff to his employer, resulting in plaintiff's discharge]) or intentional infliction of emotional distress (*see Kiseskey v. Carpenters' Trust for So. California* (1983) 144 Cal. App. 3d 222, 229-230, [192 Cal. Rptr. 492] [agents of defendant union threatened life, health, and family of employer if he did not sign agreement with union].) And, of course, as with any other means of publication, third party subjects of e-mail communications may under appropriate facts make claims for defamation, publication of private facts, or other speech-based torts. (*See, e.g., Southridge Capital Management v. Lowry* (S.D.N.Y. 2002) 188 F. Supp. 2d 388, 394-396 [allegedly false statements in e-mail sent to several of plaintiff's clients support actions for defamation and interference with contract].) Intel's claim fails not because e-mail transmitted through the Internet enjoys unique immunity, but because the trespass to chattels tort -- unlike the causes of action just mentioned -- may not, in California, be proved without evidence of an injury to the plaintiff's personal property or legal interest therein.

Nor does our holding affect the legal remedies of Internet service providers (ISPs) against senders of unsolicited commercial bulk e-mail (UCE), also known as "spam." (*See Ferguson v. Friendfinders, Inc.* (2002) 94 Cal. App. 4th 1255, 1267, [115 Cal. Rptr. 2d 258].) A series of federal district court decisions, beginning with *CompuServe, Inc. v. Cyber Promotions, Inc.* (S.D. Ohio 1997) 962 F. Supp. 1015, has approved the use of trespass to chattels as a theory of spammers' liability to ISP's, based upon evidence that the vast quantities of mail sent by spammers both overburdened the ISP's own computers and made the entire computer system harder to use for recipients, the ISP's customers. (*See id. at* pp. 1022-1023.) In those cases, discussed in greater detail below, the underlying complaint was that the extraordinary *quantity* of UCE impaired the computer system's functioning. In the present case, the claimed injury is located in the disruption or distraction caused to recipients by the *contents* of the e-mail messages, an injury entirely separate from, and not directly affecting, the possession or value of personal property.

FACTUAL AND PROCEDURAL BACKGROUND

... Hamidi, a former Intel engineer, together with others, formed an organization named Former and Current Employees of Intel (FACE-Intel) to disseminate information and views critical of Intel's employment and personnel policies and practices. FACE-Intel maintained a Web site (which identified Hamidi as Webmaster and as the organization's spokesperson) containing such material. In addition, over a 21-month period Hamidi, on behalf of FACE-Intel, sent six mass e-mails to employee addresses on Intel's electronic mail system. The messages criticized Intel's employment practices, warned employees of the dangers those practices posed to their careers, suggested employees consider moving to other companies, solicited employees' participation in FACE-Intel, and urged employees to inform themselves further by visiting FACE-Intel's Web site. The messages stated that recipients could, by notifying the sender of their wishes, be removed from FACE-Intel's mailing list; Hamidi did not subsequently send messages to anyone who requested removal.

Each message was sent to thousands of addresses (as many as 35,000 according to FACE-Intel's Web site), though some messages were blocked by Intel before reaching employees. Intel's attempt to block internal transmission of the messages succeeded only in part; Hamidi later admitted he evaded blocking efforts by using different sending computers. When Intel, in March 1998, demanded in writing that Hamidi and FACE-Intel stop sending e-mails to Intel's computer system, Hamidi asserted the organization had a right to communicate with willing Intel employees; he sent a new mass mailing in September 1998.

The summary judgment record contains no evidence Hamidi breached Intel's computer security in order to obtain the recipient addresses for his messages; indeed, internal Intel memoranda show the company's management concluded no security breach had occurred.[1] Hamidi stated he created the recipient address list using an Intel directory on a floppy disk anonymously sent to him. Nor is there any evidence that the receipt or internal distribution of Hamidi's electronic messages damaged Intel's computer system or slowed or impaired its functioning. Intel did present uncontradicted evidence, however, that many employee recipients asked a company official to stop the messages and that staff time was consumed in attempts to block further messages from FACE-Intel. According to the FACE-Intel Web site, moreover, the messages had prompted discussions between "excited and nervous managers" and the company's human resources department. ...

... DISCUSSION.

I. Current California Tort Law

Dubbed by Prosser the "little brother of conversion," the tort of trespass to chattels allows recovery for interferences with possession of personal property "not sufficiently important to be classed as conversion, and so to compel the defendant to pay the full value of the thing with which he has interfered." (Prosser & Keeton, *Torts* (5th ed. 1984) § 14, pp. 85-86.)

Though not amounting to conversion, the defendant's interference must, to be actionable, have caused some injury to the chattel or to the plaintiff's rights in it. Under California law, trespass to chattels "lies where an intentional interference with the possession of personal property *has proximately caused injury*." (*Thrifty-Tel, Inc. v. Bezenek* (1996) 46 Cal. App. 4th 1559, 1566, [54 Cal. Rptr. 2d 468], italics added.) In cases of interference with possession of personal property not amounting to conversion, "the owner has a cause of action for trespass or case, *and may recover only the actual damages suffered by reason of the impairment of the property or the loss of its use*." (*Zaslow v. Kroenert, supra*, 29 Cal.2d at p. 551, italics added; *accord, Jordan v. Talbot* (1961) 55 Cal.2d 597, 610, [12 Cal. Rptr. 488, 361 P.2d 20].) In modern American law generally, "trespass remains as an occasional remedy for minor interferences, *resulting in some damage,* but not sufficiently serious or

---

[1] To the extent, therefore, that Justice Mosk suggests Hamidi breached the security of Intel's internal computer network by "circumventing" Intel's "security measures" and entering the company's "intranet," the evidence does not support such an implication. An "intranet" is "a network based on TCP/IP protocols (an internet) belonging to an organization, usually a corporation, accessible only by the organization's members, employees, or others with authorization." (<http://www.webopedia.com/TERM/i/intranet.html> [as of June 30, 2003].) Hamidi used only a part of Intel's computer network accessible to outsiders.

sufficiently important to amount to the greater tort" of conversion. (Prosser & Keeton, *Torts*, *supra*, § 15, p. 90, italics added.)

The Restatement, too, makes clear that some actual injury must have occurred in order for a trespass to chattels to be actionable. Under section 218 of the Restatement Second of *Torts*, dispossession alone, without further damages, is actionable (*See id.*, par (a) & com. d, pp. 420-421), but other forms of interference require some additional harm to the personal property or the possessor's interests in it. (*Id.*, pars. (b)-(d).) "The interest of a possessor of a chattel in its inviolability, unlike the similar interest of a possessor of land, is not given legal protection by an action for nominal damages for harmless intermeddlings with the chattel. In order that an actor who interferes with another's chattel may be liable, his conduct must affect some other and more important interest of the possessor. *Therefore, one who intentionally intermeddles with another's chattel is subject to liability only if his intermeddling is harmful to the possessor's materially valuable interest in the physical condition, quality, or value of the chattel, or if the possessor is deprived of the use of the chattel for a substantial time, or some other legally protected interest of the possessor is affected as stated in Clause (c).* Sufficient legal protection of the possessor's interest in the mere inviolability of his chattel is afforded by his privilege to use reasonable force to protect his possession against even harmless interference." (*Id.*, com. e, pp. 421-422, italics added.)

....[A]s Prosser explains, modern day trespass to chattels differs both from the original English writ and from the action for trespass to land: "Another departure from the original rule of the old writ of trespass concerns the necessity of some actual damage to the chattel before the action can be maintained. Where the defendant merely interferes without doing any harm -- as where, for example, he merely lays hands upon the plaintiff's horse, or sits in his car -- there has been a division of opinion among the writers, and a surprising dearth of authority. *By analogy to trespass to land there might be a technical tort in such a case.... Such scanty authority as there is, however, has considered that the dignitary interest in the inviolability of chattels, unlike that as to land, is not sufficiently important to require any greater defense than the privilege of using reasonable force when necessary to protect them. Accordingly it has been held that nominal damages will not be awarded, and that in the absence of any actual damage the action will not lie.*" (Prosser & Keeton, *Torts*, *supra*, § 14, p. 87, italics added, fns. omitted.)

Intel suggests that the requirement of actual harm does not apply here because it sought only injunctive relief, as protection from future injuries. But as Justice Kolkey, dissenting below, observed, "the fact the relief sought is injunctive does not excuse a showing of injury, whether actual or threatened." Indeed, in order to obtain injunctive relief the plaintiff must ordinarily show that the defendant's wrongful acts threaten to cause *irreparable* injuries, ones that cannot be adequately compensated in damages. (5 Witkin, *Cal. Procedure* (4th ed. 1997) Pleading, § 782, p. 239.)

Even in an action for trespass to real property, in which damage to the property is not an element of the cause of action, "the extraordinary remedy of injunction" cannot be invoked without showing the likelihood of irreparable harm. (*Mechanics' Foundry v. Ryall* (1888) 75 Cal. 601, 603, [17 P. 703]; *see Mendelson v. McCabe* (1904) 144 Cal. 230, 232-233, [77 P. 915] [injunction against trespass to land proper where continued trespasses threaten creation of prescriptive right and repetitive suits for damages would be inadequate remedy].)

A fortiori, to issue an injunction without a showing of likely irreparable injury in an action for trespass to chattels, in which injury to the personal property or the possessor's interest in it *is* an element of the action, would make little legal sense.

The dispositive issue in this case, therefore, is whether the undisputed facts demonstrate Hamidi's actions caused or threatened to cause damage to Intel's computer system, or injury to its rights in that personal property, such as to entitle Intel to judgment as a matter of law. To review, the undisputed evidence revealed no actual or threatened damage to Intel's computer hardware or software and no interference with its ordinary and intended operation. Intel was not dispossessed of its computers, nor did Hamidi's messages prevent Intel from using its computers for any measurable length of time. Intel presented no evidence its system was slowed or otherwise impaired by the burden of delivering Hamidi's electronic messages. Nor was there any evidence transmission of the messages imposed any marginal cost on the operation of Intel's computers. In sum, no evidence suggested that in sending messages through Intel's Internet connections and internal computer system Hamidi used the system in any manner in which it was not intended to function or impaired the system in any way. Nor does the evidence show the request of any employee to be removed from FACE-Intel's mailing list was not honored. The evidence did show, however, that some employees who found the messages unwelcome asked management to stop them and that Intel technical staff spent time and effort attempting to block the messages. A statement on the FACE-Intel Web site, moreover, could be taken as an admission that the messages had caused "excited and nervous managers" to discuss the matter with Intel's human resources department.

Relying on a line of decisions, most from federal district courts, applying the tort of trespass to chattels to various types of unwanted electronic contact between computers, Intel contends that, while its computers were not damaged by receiving Hamidi's messages, its interest in the "physical condition, quality or value" (Rest.2d *Torts*, § 218, com. e, p. 422) of the computers was harmed. We disagree. The cited line of decisions does not persuade us that the mere sending of electronic communications that assertedly cause injury only because of their contents constitutes an actionable trespass to a computer system through which the messages are transmitted. Rather, the decisions finding electronic contact to be a trespass to computer systems have generally involved some actual or threatened interference with the computers' functioning.

… That Intel does not claim the type of functional impact that spammers and robots have been alleged to cause is not surprising in light of the differences between Hamidi's activities and those of a commercial enterprise that uses sheer quantity of messages as its communications strategy. Though Hamidi sent thousands of copies of the same message on six occasions over 21 months, that number is minuscule compared to the amounts of mail sent by commercial operations. … The functional burden on Intel's computers, or the cost in time to individual recipients, of receiving Hamidi's occasional advocacy messages cannot be compared to the burdens and costs caused ISP's and their customers by the ever-rising deluge of commercial e-mail.

… Intel's theory would expand the tort of trespass to chattels to cover virtually any unconsented-to communication that, solely because of its content, is unwelcome to the recipient or intermediate transmitter. As the dissenting justice below explained, "'Damage' of this nature -- the distraction of reading or listening to an unsolicited communication -- is not within the scope of the injury against which the trespass-to-chattel tort protects, and indeed trivializes it. After all, 'the property interest protected by the old action of trespass was that of possession; and this has continued to affect the character of the action.' (Prosser & Keeton on *Torts*, *supra*, § 14, p. 87.) Reading an e-mail transmitted to equipment designed to receive it, in and of itself, does not affect the possessory interest in the equipment. Indeed, if a chattel's receipt of an electronic communication constitutes a trespass to that chattel, then not only are unsolicited telephone calls and faxes trespasses to chattel, but unwelcome radio waves and television signals also constitute a trespass to chattel every time the viewer inadvertently sees or hears the unwanted program." We agree. While unwelcome communications, electronic or otherwise, can cause a variety of injuries to economic relations, reputation and emotions, those interests are protected by other branches of tort law; in order to address them, we need not create a fiction of injury to the communication system.

Nor may Intel appropriately assert a *property* interest in its employees' time. ... Whatever interest Intel may have in preventing its employees from receiving disruptive communications, it is not an interest in personal property, and trespass to chattels is therefore not an action that will lie to protect it. Nor, finally, can the fact Intel staff spent time attempting to block Hamidi's messages be bootstrapped into an injury to Intel's possessory interest in its computers. ...

Intel connected its e-mail system to the Internet and permitted its employees to make use of this connection both for business and, to a reasonable extent, for their own purposes. In doing so, the company necessarily contemplated the employees' receipt of unsolicited as well as solicited communications from other companies and individuals. That some communications would, because of their contents, be unwelcome to Intel management was virtually inevitable. Hamidi did nothing but use the e-mail system for its intended purpose -- to communicate with employees. The system worked as designed, delivering the messages without any physical or functional harm or disruption. These occasional transmissions cannot reasonably be viewed as impairing the quality or value of Intel's computer system. We conclude, therefore, that Intel has not presented undisputed facts demonstrating an injury to its personal property, or to its legal interest in that property, that support, under California tort law, an action for trespass to chattels.

II. Proposed Extension of California Tort Law

We next consider whether California common law should be *extended* to cover, as a trespass to chattels, an otherwise harmless electronic communication whose contents are objectionable. We decline to so expand California law. Intel, of course, was not the recipient of Hamidi's messages, but rather the owner and possessor of computer servers used to relay the messages, and it bases this tort action on that ownership and possession. The property rule proposed is a rigid one, under which the sender of an electronic message would be strictly liable to the owner of equipment through which the communication passes -- here, Intel -- for any consequential injury flowing from the *contents* of the communication. ...

....[T]he metaphorical application of real property rules would not, by itself, transform a physically harmless electronic intrusion on a computer server into a trespass.

That is because, under California law, intangible intrusions on land, including electromagnetic transmissions, are not actionable as trespasses (though they may be as nuisances) unless they cause physical damage to the real property. (*San Diego Gas & Electric Co. v. Superior Court* (1996) 13 Cal.4th 893, 936-937, [55 Cal. Rptr. 2d 724, 920 P.2d 669].)

Since Intel does not claim Hamidi's electronically transmitted messages physically damaged its servers, it could not prove a trespass to land even were we to treat the computers as a type of real property. Some further extension of the conceit would be required, under which the electronic signals Hamidi sent would be recast as tangible intruders, perhaps as tiny messengers rushing through the "hallways" of Intel's computers and bursting out of employees' computers to read them Hamidi's missives. But such fictions promise more confusion than clarity in the law. ...

The plain fact is that computers, even those making up the Internet, are -- like such older communications equipment as telephones and fax machines -- personal property, not realty. Professor Epstein observes that "although servers may be moved in real space, they cannot be moved in cyberspace," because an Internet server must, to be useful, be accessible at a known address. But the same is true of the telephone: to be useful for incoming communication, the telephone must remain constantly linked to the same number (or, when the number is changed, the system must include some forwarding or notification capability, a qualification that also applies to computer addresses). Does this suggest that an unwelcome message delivered through a telephone or fax machine should be viewed as a trespass to a type of real property? We think not: As already discussed, the contents of a telephone communication may cause a variety of injuries and may be the basis for a variety of tort actions (e.g., defamation, intentional infliction of emotional distress, invasion of privacy), but the injuries are not to an interest in property, much less real property, and the appropriate tort is not trespass.

... Creating an absolute property right to exclude undesired communications from one's e-mail and Web servers might help force spammers to internalize the costs they impose on ISP's and their customers. But such a property rule might also create substantial new costs, to e-mail and e-commerce users and to society generally, in lost ease and openness of communication and in lost network benefits. In light of the unresolved controversy, we would be acting rashly to adopt a rule treating computer servers as real property for purposes of trespass law.

The Legislature has already adopted detailed regulations governing UCE. (Bus. & Prof. Code, §§ 17538.4, 17538.45; *see generally Ferguson v. Friendfinders, Inc.*, *supra*, 94 Cal. App. 4th 1255.) It may see fit in the future also to regulate noncommercial e-mail, such as that sent by Hamidi, or other kinds of unwanted contact between computers on the Internet.... But we are not persuaded that these perceived problems call at present for judicial creation of a rigid property rule of computer server inviolability. We therefore decline to create an exception, covering Hamidi's unwanted electronic messages to Intel employees, to the general rule that a trespass to chattels is not actionable if it does not involve actual or threatened injury to the personal property or to the possessor's legally protected interest in the personal property. No such injury having been shown on the undisputed facts, Intel was not entitled to summary judgment in its favor.

III. Constitutional Considerations

Because we conclude no trespass to chattels was shown on the summary judgment record, making the injunction improper on common law grounds, we need not address at length the dissenters' constitutional arguments. A few clarifications are nonetheless in order.

Justice Mosk asserts that this case involves only "a private entity seeking to enforce private trespass rights." But the injunction here was issued by a state court.

While a private refusal to transmit another's electronic speech generally does not implicate the First Amendment, because no governmental action is involved (*see Cyber Promotions, Inc. v. America Online, Inc.* (E.D. Penn. 1996) 948 F. Supp. 436, 441-445 [spammer could not force private ISP to carry its messages]), the use of government power, whether in enforcement of a statute or ordinance *or by an award of damages or an injunction in a private lawsuit*, is state action that must comply with First Amendment limits. (*Cohen v. Cowles Media Co.* (1991) 501 U.S. 663, 668, [115 L.Ed.2d 586, 111 S. Ct. 2513]; *NAACP v. Claiborne Hardware Co.* (1982) 458 U.S. 886, 916, fn.51, [73 L.Ed.2d 1215, 102 S. Ct. 3409]; *New York Times v. Sullivan* (1964) 376 U.S. 254, 265, [11 L.Ed.2d 686, 84 S. Ct. 710].) Nor does the nonexistence of a "constitutional right to trespass" (dis. opn. of Mosk, J.) make an injunction in this case *per se* valid.

Unlike, for example, the trespasser-to-land defendant in *Church of Christ in Hollywood v. Superior Court* (2002) 99 Cal. App. 4th 1244, [121 Cal. Rptr. 2d 810], Hamidi himself had no tangible presence on Intel property, instead speaking from his own home through his computer. He no more invaded Intel's property than does a protester holding a sign or shouting through a bullhorn outside corporate headquarters, posting a letter through the mail, or telephoning to complain of a corporate practice. (*See Madsen v. Women's Health Center* (1994) 512 U.S. 753, 765, [129 L.Ed.2d 593, 114 S. Ct. 2516] [injunctions restraining such speakers must "burden no more speech than necessary to serve a significant government interest"].)

Justice Brown relies upon a constitutional "right not to listen," rooted in the listener's "personal autonomy" (dis. opn. of Brown), as compelling a remedy against Hamidi's messages, which she asserts were sent to "unwilling" listeners. Even assuming a corporate entity could under some circumstances claim such a personal right, here the intended and actual recipients of Hamidi's messages were individual Intel employees, rather than Intel itself. The record contains no evidence Hamidi sent messages to any employee who notified him such messages were unwelcome. In any event, such evidence would, under the dissent's rationale of a right not to listen, support only a *narrow* injunction aimed at protecting individual recipients who gave notice of their rejection. (*See Bolger v. Youngs Drug Products Corp.* (1983) 463 U.S. 60, 72, [77 L.Ed.2d 469, 103 S. Ct. 2875] [government may not act on behalf of all addressees by generally prohibiting mailing of materials related to contraception, where those recipients who may be offended can simply ignore and discard the materials]; *Martin v. City of Struthers* (1943) 319 U.S. 141, 144, [87 L.Ed. 1313, 63 S. Ct. 862] [anti-canvassing ordinance improperly "substitutes the judgment of the community for the judgment of the individual householder"]; cf. *Rowan v. U.S. Post Office Dept.* (1970) 397 U.S. 728, 736, [25 L.Ed.2d 736, 90 S. Ct. 1484] ["householder" may exercise "individual autonomy" by refusing delivery of offensive mail].) The principal of a right not to listen, founded in personal autonomy, cannot justify the sweeping injunction issued here against all communication to Intel addresses, for such a right, logically, can be exercised only by, or at the behest of, the recipient himself or herself.

DISPOSITION

The judgment of the Court of Appeal is reversed.

MOSK, J., dissenting

The majority hold that the California tort of trespass to chattels does not encompass the use of expressly unwanted electronic mail that causes no physical damage or impairment to the recipient's computer system. They also conclude that because a computer system is not like real property, the rules of trespass to real property are also inapplicable to the circumstances in this case. Finally, they suggest that an injunction to preclude mass, noncommercial, unwelcome e-mails may offend the interests of free communication.

I respectfully disagree and would affirm the trial court's decision. In my view, the repeated transmission of bulk e-mails by appellant Kourosh Kenneth Hamidi (Hamidi) to the employees of Intel Corporation (Intel) on its proprietary confidential e-mail lists, despite Intel's demand that he cease such activities, constituted an actionable trespass to chattels. The majority fail to distinguish open communication in the public "commons" of the Internet from unauthorized intermeddling on a private, proprietary intranet. Hamidi is not communicating in the equivalent of a town square or of an unsolicited "junk" mailing through the United States Postal Service. His action, in crossing from the public Internet into a private intranet, is more like intruding into a private office mailroom, commandeering the mail cart, and dropping off unwanted broadsides on 30,000 desks. Because Intel's security measures have been circumvented by Hamidi, the majority leave Intel, which has exercised all reasonable self-help efforts, with no recourse unless he causes a malfunction or systems "crash." Hamidi's repeated intrusions did more than merely "prompt[] discussions between 'excited and nervous managers' and the company's human resource department" (maj. opn.); they also constituted a misappropriation of Intel's private computer system contrary to its intended use and against Intel's wishes.

The law of trespass to chattels has not universally been limited to physical damage. I believe it is entirely consistent to apply that legal theory to these circumstances -- that is, when a proprietary computer system is being used contrary to its owner's purposes and expressed desires, and self-help has been ineffective. Intel correctly expects protection from an intruder who misuses its proprietary system, its nonpublic directories, and its supposedly controlled connection to the Internet to achieve his bulk mailing objectives -- incidentally, without even having to pay postage.

I.

Intel maintains an intranet -- a proprietary computer network -- as a tool for transacting and managing its business, both internally and for external business communications.

The network and its servers constitute a tangible entity that has value in terms of the costs of its components and its function in enabling and enhancing the productivity and efficiency of Intel's business operations. Intel has established costly security measures to protect the integrity of its system, including policies about use, proprietary internal e-mail addresses that it does not release to the public for use outside of company business, and a gateway for blocking unwanted electronic mail -- a so-called firewall.

The Intel computer usage guidelines, which are promulgated for its employees, state that the computer system is to be "used as a resource in conducting business. Reasonable personal use is permitted, but employees are reminded that these resources are the property of Intel and all information on these resources is also the property of Intel." Examples of personal use that would not be considered reasonable expressly include "use that adversely affects productivity." Employee e-mail communications are neither private nor confidential.

Hamidi, a former Intel employee who had sued Intel and created an organization to disseminate negative information about its employment practices, sent bulk electronic mail on six occasions to as many as 35,000 Intel employees on its proprietary computer system, using Intel's confidential employee e-mail lists and adopting a series of different origination addresses and encoding strategies to elude Intel's blocking efforts. He refused to stop when requested by Intel to do so, asserting that he would ignore its demands: "I don't care. I have grown deaf." Intel sought injunctive relief, alleging that the disruptive effect of the bulk electronic mail, including expenses from administrative and management personnel, damaged its interest in the proprietary nature of its network.

The trial court, in its order granting summary judgment and a permanent injunction, made the following pertinent findings regarding Hamidi's transmission of bulk electronic mail: "Intel has requested that Hamidi stop sending the messages, but Hamidi has refused, and has employed surreptitious means to circumvent Intel's efforts to block entry of his messages into Intel's system.... The e-mail system is dedicated for use in conducting business, including communications between Intel employees and its customers and vendors. Employee e-mail addresses are not published for use outside company business.... The intrusion by Hamidi into the Intel e-mail system has resulted in the expenditure of company resources to seek to block his mailings and to address employee concerns about the mailings. Given Hamidi's evasive techniques to avoid blocking, the self help remedy available to Intel is ineffective." The trial court concluded that "the evidence establishes (without dispute) that Intel has been injured by diminished employee productivity and in devoting company resources to blocking efforts and to addressing employees about Hamidi's e-mails." The trial court further found that the "massive" intrusions "impaired the value to Intel of its e-mail system."

The majority agree that an impairment of Intel's system would result in an action for trespass to chattels, but find that Intel suffered no injury. As did the trial court, I conclude that the undisputed evidence establishes that Intel was substantially harmed by the costs of efforts to block the messages and diminished employee productivity. Additionally, the injunction did not affect Hamidi's ability to communicate with Intel employees by other means; he apparently continues to maintain a Web site to publicize his messages concerning the company. Furthermore, I believe that the trial court and the Court of Appeal correctly determined that the tort of trespass to chattels applies in these circumstances.

... The Restatement explains that the rationale for requiring harm for trespass to a chattel but not for trespass to land is the availability and effectiveness of self-help in the case of trespass to a chattel. "Sufficient legal protection of the possessor's interest in the mere inviolability of his chattel is afforded by his privilege to use reasonable force to protect his possession against even harmless interference." (Rest.2d *Torts*, § 218, com. (e), p. 422.) Obviously, "force" is not available to prevent electronic trespasses. As shown by Intel's inability to prevent Hamidi's intrusions, self-help is not an adequate alternative to injunctive relief.

The common law tort of trespass to chattels does not require physical disruption to the chattel. It also may apply when there is impairment to the "quality" or "value" of the chattel. (Rest.2d *Torts*, § 218, subd. (b), p. 420; *see also id.*, com. (e), pp. 421-422 [liability if "intermeddling is harmful to the possessor's materially valuable interest in the physical condition, quality, or value of the chattel"].) Moreover, as we held in *Zaslow v. Kroenert*

(1946) 29 Cal.2d 541, 551, [176 P.2d 1], it also applies "where the conduct complained of does not amount to a substantial interference with possession or the right thereto, but consists of intermeddling with or use of or damages to the personal property."

Here, Hamidi's deliberate and continued intermeddling, and threatened intermeddling, with Intel's proprietary computer system for his own purposes that were hostile to Intel, certainly impaired the quality and value of the system as an internal business device for Intel and forced Intel to incur costs to try to maintain the security and integrity of its server -- efforts that proved ineffective. These included costs incurred to mitigate injuries that had already occurred. It is not a matter of "bootstrapping" (maj. opn.) to consider those costs a damage to Intel. Indeed, part of the value of the proprietary computer system is the ability to exclude intermeddlers from entering it for significant uses that are disruptive to its owner's business operations.

If Intel, a large business with thousands of former employees, is unable to prevent Hamidi from continued intermeddling, it is not unlikely that other outsiders who obtain access to its proprietary electronic mail addresses would engage in similar conduct, further reducing the value of, and perhaps debilitating, the computer system as a business productivity mechanism. Employees understand that a firewall is in place and expect that the messages they receive are from senders permitted by the corporation. Violation of this expectation increases the internal disruption caused by messages that circumvent the company's attempt to exclude them. The time that each employee must spend to evaluate, delete or respond to the message, when added up, constitutes an amount of compensated time that translates to quantifiable financial damage.[3]

All of these costs to protect the integrity of the computer system and to deal with the disruptive effects of the transmissions and the expenditures attributable to employee time, constitute damages sufficient to establish the existence of a trespass to chattels, even if the computer system was not overburdened to the point of a "crash" by the bulk electronic mail.

The several courts that have applied the tort of trespass to chattels to deliberate intermeddling with proprietary computer systems have, for the most part, used a similar analysis. Thus, the court in *CompuServe Inc. v. Cyber Promotions, Inc.* (S.D. Ohio 1997) 962 F. Supp. 1015, 1022, applied the Restatement to conclude that mass mailings and evasion

---

[3] As the recent spate of articles on "spam" -- unsolicited bulk e-mail -- suggests, the effects on business of such unwanted intrusions are not trivial. "Spam is not just a nuisance. It absorbs bandwidth and overwhelms Internet service providers. Corporate tech staffs labor to deploy filtering technology to protect their networks. The cost is now widely estimated (though all such estimates are largely guesswork) at billions of dollars a year. The social costs are immeasurable.... 'Spam has become the organized crime of the Internet.' ... 'More and more it's becoming a systems and engineering and networking problem.'" (Gleick, *Tangled Up in Spam*, N.Y. Times (Feb. 9, 2003) magazine p. 1 [as of June 30, 2003]; *see also* Cooper & Shogren, *U.S., States Turn Focus to Curbing Spam*, L.A. Times (May 1, 2003) p. A21, col. 2 ["Businesses are losing money with every moment that employees spend deleting"]; Turley, *Congress Must Send Spammers a Message*, L.A. Times (Apr. 21, 2003) p. B13, col. 5 ["Spam now costs American businesses about $9 billion a year in lost productivity and screening"]; Taylor, *Spam's Big Bang!* (June 16, 2003) *Time Magazine*, at p. 51 ["The time we spend deleting or defeating spam costs an estimated $8.9 billion a year in lost productivity"].) But the occasional spam addressed to particular employees does not pose nearly the same threat of impaired value as the concerted bulk mailings into one e-mail system at issue here, which mailings were sent to thousands of employees with the express purpose of disrupting business as usual.

of the server's filters diminished the value of the mail processing computer equipment to CompuServe "even though it is not physically damaged by defendant's conduct." The inconvenience to users of the system as a result of the mass messages "decreased the utility of CompuServe's e-mail service" and was actionable as a trespass to chattels. (*Id. at* p. 1023.)

The court in *America Online, Inc. v. IMS* (E.D. Va. 1998) 24 F. Supp. 2d 548, on facts similar to those in the present case, also applied the Restatement in a trespass to chattels claim. There, defendant sent unauthorized e-mails to America Online's computer system, persisting after receiving notice to desist and causing the company "to spend technical resources and staff time to 'defend' its computer system and its membership" against the unwanted messages. (*Id. at* p. 549.) The company was not required to show that its computer system was overwhelmed or suffered a diminution in performance; mere use of the system by the defendant was sufficient to allow the plaintiff to prevail on the trespass to chattels claim. …

These cases stand for the simple proposition that owners of computer systems, like owners of other private property, have a right to prevent others from using their property against their interests. That principle applies equally in this case. By his repeated intermeddling, Hamidi converted Intel's private employee e-mail system into a tool for harming productivity and disrupting Intel's workplace. Intel attempted to put a stop to Hamidi's intrusions by increasing its electronic screening measures and by requesting that he desist. Only when self-help proved futile, devolving into a potentially endless joust between attempted prevention and circumvention, did Intel request and obtain equitable relief in the form of an injunction to prevent further threatened injury.

The majority suggest that Intel is not entitled to injunctive relief because it chose to allow its employees access to e-mail through the Internet and because Hamidi has apparently told employees that he will remove them from his mailing list if they so request. They overlook the proprietary nature of Intel's intranet system; Intel's system is not merely a conduit for messages to its employees. As the owner of the computer system, it is Intel's request that Hamidi stop that must be respected. The fact that, like most large businesses, Intel's intranet includes external e-mail access for essential business purposes does not logically mean, as the majority suggest, that Intel has forfeited the right to determine who has access to its system. Its intranet is not the equivalent of a common carrier or public communications licensee that would be subject to requirements to provide service and access. Just as Intel can, and does, regulate the use of its computer system by its employees, it should be entitled to control its use by outsiders and to seek injunctive relief when self-help fails.

The majority also propose that Intel has sufficient avenues for legal relief outside of trespass to chattels, such as interference with prospective economic relations, interference with contract, intentional infliction of emotional distress, and defamation; Hamidi urges that an action for nuisance is more appropriate. Although other causes of action may under certain circumstances also apply to Hamidi's conduct, the remedy based on trespass to chattels is the most efficient and appropriate. It simply requires Hamidi to stop the unauthorized use of property without regard to the content of the transmissions. Unlike trespass to chattels, the other potential causes of action suggested by the majority and Hamidi would require an evaluation of the transmissions' content and, in the case of a nuisance action, for example, would involve questions of degree and value judgments based on competing interests. (*See Hellman v. La Cumbre Golf & Country Club* (1992) 6 Cal. App. 4th 1224, 1230-1231, [8 Cal. Rptr. 2d 293]; 11 Witkin, *Summary of Cal. Law* (9th ed. 1990) Equity, § 153, p. 833; Rest.2d *Torts*, § 840D).

II.

As discussed above, I believe that existing legal principles are adequate to support Intel's request for injunctive relief. But even if the injunction in this case amounts to an extension of the traditional tort of trespass to chattels, this is one of those cases in which, as Justice Cardozo suggested, "the creative element in the judicial process finds its opportunity and power" in the development of the law. (Cardozo, *Nature of the Judicial Process* (1921) p. 165.)[5]

The law has evolved to meet economic, social, and scientific changes in society. The industrial revolution, mass production, and new transportation and communication systems all required the adaptation and evolution of legal doctrines.

The age of computer technology and cyberspace poses new challenges to legal principles. As this court has said, "the so-called Internet revolution has spawned a host of new legal issues as courts have struggled to apply traditional legal frameworks to this new communication medium." (*Pavlovich v. Superior Court* (2002) 29 Cal.4th 262, 266, [127 Cal. Rptr. 2d 329, 58 P.3d 2].) The court must now grapple with proprietary interests, privacy, and expression arising out of computer-related disputes. Thus, in this case the court is faced with "that balancing of judgment, that testing and sorting of considerations of analogy and logic and utility and fairness" that Justice Cardozo said he had "been trying to describe." (Cardozo, *Nature of the Judicial Process, supra,* at pp. 165-166.) Additionally, this is a case in which equitable relief is sought. As Bernard Witkin has written, "equitable relief is *flexible and expanding*, and the theory that 'for every wrong there is a remedy' [Civ. Code, § 3523] may be invoked by equity courts to justify the invention of new methods of relief for new types of wrongs." (11 Witkin, *Summary of Cal. Law, supra,* Equity, § 3, p. 681.) That the Legislature has dealt with some aspects of commercial unsolicited bulk e-mail (Bus. & Prof. Code, §§ 17538.4, 17538.45) should not inhibit the application of common law tort principles to deal with e-mail transgressions not covered by the legislation. (*Cf. California Assn. of Health Facilities v. Department of Health Services* (1997) 16 Cal.4th 284, 297, [65 Cal. Rptr. 2d 872, 940 P.2d 323]; *I.E. Associates v. Safeco Title Ins. Co.* (1985) 39 Cal.3d 281, 285, [216 Cal. Rptr. 438, 702 P.2d 596].)

Before the computer, a person could not easily cause significant disruption to another's business or personal affairs through methods of communication without significant cost. With the computer, by a mass mailing, one person can at no cost disrupt, damage, and interfere with another's property, business, and personal interests. Here, the law should allow Intel to protect its computer-related property from the unauthorized, harmful, free use by intruders.

III.

As the Court of Appeal observed, connecting one's driveway to the general system of roads does not invite demonstrators to use the property as a public forum. Not mindful of this precept, the majority blur the distinction between public and private computer networks in the interest of "ease and openness of communication." (Maj. opn.) By upholding Intel's right to exercise self-help to restrict Hamidi's bulk e-mails, they concede that he did not have

---

[5] "It is revolting to have no better reason for a rule of law than that so it was laid down in the time of Henry IV." (Holmes, *The Path of the Law* (1897) 10 Harv. L. Rev. 457, 469.)

a right to send them through Intel's proprietary system. Yet they conclude that injunctive relief is unavailable to Intel because it connected its e-mail system to the Internet and thus, "necessarily contemplated" unsolicited communications to its employees. (Maj. opn.) Their exposition promotes unpredictability in a manner that could be as harmful to open communication as it is to property rights. It permits Intel to block Hamidi's e-mails entirely, but offers no recourse if he succeeds in breaking through its security barriers, unless he physically or functionally degrades the system.

By making more concrete damages a requirement for a remedy, the majority has rendered speech interests dependent on the impact of the e-mails. The sender will never know when or if the mass e-mails sent by him (and perhaps others) will use up too much space or cause a crash in the recipient system, so as to fulfill the majority's requirement of damages. Thus, the sender is exposed to the risk of liability because of the possibility of damages. If, as the majority suggest, such a risk will deter "ease and openness of communication" (maj. opn.), the majority's formulation does not eliminate such deterrence. Under the majority's position, the lost freedom of communication still exists. In addition, a business could never reliably invest in a private network that can only be kept private by constant vigilance and inventiveness, or by simply shutting off the Internet, thus limiting rather than expanding the flow of information.

Moreover, Intel would have less incentive to allow employees reasonable use of its equipment to send and receive personal e-mails if such allowance is justification for preventing restrictions on unwanted intrusions into its computer system. I believe the best approach is to clearly delineate private from public networks and identify as a trespass to chattels the kind of intermeddling involved here.

... Finally, with regard to alleged constitutional free speech concerns raised by Hamidi and others, this case involves a private entity seeking to enforce private rights against trespass. Unlike the majority, I have concluded that Hamidi did invade Intel's property. His actions constituted a trespass -- in this case a trespass to chattels. There is no federal or state constitutional right to trespass. (*Adderley v. Florida* (1966) 385 U.S. 39, 47, [17 L.Ed.2d 149, 87 S. Ct. 242] ["Nothing in the Constitution of the United States prevents Florida from even-handed enforcement of its general trespass statute...."]; *Church of Christ in Hollywood v. Superior Court* (2002) 99 Cal. App. 4th 1244, 1253-1254, [121 Cal. Rptr. 2d 810] [affirming a restraining order preventing former church member from entering church property: "[the United States Supreme Court] has never held that a trespasser or an uninvited guest may exercise general rights of free speech on property privately owned"]; *see also CompuServe Inc. v. Cyber Promotions, Inc., supra,* 962 F. Supp. at p. 1026 ["the mere judicial enforcement of neutral trespass laws by the private owner of property does not alone render it a state actor"]; *Cyber Promotions, Inc. v. America Online, Inc.* (E.D. Pa. 1996) 948 F. Supp. 436, 456 ["a private company such as Cyber simply does not have the unfettered right under the First Amendment to invade AOL's private property...."].) Accordingly, the cases cited by the majority regarding restrictions on speech, not trespass, are not applicable. Nor does the connection of Intel's e-mail system to the Internet transform it into a public forum any more than any connection between private and public properties. Moreover, as noted above, Hamidi had adequate alternative means for communicating with Intel employees so that an injunction would not, under any theory, constitute a free speech violation. (*Lloyd Corp. v. Tanner* (1972) 407 U.S. 551, 568-569, [33 L.Ed.2d 131, 92 S. Ct. 2219].)

IV.

The trial court granted an injunction to prevent threatened injury to Intel. That is the purpose of an injunction. (*Ernst & Ernst v. Carlson* (1966) 247 Cal. App. 2d 125, 128, [55 Cal. Rptr. 626].) Intel should not be helpless in the face of repeated and threatened abuse and contamination of its private computer system. The undisputed facts, in my view, rendered Hamidi's conduct legally actionable. Thus, the trial court's decision to grant a permanent injunction was not "a clear abuse of discretion" that may be "disturbed on appeal." (*Shapiro v. San Diego City Council* (2002) 96 Cal. App. 4th 904, 912, [117 Cal. Rptr. 2d 631]; *see also City of Vernon v. Central Basin Mun. Water Dist.* (1999) 69 Cal. App. 4th 508, 516, [81 Cal. Rptr. 2d 650] [in an appeal of summary judgment, the trial court's decision to deny a permanent injunction was "governed by the abuse of discretion standard of review"].)

The injunction issued by the trial court simply required Hamidi to refrain from further trespassory conduct, drawing no distinction based on the content of his e-mails. Hamidi remains free to communicate with Intel employees and others outside the walls -- both physical and electronic -- of the company.

For these reasons, I respectfully dissent.

* * * * *

Did Intel suffer injury beyond the "affront to its dignitary interest in ownership but tangible economic loss"? *Intel Corp. v. Hamidi,* 30 Cal. 4th 1342, 1385, 71 P.3d 296, 322, 1 Cal. Rptr. 3d 32, 66 (Cal. 2003) (Brown, J., dissenting). Judge Brown, dissenting, considered the economic aspects of the relationship between property rights and free speech interests:

> Those who have contempt for grubby commerce and reverence for the rarified heights of intellectual discourse may applaud today's decision, but even the flow of ideas will be curtailed if the right to exclude is denied. As the *Napster* controversy revealed, creative individuals will be less inclined to develop intellectual property if they cannot limit the terms of its transmission. Similarly, if online newspapers cannot charge for access, they will be unable to pay the journalists and editorialists who generate ideas for public consumption.
>
> This connection between the property right to objects and the property right to ideas and speech is not novel. James Madison observed, "a man's land, or merchandize, or money is called his property." Likewise, "a man has a property in his opinions and the free communication of them." Accordingly, "freedom of speech and property rights were seen simply as different aspects of an indivisible concept of liberty."
>
> The principles of both personal liberty and social utility should counsel us to usher the common law of property into the digital age.

Id., 30 Cal. 4th at 1385, 71 P.3d at 325-26, 1 Cal. Rptr. 3d at 66 (citing (Madison, *Property,* Nat. Gazette (Mar. 27, 1792), *reprinted in The Papers of James Madison* (Robert A. Rutland, *et al.* eds. 1983) p. 266, *quoted in* McGinnis, *The Once and Future Property-Based Vision of the First Amendment* (1996), 63 U. Chi. L. Rev. 49, 63, 65.))

Some have argued that a rule of computer server inviolability will "create 'the right social result'" through the formation or extension of a market in computer-to-computer access. *Id.,* 30 Cal. 4th at 1362, 71 P.3d at 310, 1 Cal. Rptr. 3d at 48 (quoting Professor Richard A. Epstein). Under this theory, "[i]n most circumstances, ... companies with computers on the Internet will continue to authorize transmission of information through e-mail, Web site searching, and page linking because they benefit by that open access. When a Web site owner does deny access to a particular sending, searching, or linking computer, a system of 'simple one-on-one negotiations' will arise to provide the necessary individual licenses." *Id.,* 30 Cal. 4th at 1362, 71 P.3d at 310, 1 Cal. Rptr. at 48-49.

Others argue that a property rule of server inviolability will require Internet users to secure permission from, among others, those who own servers, before communicating. A marked reduction in free electronic communication could result if computer owners through which electronic messages pass were entitled to impose restrictions. *See id.* (citing Professor Mark Lemley). "Web site linking ...'would exist at the sufferance of the linked-to party, because a Web user who followed a "disapproved" link would be trespassing on the plaintiff's server, just as sending an e-mail is trespass under the [lower] court's theory.'" *Id.,* 30 Cal. 4th at 1363, 71 P.3d at 310, 1 Cal. Rptr. at 49.

Some commentators have concluded that "[a]lthough *Intel v. Hamidi* may appear to reverse what some have characterized as a growing trend toward the liberalization of the trespass to chattels tort in the Internet context, it does not significantly change the law. The majority opinion purported simply to affirm the requirement, applied in previous Internet trespass cases, that there either must be physical damage or diminished capacity, or significantly, the potential for such damage, to the plaintiff's computer hardware or software." Bruce P. Keller and Robert D. Carroll, *Electronic Trespass Requires Physical, Not Economic, Injury,* MLRC MediaLawLetter (July 2003), at 46, 48. Others viewed the appellate court's decision as sound: "'This wasn't comparable to Mr. Hamidi standing outside Intel's property and shouting at employees using a bullhorn. It was as though he took Intel's bullhorn to do it.'" Jill Andresky Fraser, *Fighting for the Right to Communicate,* N.Y. Times, July 13, 2003, § 3 at 1 (quoting Professor Epstein).

In the wake of the California Supreme Court's decision, a Congressman indicated that he planned to introduce legislation to overturn the decision. "'Trespassing is trespassing, whether it's on land or on a computer server,'" he said. *See* Declan McCullagh, *Lawmaker Slams Bulk E-Mail Ruling,* CNet News.com (July 9, 2003), *available at* <http://news.com.com/2100-1028_3-1024339.html> (quoting U.S. Representative Christopher Cox). Federal legislation regulating spam was enacted in 2003. *See* Supplement *infra* at 318.

* * * * *

Notes and Questions

1. Will the implementation of technological filters likely result in the privatization of Internet access? What are the implications for speech from a defense of consent to a trespass to chattels case? Would Intel likely have brought suit against Hamidi if his messages lauded Intel's products or human resources practices? Are extant causes of action, such as those grounded in defamation and product disparagement, adequate to protect Intel's interests?

2. If a company's server has a very large capacity, would it suffer less harm from spam? Should the size of the server be a factor in determining the cognizability of a trespass to chattels tort or a factor in determining the quantity of any damages awarded?

3. Is there a difference between sending unwanted commercial bulk e-mail message and placing unsolicited telephone calls to the employees of a company or sending unsolicited marketing materials through the post? Would the company that employees the recipients have a cognizable trespass to chattels claim in all circumstances?

4. "Spim" refers to spam-type messages that are conveyed over instant messaging. Spim often includes a link to a web-site that the sender is trying to market. *See generally Spim, Internet.com Webopedia, available at* <http://www.webopedia.com/TERM/s/spim.html>. "Spit" refers to spam over Internet telephony. *See generally Spit,* Internet.com Webopedia, *available at* <http://www.webopedia.com/TERM/s/spit.html>.

* * * * *

SCHOOL OF VISUAL ARTS and LAURIE PEARLBERG,
Plaintiffs
v.
DIANE KUPREWICZ and JOHN DOES 1-100, Defendants

Supreme Court of New York, New York County

No. 115172-03, 3 Misc. 3d 278, 771 N.Y.S.2d 804

December 22, 2003

In this action, plaintiffs School of Visual Arts ("SVA") and Laurie Pearlberg, SVA's Director of Human Resources, contend that defendant Diane Kuprewicz, a former employee at SVA, engaged in a campaign of unlawful harassment against plaintiffs. Specifically, plaintiffs allege that Kuprewicz posted two false job listings on Craigslist.com, an internet website, stating that SVA was seeking applications for Pearlberg's position, which was not in fact vacant. These job postings, which contain accurate contact information for the purported position and otherwise appear legitimate, direct applicants to send a resume and cover letter to Pearlberg's supervisor at SVA. Plaintiffs further contend that Kuprewicz sent an e-mail to SVA's human resources department's e-mail address containing a similar job listing for Pearlberg's position, formatted to appear as if it were posted at Monster.com, a legitimate website for employment listings.[1]

Plaintiffs also allege that Kuprewicz provided Pearlberg's SVA e-mail address to various pornographic websites which resulted in Pearlberg's receipt of large volumes of unwanted sexually explicit e-mails. Similarly, plaintiffs maintain that Kuprewicz was responsible for Pearlberg's receipt, by regular mail at her work address, of unwanted catalogs offering pornographic materials. Finally, plaintiffs contend that Kuprewicz sent Pearlberg a number of "electronic cards" at her SVA e-mail address. Several of these cards were pornographic in

---

[1] It is conceded that no such job posting ever appeared on Monster.com.

nature, and one was purportedly sent by SVA's Associate Human Resources Director. Plaintiffs' complaint [includes a cause of action grounded in] trespass to chattels....

... To establish a trespass to chattels, SVA must prove that Kuprewicz intentionally, and without justification or consent, physically interfered with the use and enjoyment of personal property in SVA's possession, and that SVA was harmed thereby. PJI 3:9. Thus, one who intentionally interferes with another's chattel is liable only if there results in harm to "the [owner's] materially valuable interest in the physical condition, quality, or value of the chattel, or if the [owner] is deprived of the use of the chattel for a substantial time." Restatement (Second) of *Torts* § 218, com. e. Furthermore, to sustain this cause of action, the defendant must act with the intention of interfering with the property or with knowledge that such interference is substantially certain to result. *Buckeye Pipeline Co., Inc. v. Congel-Hazard, Inc.,* 41 A.D.2d 590 (4th Dept. 1973); 2 NY PJI2d 86 (2003).

In its complaint, SVA alleges that Kuprewicz caused "large volumes" of unsolicited job applications and pornographic e-mails to be sent to SVA and Pearlberg by way of SVA's computer system, without their consent. The complaint further alleges that these unsolicited e-mails have "depleted hard disk space, drained processing power, and adversely affected other system resources on SVA's computer system." The Court concludes that accepting these factual allegations as true, SVA has sufficiently stated a cause of action for trespass to chattels, and has alleged facts constituting each element of this claim. *See, e.g., CompuServe, Inc. v. Cyber Promotions, Inc.,* 962 F. Supp. 1015 (S.D. Ohio 1997) (sending unsolicited commercial bulk e-mail states claim for trespass to chattels where it was shown that processing power and disk space were adversely affected); *Hotmail* Corp. *v. Van$ Money Pie, Inc.,* 1998 U.S. Dist. LEXIS 10729 (N.D. Cal., Apr. 16, 1998) (plaintiff likely to prevail on trespass to chattels claim upon showing that defendant's unsolicited e-mails filled up plaintiff's computer storage space); *America Online, Inc. v. IMS,* 24 F. Supp. 2d 548 (E.D. Va. 1998); *America Online, Inc. v. LCGM, Inc.,* 46 F. Supp. 2d 444 (E.D.Va. 1998). Thus, Kuprewicz's motion to dismiss SVA's claim for common law trespass to chattels must be denied.

Intel Corporation v. Hamidi, 30 Cal. 4th 1342, 1 Cal. Rptr. 3d 32, 71 P.3d 296 (2003), upon which Kuprewicz relies, does not require a contrary result. In that case, the defendant's e-mail communications "caused neither physical damage nor functional disruption to the [plaintiff's] computers, nor did they at any time deprive [the plaintiff] of the use of its computers." 30 Cal. 4th at 1346. Thus, the court held that in the absence of any actual damage, the tort of trespass to chattels did not lie. Here, to the contrary, SVA's complaint alleges that such physical damage occurred so as to sustain the trespass claim. SVA maintains that Kuprewicz's conduct is "particularly intrusive" because of the substance, content and nature of the unsolicited e-mails, *i.e.,* pornographic material. However, this Court's decision to sustain the trespass to chattels claim is not based upon the content of the e-mails, but rather, is predicated upon plaintiffs' allegation that its receipt of large volumes of e-mails have caused significant detrimental effects on SVA's computer systems. It is important to note that by this decision, the Court does not hold that the mere sending of unsolicited e-mail communications will automatically subject the sender to tort liability. The Court merely concludes that, at this early stage in the litigation, accepting SVA's factual allegations of damage to its computer systems, the complaint states a valid cause of action for trespass to chattels.

... ORDERED that defendant Kuprewicz's cross-motion to dismiss the complaint is denied as to plaintiffs' claim for common law trespass to chattels (cause of action five)....

* * * * *

The Controlling the Assault of Non-Solicited Pornography and Marketing Act of 2003, 15 U.S.C. § 7701, *et seq.*, took effect on January 1, 2004. The legislation is known by its ambiguous-sounding acronym, the "CAN SPAM Act." The statute regulates, among other practices, the transmission of marketing e-mails to individuals; the retention of third-party services to send marketing e-mails on behalf of a company; the provision of consideration or other inducements to a third party to send e-mails promoting a company's products or services; the acquisition of e-mail addresses from third parties for purposes of sending marketing e-mails; and the inclusion of advertisements or promotions in another company's commercial e-mail messages. As a general matter, the Act:

> ~ requires opt-out notices to be included in commercial e-mails, *see id.* at §§ 4(a)(5)(A)(ii)

> ~ requires compliance with opt-out requests, *see id.* at § 4(a)(4)

> ~ prohibits the transmission of e-mail messages with false or misleading header information or subject headings, the registration of e-mail or user accounts or domain names using a false identity to send multiple commercial e-mails, and the false representation as the registrant of, or successor to, IP addresses to send multiple commercial e-mails, *see id.* at §§ 4(a)(1), (2)

> ~ prohibits the harvesting of e-mail addresses or "dictionary attacks,"[*] *see id.* at § 4(b)(1)

> ~ regulates the labeling of e-mail with sexual content, *see id.* at § 4(d)

The Act imposes both criminal and civil liabilities and may be enforced by certain governmental entities and by ISPs. *See id.* at §§ 4, 7. The FTC adopted a final rule governing the determination of what constitutes the "primary purpose" of an e-mail message. *See* 69 Fed. Reg. 55765 (Sept. 16, 2004). Under the Act, the term "commercial content" refers to "the commercial advertisement or promotion of a commercial product or service," rather than an isolated e-mail sent by one who is not engaged in commerce who wants to sell something to an acquaintance. *See id.*

Hypertouch Inc., an ISP, filed one of the first civil lawsuits under the CAN SPAM Act. *See Hypertouch, Inc. v. BVWebTies, LLC,* No. C040880MMC (N.D. Cal. 2004), *cited by* Brown Raysman, *The "Can-Spam" Act* (March 2005) at 26. The complaint alleged that the defendants sent commercial e-mail through the plaintiff's e-mail servers that included false or misleading information, used a domain name that was registered to a false entity that had

---

[*] A "dictionary attack" is a mass e-mail dispatch sent to automatically-generated e-mail addresses at common domain names; typically, the sender anticipates that at least some of the addresses will, fortuitously, be actual user addresses.

been obtained through false representations, were sent notwithstanding opt-out requests, and had utilized a dictionary attack. In addition, ISPs America Online, Inc., EarthLink Inc., Microsoft Corp., and Yahoo! Inc. coordinated to initiate suit against numerous spammers. *See, e.g.,* Press Release, Microsoft Corp., *Microsoft Files More Anti-Spam Lawsuits in Conjunction with Leading ISPs,* (Oct. 28, 2004), *available at* <http://www.microsoft.com/presspass/press/2004/oct04/10-28CANSPAMFollowUpPR.ms px.asp>. Microsoft Corp. filed additional suits against other alleged spammers. *See, e.g.,* Grant Gross, *Microsoft Sues Eight Alleged Spammers,* Computer World (June 11, 2004), *available at* <http://www.computerworld.com/softwaretopics/software/groupware/story/0, 10801,93784,00.html>.

The first criminal action was initiated by the U.S. Attorney in conjunction with the FTC. *See FTC v. Phoenix Avatar LLC,* No. 80383 (N.D. Ill. filed Apr. 23, 2004), *available at* <http://www.ftc.gov/os/2004/04/040429phhoenixavatarcriminalcmplt.pdf>. The defendants were charged with having falsified e-mail header information in a marketing scheme relating to diet products in violation of the CAN SPAM Act. *See id.* The individual defendants maintained that they could not be held liable under the CAN SPAM Act because the FTC could not prove that they had sent the spam. *See* Press Release, FTC, *Diet Patch Sellers Settle Can-Spam Charges* (Mar. 31, 2005), *available at* <http://www.ftc.gov/ opa/2005/03/phoenix.htm>. The FTC argued that the defendants were responsible because they either had sent the e-mail messages or had caused the messages to be sent by affiliates. *See id.*

In July 2004, the federal court issued an order finding that CAN SPAM liability "is not limited to those who physically cause spam to be transmitted, but also extends to those who 'procure the origination' of offending spam." The court held that the FTC had "amassed a 'persuasive chain of evidence' connecting the defendants to violations of the FTC Act and CAN-SPAM." *Federal Trade Comm'n v. Phoenix Avatar LLC*, No. 04 C 2897, 2004 U.S. Dist. LEXIS 14717, *46 (N.D. Ill. 2004). A stipulated order for permanent injunction and final judgment as to the individual defendants was entered into, prohibiting them from making false or misleading oral or written statements in connection with weight-loss products and other products or services, or from violating sections 5 and 6 of the CAN SPAM Act, 15 U.S.C. §§ 7704, 7705. *See Federal Trade Comm'n v. Phoenix Avatar, LLC,* Stipulated Order for Permanent Injunction and Final Judgment as to Defendants Daniel J. Lin, Mark M. Sadek, James Lin, and Christopher M. Chung, No. 04C 2897 (N.D. Ill. Mar. 29, 2005), *available at* <http://www.ftc.gov/os/caselist/0423084/050331stip0423084.pdf>.

* * * * *

Data Mining and Data Protection Directives, Polices, and Legislation
Data Mining Controversies

insert the following before the first full paragraph on page 434 of Law of Internet Speech:

Should persons and entities that collect data have an obligation to notify consumers when security measures have been compromised? As of early 2005, data security breach notification legislation had been enacted in Arkansas, California, Montana, North Dakota, and Washington. *See* S.B. 1167, 85th Gen. Assem., Reg. Sess. (Ark. 2005), *available at*

<http://www.arkleg.state.ar.us/ftproot/acts/2005/public/act1526.pdf>; Cal. Civ. Code §§ 1798.29, 1798.82, 1798.84, *available at* <http://www.leginfo.ca.gov./cgi-bin/calawquery? codesection=civ&codebody>; S.B.. 230, 2005-2006 Gen. Assem. Reg. Sess. (Ga. 2005), *available at* <http://www.legis.state.ga.us/legis/2005_06/pdf/sb230.pdf>; H.R. 732, 2005 Leg., Reg. Sess. (Mont. 2005), *available at* <http://data.opi.state.mt.us/bills/2005/billhtml/ HB0732.htm>; S.B. 2251, 59th Leg. Assem., Reg. Sess. (N.D. 2005), *available at* <http://www.state.nd.us/lr/assembly/59-2005/bill-text/FRBS0500.pdf>; S.B. 6043, 59th Leg., Reg. Sess. (Wash. 2005), *available at* <http://www.leg.wa.gov/pub/billinfo/2005-06/Htm/Bills/Senate%20Passed%20Legislature/6043-S.PL.htm>*; cf. also* S.B. 503, 114th Gen. Assem., 1st Reg. Sess. (Ind. 2005), *available at* <http://www.in.gov/legislative /bills/2005/SE/SE0503.1.html> (applying the breach notification requirements to state agencies). As a general matter, the statutes require persons and entities that maintain personal information about state residents to notify affected individuals of a security breach, such as the unauthorized acquisition of computerized data that compromises the security, confidentiality, or integrity of personal information.

In addition, the Federal Trade Commission announced a Disposal Rule as part of the Fair and Accurate Credit Transactions Act of 2003, to go into effect on June 1, 2005. *See* FTC, Press Release, *FACTA Disposal Rule Goes Into Effect June 1,* June 1, 2005, *available at* <http://www.ftc.gov/opa/2005/06/disposal.htm>. The Rule requires individuals and both small and large businesses to take appropriate measures to dispose of sensitive information derived from consumer reports. *See* 69 Fed. Reg. 68690, *available at* <www.ftc.gov/os/ 2004/11/041118disposalfrn.pdf>.

* * * * *

Data Protection Paradigms

insert the following after the first full paragraph on page 460 of Law of Internet Speech:

A more recent example of advertising practices challenged by the FTC concerned Petco.com, an on-line retailer catering to pet owners. In this case, the Commission was concerned about the lack of encryption. The FTC alleged that the company breached express promises to secure customer data by maintaining it in encrypted form. The FTC contended that the failure rendered the web-site vulnerable to security flaws that could have been addressed by "reasonable and appropriate security measures." *See In the Matter of Petco Animal Supplies, Inc.,* File No. 032-3221 (FTC Nov. 17, 2004); *see also* Press Release, *Petco Settles FTC Charges,* FTC (Nov. 17, 2004), *available at* <http://www.ftc.gov/opa/2004/11/ petco.htm>. The on-line store settled the charges with the FTC, agreeing, among other things, to adopt a comprehensive information security program with specified features, to designate appropriate employees to coordinate the program, and to obtain periodic and independent security audits. *See id.*

* * * * *

insert the following at the end of Notes and Questions # 4 on page 462 of Law of Internet Speech:

Thereafter, the U.S. Court of Appeals for the First Circuit expressed doubt about the utility of a reasonable expectations test for assessing authorization for access under the Computer Fraud and Abuse Act, 18 U.S.C. § 1030 (2000). *See EF Cultural Travel BV v.*

Zefer Corp., 318 F.3d 58 (1st Cir. 2003). The appellate court instead endorsed explicit prohibitions by public web-site providers, such as a statement on their home pages or in their terms of use. Such express provisions would avoid "putting users at the mercy of a highly imprecise, litigation-spawning standard like 'reasonable expectations.'" *Id.* at 63.

* * * * *

insert the following after Notes and Questions # 5 on page 462 of Law of Internet Speech:

Notes and Questions

6. Is it legally permissible to profess adherence to a privacy policy while disclaiming liability for security breaches or other problems?

7. The first case brought by the Federal Trade Commission challenging deceptive and unfair practices in connection with a company's material change to its privacy policy concerned Gateway Learning Corp. *See* Press Release, *Gateway Learning Settles FTC Privacy Charges* (July 7, 2004), *available at* <http://www.ftc.gov/opa/2004/07/gateway.htm>. The FTC claimed the company had engaged in an unfair and deceptive trade practice when it retroactively revised its privacy policy to allow the rental of consumers' personal information to marketing companies without notifying consumers of the changes. *See* Complaint, *In re Gateway Learning Corp.,* No. C-4120, FTC File 042-3047 (FTC July 7, 2004), *available at* <http://www.ftc.gov/os/caselist/0423047/040917comp0423047.pdf>. The parties settled the matter; the settlement requires Gateway Learning to comply with its previous privacy policy with respect to information it collected under that policy absent express, affirmative, opt-in consent to modifications. The settlement also requires Gateway Learning to disgorge the income obtained from the sale of the information to marketers. *See* Press Release, FTC, *Gateway Learning Settles FTC Privacy Charges,* July 7, 2004, *available at* <http://www. ftc.gov/opa/2004/07/gateway.htm>.

* * * * *

Data Collection Protections Relating to Children

insert the following before Notes and Questions on page 467 of Law of Internet Speech:

In April 2005, the Federal Trade Commission announced that it was seeking public comment on its implementation of the Children's Online Privacy Protection Act through the Children's Online Privacy Protection Rule. The FTC also sought comment on COPPA Rule's sliding scale approach to obtaining parental consent, which takes into account how information obtained from children will be used. *See* FTC, Press Release, *FTC Seeks Comment on Children's Online Privacy Rule,* Apr. 21, 2005, *available at* <http://www.ftc. gov/opa/2005/04/coppacomments.htm>. The sliding scale approach is designed to offer a flexible approach to obtaining parental consent before collecting personal information from children. Web-site operators and operators of on-line services that collect children's personal information solely for internal use can obtain parental consent through e-mail with the parent plus an additional step to provide assurance that the person providing the consent is actually the parent. Operators that want to disclose children's information publicly or to third parties must employ more reliable methods of obtaining parental consent, such as the use of a print-

and-send consent form, a credit card transaction, a toll-free telephone number staffed by trained personnel, a digital certificate using public key technology, or an e-mail with a password or PIN obtained by one of the other methods described. *Id.*

* * * * *

Legislative Privacy Protections
The Electronic Communications Privacy Act

substitute the following for Richard Fraser, et al. v. Nationwide Mutual Insurance Co., et al. on page 488 of Law of Internet Speech:

RICHARD FRASER a/b/a R.A. FRASER AGENCY; DEBORAH FRASER, Appellants

v.

NATIONWIDE MUTUAL INSURANCE CO., *et al.,* Appellees

United States Court of Appeals for the Third Circuit

No. 01-2921, 352 F.3d 107

December 10, 2003

Richard Fraser, an independent insurance agent for Nationwide Mutual Insurance Company, was terminated by Nationwide as an agent. We decide whether: ... he is entitled to damages under the Electronic Communications Privacy Act and parallel Pennsylvania law for Nationwide's alleged unauthorized access to his e-mail account.... We affirm the District Court on [that claim].

Background

This dispute stems from Nationwide's September 2, 1998 termination of Fraser's Agent's Agreement (the "Agreement"). It provided that Fraser sell insurance policies as an independent contractor for Nationwide on an exclusive basis. The relationship was terminable at will by either party.

The parties disagree on the reason for Fraser's termination. Fraser argues Nationwide terminated him because he filed complaints with the Pennsylvania Attorney General's office regarding Nationwide's allegedly illegal conduct, including its discriminatory refusal to write car insurance for unmarried and new drivers. Fraser also contends that he was terminated for criticizing Nationwide while acting as an officer of the Nationwide Insurance Independent Contractors Association (the "Contractors Association") and for attempting to obtain the passage of legislation in Pennsylvania to ensure that independent insurance agents could be terminated only for "just cause."

Nationwide argues, however, that it terminated Fraser because he was disloyal. It points out that Fraser drafted a letter to two competitors – Erie Insurance Company ("Erie") and Zurich American Insurance ("Zurich") – expressing Contractors Association members' dissatisfaction with Nationwide and seeking to determine whether Erie and Zurich would be interested in acquiring the policyholders of the agents in the Contractors Association. Fraser claims that the letters only were drafted to get Nationwide's attention and were not sent.

(Were the letters sent, however, they would constitute a violation of the "exclusive representation" provision of Fraser's Agreement with Nationwide.)

When Nationwide learned about these letters, it claims that it became concerned that Fraser might also be revealing company secrets to its competitors. It therefore searched its main file server – on which all of Fraser's e-mail was lodged – for any e-mail to or from Fraser that showed similar improper behavior. Nationwide's general counsel testified that the e-mail search confirmed Fraser's disloyalty. Therefore, on the basis of the two letters and the e-mail search, Nationwide terminated Fraser's Agreement. It is this search of his e-mail that gives rise to Fraser's claim for damages under the Electronic Communications Privacy Act of 1986 ("ECPA"), 18 U.S.C. § 2510, *et seq.*, and a parallel Pennsylvania statute, 18 Pa. Cons. Stat. § 5702, *et seq.*

... II. Discussion

... B. ECPA Claims....

Title I

Fraser argues that, by accessing his e-mail on its central file server without his express permission, Nationwide violated Title I of the ECPA, which prohibits "intercepts" of electronic communications such as e-mail. The statute defines an "intercept" as "the aural or other acquisition of the contents of any wire, electronic, or oral communication through the use of any electronic, mechanical, or other device." 18 U.S.C. § 2510(4). Nationwide argues that it did not "intercept" Fraser's e-mail within the meaning of Title I because an "intercept" can only occur contemporaneously with transmission and it did not access Fraser's e-mail at the initial time of transmission.

On this matter of statutory interpretation which we review *de novo, Moody v. Sec. Pac. Bus. Credit, Inc.*, 971 F.2d 1056, 1063 (3d Cir. 1992), we agree with Nationwide. Every circuit court to have considered the matter has held that an "intercept" under the ECPA must occur contemporaneously with transmission. *See United States v. Steiger*, 318 F.3d 1039, 1048-49 (11th Cir. 2003); *Konop v. Hawaiian Airlines, Inc.*, 302 F.3d 868 (9th Cir. 2002); *Steve Jackson Games, Inc. v. U.S. Secret Serv.*, 36 F.3d 457 (5th Cir. 1994); *see also Wesley College v. Pitts*, 974 F. Supp. 375 (D. Del. 1997), *summarily aff'd*, 172 F.3d 861 (3d Cir. 1998).

The first case to do so, *Steve Jackson Games*, noted that "intercept" was defined as contemporaneous in the context of an aural communication under the old Wiretap Act, *see United States v. Turk*, 526 F.2d 654 (5th Cir. 1976), and that when Congress amended the Wiretap Act in 1986 (to create what is now known as the ECPA) to extend protection to electronic communications, it "did not intend to change the definition of 'intercept.'" *Steve Jackson Games*, 36 F.3d at 462. Moreover, the Fifth Circuit noted that the differences in definition between "wire communication" and "electronic communication" in the ECPA supported its conclusion that stored e-mail could not be intercepted within the meaning of Title I. A "wire communication" under the ECPA was (until recent amendment by the USA Patriot Act) "any aural transfer made in whole or in part through the use of facilities for the transmission of communications by the aid of wire, cable, or other like connection between the point of origin and the point of reception ... *and such term includes any electronic storage of such communication.*" 18 U.S.C. § 2510(1) (emphasis added) (superseded by USA Patriot

Act).[8] By contrast, an "electronic communication" is defined as "any transfer of signs, signals, writing, images, sounds, data, or intelligence of any nature transmitted in whole or in part by a wire, radio, electromagnetic, photoelectronic or photooptical system ... but does *not include ... any wire or oral communication*." 18 U.S.C. § 2510(12) (emphasis added). Thus, the Fifth Circuit reasoned that because "wire communication" explicitly included electronic storage but "electronic communication" did not, there can be no "intercept" of an e-mail in storage, as an e-mail in storage is by definition not an "electronic communication." *Steve Jackson Games*, 36 F.3d at 461-62.

Subsequent cases, cited above, have agreed with the Fifth Circuit's result. While Congress's definition of "intercept" does not appear to fit with its intent to extend protection to electronic communications, it is for Congress to cover the bases untouched. We adopt the reasoning of our sister circuits and therefore hold that there has been no "intercept" within the meaning of Title I of ECPA.

Title II

Fraser also argues that Nationwide's search of his e-mail violated Title II of the ECPA. That Title creates civil liability for one who "(1) intentionally accesses without authorization a facility through which an electronic communication service is provided; or (2) intentionally exceeds an authorization to access that facility; and thereby obtains, alters, or prevents authorized access to a wire or electronic communication while it is in electronic storage in such system." 18 U.S.C. § 2701(a). The statute defines "electronic storage" as "(A) any temporary, intermediate storage of a wire or electronic communication incidental to the electronic transmission thereof; and (B) any storage of such communication by an electronic communication service for purposes of backup protection of such communication." *Id.* § 2510(17).

The District Court granted summary judgment in favor of Nationwide, holding that Title II does not apply to the e-mail in question because the transmissions were neither in "temporary, intermediate storage" nor in "backup" storage. Rather, according to the District Court, the e-mail was in a state it described as "post-transmission storage." We agree that Fraser's e-mail was not in temporary, intermediate storage. But to us it seems questionable that the transmissions were not in backup storage – a term that neither the statute nor the legislative history defines. Therefore, while we affirm the District Court, we do so through a different analytical path, assuming without deciding that the e-mail in question was in backup storage.

18 U.S.C. § 2701(c)(1) excepts from Title II seizures of e-mail authorized "by the person or entity providing a wire or electronic communications service." There is no circuit court case law interpreting this exception. However, in *Bohach v. City of Reno*, 932 F. Supp. 1232 (D. Nev. 1996), a district court held that the Reno police department could, without violating Title II, retrieve pager text messages stored on the police department's computer system because the department "is the provider of the 'service'" and "service providers [may] do as they wish when it comes to accessing communications in electronic storage." *Id.* at 1236.

---

[8] The USA Patriot Act § 209, Pub. L. No. 107-56, § 209(1)(A), 115 Stat. 272, 283 (2001), amended the definition of "wire communication" to eliminate electronic storage from the definition of wire communication.

Like the court in *Bohach*, we read § 2701(c) literally to except from Title II's protection all searches by communications service providers. Thus, we hold that, because Fraser's e-mail was stored on Nationwide's system (which Nationwide administered), its search of that e-mail falls within § 2701(c)'s exception to Title II.

... III. Conclusion

We affirm the District Court's grant of summary judgment in favor of Nationwide on Fraser's ... ECPA and parallel state claims....

* * * * *

insert the following after Notes and Questions # 3 on page 498:

4. How would the *Fraser* decision be affected by the USA PATRIOT Act's amendment to ECPA? Is there any question under the USA PATRIOT Act that ECPA governs stored wire and electronic communications?

5. The scope of privacy protection afforded to Internet users under the Electronic Communications Privacy Act of 1986, 18 U.S.C. §§ 2511, 2520 (2000), was considered by the U.S. Court of Appeals for the First Circuit in *In re Pharmatrak, Inc. Privacy Litig.,* 329 F.3d 9 (1st Cir. 2003). In that case, pharmaceutical companies had invited users to visit their web-sites to learn about their drugs and to obtain rebates. Pharmatrak sold a service to the pharmaceutical companies that accessed information about the Internet users and collected certain information about the users and was designed to permit the pharmaceutical companies to do intra-industry comparisons of web-site traffic and usage. The pharmaceutical companies indicated that they did not want personal or identifying data about their web-site users to be collected and were assured by Pharmatrak that such data collection would not occur. However, some personal and identifying data was found on Pharmatrak's computers. Plaintiffs, on behalf of a purported class of Internet users whose data Pharmatrak had collected, sued both Pharmatrak and the pharmaceutical companies, asserting, among other claims, a violation of ECPA. *See id.*

The lower court had granted summary judgment for the defendants, but the federal appellate court held that the district court had incorrectly interpreted the consent exception to ECPA. The First Circuit also concluded that Pharmatrak had "intercepted" the communication under ECPA. The appellate court reversed and remanded for further proceedings. *See id.* On remand, the Massachusetts federal court concluded that the requisite level of intent had not been shown and granted summary judgment for the defendants. *In re Pharmatrak, Inc. Privacy Litig.,* 292 F. Supp. 2d 263 (D. Mass. 2003).

6. With respect to claims passengers asserted under the Electronic Communications Privacy Act against airlines that disclosed identifiable data to governmental agencies without the prior consent of or notice to passengers, *see* Supplement *supra* at 133.

* * * * *

ROBERT C. KONOP, Plaintiff-Appellant

v.

HAWAIIAN AIRLINES, INC., Defendant-Appellee

United States Court of Appeals for the Ninth Circuit

No. 99-55106, 302 F.3d 868

August 23, 2002

Robert Konop brought suit against his employer, Hawaiian Airlines, Inc. ("Hawaiian"), alleging that Hawaiian viewed Konop's secure website without authorization, disclosed the contents of that website, and took other related actions in violation[, *inter alia,*] of the federal Wiretap Act [and] the Stored Communications Act....

On January 8, 2001, we issued an opinion, reversing the district court's decision on Konop's claims under the Wiretap Act and the Stored Communications Act.... *Konop v. Hawaiian Airlines, Inc.*, 236 F.3d 1035 (9th Cir. 2001). Hawaiian filed a petition for rehearing, which became moot when we withdrew our previous opinion. *Konop v. Hawaiian Airlines, Inc.*, 262 F.3d 972 (9th Cir. 2001). We now affirm the judgment of the district court with respect to Konop's Wiretap Act claims ... [and w]e reverse the district court's judgment with respect to Konop's claims under the Stored Communications Act....

FACTS

Konop, a pilot for Hawaiian, created and maintained a website where he posted bulletins critical of his employer, its officers, and the incumbent union, Air Line Pilots Association ("ALPA"). Many of those criticisms related to Konop's opposition to labor concessions which Hawaiian sought from ALPA. Because ALPA supported the concessions, Konop, via his website, encouraged Hawaiian employees to consider alternative union representation.

Konop controlled access to his website by requiring visitors to log in with a user name and password. He created a list of people, mostly pilots and other employees of Hawaiian, who were eligible to access the website. Pilots Gene Wong and James Gardner were included on this list. Konop programmed the website to allow access when a person entered the name of an eligible person, created a password, and clicked the "SUBMIT" button on the screen, indicating acceptance of the terms and conditions of use. These terms and conditions prohibited any member of Hawaiian's management from viewing the website and prohibited users from disclosing the website's contents to anyone else.

In December 1995, Hawaiian vice president James Davis asked Wong for permission to use Wong's name to access Konop's website. Wong agreed. Davis claimed he was concerned about untruthful allegations that he believed Konop was making on the website. Wong had not previously logged into the website to create an account. When Davis accessed the website using Wong's name, he presumably typed in Wong's name, created a password, and clicked the "SUBMIT" button indicating acceptance of the terms and conditions.

Later that day, Konop received a call from the union chairman of ALPA, Reno Morella. Morella told Konop that Hawaiian president Bruce Nobles had contacted him regarding the contents of Konop's website. Morella related that Nobles was upset by Konop's accusations that Nobles was suspected of fraud and by other disparaging statements published on the website. From this conversation with Morella, Konop believed Nobles had obtained the

326

contents of his website and was threatening to sue Konop for defamation based on statements contained on the website.

After speaking with Morella, Konop took his website offline for the remainder of the day. He placed it back online the next morning, however, without knowing how Nobles had obtained the information discussed in the phone call. Konop claims to have learned only later from the examination of system logs that Davis had accessed the website using Wong's name.

In the meantime, Davis continued to view the website using Wong's name. Later, Davis also logged in with the name of another pilot, Gardner, who had similarly consented to Davis' use of his name. Through April 1996, Konop claims that his records indicate that Davis logged in over twenty times as Wong, and that Gardner or Davis logged in at least fourteen more times as Gardner.

... DISCUSSION

... I. Electronic Communications Privacy Act Claims

We first turn to the difficult task of determining whether Hawaiian violated either the Wiretap Act, 18 U.S.C. §§ 2510-2522 (2000) or the Stored Communications Act, 18 U.S.C. §§ 2701-2711 (2000),[2] when Davis accessed Konop's secure website. In 1986,

Congress passed the Electronic Communications Privacy Act (ECPA), Pub. L. No. 99-508, 100 Stat. 1848, which was intended to afford privacy protection to electronic communications. Title I of the ECPA amended the federal Wiretap Act, which previously addressed only wire and oral communications, to "address[ ] the interception of ... electronic communications." S. Rep. No. 99-541, at 3 (1986), *reprinted in* 1986 U.S.C.C.A.N. 3555, 3557. Title II of the ECPA created the Stored Communications Act (SCA), which was designed to "address[ ] access to stored wire and electronic communications and transactional records." *Id.*

As we have previously observed, the intersection of these two statutes "is a complex, often convoluted, area of the law." *United States v. Smith*, 155 F.3d 1051, 1055 (9th Cir. 1998). In the present case, the difficulty is compounded by the fact that the ECPA was written prior to the advent of the Internet and the World Wide Web. As a result, the existing statutory framework is ill-suited to address modern forms of communication like Konop's secure website. Courts have struggled to analyze problems involving modern technology within the confines of this statutory framework, often with unsatisfying results. ... We observe that until Congress brings the laws in line with modern technology, protection of the Internet and websites such as Konop's will remain a confusing and uncertain area of the law.

A. The Internet and Secure Websites

... While most websites are public, many, such as Konop's, are restricted. For instance, some websites are password protected, require a social security number, or require the user to purchase access by entering a credit card number. *See Reno* [*v. American Civil Liberties Union,* 521 U.S. 844, 852-53 (1997)]. The legislative history of the ECPA suggests that Congress wanted to protect electronic communications that are configured to be private, such

---

[2] The Wiretap Act and SCA have since been amended by the Uniting and Strengthening America by Providing Appropriate Tools Required to Intercept and Obstruct Terrorism Act (USA PATRIOT Act), Pub. L. No. 107-56, 115 Stat. 272 (October 26, 2001).

as email and private electronic bulletin boards. *See* S. Rep. No. 99-541, at 35-36 ("This provision [the SCA] addresses the growing problem of unauthorized persons deliberately gaining access to ... electronic or wire communications that are not intended to be available to the public."); H.R. Rep. No. 99-647 at 41, 62-63 (1986) (describing the Committee's understanding that the configuration of the electronic communications system would determine whether or not an electronic communication was readily accessible to the public). The nature of the Internet, however, is such that if a user enters the appropriate information (password, social security number, etc.), it is nearly impossible to verify the true identity of that user. *Cf. Reno*, 521 U.S. at 855-56 (discussing the difficulty of verifying the age of a website user by requiring a credit card number or password).

We are confronted with such a situation here. Although Konop took certain steps to restrict the access of Davis and other managers to the website, Davis was nevertheless able to access the website by entering the correct information, which was freely provided to Davis by individuals who were eligible to view the website.

B. Wiretap Act

Konop argues that Davis' conduct constitutes an interception of an electronic communication in violation of the Wiretap Act. The Wiretap Act makes it an offense to "intentionally intercept[ ] ... any wire, oral, or electronic communication." 18 U.S.C. § 2511(1)(a). We must therefore determine whether Konop's website is an "electronic communication" and, if so, whether Davis "intercepted" that communication.

An "electronic communication" is defined as "any transfer of signs, signals, writing, images, sounds, data, or intelligence of any nature transmitted in whole or in part by a wire, radio, electromagnetic, photoelectronic or photooptical system." *Id.* § 2510(12). As discussed above, website owners such as Konop transmit electronic documents to servers, where the documents are stored. If a user wishes to view the website, the user requests that the server transmit a copy of the document to the user's computer. When the server sends the document to the user's computer for viewing, a transfer of information from the website owner to the user has occurred. Although the website owner's document does not go directly or immediately to the user, once a user accesses a website, information is transferred from the website owner to the user via one of the specified mediums. We therefore conclude that Konop's website fits the definition of "electronic communication."

The Wiretap Act, however, prohibits only "interceptions" of electronic communications. "Intercept" is defined as "the aural or other acquisition of the contents of any wire, electronic, or oral communication through the use of any electronic, mechanical, or other device." *Id.* § 2510(4). Standing alone, this definition would seem to suggest that an individual "intercepts" an electronic communication merely by "acquiring" its contents, regardless of when or under what circumstances the acquisition occurs. Courts, however, have clarified that Congress intended a narrower definition of "intercept" with regard to electronic communications.

In *Steve Jackson Games, Inc. v. United States Secret Service*, 36 F.3d 457 (5th Cir. 1994), the Fifth Circuit held that the government's acquisition of email messages stored on an electronic bulletin board system, but not yet retrieved by the intended recipients, was not an "interception" under the Wiretap Act. The court observed that, prior to the enactment of the ECPA, the word "intercept" had been interpreted to mean the acquisition of a communication contemporaneous with transmission. *Id.* at 460 (*citing United States v. Turk*, 526 F.2d 654, 658 (5th Cir. 1976)). The court further observed that Congress, in passing the ECPA, intended to retain the previous definition of "intercept" with respect to wire and oral communications, while amending the Wiretap Act to cover interceptions of electronic communications. *See Steve Jackson Games*, 36 F.3d at 462; S. Rep. No. 99-541, at 13; H.R. Rep. No. 99-647, at 34. The court reasoned, however, that the word "intercept" could not describe the exact same conduct with respect to wire and electronic communications, because wire and electronic communications were defined differently in the statute. Specifically, the term "wire communication" was defined to include storage of the communication, while "electronic communication" was not. The court concluded that this textual difference evidenced Congress' understanding that, although one could "intercept" a *wire* communication in storage, one could not "intercept" an *electronic* communication in storage:

> Critical to the issue before us is the fact that, unlike the definition of "wire communication," the definition of "electronic communication" does not include electronic storage of such communications. ... Congress' use of the word "transfer" in the definition of "electronic communication," and its omission in that definition of the phrase "any electronic storage of such communication" ... reflects that Congress did not intend for "intercept" to apply to "electronic communications" when those communications are in "electronic storage."

Steve Jackson Games, 36 F.3d at 461-62; *Wesley Coll. v. Pitts*, 974 F. Supp. 375, 386 (D. Del. 1997) ("By including the electronic storage of wire communications within the definition of such communications but declining to do the same for electronic communications ... Congress sufficiently evinced its intent to make acquisitions of electronic communications unlawful under the Wiretap Act only if they occur contemporaneously with their transmissions."), *aff'd*, 172 F.3d 861 (3d Cir. 1998); *United States v. Reyes*, 922 F. Supp. 818, 836 (S.D.N.Y. 1996) ("Taken together, the definitions thus imply a requirement that the acquisition of [electronic communications] be simultaneous with the original transmission of the data."); *Bohach v. City of Reno*, 932 F. Supp. 1232, 1236-37 (D. Nev. 1996) (requiring acquisition during transmission). The *Steve Jackson* Court further noted that the ECPA was deliberately structured to afford electronic communications *in storage* less protection than other forms of communication. *See Steve Jackson Games*, 36 F.3d at 462-64.

The Ninth Circuit endorsed the reasoning of *Steve Jackson Games* in *United States v. Smith*, 155 F.3d at 1051. The question presented in *Smith* was whether the Wiretap Act covered wire communications in storage, such as voicemail messages, or just wire communications in transmission, such as ongoing telephone conversations. Relying on the same textual distinction as the Fifth Circuit in *Steve Jackson Games*, we concluded that wire communications in storage could be "intercepted" under the Wiretap Act. We found that Congress' inclusion of storage in the definition of "wire communication" militated in favor of a broad definition of the term "intercept" with respect to wire communications, one that included acquisition of a communication subsequent to transmission. We further observed that, *with respect to wire communications only*, the prior definition of "intercept" -- acquisition contemporaneous with transmission -- had been overruled by the ECPA. *Smith*, 155 F.3d at 1057 n.11. On the other hand, we suggested that the narrower definition of "intercept" was still appropriate with regard to electronic communications:

> In cases concerning "electronic communications" -- the definition of which specifically includes "transfers" and specifically excludes

"storage" -- the "narrow" definition of "intercept" fits like a glove; it is natural to except non-contemporaneous retrievals from the scope of the Wiretap Act. In fact, a number of courts adopting the narrow interpretation of "interception" have specifically premised their decisions to do so on the distinction between § 2510's definitions of wire and electronic communications.

Smith, 155 F.3d at 1057 (citations and alterations omitted).

We agree with the *Steve Jackson* and *Smith* courts that the narrow definition of "intercept" applies to electronic communications. Notably, Congress has since amended the Wiretap Act to eliminate storage from the definition of wire communication, *see* USA PATRIOT Act § 209, 115 Stat. at 283, such that the textual distinction relied upon by the *Steve Jackson* and *Smith* courts no longer exists. This change, however, supports the analysis of those cases. By eliminating storage from the definition of wire communication, Congress essentially reinstated the pre-ECPA definition of "intercept" -- acquisition contemporaneous with transmission -- with respect to wire communications. *See Smith*, 155 F.3d at 1057 n.11. The purpose of the recent amendment was to reduce protection of voice mail messages to the lower level of protection provided other electronically stored communications. *See* H.R. Rep. 107-236(I), at 158-59 (2001). When Congress passed the USA PATRIOT Act, it was aware of the narrow definition courts had given the term "intercept" with respect to electronic communications, but chose not to change or modify that definition. To the contrary, it modified the statute to make that definition applicable to voice mail messages as well. Congress, therefore, accepted and implicitly approved the judicial definition of "intercept" as acquisition contemporaneous with transmission.

We therefore hold that for a website such as Konop's to be "intercepted" in violation of the Wiretap Act, it must be acquired during transmission, not while it is in electronic storage. This conclusion is consistent with the ordinary meaning of "intercept," which is "to stop, seize, or interrupt in progress or course before arrival." *Webster's Ninth New Collegiate Dictionary* 630 (1985). More importantly, it is consistent with the structure of the ECPA, which created the SCA for the express purpose of addressing "access to *stored* ... electronic communications and transactional records." S. Rep. No. 99-541 at 3 (emphasis added). The level of protection provided stored communications under the SCA is considerably less than that provided communications covered by the Wiretap Act. Section 2703(a) of the SCA details the procedures law enforcement must follow to access the contents of stored electronic communications, but these procedures are considerably less burdensome and less restrictive than those required to obtain a wiretap order under the Wiretap Act. *See Steve Jackson Games*, 36 F.3d at 463. Thus, if Konop's position were correct and acquisition of a stored electronic communication were an interception under the Wiretap Act, the government would have to comply with the more burdensome, more restrictive procedures of the Wiretap Act to do exactly what Congress apparently authorized it to do under the less burdensome procedures of the SCA.

Congress could not have intended this result. As the Fifth Circuit recognized in *Steve Jackson Games*, "it is most unlikely that Congress intended to require law enforcement officers to satisfy the more stringent requirements for an intercept in order to gain access to the contents of stored electronic communications." *Id.; see also Wesley Coll.*, 974 F. Supp. at 388 (same).

Because we conclude that Davis' conduct did not constitute an "interception" of an electronic communication in violation of the Wiretap Act, we affirm the district court's grant of summary judgment against Konop on his Wiretap Act claims.

C. Stored Communications Act

Konop also argues that, by viewing his secure website, Davis accessed a stored electronic communication without authorization in violation of the SCA. The SCA makes it an offense to "intentionally access[ ] without authorization a facility through which an electronic communication service is provided ... and thereby obtain[] ... access to a wire or electronic communication while it is in electronic storage in such system." 18 U.S.C. § 2701(a)(1). The SCA excepts from liability, however, "conduct authorized ... by a user of that service with respect to a communication of or intended for that user." 18 U.S.C. § 2701(c)(2). The district court found that the exception in § 2701(c)(2) applied because Wong and Gardner consented to Davis' use of Konop's website. It therefore granted summary judgment to Hawaiian on the SCA claim.

The parties agree that the relevant "electronic communications service" is Konop's website, and that the website was in "electronic storage." In addition, for the purposes of this opinion, we accept the parties' assumption that Davis' conduct constituted "access without authorization"[8] to "a facility through which an electronic communication service is provided."

We therefore address only the narrow question of whether the district court properly found Hawaiian exempt from liability under § 2701(c)(2). Section 2701(c)(2) allows a person to authorize a third party's access to an electronic communication if the person is 1) a "user" of the "service" and 2) the communication is "of or intended for that user." *See* 18 U.S.C. § 2701(c)(2). A "user" is "any person or entity who -- (A) uses an electronic communications service; and (B) is duly authorized by the provider of such service to engage in such use." 18 U.S.C. § 2510(13).

The district court concluded that Wong and Gardner had the authority under § 2701(c)(2) to consent to Davis' use of the website because Konop put Wong and Gardner on the list of eligible users. This conclusion is consistent with other parts of the Wiretap Act and the SCA which allow intended recipients of wire and electronic communications to authorize third parties to access those communications.[9] In addition, there is some indication in the

---

[8] The term "without authorization" is not defined in the statute. *Cf. EF Cultural Travel BV v. Explorica, Inc.*, 274 F.3d 577, 581-82 & n.10 (1st Cir. 2001) (explaining, with respect to alleged unauthorized use of a website, Congress' failure to define "without authorization" in the Computer Fraud and Abuse Act, and discussing some possible, practicable definitions of the term). There is some indication in the legislative history that Congress intended the configuration of the electronic communication system to "establish an objective standard [for] determining whether a system receives privacy protection." H.R. Rep. No. 99-647, at 41. Since the issue is not properly before us, however, we express no opinion on how the term "without authorization" should be defined with respect to a non-public website such as Konop's.

[9] For instance, § 2702(b)(1) permits service providers to divulge the contents of stored communications "to an addressee or intended recipient of such communication or an agent of such addressee or intended recipient." *See also id.* § 2702(b)(3) (providing a similar exception with respect to remote computing services). Similarly, the "consent" exception to the Wiretap Act allows one party to a wire communication to authorize a third party to intercept the communication. *See* 18 U.S.C. § 2511(2)(c) & (d).

legislative history that Congress believed "addressees" or "intended recipients" of electronic communications would have the authority under the SCA to allow third parties access to those communications. *See* H.R. Rep. No. 99-647, at 66-67 (explaining that "an addressee [of an electronic communication] may consent to the disclosure of a communication to any other person" and that "[a] person may be an 'intended recipient' of a communication ... even if he is not individually identified by name or otherwise").

Nevertheless, the plain language of § 2701(c)(2) indicates that only a "user" of the service can authorize a third party's access to the communication. The statute defines "user" as one who 1) *uses* the service and 2) is duly authorized to do so. Because the statutory language is unambiguous, it must control our construction of the statute, notwithstanding the legislative history. *See United States v. Daas*, 198 F.3d 1167, 1174 (9th Cir. 1999). The statute does not define the word "use," so we apply the ordinary definition, which is "to put into action or service, avail oneself of, employ." *Webster's* at 1299; *see Daas*, 198 F.3d at 1174 ("If the statute uses a term which it does not define, the court gives that term its ordinary meaning.").

Based on the common definition of the word "use," we cannot find any evidence in the record that Wong ever used Konop's website. There is some evidence, however, that Gardner may have used the website, but it is unclear when that use occurred. At any rate, the district court did not make any findings on whether Wong and Gardner actually used Konop's website -- it simply assumed that Wong and Gardner, by virtue of being eligible to view the website, could authorize Davis' access. The problem with this approach is that it essentially reads the "user" requirement out of § 2701(c)(2). Taking the facts in the light most favorable to Konop, we must assume that neither Wong nor Gardner was a "user" of the website at the time he authorized Davis to view it. We therefore reverse the district court's grant of summary judgment to Hawaiian on Konop's SCA claim.

... CONCLUSION

For the foregoing reasons, we affirm the district court's judgment with respect to Konop's Wiretap Act claims.... We reverse the district court's judgment on Konop's Stored Communications Act claims....

AFFIRMED IN PART, REVERSED IN PART, and REMANDED.

* * * * *

Does service of a "patently unlawful" subpoena to gain access to e-mail stored by another's ISP violate the ECPA? The U.S. Court of Appeals for the Ninth Circuit considered this issue:

GEORGE THEOFEL, *et al.,* Plaintiffs-Appellants
v.
ALWYN FAREY-JONES; IRYNA A. KWASNY, Defendants-
Appellees

United States Court of Appeals for the Ninth Circuit

No. 02-15742, No. 03-15301, 341 F.3d 978,
amended by 359 F.3d 1066

August 28, 2003

... Background

Plaintiffs Wolf and Buckingham, officers of Integrated Capital Associates, Inc. (ICA), are embroiled in commercial litigation in New York against defendant Farey-Jones. In the course of discovery, Farey-Jones sought access to ICA's e-mail. He told his lawyer Iryna Kwasny to subpoena ICA's ISP, NetGate.

Under the Federal Rules, Kwasny was supposed to "take reasonable steps to avoid imposing undue burden or expense" on NetGate. Fed. R. Civ. P. 45(c)(1). One might have thought, then, that the subpoena would request only e-mail related to the subject matter of the litigation, or maybe messages sent during some relevant time period, or at the very least those sent to or from employees in some way connected to the litigation. But Kwasny ordered production of "all copies of e-mails sent or received by anyone" at ICA, with no limitation as to time or scope.

NetGate, which apparently was not represented by counsel, explained that the amount of e-mail covered by the subpoena was substantial. But defendants did not relent. NetGate then took what might be described as the "Baskin-Robbins" approach to subpoena compliance and offered defendants a "free sample" consisting of 339 messages. It posted copies of the messages to a NetGate website where, without notifying opposing counsel, Kwasny and Farey-Jones read them. Most were unrelated to the litigation, and many were privileged or personal.

When Wolf and Buckingham found out what had happened, they asked the court to quash the subpoena and award sanctions. Magistrate Judge Wayne Brazil soundly roasted Farey-Jones and Kwasny for their conduct, finding that "the subpoena, on its face, was massively overbroad" and "patently unlawful," that it "transparently and egregiously" violated the Federal Rules, and that defendants "acted in bad faith" and showed "at least gross negligence in the crafting of the subpoena." He granted the motion to quash and socked defendants with over $9000 in sanctions to cover Wolf and Buckingham's legal fees. Defendants did not appeal that award.

Wolf, Buckingham and other ICA employees whose e-mail was included in the sample also filed this civil suit against Farey-Jones and Kwasny. They claim defendants violated[, *inter alia,*] the Stored Communications Act, 18 U.S.C. § 2701, *et seq.,* the Wiretap Act, 18 U.S.C. § 2511, *et seq....* The district court held that ... [neither] of the federal statutes applied, and dismissed the claims without leave to amend. ... Plaintiffs now appeal.

Analysis

1. The Stored Communications Act provides a cause of action against anyone who "intentionally accesses without authorization a facility through which an electronic communication service is provided ... and thereby obtains, alters, or prevents authorized access to a wire or electronic communication while it is in electronic storage." 18 U.S.C. §§ 2701(a)(1), 2707(a). "Electronic storage" means either "temporary, intermediate storage ... incidental to ... electronic transmission," or "storage ... for purposes of backup protection." *Id.* § 2510(17). The Act exempts, *inter alia*, conduct "authorized ... by the person or entity providing a wire or electronic communications service," *id.* § 2701(c)(1), or "by a user of that service with respect to a communication of or intended for that user," *id.* § 2701(c)(2).

The district court dismissed on the ground that NetGate had authorized defendants' access. It held that this consent was not coerced, because the subpoena itself informed NetGate of its right to object. Plaintiffs contend that NetGate's authorization was nonetheless invalid because the subpoena was patently unlawful. Their claim turns on the meaning of the word "authorized" in section 2701. We have previously reserved judgment on this question, *see Konop v. Hawaiian Airlines, Inc.*, 302 F.3d 868, 879 n.8 (9th Cir. 2002), while other circuits have considered related issues, *see, e.g., EF Cultural Travel BV v. Explorica, Inc.*, 274 F.3d 577, 582 n.10 (1st Cir. 2001) (holding access might be "unauthorized" under the Computer Fraud and Abuse Act if it is "not in line with the reasonable expectations" of the party granting permission (internal quotation marks omitted)); *United States v. Morris*, 928 F.2d 504, 510 (2d Cir. 1991) (holding access unauthorized where it is not "in any way related to [the system's] intended function").

We interpret federal statutes in light of the common law. *See Beck v. Prupis*, 529 U.S. 494, 500-01, 146 L. Ed. 2d 561, 120 S. Ct. 1608 (2000). Especially relevant here is the common law of trespass. Like the tort of trespass, the Stored Communications Act protects individuals' privacy and proprietary interests. The Act reflects Congress's judgment that users have a legitimate interest in the confidentiality of communications in electronic storage at a communications facility. Just as trespass protects those who rent space from a commercial storage facility to hold sensitive documents, *cf. Prosser and Keeton on the Law of Torts* § 13, at 78 (W. Page Keeton ed., 5th ed. 1984), the Act protects users whose electronic communications are in electronic storage with an ISP or other electronic communications facility.

A defendant is not liable for trespass if the plaintiff authorized his entry. *See Prosser & Keeton* § 13, at 70. But "an overt manifestation of assent or willingness would not be effective ... if the defendant knew, or probably if he ought to have known in the exercise of reasonable care, that the plaintiff was mistaken as to the nature and quality of the invasion intended." *Id.* § 18, at 119; *cf. Restatement (Second) of Torts* §§ 173, 892B(2). ...

Not all deceit vitiates consent. "The mistake must extend to the essential character of the act itself, which is to say that which makes it harmful or offensive, rather than to some collateral matter which merely operates as an inducement." *Prosser & Keeton* § 18, at 120 (footnote omitted). In other words, it must be a "substantial mistake[ ] ... concerning the nature of the invasion or the extent of the harm." *Restatement (Second) of Torts* § 892B(2) cmt. g. ....[T]he theory is that some invited mistakes go to the essential nature of the invasion while others are merely collateral.

We construe section 2701 in light of these doctrines. Permission to access a stored communication does not constitute valid authorization if it would not defeat a trespass claim in analogous circumstances. Section 2701(c)(1) therefore provides no refuge for a defendant who procures consent by exploiting a known mistake that relates to the essential nature of his access.

Under this standard, plaintiffs have alleged facts that vitiate NetGate's consent. NetGate disclosed the sample in response to defendants' purported subpoena. Unbeknownst to NetGate, that subpoena was invalid. This mistake went to the essential nature of the invasion of privacy. The subpoena's falsity transformed the access from a *bona fide* state-sanctioned inspection into private snooping. *See Restatement (Second) of Torts* § 174 (addressing "consent induced by fraud or mistake as to the validity of purported legal authority"); *cf. Bumper v. North Carolina*, 391 U.S. 543, 549, 20 L. Ed. 2d 797, 88 S. Ct. 1788 (1968) ("A search conducted in reliance upon a warrant cannot later be justified on the basis of consent if it turns out that the warrant was invalid."). The false subpoena caused disclosure of documents that otherwise would have remained private....

Defendants had at least constructive knowledge of the subpoena's invalidity. It was not merely technically deficient, nor a borderline case over which reasonable legal minds might disagree. It "transparently and egregiously" violated the Federal Rules, and defendants acted in bad faith and with gross negligence in drafting and deploying it. They are charged with knowledge of its invalidity. *See Prosser & Kee*ton § 18, at 119 (consent likely vitiated where defendants "ought to have known in the exercise of reasonable care" of the mistake).[2]

That NetGate could have objected is immaterial. The subpoena may not have been coercive, but it was deceptive, and that is an independent ground for invalidating consent. *See Restatement (Second) of Torts* § 892B(2)-(3). It was a piece of paper masquerading as legal process. NetGate produced the sample in response and doubtless would not have done so had it known the subpoena was void -- particularly in light of its own legal obligation not to disclose such messages to third parties, *see* 18 U.S.C. § 2702(a)(1). That NetGate could have objected proves disclosure was not an inevitable consequence, but it was still a foreseeable one (and the intended one).

Allowing consent procured by known mistake to serve as a defense would seriously impair the statute's operation. A hacker could use someone else's password to break into a mail server and then claim the server "authorized" his access. Congress surely did not intend to exempt such intrusions -- indeed, they seem the paradigm of what it sought to prohibit. *Cf. Morris*, 928 F.2d at 510 (access gained by guessing someone else's password is not "authorization" under the Computer Fraud and Abuse Act).

---

[2] Prosser and Keeton say that a plaintiff's consent is probably invalid if the defendant "ought to have known in the exercise of reasonable care" about the mistake. *Prosser & Keeton* § 18, at 119. Because the Stored Communications Act defines a criminal offense and includes an explicit *mens rea* requirement, *see* 18 U.S.C. § 2701(a)(1), we do not think a defendant can be charged with constructive knowledge on a showing of mere negligence. Rather, the defendant must have consciously procured consent through improper means. In this case, the magistrate found that defendants had acted in bad faith. That is enough to charge them with knowledge of NetGate's mistake. *See Black's Law Dictionary* 139 (6th ed. 1990) (defining "bad faith" as "not simply bad judgment or negligence, but ... conscious doing of a wrong because of dishonest purpose or moral obliquity").

The subpoena power is a substantial delegation of authority to private parties, and those who invoke it have a grave responsibility to ensure it is not abused. Informing the person served of his right to object is a good start, *see* Fed. R. Civ. P. 45(a)(1)(D), but it is no substitute for the exercise of independent judgment about the subpoena's reasonableness. Fighting a subpoena in court is not cheap, and many may be cowed into compliance with even overbroad subpoenas, especially if they are not represented by counsel or have no personal interest at stake. Because defendants procured consent by exploiting a mistake of which they had constructive knowledge, the district court erred by dismissing based on that consent.

Defendants ask us to affirm on the alternative ground that the messages they accessed were not in "electronic storage" and therefore fell outside the Stored Communications Act's coverage. *See* 18 U.S.C. § 2701(a)(1). The Act defines "electronic storage" as "(A) any temporary, intermediate storage of a wire or electronic communication incidental to the electronic transmission thereof; and (B) any storage of such communication by an electronic communication service for purposes of backup protection of such communication." *Id.* § 2510(17), *incorporated by id.* § 2711(1). Several courts have held that subsection (A) covers e-mail messages stored on an ISP's server pending delivery to the recipient. *See In re Doubleclick, Inc. Privacy Litig.*, 154 F. Supp. 2d 497, 511-12 (S.D.N.Y. 2001); *Fraser v. Nationwide Mut. Ins. Co.*, 135 F. Supp. 2d 623, 635-36 (E.D. Pa. 2001); *cf. Steve Jackson Games, Inc. v. U.S. Secret Serv.*, 36 F.3d 457, 461-62 (5th Cir. 1994) (messages stored on a BBS pending delivery). Because subsection (A) applies only to messages in "temporary, intermediate storage," however, these courts have limited that subsection's coverage to messages not yet delivered to their intended recipient. *See Doubleclick*, 154 F. Supp. 2d at 512; *Fraser*, 135 F. Supp. 2d at 636.

Defendants point to these cases and argue that messages remaining on an ISP's server after delivery no longer fall within the Act's coverage. But, even if such messages are not within the purview of subsection (A), they do fit comfortably within subsection (B). There is no dispute that messages remaining on NetGate's server after delivery are stored "by an electronic communication service" within the meaning of 18 U.S.C. § 2510(17)(B). *Cf. Doubleclick*, 154 F. Supp. 2d at 511 (holding that subsection (B) did not apply because the communications at issue were not being stored by an electronic communication service). The only issue, then, is whether the messages are stored "for purposes of backup protection." 18 U.S.C. § 2510(17)(B). We think that, within the ordinary meaning of those terms, they are.

An obvious purpose for storing a message on an ISP's server after delivery is to provide a second copy of the message in the event that the user needs to download it again -- if, for example, the message is accidentally erased from the user's own computer. The ISP copy of the message functions as a "backup" for the user. Notably, nothing in the Act requires that the backup protection be for the benefit of the ISP rather than the user. Storage under these circumstances thus literally falls within the statutory definition.[3]

One district court reached a contrary conclusion, holding that "backup protection" includes only temporary backup storage pending delivery, and not any form of "post-transmission storage." *See Fraser*, 135 F. Supp. 2d at 633-34, 636. We reject this view as contrary to the plain language of the Act. In contrast to subsection (A), subsection (B) does

---

[3] That defendants did not read the messages until NetGate posted them to a website is immaterial. Defendants' unlawful subpoena caused NetGate to retrieve the messages from electronic storage and make them available. That constitutes "access" within the meaning of the Act.

not distinguish between intermediate and post-transmission storage. Indeed, *Fraser's* interpretation renders subsection (B) essentially superfluous, since temporary backup storage pending transmission would already seem to qualify as "temporary, intermediate storage" within the meaning of subsection (A). By its plain terms, subsection (B) applies to backup storage regardless of whether it is intermediate or post-transmission. ...

Because plaintiffs' e-mail messages were in electronic storage regardless of whether they had been previously delivered, the district court's decision cannot be affirmed on this alternative ground.

2. Plaintiffs also claim a violation of the Wiretap Act, which authorizes suit against those who "intentionally intercept[ ] ... any wire, oral, or electronic communication." 18 U.S.C. §§ 2511(1)(a), 2520(a). We recently held in *Konop v. Hawaiian Airlines, Inc.*, 302 F.3d 868 (9th Cir. 2002), that the Act applies only to "acquisition contemporaneous with transmission." *Id.* at 878. Specifically, "'Congress did not intend for "intercept" to apply to "electronic communications" when those communications are in "electronic storage."'" *Id.* at 877 (quoting *Steve Jackson Games*, 36 F.3d at 462). *Konop* is dispositive, and the district court correctly dismissed the claim.

... We REVERSE dismissal of the Stored Communications Act claim[and] AFFIRM dismissal of the Wiretap Act claim....

* * * * *

In *Apple Computer, Inc. v. Doe 1, an unknown individual, and Does 2-25, inclusive,* No.: 1-04-CV-032178 (Cal. Santa Clara Cty. Mar. 11, 2005), *available at* <http://www.eff.org/ Censorship/Apple_v_Does/20050311_apple_decision.pdf>; *see also* Supplement *supra* at 75, 274, the plaintiff claimed that certain individuals had leaked trade secret information about the plaintiff's products to on-line news sites. On appeal, petitioners and non-party journalists argued, among other points, that the federal Stored Communications Act, 18 U.S.C. §§ 2701-12, prohibited any civil discovery of the content of electronic communications directly from service providers. *See* Memorandum of Points and Authorities of Petitioners and Non-Party Journalists Jason O'Grady, Monish Bhatia, and Kasper Jade's Petition for a Writ of Mandate and/or Prohibition, *Apple Computer, Inc. v. Doe 1, an unknown individual, and Does 2-25, inclusive,* No.: 1-04-CV-032178 at 3, 21-24 (Cal. Ct. App. dated Mar. 22, 2005), *available at* <http://www.eff.org/Censorship/Apple_ v_Does/20050322_writ_petition.pdf>. The petitioners and non-party journalists also contended that the Stored Communications Act preempted any state law or discovery rule to the contrary. *See id.*

In response, Apple asserted that the Stored Communications Act "was not enacted to preempt civil discovery; instead, it was enacted to regulate governmental searches of email communications." Opposition of Real Party in Interest Apple Computer, Inc. to Petition for a Writ of Mandate and/or Prohibition, *Apple Computer, Inc. v. Doe 1, an unknown individual, and Does 2-25, inclusive,* No.: 1-04-CV-032178, at 33 (Cal. Ct. App. Dist. dated Apr. 7, 2005), *available at* <http://www.eff.org/Censorship/Apple_v_Does/20050407_apple_ opposition.pdf>. Apple pointed to broad statutory exemptions that authorized disclosures, including disclosures that "'may be necessarily incident ... to the protection of the rights or property of the provider of that service[,] ... 18 U.S.C. § 2702(b)(5)[; and disclosures that comply] ... with valid court process[,] ... 18 U.S.C. § 2707." *Id.* at 35 (quoting 18 U.S.C. § 2702(b)(5)).

The petitioners and non-parties sought to rebut these arguments, pointing out that at least one court had held that the Stored Communications Act "forbids even governmental entities, which are explicitly allowed under Section 2703 to use particular types of subpoenas to compel production of content in some circumstances, from using civil discovery subpoenas to obtain even non-content subscriber information." Reply of Petitioners and Non-Party Journalists Jason O'Grady, Monish Bhatia, and Kasper Jade to Apple Computer, Inc.'s Opposition, *Apple Computer, Inc. v. Doe 1, an unknown individual, and Does 2-25, inclusive* No.: 1-04-CV-032178, at 5 (Cal. Ct. App. dated Apr. 22, 2005), *available at* <http://www.eff. org/Censorship/Apple_v_Does/reply_to_opposition.pdf> (citing *Federal Trade Comm'n v. Netscape Comm'ns Corp.*, 196 F.R.D. 559, 561 (N.D. Cal. 2000)).

* * * * *

Access to Information

The Electronic Freedom of Information Improvement Act

insert the following before Quad/Graphics, Inc. v. Southern Adirondack Library System on page 510 of Law of Internet Speech:

The FBI effectively abandoned its Carnivore system. The FBI stated that instead it began using unspecified commercial software to eavesdrop on computer traffic during investigations of suspected criminals, terrorists, and spies, and has also increasingly relied on ISPs to conduct wiretaps. *See FBI Stops Using Carnivore Wiretap Software,* Mercury News.com (Jan. 18, 2005), *available at* <http://www.silconvalley.com/mld/ siliconvalley/news/editorial/10675001.htm>

* * * * *

insert the following before Notes and Questions on page 514 of Law of Internet Speech:

With respect to the appellate proceeding, *see Putnam Pit, Inc. v. City of Cookeville,* 76 Fed. Appx. 607, 2003 U.S. App. LEXIS 17775 (6th Cir. Aug. 20, 2003) (unpublished); *see* Supplement *supra* at 77.

* * * * *

Technological Privacy Protections

The *Bernstein v. United States Dep't of Justice* Decisions

insert the following before Notes and Questions on page 532 of Law of Internet Speech:

In June 2004, Professor Peter D. Junger commented on his lawsuit challenging the regulations, stating, "If I had known the years of frustration that awaited me I might have decided to simply ignore the ITAR regulations or, rather, I might have intended that my little cryptographic program not be a cryptographic program, as if that were possible, and if it were, would somehow exempt me from the criminal penalties contained in the Internation

Trafficking in Arms Regulations. But then I have never been able to really understand what the criminal bar is talking about when they talk about intent, so I guess that was not an option." Peter D. Junger, *A Bit of History: How I Came to Challenge the ITAR,* Samsara's Blog, June 26, 2004, *available at* <http://samsara.law.cwru.edu/blog/archive2/ Bit_History_How_I_Came_Chal.html>.

The U.S. District Court for the Northern District of California dismissed the case after the incumbent Bush administration said it would no longer try to enforce aspects of the encryption regulations. *See* Declan McCullagh, *Cold War Encryption Laws Stand, But Not as Firmly,* CNet News.com (Oct. 15, 2003), *available at* <http://news.com.com/2102-1028_3-5092154.html>.

CHAPTER V

PROPRIETARY INTERESTS IN CONTENT

Copyright

insert the following at the end of Notes and Question # 3 on page 546 of Law of Internet Speech:

In August 2003, the Supreme Court of California considered whether California's trade secret law, Cal. Civ. Code § 3426, *et seq.,* offended the free speech clauses of the United States and California Constitutions. The plaintiff had alleged that the defendant's web-site operator posted others' trade secrets on his Internet web-site, notwithstanding that he knew or had reason to know that the secrets had been acquired by improper means. Specifically, the plaintiff, DVD Copy Control Association, a trade association that licensed encryption and decryption technology to constrain piracy of motion picture DVDs, contended that the defendant posted a computer program known as "DeCSS" to defeat the encryption and thus render the DVDs vulnerable to piracy.

After finding that the operator misappropriated the trade secrets, the trial court issued a preliminary injunction prohibiting the operator from disclosing the secrets. California's highest court concluded that the injunction violated neither the First Amendment of the U.S. Constitution nor article I of the California Constitution. *See DVD Copy Control Ass'n, Inc. v. Bunner,* 31 Cal. 4th 864, 75 P.3d 1, 4 Cal. Rptr. 3d 69 (Cal. 2003).

The California Supreme Court stated that

> [b]ecause the injunction does not purport to restrict DVD CCA's trade secrets based on their expressive content, the injunction's restrictions on [Andrew] Bunner's speech "properly are characterized as incidental to the primary" purpose of California's trade secret law -- which is to promote and reward innovation and technological development and maintain commercial ethics.
>
> The fact that the preliminary injunction identifies the prohibited speech by its content does not make it content based. "An injunction, by its very nature, applies only to a particular group (or individuals) and regulates the activities, and perhaps the speech, of that group. It does so, however, because of the group's past actions in the context of a specific dispute between real parties. The parties seeking the injunction assert a violation of their rights; the court hearing the action is charged with fashioning a remedy for a specific deprivation, not with the drafting of a statute addressed to the general public." In this case, the specific deprivation to be remedied is the misappropriation of a property interest in *information.* Thus, any injunction remedying this deprivation must refer to the content of that information in order to identify the property interest to be protected. Such an injunction remains content neutral so long as it serves

significant governmental purposes unrelated to the content of the proprietary information. Because the preliminary injunction at issue here does not "involve government censorship of subject matter or governmental favoritism among different viewpoints," it is content neutral and not subject to strict scrutiny.

Id., 31 Cal. 4th at 878-79, 75 P.3d at 12, 4 Cal. Rptr. 3d at 82 (citations omitted). The court also held that "[b]ecause the injunction is content neutral and was issued because of Bunner's prior unlawful conduct, … it is not a prior restraint and therefore does not violate the First Amendment." *Id.*, 31 Cal. 4th at 885-86, 75 P.3d at 17, 4 Cal. Rptr. 3d at 88.

The court did not resolve whether trade secrets in fact were disclosed. In upholding the preliminary injunction, the court assumed that the plaintiff likely would prevail on the merits of its trade secret claim but remanded the case to the Court of Appeal to determine whether the evidence led to factual findings warranting an injunction under California's trade secret law. *See id.*, 31 Cal. 4th at 889, 75 P.3d at 19-20, 4 Cal. Rptr. 3d at 91.

Thereafter, the California appellate court concluded that the evidence before it did not justify the issuance of the injunction; the plaintiff had not presented evidence as to when Bunner first posted DeCSS and there was "no evidence to support the inference that the CSS technology was still a secret when he did so." *DVD Copy Control Ass'n, Inc. v. Bunner,* 116 Cal. App. 4th 241, 255, 10 Cal. Rptr. 3d 185, 196 (Cal. App. Ct. 2004). The court also took note of the "great deal of evidence" that demonstrated that by the time the plaintiff sought the preliminary injunction prohibiting disclosure of the DeCSS program, DeCSS had been so widely distributed that the CSS technology may have lost its trade secret status. *See id.* The preliminary injunction was deemed to burden more speech than was necessary to protect the plaintiff's property interests and thus was an unlawful prior restraint on Bunner's free speech rights. *See id.* Prior to the issuance of the decision, the DVD Copy Control Association had moved to dismiss as moot its trade secrets case against Bunner. *See, e.g.,* John Borland, *Hollywood Group Drops DVD-Copying Case,* CNet News.com (Jan. 22, 2004), *available at* <http://news.com.com/2100-1025_3-5145809.html>. The court denied the motion, however, concluding that the case "present[ed] important issues that could arise again and yet evade review…." *DVD Copy Control Ass'n, Inc. v. Bunner,* 116 Cal. App. 4th at 245 n.2, 10 Cal. Rptr. 3d at 187 n.2.

* * * * *

substitute the following for the first full paragraph at the end of Notes and Questions # 4 on page 547 of Law of Internet Speech:

With respect to the subsequent rulings by the California Supreme Court and the decision on remand, *see* 31 Cal. 4th 864, 4 Cal. Rptr. 3d 69, 75 P.3d 1, 2003 (Cal. 2003); 116 Cal. App. 4th 241, 10 Cal. Rptr. 3d 185 (Cal. App. Ct. 2004); *see also* Supplement *supra* at 341.

* * * * *

insert the following after Notes and Questions # 5 on page 547 of Law of Internet Speech:

6. In *Eldred v. Ashcroft,* 537 U.S. 186 (2003), the U.S. Supreme Court upheld the constitutionality of the Sonny Bono Copyright Term Extension Act of 1998, concluding that the 20-year extension of copyright constitutes the constitutionally mandated "limited time."

* * * * *

insert the following after the third full paragraph on page 548 of Law of Internet Speech:

Thereafter, the American Society of Journalists and Authors, the Authors Guild, the National Writers Union, and several freelance writers announced a proposed settlement aggregating to as much as $18 million. *See In re Literary Works in Electronic Database Copyright Litig.,* Master Docket No. M-21-90 (GBD) (S.D.N.Y. prelim. approval of settlement granted Mar. 31, 2005). The proposed settlement contemplates compensation by participating publishers and database companies of eligible freelance writers; the amount of compensation takes into account the copyright status of the work at issue and the year the work was originally published.

In *Faulkner v. National Geographic Enters., Inc.,* No. 04-0263-cv(L), 2005 U.S. App. LEXIS 3642 (2d Cir. Mar. 4, 2005), however, the U.S. Court of Appeals for the Second Circuit deemed the inclusion of copyrighted articles and photographs in the CD-ROM version of a magazine to be a "revision" under section 201(c) of the Copyright Act. The freelance authors and photographers who had provided the works in question did not prevail on their copyright claim because the CD-ROM version presented the works to users "in the same context as they were presented to users in the original versions of the magazine," and the CD-ROM version constituted "an electronic replica" of the magazine pages as they had been published originally. *See id.* at *28.

* * * * *

Copyright Infringement Claims

insert the following before A&M Records, Inc., et al. v. Napster, Inc. on page 552 of Law of Internet Speech:

Copyright infringement actions relating to the Internet have largely concerned music sound recordings and video technologies. Peer-to-peer ("P2P") file sharing and other unauthorized dissemination of copyrighted material has given rise to litigation and has led to the enactment of legislation.

Piracy in this context refers to the illegal duplication and distribution of sound recordings. The Recording Industry Association of America delimits four types of piracy:

~ pirate recordings: unauthorized duplication of only the sound of recordings

~ counterfeit recordings: unauthorized recordings of pre-recorded sound plus of original artwork, label, trademark, and packaging

~ bootleg recordings: unauthorized recordings of live concerts or musical broadcasts on radio or television

343

~ on-line piracy: unauthorized uploading or downloading of a sound recording that is protected by copyright that is then made available to the public through an Internet web-site

See generally Recording Indus. Ass'n of Am., *Anti-Piracy, available at* <http://www.riaa.com/issues/piracy/default.asp>.

Piracy concerns have been addressed in a variety of ways. In addition to the Digital Millennium Copyright Act, 17 U.S.C. §§ 512, 1201-05, 1301-22; 24 U.S.C. § 4001, *see Law of Internet Speech* at 583, statutory responses to digitization include the Audio Home Recording Act of 1992, Pub. L. No. 102-563, 106 Stat. 4237 (1992), which, among other things, requires that digital audio recording devices include a system that precludes serial copying; and the No Electronic Theft Act of 1997, Pub. L. No. 105-47, 111 Stat. 2678 (1997), which criminalizes the distribution of pirated software.

Unauthorized dissemination of content also has been addressed through technological means, notably through Digital Rights Management, known as "DRM." Such technology manages how copyright holders' intellectual property may be used, encompassing technological restrictions on using, copying, and distributing content. "Content protection technology, such as DRM software, enables a content provider to 'wrap' a set of rules around content that defines whether and how the purchaser of the copyrighted or premium content can manipulate and share it. The rules can include, for instance, how many copies of the original file a user may make, whether a back-up or archive file can be created, and whether a user can move the content to another device. Typically, content is encrypted; to get the decryption key, a user must act – for example, by paying money, providing an e-mail address or agreeing to permit tracking. DRM software vendors deliver the tools, but content owners set the conditions." Gartner G2 and The Berkman Center for Internet & Society at Harvard Law School, *Copyright and Digital Media in a Post-Napster World* (Jan. 2005) at 43, *available at* <http://cyber.law.harvard.edu/media/files/wp2005.pdf>.

Some have criticized the routine use of DRM technology as a means of addressing piracy and other security issues associated with digitization. By restricting access to content through DRM, fair use and transformative uses of content may be constrained, disfavored digital media devices and software creators potentially can be excluded, and DRM-based data processing practices may implicate privacy interests. *See id.* at 47-48. Copyright holders may be legally entitled to control access to their content under a wide range of circumstances, but critics also question the functional efficacy of DRM technology as a deterrent to piracy because "no DRM is uncrackable." *Id.* at 48.

* * * * *

Theories of Secondary Liability

insert the following before The Fair Use Defense on page 559 of Law of Internet Speech:

IN RE: AIMSTER COPYRIGHT LITIGATION,
APPEAL OF: JOHN DEEP, Defendant

United States Court of Appeals for the Seventh Circuit

No. 02-4125, 334 F.3d 643

June 30, 2003

Owners of copyrighted popular music filed a number of closely related suits, which were consolidated and transferred to the Northern District of Illinois by the Multi-District Litigation Panel, against John Deep and corporations that are controlled by him and need not be discussed separately. The numerous plaintiffs, who among them appear to own most subsisting copyrights on American popular music, claim that Deep's "Aimster" Internet service (recently renamed "Madster") is a contributory and vicarious infringer of these copyrights. The district judge entered a broad preliminary injunction, which had the effect of shutting down the Aimster service until the merits of the suit are finally resolved, from which Deep appeals. Aimster is one of a number of enterprises (the former Napster is the best known) that have been sued for facilitating the swapping of digital copies of popular music, most of it copyrighted, over the Internet. ... To simplify exposition, we refer to the appellant as "Aimster" and to the appellees (the plaintiffs) as the recording industry.

Teenagers and young adults who have access to the Internet like to swap computer files containing popular music. If the music is copyrighted, such swapping, which involves making and transmitting a digital copy of the music, infringes copyright. The swappers, who are ignorant or more commonly disdainful of copyright and in any event discount the likelihood of being sued or prosecuted for copyright infringement, are the direct infringers. But firms that facilitate their infringement, even if they are not themselves infringers because they are not making copies of the music that is shared, may be liable to the copyright owners as contributory infringers. Recognizing the impracticability or futility of a copyright owner's suing a multitude of individual infringers ("chasing individual consumers is time consuming and is a teaspoon solution to an ocean problem," Randal C. Picker, *Copyright as Entry Policy: The Case of Digital Distribution,* 47 Antitrust Bull. 423, 442 (2002)), the law allows a copyright holder to sue a contributor to the infringement instead, in effect as an aider and abettor. Another analogy is to the tort of intentional interference with contract, that is, inducing a breach of contract. *See, e.g., Sufrin v. Hosier,* 128 F.3d 594, 597 (7th Cir. 1997). If a breach of contract (and a copyright license is just a type of contract) can be prevented most effectively by actions taken by a third party, it makes sense to have a legal mechanism for placing liability for the consequences of the breach on him as well as on the party that broke the contract.

... The Aimster system has the following essential components: proprietary software that can be downloaded free of charge from Aimster's Web site; Aimster's server (a server is a computer that provides services to other computers, in this case personal computers owned or accessed by Aimster's users, over a network), which hosts the Web site and collects and organizes information obtained from the users but does not make copies of the swapped files themselves and that also provides the matching service described below; computerized tutorials instructing users of the software on how to use it for swapping computer files; and "Club Aimster," a related Internet service owned by Deep that users of Aimster's software can join for a fee and use to download the "top 40" popular-music files more easily than by using the basic, free service. The "AIM" in "Aimster" stands for AOL instant-messaging service. Aimster is available only to users of such services (of which AOL's is the most popular) because Aimster users can swap files only when both are online and connected in a chat room enabled by an instant-messaging service.

Someone who wants to use Aimster's basic service for the first time to swap files downloads the software from Aimster's Web site and then registers on the system by entering a user name (it doesn't have to be his real name) and a password at the Web site. Having done so, he can designate any other registrant as a "buddy" and can communicate directly with all his buddies when he and they are online, attaching to his communications (which are really just emails) any files that he wants to share with the buddies. All communications back and forth are encrypted by the sender by means of encryption software furnished by Aimster as part of the software package downloadable at no charge from the Web site, and are decrypted by the recipient using the same Aimster-furnished software package. If the user does not designate a buddy or buddies, then *all* the users of the Aimster system become his buddies; that is, he can send or receive from any of them.

Users list on their computers the computer files they are willing to share. (They needn't list them separately, but can merely designate a folder in their computer that contains the files they are willing to share.) A user who wants to make a copy of a file goes online and types the name of the file he wants in his "Search For" field. Aimster's server searches the computers of those users of its software who are online and so are available to be searched for files they are willing to share, and if it finds the file that has been requested it instructs the computer in which it is housed to transmit the file to the recipient via the Internet for him to download into his computer. Once he has done this he can if he wants make the file available for sharing with other users of the Aimster system by listing it as explained above. In principle, therefore, the purchase of a single CD could be levered into the distribution within days or even hours of millions of identical, near-perfect (depending on the compression format used) copies of the music recorded on the CD -- hence the recording industry's anxiety about file-sharing services oriented toward consumers of popular music. But because copies of the songs reside on the computers of the users and not on Aimster's own server, Aimster is not a direct infringer of the copyrights on those songs. Its function is similar to that of a stock exchange, which is a facility for matching offers rather than a repository of the things being exchanged (shares of stock). But unlike transactions on a stock exchange, the consummated "transaction" in music files does not take place in the facility, that is, in Aimster's server.

What we have described so far is a type of Internet file-sharing system that might be created for innocuous purposes such as the expeditious exchange of confidential business data among employees of a business firm. *See* Daniel Nasaw, *Instant Messages Are Popping Up All Over,* Wall St. J., June 12, 2003, p. B4; David A. Vise, *AOL Makes Instant-Messaging Deal,* Wash. Post, June 12, 2003, p. E5. The fact that copyrighted materials might sometimes be shared between users of such a system without the authorization of the copyright owner or a fair-use privilege would not make the firm a contributory infringer. Otherwise AOL's instant-messaging system, which Aimster piggybacks on, might be deemed a contributory infringer. For there is no doubt that some of the attachments that AOL's multitudinous subscribers transfer are copyrighted, and such distribution is an infringement unless authorized by the owner of the copyright. The Supreme Court made clear in the *Sony* decision that the producer of a product that has substantial non-infringing uses is not a contributory infringer merely because some of the uses actually made of the product (in that case a machine, the predecessor of today's videocassette recorders, for recording television programs on tape) are infringing. *Sony Corp. of America, Inc. v. Universal City Studios, Inc.*, 464 U.S. 417, 78 L. Ed. 2d 574, 104 S. Ct. 774 (1984); *see also Vault Corp. v. Quaid Software Ltd.*, 847 F.2d 255, 262-67 (5th Cir. 1988). How much more the Court held is the principal issue that divides the parties; and let us try to resolve it, recognizing of course that the Court must have the last word.

Sony's Betamax video recorder was used for three principal purposes, as Sony was well aware (a fourth, playing home movies, involved no copying). The first, which the majority opinion emphasized, was time shifting, that is, recording a television program that was being shown at a time inconvenient for the owner of the Betamax for later watching at a convenient time. The second was "library building," that is, making copies of programs to retain permanently. The third was skipping commercials by taping a program before watching it and then, while watching the tape, using the fast-forward button on the recorder to skip over the commercials. The first use the Court held was a fair use (and hence not infringing) because it enlarged the audience for the program. The copying involved in the second and third uses was unquestionably infringing to the extent that the programs copied were under copyright and the taping of them was not authorized by the copyright owners -- but not all fell in either category. Subject to this qualification, building a library of taped programs was infringing because it was the equivalent of borrowing a copyrighted book from a public library, making a copy of it for one's personal library, then returning the original to the public library. The third use, commercial-skipping, amounted to creating an unauthorized derivative work, *see WGN Continental Broadcasting Co. v. United Video, Inc.*, 693 F.2d 622, 625 (7th Cir. 1982); *Gilliam v. American Broadcasting Cos.*, 538 F.2d 14, 17-19, 23 (2d Cir. 1976); *cf. Ty, Inc. v. GMA Accessories, Inc.*, 132 F.3d 1167, 1173 (7th Cir. 1997), namely a commercial-free copy that would reduce the copyright owner's income from his original program, since "free" television programs are financed by the purchase of commercials by advertisers.

Thus the video recorder was being used for a mixture of infringing and noninfringing uses and the Court thought that Sony could not demix them because once Sony sold the recorder it lost all control over its use. *Sony Corp. of America, Inc. v. Universal City Studios, Inc.*, *supra*, 464 U.S at 438. The court ruled that "the sale of copying equipment, like the sale of other articles of commerce, does not constitute contributory infringement if the product is widely used for legitimate, unobjectionable purposes. Indeed, it need merely be capable of substantial noninfringing uses. The question is thus whether the Betamax is capable of commercially significant noninfringing uses. In order to resolve that question, we need not explore *all* the different potential uses of the machine and determine whether or not they would constitute infringement. Rather, we need only consider whether on the basis of the facts as found by the district court a significant number of them would be non-infringing. Moreover, in order to resolve this case we need not give precise content to the question of how much use is commercially significant. For one potential use of the Betamax plainly satisfies this standard, however it is understood: private, noncommercial time-shifting in the home." *Id*. at 441.

In our case the recording industry, emphasizing the reference to "articles of commerce" in the passage just quoted and elsewhere in the Court's opinion (*see id.* at 440; *cf.* 35 U.S.C. § 271(c)), and emphasizing as well the Court's evident concern that the copyright holders were trying to lever their copyright monopolies into a monopoly over video recorders, *Sony Corp. of America, Inc. v. Universal City Studios, Inc.*, *supra*, 464 U.S at 441-42 and n.21, and also remarking Sony's helplessness to prevent infringing uses of its recorders once it sold them, argues that *Sony* is inapplicable to services. With regard to services, the industry argues, the test is merely whether the provider knows it's being used to infringe copyright. The industry points out that the provider of a service, unlike the seller of a product, has a continuing relation with its customers and therefore should be able to prevent, or at least limit, their infringing copyright by monitoring their use of the service and terminating them when it is discovered that they are infringing. Although Sony could have engineered its video recorder in a way that would have reduced the likelihood of infringement, as by eliminating the fast-forward capability, or, as suggested by the dissent, *id.* at 494, by enabling broadcasters by scrambling their signal to disable the Betamax from recording their programs (for that matter, it could have been engineered to have only a play, not a recording, capability), the majority did not discuss these possibilities and we agree with the recording industry that the ability of a service provider to prevent its customers from infringing is a factor to be considered in determining whether the provider is a contributory infringer. Congress so recognized in the Digital Millennium Copyright Act, which we discuss later in this opinion.

It is not necessarily a controlling factor, however, as the recording industry believes. If a service facilitates both infringing and noninfringing uses, as in the case of AOL's instant-messaging service, and the detection and prevention of the infringing uses would be highly burdensome, the rule for which the recording industry is contending could result in the shutting down of the service or its annexation by the copyright owners (contrary to the clear import of the *Sony* decision), because the provider might find it impossible to estimate its potential damages liability to the copyright holders and would anyway face the risk of being enjoined. The fact that the recording industry's argument if accepted might endanger AOL's instant-messaging service (though the service might find shelter under the Digital Millennium Copyright Act -- a question complicated, however, by AOL's intention, of which more later, of offering an encryption option to the visitors to its chat rooms) is not only alarming; it is paradoxical, since subsidiaries of AOL's parent company (AOL Time Warner), such as Warner Brothers Records and Atlantic Recording Corporation, are among the plaintiffs in this case and music chat rooms are among the facilities offered by AOL's instant-messaging service.

We also reject the industry's argument that *Sony* provides no defense to a charge of contributory infringement when, in the words of the industry's brief, there is anything "more than a mere showing that a product may be used for infringing purposes." Although the fact was downplayed in the majority opinion, it was apparent that the Betamax was being used for infringing as well as noninfringing purposes -- even the majority acknowledged that 25 percent of Betamax users were fast forwarding through commercials, *id.* at 452 n.36 -- yet Sony was held not to be a contributory infringer. The Court was unwilling to allow copyright holders to prevent infringement effectuated by means of a new technology at the price of possibly denying noninfringing consumers the benefit of the technology. We therefore agree with Professor Goldstein that the Ninth Circuit erred in *A&M Records, Inc. v. Napster, Inc.*, 239 F.3d 1004, 1020 (9th Cir. 2001), in suggesting that actual knowledge of specific infringing uses is a sufficient condition for deeming a facilitator a contributory infringer. 2 Paul Goldstein, *Copyright* § 6.1.2, p. 6:12-1 (2d ed. 2003).

The recording industry's hostility to the *Sony* decision is both understandable, given the amount of Internet-enabled infringement of music copyrights, and manifest -- the industry in its brief offers five reasons for confining its holding to its specific facts. But it is being articulated in the wrong forum.

Equally, however, we reject Aimster's argument that to prevail the recording industry must prove it has actually lost money as a result of the copying that its service facilitates. It is true that the Court in *Sony* emphasized that the plaintiffs had failed to show that they had sustained substantial harm from the Betamax. *Id.* at 450-54, 456. But the Court did so in the context of assessing the argument that time shifting of television programs was fair use rather than infringement. One reason time shifting was fair use, the Court believed, was that it wasn't hurting the copyright owners because it was enlarging the audience for their programs. But a copyright owner who can prove infringement need not show that the infringement caused him a financial loss. Granted, without such a showing he cannot obtain compensatory damages; but he can obtain statutory damages, or an injunction, just as the owner of physical property can obtain an injunction against a trespasser without proving that the trespass has caused him a financial loss.

What is true is that when a supplier is offering a product or service that has noninfringing as well as infringing uses, some estimate of the respective magnitudes of these uses is necessary for a finding of contributory infringement. The Court's action in striking the cost-benefit trade-off in favor of Sony came to seem prescient when it later turned out that the principal use of video recorders was to allow people to watch at home movies that they bought or rented rather than to tape television programs. (In 1984, when *Sony* was decided, the industry was unsure how great the demand would be for prerecorded tapes compared to time shifting. The original Betamax played one-hour tapes, long enough for most television broadcasts but too short for a feature film. Sony's competitors used the VHS format, which came to market later but with a longer playing time; this contributed to VHS's eventual displacement of Betamax.) An enormous new market thus opened for the movie industry -- which by the way gives point to the Court's emphasis on potential as well as actual noninfringing uses. But the balancing of costs and benefits is necessary only in a case in which substantial noninfringing uses, present or prospective, are demonstrated.

We also reject Aimster's argument that because the Court said in *Sony* that mere "constructive knowledge" of infringing uses is not enough for contributory infringement, 464 U.S. at 439, and the encryption feature of Aimster's service prevented Deep from knowing what songs were being copied by the users of his system, he lacked the knowledge of infringing uses that liability for contributory infringement requires. Willful blindness is knowledge, in copyright law (where indeed it may be enough that the defendant *should* have known of the direct infringement, *Casella v. Morris*, 820 F.2d 362, 365 (11th Cir. 1987); 2 Goldstein, *supra*, § 6.1, p. 6:6), as it is in the law generally. *See, e.g., Louis Vuitton S.A. v. Lee*, 875 F.2d 584, 590 (7th Cir. 1989) (contributory trademark infringement). One who, knowing or strongly suspecting that he is involved in shady dealings, takes steps to make sure that he does not acquire full or exact knowledge of the nature and extent of those dealings is held to have a criminal intent, *United States v. Giovannetti*, 919 F.2d 1223, 1228 (7th Cir. 1990), because a deliberate effort to avoid guilty knowledge is all that the law requires to establish a guilty state of mind. *United States v. Josefik*, 753 F.2d 585, 589 (7th Cir. 1985); *AMPAT/Midwest, Inc. v. Illinois Tool Works Inc.*, 896 F.2d 1035, 1042 (7th Cir. 1990) ("to know, and to want not to know because one suspects, may be, if not the same state of mind, the same degree of fault)." In *United States v. Diaz*, 864 F.2d 544, 550 (7th Cir. 1988), the defendant, a drug trafficker, sought "to insulate himself from the actual drug transaction so that he could deny knowledge of it," which he did sometimes by absenting himself from the scene of the actual delivery and sometimes by pretending to be fussing under the hood of his car. He did not escape liability by this maneuver; no more can Deep by using encryption software to prevent himself from learning what surely he strongly suspects to be the case: that the users of his service -- maybe *all* the users of his service -- are copyright infringers.

This is not to say that the provider of an encrypted instant-messaging service or encryption software is *ipso facto* a contributory infringer should his buyers use the service to infringe copyright, merely because encryption, like secrecy generally, facilitates unlawful transactions. ("Encryption" comes from the Greek word for concealment.) Encryption fosters privacy, and privacy is a social benefit though also a source of social costs. ... Our point is only that a service provider that would otherwise be a contributory infringer does not obtain immunity by using encryption to shield itself from actual knowledge of the unlawful purposes for which the service is being used.

We also do not buy Aimster's argument that since the Supreme Court distinguished, in the long passage from the *Sony* opinion that we quoted earlier, between actual and potential noninfringing uses, all Aimster has to show in order to escape liability for contributory infringement is that its file-sharing system *could* be used in noninfringing ways, which obviously it could be. Were that the law, the seller of a product or service used *solely* to facilitate copyright infringement, though it was capable in principle of noninfringing uses, would be immune from liability for contributory infringement. That would be an extreme result, and one not envisaged by the *Sony* majority. Otherwise its opinion would have had no occasion to emphasize the fact (at least the majority thought it a fact -- the dissent disagreed, 464 U.S. at 458-59) that Sony had not in its advertising encouraged the use of the Betamax to infringe copyright. *Id.* at 438. Nor would the Court have thought it important to say that the Betamax was used "principally" for time shifting, *id.* at 421; *see also id.* at 423, which as we recall the Court deemed a fair use, or to remark that the plaintiffs owned only a small percentage of the total amount of copyrighted television programming and it was unclear how many of the other owners objected to home taping. *Id.* at 443; *see also id.* at 446.

There are analogies in the law of aiding and abetting, the criminal counterpart to contributory infringement. A retailer of slinky dresses is not guilty of aiding and abetting prostitution even if he knows that some of his customers are prostitutes -- he may even know which ones are. *See United States v. Giovannetti, supra,* 919 F.2d at 1227; *People v. Lauria,* 251 Cal. App. 2d 471, 59 Cal. Rptr. 628 (App. 1967); Rollin M. Perkins & Ronald N. Boyce, *Criminal Law* 746-47 (3d ed. 1982). The extent to which his activities and those of similar sellers actually promote prostitution is likely to be slight relative to the social costs of imposing a risk of prosecution on him. But the owner of a massage parlor who employs women who are capable of giving massages, but in fact as he knows sell only sex and never massages to their customers, is an aider and abettor of prostitution (as well as being guilty of pimping or operating a brothel). *See United States v. Sigalow,* 812 F.2d 783, 784, 785 (2d Cir. 1987); *State v. Carpenter,* 122 Ohio App. 3d 16, 701 N.E.2d 10, 13, 18-19 (Ohio App. 1997); *cf. United States v. Luciano-Mosquera,* 63 F.3d 1142, 1149-50 (1st Cir. 1995). The slinky-dress case corresponds to *Sony,* and, like *Sony,* is not inconsistent with imposing liability on the seller of a product or service that, as in the massage-parlor case, is capable of noninfringing uses but in fact is used only to infringe. To the recording industry, a single known infringing use brands the facilitator as a contributory infringer. To the Aimsters of this world, a single noninfringing use provides complete immunity from liability. Neither is correct.

To situate Aimster's service between these unacceptable poles, we need to say just a bit more about it. In explaining how to use the Aimster software, the tutorial gives as its *only* examples of file sharing the sharing of copyrighted music, including copyrighted music that the recording industry had notified Aimster was being infringed by Aimster's users. The tutorial is the invitation to infringement that the Supreme Court found was missing in *Sony*. In addition, membership in Club Aimster enables the member for a fee of $4.95 a month to download with a single click the music most often shared by Aimster users, which turns out to be music copyrighted by the plaintiffs. Because Aimster's software is made available free of charge and Aimster does not sell paid advertising on its Web site, Club Aimster's monthly fee is the only means by which Aimster is financed and so the club cannot be separated from the provision of the free software. When a member of the club clicks on "play" next to the name of a song on the club's Web site, Aimster's server searches through the computers of the Aimster users who are online until it finds one who has listed the song as available for sharing, and it then effects the transmission of the file to the computer of the club member who selected it. Club Aimster lists only the 40 songs that are currently most popular among its members; invariably these are under copyright.

The evidence that we have summarized does not exclude the *possibility* of substantial noninfringing uses of the Aimster system, but the evidence is sufficient, especially in a preliminary-injunction proceeding, which is summary in character, to shift the burden of production to Aimster to demonstrate that its service has substantial noninfringing uses. (On burden-shifting in preliminary injunction proceedings, *see FTC v. University Health, Inc.*, 938 F.2d 1206, 1218-19 (11th Cir. 1991); *cf. Johnson v. Cambridge Industries, Inc.*, 325 F.3d 892, 897 (7th Cir. 2003); *SEC v. Lipson*, 278 F.3d 656, 661 (7th Cir. 2002); *Liu v. T & H Machine, Inc.*, 191 F.3d 790, 795 (7th Cir. 1999).) As it might:

> 1. Not all popular music is copyrighted. Apart from music on which the copyright has expired (not much of which, however, is of interest to the teenagers and young adults interested in swapping music), startup bands and performers may waive copyright in the hope that it will encourage the playing of their music and create a following that they can convert to customers of their subsequent works.

> 2. A music file-swapping service might increase the value of a recording by enabling it to be used as currency in the music-sharing community, since someone who only downloads and never uploads, thus acting as a pure free rider, will not be very popular.

> 3. Users of Aimster's software might form select (as distinct from all-comers) "buddy" groups to exchange non-copyrighted information about popular music, or for that matter to exchange ideas and opinions about wholly unrelated matters as the buddies became friendlier. Some of the chat-room messages that accompany the listing of music files offered or requested contain information or opinions concerning the music; to that extent, though unremarked by the parties, some noninfringing use is made of Aimster's service, though it is incidental to the infringement.

4. Aimster's users might appreciate the encryption feature because as their friendship deepened they might decide that they wanted to exchange off-color, but not copyrighted, photographs, or dirty jokes, or other forms of expression that people like to keep private, rather than just copyrighted music.

5. Someone might own a popular-music CD that he was particularly fond of, but he had not downloaded it into his computer and now he finds himself out of town but with his laptop and he wants to listen to the CD, so he uses Aimster's service to download a copy. This might be a fair use rather than a copyright infringement, by analogy to the time shifting approved as fair use in the *Sony* case. *Recording Industry Ass'n of America v. Diamond Multimedia Systems, Inc.*, 180 F.3d 1072, 1079 (9th Cir. 1999); *cf. Vault Corp. v. Quaid Software Ltd.*, *supra*, 847 F.2d at 266-67. The analogy was sidestepped in *A&M Records, Inc. v. Napster, Inc.*, *supra*, 239 F.3d at 1019, because Napster's system did not limit downloading to music on CDs owned by the downloader. The analogy was rejected in *UMG Recordings v. MP3.com, Inc.*, 92 F. Supp. 2d 349 (S.D.N.Y. 2000), on the ground that the copy on the defendant's server was an unauthorized derivative work; a solider ground, in light of *Sony*'s rejection of the parallel argument with respect to time shifting, would have been that the defendant's method for requiring that its customers "prove" that they owned the CDs containing the music they wanted to download was too lax.

All five of our examples of actually or arguably noninfringing uses of Aimster's service are possibilities, but as should be evident from our earlier discussion the question is how probable they are. It is not enough, as we have said, that a product or service be physically capable, as it were, of a noninfringing use. Aimster has failed to produce any evidence that its service has ever been used for a noninfringing use, let alone evidence concerning the frequency of such uses. In the words of the district judge, "defendants here have provided no evidence whatsoever (besides the unsupported declaration of Deep) that Aimster is *actually* used for any of the stated non-infringing purposes. Absent is any indication from real-life Aimster users that their primary use of the system is to transfer non-copyrighted files to their friends or identify users of similar interests and share information. Absent is any indication that even a single business without a network administrator uses Aimster to exchange business records as Deep suggests." *In re Aimster Copyright Litigation*, 252 F. Supp. 2d 634, 653 (N.D. Ill. 2002) (emphasis in original). We have to assume for purposes of deciding this appeal that no such evidence exists; its absence, in combination with the evidence presented by the recording industry, justified the district judge in concluding that the industry would be likely to prevail in a full trial on the issue of contributory infringement. Because Aimster failed to show that its service is ever used for any purpose other than to infringe the plaintiffs' copyrights, the question (as yet unsettled ...) of the net effect of Napster-like services on the music industry's income is irrelevant to this case. If the *only* effect of a service challenged as contributory infringement is to enable copyrights to be infringed, the magnitude of the resulting loss, even whether there is a net loss, becomes irrelevant to liability.

Even when there are noninfringing uses of an Internet file-sharing service, moreover, if the infringing uses are substantial then to avoid liability as a contributory infringer the provider of the service must show that it would have been disproportionately costly for him to eliminate or at least reduce substantially the infringing uses. Aimster failed to make that showing too, by failing to present evidence that the provision of an encryption capability *effective against the service provider itself* added important value to the service or saved significant cost. Aimster blinded itself in the hope that by doing so it might come within the rule of the *Sony* decision.

It complains about the district judge's refusal to hold an evidentiary hearing. But his refusal was consistent with our decision in *Ty, Inc. v. GMA Accessories, Inc., supra*, 132 F.3d at 1171 (citations omitted), where we explained that "if genuine issues of material fact are created by the response to a motion for a preliminary injunction, an evidentiary hearing is indeed required. But as in any case in which a party seeks an evidentiary hearing, he must be able to persuade the court that the issue is indeed genuine and material and so a hearing would be productive -- he must show in other words that he has and intends to introduce evidence that if believed will so weaken the moving party's case as to affect the judge's decision on whether to issue an injunction." Aimster hampered its search for evidence by providing encryption. It must take responsibility for that self-inflicted wound.

Turning to the second issue presented by the appeal, we are less confident than the district judge was that the recording industry would also be likely to prevail on the issue of vicarious infringement should the case be tried, though we shall not have to resolve our doubts in order to decide the appeal. "Vicarious liability" generally refers to the liability of a principal, such as an employer, for the torts committed by his agent, an employee for example, in the course of the agent's employment. The teenagers and young adults who use Aimster's system to infringe copyright are of course not Aimster's agents. But one of the principal rationales of vicarious liability, namely the difficulty of obtaining effective relief against an agent, who is likely to be impecunious, Alan O. Sykes, *The Economics of Vicarious Liability*, 93 Yale L.J. 1231, 1241-42, 1272 (1984), has been extended in the copyright area to cases in which the only effective relief is obtainable from someone who bears a relation to the direct infringers that is analogous to the relation of a principal to an agent. *See* 2 Goldstein, *supra*, § 6.2, pp. 6:17 to 6:18. The canonical illustration is the owner of a dance hall who hires dance bands that sometimes play copyrighted music without authorization. The bands are not the dance hall's agents, but it may be impossible as a practical matter for the copyright holders to identify and obtain a legal remedy against the infringing bands yet quite feasible for the dance hall to prevent or at least limit infringing performances. And so the dance hall that fails to make reasonable efforts to do this is liable as a vicarious infringer. *Dreamland Ball Room v. Shapiro, Bernstein & Co.*, 36 F.2d 354, 355 (7th Cir. 1929), and other cases cited in *Sony Corp. of America, Inc. v. Universal City Studios, Inc., supra*, 464 U.S. at 437 n.18; 2 Goldstein, *supra*, § 6.2, pp. 6:18 to 6:20. The dance hall could perhaps be described as a contributory infringer. But one thinks of a contributory infringer as someone who benefits directly from the infringement that he encourages, and that does not seem an apt description of the dance hall, though it does benefit to the extent that competition will force the dance band to charge the dance hall a smaller fee for performing if the band doesn't pay copyright royalties and so has lower costs than it would otherwise have.

How far the doctrine of vicarious liability extends is uncertain. It could conceivably have been applied in the *Sony* case itself, on the theory that while it was infeasible for the producers of copyrighted television fare to sue the viewers who used the fast-forward button on Sony's video recorder to delete the commercials and thus reduce the copyright holders' income, Sony could have reduced the likelihood of infringement, as we noted earlier, by a design change. But the Court, treating vicarious and contributory infringement interchangeably, see *id.* at 435 and n.17, held that Sony was not a vicarious infringer either. By eliminating the encryption feature and monitoring the use being made of its system, Aimster could like Sony have limited the amount of infringement. Whether failure to do so made it a vicarious infringer notwithstanding the outcome in *Sony* is academic, however; its ostrich-like refusal to discover the extent to which its system was being used to infringe copyright is merely another piece of evidence that it was a contributory infringer. ...

AFFIRMED.

* * * * *

METRO-GOLDWYN-MAYER STUDIOS INC., *et al.*, PETITIONERS
v.
GROKSTER, LTD., *et al.*

United States Supreme Court

No. 04-480, 2005 U.S. LEXIS 5212

June 27, 2005

JUSTICE SOUTER delivered the opinion of the Court.

The question is under what circumstances the distributor of a product capable of both lawful and unlawful use is liable for acts of copyright infringement by third parties using the product. We hold that one who distributes a device with the object of promoting its use to infringe copyright, as shown by clear expression or other affirmative steps taken to foster infringement, is liable for the resulting acts of infringement by third parties.

I.

A.

Respondents, Grokster, Ltd., and StreamCast Networks, Inc., defendants in the trial court, distribute free software products that allow computer users to share electronic files through peer-to-peer networks, so called because users' computers communicate directly with each other, not through central servers. The advantage of peer-to-peer networks over information networks of other types shows up in their substantial and growing popularity. Because they need no central computer server to mediate the exchange of information or files among users, the high-bandwidth communications capacity for a server may be dispensed with, and the need for costly server storage space is eliminated. Since copies of a file (particularly a popular one) are available on many users' computers, file requests and retrievals may be faster than on other types of networks, and since file exchanges do not travel through a server, communications can take place between any computers that remain connected to the network without risk that a glitch in the server will disable the network in its entirety. Given these benefits in security, cost, and efficiency, peer-to-peer networks are employed to store and distribute electronic files by universities, government agencies, corporations, and libraries, among others.[1]

Other users of peer-to-peer networks include individual recipients of Grokster's and StreamCast's software, and although the networks that they enjoy through using the software can be used to share any type of digital file, they have prominently employed those networks in sharing copyrighted music and video files without authorization. A group of copyright holders (MGM for short, but including motion picture studios, recording companies, songwriters, and music publishers) sued Grokster and StreamCast for their users' copyright infringements, alleging that they knowingly and intentionally distributed their software to enable users to reproduce and distribute the copyrighted works in violation of the Copyright Act, 17 U.S.C. § 101 *et seq.* (2000 ed. and Supp. II). MGM sought damages and an injunction.

Discovery during the litigation revealed the way the software worked, the business aims of each defendant company, and the predilections of the users. Grokster's eponymous software employs what is known as FastTrack technology, a protocol developed by others and licensed to Grokster. StreamCast distributes a very similar product except that its software, called Morpheus, relies on what is known as Gnutella technology. A user who downloads and installs either software possesses the protocol to send requests for files directly to the computers of others using software compatible with FastTrack or Gnutella. On the FastTrack network opened by the Grokster software, the user's request goes to a computer given an indexing capacity by the software and designated a supernode, or to some other computer with comparable power and capacity to collect temporary indexes of the files available on the computers of users connected to it. The supernode (or indexing computer) searches its own index and may communicate the search request to other supernodes. If the file is found, the supernode discloses its location to the computer requesting it, and the requesting user can download the file directly from the computer located. The copied file is placed in a designated sharing folder on the requesting user's computer, where it is available for other users to download in turn, along with any other file in that folder.

... Although Grokster and StreamCast do not therefore know when particular files are copied, a few searches using their software would show what is available on the networks the software reaches. MGM commissioned a statistician to conduct a systematic search, and his study showed that nearly 90% of the files available for download on the FastTrack system were copyrighted works.[5] Grokster and StreamCast dispute this figure, raising methodological problems and arguing that free copying even of copyrighted works may be

---

[1] Peer-to-peer networks have disadvantages as well. Searches on peer-to-peer networks may not reach and uncover all available files because search requests may not be transmitted to every computer on the network. There may be redundant copies of popular files. The creator of the software has no incentive to minimize storage or bandwidth consumption, the costs of which are borne by every user of the network. Most relevant here, it is more difficult to control the content of files available for retrieval and the behavior of users.

[5] By comparison, evidence introduced by the plaintiffs in *A & M Records, Inc.* v. *Napster, Inc.*, 239 F.3d 1004 (CA9 2001), showed that 87% of files available on the Napster filesharing network were copyrighted, *id.* at 1013.

authorized by the rightholders. They also argue that potential noninfringing uses of their software are significant in kind, even if infrequent in practice. Some musical performers, for example, have gained new audiences by distributing their copyrighted works for free across peer-to-peer networks, and some distributors of unprotected content have used peer-to-peer networks to disseminate files, Shakespeare being an example. Indeed, StreamCast has given Morpheus users the opportunity to download the briefs in this very case, though their popularity has not been quantified.

As for quantification, the parties' anecdotal and statistical evidence entered thus far to show the content available on the FastTrack and Gnutella networks does not say much about which files are actually downloaded by users, and no one can say how often the software is used to obtain copies of unprotected material. But MGM's evidence gives reason to think that the vast majority of users' downloads are acts of infringement, and because well over 100 million copies of the software in question are known to have been downloaded, and billions of files are shared across the FastTrack and Gnutella networks each month, the probable scope of copyright infringement is staggering.

Grokster and StreamCast concede the infringement in most downloads, and it is uncontested that they are aware that users employ their software primarily to download copyrighted files, even if the decentralized FastTrack and Gnutella networks fail to reveal which files are being copied, and when. From time to time, moreover, the companies have learned about their users' infringement directly, as from users who have sent e-mail to each company with questions about playing copyrighted movies they had downloaded, to whom the companies have responded with guidance. And MGM notified the companies of 8 million copyrighted files that could be obtained using their software.

Grokster and StreamCast are not, however, merely passive recipients of information about infringing use. The record is replete with evidence that from the moment Grokster and StreamCast began to distribute their free software, each one clearly voiced the objective that recipients use it to download copyrighted works, and each took active steps to encourage infringement. …

The[re is] evidence that Grokster sought to capture the market of former Napster users[,] … for Grokster launched its own OpenNap system called Swaptor and inserted digital codes into its Web site so that computer users using Web search engines to look for "Napster" or "free filesharing" would be directed to the Grokster Web site, where they could download the Grokster software. And Grokster's name is an apparent derivative of Napster. … Grokster and StreamCast receive no revenue from users, who obtain the software itself for nothing. Instead, both companies generate income by selling advertising space, and they stream the advertising to Grokster and Morpheus users while they are employing the programs. As the number of users of each program increases, advertising opportunities become worth more. While there is doubtless some demand for free Shakespeare, the evidence shows that substantive volume is a function of free access to copyrighted work. Users seeking Top 40 songs, for example, or the latest release by Modest Mouse, are certain to be far more numerous than those seeking a free Decameron, and Grokster and StreamCast translated that demand into dollars.

Finally, there is no evidence that either company made an effort to filter copyrighted material from users' downloads or otherwise impede the sharing of copyrighted files. Although Grokster appears to have sent e-mails warning users about infringing content when it received threatening notice from the copyright holders, it never blocked anyone from continuing to use its software to share copyrighted files. StreamCast not only rejected another company's offer of help to monitor infringement, *id.* at 928-929, but blocked the Internet Protocol addresses of entities it believed were trying to engage in such monitoring on its networks.

... II.

A.

MGM and many of the *amici* fault the Court of Appeals's holding for upsetting a sound balance between the respective values of supporting creative pursuits through copyright protection and promoting innovation in new communication technologies by limiting the incidence of liability for copyright infringement. The more artistic protection is favored, the more technological innovation may be discouraged; the administration of copyright law is an exercise in managing the trade-off. *See Sony Corp.* v. *Universal City Studios, supra,* at 442, 78 L. Ed. 2d 574, 104 S. Ct. 774....

The tension between the two values is the subject of this case, with its claim that digital distribution of copyrighted material threatens copyright holders as never before, because every copy is identical to the original, copying is easy, and many people (especially the young) use file-sharing software to download copyrighted works. ...

The argument for imposing indirect liability in this case is ... a powerful one, given the number of infringing downloads that occur every day using StreamCast's and Grokster's software. When a widely shared service or product is used to commit infringement, it may be impossible to enforce rights in the protected work effectively against all direct infringers, the only practical alternative being to go against the distributor of the copying device for secondary liability on a theory of contributory or vicarious infringement. *See In re Aimster Copyright Litigation,* 334 F.3d 643, 645-646 (CA7 2003).

One infringes contributorily by intentionally inducing or encouraging direct infringement, *see Gershwin Pub. Corp.* v. *Columbia Artists Management, Inc.,* 443 F.2d 1159, 1162 (CA2 1971), and infringes vicariously by profiting from direct infringement while declining to exercise a right to stop or limit it, *Shapiro, Bernstein & Co.* v. *H. L. Green Co.,* 316 F.2d 304, 307 (CA2 1963). Although "the Copyright Act does not expressly render anyone liable for infringement committed by another," *Sony Corp.* v. *Universal City Studios,* 464 U.S. at 434, 78 L. Ed. 2d 574, 104 S. Ct. 774, these doctrines of secondary liability emerged from common law principles and are well established in the law, *id.* at 486, 78 L. Ed. 2d 574, 104 S. Ct. 774 (Blackmun, J., dissenting); *Kalem Co.* v. *Harper Brothers,* 222 U.S. 55, 62-63, 56 L. Ed. 92, 32 S. Ct. 20 (1911); *Gershwin Pub. Corp.* v. *Columbia Artists Management, supra,* at 1162; 3 M. Nimmer & D. Nimmer, *Copyright,* § 12.04[A] (2005).

B.

Despite the currency of these principles of secondary liability, this Court has dealt with secondary copyright infringement in only one recent case, and because MGM has tailored its principal claim to our opinion there, a look at our earlier holding is in order. In *Sony Corp.* v. *Universal City Studios, supra,* this Court addressed a claim that secondary liability for infringement can arise from the very distribution of a commercial product. There, the product, novel at the time, was what we know today as the videocassette recorder or VCR. Copyright holders sued Sony as the manufacturer, claiming it was contributorily liable for infringement that occurred when VCR owners taped copyrighted programs because it supplied the means used to infringe, and it had constructive knowledge that infringement would occur. At the trial on the merits, the evidence showed that the principal use of the VCR was for "'time-shifting,'" or taping a program for later viewing at a more convenient time, which the Court found to be a fair, not an infringing, use. *Id.* at 423-424, 78 L. Ed. 2d 574, 104 S. Ct. 774. There was no evidence that Sony had expressed an object of bringing about taping in violation of copyright or had taken active steps to increase its profits from unlawful taping. *Id.* at 438, 78 L. Ed. 2d 574, 104 S. Ct. 774. Although Sony's advertisements urged consumers to buy the VCR to "'record favorite shows'" or "'build a library'" of recorded programs, *id.* at 459, 78 L. Ed. 2d 574, 104 S. Ct. 774 (Blackmun, J., dissenting), neither of these uses was necessarily infringing, *id.* at 424, 454-455, 78 L. Ed. 2d 574, 104 S. Ct. 774.

On those facts, with no evidence of stated or indicated intent to promote infringing uses, the only conceivable basis for imposing liability was on a theory of contributory infringement arising from its sale of VCRs to consumers with knowledge that some would use them to infringe. *Id.* at 439, 78 L. Ed. 2d 574, 104 S. Ct. 774. But because the VCR was "capable of commercially significant noninfringing uses," we held the manufacturer could not be faulted solely on the basis of its distribution. *Id.* at 442, 78 L. Ed. 2d 574, 104 S. Ct. 774.

This analysis reflected patent law's traditional staple article of commerce doctrine, now codified, that distribution of a component of a patented device will not violate the patent if it is suitable for use in other ways. 35 U.S.C. § 271(c); *Aro Mfg. Co.* v. *Convertible Top Replacement Co.*, 377 U.S. 476, 485, 12 L. Ed. 2d 457, 84 S. Ct. 1526, 1964 Dec. Comm'r Pat. 760 (1964) (noting codification of cases); *id.* at 486, n. 6, 12 L. Ed. 2d 457, 84 S. Ct. 1526 (same). The doctrine was devised to identify instances in which it may be presumed from distribution of an article in commerce that the distributor intended the article to be used to infringe another's patent, and so may justly be held liable for that infringement. "One who makes and sells articles which are only adapted to be used in a patented combination will be presumed to intend the natural consequences of his acts; he will be presumed to intend that they shall be used in the combination of the patent." *New York Scaffolding Co.* v. *Whitney*, 224 F. 452, 459 (CA8 1915); *see also Janes Heekin Co.* v. *Baker*, 138 F. 63, 66 (CA8 1905); *Canda* v. *Michigan Malleable Iron Co.*, 124 F. 486, 489 (CA6 1903); *Thomson-Houston Electric Co.* v. *Ohio Brass Co.*, 80 F. 712, 720-721, 1897 Dec. Comm'r Pat. 579 (CA6 1897); *Red Jacket Mfg. Co.* v. *Davis*, 82 F. 432, 439 (CA7 1897); *Holly* v. *Vergennes Machine Co.*, 4 F. 74, 82, 1880 Dec. Comm'r Pat. 659 (CC Vt. 1880); *Renwick* v. *Pond*, 20 F. Cas. 536, 541, F. Cas. No. 11702 (No. 11,702) (CC SDNY 1872).

In sum, where an article is "good for nothing else" but infringement, *Canda* v. *Michigan Malleable Iron Co.*, *supra*, at 489, there is no legitimate public interest in its unlicensed availability, and there is no injustice in presuming or imputing an intent to infringe, *see Henry* v. *A. B. Dick Co.*, 224 U.S. 1, 48, 56 L. Ed. 645, 32 S. Ct. 364, 1912 Dec. Comm'r Pat. 575 (1912), *overruled on other grounds, Motion Picture Patents Co.* v. *Universal Film Mfg. Co.*, 243 U.S. 502, 61 L. Ed. 871, 37 S. Ct. 416, 1917 Dec. Comm'r Pat. 391 (1917). Conversely, the doctrine absolves the equivocal conduct of selling an item with substantial lawful as well as unlawful uses, and limits liability to instances of more acute fault than the mere understanding that some of one's products will be misused. It leaves breathing room for innovation and a vigorous commerce. *See Sony Corp.* v. *Universal City Studios, supra,* at 442; *Dawson Chemical Co.* v. *Rohm & Haas Co.*, 448 U.S. 176, 221, 65 L. Ed. 2d 696, 100 S. Ct. 2601 (1980); *Henry* v. *A. B. Dick Co., supra,* at 48, 56 L. Ed. 645, 32 S. Ct. 364.

... We agree with MGM that the Court of Appeals misapplied *Sony*, which it read as limiting secondary liability quite beyond the circumstances to which the case applied. *Sony* barred secondary liability based on presuming or imputing intent to cause infringement solely from the design or distribution of a product capable of substantial lawful use, which the distributor knows is in fact used for infringement. The Ninth Circuit has read *Sony's* limitation to mean that whenever a product is capable of substantial lawful use, the producer can never be held contributorily liable for third parties' infringing use of it; it read the rule as being this broad, even when an actual purpose to cause infringing use is shown by evidence independent of design and distribution of the product, unless the distributors had "specific knowledge of infringement at a time at which they contributed to the infringement, and failed to act upon that information." Because the Circuit found the StreamCast and Grokster software capable of substantial lawful use, it concluded on the basis of its reading of *Sony* that neither company could be held liable, since there was no showing that their software, being without any central server, afforded them knowledge of specific unlawful uses.

This view of *Sony*, however, was error, converting the case from one about liability resting on imputed intent to one about liability on any theory. Because *Sony* did not displace other theories of secondary liability, and because we find below that it was error to grant summary judgment to the companies on MGM's inducement claim, we do not revisit *Sony* further, as MGM requests, to add a more quantified description of the point of balance between protection and commerce when liability rests solely on distribution with knowledge that unlawful use will occur. It is enough to note that the Ninth Circuit's judgment rested on an erroneous understanding of *Sony* and to leave further consideration of the *Sony* rule for a day when that may be required.

C.

Sony's rule limits imputing culpable intent as a matter of law from the characteristics or uses of a distributed product. But nothing in *Sony* requires courts to ignore evidence of intent if there is such evidence, and the case was never meant to foreclose rules of fault-based liability derived from the common law. *Sony Corp.* v. *Universal City Studios*, 464 U.S. at 439, 78 L. Ed. 2d 574, 104 S. Ct. 774 ("If vicarious liability is to be imposed on Sony in this case, it must rest on the fact that it has sold equipment with constructive knowledge" of the potential for infringement). Thus, where evidence goes beyond a product's characteristics or the knowledge that it may be put to infringing uses, and shows statements or actions directed to promoting infringement, *Sony's* staple-article rule will not preclude liability.

The classic case of direct evidence of unlawful purpose occurs when one induces commission of infringement by another, or "entices or persuades another" to infringe, *Black's Law Dictionary* 790 (8th ed. 2004), as by advertising. ... Evidence of "active steps . . . taken to encourage direct infringement," *Oak Industries, Inc.* v. *Zenith Electronics Corp.*, 697 F. Supp. 988, 992 (ND Ill. 1988), such as advertising an infringing use or instructing how to engage in an infringing use, show an affirmative intent that the product be used to infringe, and a showing that infringement was encouraged overcomes the law's reluctance to find liability when a defendant merely sells a commercial product suitable for some lawful use, *see, e.g., Water Technologies Corp.* v. *Calco, Ltd.*, 850 F.2d 660, 668 (CA Fed. 1988) (liability for inducement where one "actively and knowingly aids and abets another's direct infringement" (emphasis omitted)); *Fromberg, Inc.* v. *Thornhill*, 315 F.2d 407, 412-413 (CA5 1963) (demonstrations by sales staff of infringing uses supported liability for inducement); *Haworth Inc.* v. *Herman Miller Inc.*, 37 USPQ 2d 1080, 1090 (WD Mich. 1994) (evidence that defendant "demonstrated and recommended infringing configurations" of its product could support inducement liability); *Sims* v. *Mack Trucks, Inc.*, 459 F. Supp. 1198, 1215 (ED Pa. 1978) (finding inducement where the use "depicted by the defendant in its promotional film and brochures infringes the ...patent"), overruled on other grounds, 608 F.2d 87 (CA3 1979). *Cf.* W. Keeton, D. Dobbs, R. Keeton, & D. Owen, *Prosser and Keeton on Law of Torts* 37 (5th ed. 1984) ("There is a definite tendency to impose greater responsibility upon a defendant whose conduct was intended to do harm, or was morally wrong").

For the same reasons that *Sony* took the staple-article doctrine of patent law as a model for its copyright safe-harbor rule, the inducement rule, too, is a sensible one for copyright. We adopt it here, holding that one who distributes a device with the object of promoting its use to infringe copyright, as shown by clear expression or other affirmative steps taken to foster infringement, is liable for the resulting acts of infringement by third parties. We are, of course, mindful of the need to keep from trenching on regular commerce or discouraging the development of technologies with lawful and unlawful potential. Accordingly, just as *Sony* did not find intentional inducement despite the knowledge of the VCR manufacturer that its device could be used to infringe, 464 U.S. at 439, n.19, 78 L. Ed. 2d 574, 104 S. Ct. 774, mere knowledge of infringing potential or of actual infringing uses would not be enough here to subject a distributor to liability. Nor would ordinary acts incident to product distribution, such as offering customers technical support or product updates, support liability in themselves. The inducement rule, instead, premises liability on purposeful, culpable expression and conduct, and thus does nothing to compromise legitimate commerce or discourage innovation having a lawful promise.

III.

   A.

The only apparent question about treating MGM's evidence as sufficient to withstand summary judgment under the theory of inducement goes to the need on MGM's part to adduce evidence that StreamCast and Grokster communicated an inducing message to their software users. The classic instance of inducement is by advertisement or solicitation that broadcasts a message designed to stimulate others to commit violations. MGM claims that such a message is shown here. It is undisputed that StreamCast beamed onto the computer screens of users of Napster-compatible programs ads urging the adoption of its OpenNap program, which was designed, as its name implied, to invite the custom of patrons of Napster, then under attack in the courts for facilitating massive infringement. Those who accepted StreamCast's OpenNap program were offered software to perform the same services, which a factfinder could conclude would readily have been understood in the Napster market as the ability to download copyrighted music files. Grokster distributed an electronic newsletter containing links to articles promoting its software's ability to access popular copyrighted music. And anyone whose Napster or free file-sharing searches turned up a link to Grokster would have understood Grokster to be offering the same file-sharing ability as Napster, and to the same people who probably used Napster for infringing downloads; that would also have been the understanding of anyone offered Grokster's suggestively named Swaptor software, its version of OpenNap. And both companies communicated a clear message by responding affirmatively to requests for help in locating and playing copyrighted materials.

   ....[E]ach company showed itself to be aiming to satisfy a known source of demand for copyright infringement, the market comprising former Napster users. StreamCast's internal documents made constant reference to Napster, it initially distributed its Morpheus software through an OpenNap program compatible with Napster, it advertised its OpenNap program to Napster users, and its Morpheus software functions as Napster did except that it could be used to distribute more kinds of files, including copyrighted movies and software programs. Grokster's name is apparently derived from Napster, it too initially offered an OpenNap program, its software's function is likewise comparable to Napster's, and it attempted to divert queries for Napster onto its own Web site. Grokster and StreamCast's efforts to supply services to former Napster users, deprived of a mechanism to copy and distribute what were overwhelmingly infringing files, indicate a principal, if not exclusive, intent on the part of each to bring about infringement.

....[T]his evidence of unlawful objective is given added significance by MGM's showing that neither company attempted to develop filtering tools or other mechanisms to diminish the infringing activity using their software. While the Ninth Circuit treated the defendants' failure to develop such tools as irrelevant because they lacked an independent duty to monitor their users' activity, we think this evidence underscores Grokster's and StreamCast's intentional facilitation of their users' infringement.[12]

[Furthermore,] ... there is a further complement to the direct evidence of unlawful objective. It is useful to recall that StreamCast and Grokster make money by selling advertising space, by directing ads to the screens of computers employing their software. As the record shows, the more the software is used, the more ads are sent out and the greater the advertising revenue becomes. Since the extent of the software's use determines the gain to the distributors, the commercial sense of their enterprise turns on high-volume use, which the record shows is infringing. This evidence alone would not justify an inference of unlawful intent, but viewed in the context of the entire record its import is clear.

The unlawful objective is unmistakable.

B.

In addition to intent to bring about infringement and distribution of a device suitable for infringing use, the inducement theory of course requires evidence of actual infringement by recipients of the device, the software in this case. As the account of the facts indicates, there is evidence of infringement on a gigantic scale, and there is no serious issue of the adequacy of MGM's showing on this point in order to survive the companies' summary judgment requests. Although an exact calculation of infringing use, as a basis for a claim of damages, is subject to dispute, there is no question that the summary judgment evidence is at least adequate to entitle MGM to go forward with claims for damages and equitable relief.

In sum, this case is significantly different from *Sony* and reliance on that case to rule in favor of StreamCast and Grokster was error. *Sony* dealt with a claim of liability based solely on distributing a product with alternative lawful and unlawful uses, with knowledge that some users would follow the unlawful course. The case struck a balance between the interests of protection and innovation by holding that the product's capability of substantial

---

[12] Of course, in the absence of other evidence of intent, a court would be unable to find contributory infringement liability merely based on a failure to take affirmative steps to prevent infringement, if the device otherwise was capable of substantial noninfringing uses. Such a holding would tread too close to the *Sony* safe harbor.

lawful employment should bar the imputation of fault and consequent secondary liability for the unlawful acts of others.

MGM's evidence in this case most obviously addresses a different basis of liability for distributing a product open to alternative uses. Here, evidence of the distributors' words and deeds going beyond distribution as such shows a purpose to cause and profit from third-party acts of copyright infringement. If liability for inducing infringement is ultimately found, it will not be on the basis of presuming or imputing fault, but from inferring a patently illegal objective from statements and actions showing what that objective was.

There is substantial evidence in MGM's favor on all elements of inducement, and summary judgment in favor of Grokster and StreamCast was error. On remand, reconsideration of MGM's motion for summary judgment will be in order.

The judgment of the Court of Appeals is vacated, and the case is remanded for further proceedings consistent with this opinion.

JUSTICE BREYER, with whom JUSTICE STEVENS and JUSTICE O'CONNOR join, concurring.

I agree with the Court that the distributor of a dual-use technology may be liable for the infringing activities of third parties where he or she actively seeks to advance the infringement. I further agree that, in light of our holding today, we need not now "revisit" *Sony Corp. of America* v. *Universal City Studios, Inc.*, 464 U.S. 417, 78 L. Ed. 2d 574, 104 S. Ct. 774 (1984). Other Members of the Court, however, take up the *Sony* question: whether Grokster's product is "capable of 'substantial' or 'commercially significant' noninfringing uses." (GINSBURG, J., concurring) (quoting *Sony, supra*, at 442, 78 L. Ed. 2d 574, 104 S. Ct. 774). And they answer that question by stating that the Court of Appeals was wrong when it granted summary judgment on the issue in Grokster's favor. I write to explain why I disagree with them on this matter.

... I.

The Court's opinion in *Sony* and the record evidence (as described and analyzed in the many briefs before us) together convince me that the Court of Appeals' conclusion has adequate legal support.

A.

... The *Sony* Court had before it a survey (commissioned by the District Court and then prepared by the respondents) showing that roughly 9% of all VCR recordings were of the type -- namely, religious, educational, and sports programming -- owned by producers and distributors testifying on Sony's behalf who did not object to time-shifting. *Sony, supra*, at 424, 78 L. Ed. 2d 574, 104 S. Ct. 774 (7.3% of all Sony VCR use is to record sports programs; representatives of the sports leagues do not object). A much higher percentage of VCR *users* had at one point taped an authorized program, in addition to taping unauthorized programs. And the plaintiffs -- not a large class of content providers as in this case -- owned only a small percentage of the total available *un*authorized programming. But of all the taping actually done by Sony's customers, only around 9% was of the sort the Court referred to as authorized.

The Court found that the magnitude of authorized programming was "significant," and it also noted the "significant potential for future authorized copying." 464 U.S. at 444, 78 L.

Ed. 2d 574, 104 S. Ct. 774. The Court supported this conclusion by referencing the trial testimony of professional sports league officials and a religious broadcasting representative. *Id.* at 444, 78 L. Ed. 2d 574, 104 S. Ct. 774, and n.24. It also discussed (1) a Los Angeles educational station affiliated with the Public Broadcasting Service that made many of its programs available for home taping, and (2) Mr. Rogers' Neighborhood, a widely watched children's program. *Id.* at 445, 78 L. Ed. 2d 574, 104 S. Ct. 774. On the basis of this testimony and other similar evidence, the Court determined that producers of this kind had authorized duplication of their copyrighted programs "in significant enough numbers to create a *substantial* market for a noninfringing use of the" VCR. *Id.* at 447, n.28, 78 L. Ed. 2d 574, 104 S. Ct. 774 (emphasis added).

The Court, in using the key word "substantial," indicated that these circumstances alone constituted a sufficient basis for rejecting the imposition of secondary liability. *See id.* at 456, 78 L. Ed. 2d 574, 104 S. Ct. 774 ("Sony demonstrated a significant likelihood that *substantial* numbers of copyright holders" would not object to time-shifting (emphasis added)). Nonetheless, the Court buttressed its conclusion by finding separately that, in any event, *un*authorized time- shifting often constituted not infringement, but "fair use." *Id.* at 447-456, 78 L. Ed. 2d 574, 104 S. Ct. 774.

B.

When measured against *Sony's* underlying evidence and analysis, the evidence now before us shows that Grokster passes *Sony's* test -- that is, whether the company's product is capable of substantial or commercially significant noninfringing uses. *Id.* at 442, 78 L. Ed. 2d 574, 104 S. Ct. 774. For one thing, petitioners' (hereinafter MGM) own expert declared that 75% of current files available on Grokster are infringing and 15% are "likely infringing." That leaves some number of files near 10% that apparently are noninfringing, a figure very similar to the 9% or so of authorized time-shifting uses of the VCR that the Court faced in *Sony.*

As in *Sony,* witnesses here explained the nature of the noninfringing files on Grokster's network without detailed quantification. Those files include:

~ Authorized copies of music by artists such as Wilco, Janis Ian, Pearl Jam, Dave Matthews, John Mayer, and others. ...

~ Free electronic books and other works from various online publishers, including Project Gutenberg. ...

~ Public domain and authorized software, such as WinZip 8.1. ...

~ Licensed music videos and television and movie segments distributed via digital video packaging with the permission of the copyright holder. ...

The nature of these and other lawfully swapped files is such that it is reasonable to infer quantities of current lawful use roughly approximate to those at issue in *Sony.* At least, MGM has offered no evidence sufficient to survive summary judgment that could plausibly demonstrate a significant quantitative difference. To be sure, in quantitative terms these uses account for only a small percentage of the total number of uses of Grokster's product. But the same was true in *Sony,* which characterized the relatively limited authorized copying market as "substantial." (The Court made clear as well in *Sony* that the amount of material then presently available for lawful copying -- if not actually copied -- was significant, *see* 464 U.S. at 444, 78 L. Ed. 2d 574, 104 S. Ct. 774, and the same is certainly true in this case.)

Importantly, *Sony* also used the word "capable," asking whether the product is "*capable of*" substantial noninfringing uses. Its language and analysis suggest that a figure like 10%, if fixed for all time, might well prove insufficient, but that such a figure serves as an adequate foundation where there is a reasonable prospect of expanded legitimate uses over time. *See ibid.* (noting a "significant potential for future authorized copying"). And its language also indicates the appropriateness of looking to potential future uses of the product to determine its "capability."

Here the record reveals a significant future market for noninfringing uses of Grokster-type peer-to-peer software. Such software permits the exchange of *any* sort of digital file -- whether that file does, or does not, contain copyrighted material. As more and more uncopyrighted information is stored in swappable form, it seems a likely inference that lawful peer-to-peer sharing will become increasingly prevalent.

And that is just what is happening. Such legitimate noninfringing uses are coming to include the swapping of: *research information* (the initial purpose of many peer-to-peer networks); *public domain films* (*e.g.*, those owned by the Prelinger Archive); *historical recordings and digital educational materials* (*e.g.*, those stored on the Internet Archive); *digital photos* (OurPictures, for example, is starting a P2P photo-swapping service); "*shareware" and "freeware*" (e.g., Linux and certain Windows software); *secure licensed music and movie files* (Intent MediaWorks, for example, protects licensed content sent across P2P networks); *news broadcasts past and present* (the BBC Creative Archive lets users "rip, mix and share the BBC"); *user-created audio and video files* (including "podcasts" that may be distributed through P2P software); *and all manner of free "open content" works collected by Creative Commons* (one can search for Creative Commons material on StreamCast). ... I can find nothing in the record that suggests that this course of events will *not* continue to flow naturally as a consequence of the character of the software taken together with the foreseeable development of the Internet and of information technology.

There may be other now-unforeseen noninfringing uses that develop for peer-to-peer software, just as the home-video rental industry (unmentioned in *Sony*) developed for the VCR. But the foreseeable development of such uses, when taken together with an estimated 10% noninfringing material, is sufficient to meet *Sony*'s standard. And while *Sony* considered the record following a trial, there are no facts asserted by MGM in its summary judgment filings that lead me to believe the outcome after a trial here could be any different. The lower courts reached the same conclusion.

Of course, Grokster itself may not want to develop these other noninfringing uses. But *Sony*'s standard seeks to protect not the Groksters of this world (which in any event may well be liable under today's holding), but the development of technology more generally. And Grokster's desires in this respect are beside the point.

II.

The real question here, I believe, is not whether the record evidence satisfies *Sony*. As I have interpreted the standard set forth in that case, it does. And of the Courts of Appeals that have considered the matter, only one has proposed interpreting *Sony* more strictly than I would do -- in a case where the product might have failed under *any* standard. *In re Aimster Copyright Litigation*, 334 F.3d 643, 653 (CA7 2003) (defendant "failed to show that its service is *ever* used for any purpose other than to infringe" copyrights (emphasis added)); *see Matthew Bender & Co. v. West Publ. Co.*, 158 F.3d 693, 706-707 (CA2 1998) (court did not *require* that noninfringing uses be "predominant," it merely found that they *were* predominant, and therefore provided no analysis of *Sony*'s boundaries); *but see ante*, at 3 n. 1 (GINSBURG, J., concurring); *see also A&M Records* v. *Napster, Inc.*, 239 F.3d 1004, 1020 (CA9 2001) (discussing *Sony*); *Cable/Home Communication Corp.* v. *Network Productions, Inc.*, 902 F.2d 829, 842-847 (CA11 1990) (same); *Vault Corp.* v. *Quaid Software, Ltd.*, 847 F.2d 255, 262 (CA5 1988) (same); *cf. Dynacore Holdings Corp.* v. *U.S. Philips Corp.*, 363 F.3d 1263, 1275 (CA Fed. 2004) (same); *see also Doe* v. *GTE Corp.*, 347 F.3d 655, 661 (CA7 2003) ("A person may be liable as a contributory infringer if the product or service it sells has no (or only slight) legal use").

Instead, the real question is whether we should modify the *Sony* standard, as MGM requests, or interpret *Sony* more strictly....

As I have said, *Sony* itself sought to "strike a balance between a copyright holder's legitimate demand for effective -- not merely symbolic -- protection of the statutory monopoly, and the rights of others freely to engage in substantially unrelated areas of commerce." [464 U.S.] at 442, 78 L. Ed. 2d 574, 104 S. Ct. 774. Thus, to determine whether modification, or a strict interpretation, of *Sony* is needed, I would ask whether MGM has shown that *Sony* incorrectly balanced copyright and new-technology interests. In particular: (1) Has *Sony* (as I interpret it) worked to protect new technology? (2) If so, would modification or strict interpretation significantly weaken that protection? (3) If so, would new or necessary copyright-related benefits outweigh any such weakening?

A.

The first question is the easiest to answer. *Sony*'s rule, as I interpret it, has provided entrepreneurs with needed assurance that they will be shielded from copyright liability as they bring valuable new technologies to market.

Sony's rule is clear. That clarity allows those who develop new products that are capable of substantial noninfringing uses to know, *ex ante*, that distribution of their product will not yield massive monetary liability. At the same time, it helps deter them from distributing products that have no other real function than -- or that are specifically intended for -- copyright infringement, deterrence that the Court's holding today reinforces (by adding a weapon to the copyright holder's legal arsenal).

Sony's rule is strongly technology protecting. The rule deliberately makes it difficult for courts to find secondary liability where new technology is at issue. It establishes that the law will not impose copyright liability upon the distributors of dual-use technologies (who do not themselves engage in unauthorized copying) unless the product in question will be used *almost exclusively* to infringe copyrights (or unless they actively induce infringements as we today describe). *Sony* thereby recognizes that the copyright laws are not intended to discourage or to control the emergence of new technologies, including (perhaps especially) those that help disseminate information and ideas more broadly or more efficiently. Thus *Sony*'s rule shelters VCRs, typewriters, tape recorders, photocopiers, computers, cassette players, compact disc burners, digital video recorders, MP3 players, Internet search engines, and peer-to-peer software. But *Sony*'s rule does not shelter descramblers, even if one could *theoretically* use a descrambler in a noninfringing way. 464 U.S. at 441-442, 78 L. Ed. 2d 574, 104 S. Ct. 774. *Compare Cable/Home Communication Corp.*, *supra*, at 837-850 (developer liable for advertising television signal descrambler), *with Vault Corp.*, *supra*, at 262 (primary use infringing but a substantial noninfringing use).

Sony's rule is forward looking. It does not confine its scope to a static snapshot of a product's current uses (thereby threatening technologies that have undeveloped future markets). Rather, as the VCR example makes clear, a product's market can evolve dramatically over time. And *Sony* -- by referring to a *capacity* for substantial noninfringing uses -- recognizes that fact. *Sony's* word "capable" refers to a plausible, not simply a theoretical, likelihood that such uses will come to pass, and that fact anchors *Sony* in practical reality. *Cf. Aimster, supra,* at 651.

Sony's rule is mindful of the limitations facing judges where matters of technology are concerned. Judges have no specialized technical ability to answer questions about present or future technological feasibility or commercial viability where technology professionals, engineers, and venture capitalists themselves may radically disagree and where answers may differ depending upon whether one focuses upon the time of product development or the time of distribution. Consider, for example, the question whether devices can be added to Grokster's software that will filter out infringing files. MGM tells us this is easy enough to do, as do several *amici* that produce and sell the filtering technology. Grokster says it is not at all easy to do, and not an efficient solution in any event, and several apparently disinterested computer science professors agree. Which account should a judge credit? *Sony* says that the judge will not necessarily have to decide.

Given the nature of the *Sony* rule, it is not surprising that in the last 20 years, there have been relatively few contributory infringement suits -- based on a product distribution theory -- brought against technology providers (a small handful of federal appellate court cases and perhaps fewer than two dozen District Court cases in the last 20 years). I have found nothing in the briefs or the record that shows that *Sony* has failed to achieve its innovation-protecting objective.

B.

The second, more difficult, question is whether a modified *Sony* rule (or a strict interpretation) would significantly weaken the law's ability to protect new technology. ...

To require defendants to provide, for example, detailed evidence -- say business plans, profitability estimates, projected technological modifications, and so forth -- would doubtless make life easier for copyrightholder plaintiffs. But it would simultaneously increase the legal uncertainty that surrounds the creation or development of a new technology capable of being put to infringing uses. Inventors and entrepreneurs (in the garage, the dorm room, the corporate lab, or the boardroom) would have to fear (and in many cases endure) costly and extensive trials when they create, produce, or distribute the sort of information technology that can be used for copyright infringement. They would often be left guessing as to how a court, upon later review of the product and its uses, would decide when necessarily rough estimates amounted to sufficient evidence. They would have no way to predict how courts would weigh the respective values of infringing and noninfringing uses; determine the efficiency and advisability of technological changes; or assess a product's potential future markets. The price of a wrong guess -- even if it involves a good-faith effort to assess technical and commercial viability -- could be large statutory damages (not less than $750 and up to $30,000 *per infringed work*). 17 U.S.C. § 504(c)(1). The additional risk and uncertainty would mean a consequent additional chill of technological development.

C.

The third question -- whether a positive copyright impact would outweigh any technology-related loss -- I find the most difficult of the three. I do not doubt that a more intrusive *Sony* test would generally provide greater revenue security for copyright holders. But it is harder to conclude that the gains on the copyright swings would exceed the losses on the technology roundabouts.

For one thing, the law disfavors equating the two different kinds of gain and loss; rather, it leans in favor of protecting technology. As *Sony* itself makes clear, the producer of a technology which *permits* unlawful copying does not himself *engage* in unlawful copying -- a fact that makes the attachment of copyright liability to the creation, production, or distribution of the technology an exceptional thing. *See* 464 U.S. at 431, 78 L. Ed. 2d 574, 104 S. Ct. 774 (courts "must be circumspect" in construing the copyright laws to preclude distribution of new technologies). Moreover, *Sony* has been the law for some time. And that fact imposes a serious burden upon copyright holders like MGM to show a need for change in the current rules of the game, including a more strict interpretation of the test.

In any event, the evidence now available does not, in my view, make out a sufficiently strong case for change. To say this is not to doubt the basic need to protect copyrighted material from infringement. The Constitution itself stresses the vital role that copyright plays in advancing the "useful Arts." Art. I, § 8, cl. 8. No one disputes that "reward to the author or artist serves to induce release to the public of the products of his creative genius." *United States* v. *Paramount Pictures, Inc.*, 334 U.S. 131, 158, 92 L. Ed. 1260, 68 S. Ct. 915 (1948). And deliberate unlawful copying is no less an unlawful taking of property than garden-variety theft. *See, e.g.*, 18 U.S.C. § 2319 (criminal copyright infringement); § 1961(1)(B) (copyright infringement can be a predicate act under the Racketeer Influenced and Corrupt Organizations Act); § 1956(c)(7)(D) (money laundering includes the receipt of proceeds from copyright infringement). But these highly general principles cannot by themselves tell us how to balance the interests at issue in *Sony* or whether *Sony's* standard needs modification. And at certain key points, information is lacking.

Will an unmodified *Sony* lead to a significant diminution in the amount or quality of creative work produced? Since copyright's basic objective is creation and its revenue objectives but a means to that end, this is the underlying copyright question. *See Twentieth Century Music Corp.* v. *Aiken*, 422 U.S. 151, 156, 45 L. Ed. 2d 84, 95 S. Ct. 2040 (1975) ("Creative work is to be encouraged and rewarded, but private motivation must ultimately serve the cause of promoting broad public availability of literature, music, and the other arts"). And its answer is far from clear.

Unauthorized copying likely diminishes industry revenue, though it is not clear by how much. ... More importantly, copyright holders at least potentially have other tools available to reduce piracy and to abate whatever threat it poses to creative production. As today's opinion makes clear, a copyright holder may proceed against a technology provider where a provable specific intent to infringe (of the kind the Court describes) is present. Services like Grokster may well be liable under an inducement theory.

In addition, a copyright holder has always had the legal authority to bring a traditional infringement suit against one who wrongfully copies. Indeed, since September 2003, the Recording Industry Association of America (RIAA) has filed "thousands of suits against people for sharing copyrighted material." Walker, *New Movement Hits Universities: Get Legal Music,* Washington Post, Mar. 17, 2005, p. E1. These suits have provided copyright holders with damages; have served as a teaching tool, making clear that much file sharing, if done without permission, is unlawful; and apparently have had a real and significant deterrent effect. *See, e.g.*, L. Rainie, M. Madden, D. Hess, & G. Mudd, *Pew Internet Project and comScore Media Metrix Data Memo: The state of music downloading and file-sharing online*, pp. 2, 4, 6, 10 (Apr. 2004), www.pewinternet.org/pdfs/PIP_Filesharing_April_04.pdf (number of people downloading files fell from a peak of roughly 35 million to roughly 23 million in the year following the first suits; 38% of current downloaders report downloading fewer files because of the suits); M. Madden & L. Rainie, *Pew Internet Project Data Memo: Music and Video Downloading Moves Beyond P2P*, p. 7 (March 2005), www.pewinternet.org/pdfs/PIP_Filesharing_March05.pdf (number of downloaders has "inched up" but "continues to rest well below the peak level"); Groennings, *Note, Costs and Benefits of the Recording Industry's Litigation Against Individuals,* 20 Berkeley Technology L. J. 571 (2005); *but see* Evangelista, *Downloading Music and Movie Files is as Popular as Ever*, San Francisco Chronicle, Mar. 28, 2005, p. E1 (referring to the continuing "tide of rampant copyright infringement," while noting that the RIAA says it believes the "campaign of lawsuits and public education has at least contained the problem").

Further, copyright holders may develop new technological devices that will help curb unlawful infringement. Some new technology, called "digital 'watermarking'" and "digital fingerprinting," can encode within the file information about the author and the copyright scope and date, which "fingerprints" can help to expose infringers. *RIAA Reveals Method to Madness,* Wired News, Aug. 28, 2003, http://www.wired.com/news/digiwood/ 0,1412,60222,00.html; Besek, *Anti-Circumvention Laws and Copyright: A Report from the Kernochan Center for Law, Media and the Arts,* 27 Colum. J. L. & Arts 385, 391, 451 (2004). Other technology can, through encryption, potentially restrict users' ability to make a digital copy. *See* J. Borland, *Tripping the Rippers,* C/net News.com (Sept. 28, 2001), http://news.com.com/Tripping+the+rippers/2009=1023_3=273619.html; *but see* Brief for Bridgemar Services Ltd. as *Amicus Curiae* 5-8 (arguing that peer-to-peer service providers can more easily block unlawful swapping).

At the same time, advances in technology have discouraged unlawful copying by making *lawful* copying (*e.g.*, downloading music with the copyright holder's permission) cheaper and easier to achieve. Several services now sell music for less than $1 per song. (Walmart.com, for example, charges $0.88 each). Consequently, many consumers initially attracted to the convenience and flexibility of services like Grokster are now migrating to lawful paid services (services with copying permission) where they can enjoy at little cost even greater convenience and flexibility without engaging in unlawful swapping. *See* Wu, *When Code Isn't Law,* 89 Va. L. Rev. 679, 731-735 (2003) (noting the prevalence of technological problems on unpaid swapping sites); K. Dean, *P2P Tilts Toward Legitimacy,* wired.com, Wired News (Nov. 24, 2004), http://www.wired.com/news/digiwood/0,1412,65836,00.html; M. Madden & L. Rainie, *March 2005 Data Memo, supra*, at 6-7 (percentage of current downloaders who have used paid services rose from 24% to 43% in a year; number using free services fell from 58% to 41%).

Thus, lawful music downloading services -- those that charge the customer for downloading music and pay royalties to the copyright holder -- have continued to grow and to produce substantial revenue. *See* ... Bruno, *Digital Entertainment: Piracy Fight Shows Encouraging Signs* (Mar. 5, 2005), *available at* LEXIS, News Library, Billboard File (in 2004, consumers worldwide purchased more than 10 times the number of digital tracks purchased in 2003; global digital music market of $330 million in 2004 expected to double in

2005); Press Release, *Informa Media Report, supra* (global digital revenues will likely exceed $3 billion in 2010); Ashton, [*International Federation of the Phonographic Industry*] *Predicts Downloads Will Hit the Mainstream, Music Week,* Jan. 29, 2005, p. 6 (legal music sites and portable MP3 players "are helping transform the digital music market" into "an everyday consumer experience").   And more advanced types of *non*-music-oriented P2P networks have also started to develop, drawing in part on the lessons of Grokster.

Finally, as *Sony* recognized, the legislative option remains available. Courts are less well suited than Congress to the task of "accommodating fully the varied permutations of competing interests that are inevitably implicated by such new technology." *Sony*, 464 U.S. at 431, 78 L. Ed. 2d 574, 104 S. Ct. 774; *see, e.g.*, Audio Home Recording Act of 1992, 106 Stat. 4237 (adding 17 U.S.C., ch. 10); Protecting Innovation and Art While Preventing Piracy: Hearing Before the Senate Comm. on the Judiciary, 108th Cong., 2d Sess. (July 22, 2004).

I do not know whether these developments and similar alternatives will prove sufficient, but I am reasonably certain that, given their existence, a strong demonstrated need for modifying *Sony* (or for interpreting *Sony*'s standard more strictly) has not yet been shown. That fact, along with the added risks that modification (or strict interpretation) would impose upon technological innovation, leads me to the conclusion that we should maintain *Sony*, reading its standard as I have read it. As so read, it requires affirmance of the Ninth Circuit's determination of the relevant aspects of the *Sony* question.

For these reasons, I disagree with JUSTICE GINSBURG, but I agree with the Court and join its opinion.

* * * * *

Notes and Questions

1. Notwithstanding some courts' acknowledgement of the impact of P2P file sharing on industry sales, *see, e.g., A&M Records, Inc. v. Napster, Inc.*, 114 F. Supp. 2d 896, 913 (N.D. Cal. 2000) (stating that the plaintiffs produced evidence that Napster use reduces audio CD sales among college students and raises barriers to plaintiffs' entry into the market for the digital downloading of music), *aff'd in part, rev'd in part*, 239 F.3d 1004 (9th Cir. 2001) some have questioned the impact of illicit P2P file sharing on the music recording industry. Researchers at Harvard University and the University of North Carolina tracked downloads of music for a 17-week period in 2002 to assess the impact of peer-to-peer file sharing on sales of CDs. *See* Felix Oberholzer and Koleman Strumpf, *The Effect of File Sharing on Record Sales: An Empirical Analysis, Working Paper,* March 2004, *available at* <http://www.unc.edu/~cigar/papers/FileSharing_March2004.pdf>.   Their study of the correlation between file-sharing and music sales indicated that on-line music trading appears to have played a less significant role in the recent slide in CD sales than some had attributed to illicit P2P practices. The researchers concluded that "[d]ownloads have an effect on sales which is statistically indistinguishable from zero, despite rather precise estimates. Moreover, these estimates are of moderate economic significance and are inconsistent with claims that file sharing is the primary reason for the recent decline in music sales." *Id.* The study concluded:

> At most, file sharing can explain a tiny fraction of th[e] decline [in music industry sales].   This result is plausible given that movies,

369

software, and video games are actively downloaded, and yet these industries have continued to grow since the advent of file sharing. While a full explanation for the recent decline in record sales [is] beyond the scope of this analysis, several plausible candidates exist. These alternative factors include poor macroeconomic conditions, a reduction in the number of album releases, growing competition from other forms of entertainment such as video games and DVDs (video game graphics have improved and the price of DVD players or movies have sharply fallen), a reduction in music variety stemming from the large consolidation in radio along with the rise of independent promoter fees to gain airplay, and possibly a consumer backlash against record industry tactics. It is also important to note that a similar drop in record sales occurred in the late 1970s and early 1980s, and that record sales in the 1990s may have been abnormally high as individuals replaced older formats with CDs.

Id. at 24 (citation and footnote omitted).

In *Metro-Goldwyn-Mayer Studios, Inc. v. Grokster, Ltd.,* No. 04-480, 2005 U.S. Lexis 5212 (U.S. June 27, 2005), Justice Breyer, concurring, questioned the degree to which the effect of illicit P2P file sharing on music sales could be measured accurately He stated:

Unauthorized copying likely diminishes industry revenue, though it is not clear by how much. *Compare* S. Liebowitz, *Will MP3 Downloads Annihilate the Record Industry? The Evidence So Far,* p. 2 (June 2003), http://www.utdallas.edu/liebowit/intprop/records.pdf ... (file sharing has caused a decline in music sales), and Press Release, Informa Media Group Report (citing Music on the Internet (5th ed. 2004)) (estimating total lost sales to the music industry in the range of $2 billion annually), at http://www.informatm.com, *with* F. Oberholzer & K. Strumpf, *The Effect of File Sharing on Record Sales: An Empirical Analysis,* p. 24 (Mar. 2004), www.unc.edu/cigar/papers/FileSharing_March2004.pdf (academic study concluding that "file sharing has no statistically significant effect on purchases of the average album"), *and* McGuire, Study: File-Sharing No Threat to Music Sales (Mar. 29, 2004), http://www.washingtonpost.com/ac2/wp-dyn/A343002004Mar29? language=printer (discussing mixed evidence).

The extent to which related production has actually and resultingly declined remains uncertain, though there is good reason to believe that the decline, if any, is not substantial. *See, e.g.,* M. Madden, Pew Internet & American Life Project, *Artists, Musicians, and the Internet,* p. 21, http://www.pewinternet.org/pdfs/PIP_Artists.Musicians_Report. pdf (nearly 70% of musicians believe that file sharing is a minor threat or no threat at all to creative industries); Benkler, *Sharing Nicely: On Shareable Goods and the Emergence of Sharing as a Modality of Economic Production,* 114 Yale L. J. 273, 351-352 (2004) ("Much of the actual flow of revenue to artists -- from performances and other sources -- is stable even assuming a complete displacement of the CD market by peer-to-peer distribution.... It would be silly to think that music, a cultural form without which no human society has existed, will cease to be in our world [because of illegal file swapping]").

Id. at *82-*83 (Breyer, J., concurring).

2. In May 2005, plaintiffs in *In re Napster, Inc. Copyright Litig.*, No. C 04-2121 MHP (N.D. Cal.), moved for leave to file a supplemental memorandum in opposition to the defendants' motion for summary judgment, asserting the Artists' Rights and Theft Prevention Act of 2005, Pub. L. No. 109-9 (Apr. 27, 2005). *See* Memorandum and Order, *In re Napster, Inc. Copyright Litig.*, No. C 04-2121 MHP (N.D. Cal. May 12 2005), *available at* <http://patelorder.notlong.com/>. The defendants contended that the legislation raised the question of whether the operator of a peer-to-peer Internet file-sharing service that maintained an index of downloadable files embodying copyrighted sound recording and musical compositions "distribute[d]" those works within the meaning of the Copyright Act, 17 U.S.C. § 106(3). *See In re Napster, Inc. Copyright Litig.*, No. C 04-2121 MHP (N.D. Cal. 2005) at 2, *available at* <http://patelorder.notlong.com/>. Among the reasons the court rejected the plaintiffs' argument were the statute's language and the absence of persuasive legislative history. *See id.* at 3-4.

3. Ruling from the bench, a federal court dismissed a suit brought by Perfect 10 Inc., which publishes an adult magazine and operates an adult content web-site. Perfect 10 had complained that hundreds of web-site operators sold images in which Perfect 10 held property interests, and that Visa International Service Association and Mastercard International Inc. knowingly provided transactional support services to infringing sites. *See* Brenda Sandburg, *Federal Judge Tosses Porn Purveyor's Copyright Suit Against Credit Card Companies,* Law.com (Nov. 16, 2004), *available at* <http://www.law.com/jsp/article.jsp?id=1100535339538>. The plaintiff claimed that Visa and Mastercard should be held accountable under contributory and vicarious copyright infringement theories for processing the sales. *See* Brenda Sandburg, *Federal Judge Tosses Porn Purveyor's Copyright Suit Against Credit Card Companies,* Nat'l L.J., Nov. 16, 2004.

* * * * *

The Fair Use Defense

insert the following before A&M Records, Inc., et al. v. Napster, Inc. on page 571 of Law of Internet Speech:

After a bench trial in which the court ruled that the defendant had willfully infringed the plaintiffs' copyrights by engaging in unauthorized copying for commercial purposes, *see UMG Recordings, Inc. v. MP3.com, Inc.,* No. 00 Civ. 472, 2000 U.S. Dist. LEXIS 13293 (S.D.N.Y. Sept. 6, 2000), the court issued rulings as to mitigating factors that substantially reduced the damages, *see UMG Recordings, Inc. v. MP3.com, Inc., judgment entered by* No. 00 Civ. 0472, 2000 U.S. Dist. LEXIS 17907 (S.D.N.Y. Nov. 16, 2000).

* * * * *

insert the following before Notes and Questions on page 582 of Law of Internet Speech:

Thereafter, in *Kelly v. Arriba Soft Corp.,* 336 F.3d 811, 822 (9th Cir. 2003), the court agreed that the defendant's use of the plaintiff's images as thumbnails in its search engine did constitute a fair use, but reversed the district court's grant of summary judgment to the defendant insofar as it concerned the use of the full-size images because the parties had not moved for summary judgment on that point and the defendant had not had an opportunity to contest the allegations of copyright infringement on that issue.

* * * * *

In *BMG Music v. Gonzalez,* No. 03 C 6276, 2005 U.S. Dist. LEXIS 910 (N.D. Ill. Jan. 12, 2005), recording companies objected to the defendant's downloading of copyrighted songs. The defendant-user argued that the downloading constituted a fair use on the grounds that she was sampling the songs to decide whether to purchase them, she already owned many of the songs she downloaded, and she did not cause any financial harm by downloading the songs. *See id.* at *2-*3. The U.S. District Court for the Northern District of Illinois granted summary judgment for the plaintiffs, however, concluding that sampling by direct infringers was not a fair use, that prior ownership of recordings was irrelevant because the plaintiffs sought redress only for songs the defendant did not own, and that the cumulative effect of direct infringers harmed the recording industry by reducing sales and raising barriers to the plaintiffs' entry into the market for digital downloading of music. *See id.* at *3.

In *Bridgeport Music, Inc. v. Dimension Films,* 401 F.3d 647 (6th Cir. 2004), the U.S. Court of Appeals for the Sixth Circuit considered the question of *de minimis* copying in the context of digital sampling. The court opined:

> To begin with, there is ease of enforcement. Get a license or do not sample. We do not see this as stifling creativity in any significant way. It must be remembered that if an artist wants to incorporate a "riff" from another work in his or her recording, he is free to duplicate the sound of that "riff" in the studio. Second, the market will control the license price and keep it within bounds. The sound recording copyright holder cannot exact a license fee greater than what it would cost the person seeking the license to just duplicate the sample in the course of making the new recording. Third, sampling is never accidental. It is not like the case of a composer who has a melody in his head, perhaps not even realizing that the reason he hears this melody is that it is the work of another which he had heard before. When you sample a sound recording you know you are taking another's work product.

> This analysis admittedly raises the question of why one should, without infringing, be able to take three notes from a musical composition, for example, but not three notes by way of sampling from a sound recording. Why is there no *de minimis* taking or why should substantial similarity not enter the equation. Our first answer to this question is what we have earlier indicated. We think this result is dictated by the applicable statute. Second, even when a small part of a sound recording is sampled, the part taken is something of value. No

further proof of that is necessary than the fact that the producer of the record or the artist on the record intentionally sampled because it would (1) save costs, or (2) add something to the new recording, or (3) both. For the sound recording copyright holder, it is not the "song" but the sounds that are fixed in the medium of his choice. When those sounds are sampled they are taken directly from that fixed medium. It is a physical taking rather than an intellectual one.

Id. at 657-58 (footnotes omitted), *amended by* Nos. 02-6521, 03-5738, 2005 U.S. App. LEXIS 10140 (6th Cir. June 3, 2005).

* * * * *

insert the following after Notes and Questions # 5 on page 583 of Law of Internet Speech:

6. The Free Expression Policy Project, a project of the Brennan Center for Justice at New York University School of Law, conducted a study of a small sample of cease and desist letters and concluded that such letters "sometimes -- but not always -- have chilling effects on speech that might qualify as fair use. Critical factors in determining whether the recipient of such a letter will comply seem to include awareness that fair use provides a defense; support from the community; and a non-risk-averse temperament." Tricia Beckles and Marjorie Heins, *The Free Expression Policy Project, A Preliminary Report on the Chilling Effects of "Cease and Desist" Letters* (Oct. 5, 2004), *available at* <http://www.fepproject.org/ commentaries/ceaseanddesist.html>.

* * * * *

Does downloading copyrighted music from a P2P file sharing system constitute an exercise of free speech under the First Amendment? The U.S. District Court for the Southern District of New York considered the question and determined that free speech considerations did not protect the identity of the downloader when the copyright holders brought a copyright infringement suit. *See Sony Music Entertainment, Inc. v. Does 1-40,* 326 F. Supp. 2d 556 (S.D.N.Y. 2004). The selection of music may be imbued with limited First Amendment protection, but did not completely immunize the downloader from the copyright holder's "right to use the judicial process to pursue what appear to be meritorious copyright infringement claims." *Id.* at 567. The downloader was "not engaging in a true expression," according to the court, because he was not "seeking to communicate a thought or convey an idea," but rather was looking to obtain music without charge or a license. *Id.* at 564.

Nevertheless, the downloader still was expressing himself by selecting music and making it available, which qualifies as speech to some degree. *See id.* In order to defeat the downloader's interest in remaining anonymous, the plaintiffs were required to make a concrete showing of a *prima facie* claim of actionable harm; a specific discovery request; the lack of an alterative source for the information sought by the subpoena; and "a central need" for the subpoenaed information to advance the claim. *See id.* at 565. The court concluded that the plaintiffs had satisfied all components of the test, *see id.* at 565-66, and were entitled to discovery because the defendants had a minimal expectation of privacy based on the Internet service provider's terms of service, *see id.* at 566-67.

* * * * *

insert the following before The Digital Millennium Copyright Act on page 583 of Law of Internet Speech:

NXIVM CORPORATION and FIRST PRINCIPLES, INC.,
Plaintiffs-Appellants
v.
THE ROSS INSTITUTE, RICK ROSS also known as RICKY
ROSS, JOHN HOCHMAN, and STEPHANIE FRANCO,
Defendants-Appellees, PAUL MARTIN and WELLSPRING
RETREAT, INC., Consolidated-Defendants-Appellees

United States Court of Appeals for the Second Circuit

No. 03-7952, 364 F.3d 471

April 20, 2004

This case presents us with an opportunity to examine the import of the Supreme Court's holding in *Harper & Row Publishers, Inc. v. Nation Enters.*, 471 U.S. 539, 85 L. Ed. 2d 588, 105 S. Ct. 2218 (1985), that "'the propriety of the defendant's conduct'" is relevant to the "'character'" of the use under the first factor of the statutory fair use test for copyright infringement. *Id.* at 562 (quoting 3 M. Nimmer, *Copyright* § 13.05[A], at 13-72 (1984)); *see* 17 U.S.C. § 107 (enumerating the fair use factors). Because a full balancing of the statutory fair use factors of § 107, including an evaluation of the propriety of defendants' conduct, favors the relevant defendants-appellees in this case, we affirm.

Plaintiffs-appellants NXIVM and First Principles, Inc. (collectively, "NXIVM"), producers of business training seminars, appeal from the decision of the United States District Court for the Northern District of New York (Thomas J. McAvoy, District Judge), denying a preliminary injunction against various defendants-appellees who were alleged to have infringed NXIVM's copyrighted course materials by posting parts of them on the internet. Although we find that the district court erred in its application of the first statutory fair use factor, we ultimately agree that NXIVM cannot show a likelihood of success on the merits. Accordingly, we affirm. ...

I. BACKGROUND

NXIVM provides a course manual for the paid subscribers to its exclusive and expensive seminar training program known as "Executive Success." The 265-page manual contains a copyright notice on virtually every page and all seminar participants sign non-disclosure agreements, purporting to bar them from releasing the manuscript or proprietary techniques learned in the seminars to others. It is unpublished in the sense that it is not available to the general public. NXIVM claims to have developed a proprietary "technology" called "Rational Inquiry,"™ a methodology to improve communication and decision-making.

Defendant Rick Ross runs nonprofit websites, www.rickross.com and www.cultnews.com, in connection with his work as a for-profit "cult de-programmer." The websites provide information to the public about controversial groups, about which complaints of mind control have been lodged. Ross allegedly learned of NXIVM's activities in the course of his de-programming services, obtaining the manuscript indirectly from defendant Stephanie Franco, a one-time NXIVM participant.

Two reports authored separately by defendants John Hochman and Paul Martin, self-styled experts on groups such as NXIVM, were commissioned by Ross; they analyze and critique the materials from the manual. The reports quote sections of the manual in support of their analyses and criticisms and were ultimately made available to the public through Ross's websites. One of the reports plainly acknowledges that NXIVM has "intellectual property rights" in its materials and that NXIVM makes an effort to keep its manual "confidential." This report seems to appreciate that its access to the copyrighted materials was unauthorized, although this is likely a disputed issue of fact.

NXIVM sued Ross and various co-defendants for[, *inter alia,*] copyright infringement under 17 U.S.C. §§ 106 & 106A.... Principally on the basis of the copyright infringement claim, NXIVM moved for a preliminary injunction to require that defendants remove the copyrighted information from Ross's websites.

The district court denied the preliminary injunction, finding no likelihood of NXIVM's success on the merits because defendants' fair use defense was likely to succeed. *See Random House, Inc. v. Rosetta Books LLC*, 283 F.3d 490, 491 (2d Cir. 2002) (*per curiam*). However, the district court preliminarily enjoined Stephanie Franco from any further release of NXIVM's materials. NXIVM appealed.

II. DISCUSSION

... B. Defendants' Fair Use Defense

At the core of this appeal is the proper weighing, in a copyright infringement suit, of the first of the four statutory fair use factors after *Harper & Row,* 471 U.S. at 539. We must decide whether the district court should have more fully and explicitly considered, in its analysis of the first factor, that defendants must have known (or at least very likely knew) that the unpublished manuscript from which quotations were taken and which was disseminated on the internet was acquired in an unauthorized fashion. We conclude that the district court did not fully analyze the impact of defendants' alleged misappropriation of the NXIVM manual in assessing fair use. Accordingly, we cannot adopt the district court's fair use analysis in whole. However, following our own review of the relevant factors, including the subfactor that the district court failed to address fully and explicitly within the first factor, we conclude that the doctrine of fair use still defeats any likelihood of plaintiffs' success on the merits. Accordingly, we affirm the denial of the preliminary injunction.

We turn to the four-factor test for fair use.

1. The "purpose and character" inquiry

The court's function, in inquiring into "the purpose and character of the use," 17 U.S.C. § 107(1), is:

> to see, in Justice Story's words, whether the new work merely "supersedes the objects" of the original creation, or instead adds something new, with a further purpose or different character, altering the first with new expression, meaning, or message ..., in other words, whether and to what extent the new work is "transformative." ... The goal of copyright, to promote science and the arts, is generally furthered by the creation of transformative works. Such [transformative] works

thus lie at the heart of the fair use doctrine's guarantee of breathing space. ...

Campbell [*v. Acuff-Rose Music, Inc.,* 510 U.S. 569, 579, 127 L. Ed. 2d 500, 114 S. Ct. 1164 (1994)] (citations omitted) (alterations in original). We agree with the district court that the websites' use of quotations from the manual to support their critical analyses of the seminars is transformative. As we held in *Wright* [*v. Warner Books, Inc.*, 953 F.2d 731, 740 (2d Cir. 1991)], "there is a strong presumption that factor one favors the defendant if the allegedly infringing work fits the description of uses described in § 107." *Wright*, 953 F.2d at 736. Where the defendants' use is for the purposes of "criticism, comment ... scholarship, or research," 17 U.S.C. § 107, factor one will normally tilt in the defendants' favor. ...

What the district court did not fully and explicitly consider, and what NXIVM correctly urges that it should have considered, is "the propriety of [a] defendant's conduct," as directed by *Harper & Row*, 471 U.S. at 562-63 (citations omitted). Our circuit has recognized that this is an integral part of the analysis under the first factor. *Wright,* 953 F.2d at 737; *see also Los Angeles News Serv. v. KCAL-TV Channel 9,* 108 F.3d 1119, 1122 (9th Cir. 1997) (finding analysis of the defendant's conduct to be relevant "at least to the extent that [the defendant] may knowingly have exploited a purloined work for free that could have been obtained for a fee"). While some have commented that this inquiry is counter-indicated by the policy interests supporting copyright and fair use protections, *see, e.g.,* Pierre N. Leval, *Toward a Fair Use Standard,* 103 Harv. L. Rev. 1105, 1126-28 (1990) (arguing against considering the defendants' good or bad faith), *Harper & Row* directs courts to consider a defendant's bad faith in applying the first statutory factor.

Thus, to the extent that Ross, Martin, or Hochman knew that his access to the manuscript was unauthorized or was derived from a violation of law or breach of duty, this consideration weighs in favor of plaintiffs. Moreover, it has been considered relevant within this subfactor that a defendant could have acquired the copyrighted manuscript legitimately; in this case, the relevant defendants could have paid the requisite fee to enroll in NXIVM's seminars. *See generally* William F. Patry, *The Fair Use Privilege in Copyright Law* 109, 130-32 (2d ed. 1995). The district court should have more fully and explicitly considered defendants' bad faith within its analysis of the first factor and did not. For the purposes of our analysis here, we assume defendants' bad faith and weigh this subfactor in favor of plaintiffs.

But just how much weight within the first factor should a court place on this subfactor of bad faith? Some courts have found *Harper & Row* to stand for the broad proposition that "to invoke the fair use exception, an individual must possess an authorized copy of a literary work." *Atari Games Corp. v. Nintendo of Am. Inc.,* 975 F.2d 832, 843 (Fed. Cir. 1992). Since we assume defendants' copy of the NXIVM manuscript was unauthorized, the rule enunciated in Atari would foreclose the fair use defense altogether based upon defendants' bad faith.

However, we read *Harper & Row's* holding more narrowly than the broad proposition suggested by *Atari.* In *Harper & Row,* the defendants knowingly acquired a "purloined manuscript" for the very purpose of preempting the plaintiff's first publication rights, rights already sold by the copyright owner, for which the defendants had an opportunity to bid. The Court wrote that the defendants' "use had not merely the incidental effect but the intended purpose of supplanting the copyright holder's commercially valuable right of first publication." 471 U.S. at 562. Ultimately, the Court rejected the fair use defense in *Harper & Row,* not just because of the defendants' bad faith, but also because the defendants had failed to make any substantial transformative use of the copyrighted work. *Id.* at 543. Here, while NXIVM urges that its first publication rights were similarly "scooped," *id.* at 542, 556, 562, defendants' use in this case was quite plainly critical and transformative. *See also Chicago Bd. of Educ. v. Substance, Inc.,* 354 F.3d 624, 628 (7th Cir. 2003) (distinguishing *Harper & Row* on the basis that *Harper & Row* did not involve criticism of the copyrighted work).

Because the *Harper & Row* Court did not end its analysis of the fair use defense after considering and ascertaining the defendants' bad faith there, we believe that the bad faith of a defendant is not dispositive of a fair use defense. Instead, we agree with the court in *Religious Tech. Ctr. v. Netcom On-Line Communication Servs., Inc.,* 923 F. Supp. 1231, 1244 n.14 (N.D. Cal. 1995), that "[nothing in *Harper & Row* indicates that [the defendants'] bad faith [is] itself conclusive of the fair use question, or even of the first factor." Moreover, "after *Campbell,* it is clear that a finding of bad faith, or a finding on any one of the four factors, cannot be considered dispositive." *Id.; see also Campbell,* 510 U.S. at 578 (emphasizing that no single fair use factor is dispositive and warning against the application of "bright-line rules" in fair use analysis); 4 Melville B. Nimmer & David Nimmer, *Nimmer on Copyright* § 13.05[A][1][d] (2003) (noting that "knowing use of a purloined manuscript militates against a fair use defense," but not suggesting that bad faith is an absolute bar to fair use).

Thus, while the subfactor pertaining to defendants' good or bad faith must be weighed, and while it was error for the district court not to have fully and explicitly considered it, we find that even if the bad faith subfactor weighs in plaintiffs' favor, the first factor still favors defendants in light of the transformative nature of the secondary use as criticism. If no statutory factor can be dispositive after *Campbell,* neither can a single subfactor be, a fortiori.

2. The "nature of the copyrighted work" inquiry

The parties do not dispute that because the copyrighted work is unpublished, the district court properly found the second factor, "the nature of the copyrighted work," to favor plaintiffs. *See Harper & Row,* 471 U.S. at 564 ("The fact that a work is unpublished is a critical element in its 'nature,'" and "the scope of fair use is narrower with respect to unpublished works.")(citations omitted); *but see* 17 U.S.C. § 107 ("The fact that a work is unpublished shall not itself bar a finding of fair use if such finding is made upon consideration of all the above factors.").

3. The "amount and substantiality" inquiry

Consideration of the third factor, "the amount and substantiality of the portion used in relation to the copyrighted work as a whole," 17 U.S.C. § 107(3), "has both a quantitative and a qualitative component," *New Era Publications Int'l ApS v. Carol Pub. Group,* 904 F.2d 152, 158 (2d Cir. 1990). The factor favors copyright holders where the portion used by the alleged infringer is a significant percentage of the copyrighted work, or where the portion used is "essentially the heart of" the copyrighted work, *Harper & Row,* 471 U.S. at 565 (internal quotation marks omitted). Courts have also considered "whether the quantity of the material used was reasonable in relation to the purpose of the copying." *Am. Geophysical Union v. Texaco Inc.,* 60 F.3d 913, 926 (2d Cir. 1994) (internal quotation marks omitted).

... The proper analogy in this case is not to separate articles in a magazine, but instead to a book by a single author containing numerous chapters, which are not separately copyrightable. *See id.* at 925-26 (treating individual articles in a journal as the appropriate level of copyright protection when the author of each article is different). The "modules" in this case were written by the same author and they combine to produce one unitary work.

... Here, ... there is no objective core of expression in the course materials that can be similarly identified. Even plaintiffs reveal their appreciation of this fact when they charge defendants principally with copying the heart of their "services." Such services, however, are not copyrightable expression. *See* 17 U.S.C. § 102(b) (withholding copyright protection from any "idea, procedure, process, system, method of operation, concept, principle, or discovery"). Moreover, by pressing their "module" argument, plaintiffs virtually concede that defendants could not have taken the core of the copyrighted work, because they do not see the manual as having a core, but rather as an assemblage of "modules."

Finally, we agree with the district court that, in order to do the research and analysis necessary to support their critical commentary, it was reasonably necessary for defendants to quote liberally from NXIVM's manual. Accordingly, we find that the third factor does not favor plaintiffs.

4. The "market" inquiry

The fourth statutory fair use factor requires us to evaluate the economic impact of the allegedly infringing use upon the copyright owner. The focus here is on whether defendants are offering a market substitute for the original. In considering the fourth factor, our concern is not whether the secondary use suppresses or even destroys the market for the original work or its potential derivatives, but whether the secondary use usurps the market of the original work. *Campbell,* 510 U.S. at 593. As we stated in *Wright,* the relevant market effect with which we are concerned is the market for plaintiffs' "expression," and thus it is the effect of defendants' use of that expression on plaintiffs' market that matters, not the effect of defendants' work as a whole. *Wright,* 953 F.2d at 739. That the fair use, being transformative, might well harm, or even destroy, the market for the original is of no concern to us so long as the harm stems from the force of the criticism offered. *See Campbell,* 510 U.S. at 591-92 ("[A] lethal parody, like a scathing theater review, kills demand for the original, [but] does not produce a harm cognizable under the Copyright Act.").

This factor weighs heavily in defendants' favor. It is plain that, as a general matter, criticisms of a seminar or organization cannot substitute for the seminar or organization itself or hijack its market. To be sure, some may read defendants' materials and decide not to attend plaintiffs' seminars. Indeed, the record reflects that soon after the dissemination of defendants' material, actress Goldie Hawn cancelled a visit with NXIVM's leader, Keith Raniere. But that sort of harm, as the district court properly recognized, is not cognizable under the Copyright Act. If criticisms on defendants' websites kill the demand for plaintiffs' service, that is the price that, under the First Amendment, must be paid in the open marketplace for ideas. *See, e.g., New Era,* 904 F.2d at 160 (citing the "fundamentally different functions" of a critique and a copyrighted original by virtue of their "opposing viewpoints") (citing *Maxtone-Graham,* 803 F.2d at 1264); *Campbell,* 510 U.S. at 591-92.

5. Summary

Recognizing that "all [factors] are to be explored, and the results weighed together, in light of the purposes of copyright," *Campbell,* 510 U.S. at 578, and that no one factor should dominate the analysis, the district court properly denied the preliminary injunction. We agree with the district court that defendants' writings "are undoubtedly transformative secondary uses intended as a form of criticism. All of the alleged harm arises from the biting criticism of this fair use, not from a usurpation of the market by ... defendants." Accordingly, we affirm the denial of the preliminary injunction on the copyright infringement claim because plaintiffs are not likely to succeed on the merits. Even a finding of bad faith by defendants would not automatically preclude finding that their use was fair use.

... III. CONCLUSION

For the foregoing reasons, the district court's denial of a preliminary injunction is affirmed.

* * * * *

With respect to the analysis of the fourth factor of fair use principles by the U.S. Court of Appeals for the Second Circuit in *NXIVM Corp. v. Ross Inst.,* consider the U.S. District Court for the Northern District of California's view in *Online Policy Group v. Diebold, Inc.:* "At most, Plaintiffs' [posting of internal e-mails from Diebold citing problems with Deibold's product] ... might have reduced Deibold's profits because it helped inform potential customers of problems with the machines. However, copyright law is not designed to prevent such an outcome." 337 F. Supp. 2d 1195, 1203 (N.D. Cal. 2004). Both decisions recognize the utility of protecting *critical* comment as fair uses.

* * * * *

The Digital Millennium Copyright Act

insert the following before Universal City Studios, Inc., et al. v. Eric Corley, also known as Emmanuel Goldstein, et al. on page 585 of Law of Internet Speech:

COSTAR GROUP, INCORPORATED; COSTAR REALTY
INFORMATION, INCORPORATED, Plaintiffs-Appellants
v.
LOOPNET, INCORPORATED, Defendant-Appellee

BMG MUSIC; EMI MUSIC, North America, *et al., Amici*
Supporting Appellants

BELLSOUTH TELECOMMUNICATIONS, INCORPORATED,
et al., Amici Supporting Appellee

United States Court of Appeals for the Fourth Circuit

No. 03-1911, 373 F.3d 544

June 21, 2004

CoStar Group, Inc. and CoStar Realty Information, Inc. (collectively "CoStar"), a copyright owner of numerous photographs of commercial real estate, commenced this copyright infringement action against LoopNet, Inc., an Internet service provider, for direct infringement under §§ 501 and 106 of the Copyright Act because CoStar's copyrighted photographs were posted by LoopNet's subscribers on LoopNet's website. CoStar contended that the photographs were copied into LoopNet's computer system and that LoopNet therefore was a copier strictly liable for infringement of CoStar's rights under § 106, regardless of whether LoopNet's role was passive when the photographs were copied into its system.

Relying on *Religious Technology Center v. Netcom On-Line Communications Services, Inc.*, 907 F. Supp. 1361 (N.D. Cal. 1995), the district court entered summary judgment in favor of LoopNet on the claim of direct infringement under § 106. We agree with the district court. Because LoopNet, as an Internet service provider, is simply the owner and manager of a system used by others who are violating CoStar's copyrights and is not an actual duplicator itself, it is not *directly* liable for copyright infringement. We therefore affirm.

I.

CoStar is a national provider of commercial real estate information, and it claims to have collected the most comprehensive database of information on commercial real estate markets and commercial properties in the United States and the United Kingdom. Its database includes a large collection of photographs of commercial properties, and CoStar owns the copyright in the vast majority of these photographs. CoStar makes its database, including photographs, available to customers through the Internet and otherwise, and each customer agrees not to post CoStar's photographs on its own website or on the website of a third party.

LoopNet is an Internet service provider ("ISP") whose website allows subscribers, generally real estate brokers, to post listings of commercial real estate on the Internet. It claims that its computer system contains over 100,000 customer listings of commercial real estate, including approximately 33,000 photographs, and that it was, during the district court proceedings, adding about 2200 listings each day, 250 of which include photographs. LoopNet does not post real estate listings on its own account. Rather it provides a "web hosting service that enables users who wish to display real estate over the Internet to post listings for those properties on LoopNet's web site."

When using LoopNet's services, a subscriber fills out a form and agrees to "Terms and Conditions" that include a promise not to post copies of photographs without authorization. If the subscriber includes a photograph for a listing, it must fill out another form and agree again to the "Terms and Conditions," along with an additional express warranty that the subscriber has "all necessary rights and authorizations" from the copyright owner of the photographs. The subscriber then uploads the photographs into a folder in LoopNet's system, and the photograph is transferred to the RAM of one of Loop-Net's computers for review. A LoopNet employee then cursorily reviews the photograph (1) to determine whether the photograph in fact depicts commercial real estate, and (2) to identify any obvious evidence, such as a text message or copyright notice, that the photograph may have been copyrighted by another. If the photograph fails either one of these criteria, the employee deletes the photograph and notifies the subscriber. Otherwise, the employee clicks an "accept" button that prompts LoopNet's system to associate the photograph with the web page for the property listing, making the photograph available for viewing.

Beginning in early 1998, CoStar became aware that photographs for which it held copyrights were being posted on LoopNet's website by LoopNet's subscribers. When CoStar informed LoopNet of the violations, LoopNet removed the photographs. In addition, LoopNet instituted and followed a policy of marking properties to which infringing photographs had been posted so that if other photographs were posted to that property, LoopNet could inspect the photographs side-by-side to make sure that the new photographs were not the infringing photographs. By late summer 1999, CoStar had discovered 112 infringing photographs on LoopNet's website, and by September 2001, it had found over 300. At that time, LoopNet had in its system about 33,000 photographs posted by its subscribers.

CoStar commenced this action in September 1999 against Loop-Net, alleging[, *inter alia,*] copyright infringement.... On cross-motions for summary judgment, the district court concluded that LoopNet had not engaged in direct infringement under the Copyright Act. It left open, however, CoStar's claims that LoopNet might have contributorily infringed CoStar's copyrights and that LoopNet was not entitled to the "safe harbor" immunity provided by the Digital Millennium Copyright Act, 17 U.S.C. § 512. When the parties stipulated to the dismissal of all claims except the district court's summary judgment in favor of Loop-Net on direct infringement, the district court entered final judgment on that issue in favor of LoopNet. From entry of the judgment, CoStar noticed this appeal.

II.

CoStar contends principally that the district court erred in providing LoopNet "conclusive immunity," as a "'passive' provider of Internet" services, from strict liability for its hosting of CoStar's copyrighted pictures on LoopNet's website. The district court based its decision on the reasoning of *Religious Technology Center v. Netcom On-Line Communication Services, Inc.*, 907 F. Supp. 1361 (N.D. Cal. 1995) (*"Netcom"*), which held that an ISP serving as a passive conduit for copyrighted material is not liable as a direct infringer. CoStar asserts that LoopNet is strictly liable for infringement of CoStar's rights protected by § 106 of the Copyright Act. According to CoStar, any immunity for the passive conduct of an ISP such as LoopNet must come from the safe harbor immunity provided by the Digital Millennium Computer Act ("DMCA"), if at all, because the DMCA codified and supplanted the *Netcom* holding. Because Loop-Net could not meet the conditions for immunity under the DMCA as to many of the copyrighted photographs, LoopNet accordingly would be liable under CoStar's terms for direct copyright infringement for hosting web pages containing the infringing photos.

Stated otherwise, CoStar argues (1) that the *Netcom* decision was a pragmatic and temporary limitation of traditional copyright liability, which would otherwise have held ISPs strictly liable, and that in view of the enactment of the DMCA, *Netcom's* limitation is no longer necessary; (2) that Congress considered *Netcom* in enacting the DMCA, codifying its principles and thereby supplanting and preempting *Netcom* as the only exemption from liability for direct infringement; and (3) that because LoopNet cannot satisfy the conditions of the DMCA, it remains strictly liable for direct infringement under §§ 106 and 501 of the Copyright Act. We will address CoStar's points, determining first the nature and applicability of the *Netcom* decision and second the impact of the DMCA on *Netcom*.

A.

In *Netcom*, the court held, among other things, that neither the ISP providing Internet access, nor the bulletin board service storing the posted material, was liable for direct copyright infringement under § 106 when a subscriber posted copyrighted materials on the Internet. The court observed that "although copyright is a strict liability statute, there should still be some element of volition or causation which is lacking where a defendant's system is merely used to use a copy by a third party." 907 F. Supp. at 1370. In responding to the argument that the ISP's computers stored and thereby "copied" copyrighted material on its system for a period of days in rendering its service, the court stated:

Where the infringing subscriber is clearly directly liable for the same act, it does not make sense to adopt a rule that would lead to the liability of countless parties whose role in the infringement is nothing more than setting up and operating a system that is necessary for the functioning of the Internet. ... The court does not find workable a theory of infringement that would hold the entire Internet liable for activities that cannot reasonable be deterred. Billions of bits of data flow through the Internet and are necessarily stored on servers throughout the network and it is thus practically impossible to screen out infringing bits from noninfringing bits. Because the court cannot see any meaningful distinction (without regard to knowledge) between what Netcom did and what every other Usenet server does, the court finds that Netcom cannot be held liable for direct infringement.

Id. at 1372-73. ...

While the court in *Netcom* did point out the dramatic consequences of a decision that would hold ISPs strictly liable for transmitting copyrighted materials through their systems without knowledge of what was being transmitted, the court grounded its ruling principally on its interpretation of § 106 of the Copyright Act as implying a requirement of "volition or causation" by the purported infringer. This construction is one for which we have already indicated our preference over the contrary decision described in *Frena*. *See ALS Scan, Inc. v. RemarQ Cmtys., Inc.*, 239 F.3d 619, 622 (4th Cir. 2001). There are several reasons to commend this approach.

"The Copyright Act grants the copyright holder 'exclusive' rights to use and to authorize the use of his work in five qualified ways, including reproduction of the copyrighted work in copies." *Sony Corp. v. Universal City Studios, Inc.*, 464 U.S. 417, 432-33, 78 L. Ed. 2d 574, 104 S. Ct. 774 (1984). And it provides that "anyone who violates any of the exclusive rights of the copyright owner ... is an infringer of the copyright." 17 U.S.C. § 501. Stated at a general level, "to establish infringement, two elements must be proven: (1) ownership of a valid copyright, and (2) copying of constituent elements of the work that are original." *Feist Publications, Inc. v. Rural Tel. Serv. Co.*, 499 U.S. 340, 361, 113 L. Ed. 2d 358, 111 S. Ct. 1282 (1991). A direct infringer has thus been characterized as one who "trespasses into [the copyright owner's] exclusive domain" established in § 106, subject to the limitations of §§ 107 through 118. *Sony*, 464 U.S. at 433; *see also* 17 U.S.C. § 106 (specifying limitations).

While the Copyright Act does not require that the infringer know that he is infringing or that his conduct amount to a willful violation of the copyright owner's rights, it nonetheless requires *conduct* by a person who causes in some meaningful way an infringement. Were this not so, the Supreme Court could not have held, as it did in *Sony*, that a manufacturer of copy machines, possessing constructive knowledge that purchasers of its machine may be using them to engage in copyright infringement, is not strictly liable for infringement. 464 U.S. at 439-42. This, of course, does not mean that a manufacturer or owner of machines used for copyright violations could not have some *indirect* liability, such as contributory or vicarious liability. But such extensions of liability would require a showing of additional elements such as knowledge coupled with inducement or supervision coupled with a financial interest in the illegal copying.

The Copyright Act does not specifically provide for such extended liability, instead describing only the party who *actually engages* in infringing conduct -- the one who directly violates the prohibitions. Yet under general principles of law, vicarious liability or contributory liability may be imposed:

> The absence of such express language in the copyright statute does not preclude the imposition of liability for copyright infringements on certain parties who have not themselves engaged in the infringing activity. For vicarious liability is imposed in virtually all areas of the law, and the concept of contributory infringement is merely a species of the broader problem of identifying the circumstances in which it is just to hold one individual accountable for the actions of another.

Sony, 464 U.S. at 435. Under a theory of contributory infringement, "one who, with knowledge of the infringing activity, induces, causes or materially contributes to the infringing conduct of another" is liable for the infringement, too. *Gershwin Publishing Corp. v. Columbia Artists Mgmt., Inc.*, 443 F.2d 1159, 1162 (2d Cir. 1971) (footnote omitted). Under a theory of vicarious liability, a defendant who "has the right and ability to supervise the infringing activity and also has a direct financial interest in such activities" is similarly liable. *Id.*

But to establish *direct* liability under §§ 501 and 106 of the Act, something more must be shown than mere ownership of a machine used by others to make illegal copies. There must be actual infringing conduct with a nexus sufficiently close and causal to the illegal copying that one could conclude that the machine owner himself trespassed on the exclusive domain of the copyright owner. The *Netcom* court described this nexus as requiring some aspect of volition or causation. 907 F. Supp. at 1370. Indeed, counsel for both parties agreed at oral argument that a copy machine owner who makes the machine available to the public to use for copying is not, without more, strictly liable under § 106 for illegal copying by a customer. The ISP in this case is an analogue to the owner of a traditional copying machine whose customers pay a fixed amount per copy and operate the machine themselves to make copies. When a customer duplicates an infringing work, the owner of the copy machine is not considered a direct infringer. Similarly, an ISP who owns an electronic facility that responds automatically to users' input is not a direct infringer. If the Copyright Act does not hold the owner of the copying machine liable as a direct infringer when its customer copies infringing material without knowledge of the owner, the ISP should not be found liable as a direct infringer when its facility is used by a subscriber to violate a copyright without intervening conduct of the ISP.

Moreover, in the context of the conduct typically engaged in by an ISP, construing the Copyright Act to require some aspect of volition and meaningful causation -- as distinct from passive ownership and management of an electronic Internet facility -- receives additional support from the Act's concept of "copying." A violation of § 106 requires copying or the making of copies. *See* 17 U.S.C. § 106(1), (3); *id.* § 102(a); *Feist Publications*, 499 U.S. at 361. And the term "copies" refers to "material objects ... in which a work *is fixed.*" 17 U.S.C. § 101 ("Definitions") (emphasis added). A work is "fixed" in a medium when it is embodied in a copy "sufficiently permanent or stable to permit it to be perceived, reproduced, or otherwise communicated for a period *of more than transitory duration." Id.* (emphasis added). When an electronic infrastructure is designed and managed as a *conduit* of information and data that connects users over the Internet, the owner and manager of the conduit hardly "copies" the information and data in the sense that it fixes a copy in its system *of more than transitory duration.* Even if the information and data are "downloaded" onto the owner's RAM or other component as part of the transmission function, that downloading is a temporary, automatic response to the user's request, and the entire system functions solely to transmit the user's data to the Internet. Under such an arrangement, the ISP provides a system that automatically transmits users' material but is itself totally indifferent to the material's content. In this way, it functions as does a traditional telephone company when it transmits the contents of its users' conversations. While temporary electronic copies may be made in this transmission process, they would appear not to be "fixed" in the sense that they are "of more than transitory duration," and the ISP therefore would not be a "copier" to make it directly liable under the Copyright Act. With additional facts, of course, an ISP could become *indirectly* liable.

In concluding that an ISP has not itself fixed a copy in its system of more than transitory duration when it provides an Internet hosting service to its subscribers, we do not hold that a computer owner who downloads copyrighted software onto a computer cannot infringe the software's copyright. *See, e.g., MAI Systems Corp. v. Peak Computer, Inc.*, 991 F.2d 511, 518-19 (9th Cir. 1993). When the computer owner downloads copyrighted software, it possesses the software, which then functions in the service of the computer or its owner, and the copying is no longer of a transitory nature. *See, e. g., Vault Corp. v. Quaid Software Ltd.*, 847 F.2d 255, 260 (5th Cir. 1988). "Transitory duration" is thus both a qualitative and quantitative characterization. It is quantitative insofar as it describes the period during which the function occurs, and it is qualitative in the sense that it describes the status of transition. Thus, when the copyrighted software is down-loaded onto the computer, because it may be used to serve the computer or the computer owner, it no longer remains transitory. This, however, is unlike an ISP, which provides a system that automatically receives a subscriber's infringing material and transmits it to the Internet at the instigation of the subscriber.

Accordingly, we conclude that *Netcom* made a particularly rational interpretation of § 106 when it concluded that a person had to engage in volitional conduct -- specifically, the act constituting infringement -- to become a direct infringer. As the court in *Netcom* concluded, such a construction of the Act is especially important when it is applied to cyberspace. There are thousands of owners, contractors, servers, and users involved in the Internet whose role involves the storage and transmission of data in the establishment and maintenance of an Internet facility. Yet their conduct is not truly "copying" as understood by the Act; rather, they are conduits from or to would-be copiers and have no interest in the copy itself. *See Doe v. GTE Corp.*, 347 F.3d 655, 659 (7th Cir. 2003) ("A web host, like a delivery service or phone company, is an intermediary and normally is indifferent to the content of what it transmits"). To conclude that these persons are copyright infringers simply because they are involved in the ownership, operation, or maintenance of a transmission facility that automatically records material -- copyrighted or not -- would miss the thrust of the protections afforded by the Copyright Act. In rejecting even contributory infringement in some of such circumstances, the Supreme Court stated:

> The staple article of commerce doctrine must strike a balance between a copyright holder's legitimate demand for effective -- not merely symbolic -- protection of the statutory monopoly, and the rights of others freely to engage in substantially unrelated areas of commerce.

Sony, 464 U.S. at 442. We thus find it an overstatement by CoStar to argue that *Netcom* represented the adoption of a new "special liability-limiting rule for Internet servers."

B.

CoStar rests its position not only on the marginalization of the *Netcom* holding, but also on the assertion that the DMCA rendered *Netcom* no longer necessary -- indeed, even codified and preempted *Netcom* -- by imposing an exclusive safe harbor for ISPs that fulfill the conditions of the DMCA. CoStar argues that because the DMCA supplanted *Netcom*, LoopNet must rely for its defense exclusively on the immunity conferred by the DMCA. This argument, however, is belied by the plain language of the DMCA itself.

The DMCA was enacted as § 512 of the Copyright Act. The relevant subsection of § 512 provides limitations on liability "for infringement of copyright by reason of the storage at the direction of a user of material that resides on a system or network controlled or operated by or for the service for the [Internet] service provider" if the ISP lacks scienter about a copyright violation by a user, does not profit directly from the violation, and responds expeditiously to a proper notice of the violation. *See* 17 U.S.C. § 512(c)(1). In order to enjoy the safe harbor provided by § 512(c), the ISP must also fulfill other conditions imposed by the DMCA. *See id.* § 512(c), (i). Even though the DMCA was designed to provide ISPs with a safe harbor from copyright liability, nothing in the language of § 512 indicates that the limitation on liability described therein is exclusive. Indeed, another section of the DMCA provides explicitly that the DMCA is *not* exclusive:

> *Other defenses not affected.* -- The failure of a service provider's conduct to qualify for limitation of liability under this section shall not bear adversely upon the consideration of a defense by the service provider that the service provider's conduct is not infringing under this title or any other defense.

Id. § 512(*l*). Thus the statute specifically provides that despite a failure to meet the safe-harbor conditions in § 512(c) and (i), an ISP is still entitled to all other arguments under the law -- whether by way of an affirmative defense or through an argument that conduct simply does not constitute a *prima facie* case of infringement under the Copyright Act.

Given that the statute declares its intent not to "bear adversely upon" any of the ISP's defenses under law, including the defense that the plaintiff has not made out a *prima facie* case for infringement, it is difficult to argue, as CoStar does, that the statute in fact precludes ISPs from relying on an entire strain of case law holding that direct infringement must involve conduct having a volitional or causal aspect. Giving such a construction to the DMCA would in fact "bear adversely upon the consideration" of this defense, in direct contravention of § 512(*l*). We conclude that in enacting the DMCA, Congress did not preempt the decision in *Netcom* nor foreclose the continuing development of liability through court decisions interpreting §§ 106 and 501 of the Copyright Act. ...

CoStar's argument that the DMCA supplanted and preempted *Netcom* is further undermined by the DMCA's legislative history. Congress actually expressed its intent that the courts would continue to determine how to apply the Copyright Act to the Internet and that the DMCA would merely create a floor of protection for ISPs. After citing the conflicting decisions in *Netcom* and *Frena*, the Senate Committee on the Judiciary explained that "rather than embarking upon a wholesale clarification of these doctrines, the Committee decided to leave current law in its evolving state and, instead, to create a series of 'safe harbors,' for certain common activities of service providers." S. Rep. No. 105-190, at 19 (1998). ...

It is clear that Congress intended the DMCA's safe harbor for ISPs to be a floor, not a ceiling, of protection. Congress said nothing about whether passive ISPs should ever be held strictly liable as direct infringers or whether plaintiffs suing ISPs should instead proceed under contributory theories. The DMCA has merely added a second step to assessing infringement liability for Internet service providers, after it is determined whether they are infringers in the first place under the preexisting Copyright Act. Thus, the DMCA is irrelevant to determining what constitutes a *prima facie* case of copyright infringement.

At bottom, we hold that ISPs, when passively storing material at the direction of users in order to make that material available to other users upon their request, do not "copy" the material in direct violation of § 106 of the Copyright Act. Agreeing with the analysis in *Netcom*, we hold that the automatic copying, storage, and transmission of copyrighted materials, when instigated by others, does not render an ISP strictly liable for copyright infringement under §§ 501 and 106 of the Copyright Act. An ISP, however, can become liable indirectly upon a showing of additional involvement sufficient to establish a contributory or vicarious violation of the Act. In that case, the ISP could still look to the DMCA for a safe harbor if it fulfilled the conditions therein.

III.

CoStar contends that even under *Netcom's* construction of copyright infringement liability for ISPs, LoopNet's conduct in this case is more than passive, in that LoopNet screens photographs posted by its subscribers. In CoStar's opinion, this screening process renders LoopNet liable for direct copyright infringement.

LoopNet, like other ISPs, affords its subscribers an Internet-based facility on which to post materials, but the materials posted are of a type and kind selected by the subscriber and at a time initiated by the subscriber. Similarly, users who wish to access a subscriber's information may do so without intervention from LoopNet. A subscriber seeking to post a listing on LoopNet's website containing only *text* fills out a form and agrees to LoopNet's "Terms and Conditions," which include the obligation to respect others' copyrights. Once the subscriber has filled out the form and agreed to the "Terms and Conditions," an identification number is automatically assigned to the listing, and a web page containing the listing and the identification number is automatically created. The web page is then hosted on LoopNet's website to be viewed by users who request the listing. CoStar does not contend that LoopNet's activity in signing up subscribers with *only* textual property listings is anything other than passive.

To argue that LoopNet loses its status as a passive ISP and therefore becomes liable for direct copyright infringement, CoStar focuses on LoopNet's gatekeeping practice with respect to photographs. To add a photograph to a listing, the subscriber must fill out another form and again agree to the "Terms and Conditions." After expressly warranting that he has "all necessary rights and authorizations from the ... copyright owner of the photographs," the subscriber uploads the photograph into a folder in LoopNet's system. The photograph is then transferred to the RAM of one of LoopNet's computers for review. A LoopNet employee reviews the photo for two purposes: (1) to block photographs that do not depict commercial real estate, and (2) to block photographs with obvious signs that they are copyrighted by a third party. If the photograph carries a copyright notice or represents subject matter other than commercial real estate, the employee deletes the photograph; otherwise, she clicks a button marked "accept," and LoopNet's system automatically associates the photograph with the subscriber's web page for the property listing, making it available for use. Unless a question arises, this entire process takes "a few seconds."

Although LoopNet engages in volitional conduct to block photographs measured by two grossly defined criteria, this conduct, which takes only seconds, does not amount to "copying," nor does it add volition to LoopNet's involvement in storing the copy. The employee's look is so cursory as to be insignificant, and if it has any significance, it tends only to lessen the possibility that LoopNet's automatic electronic responses will inadvertently enable others to trespass on a copyright owner's rights. In performing this gatekeeping function, LoopNet does not attempt to search out or select photographs for duplication; it merely *prevents* users from duplicating certain photographs. To invoke again the analogy of the shop with the copy machine, LoopNet can be compared to an owner of a copy machine who has stationed a guard by the door to turn away customers who are attempting to duplicate clearly copyrighted works. LoopNet has not by this screening process become engaged as a "copier" of copyrighted works who can be held liable under §§ 501 and 106 of the Copyright Act.

To the extent that LoopNet's intervention in screening photographs goes further than the simple gatekeeping function described above, it is because of CoStar's complaints about copyright violations. Whenever CoStar has complained to LoopNet about a particular photograph, LoopNet has removed the photograph, and the property listing with which the photograph was associated has been marked. The next time the user tries to post a photograph to accompany that listing, LoopNet conducts a manual side-by-side review to make sure that the user is not reposting the infringing photograph. CoStar and other copyright holders benefit significantly from this type of response. If they find such conduct by an ISP too active, they can avoid it by adding a copyright notice to their photographs, which CoStar does not do. CoStar can hardly request LoopNet to prevent its users from infringing upon particular unmarked photographs and then subsequently seek to hold LoopNet liable as a direct infringer when Loop-Net complies with CoStar's request.

In short, we do not conclude that LoopNet's perfunctory gatekeeping process, which furthers the goals of the Copyright Act, can be taken to create liability for LoopNet as a direct infringer when its conduct otherwise does not amount to direct infringement.

For the reasons given, we affirm the judgment of the district court.

* * * * *

On-Line Copyright Infringement Liability Limitation

insert the following before Notes and Questions on page 610 of Law of Internet Speech:

A&M RECORDS, INC., a corporation, *et al.*, Plaintiffs-Appellants

v.

NAPSTER, INC., a corporation, Defendant-Appellee

United States Court of Appeals for the Ninth Circuit

No. 01-15998, No. 01-16003, No. 01-16011, No. 01-16308, 284
F.3d 1091

March 25, 2002

This appeal involves challenges to a modified preliminary injunction entered by the district court on remand from a prior appeal, *A&M Records, Inc. v. Napster, Inc.*, 239 F.3d 1004 (9th Cir. 2001). At issue is the district court's order forcing Napster to disable its file transferring service until certain conditions are met to achieve full compliance with the modified preliminary injunction. We entered a temporary stay of the shut down order pending resolution of this appeal. We have jurisdiction pursuant to 28 U.S.C. § 1292(a)(1). We affirm both the district court's modified preliminary injunction and shut down order.

I.

Plaintiffs' action against Napster claims contributory and vicarious copyright infringement stemming from Napster's peer-to-peer music file sharing service. In the prior interlocutory appeal, we affirmed the district court's decision to issue a preliminary injunction and reversed and remanded with instructions to modify the injunction's scope to reflect the limits of Napster's potential liability for vicarious and contributory infringement. *Napster*, 239 F.3d at 1027.

We now consider the district court's modified preliminary injunction, which obligates Napster to remove any user file from the system's music index if Napster has reasonable knowledge that the file contains plaintiffs' copyrighted works. Plaintiffs, in turn, must give Napster notice of specific infringing files. For each work sought to be protected, plaintiffs must provide the name of the performing artist, the title of the work, a certification of ownership, and the name(s) of one or more files that have been available on the Napster file index containing the protected copyrighted work. Napster then must continually search the index and block all files which contain that particular noticed work. Both parties are required to adopt reasonable measures to identify variations of the file name, or of the spelling of the titles or artists' names, of plaintiffs' identified protected works.

The district court carefully monitored Napster's compliance with the modified preliminary injunction. It required periodic reports from the parties and held several compliance hearings. The district court also appointed a technical advisor to assist in evaluating Napster's compliance.

Napster was able to prevent sharing of much of plaintiffs' noticed copyrighted works. Plaintiffs nonetheless were able to present evidence that infringement of noticed works still occurred in violation of the modified preliminary injunction. After three months of monitoring, the district court determined that Napster was not in satisfactory compliance with the modified preliminary injunction. The district court ordered Napster to disable its file transferring service until certain conditions were met and steps were taken to ensure maximum compliance.

The record company plaintiffs and the music producer plaintiffs appeal the modified preliminary injunction, and Napster cross-appeals. Napster also appeals the district court's shut down order.

... III.

Plaintiffs challenge the requirement that they provide file names found on the Napster index that correspond to their copyrighted works before those works are entitled to protection. Plaintiffs argue that Napster should be required to search for and to block all files containing any protected copyrighted works, not just those works with which plaintiffs have been able to provide a corresponding file name. Napster, on the other hand, argues that the modified preliminary injunction's articulation of its duty to police is vague and fails to conform to the fair notice requirement of Federal Rule of Civil Procedure 65(d).

We are unpersuaded that the district court committed any error of law or abused its discretion. The notice requirement abides by our holding that plaintiffs bear the burden "to provide notice to Napster of copyrighted works and files containing such works available on the Napster system before Napster has the duty to disable access to the offending content." *Napster*, 239 F.3d at 1027. Napster's duty to search under the modified preliminary injunction is consistent with our holding that Napster must "affirmatively use its ability to patrol its system and preclude access to potentially infringing files listed on its search index." *Id.* The modified preliminary injunction correctly reflects the legal principles of contributory and vicarious copyright infringement that we previously articulated.

Napster's challenge on grounds of vagueness is without merit. A preliminary injunction must "be specific in terms" and "describe in reasonable detail ... the act or acts sought to be restrained." Fed. R. Civ. P. 65(d). We do not set aside injunctions under this rule "unless they are so vague that they have no reasonably specific meaning." *E. & J. Gallo Winery v. Gallo Cattle Co.*, 967 F.2d 1280, 1297 (9th Cir. 1992). Napster has a duty to police its system in order to avoid vicarious infringement. Napster can police the system by searching its index for files containing a noticed copyrighted work. The modified preliminary injunction directs Napster, in no vague terms, to do exactly that.

... V.

Napster challenges the district court's shut down order. The district court was dissatisfied with Napster's compliance despite installation of a new filtering mechanism. The new filter analyzed the contents of a file using audio fingerprinting technology and was not vulnerable to textual variations in file names. Napster had voluntarily disabled its file transferring service to facilitate installation and debugging of the new filtering mechanism. Users were still able to upload files and search the Napster index during this period. The district court ordered Napster to keep the file transferring service disabled until Napster satisfied the court "that when the new system goes back up it will be able to block out or screen out copyrighted works that have been noticed ... and do it with [a] sufficient degree of reliability and sufficient percentage [of success].... It's not good enough until every effort has been made to, in fact, get zero tolerance.... The standard is, to get it down to zero." The shut down order was issued after the parties had filed notices to appeal the modified preliminary injunction.

Napster contends that the shut down order improperly amends the modified preliminary injunction by requiring a non-text-based filtering mechanism and ordering a shut down of the system pursuant to a new "zero tolerance" standard for compliance. Napster additionally argues that the district court lacked authority to further modify the modified preliminary injunction while the injunction was pending on appeal.

A.

Napster argues that the new filtering mechanism is unwarranted as it lies beyond the scope of Napster's duty to police the system. By requiring implementation of the new filtering mechanism, the argument goes, the shut down order fails to recognize that Napster's duty to police is "cabined by the system's current architecture." *Napster*, 239 F.3d at 1024. We are not persuaded by this argument.

"Napster [ ] has the ability to locate infringing material listed on its search indices, and the right to terminate users' access to the system." *Id.* at 1024. To avoid liability for vicarious infringement, Napster must exercise this reserved right to police the system to its fullest extent. *Id.* at 1023. The new filtering mechanism does not involve a departure from Napster's reserved ability to police its system. It still requires Napster to search files located on the index to locate infringing material.

... Napster's original filtering mechanism was unsuccessful in blocking all of plaintiffs' noticed copyrighted works. The text-based filter proved to be vulnerable to user-defined variations in file names. The new filtering mechanism, on the other hand, does not depend on file names and thus is not similarly susceptible to bypass. It was a proper exercise of the district court's supervisory authority to require use of the new filtering mechanism, which may counter Napster's inability to fully comply with the modified preliminary injunction.

B.

Napster argues that the shut down order improperly imposes a new "zero tolerance" standard of compliance. The district court did not, as Napster argues, premise the shut down order on a requirement that Napster must prevent infringement of all of plaintiffs' copyrighted works, without regard to plaintiffs' duty to provide notice. The tolerance standard announced applies only to copyrighted works which plaintiffs have properly noticed as required by the modified preliminary injunction. That is, Napster must do everything feasible to block files from its system which contain noticed copyrighted works.

The district court did not abuse its discretion in ordering a continued shut down of the file transferring service after it determined that the new filtering mechanism failed to prevent infringement of all of plaintiffs' noticed copyrighted works. Even with the new filtering mechanism, Napster was still not in full compliance with the modified preliminary injunction. The district court determined that more could be done to maximize the effectiveness of the new filtering mechanism. Ordering Napster to keep its file transferring service disabled in these circumstances was not an abuse of discretion.

C.

Napster argues that the district court lacked authority to modify the injunction pending appeal. The civil procedure rules permit modifications. While a preliminary injunction is pending on appeal, a district court lacks jurisdiction to modify the injunction in such manner as to "finally adjudicate substantial rights directly involved in the appeal." *Newton v. Consolidated Gas Co.*, 258 U.S. 165, 177, 66 L.Ed. 538, 42 S. Ct. 264 (1922) (citations omitted); *Stein v. Wood*, 127 F.3d 1187, 1189 (9th Cir. 1997). Federal Rule of Civil Procedure 62(c), however, authorizes a district court to continue supervising compliance with the injunction. *See* Fed. R. Civ. P. 62(c) ("When an appeal is taken from an interlocutory or final judgment granting, dissolving, or denying an injunction, the [district] court in its discretion may suspend, modify, restore, or grant an injunction during the pendency of the appeal ... as it considers proper for the security of the rights of the adverse party.").

The district court properly exercised its power under Rule 62(c) to continue supervision of Napster's compliance with the injunction. *See Meinhold v. United States Dep't of Def.*, 34 F.3d 1469, 1480 n.14 (9th Cir. 1994) (holding modification of preliminary injunction during pendency of appeal was proper to clarify injunction and supervise compliance in light of new facts).

VI.

We affirm both the modified preliminary injunction and the shut down order. The terms of the modified preliminary injunction are not vague and properly reflect the relevant law on vicarious and copyright infringement. The shut down order was a proper exercise of the district court's power to enforce compliance with the modified preliminary injunction.

AFFIRMED.

* * * * *

IN RE: AIMSTER COPYRIGHT LITIGATION,
APPEAL OF: JOHN DEEP, Defendant

United States Court of Appeals for the Seventh Circuit

No. 02-4125, 334 F.3d 643

June 30, 2003

[For the background of this case, *see* Supplement *supra* at 345.]

... We turn now to Aimster's defenses under the Online Copyright Infringement Liability Limitation Act, Title II of the Digital Millennium Copyright Act (DMCA), 17 U.S.C. § 512; *see* [2 Paul Goldstein, *Copyright* § 6.3 (2d ed. 2003)]. The DMCA is an attempt to deal with special problems created by the so-called digital revolution. One of these is the vulnerability of Internet service providers such as AOL to liability for copyright infringement as a result of file swapping among their subscribers. Although the Act was not passed with Napster-type services in mind, the definition of Internet service provider is broad ("a provider of online services or network access, or the operator of facilities therefor," 17 U.S.C. § 512(k)(1)(B)), and, as the district judge ruled, Aimster fits it. *See* 2 Goldstein, *supra*, § 6.3.1, p. 6:27. The Act provides a series of safe harbors for Internet service providers and related entities, but none in which Aimster can moor. The Act does not abolish contributory infringement. The common element of its safe harbors is that the service provider must do what it can reasonably be asked to do to prevent the use of its service by "repeat infringers." 17 U.S.C. § 512(i)(1)(A). Far from doing anything to discourage repeat infringers of the plaintiffs' copyrights, Aimster invited them to do so, showed them how they could do so with ease using its system, and by teaching its users how to encrypt their unlawful distribution of copyrighted materials disabled itself from doing anything to prevent infringement.

... AFFIRMED.

* * * * *

insert the following at the end of Notes and Questions # 1 on page 610 of Law of Internet Speech:

With respect to *Metro-Goldwyn-Mayer Studios, Inc. v. Grokster, Ltd., see* Supplement *supra* at 354.

* * * * *
Circumvention of Technological Protection Measures

insert the following at the end of Notes and Questions # 2 on page 621 of Law of Internet Speech:

A federal jury ultimately acquitted ElcomSoft, ruling that the prosecution had failed to demonstrate the requisite intent for criminal culpability. *See, e.g.,* Lisa Bowman, *ElcomSoft Verdict: Not Guilty,* CNet News.com (Dec. 17, 2002), *available at* <http://news.com.com/ ElcomSoftverdict+Not+guilty2100-1023_3-978176.html>.

3. Jon Lech Johansen was acquitted twice of computer piracy by Oslo courts. *See, e.g., Hacker Hero Seeks Compensation After Acquittals in DVD Cracking Case,* SiliconValley.com (Jan. 27, 2004), *available at* <http://www.siliconvalley.com/mld/ siliconvallye/news/editorial/7808655.htm>.

4. Diebold, Inc. is a manufacturer of electronic voting machines. The reliability and verification procedures of the manufacturer's equipment was called into question. *See Online Policy Group v. Diebold, Inc.,* 337 F. Supp. 2d 1195, 1197 (N.D. Cal. 2004). Two Swarthmore College students posted an e-mail archive of communications among Diebold employees that indicated there were problems with the machines, and also included employees' personal identification data. *See id.* Diebold sent a notice and takedown to the students' ISP pursuant to the DMCA, alleging that Diebold's copyrights were infringed by the publication. The plaintiffs sought injunctive, declaratory, and monetary relief in a proceeding they initiated against Diebold; the plaintiffs argued that Diebold's claim of copyright infringement was premised on knowing material misrepresentations and that Deibold interfered with plaintiff's contractual rights with their ISPs.

The U.S. District Court for the Northern District of California agreed, ruling that Diebold had failed to identify specific e-mails with copyrighted content, and at least as to portions of the e-mail archive that clearly were subject to the fair use exception, Diebold "knowingly materially misrepresented" that the posters had infringed Diebold's copyright. *Id.* at 1204. The court held that Diebold was liable for damages and attorneys' fees because:

> No reasonable copyright holder could have believed that the portions of the email archive discussing possible technical problems with Diebold's voting machines were protected by copyright, and there is no genuine issue of fact that Diebold knew -- and indeed that it specifically

intended -- that its ... [notice and take-down] letters to [the posters and the college they attended that had provided Internet access] would result in prevention of publication of that content. The misrepresentations were material in that they resulted in removal of the content from websites and the initiation of the present lawsuit. The fact that Diebold never actually brought suit against any alleged infringer suggests strongly that Diebold sought to use the DMCA's safe harbor provisions -- which were designed to protect ISPs, not copyright holders -- as a sword to suppress publication of embarrassing content rather than as a shield to protect its intellectual property.

Id. at 1204-05 (footnote omitted).

Following the court's ruling, Diebold agreed to pay $125,000 in damages. *See, e.g.,* Media Release, Online Policy Group, *Diebold Coughs Up Cash in Copyright Case* (Oct. 16, 2004), *available at* <www.onlinepolicy.org/media/041016opgvdiebolddamages.shtml>.

Thereafter, Diebold and the State of California and Alameda County settled an action against Diebold. The state and county had asserted claims grounded in fraud about the security of Diebold's electronic voting machines. *See, e.g.,* Clint Boulton, *Diebold to Settle with California,* Internet News.com (Dec. 17, 2004), *available at* <http://www.internetnews. com/bus-news/article.php/3449691>. Diebold agreed to pay Alameda County $100,000 and the state $2.6 million; of the settlement proceeds, $500,000 was to be used to develop a voter education and poll worker training program in California. *See id.*

5. In *Lexmark International, Inc. v. Static Control Components, Inc.,* 387 F.3d 522 (6th Cir. 2004), *reh'g denied,* No. 03-5400, 2004 U.S. App. LEXIS 27422 (6th Cir. Dec. 29, 2004), *reh'g en banc denied,* No. 03-5400, 2005 U.S. App. LEXIS 3330 (6th Cir. Feb. 16, 2005), a manufacturer of printer toner complained that the defendant circumvented the plaintiff's cartridge authentication sequence in violation of the DMCA. The U.S. Court of Appeals for the Sixth Circuit ruled that the printer-to-printer cartridge authentication sequence allegedly circumvented by the distributor's microchip did not "effectively control access to" a copyrighted work because the copyrighted printer control program to which the microchip enabled access was freely accessible for reading and copying without the benefit of the authentication sequence. The court also noted that "[n]owhere in its deliberations over the DMCA did Congress express an interest in creating liability for the circumvention of technological measures designed to prevent consumers from using consumer goods while leaving the copyrightable content of a work unprotected." 387 F.3d at 549.

6. In *Chamberlain Group, Inc. v. Skylink Technologies, Inc.,* 381 F.3d 1178 (Fed. Cir. 2004), *cert. denied,* 125 S. Ct. 1669 (2005), the technology at issue was a copyrighted "rolling code" computer program that continuously changed the remote transmitter signal needed to open an automatic garage door. The competitor's product was a transmitter that was capable of activating garage doors that used door openers produced by the plaintiff. *See* 381 F.3d 1184. The Federal Circuit concluded that the device the plaintiff challenged enabled only authorized users to circumvent plaintiff's copyrighted software, and therefore was presumptively legal. The lower court's decision was affirmed because the plaintiff neither proved nor alleged a valid connection between the defendant's accused circumvention device

and copyright protections. Chamberlain's failure to meet this burden alone compelled a legal ruling in Skylink's favor. *See id.* at 1182.

The International Trade Commission terminated its investigation of unfair trade practice charges brought by The Chamberlain Group, Inc. against Skylink Technologies, Inc. in a related proceeding, determining that the court's ruling deserved *res judicata* effect. *See In re Certain Universal Transmitters for Garage Door Openers,* Inv. No. 337-TA-497, 2004 ITC LEXIS 498 (Int'l Trade Comm'n July 7, 2004).

7. Is it more efficacious for the law to regulate technology or conduct? Which approach leads to sound analytical principles?

* * * * *

insert the following before Realnetworks, Inc. v. Streambox, Inc. on page 621 of Law of Internet Speech:

According to the NPD Group, music downloading via P2P services began to increase again in October 2003 and remained at a higher level in November 2003. *See* Press Release, NPD Group, Inc., *NPD Group Notes Recent Increase in Peer-to-Peer Digital Music File Sharing* (Jan. 16, 2004), *available at* <http://www.npd.com/press/releases/press_040116.htm>. As of April 2005, the Recording Industry Association of America ("RIAA") had sued more than 10,000 individuals since January 2004, with more than 2,200 settlements ranging from $3,500 to $4,500. *See, e.g.,* Evan Pondel, *Song Suits Hit Sour Note: Magistrate Says Schools Need Not Reveal Student Suspects' Names,* L.A. Daily News.com (Apr. 28, 2005) at B1, *available at* <http://www.dailynews.com/Stories/0,1413,200~20950~2839478,00.html>. After the RIAA announced in June 2003 that it would initiate lawsuits against music downloaders, the Pew Internet & American Life Project registered "a dramatic drop in self-reported downloading and filing-sharing" among survey respondents. Pew Internet & American Life Project, *Pew Internet Project and Comscore Media Metrix Data Memo* (Apr. 2004), *available at* <http://www.pewinternet.org/pdfs/PIP_Filesharing_April_04.pdf>. According to the Pew Internet & American Life Project's April 2004 Data Memo, one in seven Internet users said that they no longer downloaded music files. *See id.* at 1. The survey did not, however, distinguish between authorized and unauthorized downloading or file-sharing activity. *See id.* at n.1.

The RIAA also sought to rely on the subpoena provisions of the Digital Millennium Copyright Act, 17 U.S.C. § 512(h), to identify Internet users the RIAA believed were infringing the copyrights of its members. *See* Supplement *supra* at 263. The RIAA served subpoenas on Verizon Internet Services in order to ascertain the names of two Verizon subscribers who appeared to be trading large quantities of .mp3 files of copyrighted music via peer-to-peer file sharing programs such as KaZaA. On appeal of consideration of Verizon's statutory and constitutional challenges to section 512(h) of the DMCA, the U.S. Court of Appeals for the District of Columbia Circuit agreed with Verizon's interpretation of the DMCA and concluded that Verizon does not control the content on its subscribers' computers. *See Recording Indus. Ass'n of Am., Inc. v. Verizon Internet Servs., Inc.,* 351 F.3d 1229 (D.C. Cir. 2003), *cert. denied,* 125 S. Ct. 347 (2004). The appellate court observed that "[t]he RIAA's notification identifies absolutely no material Verizon could remove or access to which it could disable, which indicates to us that § 512(c)(3)(A) [of the DMCA] concerns means of infringement other than P2P file sharing." 351 F.3d at 1236. The court agreed with Verizon that section 512(h) did not authorize the subpoenas issued by the RIAA based on the language, structure, legislative history, and purpose of the DMCA. *See id.* at 1234-39.

The U.S. Supreme Court has observed that "Congress has the constitutional authority and the institutional ability to accommodate fully the varied permutations of competing interests that are inevitably implicated by ... new technology." *Sony Corp. v. Universal City Studios, Inc.,* 464 U.S. 417, 431 (1984) (holding that Sony's marketing and sale of home videotape recorders did not constitute contributory infringement of copyrighted material purchasers recorded). In *Recording Indus. Ass'n of Am., Inc. v. Verizon Internet Servs., Inc.,* 351 F.3d at 1238, the D.C. Circuit Court of Appeals likewise deferred to the legislature, noting that the court was "not unsympathetic either to the RIAA's concern regarding the widespread infringement of its members' copyrights, or to the need for legal tools to protect those rights. It is not the province of the courts, however, to rewrite the DMCA in order to make it fit a new and unforeseen internet architecture, no matter how damaging that development has been to the music industry or threatens being to the motion picture and software industries. The plight of copyright holders must be addressed in the first instance by the Congress...."

Thereafter, the U.S. Court of Appeals for the Eighth Circuit applied the reasoning set forth in *Recording Indus. Ass'n of Am., Inc. v. Verizon Internet Servs., Inc.* to conclude that section 512(h) of the DMCA did not authorize the issuance of a subpoena to an ISP that "merely acts as a conduit for data transferred between two internet users" that allegedly used P2P file sharing software to exchange copyrighted files. *See In re Charter Communications, Inc., Subpoena Enforcement Matter,* 393 F.3d 771, 776 (8th Cir. 2005), *reh'g denied by, reh'g en banc denied by sub nom. Recording Indus. Ass'n of Am. v. Charter Communications, Inc.,* No. 03-3802, 2003 U.S. App. LEXIS 5599 (8th Cir. Apr. 6, 2005). The subpoena provisions of section 512(h) were deemed to apply only to ISPs that had the capacity to locate and remove the allegedly infringing material. 339 F.3d at 776-78.

* * * * *

With respect to efforts by Apple Computer, Inc. to ascertain the identity of individuals who were alleged to have leaked Apple's trade secret information to on-line news sites, *see Apple Computer, Inc. v. Doe 1, an unknown individual, and Does 2-25, inclusive,* No.: 1-04-CV-032178 (Cal. Super. Ct. Mar. 11, 2005), *available at* <http://www.eff.org/Censorship/Apple_v_Does/20050311_apple_decision.pdf>; *see also* Supplement *supra* at 75, 274, 337.

* * * * *

insert the following before Copyright Management Information Provisions on page 624 of Law of Internet Speech:

* * * * *

I.M.S. INQUIRY MANAGEMENT SYSTEMS, LTD., Plaintiff

v.

BERKSHIRE INFORMATION SYSTEMS, INC., Defendant

United States District Court for the Southern District of New York

03 Civ. 2183(NRB), 307 F. Supp. 2d 521

February 23, 2004

MEMORANDUM AND ORDER

Plaintiff I.M.S. Inquiry Management Systems, Ltd., ("plaintiff" or "I.M.S.") commenced this action on March 28, 2003, against defendant Berkshire Information Systems, Inc., ("defendant" or "Berkshire") seeking damages and injunctive relief for defendant's alleged unauthorized use of plaintiff's computer system and the content thereof. ... [Plaintiff claims, among other claims, that defendant violated the Digital Millennium Copyright Act.]

... I. BACKGROUND

The following factual background and allegations are derived from plaintiff's amended complaint and are taken as true for purposes of this motion.

I.M.S., a Canadian Corporation, is engaged in the service of providing advertising tracking information to publishers, advertisers, and others. I.M.S. operates a web-based service known as "e-Basket", which is used by I.M.S.'s clients to track magazine advertising. e-Basket is available exclusively to I.M.S. clients. Each I.M.S. client is issued a unique user identification and password which allows the client to access the e-Basket service and information in I.M.S.'s computers through an I.M.S. website. The e-Basket content is selected by I.M.S. and arranged into categories and sub-categories, a process which involves substantial creativity, time and effort. According to I.M.S., the e-Basket service contains copyrightable subject matter.

Berkshire has introduced and operates a competing tracking service called "Marketshareinfo.com." I.M.S. alleges that in or around March of 2002, Berkshire, or an agent thereof, intentionally and without authorization accessed I.M.S.'s e-Basket service, and gathered and copied content therefrom for use in Marketshareinfo.com. Specifically, Berkshire's unauthorized access spanned eight different webpages of e-Basket content, including that which would ordinarily be used by I.M.S. clients. Through its unauthorized access, I.M.S. contends that Berkshire copied roughly eighty-five percent of I.M.S.'s report formats. Marketshareinfo.com was launched after Berkshire accessed e-Basket, and I.M.S. alleges that Marketshareinfo.com incorporates original copyrightable elements of e-Basket, including the selection and arrangement of informational category headings and I.M.S.-compiled market data.

To gain access to e-Basket, I.M.S. alleges that Berkshire obtained a user identification and password issued to a third party, thereby knowingly inducing that third party to breach an agreement it had with I.M.S.

According to I.M.S., Berkshire's unauthorized access of I.M.S.'s computers is causing I.M.S. irreparable harm, has impaired the integrity and availability of I.M.S.'s data, and has caused I.M.S. to incur costs of more than $5,000 in damage assessment and remedial measures.

... V. DIGITAL MILLENNIUM COPYRIGHT ACT

Congress enacted the Digital Millennium Copyright Act ("DMCA") in 1998 to "strengthen copyright protection in the digital age." *Universal City Studios, Inc. v. Corley*, 273 F.3d 429, 435 (2d Cir. 2001). Plaintiff claims that defendant, by accessing I.M.S.'s computer system through the unauthorized use of a password issued to a party other than defendant, violated the DMCA's bar on circumventing a technological measure that effectively controls access to protected work. The DMCA's "anti-circumvention" provisions, as they are commonly known, read in pertinent part:

> No person shall circumvent a technological measure that effectively controls access to a work protected under this title. 17 U.S.C. § 1201(a)(1)(A). ...

> As used in this subsection ... to "circumvent a technological measure" means to descramble a scrambled work, to decrypt an encrypted work, or otherwise to avoid, bypass, remove, deactivate, or impair a technological measure, without the authority of the copyright owner; and ... a technological measure "effectively controls access to a work" if the measure, in the ordinary course of its operation, requires the application of information, or a process or a treatment, with the authority of the copyright owner, to gain access to the work.

17 U.S.C. § 1201(a)(3).

Defendant challenges whether the facts as alleged manifest a "circumvention" as that term is defined in the subsection. According to defendant, the DMCA was passed to combat unauthorized disabling of digital walls which otherwise safeguard copyrighted materials available on the Internet and the decryption of encrypted content, such as that found on a DVD. Defendant argues that it is not accused of having "hacked" into plaintiff's website, and that "the disconnect between the harm the statute is designed to address and the acts of which plaintiff complains" warrants dismissal of this claim.

Whether accessing copyrighted work by unauthorized use of an otherwise legitimate, owner-issued password qualifies as circumvention under the DMCA appears to be a question of first impression in this Circuit and in all others.

A. Was An Effective Technological Measure In Place?

An action under the DMCA requires "circumvent[ion of] a technological measure that effectively controls access to a work protected under this title." 17 U.S.C. § 1201(a). A "technological measure that effectively controls access" is defined as one that "in the ordinary course of its operation ... requires the application of information, or a process or a

treatment, with the authority of the copyright owner, to gain access to the work." *Id.* at §
1201(a)(3).

I.M.S.'s password protection fits within this definition. In order to gain access to the e-
Basket service, a user in the ordinary course of operation needs to enter a password, which is
the application of information. Indeed, the Second Circuit in Universal Studios confirmed
that "the DMCA ... backed with legal sanctions the efforts of copyright owners to protect
their works from piracy behind digital walls such as encryption codes or password
protections." *Universal Studios*, 273 F.3d at 435.

B. Was The Technological Measure Circumvented?

It is of course the case, as defendant propounds, that the DMCA addresses activity such
as decryption, descrambling, deactivation and impairment, and that these are all forms of
circumvention under the subsection commonly involving technologically-sophisticated
maneuvers. One might associate these activities with the breaking and entering (or hacking)
into computer systems.

On the other hand, other actions proscribed by the DMCA, connote broader application
of the anti-circumvention prohibition, such as the terms "avoid" and "bypass." These actions
are far more open-ended and mundane, and do not necessarily involve some kind of tech-
based execution. Notwithstanding this, defendant argues that it has not even committed any
act of avoidance or bypass, as it is accused of confronting IMS's password-controlled access
in the way precisely intended: "All [I.M.S.] accuses Berkshire of doing is using IMS's own
customer's valid password and user [identification] to view IMS's e-Basket system exactly as
the customer itself might have done."

We agree that plaintiff's allegations do not evince circumvention as that term is used in
the DMCA. Circumvention requires either descrambling, decrypting, avoiding, bypassing,
removing, deactivating or impairing a technological measure qua technological measure. In
the instant matter, defendant is not said to have avoided or bypassed the deployed
technological measure in the measure's gatekeeping capacity. The Amended Complaint
never accuses defendant of accessing the e-Basket system without first entering a plaintiff-
generated password.

More precisely and accurately, what defendant avoided and bypassed was permission to
engage and move through the technological measure from the measure's author. Unlike the
[Computer Fraud and Abuse Act], a cause of action under the DMCA does not accrue upon
unauthorized and injurious access alone; rather, the DMCA "targets the circumvention of
digital walls guarding copyrighted material." *Universal Studios*, 273 F.3d 429, 443.

Although whether an activity qualified as circumvention was not the question posed to
the court, Universal Studios is instructive as a matter of reference. There, the offending
circumvention was a DVD decryption program, DeCSS, which enabled the viewing of
movies without using a DVD player. *See Universal Studios,* 273 F.3d at 452. The security
device that prevented access to DVD movies without a DVD player, CSS, was described "in
its basic function ... [as] a lock on a homeowner's door, a combination of a safe, or a security
device attached to a store's products." *Id.* at 452-53. Likewise, "in its basic function,
[DeCSS, the decryption program] is like a skeleton key that can open a locked door, a
combination that can open a safe, or a device that can neutralize the security device attached
to a store's products. DeCSS enables anyone to gain access to a DVD movie without using a
DVD player." *Universal Studios,* 273 F.3d at 453.

Defendant is alleged to have accessed plaintiff's protected website without plaintiff's authorization. Defendant did not surmount or puncture or evade any technological measure to do so; instead, it used a password intentionally issued by plaintiff to another entity. As an analogy to Universal Studios, the password defendant used to enter plaintiff's webservice was the DVD player, not the DeCSS decryption code, or some alternate avenue of access not sponsored by the copyright owner (like a skeleton key, or neutralizing device). Plaintiff, however, did not authorize defendant to utilize the DVD player. Plaintiff authorized someone else to use the DVD player, and defendant borrowed it without plaintiff's permission. Whatever the impropriety of defendant's conduct, the DMCA and the anti-circumvention provision at issue do not target this sort of activity.

… CONCLUSION

For the foregoing reasons, defendant's motion is … granted for plaintiff's … DMCA claims. Defendant's motion for a more definite statement is denied. …

* * * * *

insert the following before Trademarks on page 625 of Law of Internet Speech:

With respect to a subsequent ruling in *Kelly v. Arriba Soft Corp., withdrawn by, aff'd in part, rev'd in part, remanded,* 336 F.3d 811, 822 (9th Cir. 2003); *see* Supplement *supra* at 372.

* * * * *

Trademarks
Trademark Infringement and Dilution Claims

Insert the following before Bigstar Entertainment, Inc. v. Next Big Star, Inc., et al. on page 645 of Law of Internet Speech:

BROOKFIELD COMMUNICATIONS, INC., Plaintiff
v.
WEST COAST ENTERTAINMENT CORPORATION, Defendant

United States District Court for the Central District of California

No. CV 98-9074 CM, 1999 U.S. Dist. LEXIS 23251

June 10, 1999

ORDER ON MOTIONS

… Plaintiff Brookfield sells sophisticated software and specialized information regarding the entertainment industry. Among the Plaintiff's products are MovieBuff (for which they hold a trademark), which offers comprehensive listings of films and their credits; The Hollywood Connection Kit, which includes contact information on entertainment executives; and Development Tracker, a database tracking the progress of thousands of film projects. In addition to selling these applications through traditional retail outlets, Brookfield Communications has also launched several web sites that afford users the opportunity to sample the software, email the company, and order its products.

On August 19, 1997, Brookfield applied to the Patent and Trademark Office (PTO) for federal registration of "MovieBuff" as a mark to designate both goods and services. Its trademark application describes its product as "computer software providing data and information in the field of the motion picture and television industries." Its service mark application describes its service as "providing multiple-user access to an on-line network database offering data and information in the field of the motion picture and television industries." Both federal trademark registrations issued on September 29, 1998. Brookfield had previously obtained a California state trademark registration for the mark "MovieBuff" covering "computer software" in 1994.

The Defendant, West Coast Entertainment Corporation (hereafter "WCE" or "West Coast") operates a sizeable chain of video stores, and has recently decided to expand its marketing efforts to the Internet. Consequently, it expended substantial sums to create and develop a "virtual video outlet" accessible through its moviebuff.com website. From this site, West Coast attempted to provide services similar to those presently found in its stores, namely, information about new and old movies and provide customers with an opportunity to purchase videos through the internet.

West Coast's slogan is "The Movie Buff's Movie Store" and possessed a domain name of "www.moviebuff.com" that it had registered in 1996. WCE also owns an incontestable service mark for The Movie Buff's Movie Store, which was registered with the United States Patent and Trademark Office on February 12, 1991 (U.S. Registration No. 1,635,042).

The substance of this action involves Brookfield's allegations that the Defendant's use of the term "moviebuff" as a domain name infringes upon the Plaintiff's trademark. In its First Amended Complaint filed on November 18, 1998, Brookfield alleged that West Coast's proposition of online services constitutes trademark infringement and unfair competition in violation of sections 32 and 43(a) of the Lanham Act, 15 U.S.C. §§ 1114, 1125(a).

In its counterclaims, however, WCE alleges that it also owns rights to the mark in connection with its retail video stores and related services, and has used the mark since approximately 1986. According to WCE, Brookfield allegedly commenced its use of the mark MovieBuff in 1994, several years after WCE began using the mark. West Coast, therefore, argues that Brookfield is the junior user of the mark, and adopted its alleged marks with constructive and actual notice of West Coast's prior use. Consequently, WCE has brought numerous counterclaims against Brookfield[, including]: (1) trademark infringement under 15 U.S.C. § 1114; (2) trademark infringement under Section 43(a) of the Lanham Act; [and] (3) federal trademark dilution under 15 U.S.C. § 1125(c)....

I. Motion to Dismiss Defendant's First Amended Counterclaim

... C. Analysis

In bringing this motion, Brookfield contends[, *inter alia,*] that WCE cannot premise its cancellation claim on the allegation that Brookfield's registered trademark causes confusion with WCE's registered trademark....

... 2. Likelihood of Confusion

WCE's second ground for cancellation involves its claim that Brookfield's use of the mark Movie Buff causes a likelihood of confusion with its own mark, "The Movie Buff's Movie Store," which it has used since 1986. "Brookfield's claimed use and proposed use of the mark [MovieBuff] is likely to cause confusion, mistake, or deception as to an affiliation, connection, or association of Brookfield with West Coast, or as to the origin, sponsorship, or approval of Brookfield's goods, services, or commercial activities by West Coast."

... V. Plaintiff's Motion for Summary Adjudication on Likelihood of Confusion

In this motion for summary judgment, Plaintiff moves for summary adjudication on the issue of likelihood of confusion. Plaintiff argues that WCE has alleged in its pleadings that there is a likelihood of confusion between Brookfield's MOVIEBUFF product and WCE's own use of the term "movie buff," and therefore WCE should be judicially estopped from arguing that a likelihood of confusion is not present.

....WCE alleges that "Brookfield's claimed use and proposed use of the mark [MOVIE BUFF] is likely to cause confusion, mistake or deception as to an affiliation, connection or association of Brookfield with West Coast, or as to the origin, sponsorship, or approval of Brookfield's goods, services or commercial activities by West Coast." WCE's [First Amended Complaint] further alleges that "Brookfield's use and proposed use of the MOVIE BUFF MARKS constitutes false designation of origin and false description under 15 U.S.C. § 1125 and is likely to cause confusion, mistake or to deceive the public that there is an affiliation, connection or association between BROOKFIELD and WEST COAST, or that West Coast produces, sponsors or approves of BROOKFIELD's products or services."

Brookfield's central argument in support of its motion is that WCE has essentially admitted a likelihood of confusion by accusing Brookfield of this possibility in its counterclaims. In response, WCE contends that it has alleged that:

> Brookfield's use of Movie Buff is likely to cause confusion. West Coast has consistently denied that West Coast and Brookfield are competitors and that West Coast's "use of Movie Buff has caused confusion and mistake and to deceive the public into believing that West Coast and West Coast products and services are associated with and/or authorized by Brookfield."

Put another way, West Coast argues that it is Brookfield's use of the term Movie Buff that creates the likelihood of confusion, not West Coast. According to WCE, "there is nothing inconsistent between West Coast's denial that it has created confusion and that Brookfield has."

However, the crux of WCE's assertions regarding likelihood of confusion rest on its proposition that Brookfield is the junior user of the mark. ... The Court has already disposed of this argument in prior motions.

Under section 43(a) of the Lanham Act, the "basic test" is "whether the use of the mark is likely to cause confusion as to the source of the goods or services." *Films of Distinction, Inv. v. Allegro Film Productions, Inc.*, 12 F. Supp. 2d 1068, 1998 WL 372350, *3 (C.D. Cal. June 1, 1998); *see also Dr. Seuss Enterprises, L.P. v. Penguin Books USA, Inc.*, 109 F.3d 1394, 1403 (9th Cir. 1997). To be more precise, section 43(a) requires Brookfield to establish that Defendants (1) use a "word, term, name, symbol or device," (2) in commerce, (3) "in connection with any goods or services," (4) in a manner that is "likely to cause confusion," and, as a result, (5) Brookfield is "likely to be damaged." 15 U.S.C. § 1125(a).

Even assuming that WCE is not judicially estopped from asserting its own position with respect to likelihood of confusion, it has failed to create a genuine issue of material fact over whether or not such confusion exists. The Ninth Circuit, in its analysis on this very topic, concluded that Brookfield had made a strong showing that likelihood of confusion existed. In analyzing the conclusions set forth in its opinion, the Court has concluded that summary judgment on the issue of likelihood of confusion is warranted in favor of Plaintiff. It bears noting that the Ninth Circuit performed an extensive analysis in employing the eight "*Sleekcraft*" factors to these circumstances, namely: likelihood of confusion, similarity of the conflicting designations, relatedness or proximity of the two companies' products or services, strength of mark, marketing channels used, degree of care likely to be exercised by purchasers in selecting goods, the parties' intent, evidence of actual confusion, and likelihood of expansion in product lines. *Brookfield,* 174 F.3d 1036, 1999 WL 232014 at *13, citations omitted.

> First, the Ninth Circuit observed that it is readily apparent that West Coast's allegedly infringing mark is essentially identical to Brookfield's mark "MovieBuff." In terms of appearance, there are differences in capitalization and the addition of ".com" in West Coast's complete domain name, but these differences are inconsequential in light of the fact that Web addresses are not caps-sensitive and that the ".com" top-level domain signifies the site's commercial nature.

[*Id.*] at *14. It further concluded that "as 'MovieBuff' and 'moviebuff.com' are, for all intents and purposes, identical in terms of sight, sound, and meaning, we conclude that the similarity factor weighs heavily in favor of Brookfield." [*Id.*] at *15.

Second, it found that West Coast and Brookfield are not non-competitors, [*id.*] at *16, and that

> the competitive proximity of their products is actually quite high. Just as Brookfield's "MovieBuff" is a searchable database with detailed information on films, West Coast's web site features a similar searchable database, which Brookfield points out is licensed from a direct competitor of Brookfield.

Id. The Ninth Circuit concluded that the use of similar marks to offer similar products weighs heavily in favor of likelihood of confusion. *Id.*

Third, the Court, upon recognizing the "virtual identicality" of "moviebuff.com" and "MovieBuff," the relatedness of the products and services accompanied by the marks, and the companies' use of the Web as a marketing and advertising tool, predicted that "many forms of consumer confusion are likely to result." [*Id.*] at *17. Indeed, it predicted a host of situations in which confusion is likely: individuals searching for Brookfield's site may reach West Coast's site and mistakenly assume that they have reached Brookfield; conclude that West Coast may have licensed "MovieBuff" from Brookfield; assume that the "MovieBuff" database is no longer offered and has since been replaced by West Coast's service; or might take advantage of West Coast's services, thereby permitting West Coast to misappropriate any goodwill that Brookfield has developed in its mark. *Id.*

Although the Ninth Circuit recognized, as this Court found, that Brookfield's mark is weak, [*id.*] at *18, it observed that the mark's strength was of diminished importance, given the relatedness of the products and the virtual identicality of the marks. [*Id.*] at *18, quoting

McCarthy ¶ 11:76 ("Whether a mark is weak or not is of little importance where the conflicting mark is identical and the goods are closely related.") Turning to intent, the Ninth Circuit found that this factor appeared "indeterminate," but noted that an intent to confuse consumers is not required for a finding of trademark infringement and is largely irrelevant to a finding of likelihood of confusion. *Brookfield*, 174 F.3d 1036, at *19, citation omitted.

As for the final three *Sleekcraft* factors -- evidence of actual confusion, likelihood of expansion in product lines, and purchaser care, the Court found that they failed to affect the ultimate conclusion reached regarding the likelihood of confusion. [*Id.*] at *20. It found actual confusion to be irrelevant because Brookfield filed suit before West Coast actively used the "moviebuff.com" mark; and that it was "neither exceedingly likely nor unlikely that West Coast will enter more directly into Brookfield's principal market, or vice versa." *Id.*

Last, the Court never actually reached a definitive conclusion regarding the degree of care potentially exercised by consumers of the product in question. The Court cited a Third Circuit case for the proposition that "the standard of care to be exercised by the reasonably prudent purchaser will be equal to that of the least sophisticated consumer." *Id.*, quoting *Ford Motor Co. v. Summit Motor Prods., Inc.,* 930 F.2d. 277, 283 (3d Cir. 1991). Although it found some indeterminacy as to the standard of care that consumers might exercise in accessing MovieBuff, the Court declined to decide the question. It found that the "purchaser confusion factor, even considered in the light most favorable to West Coast, is not sufficient to overcome the likelihood of confusion strongly established by the other factors" it had just analyzed. *Id.*

Taking the Ninth Circuit's findings into account, this Court concludes that West Coast has failed to offer evidence to create a triable issue over the existence of the likelihood of confusion. Indeed, many of the "issues" West Coast identifies in its Opposition appear irrelevant (like whether Brookfield's inhollywood or moviebuffonline website addresses create any likelihood of confusion with any or all of West Coast's family of MOVIE BUFF marks), or have previously been exhaustively analyzed by the reviewing court.

Given the absence of evidence creating a triable issue over likelihood of confusion, the Court finds that summary judgment in Plaintiff's favor is warranted. "Where, as here, the defendant uses the identical mark on competitive goods as plaintiff, the confusion test under 15 U.S.C. Section 1114 is 'open and shut.'" *Lozano Enterprises v. La Opinion Publishing Co.,* 1997 U.S. Dist. LEXIS 20372, 44 U.S.P.Q.2d 1764, 1767 (C.D. Cal. 1997), quoting *Opticians Ass'n. v. Independent Opticians,* 920 F.2d 187, 193 (3d Cir. 1990) ("cases where a defendant uses an identical mark on competitive goods hardly ever find their way into the appellate reports. Such cases are "open and shut" and do not involve protracted litigation to determine liability for trademark infringement."). Although the Court echoes the Ninth Circuit's apt observation that "we must be acutely aware of excessive rigidity when applying the law in the Internet context; emerging technologies require a flexible approach," *Brookfield*, 174 F.3d 1036, at *14, this principle alone fails to create a triable issue with respect to the potential for consumer confusion on the Web. Accordingly, summary judgment is granted in favor of the Plaintiff on the issue of likelihood of confusion.

VI. Conclusion

... The Court grants Plaintiff's Motions for Summary Adjudication on the issues of trademark priority and likelihood of confusion, in light of the Ninth Circuit's analysis of these issues.

RETAIL SERVICES INC., FREEBIE, INCORPORATED, Plaintiffs-Appellees

v.

FREEBIES PUBLISHING, EUGENE F. ZANNON; GAIL
ZANNON, Defendants-Appellants

United States Court of Appeals for the Fourth Circuit

No. 03-1272, No. 03-1317, 364 F.3d 535

April 13, 2004

Retail Services, Inc. and Freebie, Inc. (collectively "RSI") brought this action for declaratory relief against Freebies Publishing, Eugene F. Zannon, and Gail Zannon (collectively "defendants") seeking an order declaring[, *inter alia,*] ... that RSI's use of the term "freebie" in its domain name did not infringe upon defendants' registered FREEBIES trademark under the Lanham Act, *see* 15 U.S.C.A. § 1114 (West 1997 & Supp. 2003), and that the term "freebies" is generic and therefore not protectible as a trademark. In response, defendants filed a counterclaim under the Lanham Act based on RSI's use of the word "freebie" in its domain name, asserting claims for trademark infringement and cybersquatting. Additionally, defendants included Lanham Act claims for unfair competition and trademark dilution. *See* 15 U.S.C.A. § 1125(a), (c) (West 1998 & Supp. 2003). ...

... I.

Before we recount the facts of this case, a brief discussion of the legal context in which the facts arise is helpful. Trademarks "identify and distinguish" goods produced by one person "from those manufactured or sold by others and ...indicate the source of the goods." 15 U.S.C.A. § 1127 (West Supp. 2003). To the purchasing public, a trademark "signifies that all goods bearing the trademark" originated from the same source and "that all goods bearing the trademark are of an equal level of quality." 1 J. Thomas McCarthy, *McCarthy on Trademarks and Unfair Competition* § 3.2 (4th ed. 2003) [hereinafter McCarthy]. Because of its role in assuring consumers of the origin and quality of the associated goods, a trademark is also "a prime instrument in advertising and selling the goods." *Id.*

Thus, a proposed mark cannot acquire trademark protection unless the mark is distinctive, that is, unless it serves the traditional trademark functions of "distinguishing the applicant's goods from those of others" and identifying the source of the goods. *Two Pesos, Inc. v. Taco Cabana, Inc.*, 505 U.S. 763, 768, 120 L. Ed. 2d 615, 112 S. Ct. 2753 (1992); *see* 15 U.S.C.A. § 1052 (West 1997). The antithesis of a distinctive mark is a "generic" mark which merely employs "the common name of a product or service," *Sara Lee Corp. v. Kayser-Roth Corp.*, 81 F.3d 455, 464 (4th Cir. 1996), or "refers to the genus of which the particular product is a species," *Park 'N Fly, Inc. v. Dollar Park & Fly, Inc.*, 469 U.S. 189, 194, 83 L. Ed. 2d 582, 105 S. Ct. 658 (1985). Because a generic mark, by definition, neither signifies the source of goods nor distinguishes the particular product from other products on the market, a generic term cannot be protected as a trademark nor registered as one. *See Two Pesos*, 505 U.S. at 768; *Sara Lee*, 81 F.3d at 464; *Larsen v. Terk Techs. Corp.*, 151 F.3d 140, 148 (4th Cir. 1998) (noting that "'generic marks' are accorded no protection at all ...."). "The concepts of 'generic name' and 'trademark' are mutually exclusive" because a generic term "can never function as a mark to identify and distinguish the products of only one seller." 2 McCarthy at

§ 12:1. From a policy standpoint, of course, if a business were permitted to appropriate a generic word as its trademark, it would be "difficult for competitors to market their own brands of the same product. Imagine being forbidden to describe a Chevrolet as a 'car' or an 'automobile' because Ford or Chrysler or Volvo had trademarked these generic words." *Blau Plumbing, Inc. v. S.O.S. Fix-It, Inc.*, 781 F.2d 604, 609 (7th Cir. 1986).

Whether trademark protection extends to a proposed mark is tied to the mark's distinctiveness. *See Sara Lee*, 81 F.3d at 464. In determining the distinctiveness of a given mark, courts use a categorical approach, placing the mark in one of four classifications that increase in distinctiveness as follows: generic, descriptive, suggestive, and arbitrary or fanciful. *See Pizzeria Uno Corp. v. Temple*, 747 F.2d 1522, 1527 (4th Cir. 1984). On the opposite end of the spectrum from the generic category are marks that are fanciful or arbitrary -- inherently distinctive marks. Fanciful marks are, for the most part, nonsense "words expressly coined for serving as a trademark." *Sara Lee*, 81 F.3d at 464 (offering "Clorox™, Kodak™, Polaroid™, and Exxon™" as examples). Arbitrary marks consist of recognizable words used in connection with products for which "they do not suggest or describe any quality, ingredient, or characteristic," as if the trademark was "arbitrarily assigned." *Id.* (citing "Camel™ cigarettes" and "Apple™ computers" as examples).

Between the generic and the arbitrary or fanciful categories are descriptive marks and suggestive marks, which are often difficult to distinguish from each other. Descriptive marks "merely describe a function, use, characteristic, size, or intended purpose of the product." *Id.* (mentioning "After Tan post-tanning lotion" and "5 Minute Glue"). Descriptive marks are not inherently distinctive; the Lanham Act "accords protection only if they have acquired a 'secondary meaning.'" *Larsen*, 151 F.3d at 148; *see* 15 U.S.C.A. § 1052(e)(1) (registration may be refused if the proposed mark, "when used on or in connection with the goods of the applicant[,] is merely descriptive or deceptively misdescriptive of them"). Saying that a trademark has acquired "secondary meaning" is shorthand for saying that a descriptive mark *has become* sufficiently distinctive to establish "a *mental association* in buyers' minds between the alleged mark and a single source of the product." 2 McCarthy at § 15: 5; *see Two Pesos*, 505 U.S. at 769 ("This acquired distinctiveness" necessary for a descriptive mark to be protected "is generally called 'secondary meaning.'"); *Sara Lee*, 81 F.3d at 464 (explaining that "secondary meaning" exists when, "in the minds of the public, the primary significance of a product feature or term is to identify the source of the product rather than the product itself" (internal quotation marks omitted)).

In contrast to descriptive marks, suggestive marks are inherently distinctive and, like arbitrary or fanciful marks, qualify for registration without any showing of "secondary meaning." *See Pizzeria Uno*, 747 F.2d at 1529. A mark is suggestive if it "connotes, without describing, some quality, ingredient, or characteristic of the product." *Sara Lee*, 81 F.3d at 464 (providing the following examples: "Coppertone™, Orange Crush™, and Playboy™"). A helpful rule of thumb is that "'if the mark imparts information directly, it is descriptive,'" but "'if it stands for an idea which requires some operation of the imagination to connect it with the goods, it is suggestive.'" *Pizzeria Uno*, 747 F.2d at 1528 (quoting *Union Carbide Corp. v. Ever-Ready, Inc.*, 531 F.2d 366, 379 (7th Cir. 1976)).

With these concepts in mind, we consider the facts.

II.

In 1979, the Zannons purchased the right to publish *Freebies Magazine*, a periodical providing information about free mail-order offerings. The Zannons also acquired ownership rights to the stylized trademark FREEBIES, which the previous publisher registered in 1978 to use as a logo for the magazine. Apparently, the Zannons abandoned this particular mark for a period of time beginning in June 1985; however, in March 1992, the Zannons filed an application, on behalf of Freebies Publishing, with the PTO for a new certificate of registration for a different rendition of the stylized FREEBIES mark. Although the PTO eventually issued a certificate of registration for the mark, the application process was not without difficulty. The PTO's examining attorney initially refused the application because, among other reasons, "the proposed mark merely describes the goods ... the mark describes the subject matter of applicant's publication." Freebies Publishing submitted a response but was unable to convince the PTO that the proposed FREEBIES trademark was suggestive rather than merely descriptive.

In December 1992, having received no evidence demonstrating that defendants' mark had "acquired secondary meaning," the PTO finalized its refusal of registration. This refusal was withdrawn, however, after Eugene Zannon filed an affidavit under 37 C.F.R. § 2.41(b), which allows the PTO to accept as evidence of distinctiveness a declaration that the proposed mark has been in "substantially exclusive and continuous use in commerce ...by [the] applicant for ...five years." Thus, the FREEBIES mark was finally registered on November 30, 1993, for use in connection with "periodicals; namely, magazines and newspapers with information about mail order offerings."

Defendants continued publishing *Freebies Magazine* until March 2001. After that time, Freebies Publishing shifted its focus from traditional printed media to cyberspace, offering its mail order information over the Internet under the domain name <freebies.com>. Defendants apparently anticipated this change well prior to 2001, having registered the domain name in November 1997.

RSI provides "customer management services" to retailers, which RSI delivers to its clients through computer products designed to instantly profile any given customer making a retail purchase. When a customer makes a purchase from an RSI client, the RSI product enables information to be sent from the point of sale to RSI's database of customer transactions. The system then instantaneously identifies a potential "incentive offer," described by RSI as "a freebie," which is printed out and presented to the customer along with the purchase receipt.

In 1991, between the time that the defendants abandoned the original FREEBIES trademark and applied for the new registration, RSI received legal advice that the term "freebie" was available for use and could be legally protected. RSI took no further action, however, until 1995, when it registered the domain name <freebie.com> for later use, two years before defendants registered the <freebies.com> domain name. By that time, of course, FREEBIES was a registered trademark.

In 1998, RSI agreed to perform customer management services for Blockbuster, Inc., a large and well-established corporation in the retail business of video and DVD rentals and sales. In order to service the Blockbuster account, Frank Byerley, RSI's owner, formed Freebie, Inc., drawing the corporate name from a promotional scheme for Blockbuster customers to earn "Freebie Points" which they could cash in for rent-free viewing. In August 2001, RSI began operating its website at <www.freebie.com> so that Blockbuster customers could manage their Freebie Points online. Meanwhile, defendants had been offering their mail-order information online at <www.freebies.com> for five months. ...

RSI ... fil[ed] this action against defendants for a declaration[, *inter alia,*] that RSI's use of the word "freebie" as part of its domain name ... does not constitute trademark infringement, *see* 15 U.S.C.A. § 1114(1)(a), trademark dilution, *see* 15 U.S.C.A. § 1125(c), or unfair competition, *see* 15 U.S.C.A. § 1125(a). RSI also asked the district court to rule that the word "freebies" is generic and to cancel the FREEBIES registration, rendering the arbitration order null and void. Defendants counterclaimed[, *inter alia,*] for trademark infringement and dilution....

... III.

We turn first to defendants' argument that their certificate of registration alone creates an issue of fact as to whether the word "freebies" is generic and thereby precludes summary judgment in favor of RSI. For the reasons that follow, we cannot agree.

Under the Lanham Act, the issuance of a certificate of registration arms the registrant with "*prima facie* evidence of the validity of the registered mark and of the registration of the mark, of the registrant's ownership of the mark, and of the registrant's exclusive right to use the registered mark." 15 U.S.C.A. § 1057(b) (West 1997). Because the PTO may not register a generic mark, the fact that a mark is registered is strong evidence that the mark satisfies the statutory requirements for the distinctiveness necessary for trademark protection. *See* 15 U.S.C.A. §§ 1052(e), 1057(b); 15 U.S.C.A. § 1064(3) (West 1997). The certificate of registration supplies "the registrant [with] ... *prima facie* evidence that its mark is not generic in the eyes of the relevant public ... and that its mark ... at a minimum is descriptive *and* has obtained secondary meaning." *America Online, Inc. v. AT&T Corp.*, 243 F.3d 812, 816 (4th Cir. 2001); *see U.S. Search*, 300 F.3d at 524. This is a significant procedural advantage for the registrant. Without a certificate of registration, the owner would be required to establish that the disputed mark was sufficiently distinctive to warrant trademark protection in the first place. *See Pizzeria Uno*, 747 F.2d at 1529. The effect of the presumption is to satisfy that burden in the absence of rebutting evidence. *See America Online*, 243 F.3d at 818; *see also Tie Tech, Inc. v. Kinedyne Corp.*, 296 F.3d 778, 783 (9th Cir. 2002) ("In trademark terms, the registration is not absolute but subject to rebuttal" and "discharges the plaintiff's original common law burden of proving validity in an infringement action.").

The presumption of validity flowing from trademark registration, therefore, has a burden-shifting effect, requiring the party challenging a registered mark to produce sufficient evidence to establish that the mark is generic by a preponderance of evidence. *See Glover v. Ampak, Inc.*, 74 F.3d 57, 59 (4th Cir. 1996); *Pizzeria Uno*, 747 F.2d at 1529. ....[W]e reject the defendants' contention.

IV.

Having decided that the certificate of registration alone does not immunize defendants' claims from dispositive motions prior to trial, we turn to the district court's conclusion that there was no genuine issue of material fact on the issue of genericness and that RSI was thus entitled to summary judgment.

A. RSI's Evidence of Genericness

To rebut the presumption that the mark is not generic, RSI must offer sufficient proof that "the *primary* significance of the mark [is] its indication of the nature or class of the product or service, rather than an indication of source." *Glover*, 74 F.3d at 59. Additionally, the evidence must demonstrate the generic understanding of the mark from the viewpoint of the "'relevant public.'" *Id.* (quoting 15 U.S.C.A. § 1064(3)). The district court determined that the relevant consuming public "includes Internet users seeking information about mail order offerings." *Retail Servs.*, 247 F. Supp. 2d at 826. We agree with this conclusion, and defendants do not take issue with it.

Defendants' mark was registered for use in connection with "magazines and newspapers with information about mail order offerings." Although the publication of the printed *Freebies Magazine* ceased in 2001, defendants continued to offer the same kinds of information on their website, hoping to attract Internet users looking for mail-order material. Thus, the issue boils down to this: whether RSI has offered sufficient evidence that, in the minds of Internet users interested in online free mail-order information, the term "freebie" or "freebies" does not give "an indication of source," *Glover*, 74 F.3d at 59, but rather identifies the nature or general class of goods or services, *i.e.*, employs the "common name of a product or service." *Sara Lee*, 81 F.3d at 464.

Evidence offered to rebut the presumption of validity may come from any number of sources, including "purchaser testimony, consumer surveys, listings and dictionaries, trade journals, newspapers, and other publications." *Glover*, 74 F.3d at 59; *see In re Merrill Lynch, Pierce, Fenner & Smith, Inc.*, 828 F.2d 1567, 1570 (Fed. Cir. 1987) ("Evidence of the public's understanding of the term may be obtained from any competent source ...."). Other common sources include evidence of "generic use by competitors, generic use of the term by the mark's owners, and use of the term by third parties in trademark registrations." *Nartron*, 305 F.3d at 406.

The district court considered various dictionary definitions that were roughly uniform in defining "freebie" as a slang term meaning "'something ...given or received without charge.'" *Retail Servs.*, 247 F. Supp. 2d at 826 (quoting *Webster's Ninth Collegiate Dictionary* 491 (1988)); *see, e.g.*, The American Heritage College Dictionary 542 (3d ed. 1997) ("An article or service given free."); *Webster's II New Riverside University Dictionary* 504 (1988) ("Something given or received gratis ...."); *Cambridge International Dictionary of English*, Online Edition, *available at* http://dictionary.cambridge.org ("Something which is given to you without you having to pay for it, esp. as a way of attracting your support for or interest in something."). The district court noted that, according to the *Oxford English Dictionary*, "freebie" has been understood to mean "'something that is provided free'" since its 1942 inclusion "in *The American Thesaurus of Slang: A Complete Reference Book of Colloquial Speech*." *Retail Servs.*, 247 F. Supp. 2d at 826-27. Although not controlling, "dictionary definitions are relevant and sometimes persuasive" on the issue of genericness "based upon the assumption that dictionary definitions usually reflect the public's perception of a word's meaning and its contemporary usage." 2 McCarthy at § 12.13 (internal quotation marks omitted); *see Harley-Davidson, Inc. v. Grottanelli*, 164 F.3d 806, 810 (2d Cir. 1999) ("Dictionary definitions of a word to denote a category of products are significant evidence of genericness."); *Mil-Mar Shoe Co. v. Shonac Corp.*, 75 F.3d 1153, 1158 (7th Cir. 1996) ("Because generic use implies use consistent with common understanding, we have often looked to dictionaries as a source of evidence on genericness.").

Furthermore, as noted above, evidence of the owner's generic use, in particular, "is strong evidence of genericness." 2 McCarthy at § 12.13. The district court highlighted the contents of defendants' own <freebies.com> website, which undercut their position that "freebies" is not a generic term. *See Retail Servs. Inc.*, 247 F. Supp. 2d at 827. For example, the <freebies.com> home page included a banner announcing that the website was "BRINGING YOU THE BEST FREE AND ALMOST FREE OFFERS SINCE 1977" and stating that "Freebies.com is the best place on the web for free and almost free offers that you won't find

408

anywhere else." The stylized freebies logo at the top of the home page appeared above the same slogan that had been emblazoned on the printed version of *Freebies Magazine*: "The Magazine with Something for Nothing."

The actual offers included on <freebies.com> or in *Freebies Magazine* used the term "freebies" in this same sense -- items that the reader would ordinarily expect to pay for but could obtain for free with the information provided by the magazine or website. For example, the September-October 1983 edition of *Freebies Magazine* included a section entitled "Football Freebies" which explained how to obtain "fabulous freebies offered by your own special team." The section was divided into two columns. One column, under the heading TEAM, listed addresses for various National Football League franchises, and the other column, under the heading FREEBIE, listed items that could be obtained for no cost (such as bumper stickers or posters) upon request. Likewise, on the website, typical items might include American flag lapel pins or tie tacks, like those offered on January 9, 2003, which could be obtained by sending the specified postage and handling costs to the address provided by <freebies.com>. Gail and Eugene Zannon, moreover, both gave deposition testimony confirming that their use of the term "freebies" was consistent with the commonly understood meaning of the word, referring to free goods and services, and that their primary business is "the distribution of [information about] free or almost free goods and services."
...

The district court concluded that the evidence of genericness was so one-sided that no genuine issue of fact existed as to whether, "in the public's mind, 'freebies' indicates free or almost free products and is not identified with defendants or their website in particular." *Retail Servs.*, 247 F. Supp. 2d at 827. Such one-sided evidence necessarily rebuts the presumption of non-genericness.

B. Defendants' Arguments

1. Additional Evidence that "Freebies" Is Not Generic.

Defendants contend that the district court failed to take into consideration any of their evidence, in addition to the certificate of registration, that created an issue of fact by demonstrating the distinctive, non-generic nature of the mark. First, defendants point out that in reviewing defendants' application for trademark registration, the PTO's examining attorney considered one of the same dictionary definitions of "freebie" that the district court found persuasive on the issue of genericness. Defendants argue the fact that the PTO ultimately issued the certificate of registration seriously undercuts the value of the dictionary definition. This is not additional evidence; it is part and parcel of the certificate of registration which, as we explained at length, is itself evidence the word or phrase in question is not generic. We fail to see how this part of the registration process offers anything that the whole does not. The district court, of course, took the registration into account and acknowledged its presumptive effect, but simply concluded it was not enough to prevent summary judgment for RSI. *See Retail Servs.*, 247 F. Supp. 2d at 826.

Defendants also contend that the district court all but ignored substantial evidence demonstrating that the registered term was not only not generic, but was a strong, commercially successful mark with a well-established secondary meaning. In particular, defendants highlight that <freebies.com> receives an average of "100,000 visits per month from consumers around the world;" that *Freebies Magazine* in print form had millions of paying subscribers; and that defendants sold more than 385,000 books offering information similar to that provided in *Freebies Magazine*. Evidence of an acquired secondary meaning, however, has no relevance unless the mark in question has been found not to be generic. *See, e. g., Home Builders Ass'n of Greater St. Louis v. L & L Exhibition Mgmt., Inc.*, 226 F.3d 944, 949 (8th Cir. 2000) ("A 'generic' mark is the common name of a product or service.... It may not be registered nor used exclusively by one competitor, even if it has acquired secondary meaning."); *A & H Sportswear, Inc. v. Victoria's Secret Stores, Inc.*, 237 F.3d 198, 222 (3rd Cir. 2000) (same).

For these same reasons, we also discount defendants' reliance on the evidence of actual and potential confusion -- according to defendants, for example, there were several hundred complaints from consumers who were seeking defendants' website but ended up in RSI's site, or vice-versa. Evidence establishing a likelihood of confusion simply "does not bear upon the question of whether [a] trademark ... [is] generic." *Ale House Mgmt., Inc. v. Raleigh Ale House, Inc.*, 205 F.3d 137, 144-45 (4th Cir. 2000). In sum, defendant has failed to highlight any significant evidence, outside of the certificate of trademark registration, that would create a genuine issue of fact on genericness.

2. Non-Generic Use of "Freebies"

Defendants contend that, even if the word "freebies" is generic, they were not using this term generically *in connection with their business*, which defendants carefully describe as the provision of "information about no-cost or low cost promotional offers." Defendants emphasize that they do not actually distribute or offer the free products or samples, which they concede would constitute a generic use of "freebies," but simply tell consumers how to obtain such items from others, which they claim does not. In essence, defendants argue that this distinction transforms their use of FREEBIES from generic to descriptive.

In our view, this razor-thin distinction is not significant. Of course, it is certainly possible for a term to serve as a generic description for one category of products but function as a distinctive mark for unrelated products in a different context. *See, e. g., In re Seats, Inc.*, 757 F.2d 274, 277 (Fed. Cir. 1985) (holding that the word "SEATS" was not generic for ticket reservations services even though it could not be registered in connection with chairs or couches). Even though defendants do not directly distribute free products or "freebies," their business nonetheless revolves around "freebies" in the generic sense of the word. As defendants' website proclaims, they are "BRINGING YOU THE BEST FREE AND ALMOST FREE OFFERS SINCE 1977!" Accordingly, we reject defendants' contention that they were not using the term *in its generic sense*.

3. The Incontestable Status of FREEBIES

Defendants suggest that, even if we do not agree that FREEBIES is, at the very least, a descriptive mark that has acquired secondary meaning, it is beyond dispute that FREEBIES has become incontestible, and therefore is not subject to challenge with regard to its secondary meaning. This argument misses the mark.

If a registered trademark becomes incontestable, the rebuttable presumption that a registered mark has acquired secondary meaning becomes "conclusive evidence of the registrant's exclusive right to use the registered mark" subject to a number of affirmative defenses enumerated in the Lanham Act. 15 U.S.C.A. § 1115(b) (West 1998 & Supp. 2003). This list, however, does not include a defense based upon a mark's lack of secondary meaning -- a merely descriptive mark, then, is subject to challenge based on its lack of distinctiveness until it acquires incontestable status. *See Park 'N Fly*, 469 U.S. at 196. Thus, a presumption arises from the registration of a trademark that the mark is entitled to trademark protection because of either the mark's inherently distinctive nature or its secondary meaning, but the mark is subject to challenge on the basis that it is merely descriptive. *See id.; America On Line*, 243 F.3d at 817-18. The validity of the same registered mark, after qualifying for incontestable status, is conclusively presumed and may not be challenged as merely descriptive. *See Park 'N Fly*, 469 U.S. at 196. The Supreme Court provided this concise summary:

> A mark that is merely descriptive of an applicant's goods or services is not registrable unless the mark has secondary meaning. Before a mark achieves incontestable status, registration provides *prima facie* evidence of the registrant's exclusive right to use the mark in commerce. The Lanham Act expressly provides that before a mark becomes incontestable an opposing party may prove any ... defense which might have been asserted if the mark had not been registered ... [including a] challenge [to the] mark as merely descriptive.... With respect to incontestable marks, ... registration is *conclusive* evidence of the registrant's exclusive right to use the mark.... Mere descriptiveness is not recognized by [the relevant provisions of the Lanham Act] as a basis for challenging an incontestable mark.

Id. (internal citations omitted).

Here, however, the issue is not whether the mark is merely descriptive, but whether it is generic. And incontestability is never a shield for a mark that is generic. Although § 1115(b) does not enumerate the generic nature of a trademark as a basis for challenging an incontestable mark, a registration is subject to cancellation at any time "if the registered mark becomes the generic name for the goods or services ...for which it is registered." 15 U.S.C.A. § 1064(3). As we observed before, a generic word can never function as a trademark or receive a certificate of registration as one. Even an incontestable mark, therefore, comes within the reach of § 1064(3) and may be canceled if it becomes generic. *See Park 'N Fly*, 469 U.S. at 195.

4. Stylized Lettering in the FREEBIES Trademark

Finally, defendants contend that, separate and apart from their rights in the word FREEBIES, the stylized rendering of the letters is sufficiently distinctive to merit registration. Assuming the registered *display* of FREEBIES is distinctive (which is far from clear), that fact does not aid defendants – "such a registration does not give any exclusive right to use the generic word *per se*" - "the only exclusive right from such a 'picture' registration is the use of that exact 'picture' which happens to spell out a generic name." 2 McCarthy at § 12: 40 (citing *Time, Inc. v. Petersen Publ. Co.*, 173 F.3d 113 (2d Cir. 1999)). We have no difficulty concluding that the modest stylized lettering of the FREEBIES mark in no way affords defendants ownership rights in the generic word "freebies." And, defendants do not guide us to anything in the record to suggest that the stylized rendition of the word is "so distinctive as to create a commercial impression separate and apart from the [generic] term." *In re Northland Aluminum Prods., Inc.*, 777 F.2d 1556, 1561 (Fed. Cir. 1985) (internal quotation marks omitted). The district court properly rejected this argument. ...

VII.

For the foregoing reasons, we affirm the decision of the district court in its entirety.

* * * * *

NISSAN MOTOR CO., a Japanese corporation; NISSAN NORTH
AMERICA, INC., a California corporation, Plaintiffs-Appellees
v.
NISSAN COMPUTER CORPORATION, a North Carolina
corporation, Defendant-Appellant

United States Court of Appeals for the Ninth Circuit

No. 02-57148, No. 03-55017, No. 03-55144, No. 03-55236, 378
F.3d 1002

August 6, 2004

This appeal raises a number of trademark issues arising out of the use by Uzi Nissan of his last name for several business enterprises since 1980, his use beginning in 1991 of "Nissan" as part of the name of a North Carolina computer store he owned -- Nissan Computer Corp. -- and his registration in 1994 of "nissan.com" as a domain name and website for advertising various products including for a period in 1999, automobile-related products and services. Nissan Motor Co., Ltd., a Japanese automobile manufacturer that registered the mark "NISSAN" in 1959, and its subsidiary, Nissan North America, Inc., began using that name, rather than "DATSUN," to identify and market their vehicles in the United States in 1983. They filed this action in 1999 complaining that "nissan.com" diluted the NISSAN mark under the Federal Trademark Dilution Act (FTDA), 15 U.S.C. § 1125(c), as well as the California analogue, Cal. Bus. & Prof. Code § 14330, and infringed it under the Lanham Act, 15 U.S.C. § 1114.

In a series of summary judgment rulings, the district court held that Nissan Computer's automobile-related advertising constituted trademark infringement on the basis of initial interest confusion, but that non-automobile-related advertising did not. The court determined that Nissan Motor's dilution suit was not barred by laches, that Nissan Computer's first commercial use of "nissan" was in 1994 when it registered the website "nissan.com" because that was the only use identical to the NISSAN mark, that by then Nissan Motor's NISSAN mark had become famous, and that Nissan Computer's use of "nissan.com" dilutes the quality of Nissan Motor's mark. Accordingly, the court enjoined Nissan Computer (and its alter ego, The Internet Center Inc.) from posting any commercial content at nissan.com and from placing links to other websites that contain disparaging remarks or negative commentary about Nissan Motor.

Neither side is entirely happy and both appeal. On the main issues, we hold:

Initial interest confusion exists as a matter of law as to Nissan Computer's automobile-related use of "nissan.com" because use of the mark for automobiles captures the attention of consumers interested in Nissan vehicles. To this extent "nissan.com" trades on Nissan Motor's goodwill in the NISSAN mark and infringes it, but other uses do not because there is no possibility of confusion as to them.

Even though the NISSAN mark was distinctive and incontestible within five years of registration, it must also have become "famous" before Nissan Computer's first commercial

412

use in order to be entitled to protection against dilution. The first use for purposes of the FTDA is that use which is arguably offending, here, "Nissan Computer," because *any* commercial use of a *famous* mark is diluting regardless of whether it is confusing or combined with other identifiers. As such a use occurred in 1991, and because the district court believed that triable issues of fact exist about fame of the NISSAN mark before 1994, summary judgment on the dilution claim cannot be sustained.

Finally, to enjoin Nissan Computer from providing visitors to nissan.com a link to sites with disparaging or negative commentary about Nissan Motor is a content-based restriction on non-commercial speech that is inconsistent with the First Amendment.

As a result of our conclusion on these and other issues, we affirm in part (on the infringement claim), reverse in part (on the dilution claim), and remand.

I.

It is uncontroverted that Nissan Motor Co. and its subsidiary Nissan North America, Inc. (collectively, Nissan Motor) have marketed and distributed automobiles in the United States since 1960. Nissan Motor registered the NISSAN mark for ships and vehicles on the Principal Register in 1959. Vehicles were sold in the United States under the name "Datsun" until 1983, when Nissan Motor began marketing its vehicles under the name "Nissan." For a while the two names were used together, but since 1985 only the "Nissan" name has been used.

Uzi Nissan used his last name for various businesses, including "Nissan Foreign Car Mobile Repair Service" (1980), an import/export business "Nissan International, Ltd." (1987), and "Nissan Computer Corp." established in 1991 to engage in the business of computer sales and services. On June 4, 1994, Nissan Computer registered the domain name nissan.com and established a website at that address to advertise its computer-related goods and services. In July 1995 Nissan Motor sent Nissan Computer a letter expressing "great concern" about use of the word "Nissan" in Nissan Computer's domain name; Nissan Computer made no response and nothing further happened until Nissan Motor contacted Uzi Nissan in October 1999.

Meanwhile, Nissan Computer registered "nissan.net" to offer services as an Internet Service Provider in 1996. In August 1999, it altered the nissan.com website by adding a new logo with the name "nissan.com," sold space for advertising, and registered with a website for banner advertising. Nissan Computer received a payment for each time a user clicked through to an advertiser's website. The first links (in August and September) were for goto.com, Barnes & Noble, CNet.com, and Netradio.com. Automobile-related ads appeared in late September. Within several weeks Nissan Computer signed up cartrackers.com, priceline.com, tunes.com, askjeeves.com, directhit.com, safari.com, lycos.com, asimba.com, ameritech.com, and about.com; by December, 1stopauto.com, hotlinks.com, shabang.com, fastweb.com, remarq.com, carprices.com and stoneage.com had been added.

In October 1999, Nissan Motor told Uzi Nissan that it wished to purchase nissan.com, but negotiations came to naught. This action was filed against Nissan Computer on December 10, 1999. The complaint asserts claims for trademark dilution in violation of federal and state law; trademark infringement; [and] domain name piracy.... Nissan Motor moved for a preliminary injunction, which the district court granted in a published opinion, *Nissan Motor Co., Ltd. v. Nissan Computer Corp.*, 89 F. Supp. 2d 1154 (C.D. Cal. 2000), and which we affirmed. The injunction ordered Nissan Computer to post prominent captions on the first web page of the nissan.com and nissan.net websites identifying them as affiliated with Nissan Computer Corporation and disclaiming affiliation with Nissan Motor, and to refrain from displaying automobile-related information, advertisements, and links.

In March 2000, Nissan Computer posted a link on nissan.com and nissan.net that stated "Nissan Motor's Lawsuit Against Nissan Computer." Clicking this link transferred the user to ncchelp.org. A banner at ncchelp.org stated "We Are Being Sued!!!"; and included links entitled (1) "story," which contained Uzi Nissan's description of this litigation, (2) "FAQ," (3) "news," which contained links to media reports, (4) "people's opinions," which contained emails received by Uzi Nissan, and (5) "how you can help," which contained links via banner advertising, including a link to a site operated by The Internet Center (TIC), which had auto-related advertising. TIC was owned and operated by Uzi Nissan, and was added as a defendant in Nissan Motor's First Amended Complaint.

... II.

... A.

"Injunctive relief is available under the Federal Trademark Dilution Act if a plaintiff can establish that (1) its mark is famous; (2) the defendant is making commercial use of the mark in commerce; (3) the defendant's use began after the plaintiff's mark became famous;" *Avery Dennison Corp. v. Sumpton*, 189 F.3d 868, 873-74 (9th Cir. 1999), and there is actual harm to the trademark holder, *Moseley v. V Secret Catalogue, Inc.*, 537 U.S. 418, 433-34, 155 L. Ed. 2d 1, 123 S. Ct. 1115 (2003). Noncommercial use of a mark is excepted. *See* 15 U.S.C. § 1125(c)(4)(B).

The FTDA's "grandfathering" clause lies at the heart of this dispute. It provides:

> The owner of a famous mark shall be entitled, subject to the principles of equity and upon such terms as the court deems reasonable, to an injunction against another person's commercial use in commerce of a mark or trade name, if such use begins after the mark has become famous and causes dilution of the distinctive quality of the mark, and to obtain such other relief as is provided in this subsection.

15 U.S.C. § 125(c)(1).

In Nissan Computer's view, the "first use" principle requires that fame be measured as of the defendant's actual first use of the mark, not the use that the plaintiff finds objectionable. This would be no later than 1991, when Nissan Computer was incorporated and used the name to sell computers. Not surprisingly, Nissan Motor has a different view, that the date to determine famousness of its NISSAN mark is the first time that Nissan Computer used "nissan" by itself as a trade or company name instead of as a composite trade or company name. This would be 1994, when Nissan Computer registered nissan.com as a domain name and opened a website for advertising. Nissan Motor points out that the text of the statute refers to "*such* use," which Nissan Motor interprets to mean not just any use -- but the "commercial use in commerce of a mark." Drawing on the anti-dissection rule from trademark infringement law, Nissan Motor also posits that use of "Nissan" by itself is a different "commercial use in commerce" of the NISSAN mark than is "Nissan Computer Corp."

We believe "such use" for purposes of § 1125(c) is a use that, assuming it occurs after another's mark has become famous, would arguably dilute the mark. This follows from the text of the statute as well as its purpose. The FTDA protects the holder of a trademark from dilution, which is different from, and broader than, infringement in that neither confusion nor competition is required and the protection is nationwide in scope. *See Avery*, 189 F.3d at 873. Dilution is "the lessening of the capacity of a famous mark to identify and distinguish goods or services, regardless of the presence or absence of-(1) competition between the owner of the famous mark and other parties, or (2) likelihood of confusion, mistake, or deception." 15 U.S.C. § 1127. As the Supreme Court explained, the purpose of the FTDA "is to protect famous trademarks from subsequent uses that blur the distinctiveness of the mark or tarnish or disparage it, even in the absence of a likelihood of confusion." *Moseley*, 537 U.S. at 431 (quoting H.R. Rep. No. 104-374, p.2 (1995), U.S. Code Cong. & Admin. News 1995, pp 1029, 1030). "Dilution refers to the whittling away of the value of a trademark when it's used to identify different products." *Mattel, Inc. v. MCA Records, Inc.*, 296 F.3d 894, 903 (9th Cir. 2002) (citation and quotation marks omitted). Because protection from dilution comes close to being a "right[ ] in gross," it is a cause of action "reserved for a select class of marks--those marks with such powerful consumer associations that even non-competing uses can impinge on their value." *Avery Dennison*, 189 F.3d at 875. For this reason, the FTDA extends dilution protection only to those whose mark is a "household name." *Thane Int'l., Inc. v. Trek Bicycle Corp.*, 305 F.3d 894, 911 (9th Cir. 2002).

"The mark used by the alleged diluter must be identical, or nearly identical, to the protected mark" for a dilution claim to succeed. *Id.* at 905. This means that the mark itself must be identical, or nearly identical, not that it cannot be used in combination with some other identifier. For example, as the Report of the Subcommittee on Courts and Intellectual Property of the House Judiciary Committee observes of the FTDA, "the use of DUPONT shoes, BUICK aspirin, and KODAK pianos would be actionable under this legislation." *See Moseley*, 537 U.S. at 431 (citing H.R.Rep. No 104-374, p.3 (1995), U.S.Code Cong. & Admin. News 1995, pp 1029, 1030); *Thane*, 305 F.3d at 906, 910-11 (citing the same examples in the Senate Report, S. Rep. No. 100-515, at 7 (1988), *reprinted in* 1988 U.S.C.C.A.N. 5577, 5583). We conjured others in *Mattel*, "for example, Tylenol snowboards, Netscape sex shops and Harry Potter dry cleaners would all weaken the commercial magnetism of these marks and diminish their ability to evoke their original associations. These uses dilute the selling power of these trademarks by blurring their uniqueness and singularity, and/or by tarnishing them with negative associations." 296 F.3d at 903 (internal quotations and citations omitted).

The point of dilution law is to protect the owner's investment in his mark. *See, e.g., Thane*, 305 F.3d at 904. This is why it is actionable for a store to call itself KODAK Pianos, as well as KODAK. As the use of KODAK pianos would dilute KODAK, then NISSAN pianos would dilute NISSAN if the NISSAN mark were as famous as KODAK. It follows that NISSAN Computers is a use that arguably dilutes the NISSAN mark. Whether it does in fact, of course, depends upon whether the capacity of the NISSAN mark to identify and distinguish goods or services sold by Nissan Motor has been lessened; however, for purposes of settling the date by which fame must be measured, Nissan Computer's use of the NISSAN mark is arguably diluting even though the word "Nissan" is used in combination with another identifier. *See Mattel*, 296 F.3d at 903-04 (holding that "Barbie Girl" diluted Mattel's "Barbie" mark); *see also Moseley*, 537 U.S. at 433-34 (suggesting that the evidence required to prove dilution may differ depending upon whether the junior and senior marks are identical). In sum, just as the TYLENOL mark, the BARBIE mark, and the KODAK mark are used in commerce when "snowboards," "Girl," and "pianos" are added, the NISSAN mark is used in commerce when other words are added to it such that if NISSAN were a famous mark, then "NISSAN Computer" could be a dilutive commercial use. ...

Nissan Motor's reliance on the anti-dissection rule is also unhelpful. That doctrine prescribes that "a composite mark is tested for its validity and distinctiveness by looking at it as a whole, rather than dissecting it into its component parts." 2 J. Thomas McCarthy, *McCarthy on Trademarks and Unfair Competition* § 11:27 (4th ed. 2003); *GoTo.com, Inc. v. Walt Disney Co.*, 202 F.3d 1199, 1207 (9th Cir. 2000) ("It is the mark in its entirety that must be considered--not simply individual elements of that mark.") (citation omitted). However, our task here is not to test distinctiveness but to determine famousness.

Accordingly, we hold that any commercial use of a famous mark in commerce is arguably a diluting use that fixes the time by which famousness is to be measured. In this respect as in others, a dilution claim differs from a claim for infringement, because not all uses of a mark are actionable. *See Interstellar Starship Servs., Ltd. v. EPIX, Inc.*, 304 F.3d 936, 943-44 (9th Cir. 2002) (explaining why companies using the same mark for different products with different consumer expectations may not cause initial interest confusion). For purposes of the FTDA, however, the commercial use of "Nissan" for computers in Nissan Computer was a use of the NISSAN mark in commerce that was arguably diluting. "Such use" occurred in 1991. Therefore, fame of the NISSAN mark must be measured as of 1991.

B.

Nissan Motor argues that even if the fame of its mark must be measured as of 1991 rather than 1994, reversal is not required because the NISSAN mark was also famous as of 1991. However, the district court found that there were triable issues of fact when it was of the view that fame should be determined as of 1991. The record is not so clear that we can affirm notwithstanding the district court's conclusion.

The FTDA lists eight non-exclusive factors for a court to consider in determining whether a mark is distinctive and famous. They are:

(A) the degree of inherent or acquired distinctiveness of the mark;

(B) the duration and extent of use of the mark in connection with the goods or services with which the mark is used;

(C) the duration and extent of advertising and publicity of the mark;

(D) the geographical extent of the trading area in which the mark is used;

(E) the channels of trade for the goods or services with which the mark is used;

(F) the degree of recognition of the mark in the trading areas and channels of trade used by the mark's owner and the person against whom the injunction is sought;

(G) the nature and extent of use of the same or similar marks by third parties; and

(H) whether the mark was registered ... or on the principal register.

15 U.S.C. § 1125(c)(1).

Without going into detail because we must remand in any event, there is no question that the NISSAN mark is distinctive because it became incontestible five years after being registered, yet "to be capable of being diluted, a mark must have a *degree* of distinctiveness and 'strength' beyond that needed to serve as a trademark." *Avery Dennison*, 189 F.3d at 876 (citations and quotations omitted) (emphasis added). "Famousness requires more than mere distinctiveness." *Id*. at 879.

Nissan Motor introduced evidence through surveys, studies, and expert opinion that the NISSAN mark had considerable public recognition, however Nissan Computer questioned their methodology and import, and we have no ruling on these issues from the district court. For example, an Allison-Fisher survey found that NISSAN enjoyed 55% awareness among consumers in 1985, 60% in 1986, and 65% in 1991, but Nissan Computer's experts counter that the survey measured only the attitude of people who intended to buy a new car, thereby skewing the results in favor of Nissan Motor, and claim that there are methodological errors in the survey's analysis. The same applies to the Landor Research Survey, which concluded that Nissan Motor was one of the 200 most powerful brands in America in 1988; Nissan Computer's experts point out that the survey was a newspaper account without a description of methodology, universe of respondents, or statistical reliability of results. Another public opinion survey that reported consumer familiarity with "Nissan" was conducted between 1999 and January 2000 and spoke as of that time frame, which sheds no light on public perception in 1991. Although Nissan Motor's promotional expenditures for vehicles bearing the NISSAN mark -- more than $898 million during the period 1985-1991 -- weigh in its favor, we cannot say as a matter of law, on this record, that the survey, expert, and advertising evidence permit only the conclusion that the NISSAN mark was famous as of 1991.

The record is further clouded by what it shows about the word "Nissan" and its third-party use. "Nissan" is a common Jewish/Israeli last name, a Biblical term originally identifying the first month in the calendar, the contemporary name of the seventh month in the Jewish calendar, the Arabic word for April, and is part of the trademark or trade name of more than 190 unaffiliated businesses in the United States including "Nissan Thermos," "Nissan Chemical," and "Nissan Fire and Marine Insurance Company." The word "Nissan" is an acronym in Japanese for "Japanese Industries KK." Nissan Motor itself is a party to a Trademark Basic Agreement with "Nissan Chemical," "Nissan Agriculture and Forestry," "Nippon Oxygen Co.," "Nippon Fisheries Co.," and "Nippon Oil and Fat Co.," in which each agrees to cooperate to ensure the proper use and protection of the "Nissan" related trademark. And there are thousands of domain names that use the word "Nissan." All of this is relevant, because "when 'a mark is in widespread use, it may not be famous for the goods or services of one business.'" *Avery Dennison*, 189 F.3d at 878 (quoting Trademark Review Commission, *Report & Recommendation*, 77 Trademark Rep. 375, 461 (Sept.-Oct.1987)). That other unaffiliated companies use "Nissan" in their names at a minimum raises a question whether the mark can be considered a famous mark eligible for dilution protection. *See id*.

(stating that widespread use of the mark in the name of other companies makes fame unlikely).

In sum, we cannot say on this record that genuine issues of material fact do not exist as to the degree of distinctiveness of the NISSAN mark, the weight to be given and the conclusions to be drawn from the experts' reports and surveys, the impact of third party uses of NISSAN, and the overall fame of the NISSAN mark in 1991.

C.

After the district court's final decision in this case, the Supreme Court held in *Moseley v. V Secret Catalogue*, 537 U.S. 418, 155 L. Ed. 2d 1, 123 S. Ct. 1115 (2003), that actual dilution must be shown for a dilution claim to succeed. Based on *Moseley*, Nissan Computer and TIC argue that summary judgment on the FTDA claim must be reversed because Nissan Motor presented no evidence of actual harm to the NISSAN mark. Nissan Motor argues otherwise, relying on *Moseley*'s statement that "direct evidence of dilution such as consumer surveys will not be necessary if actual dilution can reliably be proved through circumstantial evidence -- the obvious case is one where the junior and senior marks are identical." *Id.* at 434. However, it is not entirely clear what the Court meant by this, *see Ty Inc. v. Softbelly's Inc.*, 353 F.3d 528, 536 (7th Cir. 2003), and appellate review would be aided by a record developed in light of *Moseley* and the district court's analysis of it. Therefore, we follow the lead of *Horphag Research Ltd. v. Pellegrini*, 337 F.3d 1036, 1041 (9th Cir. 2003), and remand to give the district court an opportunity to consider in the first instance whether there has been actual dilution within the meaning of *Moseley*. ...

... III.

Nissan Computer argues that it did not infringe the NISSAN mark because it did nothing to draw potential Nissan Motor customers to its website or to divert customers who were looking for Nissan vehicles, and that there is at least a factual dispute whether Nissan Computer "captured" the initial interest of internet users looking for Nissan Motor products. Nissan Computer reasons that it did not offer automobiles or automobile-related services, rather it posted advertisements on its website much as a newspaper does. Nissan Motor responds that we already concluded that Nissan Computer altered its website to capitalize on the initial interest confusion of consumers who were looking for Nissan Motor's products when we affirmed the preliminary injunction entered in this case. We agree with Nissan Motor's position, but not for this reason. A determination that the district court did not abuse its discretion in granting preliminary relief is not binding on appeal from a final judgment. *See, e.g., Rodde v. Bonta*, 357 F.3d 988, 995 (9th Cir. 2004). Nissan Motor also submits that the district court should have found trademark infringement based on Nissan Computer's non-automobile-related advertising given consumer expectations, identicalness of the internet domain names and its MARK, and the simultaneous use of the Web as a marketing channel by Nissan Computer and Nissan Motor. We disagree that reversal is indicated.

"The core element of trademark infringement is whether the similarity of the marks is likely to confuse customers about the source of the products. ... Initial interest confusion occurs when the defendant uses the plaintiff's trademark 'in a manner calculated to capture initial consumer attention, even though no actual sale is finally completed as a result of the confusion.'" *Interstellar*, 304 F.3d at 941 (quoting *Brookfield Communs., Inc. v. West Coast Entertainment Corp.*, 174 F.3d 1036, 1062 (9th Cir. 1999) (quoting *Dr. Seuss Enters., L.P. v. Penguin Books USA, Inc.*, 109 F.3d 1394, 1405 (9th Cir. 1997) (internal quotation marks omitted))). As we hypothesized initial interest confusion in *Brookfield*, it would occur if

Blockbuster Video put up a billboard that advertised West Coast Video at Exit 7, when in actuality West Coast was located at Exit 8, but Blockbuster was at Exit 7. Customers looking for West Coast would leave the freeway at Exit 7, but after not finding it, rent from Blockbuster rather than reentering the freeway in search of West Coast. Customers are not confused that they are renting from Blockbuster instead of West Coast, but Blockbuster misappropriates West Coast's acquired goodwill through the initial consumer confusion. *See Brookfield*, 174 F.3d at 1064.

"To evaluate the likelihood of confusion, including initial interest confusion, the so-called *Sleekcraft* factors provide non-exhaustive guidance." *Interstellar*, 304 F.3d at 942 (citing *AMF Inc. v. Sleekcraft Boats*, 599 F.2d 341, 346 (9th Cir. 1979)). They are well known, and are: "(1) the similarity of the marks; (2) the relatedness or proximity of the two companies' products or services; (3) the strength of the registered mark; (4) the marketing channels used; (5) the degree of care likely to be exercised by the purchaser in selecting goods; (6) the accused infringers' intent in selecting its mark; (7) evidence of actual confusion; and (8) the likelihood of expansion in product lines. *Sleekcraft*, 599 F.2d at 346." *Interstellar*, 304 F.3d at 942. In the context of the internet, the three most important factors are the similarity of the marks, the relatedness of the goods or services, and the parties' simultaneous use of the internet in marketing. *See id.* (citing *GoTo.com*, 202 F.3d at 1205).

Nissan Computer's use of nissan.com to sell non-automobile-related goods does not infringe because Nissan is a last name, a month in the Hebrew and Arabic calendars, a name used by many companies, and "the goods offered by these two companies differ significantly." *Id.* at 944. However, Nissan Computer traded on the goodwill of Nissan Motor by offering links to automobile-related websites. Although Nissan Computer was not directly selling automobiles, it was offering information about automobiles and this capitalized on consumers' initial interest. An internet user interested in purchasing, or gaining information about Nissan automobiles would be likely to enter nissan.com. When the item on that website was computers, the auto-seeking consumer "would realize in one hot second that she was in the wrong place and either guess again or resort to a search engine to locate" Nissan Motor's site. *Id.* at 946. A consumer might initially be incorrect about the website, but Nissan Computer would not capitalize on the misdirected consumer. However, once nissan.com offered links to auto-related websites, then the auto-seeking consumer might logically be expected to follow those links to obtain information about automobiles. Nissan Computer financially benefited because it received money for every click. Although nissan.com itself did not provide the information about automobiles, it provided direct links to such information. Due to the ease of clicking on a link, the required extra click does not rebut the conclusion that Nissan Computer traded on the goodwill of Nissan Motor's mark.

The marks are legally identical; the goods or services are related as to auto-related advertising, but not related as to anything else; and the parties simultaneously use the internet in marketing. The NISSAN mark is an incontestible mark, but it is also used in many channels of commerce, is a last name, and is a month. The degree of care exercised by a purchaser is disputable. Whereas a consumer purchasing an automobile will exercise great care, a consumer searching for information about automobiles on the internet may exercise little care and will click on all information about automobiles. The intent of Nissan Computer in selecting the mark weighs to some extent in favor of Nissan Computer because Uzi Nissan chose a domain name to correspond with his own name, but its intent in posting automobile-related links cuts the other way. There is evidence of actual confusion in that consumers have clicked on nissan.com to find out information about Nissan Motor. The likelihood of expansion in product lines can again cut both ways. Nissan Computer is unlikely to enter the automobile sales business, however, it is likely to advertise more auto-related products.

On balance we agree with the district court that Nissan Motor is entitled to summary judgment on trademark infringement as to automobile-related advertisements, and that Nissan Computer is entitled to summary judgment as to non-auto-related advertisements.

IV.

What we have already held largely disposes of Nissan Motor's cross-appeal asking that the injunction be *broadened* to require transfer of nissan.com and nissan.net. The district court declined to enter such an order and did not abuse its discretion in doing so. *See Interstellar*, 304 F.3d at 948 (emphasizing discretion to fashion relief, and noting that only upon proving the rigorous elements of cybersquatting under the Anticybersquatting Consumer Protection Act, 15 U.S.C. § 1125(d), have plaintiffs successfully forced the transfer of an infringing domain name). To the extent that Nissan Motor requests broader relief on account of infringement through initial interest confusion, it is a request better directed to the district court because the injunction was granted on the basis of dilution under the FTDA, not on the basis of infringement.

V. Conclusion

Having held that the first use of a mark for purposes of the Federal Trademark Dilution Act is that use which is arguably offending, and such use in this case occurred when NISSAN was used in "Nissan Computer" in commerce, we must reverse and remand the partial summary judgment on dilution for the district court to consider the fame of the NISSAN mark as of 1991. On remand, it must also consider whether Nissan Computer "actually diluted" the NISSAN mark as required by *Moseley*. ... On all other issues [discussed above], we affirm.

Each party shall bear its own costs.

AFFIRMED IN PART; REVERSED IN PART; AND REMANDED.

* * * * *

SAVIN CORPORATION, Plaintiff-Appellant
v.
THE SAVIN GROUP, SAVIN ENGINEERS, P.C., SAVIN CONSULTANTS, INC. d/b/a Savin Engineers, P.C., and JMOA ENGINEERING, P.C., Defendants-Appellees

United States Court of Appeals for the Second Circuit

No. 03-9266, 391 F.3d 439

December 10, 2004

Plaintiff-appellant, Savin Corporation, appeals from a summary judgment entered in the United States District Court for the Southern District of New York (Scheindlin, J.) dismissing Savin Corporation's claims alleging[, *inter alia,*]: (1) trademark dilution, in violation of ...

the Federal Trademark Dilution Act ("FTDA"), 15 U.S.C. § 1125(c) ..., and (2) trademark infringement, in violation of the Lanham Act, 15 U.S.C. § 1114. On appeal, Savin Corporation argues that the District Court erred[, among other ways, by] holding that the FTDA requires a plaintiff to demonstrate evidence of actual dilution even where the court finds that the at-issue marks are identical....

BACKGROUND

A. The Parties

... Plaintiff is engaged in the business of marketing, selling, and distributing state-of-the-art business equipment for commercial, business, and home-office use. Plaintiff's products include color and digital-imaging technology for photocopying, printing, facsimile, and other systems. Plaintiff also offers consulting and support services related to information technology and office management. ... Plaintiff's largest customers are in the government, education, and military sectors.

Max Lowe, Savin Corporation's founder, named the company after his brother-in-law, Robert Savin. Since 1959, the company has used the trade name "Savin" or "SAVIN" in various forms in connection with various products and services. Plaintiff's ownership of the "Savin" mark is incontestable with respect to: (i) copy paper and developing liquid; (ii) photocopying machines and parts thereof; and (iii) maintenance and repair services for photocopiers and word processors. The company also owns the mark "SAVIN" for facsimile machines.

During 2002 alone, Plaintiff spent over $20 million in advertising its products and services, which are regularly featured in print and television advertisements, trade magazines, and tradeshow promotions worldwide. Plaintiff's advertisements have appeared in magazines such as *Newsweek, Time*, and *Business Week*. Plaintiff also maintains an active website -- www.savin.com -- through which Plaintiff markets and promotes its products and services. This website address is featured prominently in many of Plaintiff's advertisements.

Defendants-appellees are The Savin Group; Savin Engineers, P.C.; Savin Consultants, Inc. d/b/a Savin Engineers, P.C. ("Savin Consultants"); and JMOA Engineering, P.C. ("JMOA") (collectively, "Defendants" or "Savin Engineers"). JMOA and Savin Engineers, P.C. are New York-based professional engineering corporations with offices in Pleasantville, Syracuse, and Hauppauge, New York; together, the two corporations comprise The Savin Group. Savin Consultants is a New Jersey-based corporation that was incorporated in 1987 and that ceased to be actively engaged in business after Savin Engineers, P.C. was incorporated in 1988. Defendants provide professional engineering consulting services, in particular, civil-engineering consulting services to entities concerned with environmental waste management. Defendants also offer professional engineering services in connection with inspecting buildings and providing building-maintenance plans.

Dr. Rengachari Srinivasaragahavan, whose nickname since college has been "Nivas" (referred to in this opinion as "Dr. Nivas"), is the founder and sole shareholder of each of the defendant-appellee corporations. Dr. Nivas chose the name "Savin" by spelling "Nivas" backwards. Since 1987, Defendants have continually used the name "Savin" in commerce. Defendants did not perform a search or investigation prior to adopting and launching their trade names, and only became aware of Plaintiff's products and services about ten years ago.

Defendants have registered the Internet domain names www.thesavingroup.com and www.savinengineers.com. These websites, which became accessible after June 2001, provide information about the engineering services offered by Dr. Nivas' companies. Defendants did not perform a search or investigation prior to adopting and launching these websites, but were aware of Plaintiff's www.savin.com domain name prior to registering Defendants' domain names. Other than through these websites, Defendants have not advertised their services in any general interest media.

... Presently, there are several hundred other businesses using the name "Savin" in various industries and capacities, including, for example, a general contractor in Newington, Connecticut (Savin Brothers, Inc.), a dry cleaner in Chesapeake, Virginia (Savin Cleaners), and a dentist in Glencoe, New York (Savin Dental Associates). Plaintiff has been aggressive in protecting its marks, with respect to both traditional media and the Internet.

... DISCUSSION

I. The FTDA Claim

Plaintiff argues that the District Court "erred in holding that, even though the marks at issue are identical, [Plaintiff] was required to demonstrate circumstantial evidence of actual dilution ... to maintain its claim under the [FTDA]." Defendants, on the other hand, argue that the District Court was correct in dismissing the FTDA claim because Plaintiff had "failed to tender admissible evidence to *prima facie* prove any of [the requisite] elements" of a claim under the FTDA.

The FTDA "permits the owner of a qualified, famous mark to enjoin junior uses throughout commerce, regardless of the absence of competition or confusion." *TCPIP Holding Co. v. Haar Communications Inc.,* 244 F.3d 88, 95 (2d Cir. 2001); *see* 15 U.S.C. § 1127. Indeed, "one circuit has characterized the Dilution Act as coming 'very close to granting rights in gross in a trademark.'" *TCPIP Holding Co.,* 244 F.3d at 95 (quoting *Avery Dennison Corp. v. Sumpton,* 189 F.3d 868, 875 (9th Cir. 1999)). Specifically, the FTDA provides that "the owner of a famous mark shall be entitled ... to an injunction against another person's commercial use in commerce of a mark or trade name, if such use begins after the mark has become famous and causes dilution of the distinctive quality of the mark." 15 U.S.C. § 1125(c)(1). Thus, to establish a violation of the FTDA, a plaintiff must show that:

> (1) its mark is famous; (2) the defendant is making commercial use of the mark in commerce; (3) the defendant's use began after the mark became famous; and (4) the defendant's use of the mark dilutes the quality of the mark by diminishing the capacity of the mark to identify and distinguish goods and services.

Pinehurst, Inc. v. Wick, 256 F. Supp. 2d 424, 431 (M.D.N.C. 2003); *see* 15 U.S.C. § 1125(c); *Ringling Bros. v. Utah Div. of Travel Dev.,* 170 F.3d 449, 452 (4th Cir. 1999); *Panavision Int'l L.P. v. Toeppen,* 141 F.3d 1316, 1324 (9th Cir. 1998).

The Supreme Court has made clear that a plaintiff seeking to take advantage of the broad rights afforded under the FTDA must show, as an essential element of an FTDA claim, "actual dilution, rather than a likelihood of dilution." *Moseley v. V Secret Catalogue, Inc.,* 537 U.S. 418, 433, 155 L. Ed. 2d 1, 123 S. Ct. 1115 (2003). The theory of "dilution by blurring," the form of dilution particularly relevant to the case at bar, has been described by Professor McCarthy as follows:

If one small user can blur the sharp focus of the famous mark to uniquely signify one source, then another and another small user can and will do so. Like being stung by a hundred bees, significant injury is caused by the cumulative effect, not by just one. ... This is consistent with the classic view that the injury caused by dilution is the gradual diminution or whittling away of the value of the famous mark by blurring uses by others. It is also consistent with the rule in the [likelihood-of-confusion] cases that even a small infringer will not be permitted to "nibble away" at the plaintiff's reputation and goodwill.

4 J. Thomas McCarthy, *McCarthy on Trademarks and Unfair Competition* § 24:94 (4th ed. Supp. 2004) (footnotes omitted); *accord General Motors Corp. v. Autovation Techs., Inc.*, 317 F. Supp. 2d 756, 764 (E.D. Mich. 2004).

A. Fame and Distinctiveness

In this Circuit, to sustain a claim under the FTDA, in addition to actual dilution, a plaintiff must show that the senior mark possesses both a "significant degree of inherent distinctiveness" and, to qualify as famous, "a high degree of ... acquired distinctiveness." *TCPIP Holding Co.*, 244 F.3d at 97, 98. Although a plaintiff must show a preponderance of evidence on each element of a claimed violation of the FTDA in order ultimately to prevail on such a claim, *see Moseley*, 537 U.S. at 434, the element of fame is the key ingredient. This is because, among the various prerequisites to an FTDA claim, the one that most narrows the universe of potentially successful claims is the requirement that the senior mark be truly famous before a court will afford the owner of the mark the vast protections of the FTDA.[5]

Indeed, actionable dilution under the FTDA is defined as "the lessening of the capacity of a famous mark to identify and distinguish goods or services, regardless of the presence or absence of (1) competition between the owner of the famous mark and other parties, or (2) likelihood of confusion, mistake, or deception." 15 U.S.C. § 1127. This requirement reflects the purpose of the FTDA, which "is to protect famous trademarks from subsequent uses that blur the distinctiveness of the mark or tarnish or disparage it, even in the absence of a likelihood of confusion." *Genovese Drug Stores, Inc. v. TGC Stores, Inc.*, 939 F. Supp. 340, 349 (D.N.J. 1996) (internal quotation marks omitted). Accordingly, where it is possible for a district court to determine in the first instance the issue of the famousness of a senior mark, the court would be well advised to do so. Indeed, this will often obviate the costly litigation of potentially much thornier issues, such as whether actual blurring or tarnishing of the senior mark has in fact occurred or, as in the instant case, whether a junior and senior mark that are each used in varying ways in different contexts and media are in fact "identical" for purposes of the FTDA. ...

---

[5] In other words, a plaintiff owning only less-than-famous marks will receive no protection under the FTDA, even if that plaintiff can prove that the use of an identical junior mark has in fact lessened the capacity of the senior mark to identify and distinguish the plaintiff's goods or services -- i.e., that actual dilution has occurred. *See TCPIP Holding Co.*, 244 F.3d at 97-98.

With respect to fame, or acquired distinctiveness, we recognize that the at-issue marks ultimately may be found to possess only a degree of "niche fame." Nevertheless, we agree with the District Court's conclusion that Plaintiff has shown "more than a mere scintilla of evidence" of fame, which is a sufficient quantum of proof to submit the question to the finder of fact. In particular, the court found that:

> [Plaintiff] spent over $20 million on advertising in 2002 and has achieved annual revenues of $675 million. Further, Plaintiff's products and services are regularly featured in print advertisements, trade magazines[,] and tradeshow promotions. Plaintiff's advertisements have appeared in well known magazines such as *Newsweek, Time,* and *Business Week.*

These are sufficient indicators of fame to withstand a summary judgment challenge to a claim under the FTDA. *Cf. Nabisco, Inc. v. PF Brands, Inc.,* 50 F. Supp. 2d 188, 202 (S.D.N.Y. 1999) (finding top ranking sales dollars and advertising expenses of more than $120 million in a three-year period to be significant indicators of the fame of the mark), *aff'd,* 191 F.3d 208 (2d Cir. 1999).

With regard to inherent distinctiveness, the District Court was correct to conclude that Plaintiff's marks are entitled to a presumption of inherent distinctiveness by virtue of their incontestability. *See Sporty's Farm,* 202 F.3d at 497; *Equine Techs., Inc. v. Equitechnology, Inc.,* 68 F.3d 542, 545 (1st Cir. 1995). Defendants assert that this presumption should not apply to the marks at issue because they are "merely descriptive" marks, which can never possess inherent distinctiveness. *See TCPIP Holding Co.,* 244 F.3d at 96 ("Descriptive marks, which possess no distinctive quality, or at best a minimal degree, do not qualify for the [Dilution] Act's protection."). Defendants' argument is unavailing, however, because Plaintiff's marks are not, as a matter of law, merely descriptive marks.

While it is true that "Savin" is a surname and that Savin Corp. was named after Robert Savin, the brother-in-law of Plaintiff's founder, the word "savin" also has a dictionary meaning.[7] Admittedly, the "Savin" mark is not as obviously distinctive as, for example, "Honda" or "Acura." But it is still entirely possible for a reasonable fact-finder to determine that the "Savin" mark possesses a sufficient degree of distinctiveness to sustain a finding of dilution, especially given that Plaintiff's marks are "not patently used as a surname." *Lane Capital Mgmt., Inc. v. Lane Capital Mgmt., Inc.,* 192 F.3d 337, 347 (2d Cir. 1999); *see, e.g., IMAF, S.P.A. v. J.C. Penney Co.,* 806 F. Supp. 449, 455 (S.D.N.Y. 1992) ("The name (or word) Adiansi is not likely to be immediately identified with a person by an average buyer of a sweater at J.C. Penney. Thus, the fact that Adiansi is a surname is not dispositive on the issue of inherent distinctiveness.").

B. Evidence of Actual Dilution

In *Moseley,* the Supreme Court stated that "direct evidence of dilution such as consumer surveys will not be necessary if actual dilution can reliably be proved through circumstantial

---

[7] *See Merriam-Webster's Third New International Dictionary Unabridged* (2002) (defining "savin" as (1) "a mostly prostrate Eurasian evergreen juniper (Juniperus sabina) with dark foliage and small berries having a glaucous bloom and with bitter acrid tops that are sometimes used in folk medicine (as for amenorrhea or as an abortifacient) - called also cover-shame, sabina"; (2) "creeping juniper" or "red cedar;" or (3) "any of several trees, shrubs, or shrubby herbs somewhat resembling plants of the genus Juniperus").

evidence - the obvious case is one where the junior and senior marks are identical." 537 U.S. at 434. The Court cautioned, however, that "whatever difficulties of proof may be entailed, they are not an acceptable reason for dispensing with proof of an essential element of a statutory violation." *Id.* ...

We interpret *Moseley* to mean that where a plaintiff who owns a famous senior mark can show the commercial use of an identical junior mark, such a showing constitutes circumstantial evidence of the actual-dilution element of an FTDA claim. Thus, for example, a store owner who loses a 7-Eleven franchise yet continues to use the famous "7-Eleven" mark, in so doing, violates the FTDA and may be enjoined thereunder from using the mark. *See 7-Eleven,* 300 F. Supp. 2d at 357. Indeed, a number of commentators have suggested that this is precisely what the Supreme Court was getting at in *Moseley* -- i.e., that an identity of marks creates a presumption of actual dilution. This would comport with the holdings of other courts in analogous contexts. *See, e.g., Am. Honda Motor Co.,* 325 F. Supp. 2d at 1085 ("When identical marks are used on similar goods, dilution ... obviously occurs.").

It cannot be overstated, however, that for the presumption of dilution to apply, the marks must be identical. In other words, a mere similarity in the marks -- even a close similarity -- will not suffice to establish *per se* evidence of actual dilution. Further, "where the marks at issue are not identical, the mere fact that consumers mentally associate the junior user's mark with a famous mark is not sufficient to establish actionable dilution." *Moseley,* 537 U.S. at 433. "Such mental association will not necessarily reduce the capacity of the famous mark to identify the goods of its owner, the statutory requirement for dilution under the FTDA." *Id.* Strictly enforcing the identity requirement comports well with the purposes of the FTDA and with the principle previously elucidated by this Court that the class of parties protected by the federal dilution statute is narrow indeed. *See TCPIP Holding Co.,* 244 F.3d at 95 ("The [FTDA] further differs from traditional trademark law in that the class of entities for whose benefit the law was created is far narrower.").

Oftentimes, the issue of whether the marks are identical will be context- and/or media-specific and factually intensive in nature. For instance, marks that are textually identical may appear very different from one another (e.g., in terms of font, size, color, etc.) where they are used in the form of dissimilar corporate logos, either in traditional media or on the Internet. Depending on the circumstance, this may or may not determine the outcome of the identity analysis. Similarly, marks that are textually identical may be pronounced differently, which also could be relevant under certain circumstances, such as, for example, where the marks are used in radio advertising. Indeed, the need for careful and exacting analysis of the identity issue highlights the basis for our emphasis on the famousness factor as a more expeditious avenue of resolution, given the case law in this Circuit limiting application of the FTDA to only the most famous of marks. *See id.*

Here, the marks at issue may be identical in some contexts but not in others. Where the senior and junior "Savin" marks both are used in website addresses, the marks may be identical. On the other hand, where the "Savin" marks at issue appear in stylized graphics on webpages, the competing marks may be found merely to be very similar. For its part, the District Court appears to have concluded, without analysis, that the at-issue marks are identical: "Plaintiff offers no circumstantial evidence of any kind tending to show actual dilution other than the fact that the marks are identical." In analyzing the similarity of the marks in the context of assessing Plaintiff's infringement claim, however, the court found as follows:

425

Plaintiff and Defendants both use the name "Savin," and their logos display similar block letter fonts, with one arm of the letter "V" slanted at a greater angle than the other. The only apparent difference in the marks is that Defendants' logo incorporates four squares, one slightly tilted, to the left of the name. Given that both marks feature the same name, such a difference is inconsequential.

We find the District Court's language in this regard to be somewhat ambiguous. In particular, we are uncertain whether, in analyzing the FTDA claim, the court (a) concluded that "the marks are identical," based on its previous determination regarding the similarity of the marks in the infringement context; (b) simply assumed them to be identical, arguendo; or (c) arrived at its determination by some altogether different route, perhaps as an effect of choices made by Plaintiff in pleading its case and presenting its evidence. In light of the lack of any detailed analysis in the opinion of the District Court regarding the issue of the identity of the marks for purposes of the FTDA claim, we deem it necessary to remand the issue to the District Court for clarification and specific findings as to whether the junior and senior marks are identical.

In this regard, we caution that although the differences between the marks noted by the court in the infringement context may be inconsequential in that context, such differences may indeed be relevant in the analysis of the dilution issue. The fact that Defendants have used the marks somewhat differently than has Plaintiff -- e.g., by registering the domain name www.thesavingroup.com as opposed to simply www.savin.com -- may also be relevant. We emphasize, however, that it is the identity of the marks themselves that is germane in the dilution context, and the modifying of the mark -- by adding one or more generic descriptors to the mark in a website address, for example -- will not necessarily defeat a showing that the marks themselves are identical in specific contexts. *See, e.g., A.C. Legg Packing Co. v. Olde Plantation Spice Co.,* 61 F. Supp. 2d 426, 430-31 (D. Md. 1999) ("OPSC's OLDE PLANTATION SPICE mark is nearly identical in appearance to A.C. Legg's OLD PLANTATION mark, differing only in the spelling of 'olde' and the addition of the generic word 'spice.'" The marks are identical in sound and connotation;" *cf. Golden Door, Inc. v. Odisho,* 646 F.2d 347, 350 (9th Cir. 1980) (focusing, in the infringement context, on identical portions of a junior and senior mark).

For all of the foregoing reasons, we vacate that portion of the judgment of the District Court dismissing Plaintiff's claim of a violation of the FTDA, and remand for proceedings consistent with this opinion.

… III. The Trademark Infringement Claim

"A claim of trademark infringement … is analyzed under [a] familiar two-prong test[.] … The test looks first to whether the plaintiff's mark is entitled to protection, and second to whether [the] defendant's use of the mark is likely to cause consumers confusion as to the origin or sponsorship of the defendant's goods." *Virgin Enters., Ltd. v. Nawab,* 335 F.3d 141, 146 (2d Cir. 2003) (citing *Gruner + Jahr USA Publ'g v. Meredith Corp.,* 991 F.2d 1072, 1074 (2d Cir. 1993)).

A. Validity of Plaintiff's Marks

Defendants admit that three of Plaintiff's marks are incontestable. Accordingly, we need not tarry with the first prong of the infringement test.

B. Likelihood of Confusion

"The crucial issue in an action for trademark infringement ... is whether there is any likelihood that an appreciable number of ordinarily prudent purchasers are likely to be misled, or indeed simply confused, as to the source of the goods in question." *Mushroom Makers, Inc. v. R. G. Barry Corp.*, 580 F.2d 44, 47 (2d Cir. 1978); *Maternally Yours, Inc. v. Your Maternity Shop, Inc.*, 234 F.2d 538, 542 (2d Cir. 1956). "The court, in making this determination and fashioning suitable relief, must look ... to a host of other factors." *Mushroom Makers*, 580 F.2d at 47. First articulated in the seminal case *Polaroid Corp. v. Polarad Electronics Corp.*, 287 F.2d at 495, the eight principal factors, known as the Polaroid factors, are as follows: (1) the strength of the senior mark; (2) the degree of similarity between the two marks; (3) the proximity of the products; (4) the likelihood that the prior owner will "bridge the gap"; (5) actual confusion; (6) the defendant's good faith (or bad faith) in adopting its own mark; (7) the quality of defendant's product; and (8) the sophistication of the buyers. *Id.* Moreover, depending on the complexity of the issues, "the court may have to take still other variables into account." *Id.*

Here, Plaintiff argues that the District Court erred in its application of the first and sixth factors -- i.e., in assessing (i) the strength of Plaintiff's mark and (ii) the good faith of Defendants in adopting their own mark. Plaintiff also notes that if the District Court erred in assessing the strength of the senior mark, then error would be implied in the court's analysis of proximity as well. For their part, Defendants argue that even if the court erred in analyzing the strength of the senior mark and the good faith of Defendants, any "such error would be insufficient to overturn the ruling of the District Court on likelihood of confusion, as five of the other *Polaroid* factors weigh in favor of [Defendants], and no single factor of the analysis is dispositive."

"In reviewing the District Court's evaluation of the *Polaroid* factors, each individual factor is reviewed under a clearly erroneous standard, but the ultimate determination of the likelihood of confusion is a legal issue subject to de novo review." *Brennan's, Inc. v. Brennan's Rest. L.L.C.*, 360 F.3d 125, 130 (2d Cir. 2004).

1. Strength of the Senior Mark

"The strength of a mark depends ultimately on its distinctiveness, or its 'origin-indicating' quality, in the eyes of the purchasing public." *McGregor-Doniger Inc. v. Drizzle, Inc.*, 599 F.2d 1126, 1131-32 (2d Cir. 1979), *overruled on other grounds by Bristol-Myers Squibb Co. v. McNeil-P.P.C., Inc.*, 973 F.2d 1033, 1043-44 (2d Cir. 1992). As noted above, an incontestible registered trademark enjoys a conclusive presumption of distinctiveness. *See Park 'N Fly, Inc. v. Dollar Park and Fly, Inc.*, 469 U.S. 189, 204-05, 83 L. Ed. 2d 582, 105 S. Ct. 658 (1985).... Yet even if a mark is registered and, thus, afforded the utmost degree of protection, *Lois Sportswear, U.S.A., Inc. v. Levi Strauss & Co.*, 799 F.2d 867, 871 (2d Cir. 1986), the presumption of an exclusive right to use the mark extends only so far as the goods or services noted in the registration certificate, *Mushroom Makers*, 580 F.2d at 48.

Here, the District Court made the following findings:

> Three of Plaintiff's marks are incontestable and hence are presumptively strong as applied to the goods and services listed on the registrations, namely: Liquid and paper for photocopiers; photocopiers and parts thereof; and maintenance and repair services for photocopiers and word

processors. Plaintiff is also able to show that its marks possess secondary meaning in the market for high-quality business machinery and related services. Plaintiff has submitted evidence that it sells it [sic] products through seventeen branches and over trained dealers throughout the United States; spent over $20 million in advertising in 2002; and realized annual revenues of over $675 million. Such evidence is sufficient to establish that Plaintiff's marks possess secondary meaning in Plaintiff's market.

Critically, however, the court also found that Plaintiff had not shown "that its marks [were] strong in the market for professional engineering" services, and had not "submitted [any] evidence that its marks possessed secondary meaning in the market for professional engineering" services.

As we find no clear error in these findings, we conclude that the District Court did not err in determining that the presumption of the strength of Plaintiff's mark does not extend to the field of professional engineering. *See Mushroom Makers,* 580 F.2d at 48; *Paco Sport, Ltd. v. Paco Rabanne Parfums,* 86 F. Supp. 2d 305, 312 (S.D.N.Y. 2000). Accordingly, we also agree with the court's ultimate determination that the first *Polaroid* factor, strength of the mark, weighs in favor of Defendants.

2. Similarity of the Marks

"Even close similarity between two marks is not dispositive of the issue of likelihood of confusion." *McGregor-Doniger,* 599 F.2d at 1133. "Rather, the crux of the issue is whether the similarity is likely to cause confusion among numerous customers who are ordinarily prudent." *Swatch Group (U.S.) Inc. v. Movado Corp.,* 01 Civ. 0286, 2003 U.S. Dist. LEXIS 6015, at *11 (S.D.N.Y. Apr. 10, 2003) (citing *Morningside Group Ltd. v. Morningside Capital Group L.L.C.,* 182 F.3d 133, 139-40 (2d Cir. 1999)). Thus, "an inquiry into the degree of similarity between two marks does not end with a comparison of the marks themselves." *Spring Mills, Inc. v. Ultracashmere House, Ltd.,* 689 F.2d 1127, 1130 (2d Cir. 1982). As this Court has stated, "the setting in which a designation is used affects its appearance and colors the impression conveyed by it." *McGregor-Doniger,* 599 F.2d at 1133 (internal quotation marks omitted). Indeed, the "'impression' conveyed by the setting in which the mark is used is often of critical importance." *Spring Mills,* 689 F.2d at 1130.

Here, the District Court found that:

> Plaintiff and Defendants both use the name "Savin," and their logos display similar block letter fonts, with one arm of the letter "V" slanted at a greater angle than the other. The only apparent difference in the marks is that Defendants' logo incorporates four squares, one slightly tilted, to the left of the name. Given that both marks feature the same name, such a difference is inconsequential.

In addition, one of the settings in which the junior mark has allegedly infringed the senior mark is the Internet, where the subtle differences in font and other characteristics noted by the District Court are of even less significance, given that the overarching concern of the individual searching the Internet is to arrive at the correct website, which is ultimately identified by a purely text-based website address. We find no clear error in the District

Court's determinations on this point and, in light of the foregoing, agree that this factor weighs in Plaintiff's favor.

3. Proximity of the Entities' Products and/or Services

"This factor focuses on whether the two products compete with each other. To the extent goods (or trade names) serve the same purpose, fall within the same general class, or are used together, the use of similar designations is more likely to cause confusion." *Lang v. Ret. Living Pub. Co.*, 949 F.2d 576, 582 (2d Cir. 1991). In assessing this factor, "the court may consider whether the products differ in content, geographic distribution, market position, and audience appeal." *W.W.W. Pharm. Co. v. Gillette Co.*, 984 F.2d 567, 573 (2d Cir. 1993); *see, e.g., Arrow Fastener Co. v. Stanley Works*, 59 F.3d 384, 396 (2d Cir. 1995) (holding that customers were not likely to be confused when both parties sold staplers in the same stores, but one party sold a pneumatic stapler and the other a lightweight small stapler).

Here, the District Court found, *inter alia*, as follows:

> The [proportional] difference in price between Plaintiff's back office facilities management services and Defendants' professional engineering services is at least as great as, if not greater than, that between the two types of staplers in Arrow Fastener. Similarly, the expertise of Plaintiff's engineers in information technology and that of Defendants' [engineering professionals] in construction and waste management projects serve very different needs within the sectors from which both parties draw their customers.

> … Even though Plaintiff's marks may be strong in the market for sophisticated business equipment and services, professional engineering services do not reasonably fall within the broadly defined market of potentially related services. Although the marks are very similar, consumers are unlikely to be confused as to source because [of] the competitive distance between the parties' services.…

We discern no clear error in the District Court's findings on this point, and thus we concur in the court's determination that the at-issue products and services are not proximate as a matter of law.

4. Actual Confusion

"It is black letter law that actual confusion need not be shown to prevail under the Lanham Act, since actual confusion is very difficult to prove and the Act requires only a likelihood of confusion as to source." *Lois Sportswear*, 799 F.2d at 875. Nonetheless, it has been noted that:

> There can be no more positive or substantial proof of the likelihood of confusion than proof of actual confusion. Moreover, reason tells us that while very little proof of actual confusion would be necessary to prove the likelihood of confusion an almost overwhelming amount of proof would be necessary to refute such proof.

World Carpets, Inc. v. Dick Littrell's New World Carpets, 438 F.2d 482, 489 (5th Cir. 1971).

In the instant case, the District Court found that Plaintiff had submitted as evidence of actual confusion only the single incident at the chamber of commerce meeting, where "someone who had previously sold an exhibit to Defendants mistakenly concluded that one of Plaintiff's executives was associated with [Savin Engineers]." A single "anecdote[ ] of confusion over the entire course of competition," however, "constitutes *de minimis* evidence insufficient to raise triable issues." *See Nora Beverages, Inc. v. Perrier Group of Am., Inc.*, 269 F.3d 114, 124 (2d Cir. 2001). The District Court's presentation of background facts, on this point are not clearly erroneous, and we find that the court committed no error in concluding that this factor weighs in Defendants' favor.

5. Bridging the Gap

The question under this factor is the likelihood that Plaintiff will enter the market for professional engineering services relating to the construction industry. *See W.W.W. Pharm. Co.*, 984 F.2d at 574. "This factor is designed to protect the senior user's 'interest in being able to enter a related field at some future time.'" *Id.* (quoting *Scarves by Vera, Inc. v. Todo Imports Ltd.*, 544 F.2d 1167, 1172 (2d Cir. 1976)).

Here, the District Court found that:

> Plaintiff claims that it intends to expand its involvement in the area of facilities management, but the only evidence Plaintiff presents to support this allegation is a statement [by Thomas Salierno, Plaintiff's President and Chief Operating Officer,] that Plaintiff intends to "work[ ] in an office environment and expand[ ] [into] whatever the customer needs." This statement fails to support any inference that Plaintiff intends to enter Defendants' market.

We agree with the District Court's conclusion that even drawing all inferences in Plaintiff's favor, this bare assertion fails to raise a genuine issue of material fact that Plaintiff is likely to enter Defendants' corner of the marketplace.

6. Good Faith

The good-faith factor "considers whether the defendant adopted its mark with the intention of capitalizing on [the] plaintiff's reputation and goodwill and [on] any confusion between his and the senior user's product." *W.W.W. Pharm. Co.*, 984 F.2d at 575 (internal quotation marks omitted).

Here, Plaintiff asserts that Defendants acted in bad faith because (i) Dr. Nivas "had knowledge of [Plaintiff's] products and services for approximately ten years"; (ii) Savin Engineers "never performed a search or investigation prior to adopting and launching their trade names incorporating the term SAVIN"; and (iii) Savin Engineers were aware of Plaintiff's "savin.com domain name prior to registering their thesavingroup.com and savinengineers.com domains." Therefore, Plaintiff argues, the District Court clearly erred in finding that Defendants did not act in bad faith.

Notably, however, the District Court also found, in particular, that Defendants:

> had no reason to believe that they might be infringing another's marks[,] because they were not copying the mark from another entity. In fact,

Defendants' founder was not even aware of Plaintiff's existence at the time he adopted his mark, and arrived at the name "Savin" independently by reversing the spelling of his nickname "Nivas."

Moreover, as the District Court observed, even if Defendants had conducted a trademark search, they would have discovered only that the "Savin" mark was registered for photocopiers and related goods and services and, hence, would have had no reason to believe that using the same name for professional engineering services would infringe Plaintiff's marks.

In any event, "failure to perform an official trademark search, ... does not[,] standing alone[,] prove that [Defendants] acted in bad faith." *Streetwise Maps, Inc. v. VanDam, Inc.,* 159 F.3d 739, 746 (2d Cir. 1998). Nor is "prior knowledge of a senior user's trade mark" inconsistent with good faith. *See Arrow Fastener*, 59 F.3d at 397. Accordingly, we conclude that the District Court was correct in determining that Plaintiff has failed to raise a material issue of fact regarding Defendants' alleged bad faith.

7. Quality of the Entities' Product and/or Services

"The next factor, quality of the junior user's product, is the subject of some confusion." *Hasbro, Inc. v. Lanard Toys, Ltd.*, 858 F.2d 70, 78 (2d Cir. 1988). Essentially, there are two issues with regard to quality, but only one has relevance to determining the likelihood of confusion. If the quality of the junior user's product is low relative to the senior user's, then this increases the chance of actual injury where there is confusion, i.e., through dilution of the senior user's brand. *Id.; see, e.g., Lois Sportswear*, 799 F.2d at 875. A marked difference in quality, however, actually tends to reduce the likelihood of confusion in the first instance, because buyers will be less likely to assume that the senior user whose product is high-quality will have produced the lesser-quality products of the junior user. Conversely, where the junior user's products are of approximately the same quality as the senior user's, there is a greater likelihood of confusion, but less possibility of dilution. *Hasbro,* 858 F.2d at 78; *see, e.g., Lois Sportswear,* 799 F.2d at 875.

In this case, the District Court found that as Defendants' services were "not closely similar to those provided by Plaintiff," any equivalence in "quality between their products [was] unlikely to cause confusion." This finding is neither clearly erroneous nor, for that matter, even challenged on appeal.

8. Sophistication of Purchasers

As the theory goes, the more sophisticated the purchaser, the less likely he or she will be confused by the presence of similar marks in the marketplace. *See Maxim's, Ltd. v. Badonsky,* 772 F.2d 388, 393 (7th Cir. 1985) ("In general, where 'the cost of the defendant's trademarked product is high, the courts assume that purchasers are likely to be more discriminating than they might otherwise be.'" (quoting Jerome Gilson, *Trademark Protection and Practice* § 5.08 (1985))).

Here, the District Court found that both Plaintiff and Defendants:

> offer highly priced services that do not usually invite impulse buying and are ordinarily purchased by experienced professionals in the course of business. The decision to invest in new business equipment or to engage professional engineers is often the result of careful deliberation

by more than one individual in the purchasing organization. The likelihood that such sophisticated consumers will be confused as to the source of the services is remote.

On appeal, Plaintiff does not so much challenge this finding as sidestep it, implying that the District Court erred because "most individuals, whether they are sophisticated or unsophisticated, come into contact with the type of office equipment manufactured by [Plaintiff]." Indeed, notes Plaintiff, "everyone uses photocopiers and fax machines."

Of course, the relevant inquiry is not whether daily users, or, even more amorphously, "individuals ... coming into contact" with Plaintiff's products, would likely confuse them with those of Defendants. Rather, the pertinent question is whether "numerous ordinary prudent purchasers" would likely "be misled or confused as to the source of the product in question because of the entrance in the marketplace of [Defendants'] mark." *Gruner + Jahr USA Publ'g,* 991 F.2d at 1077; *see also Brennan's,* 360 F.3d at 134 ("To succeed on an infringement claim, plaintiff must show that it is probable, not just possible, that consumers will be confused."). The District Court's findings on this point, which are not squarely challenged on appeal, may have been somewhat in the nature of "common sense" assumptions, but this does not make them clearly erroneous. In any event, we find no error in the court's determination that this factor weighs in Defendants' favor.

C. Balancing the Factors

As the District Court found, one of the *Polaroid* factors -- similarity of marks -- weighs in Plaintiff's favor, while the other factors weigh in favor of Defendants.[13] Having undertaken our own, *de novo* review of the balancing of the various factors, we find nothing to quarrel with in the District Court's analysis of the Lanham Act infringement claim and ultimate conclusion that that claim cannot survive summary judgment. In sum, Plaintiff "has not at this point demonstrated a likelihood of confusion." *Brennan's,* 360 F.3d at 130. Accordingly, we affirm that portion of the District Court's judgment dismissing the infringement claim.

We have considered the parties' remaining arguments and find them to be without merit.

---

[13] The District Court also included an "Internet initial interest confusion factor" in the *Polaroid* balancing test. Such confusion arises when a consumer who searches for the plaintiff's website with the aid of a search engine is directed instead to the defendant's site because of a similarity in the parties' website addresses. *See BigStar Entertainment, Inc. v. Next Big Star, Inc.,* 105 F. Supp. 2d 185, 207 (S.D.N.Y. 2000). Because consumers diverted on the Internet can more readily get back on track than those in actual space, thus minimizing the harm to the owner of the searched-for site from consumers becoming trapped in a competing site, Internet initial interest confusion requires a showing of intentional deception. *See id.; see also Bihari v. Gross,* 119 F. Supp. 2d 309, 319 (S.D.N.Y. 2000). Here, the District Court found that Plaintiff had failed to raise a triable issue of fact with regard to either a likelihood of confusion or intentional deception, and, accordingly, the court concluded that this factor, too, weighs in Defendants' favor. We find no error in the court's determination on this issue, which, in any event, Plaintiff does not directly challenge on appeal.

CONCLUSION

For the foregoing reasons, we vacate those portions of the judgment of the District Court dismissing Plaintiff's FTDA ...; remand for further proceedings consistent with this opinion; and affirm the judgment in all other respects.

* * * * *

insert the following after the fourth paragraph on page 626 of Law of Internet Speech:

May a book use the phrase "fair and balanced" as part of its title without infringing on or diluting the rights of a broadcast network's use of the phrase as part of a program it airs? Fox News objected to the use by Dutton (part of the Penguin Group) of the phrase as part of a work it published by Al Franken, entitled, *Lies, and the Lying Liars Who Tell Them: A Fair and Balanced Look at the Right.* U.S. District Judge Denny Chin unhesitatingly denied Fox's motion for a preliminary injunction to enjoin use of the phrase "fair and balanced" in connection with the book, noting that "[t]here are hard cases and there are easy cases. This is an easy case, for in my view the case is wholly without merit." *Fox News Network, LLC v. Penguin Group (USA), Inc., and Alan S. Franken,* 03 Civ. 6162 (RLC) (DC), Hearing on the Plaintiff's Motion for a Preliminary Injunction, Transcript (S.D.N.Y. Aug. 22, 2003) at 20. The court also observed, "Of course, it is ironic that a media company, that should be seeking to protect the First Amendment, is seeking to undermine it by claiming a monopoly on the phrase 'fair and balanced.'" *Id.* at 23. Three days later, Fox dropped its suit, but not before Franken's book rocketed to the top of amazon.com's bestseller list. *See* Erin McClam, *Fox News Drops Suit vs. Franken Over Book,* Yahoo! News.com (Aug. 25, 2003), *available at* <http://story.news.yahoo.com/news?tmpl=story&u=/ap/20030825/ap_en_ce/fox_franken_lawsuit_3>; *see also Judge Rejects Fox News' Request for Injunction on Franken Book,* Fox News Channel, FoxLife (Aug. 22, 2003), *available at* <http://www.foxnews.com/story/0,2933,95484,00.html>.

* * * * *

insert the following before Defenses on page 630 of Law of Internet Speech:

With respect to the appellate ruling in *Playboy Enters., Inc. v. Netscape Communications Corp.,* 354 F.3d 1020 (9th Cir. 2004), Supplement *infra* at 440.

* * * * *

PLAYBOY ENTERPRISES, INC., a Delaware corporation,
Plaintiff-Appellant

v.

TERRI WELLES, *et al.,* Defendants-Appellees

United States Court of Appeals for the Ninth Circuit

No. 00-55009, No. 00-55229, No. 00-55537, No. 00-55538, 279
F.3d 796

February 1, 2002

Playboy Enterprises, Inc. (PEI), appeals the district court's grant of summary judgment as to its claims of[, *inter alia,*] trademark infringement ... against Terri Welles; Terri Welles, Inc.; Pippi, Inc.; and Welles' current and former "webmasters," Steven Huntington and Michael Mihalko. ... [W]e affirm in part and reverse in part.

... I. Background

Terri Welles was on the cover of *Playboy* in 1981 and was chosen to be the Playboy Playmate of the Year for 1981. Her use of the title "Playboy Playmate of the Year 1981," and her use of other trademarked terms on her website are at issue in this suit. During the relevant time period, Welles' website offered information about and free photos of Welles, advertised photos for sale, advertised memberships in her photo club, and promoted her services as a spokesperson. A biographical section described Welles' selection as Playmate of the Year in 1981 and her years modeling for PEI. After the lawsuit began, Welles included discussions of the suit and criticism of PEI on her website and included a note disclaiming any association with PEI.

PEI complains of ... different uses of its trademarked terms on Welles' website[, including]: the phrase "Playmate of the Year 1981" on the masthead of the website[and] the phrases "Playboy Playmate of the Year 1981 "and "Playmate of the Year 1981" on various banner ads, which may be transferred to other websites.... PEI claimed that these uses of its marks constituted trademark infringement, dilution, false designation of origin, and unfair competition. The district court granted defendants' motion for summary judgment. PEI appeals the grant of summary judgment on its infringement and dilution claims. We affirm in part and reverse in part.

... III. Discussion

A. Trademark Infringement

Except for the use of PEI's protected terms in the wallpaper of Welles' website, we conclude that Welles' uses of PEI's trademarks are permissible, nominative uses. They imply no current sponsorship or endorsement by PEI. Instead, they serve to identify Welles as a past PEI "Playmate of the Year."

We articulated the test for a permissible, nominative use in *New Kids On The Block v. New America Publishing, Inc.*[8] The band, New Kids On The Block, claimed trademark

---

[8] 971 F.2d 302 (9th Cir. 1992).

infringement arising from the use of their trademarked name by several newspapers. The newspapers had conducted polls asking which member of the band New Kids On The Block was the best and most popular. The papers' use of the trademarked term did not fall within the traditional fair use doctrine. Unlike a traditional fair use scenario, the defendant newspaper was using the trademarked term to describe not its own product, but the plaintiff's. Thus, the factors used to evaluate fair use were inapplicable. The use was nonetheless permissible, we concluded, based on its nominative nature.

We adopted the following test for nominative use:

> First, the product or service in question must be one not readily identifiable without use of the trademark; second, only so much of the mark or marks may be used as is reasonably necessary to identify the product or service; and third, the user must do nothing that would, in conjunction with the mark, suggest sponsorship or endorsement by the trademark holder.[12]

We noted in *New Kids* that a nominative use may also be a commercial one.

In cases in which the defendant raises a nominative use defense, the above three-factor test should be applied instead of the test for likelihood of confusion set forth in *Sleekcraft*.[14] The three-factor test better evaluates the likelihood of confusion in nominative use cases. When a defendant uses a trademark nominally, the trademark will be identical to the plaintiff's mark, at least in terms of the words in question. Thus, application of the *Sleekcraft* test, which focuses on the similarity of the mark used by the plaintiff and the defendant, would lead to the incorrect conclusion that virtually all nominative uses are confusing. The three-factor test -- with its requirements that the defendant use marks only when no descriptive substitute exists, use no more of the mark than necessary, and do nothing to suggest sponsorship or endorsement by the mark holder -- better addresses concerns regarding the likelihood of confusion in nominative use cases.

... To satisfy the first part of the test for nominative use, "the product or service in question must be one not readily identifiable without use of the trademark[.]"[15] This situation arises "when a trademark also describes a person, a place or an attribute of a product"[16] and there is no descriptive substitute for the trademark. In such a circumstance, allowing the trademark holder exclusive rights would allow the language to "be depleted in much the same way as if generic words were protectable."[17] In *New Kids*, we gave the example of the trademarked term, "Chicago Bulls." We explained that "one might refer to the 'two-time world champions' or 'the professional basketball team from Chicago,' but it's far simpler (and

---

[12] *New Kids*, 971 F.2d at 308 (footnote omitted).

[14] 599 F.2d at 348-49.

[15] *New Kids*, 971 F.2d at 308.

[16] *Id.* at 306.

[17] *Id.*

more likely to be understood) to refer to the Chicago Bulls."[18] Moreover, such a use of the trademark would "not imply sponsorship or endorsement of the product because the mark is used only to describe the thing, rather than to identify its source."[19] Thus, we concluded, such uses must be excepted from trademark infringement law.

... No descriptive substitute exists for PEI's trademarks in this context....

The second part of the nominative use test requires that "only so much of the mark or marks may be used as is reasonably necessary to identify the product or service[.]"[21] *New Kids* provided the following examples to explain this element: "[A] soft drink competitor would be entitled to compare its product to Coca-Cola or Coke, but would not be entitled to use Coca-Cola's distinctive lettering."[22] Similarly, in a past case, an auto shop was allowed to use the trademarked term "Volkswagen" on a sign describing the cars it repaired, in part because the shop "did not use Volkswagen's distinctive lettering style or color scheme, nor did he display the encircled 'VW' emblem."[23] Welles' banner advertisements and headlines satisfy this element because they use only the trademarked words, not the font or symbols associated with the trademarks.

The third element requires that the user do "nothing that would, in conjunction with the mark, suggest sponsorship or endorsement by the trademark holder."[24] As to this element, we conclude that aside from the wallpaper, which we address separately, Welles does nothing in conjunction with her use of the marks to suggest sponsorship or endorsement by PEI. The marks are clearly used to describe the title she received from PEI in 1981, a title that helps describe who she is. It would be unreasonable to assume that the Chicago Bulls sponsored a website of Michael Jordan's simply because his name appeared with the appellation "former Chicago Bull." Similarly, in this case, it would be unreasonable to assume that PEI currently sponsors or endorses someone who describes herself as a "Playboy Playmate of the Year in 1981." The designation of the year, in our case, serves the same function as the "former" in our example. It shows that any sponsorship or endorsement occurred in the past.

In addition to doing nothing in conjunction with her use of the marks to suggest sponsorship or endorsement by PEI, Welles affirmatively disavows any sponsorship or endorsement. Her site contains a clear statement disclaiming any connection to PEI. Moreover, the text of the site describes her ongoing legal battles with the company.

For the foregoing reasons, we conclude that Welles' use of PEI's marks in her headlines and banner advertisements is a nominative use excepted from the law of trademark infringement.

---

[18] *Id.*

[19] *Id.*

[21] [*Id.*] at 308.

[22] *Id.* at n.7.

[23] *Id.* (quoting *Volkswagenwerk Aktiengesellschaft v. Church*, 411 F.2d 350 (9th Cir. 1969)).

[24] *Id.* 971 F.2d at 308.

... B. Trademark Dilution

The district court granted summary judgment to Welles as to PEI's claim of trademark dilution. We affirm on the ground that all of Welles' uses of PEI's marks, with the exception of the use in the wallpaper which we address separately[, *see* Supplement *infra* at 454], are proper, nominative uses. We hold that nominative uses, by definition, do not dilute the trademarks.

Federal law provides protection against trademark dilution:

> The owner of a famous mark shall be entitled, subject to the principles of equity and upon such terms as the court deems reasonable, to an injunction against another person's commercial use in commerce of a mark or trade name, if such use begins after the mark has become famous and causes dilution of the distinctive quality of the mark...[33]

Dilution, which was not defined by the statute, has been described by the courts as "the gradual 'whittling away' of a trademark's value."[34] Traditionally, courts have recognized two forms of dilution: blurring and tarnishment. Blurring occurs when another's use of a mark creates "the possibility that the mark will lose its ability to serve as a unique identifier of the plaintiff's product."[35] Tarnishment, on the other hand, occurs "when a famous mark is improperly associated with an inferior or offensive product or service."[36] As we recognized in *Panavision*, dilution may occur through uses on the internet as well as elsewhere.[37]

Dilution works its harm not by causing confusion in consumers' minds regarding the source of a good or service, but by creating an association in consumers' minds between a mark and a different good or service. As explained in a First Circuit case, in dilution (as compared to infringement) "an entirely different issue is at stake -- not interference with the source signaling function but rather protection from an appropriation of or free riding on the investment [the trademark holder] has made in its [trademark]."[39] Thus, for example, if a cocoa maker began using the "Rolls Royce" mark to identify its hot chocolate, no consumer confusion would be likely to result. Few would assume that the car company had expanded into the cocoa making business. However, the cocoa maker would be capitalizing on the investment the car company had made in its mark. Consumers readily associate the mark with highly priced automobiles of a certain quality. By identifying the cocoa with the Rolls Royce mark, the producer would be capitalizing on consumers' association of the mark with high quality items. Moreover, by labeling a different product "Rolls Royce," the cocoa

---

[33] 15 U.S.C. § 1125(c)(1).

[34] *Academy of Motion Picture Arts & Sciences v. Creative House Promotions, Inc.*, 944 F.2d 1446, 1457 (9th Cir. 1991) (citing J. McCarthy, *Trademarks and Unfair Competition*, § 24:13 (2d ed. 1984)).

[35] *Panavision Int'l, L.P. v. Toeppen,* 141 F.3d 1316, 1326 n.7 (9th Cir. 1998).

[36] *Id.*

[37] *Id.* at 1326-27.

[39] *I.P. Lund Trading ApS v. Kohler Co.* 163 F.3d 27, 50 (1st Cir. 1998).

company would be reducing the ability of the mark to identify the mark holder's product. If someone said, "I'm going to get a Rolls Royce," others could no longer be sure the person was planning on buying an expensive automobile. The person might just be planning on buying a cup of cocoa. Thus, the use of the mark to identify the hot chocolate, although not causing consumer confusion, would cause harm by diluting the mark.

Uses that do not create an improper association between a mark and a new product but merely identify the trademark holder's products should be excepted from the reach of the anti-dilution statute. Such uses cause no harm. The anti-dilution statute recognizes this principle and specifically excepts users of a trademark who compare their product in "commercial advertising or promotion to identify the competing goods or services of the owner of the famous mark."[40]

For the same reason uses in comparative advertising are excepted from anti-dilution law, we conclude that nominative uses are also excepted. A nominative use, by definition, refers to the trademark holder's product. It does not create an improper association in consumers' minds between a new product and the trademark holder's mark.

When Welles refers to her title, she is in effect referring to a product of PEI's. She does not dilute the title by truthfully identifying herself as its one-time recipient any more than Michael Jordan would dilute the name "Chicago Bulls" by referring to himself as a former member of that team, or the two-time winner of an Academy Award would dilute the award by referring to him or herself as a" two-time Academy Award winner." Awards are not diminished or diluted by the fact that they have been awarded in the past.

Similarly, they are not diminished or diluted when past recipients truthfully identify themselves as such. It is in the nature of honors and awards to be identified with the people who receive them. Of course, the conferrer of such honors and awards is free to limit the honoree's use of the title or references to the award by contract. So long as a use is nominative, however, trademark law is unavailing.

... IV. Conclusion

For the foregoing reasons, we affirm the district court's grant of summary judgment as to PEI's claims for trademark infringement and trademark dilution, with the sole exception of the use of the abbreviation "PMOY." We reverse as to the abbreviation and remand for consideration of whether it merits protection under either an infringement or a dilution theory. ...

AFFIRMED in part, REVERSED and REMANDED in part. Costs to Terri Welles and Terri Welles, Inc.

* * * * *

---

[40] 15 U.S.C. § 1125(c)(4)(A).

Defenses

insert the following after People for the Ethical Treatment of Animals v. Doughney on page 635 of Law of Internet Speech:

The U.S. Court of Appeals for the Ninth Circuit held that non-commercial use of a trademark as the domain name of a web-site that did not belong to the trademark owner was not actionable under the Lanham Act, when the web-site consisted of criticism by a consumer about the trademark owner's products and services. *See Bosley Med. Inst., Inc. v. Kremer*, 403 F.3d 672 (9th Cir. 2005). The court affirmed the district court's dismissal of the trademark owner's trademark infringement and dilution claims, concluding that the use of the mark was not "in connection with the sale of goods or services" and therefore was "noncommercial." *Id.* The court rejected the argument that the commercial use requirement was satisfied because the web-site was designed to encourage other consumers to refrain from using the plaintiff's goods and services, thereby disagreeing with the reasoning of the Fourth Circuit in *People for the Ethical Treatment of Animals v. Doughney*, 263 F.3d 359 (4th Cir. 2001); *see Law of Internet Speech* at 631, 634. *See Bosley Med. Inst., Inc. v. Kremer*, 403 F.3d at 678-79. The Ninth Circuit observed:

> The Lanham Act, expressly enacted to be applied in commercial contexts, does not prohibit all unauthorized uses of a trademark. [The defendant's] use of the Bosley Medical mark simply cannot mislead consumers into buying a competing product -- no customer will mistakenly purchase a hair replacement service from [the defendant] under the belief that the service is being offered by Bosley. Neither is [the defendant] capitalizing on the good will Bosley has created in its mark. Any harm to Bosley arises not from a competitor's sale of a similar product under Bosley's mark, but from [the defendant's] criticism of their services. Bosley cannot use the Lanham Act either as a shield from [the defendant's] criticism, or as a sword to shut [the defendant] up.

Id. at 679-80 (deciding at the time not to reject the plaintiff's claim under the Anticybersquatting Consumer Protection Act).

* * * * *

insert the following after Notes and Questions # 2 on page 636 of Law of Internet Speech:

3. In *KP Permanent Make-Up, Inc. v. Lasting Impression I, Inc.*, 125 S. Ct. 542 (2004), the U.S. Supreme Court held that the fair use doctrine does not require the party asserting it to prove the absence of consumer confusion. A party may defeat a trademark infringement claim on the grounds that the use of the mark was fair, even if the use results in a likelihood of consumer confusion. *See id.*

4. How do the defenses of fair use and parody compare when analyzed under copyright and trademark law?

5. Does trademark law primarily redress harm to the consumer or harm to the trademark holder? Is the latter effectively the proxy for the consumer?

* * * * *

insert the following before Issues Relating to Domain Names on page 636 of Law of Internet Speech:

A search engine that used key words containing a trademark to trigger unlabeled targeted banner advertisements asserted the defense of nominative fair use. *See Playboy Enters., Inc. v. Netscape Communications Corp.,* 354 F.3d 1020 (9th Cir. 2004). The U.S. Court of Appeals for the Ninth Circuit determined, however, that such uses of the plaintiff's trademarks "playboy" and "playmate" as triggers for banner ads did not qualify as a nominative fair use because the product or service that was advertised was not one "readily identifiable" without the use of the trademark. *Id.* at 1050. After ruling that a genuine issue of material fact existed as to the substantial likelihood of confusion, *see id.* at 1029, the court considered various defenses.

As to the nominative fair use defense, the use of the mark must meet a tripartite test: (1) the product or service in question must be one not readily identifiable without use of the trademark; (2) only as much of the mark may be used as is reasonably necessary to identify the product or service; and (3) the user must do nothing that would suggest sponsorship or endorsement by the trademark holder. *See id.* at 1029-30. The Ninth Circuit acknowledged that the defendants' use of the plaintiff's marks to trigger a listing of the plaintiff's sites and other web-sites that legitimately used plaintiff's marks was not at issue. *See id.* at 1030. But the situation at bar was ruled to have contravened the first requirement of the nominative fair use test. The court noted that the defendants could have utilized other terms to identify consumers who might be interested in advertisements for adult-oriented products and services; "[t]here is nothing indispensable, in this context, about [the plaintiff's] marks. Defendants do not wish to identify [the plaintiff] or its products when they key banner advertisements to [the plaintiff's] marks. Rather, they wish to identify consumers who are interested in adult-oriented entertainment so they can draw them to competitors' web-sites. Accordingly, their use is not nominative." *Id.*

Netscape and Playboy Enterprises reportedly settled the case days after the court ruled. *See, e.g.,* Stefanie Olsen, *Netscape, Playboy Settles Search Trademark Case,* CNet News.com (Jan. 23, 2004), *available at* <http://news.com.com/2102-1024_3-5146502. html?tag=st.util.print>. The terms of the settlement were not made public. *See id.*

Thereafter, it was determined that the sale of a plaintiff's trademark terms by Google, a search engine, as search terms linking to competitors might give rise to trademark infringement claims. *See Google, Inc. v. American Blinds & Wallpaper Factory, Inc.,* No. C 03-05340 JF, 2005 U.S. Dist. LEXIS 6228 (N.D. Cal. Mar. 30, 2005). Do such sales constitute a "use" of the trademarks?

* * * * *

440

Issues Relating to Domain Names

The Nature of Domain Names

substitute the following for the first paragraph of The Nature of Domain Names on page 636 of Law of Internet Speech:

Locations of web-sites within the Internet are recognized by their IP addresses. Domain names help identify the site and direct visitors to it. Domain names consist of multiple levels; as the levels progressive to the left, each delimits the site with more specificity. Top-level domains indicate the general classification of the web-site and include ".com" (denoting a commercial site); ".edu" (denoting an educational site); ".org" (denoting, among other organizations, not-for-profit sites); ".gov" (denoting a government site); ".net" (denoting a networking provider); and ".mil" (denoting a military site). In November 2000, the Internet Corporation for Assigned Names and Numbers ("ICANN") announced additional top level domain names, such as ".biz" (connoting a business site); ".info" (denoting an informational site); and ".mu" (denoting a museum site).

Second-level domains consist of a term or a series of terms that specify with more particularity the domain name address. The second-level domain is the part of the Uniform Resource Locator, or "url," that identifies the specific owner or operator who is associated with the web-site address. Thus, while the top-level domain name indicates the nature or purpose of the web-site, the second-level domain more particularly identifies the organization or entity. To illustrate, the web-site "CNN.com" has as its top-level domain ".com" and as its second-level domain "CNN."

A ".xxx" domain was approved to connote sexually explicit material existed in the web-site. In addition, the Dot Kids Implementation and Efficiency Act of 2002, 47 U.S.C. § 941, created a ".kids" domain name for web-sites that provide access to material that is suitable for and not harmful to children under 13 years of age. But according to press reports, approximately a year and half after the "dot kids" legislation became effective, few had registered dot kids domain names. As of February 2004, only 1,500 had taken advantage of dot kids addresses, a sharp contrast with more than 2 million ".info" and ".biz" addresses that had been added to the system in the prior three year period. *See, e.g.,* David McGuire, *Firms Ignore Kids-Only Internet Domain Names,* Washington Post.com (Feb. 20, 2004), *available at* <http://www.washingtonpost.com/ac2/wp-dyn/A56963-2004Feb20>. As of the first half of 2005, only twenty web-sites reportedly actually used the ".kids" domain. *See* Reuters, *Not Much to Do in Kids' Online Domain,* CNet News.com (June 3, 2005), *available at* <http://news.com.com/Not+much+do+in+kids+online+domain/2100-1028_3-5731209.html>.

* * * * *

Cybergriping

insert the following before Cybersquatting on page 662 of Law of Internet Speech:

How may the tension between proprietary and free speech interests be reconciled effectively? One commentator opined that a balance could be achieved through appropriate allocation of procedural recourse; "the very nature of litigation would require companies to challenge only those critics who present a serious, credible threat to their trademark interests, leaving those who are merely exercising their free-speech rights at liberty to do so." Deborah Salzberg, *TrademarkSucks.com: Free Speech, Confusion and the Right to Cybergripe*, N.Y. State Bar Ass'n Bright Ideas, vol. 12, no. 1, at 22, 30 (Spring/Summer 2002). Are adequate legal safeguards available in existing causes of action such as defamation and product disparagement, trademark infringement, and trademark dilution for those who provide products and services?

* * * * *

Cybersquatting

insert the following after Notes and Questions # 5 on page 667 of Law of Internet Speech:

6. In December 2003, John Zuccarini pleaded guilty to charges that he used misleading domain names on the Internet to deceive minors into logging onto web-sites that contained pornographic content in violation of the Truth in Domain Names Act, which was enacted on April 30, 2003 as part of the "Amber Alert" legislation. *See* Press Release, U.S. Attorney's Office, S.D.N.Y., *"Cyberscammer" Sentenced to 30 Months for Using Deceptive Internet Names to Mislead Minors to X-Rated Sites,* Feb. 26, 2004, at 1, 4, *available at* <http://www.usdoj.gov/usao/nys/Press%20Releases/FEBRUARY04/zuccarini%20sentence%20pr.pdf>; *see also Florida Man Pleads Guilty to Directing Kids to Porn Sites,* SiliconValley.com (Dec. 10, 2003), *available at* <http://www.siliconvalley. com/mld/siliconvalley/news/editorial/7461505.htm>. According to the Information and Complaint, Zuccarini used various Internet registries to register domain names that included misspellings of popular legitimate domain names and registered multiple misspellings of the same legitimate domain name. *See* Press Release, U.S. Attorney's Office, S.D.N.Y., *"Cyberscammer" Sentenced to 30 Months for Using Deceptive Internet Names to Mislead Minors to X-Rated Sites* (Feb. 26, 2004), at 1-2, *available at* <http://www.usdoj. gov/usao/nys/Press%20Releases/FEBRUARY04/zuccarini%20sentence%20pr.pdf>. In the course of civil lawsuits, Zuccarini admitted that he earned between 10 cents and 25 cents for each visitor who he led to a pornographic site, and took in as much as $800,000 to $1 million annually from the use of misleading domain names. *See id.* at 4-5.

7. Among the factors the Anticybersquatting Consumer Protection Act lists for consideration is whether the defendant made a *"bona fide noncommercial or fair use"* of a trademark. *See* 15 U.S.C. § 1125(d)(1)(B)(i). What are the implications, then, for editorial or critical uses? A federal court construed the factor as intended by Congress to protect "activities such as critical commentary." *Mayflower Transit, LLC v. Prince,* 314 F. Supp. 2d 362, 369 (D.N.J. 2004) (citation omitted). The court buttressed its conclusion by reference to ACPA's safe harbor, 15 U.S.C. § 1125(d)(1)(B)(ii), that precludes a finding of bad faith when "the court determines that the person believed and had reasonable grounds to believe that the use of the

domain name was a fair use or otherwise lawful." *Mayflower Transit, LLC v. Prince,* 314 F. Supp. 2d at 369; *see also Lucas Nursery & Landscaping, Inc. v. Grosse,* 359 F.3d 806, 810 (6th Cir. 2004) (stating that when the "paradigmatic harm that the ACPA was enacted to eradicate -- the practice of cybersquatters registering several hundred domain names in an effort to sell them to the legitimate owners of the mark -- is simply not present" the action cannot be sustained).

In addition to construing the purpose of individual factors listed in the ACPA, courts have looked beyond the specified factors when evaluating a domain name registrant's alleged bad faith. Even when the use of the domain name satisfied some of the bad faith factors enumerated in the Act, the U.S. Court of Appeals for the Sixth Circuit declined to hold the defendant accountable, observing, "[o]ne of the ACPA's main objectives is the protection of consumers from slick internet peddlers who trade on the names and reputations of established brands. The practice [in which the defendant engaged] of informing fellow consumers of one's experience with a particular service provider is surely not inconsistent with this ideal." *Id.* at 811.

* * * * *

RETAIL SERVICES INC., FREEBIE, INCORPORATED,
Plaintiffs-Appellees
v.
FREEBIES PUBLISHING; EUGENE F. ZANNON; GAIL
ZANNON, Defendants-Appellants

United States Court of Appeals for the Fourth Circuit

No. 03-1272, No. 03-1317, 364 F.3d 535

April 13, 2004

[For the background of this case, *see* Supplement *supra* at 404.]

... [RSI also sought a declaration that] its use of the word "freebie" as part of its domain name ... does not violate the Anti-cybersquatting Consumer Protection Act, *see* 15 U.S.C.A. § 1125(d)....

II.

... In December 2001, defendants demanded that RSI cease using the word "freebie" in connection with its business. RSI refused to do so, believing the word "freebies" to be generic in nature, not entitled to trademark protection, and free for public use. Defendants initiated an arbitration proceeding against RSI pursuant to the Uniform Domain Name Dispute Resolution Policy ("UDRP"), which is incorporated into all domain-name registration agreements pursuant to which a second-level domain name is issued to a member of the public. The UDRP requires the registrant to submit disputes concerning the domain name to an approved dispute resolution provider - in this case the National Arbitration Forum -- for the purpose of what is essentially non-binding arbitration. *See Dluhos v. Strasberg,* 321 F.3d 365, 372-73 (3d Cir. 2003) ("UDRP proceedings do not fall under the Federal Arbitration Act ...[and] judicial review of those decisions is not restricted to a motion to vacate arbitration award under § 10 of the FAA, which applies only to binding proceedings likely to 'realistically settle the dispute.'"). The arbitrator concluded that <freebie.com> was confusingly similar to defendants' registered trademark and that RSI had no trademark rights in the name freebie. Additionally, the arbitrator determined that RSI registered the domain name in bad faith because it used the plural term "freebies" as a metatag for its website, which directed an Internet search for "freebies" to RSI's site. The arbitrator was persuaded that this evidence demonstrated RSI's awareness of defendants' FREEBIES trademark and, therefore, bad faith in acquiring its domain name. Accordingly, RSI was ordered to transfer the domain name <freebie.com> to defendants. ...

IV.

... Defendants' use of the term "freebies" is consistent with the use of that term by scores of other websites on the Internet. Typical of these domain names are <weeklyfreebie.com>, which compiles categorized lists of "freebie" products and where to get them, <coolfreebielinks.com>, which uses a banner announcing "Freebies, free stuff, giveaways ... call them what you want, they all break down to the same thing ...getting something for nothing," <freebies24x7.com>, which "offers one of the Web's largest collection of freebies.... If it's freebies you want, then it's freebies you got. ...so put away your wallet and grab some Freebies!"; and <freebiedirectory.com>, the domain name for a website describing itself as "Your searchable source for FREEBIES" and providing information about a wide variety of free products and services. There is also <freebiedot.com>, "your source for freebies and free stuff ... daily for freebies hunters like you;" <freebies4all.net>, which claims to be "the # 1 resource for FREE stuff on the web ... only top notch freebies are listed;" and <alwaysfreebies.com>, which also claims to be the Internet's "leading resource for free stuff" with "the latest and greatest freebies."

Defendants' website, and those listed above, are but a few of the 1,600-plus websites (or more) that incorporate the word "freebie" or "freebies" into their domain names. These websites are now so common that the term "freebie site" is often used by these sites to refer to other sites that, like defendants, offer information about free products or services. In addition to this voluminous information pulled directly from these websites, the record contains declarations from competitor sites. Glenda McGarity, the owner of a website called "Killer Freebies & Deals," <killerfreebies.com>, understands "the word 'freebies' to refer to free or almost free goods and services," supplies "information about freebies offered by other individuals or companies," and is aware of many such Internet businesses that offer freebies. Likewise, Lee Seats, who operates About.com's section on the topic of freebies, <freebies.about.com>, uses "freebies" on his website "to refer to free or almost free goods and services" and is "in the business of providing information, tips and advice about how to obtain free or almost free goods and services (i. e., freebies) offered by other companies or individuals." Finally, RSI offered a list of fifty-one newspaper or news media reports using the phrase "freebie site" to refer to websites similar to defendants' freebies.com. ...

V.

Under the Anticybersquatting Consumer Protection Act (ACPA), the owner of a protected mark has a cause of action "against anyone who registers, traffics in, or uses a domain name that is identical or confusingly similar to [the owner's] trademark with the bad faith intent to profit from the good will associated with the trademark." *Hawes v. Network Solutions, Inc.*, 337 F.3d 377, 383 (4th Cir. 2003); *see* 15 U.S.C.A. § 1125(d)(1). The district court concluded that because it "found defendants' trademark ineligible for protection, there can be no ACPA violation." *Retail Servs.*, 247 F. Supp. 2d at 827. Nevertheless, the court also analyzed whether RSI had violated the ACPA as if the FREEBIES mark were not generic, concluding that "there was insufficient evidence ... in this record to sustain a finding that [RSI] registered the domain name in bad faith." *Id.* at 828. We need go no farther than the district court's initial conclusion that defendants cannot state a claim under the ACPA without a valid trademark. This conclusion is compelled from the statutory language.

In pertinent part, the ACPA provides that "[a] person shall be liable in a civil action by the *owner of a mark*, ... if, without regard to the goods or services of the parties, that person ... (i) has a bad faith intent to profit from that *mark* ... and (ii) registers, traffics in, or uses a domain name that ... is identical or confusingly similar to that *mark*." 15 U.S.C.A. § 1125(d)(1)(A) (emphasis added). Under the statute, the term "mark" includes "trademark," which is defined as "identifying and distinguishing [the owner's] goods ... from those manufactured or sold by others and to indicate the source of the goods." 15 U.S.C.A. § 1127. As we noted before, a generic term cannot function as a trademark; in fact, to say "generic mark" is to utter an oxymoron. "By definition, something that is generic cannot serve as a trademark because it cannot function as an indication of source." *Sunrise Jewelry Mfg. Corp. v. Fred S.A.*, 175 F.3d 1322, 1325 (Fed. Cir. 1999). Thus, a prerequisite for bringing a claim under the ACPA is establishing the existence of a valid trademark and ownership of that mark. As we have already determined that "freebies" is generic and not entitled to trademark protection, defendants cannot surmount this threshold barrier. We therefore affirm the district court's entry of summary judgment against defendants on their cybersquatting counterclaim, and its declaration that RSI's "use of the domain name www.freebie.com does not violate the Anti-Cybersquatting Consumer Protection Act." *Retail Servs.*, 247 F. Supp. 2d at 829. ...

VII.

For the foregoing reasons, we affirm the decision of the district court in its entirety.

AFFIRMED

* * * * *

Special Applications to Internet Technologies

Background

insert the following after the first full paragraph on page 668 of Law of Internet Speech:

An example of technology that has been controversial is "overlay" technology. Such technology permits the placement of content other than that selected by the web-site owner or operator on top of Web pages, and has been used to facilitate, for example, price comparison among particular products. "Pop-up" and "pop-under" advertisements are those that appear automatically, usually in a new browser window on a user's computer. The ads are generated by software downloaded onto the user's computer that obscures the advertising content that was displayed prior to the pop-up or pop-under ad's appearance. Such software has been referred to as "adware," and when it contains software or scripts that enables a remote party to monitor the user's computer, it has been referred to as "spyware."

Law and technology experts described "spyware" as

Internet technologies that enable the gathering and transmission of information from a computer to a remote party over the Internet, particularly when software is downloaded or installed on a user's computer without "transparency." Some relatively non-controversial uses of these technologies include, for example, the transmission of error messages in connection with provision of sortware support services. But this kind of technology has also been adapted to other uses, including the delivery of 'pop-up' and 'pop-over' messages (in which case the software may be referred to as "adware"). Some implementations of the technology, referred to as "malware," enable the remote user to alter the settings on a user's computer, making it difficult to remove the technology at the election of the computer user, or may redirect a user's browser to an unwanted or unexpected location, or install unwanted or malicious software.

Brown Raysman Millstein Felder & Steiner LLP, *Technology, the Internet and Electronic Commerce: Staying Interactive in the High-Tech Environment,* Mar. 31, 2005 at 33 (footnote omitted). Companies often are chagrined when their competitors' advertisements appear on screens.

Gator.com,[*] for example, is the proprietor of a software program that enables computer users to store personal information, including addresses, credit card numbers, and passwords, in a "digital wallet." When a web-site prompted the user for such information, Gator's digital wallet input the user's information automatically, and the software provided the user with discounts and other offers that "popped up" on the computer screen when the user visited certain web-sites Gator had pre-selected. *See, e.g., Gator.com Corp. v. L.L. Bean, Inc.,* 398 F.3d 1125, 1127 (9th Cir. 2005).

In March 2001, Gator brought an action in the U.S. District Court for the Northern District of California, seeking a declaration that Gator.com was not infringing or diluting L.L. Bean's trademarks or other proprietary rights when Gator's software program triggered a discount coupon for Eddie Bauer, a competitor of L.L. Bean. *See Gator.com Corp. v. L.L. Bean, Inc.,* No. C-10-1126 (MEJ) (N.D. Cal. filed Mar. 19, 2001). In August 2001, after the Interactive Advertising Bureau ("IAB") reportedly questioned Gator's practices, Gator filed suit for a declaration that its practices were lawful, and for other relief based on what Gator alleged were IAB's commercial falsehood, product disparagement, trade libel, and injury to business reputation. *See Gator Corp. v. Interactive Adver. Bureau,* No. C-01-3279 (PJH) (N.D. Cal. filed Aug. 27, 2001).

A few months later, Gator and the IAB announced that they intended to work together to resolve their dispute. *See, e.g.,* Steven Bonisteel, *Gator, Ad Industry Call Truce Over "Pop-Over" Ads,* Newbytes News Network (Nov. 29, 2001), *available at* <http://www.findarticles. com/p/articles/mi_m0NEW/is_2001_Nov_29/ai_80409225>. The parties' settlement contemplated that Gator would permanently discontinue its use of pop-up advertisements on L.L. Bean's web-site and L.L. Bean released Gator from liability associated with the advertising practice. *See id.; see also Gator.com Corp. v. L.L. Bean, Inc.,* 398 F.3d at 1130-31. In February 2005, the U.S. Court of Appeals declined to entertain the action for

---

[*] The Gator Corporation subsequently became known as Claria Corporation. *See* Claria Corp., *Corporate Overview, available at* <http://www.claria.com/companyinfo/>.

declaratory relief on the ground that the parties' settlement agreement "wholly eviscerated the dispute" that gave rise to the request for a declaratory judgment and no longer presented a live case or controversy. *Id.* at 1131.

The use of pop-up technology has been challenged under the Lanham Act; such challenges have, with one exception, been rejected. *Compare Wells Fargo & Co. v. WhenU.com, Inc.,* 293 F. Supp. 2d 724 (E.D. Mich. 2003) (denying the plaintiff's motion for preliminary relief, noting that the defendant did not "use" the plaintiff's marks in "commerce," and the defendant had been engaged in legitimate comparative advertising), *and U-Haul Int'l, Inc. v. WhenU.com, Inc.,* 279 F. Supp. 2d 723 (E.D. Va. 2003) (holding that pop-up ad was not used in commerce and did not interfere with trademark holder's right to display its copyrighted works, and also ruling that no derivative work was created under the Copyright Act); *accord Wells Fargo & Co. v. WhenU.com, Inc.,* 293 F. Supp. 2d 734 (E.D. Mich. 2003), *with 1-800 Contacts, Inc. v. WhenU.com,* 309 F. Supp. 2d 467 (S.D.N.Y. 2003) (concluding that the defendant's software used the plaintiff's mark by generating competitive pop-up ads when a user entered the url of the web-site on which the plaintiff's marks appeared, and by including the plaintiff's mark in a directory of terms that triggered competitive pop-up ads; and rejecting the plaintiff's contention that the defendant's pop-up ads infringed the plaintiff's right of display in its copyrighted web-site by creating an infringing derivative work).

But even the exceptional case from a New York federal court fell in line with other courts' analysis when the action was heard on an interlocutory appeal. In *1-800 Contacts, Inc. v. WhenU.com,* the U.S. Court of Appeals for the Second Circuit held "that, as a matter of law, WhenU does not 'use' 1-800's trademarks within the meaning of the Lanham Act, 15 U.S.C. § 1127, when it (1) includes 1-800's website address, which is almost identical to 1-800's trademark, in an unpublished directory of terms that trigger delivery of WhenU's contextually relevant advertising to [computer users]; or (2) causes separate, branded pop-up ads to appear on a [computer user's] computer screen either above, below, or along the bottom edge of the 1-800 website window." Docket Nos. 04-0026-cv(L), 04-0446-cv(CON), 2005 U.S. App. LEXIS 12711 (2d Cir. June 27, 2005) at *5. The appellate court reversed the district court's entry of a preliminary injunction. *See id.*

In *Federal Trade Comm'n v. D Squared Solutions LLC,* No. 03 CV 3108, Slip Op. at 6 (D. Md. Oct. 30, 2003) (Temporary Restraining Order and Order to Show Cause), at 6, *available at* <http://www.ftc.gov/os/2003/11/0323223tro.pdf>, an injunction was issued against a pop-up advertising company prohibiting it from directly or indirectly causing a Windows Messenger Service message that, *inter alia,* advertises, promotes, markets, offers for sale or license, or sells or licenses any product or service, to appear on a computer user's computer screen. The FTC characterized D Squared's scheme as "[a]n operation that used a feature called the 'Windows Messenger Service,' which is part of the Microsoft Windows operating system, to barrage consumers' computers with pop-up ads...." *See* Press Release, FTC, *Pop-Up Ad Spammers Settle FTC Charges,* Aug. 9, 2004, *available at* <http://www.ftc.gov/opa/2004/08/dsquared.htm>. D Squared Solutions and the individual defendants settled with the FTC, agreeing that they would not send Windows Messenger Service pop-up advertising or instant message advertising. In addition, the settlement required the defendants to provide an opt-out mechanism for electronic advertising and prohibited them from using deceptive return addresses in e-mail messages they sent. *See id.*

The FTC offers consumers instructions on how to block unwanted pop-up messages. *See* FTC, *FTC Consumer Alert, available at* <http://www.ftc.gov/bcp/conline/ pubs/alerts/popalrt.htm>. California and Utah have pioneered legislative action against spyware. The California Consumer Protection Against Computer Spyware Act, Cal. Bus. & Prof. Code § 22947 (2004), *available at* <http://www.leginfo.ca.gov/pub/03-04/bill/sen/sb_1401-1450/sb_1436_bill_20040826_enrolled.pdf>, prohibits anyone other than an authorized user of a computer owned by a person in California from installing software with certain types of spyware functionality. Utah's Spyware Control Act, Utah Code Ann. § 13-39-101 to 401 (2004), *available at* <http://www.le.state.ut.us/~2004/ bills/hbillenr/hb0323.htm>, likewise prohibits the installation of spyware on others' computers. Enforcement of the Utah statute was preliminarily enjoined on the ground that the legislation violates the commerce clause of the U.S. Constitution. *See WhenU.com, Inc. v. State*, No. 040907578 (Utah 3d Jud. Dist. Ct. June 22, 2004). Thereafter, the statute was modified, *see* H.R. 104, 2005 Gen. Sess. (Utah 2005), *available at* <http://www.le.state.ut.us/~2005/bills/hbillenr/hb0104.pdf S.B. 1436 (Cal. 2004), *available at* <http://www.leginfo.ca.gov/pub/sen/sb_1401-1450/sb_1436_bill_20040816_enrolled .pdf>, defining the term "spyware" as software on the computer of a Utah resident that "collects information about an Internet website at the time the Internet website is being viewed" in Utah, and when the information is used "contemporaneously to display pop-up advertising on the computer."

* * * * *

insert the following before the first full paragraph on page 669 of Law of Internet Speech:

Technology may resolve or ameliorate a number of issues in a variety of contexts. Professor Jonathan Zittrain opined that "thinking in terms of privication architectures might help negotiate the allocation of rights to medical data to account for the interests of individual 'producers' of personal data in ways that need not disparage the legitimate interests of the sophisticated institutional players who wish to consume that data." Jonathan Zittrain, *Symposium: Cyberspace and Privacy: A New Legal Paradigm? -- What the Publisher Can Teach the Patient: Intellectual Property and Privacy in an Era of Trusted Privication*, 52 Stan. L. Rev. 1201, 1203 (2000). Can intellectual property and/or privacy concerns arising from digitization be mitigated by augmenting legal protections with systems technologies?

* * * * *

Linking

Objections to Linking Practices

insert the following before Deep Linking on page 680 of Law of Internet Speech:

NISSAN MOTOR CO., a Japanese corporation; NISSAN NORTH AMERICA, INC., a California corporation, Plaintiffs-Appellees

v.

NISSAN COMPUTER CORPORATION, a North Carolina corporation, Defendant-Appellant

United States Court of Appeals for the Ninth Circuit

No. 02-57148, No. 03-55017, No. 03-55144, No. 03-55236, 378 F.3d 1002

August 6, 2004

[For the background of this case, *see* Supplement *supra* at 412.]

... D

Nissan Computer seeks relief from the provision of the permanent injunction that restrains it from placing links on nissan.com and nissan.net to other websites containing disparaging remarks or negative commentary about Nissan Motor. It contends that such speech is non-commercial, thus not diluting under the FTDA. Nissan Computer also maintains that the disclaimer ordered in the preliminary injunction is sufficient to assure there is no dilution. Finally, it submits that the injunction does not control the uses of the domain names but instead, prohibits a particular type of content posted at the website.

Nissan Motor argues that we need not revisit Nissan Computer's First Amendment challenge to the permanent injunction because we already considered and rejected it by denying Nissan Computer's motion to stay. We disagree, as the standards for a stay differ from the review on the merits that is now before us. Beyond this, Nissan Motor defends the injunction as narrowly tailored, arguing that it restricts use of just two websites identical to the NISSAN mark. These restrictions, in its view, constitute regulation of nothing more than non-expressive trademark-equivalent domain names that do not express or communicate any views at all. For this reason, Nissan Motor asks us to hold that the First Amendment is not implicated because it is only when a trademark is used as part of a communicative message and not as a source identifier (which is what a domain name functions as in cyberspace) that the First Amendment is implicated. We disagree with this as well.

Prohibiting Nissan Computer from placing links to other sites with disparaging commentary goes beyond control of the Nissan name as a source identifier. The injunction does not enjoin use of nissan.com, but enjoins certain content on the nissan.com website. Thus, it is not the source identifier that is controlled, but the communicative message that is constrained. Consequently, the First Amendment is implicated.

The prohibited use of the mark is a content-based restriction because the purpose behind it is to control the message and it is not "justified without reference to the content of the regulated speech." *See, e.g., Ward v. Rock Against Racism*, 491 U.S. 781, 791, 105 L. Ed. 2d 661, 109 S. Ct. 2746 (1989) (citation and quotation omitted). "Content-based regulations pass constitutional muster only if they are the least restrictive means to further a compelling interest." *S.O.C., Inc. v. County of Clark*, 152 F.3d 1136, 1145 (9th Cir. 1998) (citing *Sable Communications of Cal. v. F.C.C.*, 492 U.S. 115, 126, 106 L. Ed. 2d 93, 109 S. Ct. 2829 (1989)). As a content-based restriction, the injunction is presumptively invalid, *see R.A.V. v. City of St. Paul*, 505 U.S. 377, 382, 120 L. Ed. 2d 305, 112 S. Ct. 2538 (1992), and not subject to a "time, place, and manner" analysis, *see Reno v. ACLU*, 521 U.S. 844, 879, 138 L. Ed. 2d 874, 117 S. Ct. 2329 (1997). Thus, it is immaterial whether there are alternative places on the web that negative commentary about Nissan Motor can be posted. The injunction is also viewpoint based because it only prohibits *disparaging* remarks and *negative* commentary. *See R.A.V.*, 505 U.S. at 391.

The FTDA anticipates the constitutional problem where the speech is not commercial but is potentially dilutive by including an exception for noncommercial use of a mark. *See* 15 U.S.C. § 1125(c)(4)(B); *Mattel*, 296 F.3d at 905-06 (recognizing that the "noncommercial use" exemption in the FTDA was designed to prevent courts from issuing injunctions that collide with the First Amendment). So, the relevant question is whether linking to sites that contain disparaging comments about Nissan Motor on the nissan.com website is commercial.

"Although the boundary between commercial and non-commercial speech has yet to be clearly delineated, the core notion of commercial speech is that it does no more than propose a commercial transaction." *Mattel*, 296 F.3d at 906 (quoting *Hoffman v. Capital Cities/ABC, Inc.*, 255 F.3d 1180, 1184 (9th Cir. 2001)) (quotation marks omitted). "If speech is not 'purely commercial' -- that is, if it does more than propose a commercial transaction -- then it is entitled to full First Amendment protection." *Id.* Negative commentary about Nissan Motor does more than propose a commercial transaction and is, therefore, non-commercial.

Nissan Motor argues that disparaging remarks or links to websites with disparaging remarks at nissan.com is commercial because the comments have an effect on its own commerce. *See Jews for Jesus v. Brodsky*, 993 F. Supp. 282, 308 (D.N.J. 1998) ("The conduct of the Defendant also constitutes a commercial use of the Mark and the Name of the Plaintiff Organization because it is designed to harm the Plaintiff Organization commercially by disparaging it and preventing the Plaintiff Organization from exploiting the Mark and the Name of the Plaintiff Organization."). However, we have never adopted an "effect on commerce" test to determine whether speech is commercial and decline to do so here.

We are persuaded by the Fourth Circuit's reasoning in a similar case involving negative material about Skippy Peanut Butter posted on skippy.com, a website hosted by the owner of the trademark SKIPPY for a cartoon comic strip. CPC, which makes Skippy Peanut Butter, successfully sought an injunction that ordered removal of the material. The court of appeals reversed. *CPC Int'l, Inc. v. Skippy Inc.*, 214 F.3d 456, 461-63 (4th Cir. 2000). Recognizing that criticism was vexing to CPC, the court emphasized how important it is that "trade-marks not be 'transformed from rights against unfair competition to rights to control language.'" *Id.* at 462 (quoting Mark A. Lemley, *The Modern Lanham Act and the Death of Common Sense*, 108 Yale L.J. 1687, 1710-11 (1999)). It held that speech critical of CPC was informational, not commercial speech. Likewise here, links to negative commentary about Nissan Motor, and about this litigation, reflect a point of view that we believe is protected.

Nissan Motor relies on *San Francisco Arts & Athletics, Inc. v. USOC*, 483 U.S. 522, 97 L. Ed. 2d 427, 107 S. Ct. 2971 (1987), to argue that it has obtained a limited property right in the NISSAN mark which Nissan Computer does not have a First Amendment right to appropriate to itself. In that case, the Court held that the Amateur Sports Act of 1978 did not unconstitutionally prohibit certain commercial and promotional uses of the word "Olympic" because Congress has a broader public interest than in traditional trademark law -- promoting the "physical and moral qualities which are the basis of sport" and "the participation of amateur athletes from the United States in 'the great four-yearly sport festival, the Olympic Games.'" *Id.* at 537 (quoting Olympic Charter, Rule 1 (1985)). For this reason the application of the Act to commercial speech was not broader than necessary to protect the legitimate congressional interest and therefore did not violate the First Amendment. But the Olympics are different, and there is no similar legislative interest at stake in this case.

Therefore, we conclude that the permanent injunction violates the First Amendment to the extent that it enjoins the placing of links on nissan.com to sites with disparaging comments about Nissan Motor.

… Conclusion

… Injunctive relief may not restrain Nissan Computer from placing links on nissan.com and nissan.net to other sites that post negative commentary about Nissan Motor; to this extent, the relief granted is overbroad, reaches non-commercial speech, and runs afoul of the FTDA and the First Amendment.

* * * * *

A controversial policy established by National Public Radio initially prohibited unapproved links to its web-site, but subsequently encouraged and permitted links, provided that there was no implication that the linked-to report endorsed any third party's causes, ideas, sites, products, or services and that NPR's content would not be used for "'inappropriate commercial purposes.'" *See* John Giuffo, *The Web: Unlock Those Links,* Colum. Journalism Rev. (Sept./Oct. 2002) at 9 (quoting NPR's policy).

Is it unlawful to deep link to a web-site that requires registration through a caching feature? Does the DMCA's safe harbor provisions exempt such caching? Would the site engaged in such deep linking be liable in the event the site it cached revised its content to delete or modify false and defamatory or infringing content?

* * * * *

insert the following at the end of Notes and Questions # 8 on page 689 of Law of Internet Speech:

See Supplement *supra* at 445.

* * * * *

insert the following after Notes and Questions on page 690 of Law of Internet Speech:

Can linking practices constitute evidence of bad faith intent to profit under the Anticybersquatting Act? In *Coca-Cola, Co. v. Purdy,* 382 F.3d 774 (8th Cir. 2004), the defendant had registered domain names that incorporated distinctive, famous, and protected trademarks owned by the plaintiffs, such as "drinkcoke.org," "mycoca-cola.com," "mymcdonalds.com," "mypepsi.org," and "my-washingtonpost.com." The defendant then linked the domain names to an anti-abortion web-site. *See id.* at 779.

The U.S. Court of Appeals for the Eighth Circuit declined to characterize the web-sites as entirely non-commercial because they directly solicited monetary contributions and offered various anti-abortion merchandise for sale. *See id.* at 786. "Even after [the defendant] attached the domain names to his own critical commentary sites, he continued to provide links to sites that solicited funds for the antiabortion movement and sold merchandise[,] ... apparently profit[ing] the organizations of [the defendant's] choice." *Id.* at 786 (citation omitted). The court noted that "nothing in the ACPA suggests that Congress intended to allow cybersquatters to escape the reach of the act by channeling profits to third parties. These factors support the district court's finding that plaintiffs were likely to establish Purdy's bad faith intent to profit from the marks." *Id.* The defendant's bad faith intent to profit also was evidenced by his offer to exchange the domain names that included the mark of the *Washington Post* for space on the newspaper's editorial page. *See id.*

* * * * *

In-Line Linking and Framing

insert the following before Leslie A. Kelly, an individual, dba Les Kelly Publications, dba Les Kelly Enters., dba Show Me The Gold v. Arriba Soft Corporation, an Illinois Corporation on page 696 of Law of Internet Speech:

In a subsequent unpublished opinion, the Ninth Circuit affirmed the decision and rejected Futuredontics' free speech claim. "[T]he First Amendment protects commercial speech only when it concerns lawful activity and is not misleading," remarked the court. *Futuredontics, Inc. v. Goodman,* No. 98-55801, 1999 U.S. App. LEXIS 26257, at *4-*5 (9th Cir. Oct. 14, 1999) (unpublished). "Any use of the mark in connection with a dental product violates the ... [licensing a]greement and is therefore unlawful. Furthermore, to the extent that such use suggests Applied Anagramics' endorsement of such a product, that use would also be misleading. For these reasons, the injunction does not abridge Futuredontics' First Amendment rights." *Id.* at *5.

* * * * *

insert the following before Metatags on page 699 of Law of Internet Speech:

With respect to a subsequent ruling in *Kelly v. Arriba Soft Corp., withdrawn by, aff'd in part, rev'd in part, remanded,* 336 F.3d 811, 822 (9th Cir. 2003); *see* Supplement *supra* at 372.

* * * * *

Metatags

insert the following before Notes and Questions on page 714 of Law of Internet Speech:

PLAYBOY ENTERPRISES, INC., a Delaware corporation,
Plaintiff-Appellant
v.
TERRI WELLES, an individual, *et al.,* Defendants-Appellees

United States Court of Appeals for the Ninth Circuit

No. 00-55009, No. 00-55229, No. 00-55537, No. 00-55538, 279
F.3d 796

February 1, 2002

[For the background of this case, *see* Supplement *supra* at 434.]

… PEI complains of … different uses of its trademarked terms on Welles' website[, including]: the terms "Playboy "and "Playmate" in the metatags of the website; … the repeated use of the abbreviation "PMOY '81" as the watermark on the pages of the website. PEI claimed that these uses of its marks constituted trademark infringement, dilution, false designation of origin, and unfair competition. …

Welles includes the terms "playboy" and "playmate" in her metatags. Metatags describe the contents of a website using keywords. Some search engines search metatags to identify websites relevant to a search. Thus, when an internet searcher enters "playboy" or "playmate" into a search engine that uses metatags, the results will include Welles' site. Because Welles' metatags do not repeat the terms extensively, her site will not be at the top of the list of search results. Applying the three-factor test for nominative use, we conclude that the use of the trademarked terms in Welles' metatags is nominative.

As we discussed above with regard to the headlines and banner advertisements, Welles has no practical way of describing herself without using trademarked terms. In the context of metatags, we conclude that she has no practical way of identifying the content of her website without referring to PEI's trademarks.

A large portion of Welles' website discusses her association with Playboy over the years. Thus, the trademarked terms accurately describe the contents of Welles' website, in addition to describing Welles. Forcing Welles and others to use absurd turns of phrase in their metatags, such as those necessary to identify Welles, would be particularly damaging in the internet search context. Searchers would have a much more difficult time locating relevant websites if they could do so only by correctly guessing the long phrases necessary to substitute for trademarks. We can hardly expect someone searching for Welles' site to imagine the same phrase proposed by the district court to describe Welles without referring to Playboy -- "the nude model selected by Mr. Hefner's organization...." Yet if someone could not remember her name, that is what they would have to do. Similarly, someone searching for critiques of Playboy on the internet would have a difficult time if internet sites could not list the object of their critique in their metatags.

There is simply no descriptive substitute for the trademarks used in Welles' metatags. Precluding their use would have the unwanted effect of hindering the free flow of information on the internet, something which is certainly not a goal of trademark law. Accordingly, the use of trademarked terms in the metatags meets the first part of the test for nominative use.

We conclude that the metatags satisfy the second and third elements of the test as well. The metatags use only so much of the marks as reasonably necessary and nothing is done in conjunction with them to suggest sponsorship or endorsement by the trademark holder. We note that our decision might differ if the metatags listed the trademarked term so repeatedly that Welles' site would regularly appear above PEI's in searches for one of the trademarked terms.

[With respect to t]he background, or wallpaper, of Welles' site[, we note that it] consists of the repeated abbreviation "PMOY '81," which stands for "Playmate of the Year 1981." Welles' name or likeness does not appear before or after "PMOY '81." The pattern created by the repeated abbreviation appears as the background of the various pages of the website. Accepting, for the purposes of this appeal, that the abbreviation "PMOY" is indeed entitled to protection, we conclude that the repeated, stylized use of this abbreviation fails the nominative use test.

The repeated depiction of "PMOY '81" is not necessary to describe Welles. "Playboy Playmate of the Year 1981" is quite adequate. Moreover, the term does not even appear to describe Welles -- her name or likeness do not appear before or after each "PMOY '81." Because the use of the abbreviation fails the first prong of the nominative use test, we need not apply the next two prongs of the test.

Because the defense of nominative use fails here, and we have already determined that the doctrine of fair use does not apply, we remand to the district court. The court must determine whether trademark law protects the abbreviation "PMOY," as used in the wallpaper.

... The one exception to the above analysis in this case is Welles' use of the abbreviation "PMOY" on her wallpaper. Because we determined that this use is not nominative, it is not excepted from the anti-dilution provisions. Thus, we reverse as to this issue and remand for further proceedings. We note that if the district court determines that "PMOY" is not entitled to trademark protection, PEI's claim for dilution must fail. The trademarked term, "Playmate of the Year" is not identical or nearly identical to the term "PMOY." Therefore, use of the term "PMOY" cannot, as a matter of law, dilute the trademark "Playmate of the Year."

AFFIRMED in part, REVERSED and REMANDED in part. Costs to Terri Welles and Terri Welles, Inc.

* * * * *